Modern Personality Psychology

Critical Reviews and New Directions

Edited by
Gian-Vittorio Caprara
University of Rome 'La Sapienza', Italy
Guus L. Van Heck
Tilburg University, The Netherlands

HARVESTER
WHEATSHEAF

New York   London   Toronto   Sydney   Tokyo   Singapore

First published 1992 by
Harvester Wheatsheaf
Campus 400, Maylands Avenue
Hemel Hempstead
Hertfordshire, HP2 7EZ
A division of
Simon & Schuster International Group

Typeset in 10/12pt Times
by MHL Typesetting Ltd.

Printed and bound in Great Britain by
Hartnolls Limited, Bodmin, Cornwall.

British Library Cataloguing in Publication Data

A catalogue record for this book is available from
the British Library

ISBN 0-7450-1067-9 (hbk)

1 2 3 4 5 96 95 94 93 92

Contents

Modern Personality Psychology

Preface

During one of the biannual conferences of the European Association of Personality Psychology (EAPP) the idea of a book covering important topics in current personalilty psychology was born.

While toying with the idea of producing such a book, several criteria were formulated. First of all, the EAPP conference suggested that the volume should show a reasonable balance between non-European and European writers and, within Europe, a reasonable spread of nations. In any case, what we had in mind was a book that would do justice to the pluralism of approaches and the complexity of the field of personality psychology.

Moreover, we felt that the book should focus on selected topics currently of interest in personality psychology. Rather than trying to cover the whole field in thirty to forty chapters of the 'Personality and . . . '-type, we opted for a smaller number on what we called 'those topics that show, more than others, that the field of personality psychology is very much alive nowadays'.

Furthermore, in discussing how to create a book containing chapters of an unusual freshness, we thought it a good idea to invite duos, preferably duos consisting of persons working on closely related research questions using models having a more or less common descent or origin. We were fully aware that, in following this strategy, we were asking for trouble, and that unavoidably we would overstep some of our deadlines — not unusual in the publication of handbooks on personality and related fields, as can be seen from the prefaces of such books. However, we felt strongly that it was worth a try.

Finally, we not only wanted to balance the book at the geographical and cultural level, but also with respect to the age of the authors. A good mixture of young and old, a delicate balance of some *éminence grise* and some new blood would in our view depict most convincingly the vitality of the field of personality psychology.

Now, looking back, we are satisfied that we were able to realize most of the goals we had set for ourselves. The book contains seventeen chapters and covers some of the most hotly debated issues in current personality psychology. In total, thirty-one authors contributed to the volume, stemming from nine countries and four continents. Several chapters are written by authors who have never before worked together on the same publication.

The book is designed for an advanced graduate level course in personality psychology. While the text is oriented towards students of personality, it may very well be applicable to other settings as well — for instance, classes in health psychology, clinical psychology, and organizational and personnel psychology.

We want to express our gratitude to the University of Rome 'La Sapienza' and Tilburg University for making available all the time we needed for the preparation of the book.

Finally, we express our appreciation to Harvester Wheatsheaf for the excellent assistance of Alison Stanford. We are especially grateful to our editor, Farrell Burnett, for her never waning enthusiasm and assistance.

GIAN-VITTORIO CAPRARA
University of Rome 'La Sapienza', Italy

GUUS L. VAN HECK
Tilburg University, The Netherlands

Contributors

Craig A. Anderson
University of Missouri
Department of Psychology
Columbia, MO 65211
USA

Alois Angleitner
University of Bielefeld
Department of Psychology
PO Box 100131
4800 Bielefeld 1
Germany

Peter Borkenau
University of Bielefeld
Department of Psychology
PO Box 100131
4800 Bielefeld 1
Germany

G. Leonard Burns
Washington State University
Department of Psychology
Pullman, WA 99164-4820
USA

Gian-Vittorio Caprara
University of Rome 'La Sapienza'
Department of Psychology
Via dei Marsi 78
00185 Rome
Italy

Daniel Cervone
University of Illinois at Chicago
Department of Psychology (M/C 285)
1009 Behavioral Sciences Building
PO Box 4348
Chicago, IL 60680
USA

Nino Dazzi
University of Rome 'La Sapienza'
Department of Psychology of
Developmental and
Socialization Processes
Via dei Marsi 78
00185 Rome
Italy

Alessandra De Coro
University of Rome 'La Sapienza'
Department of Psychology
Via dei Marsi 78
00185 Rome
Italy

Boele De Raad
University of Groningen
Department of Psychology
Grote Kruisstraat 2/1
9712 TS Groningen
The Netherlands

Joseph P. Forgas
The University of New South Wales
School of Psychology
PO Box 1
Kensington, NSW 2033
Australia

John H. Gruzelier
Department of Psychiatry
Charing Cross Hospital
Medical School
The Reynolds Building
St Dunstan's Road
London W6 8RF
England

Joop Hettema
Tilburg University
Department of Psychology
PO Box 90153
5000 LE Tilburg
The Netherlands

Willem K.B. Hofstee
University of Groningen
Department of Psychology
Grote Kruisstraat 2/1
9712 TS Groningen
The Netherlands

Douglas T. Kenrick
Arizona State University
Department of Psychology
Tempe, AZ 85287
USA

Barbara Krahé
Free University of Berlin
Department of Psychology (WE 7)
Habelschwerdter Allee 45
1000 Berlin 33
Germany

Hans Kreitler
University of Tel Aviv
Department of Psychology
39040 Ramat Aviv
Tel Aviv 69978
Israel

Shulamith Kreitler
University of Tel Aviv
Department of Psychology
39040 Ramat Aviv
Tel Aviv 69978
Israel

John C. Loehlin
University of Texas
Department of Psychology
Austin, TX 78712
USA

Luciano Mecacci
University of Rome 'La Sapienza'
Department of Psychology
Via dei Marsi 78
00185 Rome
Italy

Fritz Ostendorf
University Koblenz-Landau
Department of Psychology
Im Fort 7
6740 Landau
Germany

Robert Plomin
The Pennsylvania State University
Institute for the Study of
Human Development
211 Henderson Building South
University Park, PA 16802
USA

David Rowe
The University of Arizona
School of Family and
Consumer Resources
College of Agriculture
Tucson, AZ 85721
USA

Manfred Schmitt
University of Trier
Department of Psychology
PO Box 3825
W-5500 Trier
Germany

Gün R. Semin
The Free University of Amsterdam
Department of Psychology
De Boelelaan 1081
1081 HV Amsterdam
The Netherlands

Gudmund J.W. Smith
University of Lund
Department of Psychology
Paradisgatan 5
223 50 Lund
Sweden

Arthur W. Staats
University of Hawaii at Manoa
Department of Psychology
2430 Campus Road
Honolulu, HI 96822
USA

Jan Strelau
University of Warsaw
Department of Psychology
Stawki 5/7
00-183 Warsaw
Poland

Guus L. Van Heck
Tilburg University
Department of Psychology
PO Box 90153
5000 LE Tilburg
The Netherlands

Bernard Weiner
University of California
Department of Psychology
Los Angeles, CA 90024
USA

Bert Westerlundh
University of Lund
Department of Psychology
Paradisgatan 5
223 50 Lund
Sweden

S. Lloyd Williams
Lehigh University
Department of Psychology
Chandler 7
Bethlehem, PA 18015
USA

PART I
Introduction

1/ Personality psychology
Some epistemological assertions and historical considerations

Gian-Vittorio Caprara
University of Rome 'La Sapienza', Italy

Guus L. Van Heck
Tilburg University, The Netherlands

Introduction

Although we are not historians, we cannot avoid touching upon some historical considerations regarding the content and the theoretical status of the discipline of psychology as it has developed in time. It seems particularly compelling for personality psychology to ascertain whether any real progress has taken place and, if so, to identify significant cues which indicate this progress.

In spite of a resurgent interest in the discipline, one may cite Meehl's (1978) criticism with regard to noteworthy questions which remain the same and innovations which seem mere, and still incorrect, reformulations of old problems. In this regard, we agree with Pervin's (1990) re-proposal of Sanford's (1963) opinion regarding the value of a longer time perspective and an awareness of the history of the field. However, we are not completely sure that we share their view concerning the length of the time perspective and the meaning of the awareness. For instance, we doubt that the recent history of personality psychology, which has developed over the past 60 years, should be primarily confined to the history of North American personality psychology, without questioning the reasons for and the consequences of this restriction. We also have difficulty in agreeing that the issues that have remained noteworthy are entirely the same.

In tracing the history of a discipline, the *ideological-cultural* determinants which provide the background for the scientists' reflection must be taken into consideration. This implies scrutinizing the variables of the economic and social context in which a certain type of research question is posed and in which investigations aiming at clarifying that type of question develop and mature.

In this perspective, we believe that an examination of the reasons why much of recent personality psychology is that of the 'new continent' should not be disregarded;

nor should an examination of the characteristics of that context which have marked the course of personality psychology in the past 60 years be neglected.

We also believe that the emphasis on the resemblance of enunciations should not obscure the diversity of implications, when the conditions which form the basis and provide the framework for the development of the scientific investigation are different. For instance, Spinoza's (1677) reflections on passions are only metaphorically somewhat analogous to the issues which can be found at the centre of today's study of emotions. Also, the unconscious in Leibniz's and Kant's work has only metaphorical resemblance to the Freudian unconscious or to the unconscious of modern cognitivism. Moreover, the current interrogatives at the centre of the study of personality (for example, those regarding traits, needs, and mind—body linkages) are only apparently the same as those posed by Allport (1937) or Murray (1938) over 50 years ago. Parsimony of language cannot make us neglect the accumulation of cognitive elements which have significantly *modified* the importance of the same concepts over time.

In this regard, we believe that attention to *differences*, more than an analysis of *resemblances*, can help us single out the elements to which the progress of personality psychology is closely linked.

Therefore, it is from this perspective that we present in the following paragraphs a series of considerations which favour the examination of the elements of *discontinuity* which have characterized the theoretical debate and the methodological developments of the discipline. Based upon these premises, we will first present some metatheoretical considerations and views on theory development. Then we will describe a three-stage model of progress of the discipline. Moreover, we will briefly sketch some main issues and trends within the recent history of personality psychology.

Metatheoretical considerations

As Burnham (1968) observed, from the time of ancient Greece up until the nineteenth century, the history of systematic reflection on human nature and on personality corresponds with a series of events marking the development of naturalism. At least, this seems to be true for modern western psychology which has its roots in classical thought.

In the context of western culture, the history of psychology is comparable to a long march toward a conception of humankind as part of nature and, as such, the object of scientific investigation. This march indeed has been long, moving from systematic investigations of laws which govern the external world to investigations of the elements which characterize internal psychic reality. This seems particularly true for personality psychology. Its history has been characterized by the emancipation from mere philosophical speculation to a systematic examination of mental processes and products discovering the regularities upon which their organization relies.

Psychology more than other disciplines, and personality psychology, more than other psychologies, were affected by various forms of conditioning associated with specific world views reflecting particular philosophical systems and socio-political organizations. In an era in which the pathologist ran the risk of being buried alive, because investigating the human body was conceived of as a profanation of a creature of God, it was even more dangerous to question the real nature of mind and soul. So it is not surprising that psychology developed much later than physics, chemistry, and biology in that long march leading from knowledge of the external reality to an ever-increasing understanding of the internal reality, swinging back and forth between the opposite temptations of rational and physical reductionism. Nor should the long-term effects of reductionism upon the new-born personality psychology be underestimated.

There is no doubt that in many cases only a mask of originality sustains the illusion of novelty and progress. However, it would be misleading to overlook the different attitudes which derive from the various possibilities of modern personality psychology for isolating variables under investigation and examining their relationships.

In this regard, we are convinced that great progress has been made; in spite of the fact that the primary questions are only apparently the same. For instance, Descartes's interactionism has very little in common with modern interactionism; and the debates of the 1920s on what is innate and what is learned are rather distant from the topics of the current debate. So the ways of scrutinizing questions that are considered relevant are currently rather different. Note, however, that the concern with subjectivity, found in Dilthey (1894) and Allport (1937), seems to be much less incompatible with recent person-oriented strategies than it was with the scientific psychology of the nineteenth century or with the radical behaviourism of the 1930s. Furthermore, it seems to be grounded on a much more solid base.

After more than 20 years even Burnham's (1968) brilliant analysis must be revised. We strongly feel that it can be misleading to *overemphasize* the association between the development of personality psychology and the development of naturalism. Personality psychology should go beyond naturalism, or at least it should be very cautious in taking on the assumptions of naturalism, just as it should be in wondering about new forms of spiritualism. The naturalism one should wonder about is that of a psychology of mere facts, incapable of capturing the underlying processes and recognizing subjectivity as an essential property of psychic functioning. This concern, in our opinion, should be particularly relevant for much of the psychology that has developed within a theoretical tradition under the protection of logical positivism and radical empiricism.

Considerations on theory development

In the cultural tradition which extended from the seventeenth century and through most of the nineteenth century, knowledge was essentially devoted to the search for the stable and ultimate truth. Science's commitment to absolute certainties has continued to pervade much of the thinking of our century, precluding the idea of the dialectic process of scientific knowledge. The scientific enterprise was understood as a cumulative process; its discontinuities were largely disregarded and its hypothetical nature was finally recognized only recently and reluctantly.

The idea of *knowledge as a hypothetical construction* is relatively new among scientists of various disciplines. For a long time it was difficult to recognize any compatibility between accumulation and discontinuity, to assimilate the notion of the probabilistic nature of knowledge without making any concessions to mere relativism and scepticism, and to be aware of the transitoriness of any solution without losing confidence in the progress of science.

Today, acceptance of the hypothetical nature of knowledge is unavoidable. It is imposed by the advance of knowledge from one increasingly complex and profound problem to another through continuous revisions of statements and conjectures. Also, the non-uniformity of progress in the various disciplines is inevitable, given the different paths taken in moving away from the common speculative matrix.

The epistemological consequences which derive from the turbulent progress of various disciplines lead to considerations of the critical role of theory under different perspectives and to revisions of the idea of common criteria capable of establishing the validity of different theories across different disciplines.

Apparently, there is no longer any hope of establishing once and for all what a scientific theory should be in order to be scientific. Theories organize what is known and disclose new ways of obtaining knowledge by predetermining what can be known. In the initial stages of scientific disciplines the creation of theories is the result of the scientist's spontaneous thinking, which takes form directly from his or her creativity and world view. In a more advanced stage of scientific development, when the issue of comparison and pre-eminence among competitive theories arises, the establishment of requisites is linked to the possibility of representing a set of conventions, shared by the scientific community, capable of connecting assumptions, hypotheses, and events, and capable of orienting and promoting the progress of science within a certain domain of knowledge.

Primarily within the tradition of logical positivism, the semantic and the syntactic aspects of a theory have been distinguished. Moreover, a number of criteria have been established for its evaluation, namely parsimony, clarity, and internal and external validity. Within this tradition, a scientific theory is basically a system of empirical propositions which can be confirmed or falsified by means of rigorous controls. The view of scientific progress that is endorsed is essentially in terms of cumulation.

Recently, these views have been criticized severely. An emphasis on complexity rather than simplicity, on diversity rather than similarity, on specificity rather than generality, and on uniqueness rather than commonality has led to a redefinition of what a theory should be. Now, more than in the past, scientists are aware that theories, in addition to being more or less ordered sets of *propositions, rules*, and *definitions*, also imply more or less explicit sets of *values, beliefs*, and *expectations*. Now many subscribe to the viewpoint that, in directing cognitive activity, every theory is characterized by the specific aspects which are investigated, the facts which are selected, the connections between events which are emphasized, and also by what is considered important or irrelevant. Nowadays, more than in the past, the scientist is concerned with the limitations that the *logic of justification* may impose upon the *logic of discovery*. Therefore, new attention is being paid to all those phenomena whose apparent lack of order represents a challenge for discovering new forms of order and regularity.

In psychology and, in particular, in personality psychology, every theory is always implicitly a theory of the person and of the society which in some ways reflects the aspirations and the cognitive limitations of the knowing subject. In this regard, it is evident that restrictive notions of *objectivity* and *validity* are untenable. The kind of objectivity and validity which can be pursued in psychology cannot correspond to the mere application of formal criteria borrowed from other disciplines, or to the mere exclusion of any evaluative component. Modelling the progress of psychology on the progress of the natural sciences may ultimately be misleading. Various criteria must be applied, taking into account the specificity of the discipline, its objects, and its methods. Everything that may represent a limitation on the objectivity of the knowing subject must become the object of awareness. In particular, *subjectivity* must be at the centre of the investigation as a property of the knowing subject as well as of the object of investigation.

For years, there has been debate over the epistemological limits of psychology. Often philosophers' criticisms have created a mixture of awe and resentment among psychologists. In recent years a new debate has developed among philosophers regarding the canons and the limits of scientific investigation, which seems to be re-establishing the conditions for mutual understanding. The content of this debate can be best and most succinctly evaluated with reference to the work of Popper (1959, 1969), Kuhn (1962), Lakatos (1970, 1978), and Laudan (1977). In the formulations of these authors one can observe the gradual abandonment of the notion that unique criteria may exist for evaluating the scientific consistency of theories across disciplines, as well as the gradual emergence of an *epistemological pluralism*. The history of this debate is very relevant for personality psychology. Popper, Kuhn, Lakatos, and Laudan may help us in increasing our understanding of what personality psychology has become thus far. In the next paragraphs we will briefly discuss their analyses.

Popper

For Popper (1959, 1969) the aim of scientific activity is to find satisfying explanations which can improve the state of acquired knowledge. Basically, a scientific explanation is a process which can be constantly modified and improved to discover the secrets of the world with the help of consistent and controllable theories.

According to Popper, the first task of the logic of knowledge is to trace a clear line of *demarcation* between science and metaphysical ideas; even though these ideas may have favoured the progress of science in earlier stages of its development. With respect to this line of demarcation, it is fundamental to ascertain how a system of empirical assertions is consistent with empirical reality.

A theory which aims at acquiring empirical character must be open to refutation or disproval. A theory is outside of empirical science when it does not allow for this. Thus, it is the *criterion of falsification* which establishes the demarcation between empirical theories and non-empirical theories. What characterizes the empirical method is not preserving the life of untenable systems but, on the contrary, exposing each theory to the most ferocious fight for survival and keeping the theory which withstands all conceivable controls. Experiments provide support for a scientific hypothesis primarily if they are valid attempts to prove the theory to be false. Observations and experiments have an essential critical function allowing for the elimination of the weaker theories and, at the same time, guaranteeing a stronger basis (even if only temporary) for the theories which have withstood all attempts to refute them.

All scientific knowledge is hypothetical and conjectural. As scientists, we stumble over some problem; we try to resolve it; we learn from our errors, especially those we have become aware of through critical discussion of our attempts at resolution. Change and progress in scientific knowledge derive from attempts at solving new and increasingly profound problems. In a comparison among theories, rather than the idea of truth, it is the idea of the *probability of truth* which plays a regulative function in stimulating critical discussions and in determining the consistency of a scientific theory. What qualifies the *scientific consistency* of a theory is not the fact of its being more or less true than others, but its showing higher or lower probability of being disconfirmed than others. However, a theory should not only explain the *explicanda*, it should also be able to lead to relevant and controllable empirical consequences. Thus, the notion of *empirical success*, in addition to the notion of scientific consistency, becomes crucial. Whereas new controls lead to the setting up of new experiments, positive results provide the conditions for continuing investigations with the aim of extending the knowledge of empirical reality.

Kuhn

According to Kuhn (1962), scientific progress does not proceed cumulatively, but is the result of a revolutionary process which always takes place following the research phases of normal science.

Kuhn's fundamental concept is the *paradigm*. This term reflects the universally recognized scientific conquests which, for a certain period, provide models of problems and solutions acceptable to those in a certain research field. On the one hand, the notion of paradigm refers broadly to the entire constellation of beliefs, values, expectations, techniques, and instruments shared by members of a given scientific community. On the other hand, paradigm refers less broadly to several elements of that constellation. For instance, it refers to the concrete solutions to 'puzzles', which, used as models and examples, can provide the explicit rules and can constitute the premises for the solution of the remaining 'puzzles' of normal science. In the first case, the notion of paradigm refers to the set of conceptual ideas which is part of the cultural patrimony of a scientific community, and to the metaphysical implications and ideologies of that patrimony. In the second case, the notion of paradigm has, above all, heuristic valence: the existence of the paradigm establishes the task to be resolved.

Paradigms determine the methods, the range of problems, and the models of solution accepted by a mature scientific community in a particular historical period. The welcoming of new paradigms is always associated with more or less extended revisions and redefinitions of a particular science. The change of paradigm assumes revolutionary connotations with the opening of a crisis period in normal science, in connection with a series of *anomalies* which sanction the end of the dominant paradigm(s) and generate the need for considering alternative ones. When a new paradigm shows greater empirical validity and overrides pre-existing paradigms in terms of its pervasiveness and independence from previous ways of thinking, a *real scientific revolution* takes place and a new phase of normal science is inaugurated.

Normal science is a scientific praxis consolidated by traditions and schools; on the basis of models, laws, theories, applications, and instruments, as well as of an implicit set of interwoven methodological beliefs and theories. The determination of relevant facts, the comparison of facts with the theory, and the articulation of the theory largely define the tasks of both empirical and theoretical normal science. In this regard, normal science is more concerned with confirmations and justifications than with discovery. The existence of consolidated paradigms marks the establishment of normal science as a fundamental stage for the emancipation and autonomous development of the various disciplines. It is, in fact, with the establishment of normal science that the object is defined, methods are set out, rules and general coordinates of a cognitive praxis are fixed, and curricula for the selection and training of researchers are defined.

The proliferation of schools (*pre-paradigmatic*) precedes the development of normal science (*paradigmatic*). Questions about its epistemological and critical identity are primarily part of the pre-paradigmatic period of a discipline, usually marked by frequent and profound discussions about the legitimacy of various methods, problems, and models of solution. The goal then is not so much producing agreement as characterizing the empirical content and the methods peculiar to the various schools.

On the whole, Kuhn's reasoning seems particularly pertinent to psychology. The history of psychology confirms that its development has not been cumulative and indicates that what limited its progress was not only the complexity of the object, but also the difficulty of freeing itself from metaphysical and ideological reasoning.

Using Kuhn's categories, one may question whether psychology is a paradigmatic discipline or still the arena of antagonistic schools. In answering this question, it can be argued that psychoanalysis, behaviourism, and cognitivism are the dominant competitive ways of turning psychology into science. They have led the field of psychology to the doors of normal science.

Lakatos

Lakatos's (1970) theory is defined as the *methodology of scientific research programmes*. The research programme is a general theory, a structure composed of several fundamental elements which intersect the various phases of the scientific process. Several methodological rules indicate that certain research directions should be avoided and that other directions should be pursued.

A *negative heuristic*, according to Lakatos (1970), refers to the methodological decision of scientists that the fundamental assumptions of the research programme which characterize the *nucleus* cannot be modified, abandoned, or refuted. The task of saving the nucleus from controls and falsifications is carried out by a *protective belt of auxiliary hypotheses*. Whereas the auxiliary hypotheses, which provide empirical support for the basic theses set forth in the nucleus, can be changed, the nucleus, which constitutes the distinctive aspect of a programme, is entirely preserved. The modification of the nucleus of a research programme is the expression of open disagreement among scientists about the conditions providing the presupposition of the scientific investigation. A new conception, incompatible with the nucleus, marks the abandonment of the programme. This occurs in the empirical sphere, when the nucleus is no longer able to assure the advance of new empirical events.

With the notion of *positive heuristic*, Lakatos (1970) refers to the variety of indications and proposals which allow for the articulation, development, and improvement of the nucleus of the research programme. The positive heuristic — given that the anomalies are never completely exhausted in a research programme — provokes suggestions on how to change and develop the refutable variants of the research programme, and on how to modify the refutable protective belt.

What decides the quality of the programme and determines empirical progress is *verification*; that is, the confirmation of the expectations established in the logical order of the research programme. A series of theories (T1, T2, T3, ...) provides the specific examples of a research programme which is theoretically progressive when the new theory has greater empirical content with respect to the theories that precede it. In this regard, Lakatos (1970) negates the scientific validity of an isolated theory. Rather, one can speak of a single theory and consider it as scientific only if it can be inserted into the developmental context of a series of theories. According to these premises, one theory is obviously superior to another with respect to the consistency of empirical content, just as a scientific research programme constitutes progress if the discovery of new facts inaugurates the empirical development of a scientific tradition.

At the core of psychology, learning theory and cognitivism, at least as developed in the North American tradition, may be seen as part of the same research programme. However, one should not overlook the significant modifications that have affected the nucleus of the programme over time. Also, to some extent, psychoanalysis and the psychology of object relations may be seen as part of the same research programme. However, in the case of psychoanalysis, what is more problematic than the modifications in the nucleus of the programme is the kind of empirical support which is provided for the basic themes set forth in the nucleus.

Laudan

According to Laudan (1977), the goal of science is primarily that of problem solving.

Consequently, scientific theories represent the final outcome or response to science's interrogatives. The function of a theory is to resolve ambiguity, to reduce irregularity to uniformity, to show that what occurs is in some way understandable and predictable. It is primarily to this set of functions that Laudan is referring when treating theories as *solutions to problems*. In this regard, Laudan (1977) differentiates empirical problems from conceptual problems. He underlines how both are important for scientific progress.

Basically, three types of empirical problem are identified: (1) unresolved problems, (2) resolved problems, and (3) anomalous problems. In comparison with resolved problems, unresolved ones are those which have not yet been resolved satisfactorily by any theory. They essentially serve as questions for further research. Anomalous problems are those empirical problems which, resolved by one or more theories, have not been resolved by a *particular* theory with which they are in opposition. It is clear that resolved problems testify in favour of a theory, anomalous problems constitute proof against a theory, and unresolved problems simply indicate the direction of future research.

When scientific theories are considered in relation to their capacity to resolve problems and in relation to anomalies which can impede their sphere of action, their evaluation becomes paramount. In the evaluation of scientific theories, conceptual problems (non-empirical) warrant greater attention than they have actually received. There are two types of conceptual problem: *internal* conceptual problems and *external* ones. Internal conceptual problems emerge when a theory has no logical coherence or when conceptual ambiguity exists within the theory. In this regard, excessive ambiguity of a theory constitutes a serious limitation for the progress of knowledge. In contrast, conceptual clarity is one of the strongest foundations for such progress. External conceptual problems originate from the contrast between theories linked to different scientific domains, from the conflict between a scientific theory and methodological theories accredited to a scientific community, and from the conflict between a scientific theory and the prevailing *Weltanschauung*.

With respect to an epistemological tendency which leads philosophers such as Popper, Kuhn, and Lakatos to neglect the importance of non-empirical factors in the development of science, Laudan (1977) approaches the definition of a conceptual model of science based on the following two fundamental assumptions:

1. The resolved problem, whether empirical or conceptual, is the basic unity of scientific progress.
2. The aim of science is that of maximizing the range of resolved empirical problems and reducing that of anomalous empirical problems and unresolved conceptual problems.

If scientific theories are formulated to solve certain empirical problems and to reduce anomalies and conceptual problems resulting from preceding theories, then those theories which are the most effective in achieving this goal are obviously the ones that should be favoured.

According to Laudan (1977), the term *theory* can be used in a specific sense to determine the principles, axioms, etc. with which we try to predict determining events or explain certain phenomena. However, the term *theory* can also be used broadly to refer to general assumptions which include more theories and have a common matrix. These general theories, which Laudan (1977) calls *research traditions*, are arrays of general assumptions regarding the entities and the processes present in a certain field of study, and the appropriate methods to be used for investigating problems and constructing theories in that field. The scientific theories which are part of different research traditions follow a 'particular form' of ontology and are often irreconcilable. It is the task of the research tradition to establish an ontology and a general methodology for confronting all problems in a given field or in a group of fields. From this derives what Laudan (1977) defines as *the constrictive role of research traditions*, which excludes all theories which are incompatible either with the ontology or with the methodology of research traditions.

Research traditions are subject to transformations which derive from modifications of theories as well as from changes of their primary aspects. Furthermore, since research traditions always relate to an entire belief system and to values inherent in a particular cultural area, they may encounter notable difficulties when incompatibility develops between theories and methods and the prevailing world view. Also, it may happen that a research tradition produces notable changes in consolidated beliefs and fundamental elements of the cultural context. However, more frequently the dominant world view successfully opposes the revolutionary tendencies of new theories, primarily with regard to their social dissemination.

Even though research traditions are in competition and one tradition must usually succumb to the other, they can also be integrated. Without destroying their respective identities such an integration can bring about remarkable scientific results.

In the case of research traditions too, the fundamental problem concerns their evaluation. Although research traditions do not directly manifest observable results, they can be the object of rational evaluation. Consequently, they can be compared. In this regard, the adequacy, acceptability, and progress of a research tradition can be evaluated on the basis of the *effectiveness* in problem solving of the theories of which it is composed. As a consequence, the evaluation of scientific theories is no longer based on normative criteria of verification, falsification, and corroboration of assertions, or on a discrimination of knowledge in terms of some sort of absolute increase. Scientific progress no longer coincides with the progressive and gradual attainment of truth, but with the efficacy of the theories and research traditions in solving specific problems in determined contexts. This position does not eliminate the possibility of considering scientific theories and scientific knowledge as true, or in terms of coming closer to the truth. Rather, the idea is that it cannot be established *with certainty* when science is true, is approaching truth, or is not true.

The model proposed by Laudan (1977) seems particularly adequate for characterizing the development of theories and research traditions. As a matter of fact, chains of theories can be singled out in psychology which are part of a particular research tradition. They share a common ontology and have the same methodological stance. During their development they have uncovered important knowledge in an area under investigation or have heuristically posed the premises for its greater specification, coherent with the solution of certain problems. In particular, Laudan's

(1977) refusal of rigid criteria of demarcation between empirical and non-empirical disciplines may appropriately fit the analysis of a vast area of personality psychology.

A three-stage model of progress in personality psychology

As mentioned previously, personality psychology is greatly dependent on the past for the interrogatives it faces, the methods it follows, and for the limitations which condition its development.

To make a long story short, the history of personality psychology in the western hemisphere has its roots in speculation about the nature of humankind by early physicians and philosophers within the context of the classical tradition. Closer to the present, three movements provided the premises for what later became personality psychology: the psychiatric concern with a taxonomy of mental illness, the development of mental testing, and the interest in instincts. In a certain way, these movements identify the various characteristics and stages which have accompanied the development of personality psychology. Description and classification remain at the core of the clinical study of normal and abnormal personality. The study of individual differences paved the way for the investigation of the structure of personality as a coherent and functional constellation of dispositions. Debate around the notion of instincts brought the dynamics and the development of personality in relation to the environment under investigation.

Modern personality psychology is usually traced to the 1930s, primarily to the work of Allport and Murray (see, for example, Pervin, 1990). Of course, this does not mean that other authors, such as Stagner (1937) or Lewin (1935), were not important. However, it is a matter of fact that Allport and Murray are the most frequently quoted and are almost universally identified with the discipline. At first sight, the exclusion of Freud may seem exaggerated. However, in our view, it accurately reflects current relations between psychoanalysis and personality psychology.

To disregard contributions which were separated from the mainstream of American psychology, such as Heymans or Steen, may seem excessively patriotic to psychologists of the new world. In this regard, it is difficult to establish whether the barriers were only linguistic, or also logistic. We leave the historians the task of rewriting the history of personality psychology and of evaluating the importance of the contributions of the rest of the world. Here, we limit ourselves to sketching a three-stage model of the development of personality psychology, once again relying on the sources which are available within the framework of 'normal science' — that is, *legitimate* science — with greater awareness of its limitations.

Emerging paradigms

There is a period at the beginning of a discipline when one can catch a glimpse of its contours, and when what should be its essential characteristics, goals, and methods are the object of debate and conflict among competing schools of thought. This is often a period when a discipline is not well differentiated with respect to other, more or less contiguous disciplines. Approaches venture in and intermingle to define its identity.

Personality psychology experienced such a period immediately preceding and following the Second World War. Within the broad meaning of paradigm, this period can be defined as *pre-paradigmatic*, since no paradigm yet existed that was the object of a consensus broad enough to ensure personality psychology, or even psychology, the status of normal science. Undoubtedly, within the narrow meaning of paradigm, behaviourism on one side, and psychoanalysis on the other, already possessed the attributes of systems able to organize scientific activity and form autonomous research traditions, not only in psychology but also in personality psychology. It is curious that personality psychology was defined, even if in an intuitive and speculative way, by authors who kept their distance from one another and assembled pieces from the various dominant *paradigms*. In various ways, Allport (1937) and Murray (1938), testify to the ambition of clarifying the most complex phenomena and resolving, at the same time, the apparent irreconcilability of the two dominant viewpoints. In particular, personality psychology appears in the work of these authors as a discipline which can act as a hinge between research on basic processes and clinical practice. Emphasis on the singular organism or psychic functioning and attention to processes and conditions which mark development and adaptation represent its distinct characteristics.

In Europe, the study of character and constitutional types has been bogged down by the ideologies of right and left with no connection to a reflection on being, whose tones are increasingly metaphysical. Thus, it was primarily on the new continent that personality became a new field of study with characteristics more congenial to it.

Over 60 years later it is impossible to appreciate the treatments of Allport and Murray without considering the context in which they worked, caught between a theory of instincts and a theory of learning which left little space for subjectivity and individuality. Reflections on self-development, character traits, motivation, and processes of socialization and acculturation have more value for the avenues they opened than for the goals they achieved. Today very little remains of the content of those reflections, just as very little remains of the theory of instincts and learning theory. Also, it seems that the era of the great theories has passed, the products of the genius and fantasy of individual authors, concomitant with the accumulation of greater knowledge, with more precise differentiation between the various fields of psychological investigation, and with a more decisive characterization of the various lines of research.

Micro-theories

From the end of the 1940s to the end of the 1960s, personality psychology had an orbital development. Despite conditions for a maximal relaunching the discipline was pushed into marginal or problematic positions. This was a period when, more than ever before, personality psychology seemed to develop principally on the

American scene. It received its initial push from wartime needs. The problems of leadership, motivation, attitudes, selection and composition of crews, identification of the most congenial individual characteristics for specific roles and missions, and the reintroduction of veterans into civilian life launched investigation on personality and directly involved the most prestigious scholars. It was probably in the 1950s, however, that the discipline achieved its greatest growth and popularity, followed by a rapid decline in the 1960s.

In 1950, Sears defined the field of personality psychology in terms of three areas of investigation: structure, dynamics, and the development of motives and traits. These domains still correspond with the ambitions of modern personality psychology. In the same year the 'new look' indicated a passage in personality, which was necessary for clarifying the functioning of perception, thought, and memory. What animated the movement was anti-separatism and the aim of combining the North American functionalist tradition, the dynamic theories of Freud (1953ff), McDougall (1926), and Lewin (1951), and the organismic theories of Goldstein (1939), Werner (1948), and Murphy (1947). On the one side, they anticipated themes and intuitions which would come much later, revived by the most recent cognitivist trends; on the other side, they built new bridges between the various traditions of personality psychology to oppose separation and isolation.

The final attempts of behaviourists, such as Dollard and Miller (1950), to find points of contact with psychoanalysis and of psychoanalytic scholars, such as Rapaport (see Gill, 1967), to reconcile psychoanalysis and general psychology took place in the same years. Following this, various centrifugal movements were reinvigorated which led to the laceration of the original project and to the pulverization of research as witness to the advancing crisis.

What were the reasons? We believe that there were many, in large part connected with the growth of psychology in general. Many of the themes which had characterized the original personality psychology were studied by other sectors of psychological research: developmental psychology, social psychology, and clinical psychology. On the one hand, it was difficult to establish whether, for instance, Lewin (1935), Sears (1950), Maslow (1954), and Rogers (1961) were personality psychologists and not social, developmental, or clinical psychologists. On the other hand, the construction of general systems able to clarify the structure, dynamics, and development of personality, not only on a speculative basis but solidly anchored to the comparisons and rigours of empirical investigation, was increasingly problematic. Respect for criteria which defined the acceptability of a scientific theory placed insurmountable limits on the formulation of large theories and necessitated turning to more limited and more accessible objects of investigation. The separation of psychoanalysis from general psychology also seemed to be a consequence of the growth process. Increasingly they seem to be two autonomous disciplines developing independently.

When psychology was becoming articulated into many different psychologies, psychoanalysis also showed different trends representing various levels of investigation within the Freudian movement. In addition to the now definite breaks with Jung, Adler, and various schools of social psychoanalysis, orthodox psychoanalysis was torn by conflicts among Hartmanians, Kleinians, and Winnicottians which resulted in deep rifts between European and North American psychoanalysis. Psychoanalysis, above all the rationalistic and phenomenological version of 'clinical theory', continued to exercise notable appeal at least to a part of European personality psychology. However, with the entry into crisis of every attempt to operationalize and validate general theory by Rapaport and his followers in North America, a sort of curtain fell between psychoanalysts, who were increasingly involved in clinical practice, and personality psychologists, who were increasingly involved in academia. The excursions of eclectics from one field to the other were not well looked upon by either group.

The consequences of the distance and incomprehension between psychoanalysis and psychology must still be overcome in large part. Whereas for psychoanalysis the speculative suggestions and the risk of returning to purely hermeneutical forms seems increasingly frequent, for psychology various neo-positivist suggestions are reducing the space for an investigation of everything which, like affect and individual differences, seems to be an element of disturbance and interference with respect to the effective control of behaviour. Thus, academia is the place where personality psychology ended up having to legitimize itself, caught between two movements which limit its aspirations: on the one hand, radical *empiricism*, as the dominating epistemological paradigm, and on the other hand, *behaviourism*, which represents the most faithful expression of the first in the area of psychological research.

With only a few exceptions of authors neglected and later reinstated, such as Kelly (1955), the renunciation of large theories together with the anxiety of finding an academic legitimation led, as also noted by Pervin (1990), to a myriad of micro-theories, topics of research, and personality measures which occasionally dominate the field, only to disappear and be replaced by other micro-theories, topics of research, and personality measures. The only tradition which preserves its own identity and ensures a measure of scientific credibility on the part of personality psychology is the psychometric tradition of Cattell (for example, 1950, 1957), Guilford (for example, 1959, 1975), and Eysenck (for example, 1967). This tradition is exposed on the one hand, to the scepticism of experimental psychologists and, on the other hand, to the intrusion of clinical and social psychologists. However, this accounts for the armature, but not for its construction and internal organization. The merits of these authors are immense, but primarily with respect to a personality psychology that is almost totally subsumed by the psychology of individual differences.

The singling out of fundamental traits and the thorough examination of their biological correlates form the basis for new perspectives of research on mind—body relationships, on the role of heredity, and on the nature of the dialogue between organism and environment. However, some central themes of personality psychology remain in the background, such as motivation, the self, and a large part of what defines strategies in person—environment transactions. Thus, Mischel made a good point when he indicated the limits of a psychology of essences which does not account for stability and flexibility of conduct, or for how the situation ends up acting on conduct. When these ideas were published by Mischel (1968), it was the start of a period of crisis in personality psychology.

Crisis and renovation: toward integration

The limits of a psychology of essences are in many respects the limits of a whole conception which ends up renouncing the context-specificity of behaviour, as well as the collection of the eminently subjective properties of psychic functioning and the interweaving of affects and cognitions which explain subjective experience and conduct.

By the late 1960s, the dominant views and core assumptions of personality psychologists were seriously challenged when reviews of the literature showed that, apart from cognitive and intellective dimensions, individuals usually show far less cross-situational consistency in their behaviour than has been assumed by trait theories. Data indicating that response patterns even in highly similar situations frequently failed to be strongly related were used to support the statement that this inconsistency must 'reflect the state of nature and not just the noise of measurement' (Mischel, 1990, p. 113). The challenges to classic dispositional assumptions formed the core of the so-called *person—situation debate*. Far from denying individual differences in personality, the criticisms

> were largely motivated to defend individuality and the uniqueness of each person
> against the tendency, prevalent in 1960s clinical and diagnostic efforts, to use a few
> ratings or few behavioral signs to categorize people into categories on an assessor's
> favorite nomothetic trait dimension. It was common practice to assume in the 1960s
> that such assessments were useful to predict not just 'average' levels of individual
> differences, but a person's specific behavior on specific criteria as well as 'in
> general'. It was not uncommon to undertake decision making about a person's life
> and future on the basis of a relatively limited sampling of personological 'signs' or
> 'trait indicators'. (Mischel, 1990, p. 115).

So the end of the 1960s and the whole of the 1970s were characterized by a debate between those who stated that the paradigm (cf. Kuhn, 1962) traditionally employed in personality psychology was fundamentally inadequate and should be replaced by newer situationist or interactionist conceptualizations, and those who maintained that the essential criticism on the dispositional model was an empirical one, and that the solution therefore should be sought in improvements of the quality of research and not in a paradigmatic shift. The attack was led by Mischel (1968), with, fighting in the front ranks, Magnusson (1976) and Endler (1973; see also Magnusson and Endler, 1977). The defence in the camp under attack was organized by, among others, Block (1977), Epstein (1977, 1979, 1980, 1984), and Bem and Allen (1974). The defenders tried to prevent the threatening scientific revolution (cf. Kuhn, 1962) in several ways.

For instance, Block (1977) stated that a foreclosure on efforts to seek lawfulness based on the results achieved by data derived from standardized, objective tests or laboratory situations was completely premature. According to Block, these so-called T-data (cf. Cattell, 1957) should be better created. In other words, personality psychologists should focus on attempts to achieve technical sophistication of T-research. Epstein (1977, 1979, 1980, 1984), on the other hand, claimed that traits could be alive and well if one employed aggregated multiple observations and measures rather than single instances. Finally, Bem and Allen (1974) revived the moderator variable strategy, earlier propagated by Ghiselli (1963) and Saunders (1956), by proposing to use self-reported consistency as a moderator (for a detailed review of the moderator variable approach, see Schmitt and Borkenau, Chapter 2 in this volume).

Now, looking back at this period of crisis that has elicited a division of opinion ranging from a 'life-giving transfusion' (Kenrick and Funder, 1988, p. 34) to an 'unfortunate era in personality research' (Carson, 1989, p. 229), some conclusions can be drawn. There seems to be some agreement about the lessons that can be learned from the person—situation controversy. Mischel (1990) summarizes this as follows:

> The data available in 1968, like the data over two decades later, do not suggest that useful predictions cannot be made. They also do not imply that different people will not act differently with some consistency in different types of situations. Rather, the data both then and now do suggest that if predictive precision is the goal, the particular classes of conditions or equivalence units have to be taken into account much more carefully and seem to be considerably narrower and more local than traditional trait theories assumed. It should be self-evident that, instead of debating the existence of dispositions, the continuing need is to specify their nature with increasing precision, to determine their organization and structure, and to identify types of if—then, condition—behavior relations that constitute them in particular contexts and populations. (1990, p. 131)

Kenrick and Funder's (1988) related summary statement, that according to Carson (1989) reads like an epitaph, points to the systematic sources of judgmental bias, systematic effects of situations, and systematic interactions between persons and situations that must be explicitly dealt with before one can predict from trait measures. In addition, Kenrick and Funder (1988) subscribe to Epstein's (1977, 1979, 1980, 1984) viewpoint that multiple behavioural observations and multiple observers are a *conditio sine qua non*. Moreover, they subscribe to the viewpoint of Houts, Cook, and Shadish (1986) that personality psychology best progresses through what they call *critical multiplism*; that is, through multiple and mutually critical attempts to understand the same problem. According to Houts *et al.* (1986), multiplism is based on the premise that no perfect options regarding question generation, research design, data manipulation, and interpretation, etc. exist. As a consequence, the multiplist stance is to implement more than one option in a research study and openly to scrutinize these selections from a wide variety of theoretical perspectives, including overtly antagonistic ones. In this respect, multiplism is fully in line with the shift that has taken place in the philosophy of science away from the *crucial experiment* that distinguishes between theories to a concern with research programmes and traditions (cf. Lakatos, 1978; Laudan, 1977). According to Houts *et al.* (1986, pp. 60−1),

> critical multiplists welcome the multiple investigators, studies, issues, and question frames that arise in research programs. But they also seek to force out and test the shared implicit assumptions of such programs, and they assume that this is more likely to occur the more numerous and intellectually heterogeneous are the outsiders who come to look in on a research program.

Houts *et al.* (1986) admit that such a multiplism could easily degenerate into a counterproductive relativism and epistemological anarchy (cf. Feyerabend, 1975). Therefore, they emphasize that multiplism does not imply equivalent utility. According to them, 'part of what makes critical multiplism critical is knowledge of the evidence in favor of the relative superiority of some options for fulfilling a research task over others. *The dilemma that necessitates multiplism arises from the imperfection of current options and not from their equivalent*' (Houts *et al.*, 1986, p. 70; italics in the original).

In the introductory chapter of their book *Personality Psychology*, with the subtitle *Recent trends and emerging directions*, Buss and Cantor (1989) state that personality psychology nowadays expands in important directions. First, they point to new middle-level units such as (1) script units (Abelson, 1981); (2) intentional units like personal projects (Little, 1983), personal strivings (Emmons, 1986), or life tasks and strategies (Cantor and Kihlstrom, 1987); (3) conditional disposition units (Wright and Mischel, 1987); and (4) social-structural and social role constraints on personality development (Caspi, 1987). Then they point to new forms of personality coherence (such as interactional continuity, Caspi, 1989; life path, Moskowitz and Schwarzman, 1989; life story, McAdams, 1987). In contrast to older conceptualizations of cross-situational and temporal consistency, these coherence approaches sketch not a static but a dynamic view on personality. It speaks for itself that these new middle-level units and these new forms of personality coherence are related to advances in personality assessment. Finally, Buss and Cantor (1989) call attention to two other recent trends (or emerging directions?): (1) the convergence on a five-factor model of personality, and (2) an expansion of the levels of explanation in personality. The latter trend highlights the fact that personality psychologists are expanding their explanatory search. Cognitive psychology, behavioural genetics and evolutionary theory, lifespan development, and social-structural analysis, according to Buss and Cantor (1989), have provided personality research with new directions. That personality psychology should encompass all these levels of explanation is appropriate, according to them, 'for this field is unique among the branches of psychology in its *integrative and wholistic focus*' (Buss and Cantor, 1989, p. 11; italics added).

The five-factor model (extraversion/surgency, agreeableness, conscientiousness, emotional stability, and intellect/openness), initially articulated by Norman (1963), is seen as an *integrative*, heuristic model for personality researchers (Hofstee and Van Heck, 1990; see also Ostendorf and Angleitner, Chapter 4 in this volume; Hofstee and De Raad, Chapter 3 in this volume). Historical reviews of the structural representation of personality descriptors (John, 1990a, 1990b; John, Angleitner and Ostendorf, 1988; Wiggins and Trapnell, in press) demonstrate the generalizability of this five-factor structure. Digman, reviewing the evidence for the 1990 *Annual Review of Psychology*, points at this rapid convergence of views regarding the structure of the concepts of personality (that is, the language of personality), and does not hesitate to call the five-factor model 'a theoretical structure of surprising generality' (Digman, 1990, p. 418). So research on the structure of the trait lexicon has converged considerably. As a result, we now have the beginnings of a consensus regarding the dimensions that should be included if one wishes systematically to sample the personality domain (Hogan, 1987; McCrae and Costa, 1987).

The integrative role of personality psychology is also stressed by Pervin (1990, p. 726):

> What is distinctive about personality is the focus on the person as a system, thereby involving the interplay between consistency and diversity, stability and change, and *integration* and conflict, as well as the study of people in a variety of contexts and over a long enough time period for patterns to emerge, in their private world of thought and feeling as well as in their public behaviors. (italics added).

This statement by Pervin summarizes in one sentence the major trends in present-day personality psychology.

First, there is a growing tendency to adopt a theoretical perspective emphasizing the process of *interaction* between the individual and the environment. According to Mischel (1990) this body of theorizing is cumulative and frankly revisable, not owned by any single theorist or school. Instead, 'it is based . . . on the most promising relevant findings from the diverse fields on which a comprehensive scientific attempt to understand personality can build. What seems to be evolving is not a single-owner, single-view theory of "what people are like," but a general shared perspective' (Mischel, 1990, p. 116). Magnusson (1990) gives the following three propositions covering the basic view of such an interactional perspective:

1. An individual develops and functions as a total, *integrated* organism.
2. An individual develops and functions in a dynamic, continuous, and reciprocal process of interaction with his or her environment.
3. The characteristic way in which an individual develops and functions, in interaction with the environment, depends on and influences the continuous reciprocal process of interaction among sub*systems* of mental and biological *systems*.

The implications of this are attempts to employ within one and the same research programme (cf. Lakatos, 1978; Laudan, 1977) mentalistic, biological, and environmental models (see Hettema and Kenrick, Chapter 15 in this volume; Magnusson, 1990). Thus, modern personality psychology focuses on information-processing models (for example, Kreitler and Kreitler, Chapter 9 in this volume; for a review see Pervin, 1985) and the relations between cognition, affect, and motivation (for example, Carver and Scheier, 1982; Hettema, 1991; for a review see Pervin, 1985); but also on biological factors (for example, Buss, 1990, 1991; Loehlin and Rowe, Chapter 13 in this volume; Gruzelier and Mecacci, Chapter 14 in this volume), and on the psychology of situations (for example, Forgas and Van Heck, Chapter 16 in this volume; Magnusson, 1981). This multiplism contributes 'to placing the interactional approach within a total perspective' (Magnusson, 1990, p. 194).

In this process towards increasing multiplism, general systems theory (von Bertalanffy, 1962, 1966, 1968) has been introduced into personality psychology by several researchers (for example, Hettema, 1979, 1989; Hettema and Kenrick, Chapter 15 in this volume; Magnusson, 1990; Powell, Royce and Voorhees, 1982). The notion of *open systems* especially has been proven useful in the analysis of the goal-directed nature of organismic functioning. Open systems are responsive to the environment, but also act upon the environment. Characteristic features are: (1) adaptive processes of self-regulation aiming at maintaining a constancy of the internal 'environment' in the face of changing external conditions, and (2) adaptive processes aiming at reducing or eliminating an antagonism between the personality system and the external environment. All these processes involve some sort of complex *interaction*.

According to Pervin (1978), the open system model has profound conceptual and research implications. The most important are an *emphasis on multivariate interaction* (that is, the interaction of many internal and external variabilities) and a concern with the *temporal aspect* of behavioural processes. The consideration of multivariate interactions reflects the conviction that modern personality psychology should keep in focus the *complexity* of the phenomena. The interest in the temporal aspect of behavioural processes has constituted some firm links between personality psychologists and developmental psychologists. According to Collins and Gunnar (1990, p. 387), 'social and personality development research is in the midst of one of the most expansionist periods in its history'. The *Annual Review of Psychology* chapter by Collins and Gunnar (1990) shows, compared with an earlier *Annual Review* chapter (Parke and Asher, 1983), that the range of problems addressed has broadened appreciably. Moreover, in recent years increasing attention is being paid to the collection and analyses of longitudinal data (see, for example, Borkenau, 1992; Magnusson, 1988, 1990). In current studies of the individuals' courses of development, there is also this regard of the complexity of the phenomena. For instance, Magnusson (1990, pp. 216–17) writes: 'In order to understand the lawful patterning of developmental stability and change in individuals by discovering the distinct configurations of psychological and biological factors ... there is a need to cover *a broad spectrum of psychological, biological, and social aspects of individual functioning*' (italics added).

One further aspect of modern personality psychology deserves attention. Personality can be defined in two different ways. These are the perspectives of the observer and the actor. According to Hogan (1987), a great deal of confusion has resulted from the failure to distinguish between these two perspectives. Personality in the first sense refers to a person's social reputation, his or her distinctive social stimulus value; personality in the second sense refers to the intrapsychic factors that explain why actors create their unique reputations. Hogan (1987), quite rightly, points to the fact that, because these two concepts of personality derive from such different realms of experience, data based on these sources will not always converge. Hogan (1987, pp. 85−6) states:

> From the perspective of an actor . . . personality consists of the inner psychological structures, qualities, and characteristics that cause him or her to generate his or her unique reputation. We can speak with some confidence about the parameters of a person's reputation. About the causes of that reputation, however, we must be a good bit more cautious. Causes lie in the domain of *verstehen*, of hermeneutics, of interpretation. This is the great, uncharted frontier of personality psychology; it is the region of the self-concept, of social aspiration and personal despair, of public claims and private reservations, of hopes, doubts, and self-delusion.

The differentiation between these two definitions of personality has major conceptual and research implications. We need methods for predicting meaningful behaviours and methods for explaining why the prediction models work as they do. According to Hogan (1987, p. 87), 'we must systematically mine the latent knowledge of observers while at the same time exploring the intentions of actors as we pursue both prediction and explanation'. Following both paths will increase the complexity of the task of personality psychologists.

The following chapters show how personality psychologists try to deal with the complexity of phenomena in a field that has much wider horizons than some decades ago. Nowadays, personality psychologists are less inclined towards simplification, separation, and reductive thought than before and are more than ever striving at cumulation of knowledge. We feel that present-day personality psychology warrants some optimism regarding the future. *It is now or never!*

References

Abelson, R.P. (1981), 'Psychological status of the script concept', *American Psychologist,* **36**, 715−29.

Allport, G.W. (1937), *Personality: A psychological interpretation*, New York, NY: Holt, Rinehart & Winston.

Bem, D.J. and Allen, A. (1974), 'On predicting some of the people some of the time: the search for cross-situational consistencies in behavior', *Psychological Review, 81,* 506−20.

Block, J. (1977), 'Advancing the science of personality: paradigmatic shift or improving the quality of research?', in D. Magnusson and N.S. Endler (eds.), *Personality at the Crossroads: Current issues in interactional psychology*, Hillsdale, NJ: Erlbaum, pp. 37−63.

Borkenau, P. (ed.) (1992), 'Longitudinal research on personality development' (Special Issue), *European Journal of Personality, 6*(2), 83−176.

Burnham, J.C. (1968), 'Historical background for the study of personality', in E.F. Borgatta and W.W. Lambert (eds.), *Handbook of Personality: Theory and research*, Chicago, IL: McNally, pp. 3−81.

Buss, D.M. (1990), 'Toward a biologically informed psychology of personality', *Journal of Personality*, **58**, 1–16.

Buss, D.M. (1991), 'Evolutionary personality psychology', *Annual Review of Psychology*, **42**, 459–91.

Buss, D.M. and Cantor, N. (eds.) (1989), 'Introduction', in D.M. Buss and N. Cantor (eds.), *Personality Psychology: Recent trends and emerging directions*, New York, NY: Springer-Verlag, pp. 1–12.

Cantor, N. and Kihlstrom, J.F. (1987), *Personality and Social Intelligence*, Englewood Cliffs, NJ: Prentice Hall.

Carson, R.C. (1989), 'Personality', in M.R. Rosenzweig and L.W. Porter (eds.), *Annual Review of Psychology*, Palo Alto, CA: Annual Reviews Inc., vol. 40, pp. 227–48.

Carver, C.S. and Scheier, M.F. (1982), 'Control theory: a useful conceptual framework in personality-social, clinical and health psychology', *Psychological Bulletin*, **92**, 111–35.

Caspi, A. (1987), 'Personality in the life course', *Journal of Personality and Social Psychology*, **53**, 1203–13.

Caspi, A. (1989), 'On the continuities and consequences of personality: a life-course perspective', in D.M. Buss and N. Cantor (eds.), *Personality Psychology: Recent trends and emerging directions*, New York, NY: Springer-Verlag, pp. 85–98.

Cattell, R.B. (1950), *Personality*, New York, NY: McGraw-Hill.

Cattell, R.B. (1957), *Personality and Motivation Structure and Measurement*, Yonkers-on-Hudson, NY: World Book Company.

Collins, W.A. and Gunnar, M.R. (1990), 'Social and personality development', *Annual Review of Psychology*, **41**, 387–416.

Digman, J. (1990), 'Personality structure: emergence of the five-factor model', *Annual Review of Psychology*, **41**, 417–40.

Dilthey, W. (1894), *Ideen über eine beschreibende und zergliedernde Psychologie* [Ideas about a Descriptive and Dissected Psychology], in W. Dilthey (1914), *Gesammelte Schriften* [Collected works], Leipzig: Teubner, vol. 5.

Dollard, J. and Miller, N.E. (1950), *Personality and Psychotherapy*, New York, NY: McGraw-Hill.

Emmons, R.A. (1986), 'Personal strivings: an approach to personality and subjective well-being', *Journal of Personality and Social Psychology*, **51**, 1058–68.

Endler, N.S. (1973), 'The person vs. situation: a pseudo issue?', *Journal of Personality*, **41**, 287–303.

Epstein, S. (1977), 'Traits are alive and well', in D. Magnusson and N.S. Endler (eds.), *Personality at the Crossroads: Current issues in interactional psychology*, Hillsdale, NJ: Erlbaum, pp. 83–98.

Epstein, S. (1979), 'The stability of behavior: I. On predicting most of the people much of the time', *Journal of Personality and Social Psychology*, **37**, 1097–26.

Epstein, S. (1980), 'The stability of behavior: II. Implications for psychological research', *American Psychologists*, **35**, 790–806.

Epstein, S. (1984), 'The stability of behavior across time and situations', in R. Zucker, J. Aronoff, and A.I. Rabin (eds.), *Personality and the Prediction of Behavior*, San Diego, CA: Academic Press, pp. 209–68.

Eysenck, H.J. (1967), *The Biological Basis of Personality*, Springfield, IL: Thomas.

Feyerabend, P.K. (1975), *Against Method: Outline of an anarchistic theory of knowledge*, London: NLB.

Freud, S. (1953ff), *The Complete Psychological Works: Standard edition* (24 vols.), J. Strachey (ed.), London: Hogarth Press.

Ghiselli, E.E. (1963), 'Moderating effects and differential reliability and validity', *Journal of Applied Psychology*, **47**, 81–6.

Gill, M. (ed.), (1967), *Collected Papers of David Rapaport*, New York, NY: Basic Books.

Goldstein, K. (1939), *The Organism*, New York, NY: American Book Co.

Guilford, J.P. (1959), *Personality*, New York, NY: McGraw-Hill.

Guilford, J.P. (1975), 'Factors and factors of personality', *Psychological Bulletin*, **82**, 802−14.

Hettema, P.J. (1979), *Personality and Adaptation*, Amsterdam: North Holland.

Hettema, P.J. (ed.), (1989), *Personality and Environment: The assessment of human adaptation*, Chichester: Wiley.

Hettema, P.J. (1991), 'Emotions and adaptation: an open-systems perspective', in C.D. Spielberger, I.G. Sarason, Z. Kulcsár and G.L. Van Heck (eds.), *Stress and Emotion: Anxiety, anger, and curiosity*, New York, NY: Hemisphere Publishing Corporation, vol. 14, pp. 47−63.

Hofstee, W.K.B. and Van Heck, G.L. (eds.) (1990), 'Personality language' (Special Issue), *European Journal of Personality*, **4**(2).

Hogan, R. (1987), 'Personality psychology: back to basics', in J. Aronoff, A.I. Rabin and R.A. Zucker (eds.), *The Emergence of Personality*, New York, NY: Springer Publishing Company, pp. 79−104.

Houts, A.C., Cook, T.D. and Shadish, W.R. (1986), 'The person−situation debate: a critical multiplist perspective', *Journal of Personality*, **54**, 52−105.

John, O.P. (1990a), 'The "Big-Five" factor taxonomy: dimensions of personality in the natural language and in questionnaires', in L.A. Pervin (ed.), *Handbook of Personality: Theory and research*, New York, NY: Guilford Press, pp. 66−100.

John, O.P. (1990b), 'The search for basic dimensions of personality: a review and critique', in P. McReynolds, J.C. Rosen and G.J. Chelune (eds.), *Advances in Psychological Assessment*, New York, NY: Plenum Press, vol. 7, pp. 1−37.

John, O.P., Angleitner, A. and Ostendorf, F. (1988), 'The lexical approach to personality: a historical review of trait taxonomic research', *European Journal of Personality*, **2**, 171−203.

Kelly, G.A. (1985), *The Psychology of Personal Constructs*, New York, NY: Norton, vols. 1 and 2.

Kenrick, D.T. and Funder, D.C. (1988), 'Profiting from controversy: lessons from the person−situation debate', *American Psychologist*, **43**, 23−34.

Kuhn, T.S. (1962), *The Structure of Scientific Revolutions*, Chicago, IL: University of Chicago Press.

Lakatos, I. (1970), 'Falsification and the methodology of scientific research programs', in L. Lakatos and A. Musgrave (eds.), *Criticism and the Growth of Knowledge*, Cambridge: Cambridge University Press, pp. 91−196.

Lakatos, I. (1978), *The Methodology of Scientific Research Programs*, Cambridge: Cambridge University Press.

Laudan, L. (1977), *Progress and its Problems: Towards a theory of scientific growth*, Berkeley, CA: University of California Press.

Lewin, K. (1935), *A Dynamic Theory of Personality*, New York, NY: McGraw-Hill.

Lewin, K. (1951), *Field Theory in Social Science: Selected theoretical papers*, New York, NY: Harper & Brothers.

Little, B.R. (1983), 'Personal projects: a rationale and method for investigation', *Environment and Behavior*, **15**, 273−309.

McAdams, D.P. (1987), 'A life-story model of identity', in R. Hogan and W.H. Jones (eds.), *Perspectives in Personality*, Greenwich, CT: JAI Press, vol. 2, pp. 15−50.

McCrae, R.R. and Costa, P.T., Jr. (1987), 'Validation of the five-factor model of personality across instruments and observers', *Journal of Personality and Social Psychology*, **52**, 81−90.

McDougall, W. (1926), *An Introduction to Social Psychology*, London: Methuen.

Magnusson, D. (1976), 'The person and the situation in an interactional model of behavior', *Scandinavian Journal of Psychology*, **17**, 81−96.

Magnusson, D. (ed.) (1981), *Toward a Psychology of Situations: An interactional perspective*, Hillsdale, NJ: Erlbaum.
Magnusson, D. (1988), *Individual Development from an Interactional Perspective. Vol. 1*, Hillsdale, NJ: Erlbaum.
Magnusson, D. (1990), 'Personality development from an interactional perspective', in L.A. Pervin (ed.), *Handbook of Personality: Theory and research*, New York, NY: Guilford Press, pp. 193–222.
Magnusson, D. and Endler, N.S. (1977), *Personality at the Crossroads: Current issues in interactional psychology*, Hillsdale, NJ: Erlbaum.
Maslow, A.H. (1954), *Motivation and Personality*, New York, NY: Harper.
Meehl, P. (1978), 'Theoretical risks and tabular asterisks: Sir Karl, Sir Ronald and the slow progress of soft psychology', *Journal of Consulting and Clinical Psychology*, **46**, 806–34.
Mischel, W. (1968), *Personality and Assessment*, New York, NY: Wiley.
Mischel, W. (1990), 'Personality dispositions revisited and revised: a view after three decades', in L.A. Pervin (ed.), *Handbook of Personality: Theory and research*, New York, NY: Guilford Press, pp. 111–34.
Moskowitz, D.S. and Schwartzman, A.E. (1989), 'Life paths of aggressive and withdrawn children', in D.M. Buss and N. Cantor (eds.), *Personality Psychology: Recent trends and emerging directions*, New York, NY: Springer-Verlag, pp. 99–114.
Murphy, G. (1947), *Personality: A biosocial approach to origins and structure*, New York, NY: Harper.
Murray, H.A. (1938), *Explorations in Personality*, New York, NY: Oxford University Press.
Norman, W. (1963), 'Toward an adequate taxonomy of personality attributes: replicated factor structures in peer nomination personality ratings', *Journal of Abnormal and Social Psychology*, **66**, 574–83.
Parke, R.D. and Asher, S.R. (1983), 'Social and personality development', *Annual Review of Psychology*, **34**, 465–509.
Pervin, L.A. (1978), 'Individual–environment interaction', in L.A. Pervin and M. Lewis (eds.), *Perspectives in Interactional Psychology*, New York, NY: Plenum Press, pp. 67–85.
Pervin, L.A. (1985), 'Personality: Current controversies, issues, and directions', *Annual Review of Psychology*, **36**, 83–114.
Pervin, L.A. (1990), 'A brief history of modern personality theory', in L.A. Pervin (ed.), *Handbook of Personality: Theory and research*, New York, NY: Guilford Press, pp. 3–18.
Popper, K.R. (1959), *The Logic of Scientific Discovery*, London: Hutchinson.
Popper, K.R. (1969), *Conjectures and Refutations*, London: Routledge & Kegan Paul.
Powell, A., Royce, J.R. and Voorhees, B. (1982), 'Personality as a complex information-processing system', *Behavioral Science*, **27**, 338–76.
Rogers, C.R. (1961), *On Becoming a Person*, Boston, MA: Houghton Mifflin.
Sanford, N. (1963), 'Personality: its place in psychology', in S. Koch (ed.), *Psychology: A study of a science*, New York, NY: McGraw-Hill, vol. 5, pp. 488–592.
Saunders, D.R. (1956), 'Moderator variables in prediction', *Educational and Psychological Measurement*, **16**, 209–22.
Sears, R.R. (1950), 'Personality', *Annual Review of Psychology*, **1**, 105–18.
Spinoza, B. (1677), *Ethica*, Amsterdam: Rieuwertz. (Dutch transl. N. Van Suchtelen, Amsterdam, Wereldbibliotheek, 1979).
Stagner, R. (1937), *Psychology of Personality*, New York, NY: McGraw-Hill.
Von Bertalanffy, L. (1962), 'General systems theory: a critical review', *General Systems*, **7**, 1–20.
Von Bertalanffy, L. (1966), 'General systems theory and psychiatry', in S. Arieti (ed.), *American Handbook of Psychiatry*, New York, NY: Basic Books, vol. 3, pp. 705–21.
Von Bertalanffy, L. (1968), *General Systems Theory: Foundations, development, applications*, New York, NY: Braziller.

Werner, H. (1948), *Comparative Psychology of Mental Development*, Chicago, IL: Follett.

Wiggins, J.S. and Trapnell, P.D. (in press), 'Personality structure: the return of the Big Five', in S.R. Briggs, R. Hogan and W.H. Jones (eds.), *Handbook of Personality Psychology*, Orlando, FL: Academic Press.

Wright, J.C. and Mischel, W. (1987), 'A conditional approach to dispositional constructs: the local predictability of social behavior', *Journal of Personality and Social Psychology*, **53**, 1159–77.

Part II
Dispositional Models

2/ The consistency of personality

Manfred Schmitt
University of Trier, Germany

Peter Borkenau
University of Bielefeld, Germany

Introduction

Suppose someone asks us to describe our personality, the personality of a friend, or the difference between our and our friend's personality. Very probably we will use trait concepts to answer this question. We may describe ourselves and others as intelligent, friendly, helpful, creative, honest, orderly, sociable, talkative, anxious, and so forth. Yet how do we know that someone is intelligent, friendly, helpful, etc.? In contrast to physical properties such as sex, eye-colour, or height, psychological characteristics like the ones mentioned cannot be directly observed. If we merely see persons, we cannot confidently know how honest, intelligent, or creative they are. Rather, we need concrete behavioural information that we consider relevant for these traits. For example, if someone comes up with an unusual solution for a difficult problem, we may perceive him or her as a creative or intelligent person. Inferring psychological traits from observable behaviours is common for both lay people and scientists. It serves two major purposes: the prediction of behaviour and the parsimonious description of individuals.

Prediction of behaviour

Trait concepts imply behavioural continuity or stability (Chaplin *et al.*, 1988). If John laughs and jokes a lot on some days but not on others, and if no reason for this variability in behaviour can be identified, we would hardly say that 'John is a cheerful person'. Rather, we would state that 'Sometimes, John is in a cheerful mood.' By contrast, if John laughs and jokes whenever we see him, we would infer from the stability of his behaviour that he is a cheerful person and that he will laugh and joke in the future as well. Moreover, we can infer conditional stability if John's behaviour depends systematically on the situation. This is so if some situations are 'more difficult' than others; for example, we may appropriately describe John as cheerful although he jokes at parties but not at funerals.

Parsimonious description of individuals

Describing individuals by listing hundreds of specific behaviours would be very inefficient. Even though we sometimes describe others in terms of specific behaviours (for example, 'Paul collects stamps'), we usually try to eliminate redundancy by searching for similarities among specific behaviours. We come up with a smaller set of traits, each of which comprises several specific behaviours. For example, we consider persons to be friendly if they greet others, listen if somebody speaks to them, do not interrupt ongoing conversations, and bring gifts when visiting friends. Since any abstraction necessarily implies a loss of information, traits that comprise related but different behaviours have to be probabilistic concepts. For example, friendly persons are more likely than unfriendly persons to greet acquaintances, but greeting acquaintances is not a *conditio sine qua non* for being appropriately described as friendly.

Traits that are inferred from various observable behaviours are summary constructs and dispositional constructs (Alston, 1975; Buss and Craik, 1983; Hirschberg, 1978). The summary view implies that friendly persons have more frequently displayed the above-mentioned behaviours in the past than unfriendly persons. The dispositional view implies that, under appropriate circumstances, friendly persons are more likely than unfriendly persons to display these behaviours in the future as well. Neither summary nor dispositional statements imply any causal relations between the trait and its behavioural indicators, although unknown psychological (or biological) causes for the covariation among behaviours are likely to exist. Factors (in the factor-analytic sense) are versions of such summary statements that are identified by algebraic routines. They are hypothetical latent variables that are derived from correlations among manifest variables. They are statistical concepts that allow us to describe individual differences objectively and parsimoniously. But they do not explain the observed individual differences in behaviour.

If trait concepts have been generated by lay people and scientists to predict individuals and to describe them parsimoniously, which criteria can be used to establish the stability of behaviour and the similarity among behaviours that constitute a trait? The questions are closely related to each other, and they are core issues in the study of individual differences from a trait perspective.

Stability of personality

Suppose we want to know whether somebody is consistently helpful; that is, a helpful person. There seems to be an easy way to figure this out: to address the same request for help to the person repeatedly. Let us assume we ask a person twice to donate money to some charity. If the person gives the same amount of money on both occasions, we would have a case of perfect intra-individual stability of behaviour. Nevertheless, we could not be sure that the person's true helpfulness has remained constant. Imagine that the person has lost his or her job in the meantime. Due to shortage of money, his or her behaviour at Time 2 would be more altruistic than his or her behaviour at Time 1. The stability of this person's behaviour may then reflect changes in personal dispositions. Maybe the person has developed a stronger motivation to help due to the experience of loss, and this experience has raised his or her empathy with needy persons and general inclination to help (Batson and Oleson, 1992; Hoffman, 1981). Thus we have to distinguish between the stability of behaviour and the stability of personality (McCrae and Costa, 1984).

Consistency of personality

A similar problem arises if we want to decide which behaviours belong together; that is, which indicators are functionally equivalent regarding a particular trait. Suppose we want to know how general the disposition to help is. In order to investigate this question, we could expose persons to different situations in which their help is required. We could ask them, for instance: (1) to donate bone marrow for a patient suffering from leukemia, and (2) to help strangers find their way on a city map. Let us suppose a person does not comply with the first request but helps in the second situation. Can we infer from this observation that the person has no generalized disposition to help? We cannot, as virtually all behaviours have multiple causes. Providing help in a particular situation depends not only on one's specific motivation to help, but on other factors as well. For example, whereas the costs of helping are very high in Situation 1, they are rather low in Situation 2. Since willingness to help depends, among other things, on the costs of helping (Seibold, 1975), the data remain ambiguous concerning how generalized the disposition to help is. Perhaps the person found it too difficult, too costly, or too dangerous to help in Situation 1 despite a strong feeling of obligations to donate one's bone marrow. Phrased in psychometric terms, this would mean that the difficulty of Situation 1 on the latent altruism dimension was higher than the person's trait level on that dimension. This interpretation is perfectly consistent with the assumption that willingness to help is a generalized disposition.

However, the behavioural pattern observed could also mean that the motivation to help is domain-specific and does not generalize across different kinds of helping behaviour. Thus we have to distinguish between the consistency of behaviour and the consistency of personality (Funder and Colvin, 1991).

The more general message from both the stability example and the consistency example is that situational variability of behaviour is perfectly compatible with the notion of broad personal dispositions. This is even more obvious in cases where the unit of measurement changes across relevant behaviours. It is not possible, for example, to compare the amount of dollars given to some charity with the number of phone calls made to raise money for the same purpose. For these reasons, absolute intra-individual stability of behaviour across time and absolute intra-individual consistency of behaviour across situations are not useful criteria on which to evaluate the consistency of personality and the appropriateness of trait concepts. Rather, more appropriate standards have to be identified to determine the stability and consistency of personality.

Relative consistency

The most widespread solution to this problem is to compare several individuals and to check the stability of inter-individual differences in behaviour across time, across situations, and across behavioural manifestations. But before we begin to elaborate this, we simplify our terminology. Because most of our arguments apply to all three types of consistency, we will not always distinguish between temporal stability, cross-situational consistency, and cross-modal consistency. Rather we use the term *consistency* in a generic sense to refer to all three varieties of trait-like patterns of behaviour.

Relative consistency of, for example, pro-social behaviour implies that the *differences* between individuals in their helping behaviour should remain constant across time, across situations, and across behavioural manifestations. This does not imply that occasions and situations have no impact on behaviour. Rather, these factors should affect the behaviour of all individuals in the same way. Phrased in analysis-of-variance terms, the main effects of persons and of situations are fully consistent with the notion of relative consistency, whereas interactions between persons and situations are not. Thus the finding of situational main effects is irrelevant for the viability of dispositional constructs.

The most frequently used measure of relative consistency (Magnusson and Endler, 1977a; Wohlwill, 1973) is the Pearson correlation coefficient. It is an appropriate measure of consistency whenever the effects of situations, occasions, and types of measurement on means and variances are irrelevant. This is true of most psychological applications. Moreover, different behavioural indicators of the same trait are often measured on arbitrary scales with different units of measurement, and thus differences in means cannot be interpreted (Herrmann, 1980). Perfect relative consistency of a particular behavioural measure exists whenever its auto-correlation across time, situations, or modes of behaviour is unity; that is, the differences between individuals are exactly the same on each of the (z-standardized) variables. In contrast, a correlation of less than 1.00 implies an interaction of persons and either situations, occasions, or types of measurement.

Individual consistency

Sometimes we want to investigate the consistency of individuals without using other individuals as a frame of reference. How can we proceed in such a situation? If we use behavioural measures with known population means and variances, we can standardize the individuals' raw scores and determine their consistency by computing their individual z-score differences, z-score variances, or any derivative of these (Asendorpf, 1990). Otherwise, we have to establish some individual frame of reference in order to decide whether inconsistencies in observed behaviours are true inconsistencies or merely differences in the properties of the measurement instruments — as was the case in the altruism example given above.

In contrast to suggestions by Lamiell (1981), we believe that the best way that such an individual frame of reference can be established is to include more than one source of intra-individual variance. For instance, one may measure different modes of behaviour in different situations. Individual consistency (Magnusson and Endler, 1977a) can then be defined as the profile similarity (for example, correlation) of modes of behaviour across situations (Schmitt, 1989), or of situations across modes of behaviour (Magnusson and Ekehammar, 1978). Individual consistency is then inferred from perfect profile similarity ($r = 1.00$), or from complete absence of any interaction between the two sources of variance under study. For a more extensive description of this approach, the reader is referred to Asendorpf (1991) or Ozer (1986).

Evidence on the stability and consistency of personality

After this discussion of several kinds of consistency, we will now address the actual extent of consistency of personality. Is behaviour stable and consistent enough to warrant trait concepts for the description of individuals and the prediction of behaviour? Given that traits are widely used both in everyday life and in scientific psychology, this question may sound superfluous. It is not. In fact, the consistency of personality is one of the most heatedly debated issues in personality and attitude research (Ajzen, 1987; Amelang and Borkenau, 1984a, 1986; Kenrick and Funder, 1988; Magnusson and Endler, 1977b; West, 1983; Zanna et al., 1982; Zucker et al., 1984). Once again, we distinguish here between stability, cross-situational consistency, and cross-modal consistency.

The longitudinal stability of personality

There is general consensus that the longitudinal stability of personality is substantial (for instance, Conley, 1985; Costa and McCrae, 1980). For example, Olweus (1979) reviewed data sets from 16 studies on the stability of aggressive reaction patterns in males, and found uncorrected stability coefficients for the various measures used in these studies (direct observations, peer ratings and nominations, teacher ratings, clinical ratings) that ranged from 0.22 to 0.80 with an average of 0.55. If these stability coefficients were corrected for unreliability of measurement, they even ranged from 0.26 to 0.98 and their average was 0.68. Thus, the longitudinal stability of personality was substantial. Moreover, Olweus (1979) identified two variables that explain most of the differences among the stability coefficients in these studies. First, the younger the subjects were, the lower were the stability coefficients. Second, there was an inverse relation between the size of stability coefficients and the time interval between the measurements: the shorter the interval in between, the higher was the stability. Both findings are reasonable from a lifespan developmental point of view. Moreover, similar phenomena have been observed in the intelligence and achievement domains (Bloom, 1964; Wilson, 1983).

The cross-situational consistency of personality

A classic study on this issue has been conducted by Hartshorne and May (1928). In an ambitious investigation of moral character in which more than 8,000 subjects were involved, these authors examined the consistency of behaviour among schoolchildren. They arranged various situations in which subjects could act either honestly or dishonestly, and where cases of dishonesty could easily be detected. It is important in the present context that the average correlation among their various tests of honesty was 0.23. Thus the cross-situational consistency of behaviour turned out to be modest at best. But Hartshorne and May must somehow have felt the ambiguity of this finding. At most places, they emphasize the specificity of behaviour, arguing, for instance, 'that honesty or dishonesty is not a unified character trait in children of the ages studied, but a series of specific responses to specific situations' (Hartshorne *et al.*, 1929, p. 243). At other places, however, they admit some support for a more global concept of honesty as a trait:

> Just as one test is an insufficient and unreliable measure in the case of intelligence, so one test of deception is quite incapable of measuring a subject's tendency to deceive. That is, we cannot predict from what a pupil does on one test what he will do on another. If we use ten tests of classroom deception, however, we can safely predict what a subject will do on the average whenever ten similar situations are presented. (Hartshorne and May, 1928, p. 135)

Despite the interactions between persons and single situations that Hartshorne and May found, act trends in one sample of situations correlated highly with act trends in other samples of situations. Stated differently, the dispositions were much more consistent than the single behaviours. Quite similar results have been reported by Mischel and Peake (1982) for conscientiousness.

A recent study by Funder and Colvin (1991) sheds additional light on this issue. These authors produced videotapes of 140 target persons in three settings and displayed these tapes to independent judges, in such a way that each judge observed each target person in only one of the three settings. The judges then provided independent judgments of the target persons, using the 62-item California Q-set. Thus the judge indicated whether the target persons spoke in a loud voice, behaved in a fearful or timid manner, tried to control the interaction, and so on. Altogether, 186 coefficients of cross-situational consistency were computed that ranged from −0.09 to 0.70 with an average of 0.26 — a figure quite similar to that reported by Hartshorne and May more than 60 years earlier. The interesting finding in Funder and Colvin's (1991) study, however, is that the cross-situational consistency was systematically higher for stylistic items like 'speaks in a loud voice' and 'speaks quickly' than for items that refer to the content of behaviour, like 'asks series of questions' and 'expresses interest in fantasy and daydreams'. Thus the cross-situational consistency of personality differed systematically for various personality domains. Perhaps the evidence in support of the cross-situational consistency of behaviour would be more convincing if the few studies on this issue had focused on extraversion instead of honesty and conscientiousness.

The cross-modal consistency of personality

The cross-modal consistency of personality was first systematically explored by Allport and Vernon (1933) who concluded that 'acts and habits of expression show a certain consistency among themselves' (p. 171). More recently, Borkenau and Liebler (1992) videotaped 100 target persons and confronted one group of judges with the visual information (silent film) and another group of judges with the acoustic information (audiotape). Although no judge had ever met any of the targets before, the ratings by the 'watchers' and the 'listeners' were substantially correlated. This finding indicates some consistency of personality expression across the visual and the acoustic channel. The uncorrected correlations between the ratings by 'watchers' and 'listeners' ranged from −0.20 to 0.40, with a mean of 0.25. When the correlations were corrected for unreliability, the correlations between the ratings by the two groups of judges went up to about 0.35.

In defence of the consistency assumption

From the evidence reported in the last sections, some authors have concluded that the consistency of personality exists only in the eye of the beholder, rather than in the behaviour of the actor. But defendants of the trait approach have argued as follows.

Lessons to be learned from psychometric principles

Critics of the trait approach emphasize the low correlations between single items or single behavioural acts. They often seem to ignore, however, that the size of correlation coefficients depends on at least three influences that attenuate correlations but are irrelevant for the consistency issue: (1) low reliabilities of the variables, (2) differences in the distributions of the correlated variables, and (3) restrictions of range. The impact of these factors is well known in statistics. Thus, they should be taken into account whenever stability and consistency coefficients are evaluated in terms of their empirical support for a trait approach to personality.

Measurement error

Virtually all psychological measures are less than perfectly reliable. If the same measure is taken twice, the observed scores usually differ. The most common solution to this problem is aggregation (Gulliksen, 1950; Lord and Novick, 1968). If several fallible measures of the same phenomenon are combined into a composite score, this composite is more reliable than its constituent elements. Proponents of the trait model have therefore argued that it would only be fair to test the consistency assumption either by using reliable composite scores or by disattenuating correlations among single items for unreliability (for example, Conley, 1984; Epstein, 1979; Epstein and O'Brien, 1985; Fishbein and Ajzen, 1974; Paunonen, 1984; Schmitt *et al.*, 1985).

Heterogeneous distributions

The correlation among variables depends on the shape of their distributions in general and the skewness of their distributions in particular (Carroll, 1961). Only variables with uniform distributions can correlate perfectly and only variables with similar distributions can correlate highly. This is a well-known phenomenon in factor analysis and test construction. If skewness differs substantially between correlated variables, a perfect correlation can never be obtained. Thus items with similar distributions tend to produce difficult factors (Ferguson, 1941). Campbell (1963) has argued that many behavioural inconsistencies reported in the literature are 'pseudo inconsistencies' due to differences in the difficulty of the 'items'.

As an example, Campbell (1963) cites a classic study by LaPierre (1934), who found a very low correspondence between the self-reported social attitudes of personnel working in hotels and restaurants and their relevant overt behaviour. Whereas more than 90 per cent of the subjects claimed that they would not accept Chinese guests in their establishment, a Chinese couple was rejected in only one of 128 places. Not surprisingly, the correlation between self-reported attitudes and overt behaviour was almost zero. Yet, given the highly dissimilar distributions of the variables and almost no variance in one of them, the correlation reached its upper limit. Thus LaPierre's (1934) data do not falsify the assumption that individuals hold trait-like social attitudes towards members of other ethnic groups. This is because the two variables under study were poor measures of this attitude: they had almost no variance and were therefore not useful to distinguish among individuals in terms of their racial attitudes. Raden (1977) has reviewed research on attitude—behaviour consistency and concluded that most studies that report low consistencies are subject to similar problems.

Restriction of range

Another source of low correlations is a restricted range of the levels of behaviour in a sample compared to the population. Most studies on the consistency of behaviour were done on students. Very probably some of the behaviours investigated in these studies varied less in this group due either to social norms or to selection processes. For instance, neatness of dress as a measure of conscientiousness and academic knowledge as a measure of cultural sophistication (Chaplin and Goldberg, 1984) are likely to vary less among college students than in the general population: neatness of dress due to social norms and academic knowledge due to selective admission to college.

Lessons to be learned from factor analysis

Hierarchical common factor models have been suggested for various domains of individual differences to account for the correlational structure among behavioural measures of hypothetical constructs (Amelang and Bartussek, 1990). Figure 2.1 illustrates a hypothetical hierarchical common factor model.

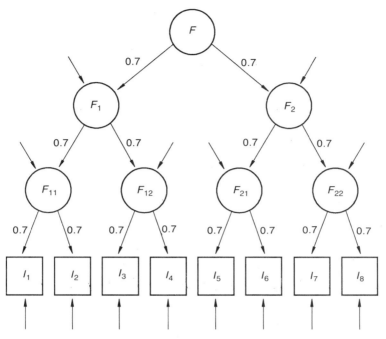

Figure 2.1 Hierarchical factor model with hypothetical loadings

Let us take intelligence as an example — more specifically, Vernon's (1961) structural model of intelligence. In this case, F is a general third-order common factor and represents intelligence as a broad construct. F_1 is a second-order common factor representing verbal-educational intelligence, F_2 is a second-order common factor representing 'kinesthetic-motorial intelligence', and F_{11}, F_{12}, F_{21} and F_{22} are first-order common factors representing lower-level constructs. We assume that each of the first-order factors is measured by two items, referred to in Figure 2.1 as I_1–I_8. For reasons of simplicity, let us assume that all manifest and all latent variables are z-standardized, and that all factor loadings are 0.7. Let us further assume that all residual variables (unique factors) are uncorrelated.

Given these assumptions, we can easily derive the correlations among all manifest variables, among all latent variables, and between all manifest and latent variables (see Table 2.1). The correlation between any two variables in Figure 2.1 is simply the product of the paths that connect them (Wright, 1934). For example, the correlation between I_1 and I_2 is $0.7^2 = 0.49$ because these two variables are connected by two paths. Furthermore, the correlation between F and I_1 is $0.7^3 = 0.34$ because there are three paths between F and I_1. Finally, the correlation between I_1 and I_8 is only 0.12 ($=0.7^6$) because it takes six paths to connect these two variables. Of course, the correlation between any two variables that are connected by only one path is 0.7.

Table 2.1 Correlations (without decimal point) between the manifest indicator variables and latent factors in Figure 2.1 (hypothetical example)

	I_1	I_2	I_3	I_4	I_5	I_6	I_7	I_8	F	F_1	F_2	F_{11}	F_{12}	F_{21}
I_2	49													
I_3	24	24												
I_4	24	24	49											
I_5	12	12	12	12										
I_6	12	12	12	12	49									
I_7	12	12	12	12	24	24								
I_8	12	12	12	12	24	24	49							
F	34	34	34	34	34	34	34	34						
F_1	49	49	49	49	24	24	24	24	70					
F_2	24	24	24	24	49	49	49	49	70	49				
F_{11}	70	70	34	34	17	17	17	17	49	70	34			
F_{12}	34	34	70	70	17	17	17	17	49	70	34	49		
F_{21}	17	17	17	17	70	70	34	34	49	34	70	24	24	
F_{22}	17	17	17	17	34	34	70	70	49	34	70	24	24	49

The proportion of variance of any dependent variable (item, first-order factor, second-order factor) explained by its common factor (first-order factor, second-order factor, third-order factor, respectively) equals 0.49 (0.7^2) because each dependent variable depends on only one common factor directly. Thus, 49 per cent of the variance of the eight manifest variables, the four first-order factors, and the two second-order factors are accounted for by higher-order latent variables or common factors represented in the model. It follows that 51 per cent of the variances of the items as well as the first- and second-order factors are unique and remain unexplained. The correlations derived from the parameters of the model have two important implications.

Functional similarity

First, there is no such thing as *the* consistency of behaviour. Rather, the correlation between two items depends on what might be called their functional similarity. I_1 is more closely related to I_2 than to I_5 because I_1 and I_2 share the same first-order factor F_{11}, whereas I_1 and I_5 share neither a first-order factor nor a second-order factor as common sources of variance. They only have the general factor F in common. In fact, F is the only source of variance common to all items $I_1–I_8$, and all items are parallel measures of F because their loadings on this factor are equal ($0.7^3 = 0.34$). Due to the hierarchical structure of factors in the model, however, the correlations among the manifest variables vary between 0.12 and 0.49.

Prototypicality

Second, there is no such thing as *the* predictability of behaviour from trait measures. One may explain the pattern of correlations in Table 2.1 from the perspective of semantic proximities in general and prototypicality in particular (Buss and Craik, 1983). Prototypicality is a measure of the semantic proximity between an exemplar and a category. For example, Item I_1 may be regarded as a prototypical examplar of those items that measure Factor F_{11}. Hence it correlates substantially with a measure of Factor F_{11}. But Item I_1 is a very untypical examplar of those items that measure Factor F_{21}. Hence a measure of Factor F_{21} would have a low correlation with Item I_1. Finally, all eight items are equally prototypical for the class of all items that measure the general Factor F. But this factor represents a broad construct; items that measure it do not have many attributes in common (Hampson *et al.*, 1986), and the upper limit of prototypicality is quite low (Borkenau and Müller, 1991). Thus items do not correlate highly with measures of the general factor.

Our hypothetical factor model might explain why the consistency controversy lasted that long: consistency and predictability of behaviour are not only a matter of empirical evidence but also a matter of choice. High consistency of behaviour is found if behaviours from the same specific psychological domain are compared (Jackson and Paunonen, 1985). By contrast, low behavioural consistency is found if behaviours from different specific domains within a highly general domain are compared (Mischel and Peake, 1982). Similarly, single acts are poorly predicted either from measures of very broad constructs or from measures of narrow but psychologically distant constructs (Ajzen and Fishbein, 1977; Buss and Craik, 1983; Fishbein and Ajzen, 1974).

The consistency debate was primarily concerned with two questions: (1) how consistent behaviour is, and (2) how useful the trait model is to describe individual differences and to predict behaviour. Considering the implications of the hierarchical factor model, both questions seem not to be well chosen. Rather, empirical investigations should identify differences between behavioural items in terms of their stability, their consistency, and their correlations with other behavioural items. Afterwards, it may be decided which behavioural items can be combined into a trait construct and used as measures of this construct. Researchers like Eysenck (Eysenck and Eysenck, 1969) who emphasize parsimony and therefore search for a small set of very broad trait constructs have to accept both: (1) low average correlations among behavioural indicators of their trait constructs, and (2) a poor prediction of behaviour from measures of their traits (Mershon and Gorsuch, 1988). By contrast, psychologists who are interested in a strong prediction of single behaviours will prefer a different solution to the bandwidth/fidelity dilemma (cf. Cronbach, 1970): they will prefer narrow constructs (for example, Zuckerman, 1977), resulting in a large set of different traits to account for the numerous aspects of individual differences in behaviour.

Multi-determination

Factor-analytic research is not only useful for grouping behaviours into more or less homogeneous sets, thereby suggesting and testing hierarchical factor models. Factor-analytic research is also helpful to investigate whether a particular behaviour depends on various hypothetical factors or latent variables. In fact, this is a highly reasonable assumption as virtually all behaviours have multiple determinants (Ahadi and Diener, 1989). Consequently, a particular behaviour may indicate more than one trait (Borkenau, 1986, 1988). The factor model in Figure 2.1 does not account for this idea. It represents only one (broad) construct and accounts for 49 per cent of the total variance of the items.

The remaining (residual) variance, however, need not only reflect random measurement error. Rather, the 51 per cent unique variances are likely to reflect random error plus systematic but specific variance that is not accounted for by the common factors in Figure 2.1. Longitudinal research is one strategy to distinguish between error variance and systematic but specific variance. If the stability coefficients of the items exceeded 0.49, we would know that the residual variances contain systematic variance in addition to error variance. This, however, would point to rather than solve a problem, because a psychological explanation of the specific variance would still be needed. One solution to this problem might be to extend the model; that is, to introduce additional constructs. Another solution might be to allow for additional paths in the model. The choice of additional constructs or additional paths should reflect substantive theoretical reasoning. By means of confirmatory factor analysis (Jöreskog and Sörbom, 1988), one could then test whether the more comprehensive model does indeed account for more variance of the items.

Consider the following example, suggested by Ehrlich (1969). The decision of white male clients to see or not to see a black female medical doctor is probably a good indicator of their attitude toward black people. A measure of this attitude might predict individual differences in the behaviour at issue above chance level. Quite certainly, however, this prediction would not be perfect because there may be other reasons as well to decide for or against black female physicians. Perhaps the decision also depends on other attitudes, maybe towards women or towards medical treatment in general. Last but not least, personality traits like neuroticism or, more specifically, hypochondria may also be important. If these hypotheses could be confirmed, the decision to see or not to see a black female physician could serve as an indicator of various constructs: attitude toward black people, attitude toward women, attitude toward medical treatment, neuroticism, and hypochondria.

Concerning the consistency controversy, two important lessons can be learned from this example. First, the poor prediction of single acts from one trait measure does not disprove the validity and usefulness of the trait approach *per se*. Rather, it may reflect the fact that behaviours depend on multiple factors. In this case, the behaviour can be used as an (imperfect) indicator or measure of each of these factors. Second, research on the correlational structure and predictability of behaviour should be conducted in as multivariate a fashion as possible. Obviously, this is neither a new insight nor a new claim (for example, Cattell, 1946). But it seems to have been overlooked or ignored by some who challenged the trait approach during the consistency debate.

Individual differences in consistency: the moderator variable approach

The statistical, psychometric, and factor-analytic arguments discussed in the last section rely on the assumption that traits are universal constructs. Thus, it is assumed that the consistency coefficients found in a subject sample apply to all other samples as well — and ultimately to each individual in the population. Similarly, the parameters of factor models — that is, factor loadings, residual variances, and factor correlations — are assumed to apply to each individual — even though they were estimated from group statistics. Ultimately, this implies that trait constructs should be equally useful to describe all persons, and that the same behaviours can be subsumed under the same trait construct for all individuals.

This assumption has been attacked repeatedly in the history of personality research, most notably by Gordon Allport (1937). This author emphasized that individuals differ not only in the degree to which they show common traits, but also in terms of which traits are even relevant. 'Strictly speaking, no two persons ever have precisely the same trait. Though each of two men may be *aggressive* (or *esthetic*), the style and range of the aggression (or estheticism) in each case is noticeably different' (Allport, 1937, p. 297). Allport's definition of personality traits makes allowance for this notion. He defines a trait as a 'generalized and focalized neuropsychic system (peculiar to the individual), with the capacity to render many stimuli functionally equivalent, and to initiate and guide consistent (equivalent) forms of adaptive and expressive behavior' (Allport, 1937, p. 295). Thus, each individual may have his or her idiosyncratic equivalence classes of situations and behaviours. Consequently, Allport criticized the use of factor analysis (Allport, 1961, p. 331) because it presumes that all dimensions are equally useful for describing each individual, and that individual differences are appropriately accounted for by different factor scores on the same set of underlying dimensions (see Eysenck and Eysenck, 1980, for this view). Taking Allport's perspective, the cross-situational consistency coefficients reported, for example, by Hartshorne and May (1928) are not particularly meaningful. 'The low correlations between the tests employed prove only that children are not consistent *in the same way*, not that they are inconsistent with *themselves*' (Allport, 1937, p. 250). By this he meant that a particular behaviour may serve various traits, the traits being more stable than cross-situational correlations indicate:

> It may be that child A steals pennies because he has a consistent personal trait of *bravado* based upon his admiration for the gangsters he reads about in the tabloids and sees on the screen; child B steals because he has a persistent interest in tools and mechanics that drives him to buy more equipment than he can honestly afford; child C, suffering from a gnawing *feeling of social inferiority*, steals pennies to purchase candy to buy his way into favor with his playmates. Child D does not steal pennies, but he lies about his cheating, not because he has a general trait of dishonesty, but because he has a general trait of *timidity* (fear of consequences); child E lies because

he is afraid of hurting the feelings of the teacher whom he adores; child F lies because he is *greedy for praise*. Each of these children behaved as he did toward these tests, not because he had specific habits, but because he had some deep-lying and characteristic trait. (Allport, 1937, pp. 251–2)

Thus Allport suggested that it is not situational factors that account for the low cross-situational consistency of particular behaviours. Rather, in this passage he is claiming that persons are consistent with themselves, and implying that such consistency is what enables others — acquaintances and psychologists alike — to predict their behaviour from knowledge of their individual dispositions. Cross-situational consistency estimates, however, presume that all subjects do possess exactly the same trait, albeit to different degrees.

Furthermore, Allport points out that there may be qualitatively important mismatches between subjects' actual traits and the trait conjectured by the investigator; these will, of course, tend to reduce the apparent consistency of personality.

The error of probing for consistency in the wrong place (and failing to find it, pronouncing in favor of specificity) has been likened by G.B. Watson to the absurdity of asking whether a person using the public library has a trait causing him to take out only books with red or with blue covers. Of course he hasn't. If only the bindings were studied, no consistency should be expected. But if the *subject-matter* of the chosen books was investigated, well-organized traits of interest would appear. (Allport, 1937, p. 256)

And concerning the problem of misinterpreting individual traits as situational specificity, he stated: 'Statistical methods are ordinarily applied only to those variables to which all people may be ordered. If many people do not happen to fit the variable then the illusion of specificity results' (Allport, 1937, p. 256).

A second line of research that challenges the general trait model dates back to the 1950s and was first concerned with individual differences in the predictability of achievement behaviour. Frederiksen and Melville (1954) found that the prediction of academic success from academic interests was better for non-compulsive students than for compulsive students. Although this particular finding could not be replicated in later research (Frederiksen and Gilbert, 1960), it gave rise to the general idea of individual differences in predictability. Depending on the problem under study, the issue has been termed *differential predictability* (Frederiksen and Melville, 1954), *differential reliability* (Ghiselli, 1963), *differential validity* (Amelang and Bartussek, 1971), *differential testability* (Jäger, 1978), *differential stability* (Montada and Schmitt, 1982), and *differential scalability* (Lanning, 1988). These concepts are equivalent in a formal sense: correlations and effect parameters like factor loadings or regression coefficients are no longer considered to be constants, but to vary between individuals or subject samples (Cleary, 1966), and to covary with other variables — so-called moderator variables (Ghiselli, 1963; Saunders 1956; see also Hofstee and De Raad, Chapter 3 in this volume). In the example given above, compulsiveness moderates the correlation between academic interest and academic achievement.

Phrased in analysis-of-variance terms, compulsiveness and academic interest exert an *interaction effect* on academic achievement.

In the context of the debate on the consistency of personality, the basic assumption underlying the moderator variables approach was rediscovered and advanced by several authors (such as Alker, 1972; Bem, 1972). These authors argued that it would be wrong to dismiss the trait approach before trying to refine it. The refinement they had in mind reflected their assumption that some individuals may be more consistent than others. Consequently, trait concepts would be more adequate for the description of some people, and the predictability of behaviour from trait measures would be better for these individuals than for others.

Prediction of individual differences in consistency

One way to refine the trait approach is to develop measures of individual consistency and to use them as moderator variables. In a study that has become a classic, Bem and Allen (1974) proposed two measures of consistency, a self-report measure and an objective index of behavioural variability across situations. These measures of consistency were used to predict individual differences in predictability for two traits, friendliness and conscientiousness. Several measures of each of these traits were used: (1) a cross-situation behavior survey (CSBS), a personality inventory consisting of 86 items, 24 for friendliness, 23 for conscientiousness, and the remaining 39 for other personality traits; (2) the subjects' self-ratings for friendliness and conscientiousness on simple adjective rating scales (for example, 'In general, how friendly and outgoing are you?'); (3) ratings by parents and peers on similar adjective rating scales; and (4) observations of several behaviours that presumably indicated friendliness or conscientiousness — for example, the frequency and duration of a subject's talking in a group discussion was used as an indicator for friendliness.

Self-reported consistency as a moderator

To measure individual consistency via self-report, Bem and Allen (1974) asked their subjects 'How much do you vary from one situation to another in how friendly and outgoing you are?' and 'How much do you vary from one situation to another in how conscientious you are?' As expected, the correlations among the various measures for friendliness were higher for those subjects who described themselves as more cross-situationally consistent than for those who reported that their friendliness would differ widely from situation to situation. The corresponding item for conscientiousness, however, failed to moderate the correlations among the various measures of conscientiousness. Several attempts to replicate and to extend these findings (for example, Borkenau, 1981; Chaplin, 1991; Chaplin and Goldberg, 1984; Mischel and Peake, 1982; Paunonen and Jackson, 1985; Zuckerman *et al.*, 1988) yielded mixed results. In some but not all of these studies, moderator effects of self-rated consistency on actual consistency and predictability were found, but even if moderator effects were found they were small (see Schmitt, 1990a; Zuckerman *et al.*, 1989, for reviews).

Furthermore, self-rated consistency was found in some studies to correlate poorly or not at all with objective measures of intra-individual consistency (Borkenau, 1981; Chaplin and Goldberg, 1984; Paunonen and Jackson, 1985). This low validity of self-reports of consistency is not surprising, given that the single items are very unreliable and thus distinguish poorly between consistent and inconsistent subjects (Borkenau, in press; Schmitt, 1992). Some authors have tried to solve this problem by aggregating self-rated consistency across various traits and then using the more reliable composite measure of consistency as a moderator of the correlations among several indicators of a specific trait. This procedure seems reasonable given that consistency measures for different traits correlate positively among each other (Amelang and Borkenau, 1981; McFarland and Sparks, 1985), suggesting that consistency is not strictly trait-specific but may be a generalized trait itself (Schmitt, 1990a). But whereas the aggregation of consistency ratings for different traits solves the reliability problem, it creates another one. For reasons explained in the section on hierarchical factor models, a measure of general consistency will probably be a less powerful moderator for a specific trait than an equally reliable measure of trait-specific consistency.

Another reason for the low validity of self-rated consistency in these studies may be that the subjects were not told which situations to compare when judging their cross-situational variability in behaviour. But if subjects select the relevant situations themselves, situational differences may be confounded with individual differences. Some subjects may choose situations that differ widely in difficulty. Consider the two kinds of pro-social behaviour given above. Subjects who choose the two situations 'donating bone marrow' and 'helping a stranger find his way on a city map' would probably infer a higher variability of their pro-social behaviour than subjects who choose two very similar situations. Yet in this case, the difference between the two subjects in their self-rated consistency would reflect differences in the situations that are imagined and compared rather than differences in cross-situational consistency of their pro-social behaviour.

Schmitt (1990b, 1990c) attempted to solve this problem for the attitude domain. He constructed a self-report scale to measure individual differences in relative consistency. The questionnaire consisted of twelve items that loaded on three moderately correlated factors: (1) centrality of consistency, (2) independence from situational factors, and (3) stability of attitudes. To assess the centrality of consistency, subjects were asked how much their behaviour depended on their attitudes. To assess their independence from situational factors, subjects were asked to indicate the extent to which situational constraints kept them from behaving in agreement with their attitudes. Finally, the stability of attitudes was assessed by asking the subjects how stable their attitudes were across time.

The three scales had acceptable internal consistencies of above 0.8. In two correlational studies of social responsibility and helping behaviour (Montada *et al.*,

1986, 1991), their construct validity was checked by comparing the subjects' self-reports with the actual consistency of their behaviour. Unfortunately, the consistency measures turned out to be invalid. For example, self-reported centrality of consistency did not moderate the correlation between pro-social attitudes and pro-social behaviour. Furthermore, self-reported stability of attitudes did not correlate with the stability of pro-social attitudes and norms over periods of 9 and 18 months, and it also did not correlate with the actual stability of voting behaviour in two subsequent federal elections (*Bundestagswahlen*). Finally, independence from situational factors did not moderate the relationship between anticipated costs of helping and the actual extent of helping.

Thus it may be concluded from the various studies on the construct validity of self-ratings of consistency that these measures do not distinguish among individuals in terms of whether or not they show trait-like consistencies of behaviour, and whether or not their behaviour can be predicted from trait measures.

Objective measures of consistency

As a second and more objective measure of behavioural consistency, Bem and Allen (1974) computed for each individual his or her variance across the CSBS-items for friendliness or conscientiousness, and divided this variance term by the subject's variance across all 86 CSBS-items. In Bem and Allen's study, this so-called *ipsatized variance index* moderated the correlations among the various measures of conscientiousness but not those among the various measures of friendliness. Bem and Allen (1974, p. 515) claim that their ipsatized variance index 'reflects the degree to which an individual "extracts" the particular trait-scale items from the total pool of items and "clusters" them into an equivalence class'. But the denominator of the fraction contains not only the subjects' cross-situational variability within each trait, but also systematic intra-individual differences between these traits, the latter being not at all relevant for the consistency issue. Despite this problem, the ipsatized variance index has been used in various subsequent studies to replicate Bem and Allen's (1974) findings. Some authors have also used the simple intra-individual variance across the items of the same scale. This measure seems to represent the notion of within-trait variability more closely. Furthermore, some authors have suggested various kinds of profile similarity coefficient to measure individual consistency (for example, Lanning, 1988; Schmitt, 1989; Tal, 1987; Tellegen, 1988).

Research on the moderating effect of these individual consistency measures on *relative* consistency and predictability is not tautological because the formal definitions of intra-individual and relative consistency are algebraically dependent only under very special but unlikely conditions (cf. Asendorpf, 1990; Schmitt, 1990a, 1992). Rather, research on the moderating effects of objective measures of intra-individual consistency tells us how apt they are to differentiate individuals or groups in terms of how well their behaviour fits a general trait model. Schmitt (1990a) has summarized this research and concluded that objective measures of individual consistency do not perform much better than subjective measures. The average moderator effects reported in the literature are either small, non-significant, or even non-existent (Chaplin and Goldberg, 1984; Paunonen and Jackson, 1985).

It is still unclear, however, whether the poor performance of objective measures of consistency is due to a lack of reliability. This would not be surprising because these measures reflect differences or composites of differences between correlated variables, and the reliability of differences has an inverse relation to the correlations among the original variables (Cronbach and Furby, 1970). Unfortunately, most authors either did not investigate the reliability of their consistency measures or did not report it. There is at least one study, however, that directly addressed this issue. Schmitt (1988) investigated the reliability of various profile similarity measures for objective individual consistency. He found very low reliability coefficients, rarely exceeding values of 0.50 and usually with a size of about 0.30. Furthermore, traditional research on response variability (Cattell, 1943; Fiske and Rice, 1955) and person reliability (Goldberg, 1978; Holden *et al.*, 1985) has revealed a rather low reliability of the variability measures that were used in this kind of research (see Schmitt, 1990a, for a review). To summarize, both subjective and objective measures of individual consistency did not identify the more consistent people, who are described more accurately by trait terms and whose behaviour can be more precisely predicted from measures of traits. Whereas subjective measures of consistency seem to lack validity even when their reliability is sufficient, objective measures of individual consistency seem to suffer from a lack of reliability. This hypothesis is not yet well confirmed, however, and needs to be addressed more systematically in future research.

Explaining individual differences in consistency

The successful prediction of individual differences in consistency would demonstrate that the general trait model can be refined and improved, resulting in stronger predictions of behaviour. But it would be theoretically more interesting to know about psychological explanations for individual differences in consistency. A general answer to this question cannot be expected, because the consistency assumption of the trait model refers to all kinds of manifest trait indicator; that is, to overt behaviour, to self-ratings, to ratings by others, to physiological indicators (such as those of anxiety), sometimes even to biographical data (such as career decisions), and archive data (such as grades). Depending on the type of trait indicator, individual differences in their correlations may have different sources. It is therefore not surprising that many different moderator constructs have been suggested to explain individual differences in consistency. These moderator constructs can be grouped into at least three categories.

Qualifying attributes of dispositions

This category comprises particular attributes of dispositions that affect the correlation of these dispositions with actual behaviour. Several such attributes have been suggested in attitude research, mainly to explain individual differences in the prediction of behaviour from self-reported attitudes (Raden, 1985). Thus there is evidence that behaviour is predicted more strongly from attitudes: (1) if subjects are certain about them (Fazio and Zanna, 1978), (2) if the attitudes are more important or central for the subjects (Nederhof, 1989), or (3) if the attitudes were formed through direct behavioural experience (Fazio, 1986). Kallgren and Wood (1986) correlated modes of environmental behaviour, such as length of participation in a recycling project, with relevant environmental attitudes. They found a significant moderator effect of the number of own past environmental behaviours that the subject recalled within two minutes.

Traits that moderate specific relations

A second class of moderator constructs comprises personality traits that explain individual differences in consistency in a specific behavioural domain only. Repression-sensitization is a classic example (Byrne, 1964), as the assumption of individual differences in consistency is crucial for this construct. Compared to the level of their physiological arousal, repressors experience or report too low levels of stress, threat, and negative emotions. By contrast, sensitizers experience or report more negative emotions than would be expected from their level of physiological arousal. For example, in a study by Otto and Bösel (1978) subjects were shown a distressing film, and their galvanic skin response was recorded during this film. Afterwards, they indicated their level of anxiety during various scenes of the film. The intra-individual z-score difference between the two behavioural modes correlated significantly (0.31) and in the expected direction with a measure of repression-sensitization.

Other personality variables that have been suggested as moderators of consistency within a specific behavioural domain include responsibility denial (for example, Schwartz and Fleishman, 1982), moral development (for example, Rholes and Bailey, 1983), idealism (Wojciszke, 1987), and need for cognition (Cacioppo et al., 1986). Yet research on the moderating effects of these constructs have either been rare or it has yielded inconclusive results (cf. Schmitt, 1990a).

Personality traits as general moderators

Several personality traits have been suggested as global moderators of various trait— behaviour and behaviour—behaviour relations. Snyder (1974, 1987) suggested the construct of self-monitoring. In behaving according to changing normative expectations, self-monitors have both a high motivation and good skills. By contrast, low self-monitors are less responsive to social norms but behave according to their actual moods, values, attitudes, and habits. Several moderator hypotheses can be derived from this definition of self-monitoring.

First, high self-monitors should behave consistently as long as the social norms remain constant across situations. If expectations change across situations, however, their behaviour should be less consistent than that of low self-monitors. In line with this assumption, Lippa (1976) found that the expressive behaviour of high self-monitors varied more than that of low self-monitors among subjects who first played an extraverted teacher, then an introverted teacher, and finally how they would prefer to behave as teachers.

Second, behaviour predictions from self-report trait measures should be poorer for high self-monitors than for low self-monitors because: (1) high self-monitors are affected by perceived expectations when answering questionnaires, thus attenuating the validity of their responses; and (2) their behaviour depends more on situational influences than the behaviour of low self-monitors. This hypothesis has been confirmed in several studies. For example, Snyder and Swann (1976) found that, in a fictitious court case involving a woman who felt discriminated against because of her sex, low self-monitors pleaded in better agreement with their attitudes towards affirmative action than high self-monitors.

Third, it is expected that high self-monitors will change their attitudes less than low self-monitors after instances of counter-attitudinal behaviour. This is because high self-monitors are more motivated to comply with situational demands than to act in agreement with their attitudes, and this should result in less cognitive dissonance after counter-attitudinal behaviour. Consequently, they should be less motivated than low self-monitors to adjust their attitudes to their actual past behaviour. In a study by Snyder and Tanke (1976), this hypothesis was confirmed. High self-monitors changed their attitudes less than low self-monitors after having complied with an experimenter's request to write a counter-attitudinal essay.

Fourth, cross-modal consistency should be lower among high self-monitors than among low self-monitors whenever the behavioural modes differ in conscious controllability (for example, verbal behaviour versus physiological responses). In a study by Lippa (1978), this hypothesis was tested and confirmed. As in his study mentioned above (Lippa, 1976), the subjects had to play teachers with different personalities. In line with expectations, high self-monitors showed more intra-individual cross-modal variability of responses than low self-monitors.

Finally, some authors have claimed that self-monitoring should also moderate the agreement of self-ratings on traits with trait ratings by knowledgeable informants, as well as the agreement among knowledgeable informants. It has been argued that lack of consistency in the behaviour of high self-monitors should make it difficult for outside observers to infer their traits. This hypothesis, however, is reasonable only under the condition that the judges have observed the target person in dissimilar situations. Unfortunately, this important factor has not been controlled in past research. It is therefore not surprising that this kind of research has yielded inconsistent results.

Another problem is that self-monitoring has been used in most studies as a unitary construct, although the items of the self-monitoring scale (Snyder, 1974) constitute several factors (for example, Briggs and Cheek, 1988), and these factors have been found to moderate behavioural consistency in different ways (Baize and Tetlock, 1985; Cheek, 1982; Nowack and Kammer, 1987; Wymer and Penner, 1985).

In addition to self-monitoring, several other personality traits have been suggested as global moderators, such as self-consciousness (Fenigstein *et al.*, 1975; Scheier *et al.*, 1978) and social desirability (Amelang and Borkenau, 1984b; Bem, 1972; Kogan and Wallach, 1964). It is beyond the scope of this chapter, however, to discuss these and other moderator constructs in detail. For a comprehensive review, see Schmitt (1990a).

Summary

Although lay people and scientists alike tend to talk about individual differences in terms of traits, and although there are thousands of trait-descriptive terms in the dictionaries of the major western languages, it has been argued that traits are merely cognitive fictions that do not have any basis in actual behaviour. The controversy brought about by this claim sharpened the view of the consistencies and inconsistencies in human behaviour and of the way that traits are useful concepts to describe individual differences.

First, the main effects of situations on behaviour as identified in numerous experimental studies are substantial, but irrelevant for the relative consistency of behaviour that is crucial for the viability of dispostional constructs. It is the interactions of persons and situations or the size of consistency coefficients that count. *Second*, low consistency coefficients reflect in part statistical sources, like limited reliabilities and skewed distributions of the measures involved. *Third*, the size of consistency and predictability coefficients depends on how specific (narrow) versus general (broad) a trait construct has been conceptualized as. *Fourth*, virtually all behaviours have multiple causes. Therefore, perfect predictability of behaviour from a single trait measure cannot be expected. *Fifth*, individual differences in consistency exist. Some individuals are less traited than others; that is, not all individuals can be described equally well with the same traits. Measures of individual consistency suffer from conceptual and methodological shortcomings and need to be improved. Various psychological explanations for individual differences in consistency and traitedness have been proposed and some have been investigated fruitfully.

References

Ahadi, S. and Diener, E. (1989), 'Multiple determinants and effect size', *Journal of Personality and Social Psychology*, **56**, 398−406.

Ajzen, I. (1987), 'Attitudes, traits and actions: dispositional prediction of behavior in personality and social psychology', in L. Berkowitz (ed.), *Advances in Experimental Social Psychology*, New York, NY: Academic Press, vol. 20, pp. 1−63.

Ajzen, I. and Fishbein, M. (1977), 'Attitude−behavior relations: a theoretical analysis and review of empirical research', *Psychological Bulletin*, **84**, 888−918.

Alker, H.A. (1972), 'Is personality situationally specific or intrapsychically consistent?', *Journal of Personality*, **40**, 1−16.

Allport, G.W. (1937), *Personality: A psychological interpretation*, New York, NY: Holt.

Allport, G.W. (1961), *Pattern and Growth in Personality*, New York, NY: Holt.

Allport, G.W. and Vernon, P.E. (1933), *Studies in Expressive Movement*, New York, NY: Macmillan.

Alston, W.P. (1975), 'Traits, consistency, and conceptual alternatives for personality theory', *Journal for the Theory of Social Behavior*, **5**, 17–48.

Amelang, M. and Bartussek, D. (1971), 'Zur differentiellen Validität von Fragebogen' [Towards differential validity of questionnaires], *Diagnostica*, **17**, 83–4.

Amelang, M. and Bartussek, D. (1990), *Differentielle Psychologie und Persönlichkeitsforschung* [Differential Psychology and Personality Research]. Stuttgart, FRG: Kohlhammer.

Amelang, M. and Borkenau, P. (1981), 'Vorhersagen für einige Personen und viele Merkmale. Oder: Konsistenz über Merkmale und Kontextbedingungen als Eigenschaft' [Prediction of some of the people and many response variables. Or: consistency across response variables and environmental contexts as a personality trait], in W. Michaelis (ed.), *Bericht über den 32. Kongreß der Deutschen Gesellschaft für Psychologie in Zürich 1980* [Report of the 32nd Congress of the German Psychological Association, Zurich 1980.] Göttingen, FRG: Hogrefe, pp. 495–8.

Amelang, M. and Borkenau, P. (1984a), 'Versuche einer Differenzierung des Eigenschaftskonzeptes: Aspekte intraindividueller Variabilität und differentieller Vorhersagbarkeit' [Attempts at differentiating the trait concept: aspects of intra-individuality and differential predictability], in M. Amelang and H.J. Ahrens (eds.), *Brennpunkte der Persönlichkeitsforschung* [Focus of Personality Research], Göttingen, FRG: Hogrefe, vol. 1, pp. 89–107.

Amelang, M. and Borkenau, P. (1984b), 'Constructing cross-situational consistency in behavior: some tests on Bem's thoughts on social desirability as a moderator variable', in H. Bonarius, G.L. Van Heck and N. Smid (eds.), *Personality Psychology in Europe: Theoretical and empirical developments*, Lisse, The Netherlands: Swets & Zeitlinger, pp. 101–10.

Amelang, M. and Borkenau, P. (1986), 'The trait concept: current theoretical considerations, empirical facts, and implications for personality inventory construction', in A. Angleitner and J.S. Wiggins (eds.), *Personality Assessment via Questionnaires: Current issues in theory and measurement*, Berlin: Springer-Verlag, pp. 7–34.

Asendorpf, J. (1990), 'The measurement of individual consistency', *Methodika*, **4**, 1–22.

Asendorpf, J. (1991), *Die differentielle Sichtweise in der Psychologie* [The Individual Differences Perspective in Psychology], Göttingen, FRG: Hogrefe.

Baize, H.R. and Tetlock, P.E. (1985), 'Self-monitoring and the attitude–behavior relationship: a closer look at the Ajzen, Timko, and White study', *Representative Research in Social Psychology*, **15**, 36–41.

Batson, C.D. and Oleson, K.C. (1992), 'Current status of the empathy-altruism hypothesis', in M.S. Clark (ed.), *Pro-social Behavior, Review of Personality and Social Psychology*, Beverly Hills, CA: Sage, vol. 12, pp. 62–85.

Bem, D.J. (1972), 'Constructing cross-situational consistencies in behavior: some thoughts on Alker's critique of Mischel', *Journal of Personality*, **40**, 17–26.

Bem, D.J. and Allen, A. (1974), 'On predicting some of the people some of the time: the search for cross-situational consistencies in behavior', *Psychological Review*, **81**, 506–20.

Bloom, B.S. (1964), *Stability and Change in Human Characteristics*, New York, NY: Wiley.

Borkenau, P. (1981), 'Intraindividuelle Variabilität und differentielle Vorhersagbarkeit' [Intra-individual variability and differential predictability], unpublished dissertation, University of Heidelberg, Heidelberg, FRG.

Borkenau, P. (1986), 'Toward an understanding of trait-interrelations: acts as instances of several traits', *Journal of Personality and Social Psychology*, **51**, 371–81.

Borkenau, P. (1988), 'The multiple classification of acts and the big five factors of personality', *Journal of Research in Personality*, **22**, 337–52.

Borkenau, P. (in press), 'To predict some of the people more of the time: individual traits and the prediction of behavior', in K.H. Craik, R. Hogan and R. Wolfe (eds.), *Fifty Years of Personality Psychology*, New York, NY: Plenum Press.

Borkenau, P. and Liebler, A. (1992), 'The cross-modal consistency of personality: inferring strangers' traits from visual or acoustic information', *Journal of Research in Personality*, **26**, 183–204.

Borkenau, P. and Müller, B. (1991), 'Breadth, bandwidth, and fidelity of personality-descriptive categories', *European Journal of Personality*, **5**, 309–22.

Briggs, S.R. and Cheek, J.M. (1988), 'On the nature of self-monitoring: problems with assessment, problems with validity', *Journal of Personality and Social Psychology*, **54**, 663–78.

Buss, D.M. and Craik, K.H. (1983), 'The act frequency approach to personality', *Psychological Review*, **90**, 105–26.

Byrne, D. (1964), 'Repression-sensitization as a dimension of personality', in B.A. Maher (ed.), *Progress in Experimental Personality Research*, New York, NY: Academic Press, vol. 1, pp. 170–220.

Cacioppo, J.T., Petty, R.E., Kao, C.F. and Rodriguez, R. (1986), 'Central and peripheral routes to persuasion: an individual difference perspective', *Journal of Personality and Social Psychology*, **51**, 1032–43.

Campbell, D.T. (1963), 'Social attitudes and other acquired behavioral dispositions', in D. Koch (ed.), *Psychology: A study of a science*, New York, NY: McGraw-Hill, vol. 6, pp. 94–172.

Carroll, J.B. (1961), 'The nature of data or how to choose a correlation coefficient', *Psychometrika*, **26**, 347–72.

Cattell, R.B. (1943), 'Fluctuations of sentiments and attitudes as a measure of character integration', *American Journal of Psychology*, **56**, 195–216.

Cattell, R.B. (1946), *Description and Measurement of Personality*, Yonkers-on-Hudson, NY: World Book Company.

Chaplin, W.F. (1991), 'The next generation of moderator research in personality psychology', *Journal of Personality*, **59**, 143–78.

Chaplin, W.F. and Goldberg, L.R. (1984), 'A failure to replicate the Bem and Allen-study of individual differences in cross-situational consistency', *Journal of Personality and Social Psychology*, **47**, 1074–90.

Chaplin, W.F., John, O.P. and Goldberg, L.R. (1988), 'Conceptions of states and traits: dimensional attributes with ideals as prototypes', *Journal of Personality and Social Psychology*, **54**, 541–57.

Cheek, J.M. (1982), 'Aggregation, moderator variables, and the validity of personality tests: a peer rating study', *Journal of Personality and Social Psychology*, **43**, 1254–69.

Cleary, T.A. (1966), 'An individual differences model for multiple regression', *Psychometrika*, **31**, 215–24.

Conley, J.J. (1984), 'Relation of temporal stability and cross-situational consistency in personality: comment on the Mischel–Epstein debate', *Psychological Review*, **91**, 491–6.

Conley, J.J. (1985), 'Longitudinal stability of personality traits: a multitrait-multimethod-multioccasion analysis', *Journal of Personality and Social Psychology*, **49**, 1266–82.

Costa, P.T., Jr. and McCrae, R.R. (1980), 'Still stable after all these years: personality as a key to some issues in adulthood and old age', in P.B. Baltes and O.G. Brim (eds.), *Life-span Development and Behavior*, New York, NY: Academic Press, pp. 66–102.

Cronbach, L.J. (1970), *Essentials of Psychological Testing*, New York, NY: Harper & Row.

Cronbach, L.J. and Furby, L. (1970), 'How should we measure "change" — or should we?', *Psychological Bulletin*, **74**, 68–80.

Ehrlich, H.J. (1969), 'Attitudes, behavior and intervening variables', *American Sociologist*, **4**, 29–34.

Epstein, S. (1979), 'The stability of behavior: I. On predicting most of the people much of the time', *Journal of Personality and Social Psychology*, **37**, 1097–126.

Epstein, S. and O'Brien, E. (1985), 'The person–situation debate in historical and current perspective', *Psychological Bulletin*, **98**, 513–37.

Eysenck, H.J. and Eysenck, S.B.G. (1969), *Personality Structure and Measurement*, London: Routledge & Kegan Paul.

Eysenck, M.W. and Eysenck, H.J. (1980), 'Mischel and the concept of personality', *British Journal of Psychology*, **71**, 191–204.

Fazio, R.H. (1986), 'How do attitudes guide behavior?', in R.M. Sorrentino and E.T. Higgins (eds.), *The Handbook of Motivation and Cognition: Foundations of Social Behavior*, New York, NY: Guilford Press, pp. 204–43.

Fazio, R.H. and Zanna, M.P. (1978), 'On the predictive validity of attitudes: the role of direct experience and confidence', *Journal of Personality*, **46**, 228–43.

Fenigstein, A., Scheier, M.F. and Buss, A.H. (1975), 'Public and private self-consciousness: assessment and theory', *Journal of Consulting and Clinical Psychology*, **42**, 522–7.

Ferguson, G.A. (1941), 'The factorial interpretation of test difficulty', *Psychometrika*, **6**, 323–9.

Fishbein, M. and Ajzen, I. (1974), 'Attitudes towards objects as predictors of single and multiple behavioral criteria', *Psychological Review*, **81**, 59–74.

Fiske, D.W. and Rice, L. (1955), 'Intra-individual response variability', *Psychological Bulletin*, **52**, 217–50.

Frederiksen, N. and Gilbert, A.C.F. (1960), 'Replication of a study of differential predictability', *Educational and Psychological Measurement*, **20**, 759–67.

Frederiksen, N. and Melville, S.D. (1954), 'Differential predictability in the use of test scores', *Educational and Psychological Measurement*, **14**, 647–56.

Funder, D.C. and Colvin, C.R. (1991), 'Explorations in behavioral consistency: properties of persons, situations, and behaviors', *Journal of Personality and Social Psychology*, **60**, 773–94.

Ghiselli, E.E. (1963), 'Moderating effects and differential reliability and validity', *Journal of Applied Psychology*, **47**, 81–6.

Goldberg, L.R. (1978), 'The reliability of reliability: the generality and correlates of intra-individual consistency in responses to structured personality inventories', *Applied Psychological Measurement*, **2**, 269–91.

Gulliksen, H. (1950), *Theory of Mental Tests*. New York, NY: Wiley.

Hampson, S.E., John, O.P. and Goldberg, L.R. (1986), 'Category breadth and hierarchical structure in personality: studies of asymmetries in judgements of trait implications', *Journal of Personality and Social Psychology*, **51**, 37–54.

Hartshorne, H. and May, M.A. (1928), *Studies in the Nature of Character. Vol. 1: Studies in deceit*. New York, NY: Macmillan.

Hartshorne, H., May, M.A. and Maller, J.B. (1929), *Studies in the Nature of Character: Vol 2: Studies in service and self-control*. New York, NY: Macmillan.

Herrmann, T. (1980), 'Die Eigenschaftskonzeption als Heterostereotyp: Kritik eines persönlichkeitspsychologischen Geschichtsklischees' [The trait concept of heterostereotype: criticism on a historical cliché in personality psychology], *Zeitschrift für Differentielle und Diagnostische Psychologie*, **1**, 7–16.

Hirschberg, N. (1978), 'A correct treatment of traits', in H. London (ed.), *Personality: A new look at metatheories*, Hillsdale, NJ: Erlbaum, pp. 45–68.

Hoffman, M.L. (1981), 'The development of empathy', in J.P. Rushton and R.M. Sorrentino (eds.), *Altruism and Helping Behavior: Social, personality, and developmental perspectives*, Hillsdale, NJ: Erlbaum, pp. 41–63.

Holden, R.R., Helmes, E., Fekken, G.C. and Jackson, D.J. (1985), 'The multidimensionality of person reliability: implications for interpreting individual test item responses', *Educational and Psychological Measurement*, **45**, 119–30.

Jackson, D.N. and Paunonen, S.V. (1985), 'Construct validity and the predictability of behavior', *Journal of Personality and Social Psychology,* **49**, 554–70.

Jäger, R. (1978), *Differentielle Diagnostizierbarkeit in der psychologischen Diagnostik* [Differential Predictability in Psychodiagnostics], Göttingen, FRG: Hogrefe.

Jöreskog, K.G. and Sörbom, D. (1988), *LISREL VII,* Chicago, IL: SPSS-Inc.

Kallgren, C.A. and Wood, W. (1986), 'Access to attitude-relevant information in memory as a determinant of attitude–behavior consistency', *Journal of Experimental Social Psychology,* **22**, 328–38.

Kenrick, D.T. and Funder, D.C. (1988), 'Profiting from controversy: lessons from the person–situation debate', *American Psychologist,* **43**, 23–34.

Kogan, N. and Wallach, M.A. (1964), *Risk Taking: A study in cognition and personality,* New York, NY: Holt, Rinehart & Winston.

Lamiell, J.T. (1981), 'Toward an idiothetic psychology of personality', *American Psychologist,* **36**, 276–89.

Lanning, K. (1988), 'Individual differences in scalability: an alternative conception of consistency for personality theory and measurement', *Journal of Personality and Social Psychology,* **55**, 142–8.

LaPierre, R.T. (1934), 'Attitudes versus actions', *Social Forces,* **13**, 230–7.

Lippa, R. (1976), 'Expressive control and the leakage of dispositional introversion-extraversion during role-played teaching', *Journal of Personality,* **44**, 541–59.

Lippa, R. (1978), 'Expressive control, expressive consistency, and the correspondence between expressive behavior and personality', *Journal of Personality,* **46**, 438–61.

Lord, F.M. and Novick, M.R. (1968), *Statistical Theories of Mental Test Scores.* Reading, MA: Addison-Wesley.

McCrae, R.R. and Costa, P.T., Jr. (1984), *Emerging Lives, Enduring Dispositions: Personality in adulthood,* Boston, MA: Little, Brown.

McFarland, S.G. and Sparks, C.M. (1985), 'Age, education, and the internal consistency of personality scales', *Journal of Personality and Social Psychology,* **49**, 1692–702.

Magnusson, D. and Ekehammar, B. (1978), 'Similar situations — similar behaviors?: a study of the intraindividual congruence between situation perception and situation reactions', *Journal of Research in Personality,* **12**, 41–8.

Magnusson, D. and Endler, N.S. (1977a), 'Interactional psychology: present status and future prospects', in D. Magnusson and N.S. Endler (eds.), *Personality at the Crossroads: Current issues in interactional psychology,* Hillsdale, NJ: Erlbaum, pp. 3–31.

Magnusson, D. and Endler, N.S. (eds.) (1977b), *Personality at the Crossroads: Current issues in interactional psychology,* Hillsdale, NJ: Erlbaum.

Mershon, B. and Gorsuch, R.L. (1988), 'Number of factors in the personality sphere: does increase in factors increase predictability of real-life criteria?, *Journal of Personality and Social Psychology,* **55**, 675–80.

Mischel, W. and Peake, P.K. (1982), 'Beyond déjà vu in the search for cross-situational consistency', *Psychological Review,* **89**, 730–55.

Montada, L. and Schmitt, M. (1982), 'Issues in applied developmental psychology: a life-span perspective', in P.B. Baltes and O.G. Brim, Jr. (eds.), *Life-span Development and Behavior,* New York, NY: Academic Press, vol. 4, pp. 1–32.

Montada, L., Schmitt, M. and Dalbert, C. (1986), 'Thinking about justice and dealing with one's own privileges: a study of existential guilt', in H.-W. Bierhoff, R.L. Cohen and J. Greenberg (eds.), *Justice in Social Relations,* New York, NY: Plenum Press, pp. 125–43.

Montada, L., Schmitt, M. and Dalbert, C. (1991), 'Prosocial commitments in the family: situational, personality, and systemic factors', in L. Montada and H.-W. Bierhoff (eds.), *Altruism in Social Systems,* Toronto, Canada: Hogrefe & Huber Publishers, pp. 177–203.

Nederhof, A.J. (1989), 'Self-involvement, intention certainty, and attitude–intention consistency', *British Journal of Social Psychology,* **28**, 123–33.

Nowack, W. and Kammer, D. (1987), 'Self-presentation: social skills and inconsistency as independent facets of self-monitoring', *European Journal of Personality*, **1**, 61–77.

Olweus, D. (1979), 'Stability of aggressive reaction patterns in males: a review', *Psychological Bulletin*, **86**, 852–75.

Otto, J. and Bösel, R. (1978), 'Angstverarbeitung und Diskrepanz zwischen Selfreport und physiologischem Streßindikator: Eine gelungene Replikation der Weinstein-Analyse [Coping with anxiety and the discrepancy between self-reports and physiological indicators of stress: a successful replication of the Weinstein analysis]', *Schweizerische Zeitschrift für Psychologie und ihre Anwendungen*, **37**, 321–30.

Ozer, D.J. (1986), *Consistency in Personality*, Berlin, FRG: Springer.

Paunonen, S.V. (1984), 'The reliability of aggregated measurements: lessons to be learned from psychometric theory', *Journal of Research in Personality*. **18**, 383–94.

Paunonen, S.V. and Jackson, D.M. (1985), 'Idiographic measurement strategies for personality and prediction: some unredeemed promissory notes', *Psychological Review*, **92**, 486–511.

Raden, D. (1977), 'Situational thresholds and attitude–behavior consistency', *Sociometry*, **40**, 123–9.

Raden, D. (1985), 'Strength-related attitude dimensions', *Social Psychology Quarterly*, **48**, 312–30.

Rholes, W.S. and Bailey, S. (1983), 'The effect of level of moral reasoning on consistency between moral attitudes and related behaviors', *Social Cognition*, **2**, 32–48.

Saunders, D.R. (1956), 'Moderator variables in prediction', *Educational and Psychological Measurement*, **16**, 209–22.

Scheier, M.F., Buss, A.H. and Buss, D.M. (1978), 'Self-consciousness, self-report of aggressiveness, and aggression', *Journal of Research in Personality*, **12**, 133–40.

Schmitt, M. (1988), 'Über die Konsistenzannahme des Eigenschaftsmodells und über Konsistenz als Eigenschaft: Theoretische, methodische und empirische Untersuchungen' [On the consistency assumption of the trait model and on consistency as a trait: theoretical, methodological, and empirical inquiries], unpublished dissertation, University of Trier, Trier, FRG.

Schmitt, M. (1989), 'Ipsative Konsistenz (Kohärenz) als Profilähnlichkeit' [Ipsative consistency (coherence) as profile similarity], *Trierer Psychologische Berichte*, **16**, Heft 2.

Schmitt, M. (1990a), *Konsistenz als Persönlichkeitseigenschaft?: Moderatorvariablen in der Persönlichkeits- und Einstellungsforschung* [Consistency as a Personality Trait?: Moderator variables in personality and attitude research], Berlin, FRG: Springer.

Schmitt, M. (1990b), 'Zur (mangelnden) Konstruktvalidität von Konsistenz-Selbstein- schätzungen' [(Lack of) Construct validity of self-reports of consistency], *Zeitschrift für Differentielle und Diagnostische Psychologie*, **11**, 149–66.

Schmitt, M. (1990c), 'Further evidence on the invalidity of self-reported consistency', in P.J.D. Drenth, J.A. Sergeant and R.J. Takens (eds.), *European Perspectives in Psychology*, New York, NY: Wiley, vol. 1, pp. 57–68.

Schmitt, M. (1992), 'Interindividuelle Konsistenzunterschiede als Herausforderung für die differentielle Psychologie' [Inter-individual consistency differences as a challenge for differential psychology], *Psychologische Rundschau*, **43**, 30–45.

Schmitt, M., Dalbert, C. and Montada, L. (1985), 'Drei Wege zu mehr Konsistenz in der Selbstbeschreibung: Theoriepräzisierung, Korrespondenzbildung und Datenaggregierung [Three ways towards more consistency in self-descriptions: theory specification, the forming of correspondences, and the aggregation of data], *Zeitschrift für Differentielle und Diagnostische Psychologie*, **6**, 147–59.

Schwartz, S.H. and Fleishman, J.A. (1982), 'Effects of negative personal norms on helping behavior', *Personality and Social Psychology Bulletin*, **8**, 81–6.

Seibold, D.R. (1975), 'Communication research and the attitude–verbal report–overt behavior relationship: a critique and theoretical reformulation', *Human Communication Research*, **2**, 3–32.

Snyder, M. (1974), 'The self-monitoring of expressive behavior', *Journal of Personality and Social Psychology,* **30**, 526–37.

Snyder, M. (1987), *Public Appearances, Private Realities: The psychology of self-monitoring,* New York, NY: Freeman.

Snyder, M. and Swann, W.B., Jr. (1976), 'When actions reflect attitudes: the politics of impression management', *Journal of Personality and Social Psychology,* **34**, 1034–42.

Snyder, M. and Tanke, E.D. (1976), 'Behavior and attitude: some people are more consistent than others', *Journal of Personality,* **44**, 501–17.

Tal, J.S. (1987), *Personality Traits and Prediction: Utilizing latent trait theory in an attempt to increase the validity of traits,* Ann Arbor, MI: University Microfilms International.

Tellegen, A. (1988), 'The analysis of consistency in personality assessment', *Journal of Personality,* **56**, 621–63.

Vernon, P.E. (1961), *The Structure of Human Abilities,* London: Methuen.

West, S.G. (1983), 'Personality and prediction: an introduction', *Journal of Personality,* **51**, 275–85.

Wilson, R.S. (1983), 'The Louisville Twin Study: developmental synchronies in behavior', *Child Development,* **54**, 298–316.

Wohlwill, J.F. (1973), *The Study of Behavioral Development,* New York, NY: Academic Press.

Wojciszke, B. (1987), 'Ideal-self, self-focus and value–behavior consistency', *European Journal of Social Psychology,* **17**, 187–98.

Wright, S. (1934), 'The method of path coefficients', *Annals of Mathematical Statistics,* **5**, 161–215.

Wymer, W.E. and Penner, L.A. (1985), 'Moderator variables and different types of predictability: do you have a match?' *Journal of Personality and Social Psychology,* **49**, 1002–15.

Zanna, M.P., Higgins, E.T. and Herman, C.P. (eds.), (1982), *Consistency in Social Behavior,* Hillsdale, NJ: Erlbaum.

Zucker, R., Aronoff, J. and Rabin, A.I. (eds.) (1984), *Personality and the Prediction of Behavior,* San Diego, CA: Academic Press.

Zuckerman, M. (1977), 'Development of a situation specific trait-state test for the prediction and measurement of affective responses', *Journal of Consulting and Clinical Psychology,* **45**, 513–23.

Zuckerman, M., Bernieri, F., Koestner, R. and Rosenthal, R. (1989), 'To predict some of the people some of the time: in search of moderators', *Journal of Personality and Social Psychology,* **57**, 279–93.

Zuckerman, M., Koestner, R., DeBoy, T., Garcia, T., Maresca, B.C. and Sartoris, J.M. (1988), 'To predict some of the people some of the time: a reexamination of the moderator variable approach in personality theory', *Journal of Personality and Social Psychology,* **54**, 1006–19.

3/ Personality structure through traits

Willem K.B. Hofstee and **Boele De Raad**
University of Groningen, The Netherlands

Introduction

What do people mean when they say that there is more to a person than a bunch
of scores? What is the meaning of terms like intra-individual consistency as opposed
to inter-individual differences, or 'the unique organization of traits within the person'?
These are important questions for anyone who cares about the back-translation of
scientific findings to professional practice and lay discourse. For it is a fact of life
that professionals and lay persons tend to go beyond the data, and invoke concepts
like individuality, internal coherence, and uniqueness.

Why ask the question about the meaning of intra-individual structure? Is not the
concept self-evident, or clearly defined in the literature? Quite to the contrary, it
is highly problematic. In psychometric terms, the person is a score vector or,
equivalently a point in a personality space, or an element of a Cartesian product.
The variables need not be test scores or quantities: we may say, for example, that
a person is a typical extravert, or used-car saleswoman, or zombie; such sayings
may be represented by a binary matrix of persons by types. A zombie gets a score
of one in the zombie column, and zeros in other columns unless the idea is to permit
multiple class membership and overlapping typologies. We can make an intensive
study of an individual and arrive at a refined and evocative description (McCrae,
1990); however, in a scientific rather than a poetic context, a legitimate question
is whether or to what extent the description would also fit other persons — in other
words, we have created a variable. Even the extent to which a person is intra-
individually consistent (Asendorpf, 1990; Bem and Allen, 1974; Ghiselli, 1963) is
a variable among other variables (Amelang and Borkenau, 1986). There is no escape
at all from the representation of the person as a score vector. Therefore, the question
of what lies beyond these scores is as exasperating as it is important.

The easy solution is to relegate the idea of personality structure to the realm of
metaphysics. However, that would not be very constructive. Instead, we shall examine
several interpretations of the concept. One of these, in which personality is conceived
as a syndrome or type, will appear to be quite viable; an illustrative empirical
elaboration will be given to tie it with the Big Five (see, for example, Digman, 1990)

tradition in trait research. To clarify the type interpretation, however, other interpretations will be discussed first.

The haunting problem of uniqueness

Dissatisfaction with the psychometric representation of the person may follow from a fundamental discontent, which is usually phrased as a concern for the uniqueness, the freedom, or the identity of the person. Our programme here is not to brush away that concern; however, we shall also not open any false perspectives on dealing scientifically with the uniqueness of the person. Rather, the argument will consist of documenting the impossibility of a scientific approach to uniqueness.

Persons may be meaningfully said to be unique and incomparable. For example, Jack may be said to be emotional in a manner that nobody else is, because his emotionality is embedded in a personality structure all his own; to call him emotional is to reshape the meaning of emotionality. The object and the attribute define each other interactively; emotionality will never be the same again for having been applied to Jack.

It should be noted that the argument is not restricted to personality traits. It extends to all attributes as applied to all humans. Nobody weighs 78 kilos the way Jack does. The reason is that we are not discussing Jack's weight in a physical context, for example, with the purpose of finding out whether he will be permitted to enter the lift, but in a psychological context. Jack's weight is embedded in a different subjective configuration to Jill's.

Strictly speaking, the uniqueness argument can be extended to make all comparison impossible. For example, counting bricks is a meaningless enterprise because it is easy to show that every brick is unique. However, this extension of the argument — or Eysenck's (1952) saying that his old shoe is unique — will generally be considered to be a sophism, whereas to stress the uniqueness of persons is not. We do not count and measure humans as freely as we do inanimate objects or even animals. So it looks as if one should at least discuss the distinction between persons and bricks, between the natural and the human sciences.

Kouwer (1973) has introduced a distinction between the person as an object of discourse and the person as a discourse partner. As an object, the individual is not systematically different from other objects. Humans, however, are distinct from other entities because they are the only ones that we talk with (to say *to someone* that you talk with your dog could be subtly insulting to that person, because the implication is that you are talking with him or her the way you talk with a dog, which would be literally quite cynical). A refined version of the argument is that in order to deny that one talks with persons, one would need a human audience for the denial to make sense (nobody goes around telling objects that talking with them is impossible); not only does the denial thus become paradoxical, but the thought experiment also emphasizes the special status of humans.

Quite analogously, we cannot deny the freedom or the subjectivity of the other person, because the act of denying presupposes a discourse partner who is free to agree or disagree with the statement: to say things only makes sense if the saying is subject to potential refutation. Evidently, one can imagine saying all sorts of things in the abstract. Kouwer's (1973) heuristic, however, consists of placing statements in the context of an actual discourse, which is a powerful way to discover the pragmatic aspects of meaning.

At a more mundane level, the analysis offers an explanation of the discontent of professional practitioners who work with individuals. A defining characteristic of professional labour is that the client is not only an object of investigation, but also a subject whose active effort is required for success. Upon talking with the client, a professional inevitably experiences the insufficiency and ineptness of person descriptions. In discussing personality disorders, for example, Millon (1990) notes that 'clinicians often claim that the better they know a patient, the greater difficulty they have in fitting him or her into a single category' (p. 349). If our analysis is correct, the increasing difficulty of diagnosis would not be specific to a classification of patients into single categories, but would hold for any diagnostic or person-descriptive system.

Does the analysis open a perspective towards a solution? Is it possible to conceive of a scientific investigation of people that does justice to their freedom and subjectivity? Kouwer's (1973) answer is emphatically negative. Absolutely nothing can be said about persons *qua* subjects (in the sense of discourse partners), as any description would automatically degenerate the person into object status. In practice, one would shift between investigative and communicative phases in a professional relationship (Hofstee, 1980); the task might even be carried out with such agility that the distinction might almost seem to dissolve. But no approach is conceivable whereby the person could simultaneously retain subject and object status, because the two are incompatible.

Psychological research is usually characterized by a protracted investigative phase, following by brief and scattered spurts of communication of an indirect kind; in psychological practice, the periodicity tends to be much shorter. While talking with a client and trying to share that client's perspective, a professional may even catch a shadow of the fleeting subjectivity of the other person, and momentarily indulge in the illusion of having grasped the true subject by the tail. In fact, however, there is a trade-off between diagnostic reliability, which requires an emphasis on methodical investigation, and not losing the client as a discourse partner, requiring extrascientific discourse.

In sum, the unique person is someone to talk with, not to try to describe; personality structure in the sense that individuals freely dispose of their traits is not an object of scientific investigation. It suits academic investigators to respect the concern of practitioners with the subject status of their clients. However, science is incapable of bridging the gap between theory and practice, description and discourse.

Moderator models

A much more technical translation of the concept of personality structure is the moderated regression equation (Saunders, 1956), or rather, a family of approaches that are captured by the moderator model. In this model, personality structure is rendered as interaction between traits: the idea that a person is more than a set of separate scores, and that the same score may mean different things in different intra-personal contexts, is expressed through addition of interaction terms to the linear terms in the regression equation that predicts behaviour from scores (see also Schmitt and Borkenau, Chapter 2 in this volume). Note that the approach is consistent with the psychometric principle that the person is represented by a vector of scores; however, relations between traits are explicitly attended to.

Moderator models come in several guises. In an early study, Frederiksen and Melville (1954) found that the relationship between interest (X_1) and grade-point average (Y) was lower for compulsive ($X_2 = 1$) than for non-compulsive ($X_2 = 0$) students. It has thus become customary to distinguish between predictor variables X_1 and moderator variables X_2, and to conceive of the moderator model as the case in which the validity of the predictor is different between sub-groups; the variable that separates the sub-groups is called the moderator variable. However, this conception is somewhat primitive. Saunders (1956) has presented the general form of the moderated regression equation:

$$Y = a + bX_1 + cX_2 + dX_1X_2, \tag{3.1}$$

of which the Frederiksen and Melville design is a special case: setting X_2 equal to 1 and 0, respectively, we obtain

$$Y = (a + c) + (b + d)X_1, \text{ and} \tag{3.2}$$

$$Y = a + bX_1, \tag{3.3}$$

that is, the two different linear regressions in the sub-groups are captured by one nonlinear moderated regression equation. The gain of this more general representation is threefold: first, the Saunders equation can handle moderator variables that are continuous, as well as dichotomous moderators. Second, the Saunders equation is symmetrical. It is thus seen that the term 'moderator *variable* is inappropriate; with respect to the Frederiksen and Melville study, the conclusion that interest moderated the relation between compulsiveness and grade-point average (GPA) is equally correct. Characteristic of the Saunders equation is a moderator or interaction *term*; if it contributes to the multiple correlation, a moderator effect has been found. Third, it appears that in the Frederiksen and Melville design, X_2 is not used as a predictor in its own right, that is, c is arbitrarily set equal to 0. That restriction can only lower the multiple correlation (see also Hofstee and Smid, 1986).

Lubinksi and Humphreys (1990) and Shepperd (1991) have emphasized the need for considering quadratic terms in addition to interaction terms. When predictors are highly correlated, the product term becomes indistinguishable from the quadratic terms. Failure to take the quadratic terms into consideration might lead one to concluding spuriously upon a moderator effect. Lubinski and Humphreys (1990) show that a seeming synergic interaction between spatial and mathematical ability in predicting exceptional mathematical sophistication is explained away by taking the quadratic terms into account. The general recommendation that ensues is to expand the Saunders model:

$$Y = aX_1 + bX_2 + cX_1^2 + dX_2^2 + eX_1X_2 \qquad (3.4)$$

Upon using this expanded regression equation, spurious moderator effects will be suppressed.

An extra benefit is that Equation (3.4) may be used to represent profile interpretation. In attending to a score profile, discrepancies among the scores of an individual are given special meaning. Implicitly, therefore, absolute or squared differences are added as predictors. (Naturally, nothing would be added when considering algebraic differences.) For two variables, the regression equation is:

$$Y + aX_1 + bX_2 + g(X_1 - X_2)^2 \qquad (3.5)$$

or $\qquad Y = aX_1 + bX_2 - 2gX_1X_2 + gX_1^2 + gX_2^2 \qquad (3.6)$

Conversely, moderator effects may be conceived as a complicated form of profile prediction in the following shape:

$$Y = aX_1 + bX_2 + g(vX_1 - wX_2)^2 \qquad (3.7)$$

which gives the full five-parameter model of Equation (3.4). The reader may wonder whether this complicated model would ever be appropriate. That objection should be understood as a comment on moderator models. It should further be noted that with more than two predictors the number of parameters rises rapidly, heightening the risk of capitalization on chance.

A slight simplification may be achieved by taking the absolute rather than the squared difference as the last term in Equation (3.5). This version is reminiscent of the Ghiselli (1956) approach to differential predictability; there, however, the discrepancy between observed and predicted criterion scores is considered rather than the discrepancies among predictor scores. Asendorpf (1990; 1991, p. 123) has called attention to the fact that absolute scores do not fit with parametric statistics such as the Pearson correlation coefficient. An appropriate coefficient of association would be the Gower (1971) coefficient, which is a linear function of the summed absolute discrepancies between two variables (see also Hofstee and Zegers, in press).

Several authors have introduced models that can be shown to be complications of the moderator model. Fiske (1986) has proposed calculating the intra-personal standard deviation over items as a consistency measure to supplement a trait score.

This proposal amounts to a cubic regression function (Hofstee and Smid, 1986). Asendorpf (1990) takes the squared discrepancy between standardized scores as a moderator 'variable'; substitution into the Saunders equation again leads to a cubic regression function. A plausible conjecture is that such treatments lead to psychometric artifacts; for example, linear correlations may be washed out or blown up by carrying outlier scores to the third power. In view of the fallibility of personological data there can hardly be any justification for using models of such sophistication and extreme lack of robustness (see also Shepperd, 1991).

Other proposals for moderator models appear not to contain moderator terms at all. Using a variable as its own moderator amounts to writing a quadratic regression equation. A case where the intercepts (but not the slopes) of the regression functions in two or more groups differ constitutes not a moderator effect, but a simple linear multiple regression with the grouping variable as an extra predictor. Not even differential validity in general (different slopes and different intercepts) means that a moderator effect is necessarily present (for a full exposition, see Hofstee and Smid, 1986).

Empirically, the status of moderator models is doubtful at best (Amelang and Borkenau, 1986; Wiggins, 1973). Brown and Scott (1966) failed to replicate Ghiselli's (1963) results on differential predictability; Bem and Allen's (1974) highly influential study has met the same fate (Amelang and Borkenau, 1981; Chaplin and Goldberg, 1984); Hofstee and Smid (1986) tried out Jackson's (1986) recommendation of using the slope of the intra-individual regression of item responses on group responses as a moderator, with negative results. Schmitt (1990), after a thorough review of the literature, concludes that the moderator approach is not very promising for predictive purposes (p. 156). It should be realized that even the Saunders equation places heavy demands on the data. As a consequence of the occurrence of outliers, one may confidently predict (1) that conspicous moderator effects will be found in samples, and (2) that these effects, if not artifactual to begin with, will melt like snow in the desert upon replication in fresh samples.

The moderator model, at first sight, would seem to contain a faithful psychometric translation of the idea of personality structure: the tenet that traits should be regarded not in isolation but also with respect to the way they interact, and that the specific profile of an individual, with its discrepancies between single scores, should be taken into consideration. However, by carrying these ideas to their formal consequence, researchers have gone the way of King Midas, who turned everything he touched into gold. With increasing numbers of variables the model becomes too heavy to be carried by fragile data; also, it cannot reflect intuitive or theoretical ideas about structure any more, as the number of interaction or discrepancy terms far exceeds human cognitive capacity. It may serve for two or maybe three trait variables. The even more sophisticated models discussed above should be scrutinized for potential artifacts, and should probably be suspended until justifications can be presented for introducing third-power terms into the regression equation.

Integrating traits and types

Instead of further pursuing sophisticated representations of the notion of personality structure, let us change tack and turn to the old notion of personality types. Older generations of psychology students vaguely remember being taught that typologies (such as extravert—introvert) have nothing to recommend them over continuous traits, especially because any personality scale shows a unimodal rather than a bimodal, typological distribution. Later generations have lost the concept of type out of sight. Typologies, however, have continued to exist in psychiatric classification (Millon, 1990), and within psychology Magnusson (1990; Bergman and Magnusson, 1990) has made vigorous pleas for a person-oriented (that is, typological) approach in addition to the dominant variable-oriented one.

Millon (1990, p. 348ff.) discusses the relative merits of the type and trait approaches. Whereas trait scores are more comprehensive and differentiated, and are more fit to account for 'atypical' cases, typologies 'restore and recompose the unity of personality by integrating seemingly diverse elements into a single coordinated syndrome. Moreover, the availability of well-established syndromes provides standard references for clinicians, who would otherwise be faced with repeated analyses and *de novo* personality constructions' (p. 349). According to this quote, typological thinking is eminently relevant for the concept of personality structure, and for the communication between investigators and practitioners that is of central concern here.

How sinful is it to discard information and to put people into boxes? The reason for phrasing the question this way is that many a psychometrician would experience feelings of guilt and revolt upon practising typology. Still, the canons of science contain no unequivocal directive towards retaining subtle distinctions. Rather, scientific description might be said to be the art of judiciously discarding information; the requirement of comprehensive representation of objects would bring all empirical sciences to an immediate standstill. The only sensible question can be what an optimal level of refinement is. Evidently, the answer depends on circumstances and purposes.

A devil's (typologist's) advocate might reason as follows: an optimistic estimate of the proportion of true trait variance of a personality scale, after subtraction of both unreliable and method variance, is 0.5, giving a standard error of measurement of 0.7. So, a standard score would have to be below -1.4 or over $+1.4$ to be significantly ($p = 0.05$) different from 0. To trichotomize a population into extraverts, introverts, and neither accordingly would be quite realistic in view of the large error of measurement.

Millon's passage quoted above contains another, positive reason for seriously reconsidering typologies. That reason, briefly, is cognitive and communicative ease. Not only health workers profit from immediate recognition of particular syndromes; other professionals, and lay persons, also have a use for distinct types. In a fully automated world — for example, when screening large numbers of applicants with written or computerized tests — one would not need typologies, or any personological concepts at all; in the end, however, decisions about humans tend to be made by humans, and the question about the optimal level of refinement is a highly practical one.

A final preliminary consideration is that there is nothing very deep about the distinction between the type and trait, person-oriented and variable-oriented approaches to personality (see also Cattell, 1970). Types are dichotomous or trichotomous variables. One may further restrict typological representations by excluding overlap between types; that is, by assigning each individual to at most one type in a typological system, which amounts to setting all other scores on the type variables to zero. That restriction seems to go beyond common sense, however, as classifications in daily life tend not to be mutually exclusive (see also Millon, 1990, p. 349; Bergman and Magnusson, 1990). Other distinctions are equally inconsequential. The favourite language for types is nouns, and for traits it is adjectives; but the difference between an extraverted person and an extravert is grammatical rather than psychological. Finally, a type or syndrome may be said to consist of a cluster of variables, or symptoms; but there is nothing inherently elemental about single traits, and we could construct a personality variable from a number of type scores (for example, endorsements of type nouns) if we would feel so contrarily inclined.

In the following, a detailed procedure for developing a typology of personality will be presented. Empirical illustrations will be drawn from studies using self- and peer-ratings on Dutch trait terms (Hofstee and De Raad, 1991); at this stage, a set of canonical translations of trait terms into other languages is not available, as dictionaries are insufficient for this purpose. The procedures, however, are generalizable.

Constructing a dimensional typology

A logical first step in constructing a typology is to define its dimensions. That definition is not necessarily the first chronological step: one might propose a certain number of types and add more as the need arises, in the manner that rooms are added on to a house as the family expands. At the current state of personological theory, however, it is quite justifiable to set the number of dimensions at five (Digman, 1990; Goldberg, 1990; John, 1990; Ostendorf, 1990). In other words, a state-of-the-art typology should be contained within the Big Five global dimensions of personality, usually if somewhat inaccurately (Hofstee *et al.*, 1992) designated as extraversion, agreeableness, conscientiousness, emotional stability, and intellect.

Persons may be represented in the Big Five space by rows of the person × factors matrix of factor scores or, equivalently, as vectors in that space. To group persons together into types, several procedures could be used. One is hierarchical cluster analysis on the correlations between persons calculated from the matrix of factor scores. With large numbers of subjects, that would be a clumsy procedure. Also, hierarchies with non-overlapping clusters do not provide a felicitous solution for typological purposes. Most importantly, however, the intimate link between persons and variables, which is part and parcel of principal component analysis (PCA), is cut by cluster analytic procedures. Another method is Q-factor analysis right from the start, which would give factor loadings for persons and factor scores for variables, or some similar procedure. We will return to that method below. First, we shall approach the problem in a roundabout manner. We present a trait taxonomy (see also Hofstee *et al.*, 1992) that has a number of desirable properties, and explore whether this taxonomy of variables can be of service in locating person types.

The AB5C taxonomy of traits

To find scales that measure the Big Five factors of personality — or any factors — is a tricky enterprise. Taking the highest-loading variables for a factor, it appears that these variables tend to have non-negligible secondary loadings: a trait loading 0.7 on one factor could easily load 0.5 on another. Moreover, these secondary loadings tend not to balance: the density of high-loading variables to the right of a socially desirable factor pole tends to be higher than to the left, assuming that the second factor is also socially desirable. (Whether this is because socially desirable traits tend to covary in nature or in our heads need not concern us here.) Consequently, scales consisting of highest-loading variables tend to correlate to a significant extent. It would be improper to designate these scales as factor scales, as the scales measure a construct at some angle with the intended factor. Also, the interpretation of the factor is problematic: for a proper interpretation, one should use the second factor as a suppressor variable, but that operation surpasses our cognitive capacity.

An obvious solution would seem to be to apply oblique rotation to simple structure rather than orthogonal rotation. However, if three or more clusters of variables are located in a plane in such a way that no two of these are opposite each other, oblique rotation does not succeed. As a matter of fact, Goldberg (1990) has observed that oblique solutions of trait structure are empirically indistinguishable from orthogonal solutions. The simple fact is that empirical structures do not conform to simple-structure models, even though variables do tend to cluster together. The availability of Varimax and other simple-structure rotation procedures has to some extent obscured the empirical facts.

Naively, one would like to draw a factor through each observed cluster of variables, thereby increasing the number of factors. A more systematic version of this approach is to slice up the factor space into small segments, and see what segments are well-filled with variables. Essentially, this is what the abridged Big Five Circumplex (AB5C) model to be set out here does. The model is thus a generalization or liberalization of simple-structure models. With two factors, for example, simple structure amounts to slicing up the plane into four quadrants, of which the four factor poles are the bisectrices; the AB5C procedure uses twelve slices of 30° each.

Not only simple-structure but also circumplex models (Wiggins, 1979) may be viewed as special cases of the AB5C model. The AB5C algorithm (see Hofstee *et al.*, 1992) essentially takes the projections of each variable on each of the ten planes that are formed by combining two factors at a time, and assigns the variable to the plane on which the projection is highest. Thus the model consists of all ten circumplexes that are two-dimensional slices of the five-space. The reason for this representation is that few variables have appreciable loadings on more than two factors (whereas many load on two, precluding simple structure). As a consequence of the AB5C approach, the classical two-dimensional circumplex models are part of the AB5C model.

Circumplex models tend to use octants or sextants rather than duodecants. There are two reasons for preferring the latter segmentation. One is empirical: Hofstee and De Raad (1991) found, for example, that traits denoting nervousness had a IV − I − profile (primary loading on the negative pole of Factor IV, emotional stability; secondary loading on the negative pole of I, extraversion), whereas traits denoting depression had a I − IV − pattern. Such clinically relevant distinctions would disappear upon coarser segmentation. The other reason for taking twelve segments is that facets of factors may be written as admixtures of other factors. For each factor pole, the model allows for a maximum of nine facets: one formed by the traits that load exclusively on that pole, and 2 × 4 facets that arise through adding secondary loadings on the positive and negative poles of the four other factors. Thus in the above example, nervousness is a facet of Factor IV −, whereas depressiveness is a facet of I −. Table 3.1 lists the facets that were found in an analysis of Dutch trait terms (Hofstee and De Raad, 1991); we repeat that translations into English should be taken with a grain of salt. A drawback of fine segmentation is that traits are more likely to shift to another segment in a different sample of subjects.

Like two-dimensional models, the AB5C structure has certain dynamic qualities that are lacking in simple-structure representations, and make it more suitable for typological purposes. For example, if a person is high on both spontaneity (I+) and peaceableness (II+), one would be searching for a single label to express the blend, rather than retaining the isolated components. Scanning the AB5C solution, we would be guided towards the I+II+ terms such as merry, jovial, and cordial, or to the II+I+ segment containing sympathetic, friendly, and helpful, among many other terms. Reiterating Millon's quote, such labels 'restore and recompose the unity of personality by integrating seemingly diverse elements into a single coordinated syndrome'. If the spontaneous person were secondarily characterized by imperturbability (IV+) rather than peaceableness, the model would suggest I+IV+ optimistic, brisk, heroic, and the like. If he or she were somewhat casual (III−) in addition to being spontaneous, we could find uninhibited, light-hearted, and forward in the I+III− segment.

Naturally, there are limits to the taxonomy's flexibility. Like any system, it represents a compromise between parsimony and descriptive accuracy. Table 3.1 contains some 50 'types' out of the 90 that would be permitted by the model. The remaining segments are empty or near-empty, meaning that these types, if they exist, have not been sufficiently recognized to deserve a labelling. A complementary objection could be that the number of types is far too large. However, the conceptual parsimony and coherence of the model are such that only five bipolar concepts are needed to create and understand the typology.

Of paramount importance is the fact that AB5C types emerge, not through

Table 3.1 Facets of personality resulting from the AB5C analysis of Dutch trait terms

Facet	Term		Facet	Term
I+	Spontaneous	vs.	I−	Introverted
I+II+	Cheerful	vs.	I−II−	Mistrustful
I+IV+	Optimistic	vs.	I−IV−	Depressive
I+V+	Lively	vs.	I−V−	Shy
I+III−	Uninhibited	vs.	I−III+	Reserved
II+	Peaceable	vs.	II−	Bossy
II+I+	Sympathetic	vs.	II−I−	Selfish
II+III+	Modest	vs.	II−III−	Conceited
II+IV+	Patient	vs.	II−IV−	Impatient
II+V+	Liberal	vs.	II−V−	Greedy
II+IV−	Soft-hearted	vs.	II−IV+	Imperious
II+V−	Mild	vs.	II−V+	Aggressive
III+	Precise	vs.	III−	Nonchalant
III+II+	Conscientious			
III+IV+	Consistent	vs.	III−IV−	Thoughtless
III+I−	Serious	vs.	III−I+	Rash
III+II−	Perfectionistic	vs.	III−II+	Impish
III+V−	Disciplined	vs.	III−V+	Reckless
IV+	Imperturbable	vs.	IV−	Emotional
IV+I+	Self-assured	vs.	IV−I−	Nervous
IV+II+	Stable	vs.	IV−II−	Irritable
IV+III+	Steadfast	vs.	IV−III−	Unsteadfast
IV+V+	Resolute	vs.	IV−V−	Credulous
IV+I−	Rational	vs.	IV−I+	Impulsive
IV+II−	Hard	vs.	IV−II+	Vulnerable
V+I+	Dynamic	vs.	V−I−	Sedate
			V−III−	Superficial
V+IV+	Inventive	vs.	V−IV−	Submissive
V+II−	Explosive	vs.	V−II+	Meek
V+III−	Rebellious	vs.	V−III+	Obedient

sophisticated but fragile and opaque nonlinear combinations of data, but simply by applying the additive model, which is the most robust and transparent of all quantitative models. In our experience, the result of the application of the AB5C procedure, represented by a set of circumplex figures or by a table comparable to a full tournament schedule (home game, primary loading; away game, secondary loading), is easy to explain to practitioners, students, and interested lay persons.

Before returning to the question of how to cluster persons, a number of reservations should be made explicit. First, the empirical data in the trait domain are very shaky. Our educated guess is that less than 50 per cent of the variance of a trait term is common variance, the remainder consisting of specific and idiosyncratic interpretations of term meaning. Samples of many hundreds of subjects are therefore needed for stable results. Second, the solutions are language-dependent: we expect AB5C solutions in different sets of traits and/or different languages to be rotations of each other, but this expectation has not yet been tested. Third, the model has arisen in the context of the lexical approach to personality; no explicit attempt has as yet been made to apply it to scientific or professional vocabularies. However, none of these limitations is specific to the AB5C approach; the taxonomic properties are independent of the particular illustrations that were given.

Back to the person

Thus far, we have been clustering traits rather than people. In the abstract, there need not be correspondence between the two clusterings. In terms of the factor-analytic model: a matrix of factor *scores* could be rotated to simple structure; the corresponding rotation matrix will generally not be the same as the matrix that rotates the factor loadings to simple structure. However, the lexical hypothesis implies a more optimistic view on the relationship: if it is true that the language community tends to invent labels for personological syndromes that are frequent and salient enough, then the *a posteriori* conclusion would be justified that such labels represent types of person. Here, we will explore the relation between person clusters and variable clusters in a more detailed manner.

Principal components analysis (PCA) is eminently suited to investigate the relation between the structures of variables and persons (Hofstee and Ten Berge, 1988). Unlike other factor-analytic models, PCA is quite impartial in its treatment of the two sides of the coin (see, most notably, Horst, 1965). Even though factor scores are not usually attended to — presumably because subjects are anonymous whereas variables have labels — they have the same formal status as the loadings, and the two sets are intimately connected. For example, when factor loadings are rotated, implicitly the matrix of factor scores is post-multiplied with the same rotation matrix.

There are close correspondences between PCA of persons and of variables. A Q-type analysis of raw scores would give exactly the same solution as a regular R-analysis, except for the fact that the scales of the factor scores and loadings would be complementary: in Q-analysis, the sum of squares of the person loadings would be the eigenvalue of the factor rather than the number of persons. The symmetry gets lost when variables are standardized in one direction or another, as happens automatically in routine applications. However, there is every reason to try for standardization in both directions (with the reservation that exact double standardization is generally not possible): in ordinary factor analysis, differences between subjects in mean and standard deviation are often a nuisance, as these differences represent differential response sets rather than substantive variance; in Q-analysis, differences between means and/or variances of variables usually have no substantive meaning. With approximate double standardization, the symmetry of the treatments would be restored. In sum, there is no substantive difference between Q-PCA and R-PCA, and the choice of direction may depend on practical considerations.

For a closer empirical look, we carried out separate rotations of the factor loadings and factor scores matrices of the same data set. Self-ratings and ratings by a peer on 75 trait-descriptive adjectives were obtained from 197 paid subjects, as part of a larger investigation. The traits were carefully selected to cover the 25 best-filled positive segments (that is, from I+I+ to V+II−) of the AB5C solution of Dutch trait terms (Hofstee and De Raad, 1991); per segment, three terms were selected. Self-ratings and peer-ratings were treated separately. Five principal components were extracted for each set.

Treatment P (for persons) of the data consisted of rotating the matrix of factor scores to simple structure according to the Varimax criterion, and rotating the matrix of factor loadings with the same rotation matrix. Subsequently, the AB5C algorithm assigning each variable and each person to the segment with the largest projection was applied to both matrices. Treatment V (for variables) rotated the matrix of factor loadings to maximum correspondence with the intended structure; subsequently, the AB5C algorithm was applied to the factor scores and loadings.

The treatments gave different solutions; that is, the rotation matrices were not nearly identical. The question is whether they do each other's job; that is, how well the P treatment captures the variables and the V treatment the persons. Table 3.2 gives a cross-tabulation of the AB5C-projection lengths of the variables according to both treatments. Clearly, the P treatment is quite harmful to the representation of the variables: the large majority of the variables have lower projections in the P-solution, the difference being in the order of 0.1; it should be realized that even the V-solution is not optimal for the variables, as a Varimax rotation would have been. Somewhat surprisingly, the reverse effect does not occur: as Table 3.3 shows, the sizes of the person projections (on a standard score scale) are hardly different for the two treatments. So overall, the standard V-approach is the clear winner, and rotation of factor scores matrices does not appear to be a preferable alternative, even from a typological point of view.

Somewhat enigmatically, the persons do not appear to cluster into particular AB5C segments, as the variables tend to do; rather, the persons seem to be scattered more or less randomly over segments. Most notably, many persons can be found in segments that carry few if any trait variables. This finding is difficult to reconcile

Table 3.2 Cross-tabulations of vector lengths[1] of 75 variables resulting from V-treatment (columns) and P-treatment (rows), for self-ratings and other-ratings

		P-treatment								
		Self-ratings					Other-ratings			
		0.3	0.4	0.5	0.6		0.3	0.4	0.5	0.6
V-treatment	0.4	6	5	1	—	0.4	11	4	—	—
	0.5	4	17	5	1	0.5	6	12	6	—
	0.6	—	11	10	1	0.6	—	14	13	1
	0.7	—	5	1	8	0.7	—	3	4	1

[1] Vector lengths are reported by their first digit.

Table 3.3 Cross-tabulations of vector lengths[1] of 197 subjects resulting from V-treatment (columns) and P-treatment (rows), for self-ratings and other-ratings

			Self-ratings					Other-ratings			
		0	1	2	3		0	1	2	3
V-treatment	0	15	3	—	—	0	16	6	—	—
	1	3	97	7	—	1	5	87	11	—
	2	—	8	49	2	2	—	6	46	3
	3	—	—	—	13	3	—	—	2	15

[1] Vector lengths are reported by their first digit.

with the lexical hypothesis cited above, which would seem to predict that the clusterings of persons and trait terms covary. The fact that no salient clusters of persons arise may be responsible for the lack of success of the P-treatment.

In conclusion, we have explored the formal correspondence between person-oriented and variable-oriented approaches. We have demonstrated a method that starts with structuring the persons space; from that demonstration, however, it cannot be concluded that the person-oriented approach is in any way superior. In view of the dynamic properties of the AB5C approach to variables, it may be maintained that it implements the idea of personality structure, and may serve as a useful heuristic for typological purposes. However, many persons seem to shirk from any typological system.

General conclusions

After having gone to some length in exploring philosophical and sophisticated psychometric renderings of the elusive concept of personality structure, we have arrived at a simple answer: the thing is right under our noses. Every time a professional or lay person succeeds in arriving at the most telling label for a person, unity — if not uniqueness — is created. The label need not be part of ordinary language; dedicated vocabularies have been constructed, for example, for clinical classification. The interchange between scientific and general-purpose language, however, is lively: on the one hand, the Big Five dimensions derived from everyday language are rapidly gaining scientific ground; on the other, it cannot take long before 'borderlines' become a fact of everyday life.

What may have obscured the view of trait labels as the carriers of personality structure is the fiction that traits are elemental. Few contemporary philosophers of science would still subscribe to the idea that elementary observations can be pinpointed that would form the basis of knowledge. However, the parallel notion that traits constitute personality, and that structures should be imposed upon traits to arrive at the level of the person, goes virtually undisputed in psychological science. Only upon full realization that traits themselves are summary labels — not necessarily of behavioural tendencies, but at least as much of inferences and projections — are we ready to stop looking for the phantom of an additional structure.

What is needed is not structure superimposed upon traits but a structure *of* traits; that is, a heuristic for handling the many thousands of existing and still-to-be-invented labels in a systematic manner. The lexical approach to personality, by its relative comprehensiveness on the one hand and its parsimonious five-dimensional model on the other, is the most promising in this respect. One may even judge that to classify persons into one of ten slots ranging from I + to V − is quite enough for certain purposes. However, without loss of conceptual parsimony and without using opaque nonlinear modelling, the AB5C model provides a more refined typology by pitting the ten factor poles against each other for both a home and an away game, thus producing 90 slots. Whereas about half of these slots are defined only by their place in the system rather than explicitly by a sufficient number of variables, persons seem to occupy just about all of these slots. That discrepancy may inspire a search for appropriate labels.

Finally, some may doubt whether typologies are ethical. We would agree that calling people names is no personological business. However, description of persons is; and complicated and laborious description is no more ethical, and no more scientific, than crude but efficient description.

References

Amelang, M. and Borkenau, P. (1981), 'Vorhersagen für einige Personen und viele Merkmale. Oder: Konsistenz über Merkmale und Kontextbedingungen als Eigenschaft' [Prediction of some of the people and many response variables. Or: consistency across response variables and environmental context as a personality trait], in E. Michaelis (ed.), *Bericht über den 32. Kongress der Deutschen Gesellschaft für Psychologie in Zürich, 1980* [Reports of the 32nd Congress of the German Psychological Association, Zurich 1980.] Göttingen, FRG: Hogrefe, vol. 2, pp. 495–8.

Amelang, M. and Borkenau, P. (1986), 'The trait concept: current theoretical considerations, empirical facts, and implications for personality inventory construction', in A. Angleitner and J.S. Wiggins (eds.), *Personality Assessment via Questionnaires: Current issues in theory and measurement*, Berlin, FRG: Springer-Verlag, pp. 7–34.

Asendorpf, J. (1990), 'The measurement of individual consistency', *Methodika*, **4**, 1–23.

Asendorpf, J. (1991), *Die differentielle Sichtweise in der Psychologie* [The Individual Differences Perspective in Psychology], Göttingen, FRG: Hogrefe.

Bem, D.J. and Allen, A. (1974), 'On predicting some of the people some of the time: the search for cross-situational consistencies in behavior', *Psychological Review*, **81**, 506–20.

Bergman, L.R. and Magnusson, D. (1990), 'General issues about data quality in longitudinal research', in D. Magnusson and L.R. Bergman (eds.), *Data Quality in Longitudinal Research*, Cambridge: Cambridge University Press, pp. 1–31.

Brown, F.G. and Scott, D.A. (1966), 'The unpredictability of predictability', *Journal of Educational Measurement*, **3**, 297–301.

Cattell, R.B. (1970), 'The integration of functional and psychometric requirements in a quantitative and computerized diagnostic system', in A.R. Mahrer (ed.), *New Approaches to Personality Classification*, New York, NY: Columbia University Press, pp. 9—52.

Chaplin, W.F. and Goldberg, L.R. (1984), 'A failure to replicate the Bem and Allen study of individual differences in cross-situational consistency', *Journal of Personality and Social Psychology*, **47**, 1074—90.

Digman, J.M. (1990), 'Personality structure: emergence of the five-factor model', *Annual Review of Psychology*, **41**, 417—40.

Eysenck, H.J. (1952), *The Scientific Study of Personality*, London: Routledge & Kegan Paul.

Fiske, D.W. (1986), 'The trait concept and the personality questionnaire', in A. Angleitner and J.S. Wiggins (eds.), *Personality Assessment via Questionnaires: Current issues in theory and measurement*, Berlin, FRG: Springer-Verlag, pp. 35—48.

Frederiksen, N. and Melville, S.D. (1954), 'Differential predictability in the use of test scores', *Educational and Psychological Measurement*, **14**, 647—56.

Ghiselli, E.E. (1956), 'Differentiation of individuals in terms of their predictability', *Journal of Applied Psychology*, **40**, 374—7.

Ghiselli, E.E. (1963), 'Moderating effects and differential reliability and validity', *Journal of Applied Psychology*, **47**, 81—6.

Goldberg, L.R. (1990), 'An alternative "description of personality": the big-five factor structure', *Journal of Personality and Social Psychology*, **59**, 1216—29.

Gower, J.C. (1971), 'A general coefficient of similarity and some of its properties', *Biometrics*, **27**, 857—71.

Hofstee, W.K.B. (1980), *De empirische discussie: Theorie van het sociaal-wetenschappelijk onderzoek* [The Empirical Discussion: The theory of social-scientific research], Meppel, The Netherlands: Boom.

Hofstee, W.K.B. and De Raad, B. (1991), 'Persoonlijkheidsstructuur: De AB5C-taxonomie van Nederlandse eigenschapstermen' [Personality structure: the AB5C taxonomy of Dutch trait terms], *Nederlands Tijdschrift voor de Psychologie*, **46**, 262—74.

Hostee, W.K.B. and Smid, N.G. (1986), 'Psychometric models for analysis of data from personality questionnaires', in A. Angleitner and J.S. Wiggins (eds.), *Personality Assessment via Questionnaires: Current issues in theory and measurement*, Berlin, FRG: Springer-Verlag, pp. 166—77.

Hofstee, W.K.B. and Ten Berge, J.M.F. (1988), 'Principal components analysis in longitudinal research', invited comment, Conference on Stability and Change: Methods and Models for Data Treatment, Soria Moria, 2—5 April 1988.

Hofstee, W.K.B. and Zegers, F.E. (in press), 'Idiographic correlation: modeling judgments of agreement between school grades', *Tijdschrift voor Onderwijsresearch*.

Hofstee, W.K.B., De Raad, B. and Goldberg, L.R. (1992), 'Integration of the big five and circumplex approaches to trait structure', *Journal of Personality and Social Psychology*, **63**, 146—63.

Horst, P. (1965), *Factor Analysis of Data Matrices*, New York, NY: Holt.

Jackson, D.N. (1986), 'The process of responding in personality assessment', in A. Angleitner and J.S. Wiggins (eds.), *Personality Assessment via Questionnaires: Current issues in theory and measurement*, Berlin, FRG: Springer-Verlag pp. 123—42.

John, O.P. (1990), 'The "Big Five" factor taxonomy: dimensions of personality in the natural language and in questionnaires', in L.A. Pervin (ed.), *Handbook of Personality: Theory and research*, New York, NY: Guilford Press, pp. 66—100.

Kouwer, B.J. (1973), *Existentiële psychologie: Grondslagen van het psychologisch gesprek* [Existential Psychology: Fundamentals of the psychological talk], Meppel, The Netherlands: Boom.

Lubinski, D. and Humphreys, L.G. (1990), 'Assessing spurious "moderator effects": illustrated substantively with the hypothesized ("synergistic") relation between spatial and mathematical ability', *Psychological Bulletin,* **107,** 385–93.

McCrae, R.R. (1990), 'Traits and trait names: how well is openness represented in natural languages?', *European Journal of Personality,* **4,** 119–29.

Magnusson, D. (1990), 'Personality development from an interactional perspective', in L.A. Pervin (ed.), *Handbook of Personality: Theory and research,* New York, NY: Guilford Press, pp. 193–222.

Millon, T. (1990), 'The disorders of personality', in L.A. Pervin (ed.), *Handbook of Personality: Theory and research,* New York, NY: Guilford Press, pp. 339–70.

Ostendorf, F. (1990), *Sprache und Persönlichkeitsstruktur: Zur Validität des Fünf-Faktoren-Modells der Persönlichkeit* [Language and Personality Structure: The validity of the five-factor model of personality], Regensburg, FRG: Roderer.

Saunders, D.R. (1956), 'Moderator variables in prediction', *Educational and Psychological Measurement,* **16,** 209–22.

Schmitt, M. (1990), *Konsistenz als Persönlichkeitseigenschaft?* [Consistency as a Personality Trait?], Berlin, FRG: Springer.

Shepperd, J.A. (1991), 'Cautions in assessing spurious "moderator effects" ', *Psychological Bulletin,* **110,** 315–17.

Wiggins, J.S. (1973), *Personality and Prediction: Principles of personality assessment,* Reading, MA: Addison-Wesley.

Wiggins, J.S. (1979), 'A psychological taxonomy of trait-descriptive terms: the interpersonal domain', *Journal of Personality and Social Psychology,* **37,** 395–412.

4/ On the generality and comprehensiveness of the Five-Factor model of personality
Evidence for five robust factors in questionnaire data

Fritz Ostendorf
University of Koblenz-Landau, Germany

Alois Angleitner
University of Bielefeld, Germany

Introduction

In recent years, the development of personality trait taxonomies has led to increasing research on the most reliable and most important personality factors. As a result, a 'new' model of personality structure (but see Wiggins and Trapnell, in press) has joined the old debate between the well-known but vehemently competing factor models proposed by Cattell, Eysenck, Guilford, and others. Assuming five factors, which are believed to provide a sufficient description of personality structure, the new model takes an intermediate position between the more simple three-factor PEN model proposed by Eysenck and the more complex multifactorial systems proposed by Cattell and Guilford. Because the Five-Factor model has been shown to be robust across a diversity of studies, the five factors have also been called the Big Five. With reference to the work of Norman (1963, 1967), Goldberg (1980), and McCrae and Costa (1985a,b,c), the Big Five are frequently labelled: (1) *surgency* or *extraversion*; (2) *agreeableness*; (3) *conscientiousness*; (4) *emotional stability* or, conversely, *neuroticism*; and (5) *culture, intellect,* or *openness to experience.*

Although different researchers have varied in their choice of labels, there are substantial meaning overlaps as well as strong empirical relationships between the different operationalizations of the five factors. To elucidate their meaning, Table 4.1 presents some marker variables of the Big Five selected from adjective rating inventories published by Norman (1963), McCrae and Costa (1987), and Peabody and Goldberg (1989). In addition, Table 4.1 shows the loadings of the adjective rating scales on five Varimax rotated factors that emerged from principal component

Table 4.1 Big-Five marker scales from various rating inventories and their factor loadings in analysis of self- and peer-rating data

	SU/EX		AG		CO		ES		OP/IN	
	I	II	I·	II	I	II	I	II	I	II
Factor I (surgency or extraversion)										
Talkative—silent	**78**	**71**	−05	03	02	06	−00	−06	09	05
Sociable—reclusive	**79**	**76**	09	17	02	−01	18	04	02	04
Fun-loving—sober	**61**	**53**	19	22	−24	−**30**	06	−06	18	27
Spontaneous—inhibited	**73**	**73**	02	−01	−09	−11	26	15	14	24
Frank—secretive	**76**	**65**	23	**33**	−03	−01	03	06	14	16
Active—inactive	**64**	**58**	−00	−05	**38**	**30**	19	16	17	27
Factor II (agreeableness)										
Mild, gentle—headstrong	−03	01	**69**	**68**	−05	−02	11	20	14	23
Good-natured—irritable	−13	−05	**58**	**57**	−02	12	**43**	**38**	07	09
Soft-hearted—ruthless	12	13	**71**	**68**	07	19	−13	−09	15	19
Forgiving—vengeful	25	18	**64**	**67**	10	24	17	25	07	14
Trustful—distrustful	28	25	**55**	**56**	−02	04	07	16	−02	−04
Lenient—harsh	04	−01	**68**	**69**	01	08	13	**30**	22	13
Factor III (conscientiousness)										
Responsible—undependable	15	12	17	24	**68**	**73**	−04	03	25	18
Scrupulous—unscrupulous	−15	−13	−04	−04	**68**	**65**	−03	−11	−03	11
Conscientious—negligent	13	14	07	18	**80**	**77**	07	04	07	12
Hardworking—lazy	16	20	11	17	**67**	**69**	07	04	06	06
Serious—frivolous	−25	−23	10	10	**64**	**70**	−01	09	09	14
Orderly—disorderly	04	05	07	14	**76**	**76**	18	16	−09	−01
Factor IV (emotional stability)										
Poised—nervous, tense	11	06	24	**30**	04	02	**75**	**73**	05	09
Calm—anxious	21	09	03	09	11	17	**64**	**70**	19	13
Hardy—vulnerable	12	16	−07	−03	15	10	**64**	**59**	−12	−20
Calm—worrying	11	−08	12	11	04	−03	**64**	**61**	06	02
Relaxed—tense	08	06	24	**31**	−02	−08	**70**	**63**	02	11
Contented—discontented	**39**	26	26	**32**	17	21	**55**	**54**	08	06
Factor V (culture, intellect, or openness to experience)										
Artistically sensitive—artistically insensitive	−04	05	09	15	−14	−04	−08	−06	**57**	**60**
Intellectual—unreflective, narrow	−07	−02	03	04	25	**36**	09	10	**66**	**69**
Creative—uncreative	12	19	06	14	04	04	09	02	**60**	**64**
Broad interests—narrow interests	18	**32**	09	16	18	**30**	21	13	**58**	**63**
Intelligent—unintelligent	08	16	01	07	20	**31**	09	13	**68**	**67**
Imaginative—unimaginative	27	**31**	10	12	00	05	04	05	**63**	**67**

Notes   All loadings ≥0.30 are listed in **bold**. The first two adjective rating scales listed under the heading of each factor are from Norman (1963), the next two scales from McCrae and Costa (1987), and the last two from Peabody and Goldberg (1989). The factor loadings reported in the table are loadings on five Varimax rotated principal components based on analyses of 179 rating scales (see Ostendorf, 1990) published by Norman (1963), McCrae and Costa (1987), Peabody and Goldberg (1989), Goldberg (1983, 1989), and John (1983; see John *et al.*, 1984). I: peer-ratings ($N = 383$), II: self-ratings ($N = 401$). SU/EX = surgency or extraversion, AG = agreeableness, CO = conscientiousness, ES = emotional stability, OP/IN = openness or intellect.

analyses of all 179 rating scales contained in the rating inventories from Norman (1963), McCrae and Costa (1987), Peabody and Goldberg (1989), Goldberg (1983, 1989), and John (1983; see John *et al.*, 1984). Although the adjectives listed in Table 4.1 were not selected according to their factor loadings, the patterns there are strikingly congruent and clear. Details of both analyses, which were based on samples of 383 (peer-ratings) and 401 subjects (self-ratings) are reported in Ostendorf (1990).

Most previous confirmations of the robustness of these five factors have come from studies of adjective rating data. For example, the validity of the Five-Factor model has been demonstrated on the basis of representative samples of personality-descriptive terms in various languages: Goldberg (1990) for Anglo-American; De Raad *et al.* (1988) for Dutch; and Ostendorf (1990) for German. Similar variants of the Big Five were found in studies of non-western personality languages; for example, Chinese (Yang and Bond, 1990), Filipino (Church and Katigbak, 1989), and Japanese (Isaka, 1990). These and other studies have shown that the five factors were not always the only factors that could underlie a specific data set. However, they were the only robust factors that could be replicated reliably across different languages, adjective samples, groups of raters, rating formats, and variations in the method of factor analysis.

Because it is quite likely that the range of all possible personality descriptions based on trait adjectives is not equivalent to that based on personality-descriptive sentences, it seems advisable to test the structural validity of the Five-Factor model on other data sources as well; for example, on the basis of questionnaire scales or items. If these factors are universal factors of personality language, they should be revealed not only on the basis of personality-descriptive adjectives in rating data but also on the basis of personality-descriptive phrases in questionnaire data.

McCrae and Costa explored this issue in a series of studies. For each separate study, they selected one popular personality inventory that was representative of one other major personality theory (for example, the Personality Research Form-E: Costa and McCrae, 1988; the California Q-Sort: McCrae *et al.*, 1986; the Myers-Briggs Type Indicator: McCrae and Costa, 1989a; the Adjective Check List: Piedmont *et al.*, 1991; the EPI and Psychoticism scales: McCrae and Costa, 1985b). To evaluate the comprehensiveness of the Five-Factor model, the scales of each personality inventory were correlated with the scales of the NEO Personality Inventory (NEO-PI), a questionnaire explicitly constructed for measuring the Big Five. In most studies, the common structure of both inventories was subsequently analysed in one common factor analysis. However, a more suitable test of the Five-Factor structure in questionnaire data would require the inclusion of a more comprehensive sample of questionnaires, such as a simultaneous factor analysis of scales or items from a very broad spectrum of personality questionnaires.

A basic principle underlying the major studies on the Five-Factor model in rating data has been the *comprehensiveness* and *representativeness* of the item pool analysed: proceeding from the assumption that most important individual differences are already encoded in everyday language, one first extracts a comprehensive and reasonably representative sample of the personality-descriptive terms from this language. Then, the most important factors describing personality can be determined on the basis of this representative sample of terms. Ideally, representative samples of personality-descriptive adjectives, verbs, or nouns are drawn from dictionaries containing the complete vocabulary of the language in question.

Unfortunately, no comparable sampling procedure is available for compiling personality-descriptive phrases such as questionnaire items. In principle, it is possible to construct an infinitely large number of personality-descriptive phrases. So, the number of possible questionnaire items is, at least theoretically, infinite. Previous attempts to test the validity of the Five-Factor model on the basis of questionnaire data have thus restricted their studies to a specific selection of items or scales from well-known personality questionnaires. Consequently, such a selection of questionnaire items does not represent the population of all possible personality-descriptive phrases but instead reflects the specific focuses and preferences of different researchers.

None the less, a relatively convincing solution could be provided by simultaneously analysing the items from a large set of personality questionnaires, even if representativeness cannot be ultimately achieved. With regard to the validity of the Five-Factor model, some such studies have already been performed with varying success.

In the following, we want to review a selection of such studies. Our selection is limited to studies in which a large sample of items or scales from several inventories have been factored in a common analysis. First, we will report results from factor analyses of questionnaire *scales*, which have been interpreted within the conceptual framework of the Five-Factor model either by the authors of the study in question or by other researchers. The next section explores how far the results of former extensive *item*-factor analyses have shown evidence for the Big-Five factors. Finally, we report the results of our own study, in which we examined the structural validity of the Five-Factor model on the basis of 576 items from inventories of different prominent personality theories.

Questionnaire scales and the Big Five

An overview of the many factor analytic studies of personality questionnaires is beyond the scope of this chapter. The only studies that are relevant to the structural validity of the Five-Factor model are those in which a large and comprehensive number of scales, preferably stemming from multidimensional personality inventories, have been analysed. We have also chosen a selection from this set of studies: in the following, we will report only studies whose results were originally discussed within the framework of the Five-Factor model. Table 4.2 presents a broad view of the results of such studies.

The results of a study by Amelang and Borkenau (1982) may lead to the assumption that the five rating factors can also be replicated in the domain of questionnaire data as long as a sufficiently large number of questionnaire scales from different inventories

Table 4.2 Classification of factors derived from comprehensive factor analyses of questionnaire scales

	Extraversion (I)	Agreeableness (II)	Conscientiousness (III)	Neuroticism (IV)	Openness (V)
Amelang and Borkenau (1982)	Extraversion	Dominance[R]	Self-control	Neuroticism	Independence of opinion
Noller *et al*. (1987)	Extraversion	Agreeableness	Conscientiousness	Neuroticism	—
Boyle (1989)	Extraversion	Tough poise[R]	Control	Neuroticism	Independence
Montag and Comrey (1990)	Extraversion	Agreeableness	Conscientiousness	Neuroticism	—
Conn and Ramanaiah (1990)	Extraversion	Agreeableness	Conscientiousness	Neuroticism	Openness to experience
Matthews *et al*. (1990)	Extraversion	Agreeableness	Conscientiousness	Neuroticism	Openness to experience
Zuckerman *et al*. (1988)	Sociability	Aggressive Sensation-seeking[R]	Impulsive Unsocialized Sensation-seeking[R]	Neuroticism Emotionality	—
Zuckerman *et al*. (1991)	Sociability	Aggression Hostility[R]	P-Impulsive Unsocialized Sensation-seeking[R]	Neuroticism Anxiety	—

Note: The superscript [R] means that a factor is reverse-scored in the direction opposite to that of the Big-Five label listed in the column head.

are entered into a common factor analysis. In this German study, the scales of Cattell's Sixteen Personality Factor Questionnaire (16PF; Schneewind, 1977), the Freiburg Personality Inventory (FPI; Fahrenberg and Selg, 1970), the Eysenck Personality Inventory in its two parallel forms (Eggert, 1974; Eysenck and Eysenck, 1968), and the scales of several inventories constructed by Guilford and his co-workers (GAMIN, STDCR, and GMPI, cited in Guilford *et al.*, 1976) were factor-analysed together. The extracted factors were interpreted as neuroticism, extraversion, dominance (probably similar to non-agreeableness), independence of opinion (culture/openness), and self-control (conscientiousness). Advocates of the Five-Factor model (such as Digman, 1990; McCrae and Costa, 1985b) frequently cite the results of this study as evidence for the generality and robustness of the Big Five. Other comparisons, using the factor models of Cattell, Guilford, and Eysenck, have led to outcomes that cannot be interpreted so clearly as corresponding to the Five-Factor model.

Noller, Law, and Comrey (1987) explored the common factor structure of the scales of the following inventories: the Comrey Personality Scales (CPS; Comrey, 1970), the 16PF scales (Cattell *et al.*, 1970), and the EPI scales (Eysenck and Eysenck, 1968). The factor analysis included 26 personality scales, five validity and response distortion scales, and scores for gender and age. Seven factors were extracted. According to the authors' interpretations, the most important part of the common variance of the questionnaire scales could be explained by four of the five

Norman factors. A factor identifiable as culture or openness could not be replicated. The evidence for the agreeableness factor was only weak. Costa and McCrae (1976), for example, interpreted a similar 'agreeableness' factor as openness to experience.

A quite similar picture resulted from a reanalysis of Noller *et al.*'s data conducted by Boyle (1989). Five factors resulted from a factor analysis of 25 EPI, CPS, and 16PF personality variables. In accordance with the 16PF secondaries reported by Krug and Johns (1986), Boyle (1989) interpreted the 'Big-Five' factors as extraversion, neuroticism, tough poise, independence, and control. Whereas Boyle (1989) did not discuss the possible correspondence of these factors to the Big Five, John (1990), starting from an inspection of the items of the 16PF, recently postulated a high equivalence between Cattell's second-order factors and the Big Five. We see a relatively high similarity between three factors reported by Boyle and the following three Big-Five factors: extraversion, neuroticism, and conscientiousness (Boyle's control factor). However, correspondence of the remaining two factors to the Big Five cannot be assumed without further empirical proof.

Montag and Comrey (1990) factored a subset of Noller *et al.*'s (1987) questionnaire scales in a different sample. In a common factor analysis of the 16PF and CPS scales, the authors clearly identified three of the Big-Five factors (extraversion, conscientiousness, and emotional stability). Some variants of agreeableness and openness were also identified, although not so clearly.

Conn and Ramanaiah (1990) found three factors underlying the Comrey Personality Scales (CPS) and five factors underlying the scales of the Personality Research Form-E (PRF; Jackson, 1984). The three Comrey factors were seen as similar to agreeableness, conscientiousness, and extraversion, and the five PRF factors were interpreted as being similar to those in the Five-Factor model. A combined factor analysis of the CPS and PRF factors yielded five second-order factors that were interpreted as extraversion, agreeableness, conscientiousness, neuroticism, and openness to experience. In our view, these results demonstrate that the CPS scales, and especially the PRF scales, assess a large proportion of the content of the Big Five. Besides obvious correspondences, there are also specific discrepancies. The CPS-extraversion factor, extracted by Conn and Ramanaiah (1990), appears to be a fusion of extraversion and neuroticism. However, no marker scales measuring the Big Five were included in the analysis, and, therefore, the concept of similarity used by Conn and Ramanaiah (1990) may be questioned.

Matthews, Stanton, Graham, and Brimelow (1990) analysed the structure of the Occupational Personality Questionnaire (OPQ; Saville & Holdsworth, 1984), which is based on a conceptual model claiming to provide a comprehensive coverage of personality. The authors conducted a factor analysis of the 31 OPQ scales, and the resulting pattern matrix of factor loadings showed a closer correspondence with the Big-Five dimensions of personality than with the structural model assumed by the authors of the OPQ. The similarity to the Big Five was impressive, although, as this interpretation is based on the inspection of factor loadings only, it needs further empirical proof.

Zuckerman, Kuhlman, and Camac (1988) factored a set of 46 questionnaire scales mostly measuring the constructs of biologically oriented temperament theories.[1] As can be expected from such a specific selection of variables, the following factors were clearly identifiable: sociability (or extraversion) and emotionality (neuroticism). Another factor was called impulsive-unsocialized sensation seeking. This factor was mostly marked by scales that included not only aspects of openness but also features of conscientiousness. A fourth factor called aggressive sensation seeking primarily loaded through the scales aggression (PRF) and responsibility (Jackson Personality Inventory; Jackson, 1976). This factor might possibly represent the negative pole of agreeableness.

Quite similar factors were found by Zuckerman, Kuhlman, Thornquist, and Kiers (1991) in an analysis of a selection of 33 of the 46 scales originally used by Zuckerman *et al.* (1988). The authors, however, emphasized that their interpretations required further empirical evidence. Unfortunately, the studies of Zuckerman *et al.* (1988, 1991) only analysed a highly selective sample of scales from several more or less broad personality inventories. Scales that can be considered as relatively clear markers for the factors agreeableness (such as PRF-nurturance), conscientiousness (such as the PRF scales order, achievement, endurance, impulsivity), and openness (such as PRF-understanding) were not included.

In summary, at least variants of the Big Five have been found in the majority of studies. Nevertheless, there were some clear deviations from the postulated factor structure in single cases. As one could expect, the factors extraversion and neuroticism were the most robust. With only a few exceptions, these factors could be replicated reliably in all studies. It was nearly always these factors that explained the largest part of the variance.[2] Third in order of stability was conscientiousness. This factor could be replicated particularly well in factor analyses that included the scales of the 16PF, the CPS, or the PRF. Primary marker variables for conscientiousness were the CPS-scale orderliness, and the 16PF-scales superego strength, and self-control, as well as the PRF-scales order, cognitive structure, achievement, and non-impulsivity. There was less empirical evidence for the hypothesized factor agreeableness and only little evidence for an independent and clearly interpretable fifth factor. Of course, this pattern of results is most probably due to the idiosyncratic variable selections used in the different studies. The factor openness, for instance, was only represented in a few studies through a small number of questionnaire scales (such as the 16PF-M-scale imagination, the Q1-scale radicalism, and the PRF-scale understanding). Indeed, the results of the studies reflect the fact that most personality test constructors are interested in measuring at least the (most important?) personality factors extraversion and neuroticism.

Furthermore, a common characteristic of all reported studies was that assumed correspondence between questionnaire factors and the Big-Five rating factors were always inferred by subjective interpretations but not tested via empirical analyses. Most studies interpreted the results of explorative factor analyses solely on the basis of visual inspections of factor-loading patterns. Furthermore, all former studies analysed questionnaire data on the scale level. For several reasons, we prefer to factor-analyse questionnaire data on the item level.

Item-factor analysis as an appropriate method for analysing the structure of questionnaire data

It is well-known that different personality researchers have a preference for constructs of varying breadth, abstraction, or globality. Broad, abstract, or global constructs are defined in such a way that they refer to a larger number of behaviours than do narrow ones. In factor analyses, variations in the breadth of the measured traits could be represented adequately by using large numbers of scales or items for broad traits and only one or a few for narrow traits. In fact, broad constructs are usually operationalized through a larger number of items (for example, the NEO-extraversion scale contains 48 items). In factor analyses of scales, however, these items are summed up to only one single-scale score, with the result that broad scales unwarrantedly obtain the same weight as narrow ones. That is, the different breadths of the constructs are concealed. The resulting factors represent a mixture of different levels of abstraction. In extreme cases, a new factor appears because a very specific construct has been operationalized via several narrow scales, each composed of a small number of highly similar items. If, in contrast, the complete item pool is factored, the content of all the items can be represented more adequately. In an item-factor analysis, the contents will be represented most adequately if specific constructs are operationalized through fewer items than broad constructs. This tends to be the case, because global scales frequently comprise more items than narrow ones.

As well as accounting for a broader spectrum of contents at the item level, the method of item-factor analysis is more in line with the goal of the lexical approach: a comprehensive description of the structure of personality language should include as many different personality-descriptive terms or statements as possible.

Finally, for the purpose of assigning items to scales, a factor analysis of a large number of questionnaire items may lead to item weights that are much more valid than those given by the item keys of many commonly used personality inventories. This comparison also applies to factor-analytically derived questionnaire scales if these scales have been developed on the basis of only small homogeneous item pools. It is well known that the correlation between items and scales or factors heavily depends on the kind and size of the item pool. A collection of items that appears to be quite homogeneous in a specific item sample may turn out to be much more heterogeneous in a broader item sample.

A related argument derives from the observation that factor analyses of questionnaire scales are often difficult to interpret because the labels of the scales do not refer accurately to the item contents: similar labels refer to different contents; scales labelled differently measure similar domains. Therefore, in most scale-factor analyses, the interpretation of the factors cannot be based solely upon the factor pattern of the scales but must be grasped and guided indirectly through the interpretation of items. In factor analyses of items, this problem does not exist: the factors are directly interpretable according to their item loadings.

Actually there are a number of statistical problems associated with the application of item-factor analysis (see Nunnally, 1978). None the less, some of the leading experts in factor analysis are convinced that the advantages of item-factor analysis outweigh its disadvantages. So, one can follow Cattell and Gibbons's (1968) recommendation that even the parcel-factor analysis appears to be an unsatisfactory compromise in comparison with complete item-factor analyses: 'any attempt to decide between the factor structure of two scales had best . . . break down the scales under examination ideally into single items or, if economy forbids this, into a fair number . . . [of] random "parcels" from each scale' (p. 118).

Studies based on comprehensive samples of questionnaire items

To the best of our knowledge, no study has been published in which the Five-Factor model was tested with a *comprehensive* selection of questionnaire items. Most factor-analytic studies of questionnaire items have been based on samples of items from the three prominent personality theories of Cattell, Guilford, and Eysenck. From the countless number of studies, we will review only those that have performed a factor analysis of large item samples taken from several personality questionnaires. Table 4.3 gives an overview of these studies.

Cattell and Gibbons (1968) compared the Guilford and Cattell factor markers in

Table 4.3 Classification of factors derived from comprehensive factor analyses of questionnaire items

	Extraversion (I)	Agreeableness (II)	Conscientiousness (III)	Neuroticism (IV)	Openness (V)
Cattell and Gibbons (1968)[a]	Exvia	Pathemia vs. cortertia	—	Anxiety	Independence
Sells *et al.* (1970)	Extraversion	Relaxed composure vs. suspicious excitability	Conscientiousness	Emotional stability[R]	Artistic interests
Eysenck and Eysenck (1969)	Extraversion	—	—	Neuroticism	—
Vagg and Hammond (1976)	Sociability	Community-centred morality vs. self-centred independence		Neuroticism	Sensitivity vs. practicality
Eysenck (1978)	Extraversion	—	—	Neuroticism	—
McKenzie (1988)	Extraversion	—	Superego strength	Neuroticism	—
Johnson *et al.* (1984)	Surgency	Agreeableness	Conscientiousness	Emotional stability[R]	Culture
Costa *et al.* (1985)	Extraversion	Cynicism[R]	—	Neuroticism	Intellectual interests

Notes: The superscript [R] means that a factor is reverse-scored in the direction opposite to that of the Big-Five label listed in the column head. The factors found by Browne and Howarth (1977) are not reported in Table 4.2 (see text).
[a]Cattell and Gibbons (1968) performed an item-parcel factor analysis.

a common factor analysis. The data, sampled by Gibbons (1966) in a doctoral dissertation under Guilford, involved 424 items representing 14 Cattell factors and 15 Guilford factors. The authors conducted a parcel-factor analysis based on 68 variables representing the 424 items; that is, the 68 variables were constructed out of clusters of items with homogeneous content. Eighteen primary-order factors were extracted and rotated to an oblique factor pattern. Cattell and Gibbons (1968) concluded that all 14 Cattell factors were confirmed, and that the 14 Cattell factors and 15 Guilford factors had eight dimensions in common. However, we are more interested in the second-order factors found in these studies, because the primaries have been found to be highly unreplicable (for example, Eysenck and Eysenck, 1969; Howarth and Browne, 1971a,b; Kline and Barrett, 1983). Nine second-order factors were rotated. In agreement with former studies, the four factors explaining most variance were labelled: (1) exvia vs. invia, (2) anxiety, (3) cortertia, and (4) independence. As John (1990) has recently argued, Cattell's second-order factors show a high correspondence with the Big Five. According to John (1990, p. 88), there is a high correspondence between the factors extraversion and exvia, neuroticism and anxiety, agreeableness and pathemia vs. cortertia, openness to experience and independence, as well as between conscientiousness and superego strength. In line with John's interpretation, the four second-order factors in Cattell and Gibbons (1968) can be considered as equivalent to four of the Big Five. However, Cattell and Gibbons did not report a factor superego strength. Furthermore, the loading patterns of Cattell and Gibbons's second-order factors reveal some marked deviations from the results of other studies reported by Cattell's team (see Cattell and Gibbons, 1968, pp. 115–16). For example, the factor exvia–invia not only correlated with the typical scales for this factor but also showed substantial loadings of G (superego strength), O (untroubled adequacy vs. guilt proneness), and Q1 (conservatism vs. radicalism). Further pecularities were found in the loading patterns of the other factors. Therefore, neither a high stability of the second-order factors nor a perfect correspondence with the Big Five can be assumed. Consequently, the precise level of correspondence with the Big Five needs to be tested empirically through the inclusion of appropriate marker variables.

Sells, Demaree, and Will (1970) conducted an item-factor analysis comparing the personality concepts of Cattell's and Guilford's models. This study is one of the largest item-factor analyses ever reported. A total of 600 items was factorized; 300 marker items comprised 78 marker clusters for 15 Guilford factors, and 300 items represented marker items for 17 Cattell factors. Twenty-three factors were extracted from the matrix of item correlations, and both 15 and 18 factors were rotated using both the Varimax and Promax methods. The 18 Promax factors were interpreted, but neither Guilford's nor Cattell's model was confirmed. The two most dominant factors were clearly identified as *(1) emotional stability* (primarily marked by items from the Guilford [G] and Cattell [C] scales cycloid disposition [G:C], nervousness [G:N], depression [G:D], guilt proneness [C:O], ergic tension [C:Q4], and as *(2) extraversion* (which was primarily loaded by items of the scales sociability [G:S], Parmia [C:H: venturesome, bold], surgency [C:F], and ascendance [G:A]). In terms of explained variance, the next most importance factors were *(3) artistic interests* (this factor corresponds almost completely with Guilford's Artistic Interest Scale), *(4) conscientiousness* (which shows loadings from cultural conformity [G:CC] and superego strength [C:G]) and *(5) relaxed composure vs. suspicious excitability* (primarily loaded by excitability [C:D], protension [C:L: suspicious] vs. alaxia [trusting, adaptable], agreeableness [G:A], and self-control [C:Q3].

It is probable that at least the three most dominant factors (emotional stability, extraversion, conscientiousness) are very similar to Big-Five factors, as well as to Cattell's postulated second-order factors (exvia—invia, anxiety, superego strength). Usually, artistic interests is considered to be an important facet of the fifth factor in the Five-Factor model (Costa and McCrae, 1985). For this reason, one would expect a close correspondence — although no identity — between these factors. Likewise the factor relaxed composure vs. suspicious excitability should correspond to agreeableness. The Cattell factors excitability (for example, the uncontrolled expression of anger) and suspiciousness vs. trust can be interpreted as facets of the broader factor agreeableness.

However, our speculations are just as empirically unfounded as the stability of the factors reported by Sells *et al.* (1970). For instance, the decision to extract 18 factors was made rather arbitrarily. Even using marker variables, Howarth and Browne (1971a) were able to replicate only some of the factors reported by Sells *et al.* (1970). It has often been shown that large numbers of factors are usually required to explain a reasonable proportion of the variables' common variance in a specific sample. In general, however, only those factors explaining most of the variance are found to be replicable over different studies. These factors are mostly similar to those that can be found at a higher-order level (McCormick *et al.*, 1991). A reanalysis of the data in Sells *et al.* (1970) could perhaps reveal more evidence for the Big Five by considering only the most dominant and robust factors or by extracting only higher-order factors.

An interesting detail of this study, which supports the utility of item-factor analysis, was the finding 'that analysis at the item level is highly destructive to the factors previously assembled without adequate concern for their loadings in large matrices' (Sells *et al.*, 1970, p. 419). For example, Sells *et al.*'s analysis of Cattell's and Guilford's scales indicated 'a clear need for reclassification of at least 400 of the 600 source items' (p. 421).

A further extensive analysis is reported by Eysenck and Eysenck (1969). They factored a selection of marker items from the following personality inventories: STDCR and GAMIN (Guilford), 16PF (Cattell), and EPI (Eysenck). In this study, Guilford's model was represented by 109 items, Cattell's model by 99 items, and Eysenck's model by the 114 items from the EPI. All items were administered to 600 male and 600 female students. First-, second-, and third-order Promax factor solutions were calculated separately for each inventory, and only factors from a higher level of analysis were carried over into a common factor analysis. As Vagg and Hammond (1976, p. 122) noted, 'only three factors, at most, were carried into common factoring, and since it was to be expected that two of these would be E and N, there was little chance for another factor to appear'. Unfortunately, Eysenck and Eysenck (1969) did not describe their analysis procedure in sufficient detail. None the less, the higher-order-level analyses yielded only two robust factors. One additional factor found in the male sample and two further factors in the female sample were relatively unimportant and difficult to interpret. The primary goal of Eysenck and Eysenck's (1969) study seems to have been to confirm the factors neuroticism and extraversion. This may be underlined with a citation from Eysenck and Eysenck (1985), regretting 'that at the time these analyses were done . . . no P scale was in existence; hence the analysis is concerned only with two factors. It would be interesting to repeat the work . . . and to attempt to find a third factor representing psychoticism' (p. 137). Kline and Barrett (1983) have also pointed out procedural problems in the above-mentioned study.

Vagg and Hammond (1976) designed their study as a partial replication of Eysenck and Eysenck (1969). However, they employed methods that gave smaller factors a chance to emerge. That is, Vagg and Hammond (1976) based their analysis on correlations between a larger number of primary factors extracted from each of the three questionnaires, whereas Eysenck and Eysenck's (1969) inter-inventory analysis relied on the correlations of a small number of higher-order factors from each questionnaire. As in the original study, the matrix of item correlations of each inventory was factored for the arbitrary number of 20 principal components, and each of these solutions was subsequently transformed by a Promax rotation. To arrive at a second-order solution, the authors did not calculate factor scores, but obtained scale scores for each person on the 60 primary factors by giving unit weight to each item assigned to a factor. Ten second-order factors were extracted from the correlation matrix of the 60 scales, and a four-factor Varimax solution was found to be robust across gender groups. The largest and most stable factors could be identified clearly as neuroticism and sociability or social extraversion. Factor III was called sensitivity vs. practicality, and was primarily loaded by items from the Cattell scales M+ (praxernia; imagination), I+ (harria; tender-mindedness), A− (sizothymia), and the Guilford scale T (introspectiveness). The authors speculated that this factor might also be related to the artistic interests factor of Sells *et al.* (1970). A comparison reveals that Factor III has much in common with the factor called *Unabhängigkeit der Meinungsbildung* (independence of opinion) found by Amelang and Borkenau (1982) in their common-factor analysis of the Cattell, Eysenck, and Guilford scales. McCrae and Costa (1985b), for example, viewed this factor (*Unabhängigkeit der Meinungsbildung*) as evidence for the robustness of their factor openness to experience. An inspection of the factor loadings and the item contents reported by Vagg and Hammond (1976, p. 126) reveals that this factor covers all important aspects of Costa and McCrae's (1985) factor openness to experience: openness to ideas, to aesthetics, to feelings, values, actions, and openness to fantasy. Factor IV was called community-centred morality vs. self-centred independence, and was seen as equivalent to the conscientiousness factor found by Sells *et al.* (1970) and as similar to Cattell's conception of Promethean will. In addition, the authors expected significant relations to a factor called friendliness, which was found by Bendig (1962) in a factor analysis of the Guilford–Zimmerman Temperament Survey. Therefore, community-centred morality vs. self-centred independence may be related to both the conscientiousness and the agreeableness factor of the Five-Factor model. However, further studies are needed to test these hypotheses empirically.

Because the studies of Eysenck and Eysenck (1969) and Sells *et al.* (1970) intended to provide a direct comparison of the personality systems of Cattell, Guilford, and Eysenck, their results only apply to these factor models. In contrast, Browne and Howarth (1977) started — similarly to the classic work of French (1953, 1973) — with a comprehensive sampling of scales from several personality theories.

In summary, Browne and Howarth (1977) sampled 3,029 items from 17 personality inventories. After eliminating repeated items, the pool amounted to 1,726 items. The authors selected 400 items on the basis of 20 putative factor hypotheses (PFHs). These PFHs were determined as being representative of the factor structure indicated by previous item-factor studies as well as a review of the literature.[3] Twenty factors were extracted from the correlation matrix of the 400 personality inventory items, rotated to an oblique criterion, and interpreted according to their psychological content. The authors concluded that they had recovered some 15 of the 20 PFHs with which they entered their study. We consider that the contents of these factors are mostly related to the domains of neuroticism and extraversion, and only a few may be related to conscientiousness and agreeableness. Aspects of openness to experience are probably only represented by one factor, called optimal arousal, which combines the PFHs sensation seeking (need for external arousal) and thoughtfulness (need for internal, intellectual arousal). The latter interpretation is in accordance with results reported by McCrae and Costa (in press) who found that some of the aspects of sensation seeking (Zuckerman, 1979) are highly related to openness (see also Angleitner and Ostendorf, 1991).

Eysenck (1978) used the factor inter-correlations reported by Browne and Howarth (1977) to perform a second-order factor analysis. The resulting factors were identified by Eysenck (1978) as neuroticism, extraversion, and psychoticism. The best fit resulted for N and E. Eysenck (1978) attributed the poorer fit for P to the fact that 'traditional inventories have always been preoccupied with N and E variables, and have not paid much attention to Psychoticism' (p. 478). The persuasiveness of Eysenck's results, however, is reduced by the fact that he used a target rotation procedure that probably led to a forced adjustment of the factors from Browne and Howarth (1977) to the Eysenckian model. One indication for this is the fact that the target-rotated factors correlated quite substantially (for example, E and P: -0.32). However, an inspection of the comprehensive sampling of personality inventory items by Browne and Howarth (1977, pp. 417–25) shows that one of Eysenck's arguments is highly convincing: most personality inventories primarily pick out extraversion and neuroticism as a central theme. As long as other personality traits are measured only occasionally, they have only a reduced chance of appearing as independent and significant personality factors.

In a more recent study, McKenzie (1988) subjected the items of the 16PF and the EPQ to a common-factor analysis. He concluded that the Eysenckian and Cattelian personality model is based on three common, robust factors. But, contrary to the result that the reader might expect, McKenzie (1988) found that Cattell's second-order factor superego, rather than Eysenck's psychoticism, 'may best lay claim to join neuroticism and extraversion in what may be termed the great triumvirate of the personality sphere' (p. 850). Superego is primarily defined by items from the 16PF scales superego strength (G) and self-control (Q3), and this pattern is highly compatible with an interpretation of this factor as conscientiousness. The P-dimension is only partly related to the factor superego; a finding that is in accordance with empirical results from Goldberg (1991) and McCrae and Costa (1985b), who found that psychoticism — as a measure of both Factor 2 (agreeableness) and 3 (conscientiousness) — is related more strongly to agreeableness.

Despite the psychopathological emphasis of the Minnesota Multiphasic Personality Inventory (MMPI), it is also frequently viewed as a comprehensive personality inventory. The total pool of 556 MMPI-items may be large enough to measure a broad spectrum of personality characteristics. For example, the fact that the item pool has been used to develop more than 500 sub-scales used in research and clinical applications may lead to the conviction that one could measure almost everything with the MMPI item base.

Johnson, Null, Butcher and Johnson (1984) factored the whole pool of 556 items from the MMPI and found 21 Varimax-rotated factors to be replicable across random halves of a sample of 11,138 psychiatric patients. The factors were categorized rationally according to Norman's (1963) Five-Factor model, and Johnson *et al.* (1984) concluded that the MMPI factors 'reflect a large number or range of personality traits rather than just those related to emotional stability' (p. 112). However, none of the MMPI factors could be classified to the content domain of the factor conscientiousness of the Five-Factor model. The observed similarities, however, were only defined via rational classifications. The relation between the MMPI factors and the Big Five could have been interpreted much more adequately if Johnson *et al.* (1984) had applied some sort of higher-order factor analysis.

Such an analysis was undertaken by Costa, Zonderman, McCrae, and Williams (1985). They were unable to replicate the 21 MMPI factors postulated by Johnson *et al.* (1984) in a new sample of 1,576 normal subjects. They found only 11 interpretable factors and they accepted a solution with nine Varimax-rotated factors, because this was the psychologically most interpretable solution. Five of the nine components — neuroticism, cynicism, extraversion, religious orthodoxy, and intellectual interests — correspond closely to five factors found by Johnson *et al.* (1984). From these, neuroticism and extraversion correspond to two factors of the Five-Factor model. The cynicism factor may be related to the agreeableness factor, and the fifth factor of the Five-Factor model may include the MMPI intellectual interests factor. Then, nine scale scores were computed for each subject by summing up the items with absolute loadings exceeding 0.3 on each factor. These scale scores were inter-correlated, and a component analysis followed by Varimax rotation of the nine scales yielded one major factor that was defined by five psychopathology scales. Two additional minor factors were defined by the scales (1) masculinity versus femininity and religious orthodoxy, and (2) extraversion and intellectual interests.

Costa *et al.* (1985) concluded that the MMPI appears to represent only one of the five Normal dimensions (neuroticism) and partly to represent three others. However, these speculations also require empirical proof.

As in the case of *scale*-factor analyses, the results of these extensive *item*-factor analyses lead us to conclude that at least variants of the Big-Five factors have been found in many of the studies mentioned. However, there were once more clear discrepancies in individual cases. In many studies, various facets described by the five factors were actually represented, but often to a differing extent depending on the factor. Factors represented only by a few of their facets had little chance of appearing. Nevertheless, no important and robust factor was found beyond the Big Five.

The resulting item factors and their interpretation varied not only according to the kind of sample of variables chosen but also according to the author of the study and the methods of factor analysis applied. These aspects can be seen in the discussion on the factor systems of Cattell, Guilford, and Eysenck. Whereas, for example, the study by Cattell and Gibbons (1968) could confirm only vaguely the Cattell factors exvia, anxiety, pathemia, and independence, which in our opinion correspond only weakly with the Big Five, the most dominant factors published by Sells *et al.* (1970) proved to be surprisingly similar to the Big Five. Sells *et al.*'s study was also based on a representative selection of Cattell's and Guilford's items.

Similar discrepancies can be found between the publications of those authors who examined samples of questionnaire items or scales from the three major factor analytical personality systems (Amelang and Borkenau, 1982; Eysenck and Eysenck, 1969; Vagg and Hammond, 1976). Whereas Eysenck and Eysenck (1969) discovered only the factors neuroticism and extraversion (what else was to be expected in 1969?), Vagg and Hammond (1976) found four robust factors in their replication study, three of which seem to show a high correspondence with the factors neuroticism, extraversion, and openness. Facets of the remaining two Big-Five factors were also represented in the study, although not comprehensively enough to withstand analysis as separate factors. The results of the study by Amelang and Borkenau (1982) offer the clearest evidence that the superstructure of the factor models of Cattell, Guilford, and Eysenck can be well described by the Big Five.

As Table 4.3 shows, neuroticism and extraversion appear as remarkably robust factors even in item-factor analyses. Compared to the results of the scale-factor analyses, the evidence for an independent item factor conscientiousness is relatively weak. This is most probably due to the different samples of variables analysed in the respective studies. For example, in scale analyses, the factor conscientiousness was usually represented adequately by scales from the PRF, the CPS, and the 16PF. In contrast, questionnaire items for the traits order, achievement, endurance, reliability, and self-control, which are the typical marker items for the factor conscientiousness, were poorly represented even in those studies in which extensive and supposedly representative samples of questionnaire items were factor-analysed (such as Browne and Howarth, 1977; Eysenck and Eysenck, 1969; Sells *et al.*, 1970).

In comparison with the dominant extraversion and neuroticism factors, empirical evidence for the factors agreeableness and openness is also weak. However, the relative weakness of the factors conscientiousness, agreeableness, and openness does not necessarily mean that they are less important personality dimensions. On the contrary, this weakness could possibly be explained simply by the strong *overrepresentation* of neuroticism and extraversion items in personality question-naires. This overrepresentation may, in turn, merely be a sign of the idiosyncratic preference of many researchers for the factors extraversion and neuroticism. For example, studies of the structure of representative sets of personality-descriptive terms have revealed that the factor neuroticism plays a much less important role in ordinary personality language than a review of many personality questionnaire studies might lead us to anticipate (see Ostendorf, 1990; Peabody, 1987; Peabody and Goldberg, 1989). In these representative studies, neuroticism generally explained the lowest percentage of variance compared to the other four Big-Five factors (for example, only 25—58 per cent of the variance explained by the factor agreeableness or conscientiousness). Consequently, many personality inventories do not refer adequately to some of the most important individual differences that ordinary people observe in their daily transactions.

As in the case of scale-factor analyses, a typical characteristic of the reported item-factor analyses is that the labelling of the factors depends solely on the imagination of the authors. Empirical methods such as the Recaptured Item Technique suggested by Meehl, Lykken, Schofield, and Tellegen (1971), which could enable the idiosyncratic interpretations to be made more objectively, are not yet in use even in the most up-to-date studies. Similarly, the deduced correspondence between factors found in a study and those found in earlier studies is always the result of an interpretation on behalf of the researchers involved and is not based on empirical evidence — for instance, on the use of marker items.

Of course, this criticism also applies to our own review. That is, the taxonomy of factors presented in Tables 4.2 and 4.3 is also found solely on our subjective interpretations of factor patterns reported in the studies discussed. The only way to carry out a rigorous test of the validity of the proposed classification would be to replicate all reported studies. To test the putative factor structure empirically, it would then be necessary to include additional items or scales, known as marker variables, measuring the Big Five. Unfortunately, such a comprehensive study would take a lot of time and money to perform. Instead, until now, we have chosen to test the Five-Factor model with our own set of data, which was compiled earlier for other research purposes. In the present studies, we investigated the structural validity of the Five-Factor model on the basis of 576 items taken from personality questionnaires related to different major theories of personality.

Testing the Big-Five-Factor structure on a comprehensive set of 576 questionnaire items

Each of the questionnaires used in our study purports to assess a collection of personality constructs that cover a major proportion of the personality sphere. To check the validity of the interpretation of the questionnaire factors, we correlated these factors with factors calculated from marker variables of the Big Five in the domain of rating data. Two kinds of rating datum were used for this comparison: first, questionnaire factor scores were correlated with factor scores from various standard rating inventories measuring the Big Five. Then, the questionnaire factors were correlated with the five factors that had previously been found in analyses of self- and peer-rating data obtained for a representative set of 430 German personality-descriptive adjectives (Ostendorf, 1990).

Study I: Questionnaire study

Method

The rating and questionnaire data sets were collected in two different studies.[4]

Subjects

Subjects of the questionnaire study were 300 German adults (171 females, 129 males) with a mean age of 26.4 years ($SD = 9.84$ years). They were recruited through an announcement in the local newspapers of the City of Bielefeld. They had various occupational backgrounds and were paid for their participation.

Measures

Subjects were asked to fill out the following questionnaires in addition to performing other tests: the German version of the Personality Research Form A (PRF-A; Jackson, 1984; Stumpf *et al.* 1985), the Freiburg Personality Inventory-Revised Form (FPI-R; Fahrenberg *et al.*, 1984), a personality questionnaire widely used in Germany; the Eysenck Personality Inventory Form A (EPI-A; Eggert, 1974; Eysenck and Eysenck, 1968; and the NEO Personality Inventory (Borkenau and Ostendorf, 1986; Costa and McCrae, 1985).

For the purpose of this study, all items from the control scales of the questionnaires (*SD*-scales, Lie-scales) were dropped from the analysis. All 224 items in the German adaptation of the PRF (which contains 14 of the original American scales) were included.[5] All 125 items were taken from the 11 scales of the FPI-R.[6] In addition, we used all 47 items from the neuroticism and extraversion scales of the EPI-A and all 180 items of the NEO Personality Inventory. Altogether, we analysed a sample of 576 questionnaire items.

In addition to the questionnaire items, subjects in Study I completed 20 bipolar adjective rating scales. These rating scales were translations of the scales suggested by Norman (1963). Because a different translation of the 20 Norman scales was administered five months later to subjects in Study II, we labelled the rating scales in Study I the *Norman-A scales*.

Results

To determine the factor structure of the item sample, we applied principal component analysis to the correlation matrix of the 576 questionnaire items (for the sake of simplicity, we will call components 'factors').

Eigenvalues

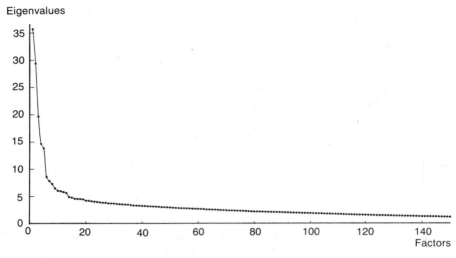

Figure 4.1 Analysis of 576 questionnaire items: plot of the first 150 eigenvalues

As shown in Figure 4.1, the plot of eigenvalues indicated five large factors, with a clear 'break' at the sixth eigenvalue. The eigenvalues for the first ten unrotated components were 35.7, 29.4, 19.6, 14.6, 13.8, 8.6, 7.8, 7.3, 6.5, and 6.0, respectively.

The first five factors were well ahead of the others in terms of percentage of explained variance. Of greater interest than the number of important factors is the correspondence between the first five dominant factors and the Big Five. In order to answer this question, we extracted five factors and rotated them according to the Varimax criterion. Those questionnaire items that loaded highest on the five factors are reported in Tables 4.4–4.8. It can be seen that all five factors could be interpreted as clear variants of the Big Five.

Table 4.4 shows the 20 items with the highest loadings on the neuroticism factor. This factor was the most dominant principal component of the analysis, accounting for 27.8 per cent of the common variance explained by all five factors. Even items loading on the neuroticism factor but belonging — according to the scoring key of a questionnaire — to conceptually different traits could be seen to be descriptive of the neuroticism dimension; for example, the item belonging to the dominance scale of the PRF: 'I feel incapable of handling many situations.'

The other factors could also be interpreted quite clearly: the factor extraversion explained 16.5 per cent of the common variance and was primarily marked by items from the different extraversion scales of the personality inventories as well as by items from the PRF-Affiliation scale (see Table 4.5). Of the 20 items with the highest loadings, 13 were from extraversion scales, four from the PRF-affiliation scale, two from the PFR-exhibition scale, and one from the PRF-play scale. Extraverted subjects with high scores on this factor 'really enjoy talking to people', they 'consider

Table 4.4 Varimax structure of 576 questionnaire items. 20 items with highest loadings on factor IV (neuroticism)

Questionnaire scale	Item	E	A	C	N	O
NEO-N	I am seldom sad or depressed.	06	−04	−01	**−67**	−19
NEO-N	I rarely feel lonely or blue.	10	−01	02	**−63**	−24
NEO-N	I often feel helpless and want someone else to solve my problems.	08	09	−25	**60**	−04
FPI-CO	I'm hardly ever in a depressed, unhappy mood.	14	00	00	**−57**	−25
NEO-N	I'm pretty stable emotionally.	00	02	19	**−56**	−15
NEO-N	Sometimes things look pretty bleak and hopeless to me.	−07	03	−10	**56**	21
EPI-N	Are you often troubled with feelings of guilt?	−07	09	−06	**56**	13
NEO-N	I feel I am capable of coping with most of my problems.	01	01	18	**−55**	03
NEO-N	It takes a lot to get me mad.	−22	06	03	**−55**	04
PRF-DO	I feel incapable of handling many situations.	−02	20	**−35**	**55**	−07
NEO-N	I rarely feel fearful or anxious.	−12	−02	−02	**−53**	−06
EPI-N	Are you troubled with feelings of inferiority?	−07	08	−12	**53**	11
FPI-PS	I'm often nervous, because too much seems to happen at once.	−02	08	17	**53**	07
NEO-N	When I'm under a great deal of stress, sometimes I feel like I'm going to pieces.	12	−00	−11	**52**	04
NEO-N	I have fewer fears than most people	00	−14	05	**−52**	06
FPI-IR	In general, I'm a very calm person and it's not easy to arouse me.	−23	27	02	**−52**	09
EPI-N	Are you an irritable person?	03	−12	13	**51**	06
FPI-CO	All in all, I am very happy with my previous life.	17	09	02	**−51**	−16
NEO-N	Too often, when things go wrong, I get discouraged and feel like giving up.	−06	04	**−32**	**50**	03
NEO-N	I am easily frightened.	16	15	−13	**50**	−09

Notes: $N = 300$. All loadings ≥ 0.30 are listed in **bold**. NEO = NEO Personality Inventory: FPI = Freiburg Personality Inventory; EPI = Eysenck Personality Inventory; PRF = Personality Research Form; Questionnaire scales: N = neuroticism; CO = contentedness; IR = irritability; PS = proneness to stress; DO = dominance.

themselves as especially light-hearted' (NEO-extraversion), they have many friendships (PRF-affiliation), and they report that other people do *not* consider them 'as a serious, reserved person' (PRF-play).

Conscientiousness was not an appropriate label for the third factor. Digman's (1990) 'will to achieve' offered a better description. This factor explained 19.1 per cent

Table 4.5 Varimax structure of 576 questionnaire items. 20 items with highest loadings on factor I (extraversion)

Questionnaire scale	Item	E	A	C	N	O
NEO-E	I like to have a lot of people around me.	**62**	−12	−09	−04	−03
FPI-E	I only make friends slowly.	**−59**	16	00	03	01
PRF-AF	My friendships are many.	**55**	−08	−00	−10	−09
NEO-E	I really enjoy talking to people.	**53**	07	03	−10	07
PRF-PL	People consider me as a serious, reserved person.	**−50**	13	08	05	−02
PRF-EX	At a party I enjoy entertaining others.	**50**	−16	−01	−01	12
NEO-E	I don't consider myself especially 'light-hearted'.	**−48**	09	−02	25	20
EPI-E	Do other people think of you as being very lively?	**48**	−28	07	−10	13
PRF-AF	I spend a lot of time visiting friends.	**48**	−07	−23	−12	−03
NEO-E	I usually prefer to do things alone.	**−47**	−09	13	−00	02
FPI-E	I'm quite a lively person.	**47**	−23	03	−15	15
NEO-E	I laugh easily.	**46**	04	−11	−11	09
NEO-E	Many people think of me as somewhat cold and distant.	**−46**	−10	05	−03	13
NEO-E	I'm known as a warm and friendly person.	**46**	21	08	−08	−17
EPI-E	Can you usually let yourself go and enjoy yourself a lot at a gay party?	**46**	−23	09	−16	25
NEO-E	I am a cheerful, high-spirited person.	**45**	01	−04	**−35**	−10
PRF-EX	Others think I am lively and witty.	**45**	−22	00	−14	05
PRF-AF	I choose hobbies I can share with other people.	**45**	04	−08	−12	−05
PRF-AF	I try to be in the company of friends as much as possible.	**45**	−08	−18	−01	−07
NEO-E	Sometimes I bubble with happiness.	**44**	02	−00	07	27

Notes: $N = 300$. All loadings ≥ 0.30 are listed in **bold**. NEO = NEO Personality Inventory: FPI = Freiburg Personality Inventory; EPI = Eysenck Personality Inventory; PRF = Personality Research Form; Questionnaire scales: E = extraversion; AF = affiliation; PL = play; EX = exhibition.

of the common variance. It was marked primarily by items from the NEO-conscientiousness scale (6 items), the PRF-endurance scale (5 items), the PRF-achievement scale (3 items), the PRF-play scale (3 items with negative loadings), and 2 items from the PRF-order and the PRF-impulsivity scales (see Table 4.6). One of the 20 items with the highest loadings was from the NEO-scale extraversion, which is clearly misclassified in the NEO-inventory: 'I have a leisurely style in work and play.' Items such as 'I work hard to accomplish my goals' and 'I strive for

Table 4.6 Varimax structure of 576 questionnaire items. 20 items with highest loadings on factor III (conscientiousness or will to achieve)

Questionnaire scale	Item	E	A	C	N	O
NEO-C	I waste a lot of time before settling down to work.	02	−09	**−56**	26	29
NEO-C	I work hard to accomplish my goals.	09	−08	**55**	−09	−15
NEO-C	I have a clear set of goals and work toward them in an orderly fashion.	07	−13	**49**	−23	−07
PRF-PL	Even if I had the money and the time, I would not feel right just playing around.	−11	19	**47**	10	−01
PRF-PL	I spend a good deal of time just having fun.	23	−20	**−47**	−04	07
PRF-EN	If I run into great difficulties on a project, I usually stop work rather than try to solve them.	12	−05	**−47**	17	−16
NEO-C	I strive for excellence in everything I do.	−07	−04	**46**	−02	−10
PRF-EN	The mere prospect of having to put in long hours working makes me tired.	01	−14	**−44**	20	04
NEO-C	I am a productive person who always gets the job done.	08	19	**43**	−21	**−32**
PRF-PL	Most of my spare moments are spent relaxing and amusing myself.	06	−19	**−43**	01	−05
PRF-IM	Often I stop in the middle of an activity in order to start something else.	09	−02	**−43**	**32**	24
PRF-EN	I do not like leaving anything unfinished.	−03	04	**43**	−19	−28
PRF-OR	I rarely clean out my bureau drawers.	−13	−03	**−42**	01	**37**
PRF-EN	When other people give up working on a problem, I usually quit too.	07	15	**−42**	15	−21
PRF-AC	I do not mind working while other people are having fun.	−22	11	**42**	−15	01
PRF-AC	I enjoy difficult work.	03	06	**42**	−01	03
PRF-EN	I will continue working on a problem even with a severe headache.	−08	−01	**41**	−14	06
PRF-AC	I enjoy work more than play.	−15	11	**41**	01	−03
NEO-E	I have a leisurely style in work and play.	−17	12	**−40**	02	05
NEO-C	I try to perform all the tasks assigned to me conscientiously.	11	24	**40**	−11	−25

Notes: *N* = 300. All loadings ≥0.30 are listed in **bold**. NEO = NEO Personality Inventory: PRF = Personality Research Form. Questionnaire scales: C = conscientiousness; PL = play; EN = endurance, IM = impulsivity; OR = order; AC = achievement; E = extraversion.

Table 4.7 Varimax structure of 576 questionnaire items. 20 items with highest loadings on factor II (agreeableness)

Questionnaire scale	Item	E	A	C	N	O
NEO-A	If necessary, I am willing to manipulate people to get what I want.	−06	**−61**	−02	−07	14
PRF-AG	I am reluctant to distress someone even if I do not like him.	04	**53**	−03	−09	13
PRF-DO	I do not have a forceful or dominating personality.	−16	**49**	−23	04	−09
FPI-RE	I prefer to remain in the background at social and public events.	**−38**	**48**	−05	07	−09
NEO-E	I have often been a leader of groups I have belonged to.	08	**−47**	18	−09	23
PRF-EX	The idea of acting in front of a large group does not appeal to me.	−23	**46**	−04	−04	−13
NEO-A	Some people think I'm selfish and egoistical.	−06	**−45**	−01	09	21
NEO-E	I like to be where the action is.	**33**	**−45**	−02	09	14
NEO-N	I am known as hot-blooded and quick-tempered.	27	**−45**	02	16	02
FPI-E	I like to take command of group activities.	13	**−43**	18	−19	12
PRF-EX	I like to be in the spotlight.	**30**	**−43**	11	01	17
PRF-DO	I have little interest in leading others.	−15	**43**	−25	05	14
NEO-A	I generally try to be thoughtful and considerate.	13	**42**	03	17	07
PRF-EX	I am more a listener than a talker.	−09	**42**	−16	−00	−17
PRF-DO	I would make a poor military leader.	03	**42**	−20	11	10
NEO-A	I would rather cooperate with others than compete with them.	09	**41**	−19	07	17
PRF-DO	I feel confident when directing the activities of others.	03	**−41**	24	−20	−05
PRF-AG	I would never start a fight with someone.	20	**41**	02	−10	−10
PRF-AG	I try to show self-restraint to avoid hurting other people.	08	**40**	15	04	03
NEO-A	Some people think of me as cold and calculating.	−28	**−39**	07	−02	15

Notes: $N = 300$. All loadings ≥ 0.30 are listed in **bold**. NEO = NEO Personality Inventory: PRF = Personality Research Form; FPI = Freiburg Personality Inventory. Questionnaire scales: A = agreeableness; AG = aggression; DO = dominance; RE = restraint; E = extraversion; EX = exhibition; N = neuroticism.

excellence in everything I do' (NEO-conscientiousness) were typically representative for the meaning of the third factor. This third questionnaire factor primarily described only one facet of the conceptually broader factor conscientiousness in the Five-Factor model: will to achieve. Further central facets, such as orderliness, honesty, punctuality, and self-control were only marginally covered by this third factor.

The factor agreeableness explained 20 per cent of the extracted variance and was marked primarily by items from the following scales: NEO-agreeableness (5 items), PRF-aggression (3 items), PRF-dominance (4 items), and PRF-exhibition (3 items; see Table 4.7). Traits such as dominance and exhibition are usually associated more strongly with the extraversion factor. Most of the items in the extraversion, dominance, and exhibition scales that loaded on the agreeableness factor referred to — at least in terms of German culture — socially *un*desirable, aggressive dominance over others (for example, 'I have a forceful or dominating personality', 'I would make a good military leader', PRF-dominance; 'I like to be in the spotlight', PRF-exhibition; 'I like to take command of group activities', FPI-extraversion). Subjects who agreed with such items as 'I would rather cooperate with others than compete with them' and 'I'm not willing to manipulate people to get what I want' from the NEO-agreeableness scale and who described themselves as 'unselfish, not egoistical, thoughtful, and considerate' tended to negate items from the extraversion, dominance, and exhibition scales. These results corresponded with our findings on the rating data domain showing that aggressive dominance and its opposite pole, unassertiveness, were important components of the agreeableness factor (Ostendorf, 1990). Such results may in fact reflect actual cultural trait differences. Whereas dominance is a more socially desirable trait in American culture and can be said to be an elementary part of North-American lifestyle, it is generally associated with aggression and seen as a negative character trait in Germany. Here, dominance is seen as an uncooperative way of imposing one's will without regard for the interests of others.

The greatest differences in opinion between authors are seen in the interpretation of the fifth factor of the Norman taxonomy. Norman (1963) himself has labelled this factor culture, while McCrae and Costa (1987, in press) refer to openness to experience. In our own studies, based on self- and peer-ratings, we have found a factor intellect (Angleitner and Ostendorf, 1989; Ostendorf, 1990) analogous to the results of Goldberg (1990) and Peabody and Goldberg (1989). In our present study, the fifth factor was also the most difficult to interpret. It explained 16.6 per cent of the common variance. As Table 4.8 shows, in line with our hypotheses, the factor was marked in most cases by items belonging to the openness construct of Costa and McCrae (1985).

However, at the same time, some items describing a lack of orderliness correlated with this factor. These correlations deviated from the Five-Factor structure usually found in rating data in which items from the trait sphere order load primarily on the third factor conscientiousness (Digman, 1989; Goldberg, 1990; Hofstee *et al.*, 1992; McCrae and Costa, 1987; Ostendorf, 1990). Consequently, it may be difficult

Table 4.8 Varimax structure of 576 questionnaire items. 20 items with highest loadings on factor V (openness)

Questionnaire scale	Item	E	A	C	N	O
PRF-OR	I feel comfortable in a somewhat disorganized room.	−02	−01	−30	−09	**47**
NEO-O	I often enjoy playing with theories or abstract ideas.	−17	−13	−07	−06	**46**
NEO-O	I find philosophical arguments boring.	12	03	−24	−16	**−44**
NEO-O	I follow the same route when I go somewhere.	−02	01	−02	08	**−42**
PRF-UN	Abstract ideas are of little use to me.	03	09	−07	−04	**−42**
PRF-OR	I seldom take the time to hang up my clothes neatly.	−15	−02	**−39**	01	**42**
NEO-O	I have a wide range of intellectual interests.	−11	−06	14	01	**41**
NEO-O	I believe that laws and social policies should change to reflect the needs of a changing world.	−08	21	−04	09	**41**
NEO-O	I believe letting students hear controversial speakers can only confuse and mislead them.	07	14	−01	−01	**−41**
NEO-C	I never seem to be able to get organized.	−04	−01	**−36**	**31**	**41**
PRF-SR	Nothing would hurt me more than to have a bad reputation.	27	14	10	10	**−41**
NEO-O	I believe that the different ideas of					

cont.

to discriminate between the fifth questionnaire factor and the rating factor conscientiousness. Subjects with high scores on the fifth questionnaire factor can be described as intellectual, imaginative, and liberal. They think critically about socio-political issues, are interested in arts, and do not take much care of their appearance or their personal belongings (such as, clothing, home). The prototype can be described as the 'absent-minded professor'.

In order to provide empirical support for the interpretation of the five questionnaire factors from the NEO Personality Inventory, the NEO-PI facets were factored and rotated by the Validimax method, as recommended by McCrae and Costa (1989b). Correlations between questionnaire-item and Validimax-factor scores ranged from 0.73 (for the conscientiousness factor) to 0.89 (for the Neuroticism factor) with a mean of 0.81. As expected, the highest hetero-factor correlation was −0.33 between the fifth questionnaire factor (openness) and the third factor from the NEO-PI (conscientiousness). On the whole, these results demonstrated that the questionnaire factors could readily be interpreted in accordance with the Big-Five factor structure.

Table 4.8 *cont.*

Questionnaire scale	Item	E	A	C	N	O
	right and wrong that people in other societies have may be valid for them.	−06	08	−08	−08	**40**
NEO-O	Sometimes when I am reading poetry or looking at a work of art, I feel a chill or wave of excitement.	−03	13	−00	13	**40**
NEO-C	I like to keep everything in its place so I know just where it is.	−14	12	12	−10	**−40**
NEO-O	I experience a wide range of emotions or feelings.	22	−01	16	11	**40**
NEO-C	I keep my belongings neat and clean.	00	12	25	−09	**−40**
PRF-EX	When I am in the crowd, I want others to notice me.	15	−21	−04	**−30**	**40**
NEO-O	I would have difficulty just letting my mind wander without control or guidance.	−04	08	13	−10	**−38**
FPI-SO	As the state already takes care of welfare, I don't have to help people personally.	−20	−24	−07	−22	**−38**
PRF-SR	I constantly try to make people think highly of me.	**39**	12	07	05	**−38**

Notes: N = 300. All loadings ≥ 0.30 are listed in **bold**. PRF = Personality Research Form; NEO = NEO Personality Inventory: FPI = Freiburg Personality Inventory. Questionnaire scales: OR = order; O = openness; UN = understanding; C = conscientiousness; SR = social recognition; EX = exhibition; SO = social orientation.

Study II: Convergence of questionnaire and adjective rating factors

Method

Subjects

Six months later, 95 of the 300 subjects from the questionnaire study took part in a second study to test the Five-Factor model on the basis of adjective rating data (Ostendorf, 1990). A total of 414 subjects participated in this rating study (170 males and 239 females; 5 did not report gender). Again, subjects were recruited through announcements in local newspapers in Bielefeld and neighbouring cities. They filled out the test material at home and were not paid for their participation. Their ages ranged from 15 to 81 years with a mean of 32.6 years ($SD = 13.3$).

Measures

The subjects filled out adjective rating inventories constructed by various authors. The marker variables consisted of German translations of the rating inventories developed by Norman (1963; Norman-B scales), Goldberg (1983, 1989), McCrae and Costa (1987), and Peabody and Goldberg (1989). The Norman-B scales contained German translations that differed from those of the Norman-A scales used in Study I. The final list was made up of 179 separate bipolar adjective rating scales. This also contained German translations of 80 adjectives from Norman's Five-Factor taxonomy (see Goldberg, 1990) published by John (1983; see John *et al.*, 1984). Because all of these Big-Five standard rating inventories use bipolar scales, we have labelled them the Bipolar Adjective Rating Scale (BARS).

Additionally, ratings on Unipolar Adjective Rating Scales (UARS) were obtained for a representative sample of 430 trait adjectives previously selected from a total pool of 5,160 German personality-descriptive adjectives (see Angleitner *et al.*, 1990; Ostendorf, 1990). A detailed description of the rating scales administered can be found in Ostendorf (1990). Because each of the rating inventories involved a separate operationalization of the Five-Factor model by a different author, diverse indicators were available to test the convergence of rating and questionnaire factors.

Results

Taking the total sample of 414 subjects as a basis, we first performed a separate principal component analysis for each list of adjective rating scales, extracted five factors, and rotated them according to the Varimax criterion. The five postulated factors were found very clearly in each of these analyses (see Ostendorf, 1990). Then, we calculated factor scores on the basis of the rating factors from Study II and the questionnaire factors from Study I. Factor scores were also computed for each subject on the basis of the self-rating inventories from Study I (Norman-A factors). Then, all adjective and questionnaire factor scores were correlated in order to perform a higher-order principal component analysis. This was done to test the congruence and discrimination of the five factors across the different methods.

The eigenvalues of the first six principal components were 9.1, 7.9, 7.6, 6.7, 6.1, and 1.7. The first five of the second-order factors explained 83 per cent of the total variance. Table 4.9 presents the loadings of the primary rating and questionnaire factors on five Varimax-rotated second-order components.

Table 4.9 shows that the second-order factors could be interpreted clearly in terms of the Big Five. All rating and questionnaire factors loaded highest on the appropriate factors and generally had only relatively low loadings on the other factors. This was particularly true for the factors from the bipolar adjective rating scales. Factors from the Norman-A scales showed somewhat smaller loadings, which — compared to the loadings of the Norman-B scales — could be attributed not only to the different kind of translation but also to temporal changes in the characteristics. Although the Norman-A scales were applied five months earlier under different conditions in Study I, the Norman-A factors generally had impressive convergent and discriminant validities.

Table 4.9 shows that factors from the total list of all bipolar rating scales (BARS179) had particularly high loadings on the secondary factors. This finding was to be expected, as the total list contained the scales from all previously mentioned rating inventories (with the exception of the Norman-A scales). None the less, the operationalizations of the five factors differed greatly: for example, Peabody's list of 57 rating scales (Peabody, 1987; Peabody and Goldberg, 1989) was developed without reference to the Five-Factor model in order to compile a representative selection of trait terms for the total vocabulary of American trait adjectives.

Similarly, the list of 430 unipolar adjective rating scales (UARS) was compiled on the basis of lexical analyses of the German language — completely independently from the Five-Factor model. This list represented a sample of prototypical trait adjectives that could be viewed as representative for the entire range of trait-descriptive terms in the German language. Ostendorf (1990) has shown that the Big Five provide an adequate description of the structure of this representative trait list. As Table 4.9 shows, with the exception of the fourth factor (emotional stability), each primary factor had a high and relatively unequivocal loading on its corresponding secondary factor. The weaker correspondence for emotional stability was probably due to the small number of German adjectives describing it. As in American studies, emotional stability explained only a small proportion of the common variance of representative adjective-rating samples in German-speaking countries (Ostendorf, 1990; Peabody and Goldberg, 1989).

An interpretation of the loadings of the primary questionnaire factors in Table 4.9 has to take account of the five-month time interval between the presentation of the questionnaires and most of the rating inventories. Three of the five questionnaire factors (extraversion/surgency, agreeableness, and neuroticism vs. emotional stability) exhibited a pattern of high convergent and discriminant validity; that is, they had their highest loadings on the corresponding second-order factors, whereas they correlated only marginally with factors from which they were expected to discriminate. In comparison, the loading of the third questionnaire factor on the second-order factor conscientiousness was lower. This outcome was expected, as the questionnaire factor primarily assesses a specific facet (will to achieve) of the conscientiousness factor. None the less, the more specific questionnaire factor could be interpreted unequivocally, as there were no significant secondary loadings on conceptually unrelated secondary factors. The fifth questionnaire factor, which primarily marked the secondary factor intellect vs. openness, exhibited an anticipated, significantly negative relationship to the second-order factor conscientiousness.

Discussion

In summary, we may conclude that our studies have revealed highly unequivocal variants of the Big Five in the domain of questionnaire data. In contrast to the common practice of factor interpretation, our findings are supported by not only a subjective inspection of factor-loading patterns but also objective empirical tests of the convergence of questionnaire and rating factors.

Our studies have examined the common structure of questionnaire items from the

Table 4.9 Higher-order Varimax-rotated factor structure calculated from first-order adjective-rating and questionnaire factors

First-order self-rating adjective factors	I SU/EX	II AG	III CO	IV N	V IN/OP
Factors from bipolar adjective rating scales					
Norman-A (20 scales)					
Surgency	**80**	−16	−05	−08	−04
Agreeableness	00	**75**	05	−16	−14
Conscientiousness	−09	11	**82**	−08	00
Emotional stability	−11	−13	−03	**82**	−11
Culture	−01	−07	−00	−00	**43**
Norman-B (20 scales)					
Surgency	**94**	−02	09	01	11
Agreeableness	−13	**89**	05	−06	09
Conscientiousness	−03	−01	**90**	11	−06
Emotional stability	−09	01	−14	**88**	−04
Culture	−02	13	04	22	**85**
NEO-R (80 scales)					
Surgency	**96**	−10	−03	−02	−04
Agreeableness	01	**97**	10	01	−03
Conscientiousness	03	05	**98**	02	10
Neuroticism	−04	04	04	**97**	02
Openness	02	06	−08	13	**96**
Peabody and Goldberg (57 scales)					
Surgency	**96**	−04	14	−10	−02
Agreeableness	−01	**95**	06	04	19
Conscientiousness	−13	11	**95**	−01	−06
Emotional stability	16	07	06	**87**	19
Intellect	01	−13	01	00	**95**
Goldberg (40 scales)					
Surgency	**91**	−27	−06	−06	07
Agreeableness	15	**95**	−02	08	00
Conscientiousness	08	11	**96**	06	−06
Emotional stability	−04	00	−02	**96**	10
Intellect	−07	06	04	05	**97**

cont.

PRF, the FPI, the EPI, and the NEO-PI. This selection of items represents a *broad* spectrum of personality characteristics as assessed by popular personality questionnaires. None the less, it certainly cannot be viewed as a representative sample drawn from the population of all conceivable personality-descriptive items. By drawing on commonly used questionnaires, it reflects far more the specific research foci of the various scientists who developed them.

Some general conclusions can be drawn from the review of comprehensive factor analyses and the results of our own studies:

1. Factors E and N are the most robust factors in nearly all of the reported studies, and in comparison to other item or scale factors, they frequently explain the

Table 4.9 *cont.*

First-order self-rating adjective factors	Higher-order factors				
	I SU/EX	II AG	III CO	IV N	V IN/OP
John (40 scales)					
Surgency	**80**	**43**	−13	20	−05
Agreeableness	**−51**	**80**	−01	15	−10
Conscientiousness	17	19	**93**	09	−12
Emotional stability	−11	−03	01	**95**	12
Culture	02	14	03	−00	**94**
BARS179 (179 scales)					
Surgency	**98**	02	09	−03	−02
Agreeableness	−13	**98**	06	00	−00
Conscientiousness	−05	08	**98**	05	01
Emotional stability	01	10	04	**98**	04
Intellect	−01	06	−02	10	**98**
Factors from 430 unipolar adjective rating scales					
Surgency	**91**	−11	−10	−20	02
Agreeableness	10	**89**	12	−05	13
Conscientiousness	−05	−09	**89**	−27	−11
Emotional stability	18	−05	25	**63**	**30**
Intellect	−14	−02	−04	−14	**87**
First-order questionnaire factors					
I	**77**	05	−05	10	−12
II	−24	**78**	17	05	−01
III	04	02	**54**	−03	11
IV	−15	−02	−16	**84**	−16
V	29	−03	**−42**	−05	**54**

Notes: $N = 98$ subjects. All loadings ≥ 0.30 are listed in **bold**. Factors from bipolar rating scales: Norman-A: scales from Norman (1963), translated by Borkenau (1988); Norman-B: scales from Norman (1963), translated by Ostendorf (1990); NEO-R: NEO Rating Inventory (McCrae and Costa, 1985a); Peabody and Goldberg: scales from Peabody and Goldberg (1989); Goldberg: scales from Goldberg (1983); John: scales from John (1982); BARS179: 179 bipolar rating scales. Factors from unipolar rating scales: these are based on a representative set of 430 trait adjectives. Questionnaire factors = factors based on 576 questionnaire items.

largest proportions of variance in questionnaire data. The dominance of the factors E and N can be attributed to the overrepresentation of both E- and N-items in the domain of questionnaire data. This overrepresentation can be found even in studies designed to sample a broad spectrum of questionnaire items and in which the largest and most comprehensive pools of questionnaire items have been analysed (see Browne and Howarth, 1977; Sells *et al.*, 1970). The item samples utilized in these studies have generally been compiled on the basis of literature surveys; that is, from popular, broad-band personality questionnaires. This sampling strategy will almost inevitably lead to an overrepresentation of E- and N-items, because most personality inventories measure at least some aspects of E and N, but either assess the domains of other factors less systematically or neglect their measurement completely.

2. Neuroticism is found to be by far the most dominant factor. However, neuroticism usually explains the smallest proportion of variance when factor analyses are based on representative samples of trait-descriptive adjectives (Ostendorf, 1990; Peabody and Goldberg, 1989). This difference may be due to many questionnaire authors preferring to measure clinical aspects of personality, while these personality features apparently receive only little consideration in the ordinary language of western cultures. In German, for instance, there are roughly three times as many adjectives describing the domain of agreeableness as adjectives describing characteristics of neuroticism.

3. On the other hand, the measurement of some major personality characteristics seems to be neglected in the domain of Q data when the range of personality features measured by an average or typical personality inventory is compared with the bandwidth of the Big-Five rating factors. This particularly applies to the factor openness, which cannot be found in Eysenck's P-E-N model of personality and has only a relatively weak representation in Guilford's and Cattell's factor models. Important facets of this factor, such as self-reports on abilities, intelligence, creativity and fantasy, gifts, talents, artistic skills, and musical as well as cultural needs and interests are rarely measured by personality questionnaires. Although there are certainly good reasons for measuring abilities through objective tests, self- or peer-reports on these characteristics are in no way less interesting or less important. Compared with the domain of trait adjectives, questionnaire items measuring openness are strongly underrepresented in our present empirical studies. Apart from relevant items in the NEO-openness scale, only the PRF-understanding scale assesses central facets of the fifth factor. The underrepresentation of relevant items may explain, first, the somewhat lower level of congruence of the openness factors across the Q- and L-data media, and second, the relatively low discrimination between the questionnaire factor openness and the adjective-rating factor conscientiousness. A long list of personality traits that correlate with openness is reported by McCrae and Costa (1985c, in press). However, most of these traits are rarely measured by the scales of very specific questionnaires.

4. Scales measuring facets of agreeableness and conscientiousness are usually underrepresented in broad-band personality inventories as well. For example, traits like pro-social behaviour, altruism, nurturance, and so forth describe important individual differences that have long been neglected in personality research (see Rushton, 1981). This is documented by the fact that many popular textbooks on personality psychology at most refer only marginally to this trait domain. As our review and results have shown, the likelihood that an independent conscientiousness factor will emerge from a common-factor analysis of several broad-band personality inventories is usually greater than that for the factors agreeableness and openness. The reason that attributes of conscientiousness are measured more frequently by personality inventories may be traced back to the important role of achievement and competition behaviour in western industrial societies. Relevant questionnaire scales are frequently rooted in (1) Freudian

theory (for example, superego strength, self-control) and (2) achievement motivation research (for example, need for achievement, need for endurance). In contrast, scales measuring related characteristics like conscientiousness, honesty, reliability and will are only seldom included in personality inventories. For example, some central facets of the conscientiousness factor represented by adjectives such as discreet, honest, deliberate, firm, thrifty, responsible, reliable, punctual, self-disciplined, strong-willed, foresighted, organized, scrupulous, and thorough have no equivalents in our pool of questionnaire scales. In the analysis, only a few core features of the construct are represented by the PRF scales need for achievement, need for endurance, and need for order, and the FPI scale achievement orientation. This may explain why the narrow questionnaire factor conscientiousness shows a high discriminant validity but only a moderate convergence with the broader adjective rating factor.

By and large, the correspondence of the five factors across the two data media is quite substantial. Observed deviations from the hypothesized, ideal structure can be explained by the different bandwidths of the factors in each data medium. An inspection of the scales and items shows that the bandwidth of the rating factors seems to be broader than that of the questionnaire factors. Further empirical studies are required to determine how far these differences in bandwidth will affect the instruments' power to predict important life criteria.

Although we have analysed a broad spectrum of questionnaire items, we are not able to present any persuasive arguments confirming the representativeness of our item selection. (Actually, the selection of personality inventories was guided by the aims of a research programme that was completely unrelated to the Five-Factor model under study.)[4] More powerful tests of the Big-Five factor structure in questionnaire data will require much larger and more representative samples of questionnaire items. For example, future studies could start by using the large item pools compiled by French and his colleagues. Taking French's (1953, 1973) comprehensive survey of the literature as a basis, Dermen, French, and Harman (1978) wrote questionnaire items to assess all the discernible, homogeneous facets of 28 factors previously identified in at least three analyses carried out in at least two different laboratories. L.R. Goldberg administered more than 1,400 of these items to large samples of subjects. Unfortunately, only preliminary results of this study have been reported (Dermen *et al.*, 1974; French and Dermen, 1974). It would be an interesting task for future research to explore the relationships between the structure of this comprehensive pool of questionnaire items and the Five-Factor model. Likewise, it may be worth reanalysing the studies of Browne and Howarth (1977), Eysenck and Eysenck (1969), and Sells *et al.* (1970).

But we anticipate that the results of such large item studies would not differ greatly from our general conclusions: extraversion and neuroticism would emerge as the most dominant factors, while the structure of all the remaining traits would be largely described by conscientiousness, agreeableness, and openness to experience. However, it would be most interesting to search for additional robust questionnaire factors beyond the first five and to test whether these factors carry a substantial meaning not already covered by the Big-Five personality factors originally found in the domain of rating data.

Authors' notes

This research was supported in part by a grant from the German science foundation to the second author (DFG-Az. 106/10-1).

We thank J. Harrow and F. Spinath for their assistance in preparing this manuscript.

Notes

1. For a discussion of differences between personality and temperament see Strelau (1987) and Hofstee (1991).
2. These restrictions refer to Conn and Ramanah's (1990) study that resulted in no clearly interpretable neuroticism and extraversion factors. Unfortunately, we cannot report any statistics on the amount of variance explained by the factors, as most authors do not provide the necessary information.
3. The use of PFHs was recommended by Guilford: 'The initial planning should emphasize the formation of hypotheses as to what factors are likely to be found in the selected domain' (1952, p. 36). Thus, Browne and Howarth (1977) expected 20 replicable factors, representative of the domain of questionnaire items.
4. We are indebted to Peter Borkenau for allowing us to use his questionnaire data.
5. PRF-scales: achievement, affiliation, aggression, dominance, endurance, exhibition, harm-avoidance, impulsivity, nurturance, order, play, social recognition, succourance, understanding.
6. FPI-R-scales: contentedness, social orientation, achievement orientation, restraint, irritability, aggression, proneness to stress, somatic complaints, health concerns, extraversion, emotionality.

References

Amelang, M. and Borkenau, P. (1982), 'Über die faktorielle Struktur und externe Validität einiger Fragebogen-Skalen zur Erfassung von Dimensionen der Extraversion und emotionalen Labilität' [On the factor structure and external validity of some questionnaire scales measuring dimensions of extraversion and emotion lability], *Zeitschrift für Differentielle und Diagnostische Psychologie*, **3**, 119−46.
Angleitner, A. and Ostendorf, F. (1989), 'Personality factors via self- and peer-ratings based

on a representative sample of German trait descriptive terms', paper presented at the First European Congress of Psychology, Amsterdam, The Netherlands, 2–7 July, 1989.

Angleitner, A. and Ostendorf, F. (1991), 'Temperament and the Big-Five factors of personality', paper presented at the Conference on the Developing Structure of Temperament and Personality in Childhood, Netherlands Institute for Advanced Study in the Humanities and Social Sciences (NIAS), Wassenaar, The Netherlands, 17–20 June, 1991.

Angleitner, A., Ostendorf, F. and John, O.P. (1990), 'Towards a taxonomy of personality descriptors in German: a psycho-lexical study', *European Journal of Personality*, **4**, 89–118.

Barrett, P.T. and Kline, P. (1980), 'The location of superfactors P, E, and N within the unexplored factor space', *Personality and Individual Differences*, **1**, 239–47.

Bendig, A.W. (1962), 'Factor analysis of the Guilford–Zimmerman Temperament Survey', *Journal of General Psychology*, **67**, 21–6.

Borkenau, P. (1988), 'The multiple classification of acts and the Big-Five factors of personality', *Journal of Research in Personality*, **22**, 337–52.

Borkenau, P. and Ostendorf, F. (1986), 'The NEO-Personality Inventory', unpublished German translation, University of Bielefeld, FRG.

Boyle, G.J. (1989), 'Re-examination of the major personality-type factors in the Cattell, Comrey and Eysenck Scales: were the factor solutions by Noller *et al.* optimal?', *Personality and Individual Differences*, **10**, 1289–99.

Browne, J.A. and Howarth, E. (1977), 'A comprehensive factor analysis of personality questionnaire items: a test of twenty putative factor hypotheses', *Multivariate Behavioral Research*, **12**, 399–427.

Cattell, R.B. and Gibbons, B.D. (1968), 'Personality factor structure of the combined Guilford and Cattell personality questionnaires', *Journal of Personality and Social Psychology*, **9**, 107–20.

Cattell, R.B., Eber, H.J. and Tatsuoka, M.M. (1970), *Handbook for the Sixteen Personality Factor Questionnaire (16PF)*, Champain, IL: Institute for Personality and Ability Testing.

Church, A.T. and Katigbak, M.S. (1989), 'Internal, external, and self-report structure of personality in a non-western culture: an investigation of cross-language and cross-cultural generalizability', *Journal of Personality and Social Psychology*, **57**, 857–72.

Comrey, A.L. (1970), *Manual for the Comrey Personality Scales*, San Diego, CA: Educational and Industrial Testing Service.

Conn, S.R. and Ramanaiah, N.V. (1990), 'Factor structure of the Comrey Personality Scales, the Personality Research Form-E, and the Five-Factor model', *Psychological Reports*, **67**, 627–32.

Costa, P.T., Jr. and McCrae, R.R. (1976), 'Age differences in personality structure: a cluster analytic approach', *Journal of Gerontology*, **31**, 564–70.

Costa, P.T., Jr. and McCrae, R.R. (1985), *The NEO Personality Inventory Manual*, Odessa, FL: Psychological Assessment Resources, Form S and Form R.

Costa, P.T., Jr. and McCrae, R.R. (1988), 'From catalog to classification: Murray's needs and the Five-Factor model', *Journal of Personality and Social Psychology*, **55**, 258–65.

Costa, P.T., Jr., Zonderman, A.B., McCrae, R.R. and Williams, R.B., Jr. (1985), 'Content and comprehensiveness in the MMPI: an item factor analysis in a normal adult sample', *Journal of Personality and Social Psychology*, **48**, 925–33.

De Raad, B., Mulder, E., Kloosterman, K. and Hofstee, W.K.B. (1988), 'Personality-descriptive verbs', *European Journal of Personality*, **2**, 81–96.

Dermen, D., French, J.W. and Harman, H.W. (1974), *Verification of Self-report Temperament Factors*, Technical Report 6, Princeton, NJ: Educational Testing Service, Report No. ED 104 912.

Dermen, D., French, J.W. and Harman, H.W. (1978), *Guide to Factor-referenced Temperament Scales*, Princeton, NJ: Educational Testing Service, Report No. NR 150 329.

Digman, J.M. (1989), 'Five robust trait dimensions: development, stability, and utility', *Journal of Personality*, **57**, 195–214.

Digman, J.M. (1990), 'Personality structure: emergence of the five-factor model', *Annual Review of Psychology*, **41**, 417–40.

Eggert, D. (1974), *Eysenck-Persönlichkeits-Inventar, EPI: Handanweisung für die Durchführung und Auswertung* [Manual of the Eysenck Personality Inventory, EPI], Göttingen, FRG: Hogrefe.

Eysenck, H.J. (1978), 'Superfactors P, E and N in a comprehensive factor space', *Multivariate Behavioral Research*, **13**, 475–81.

Eysenck, H.J. and Eysenck, M.W. (1985), *Personality and Individual Differences: A natural science approach*, New York, NY: Plenum Press.

Eysenck, H.J. and Eysenck, S.B.G. (1968), *Manual of the Eysenck Personality Inventory*, San Diego, CA: Educational and Industrial Testing Service.

Eysenck, H.J. and Eysenck, S.B.G. (1969), *Personality Structure and Measurement*, London: Routledge & Kegan Paul.

Fahrenberg, J. and Selg, H. (1970), *Das Freiburger Persönlichkeitsinventar (FPI)* [The Freiburg Personality Inventory], Göttingen, FRG: Hogrefe.

Fahrenberg, J., Hampel, R. and Selg, H. (1984), *Das Freiburger Persönlichkeitsinventar (FPI-R)* [The Freiburg Personality Inventory (FPI-R)], Göttingen, FRG: Hogrefe.

French, J.W. (1953), *The Description of Personality Measurements in Terms of Rotated Factors*, Princeton, NJ: Educational Testing Service.

French, J.W. (1973), *Toward the Establishment of Noncognitive Factors through Literature Search and Interpretation*, Princeton, NJ: Educational Testing Service.

French, J.W. and Dermen, D. (1974), *Seeking Markers for Temperament Factors among Positive and Negative Poles of Temperament Scales*, Princeton, NJ: Educational Testing Service, Report No. ED 104 909.

Gibbons, B.D. (1966), 'A study of the relationships between factors found in Cattell's 16PF questionnaire and factors found in the Guilford personality inventories', unpublished doctoral dissertation, University of Southern California.

Goldberg, L.R. (1978), *Language and Personality: Developing a taxonomy of personality-descriptive terms. A progress report and research proposal*, University of Oregon and Institute for Measurement of Personality, 1201 Oak Street, Eugene, OR 97401, USA.

Goldberg, L.R. (1980), 'Some ruminations about the structure of individual differences: developing a common lexicon for the major characteristics of human personality', a contribution to the symposium 'Personality: Beyond and Beneath the Factors', Honolulu, Hawaii, May, 1980.

Goldberg, L.R. (1983), 'The magical number five, plus or minus two: some considerations on the dimensionality of personality descriptors', paper presented at a Research Seminar, Gerontology Research Center, NIA/NIH, Baltimore, MD, June 1983.

Goldberg, L.R. (1989), 'Standard markers of the Big-Five factor structure', paper presented at the Invited Workshop on Personality Language, Groningen, The Netherlands, 26–30 June 1989.

Goldberg, L.R. (1990), 'An alternative "description of personality": the Big-Five factor structure', *Journal of Personality and Social Psychology*, **59**, 1216–29.

Goldberg, L.R. (1991), 'Comparing the Big-Five factor structure with its competitors: I. Eysenck's P-E-N model', paper presented at the Conference on the Development Structure of Temperament and Personality in Childhood, Netherlands Institute for Advanced Study in the Humanities and Social Sciences (NIAS), Wassenaar, The Netherlands, 17–20 June 1991.

Guilford, J.P. (1952), 'When not to factor analyze', *Psychological Bulletin*, **49**, 26–37.

Guilford, J.S., Zimmerman, W.S. and Guilford, J.P. (1976), *The Guilford–Zimmerman Temperament Survey Handbook: Twenty-five years of research and application*, San Diego, CA: Edits Publishers.

Hofstee, W.K.B. (1991), 'The concepts of personality and temperament', in J. Strelau and

A. Angleitner (eds.), *Explorations in Temperament: International perspectives on theory and measurement*, New York, NY: Plenum Press, pp. 177—88.

Hofstee, W.K.B., De Raad, B. and Goldberg, L.R. (1992), 'Integration of the Big Five and circumplex approaches to trait structure', *Journal of Personality and Social Psychology*, **63**, 146—63.

Howarth, E. (1980), 'Major factors of personality', *Journal of Personality*, **104**, 171—83.

Howarth, E. and Browne, J.A. (1971a), 'Investigation of personality factors in a Canadian context. I. Marker structure in personality questionnaire items', *Canadian Journal of Behavioral Science*, **3**, 161—73.

Howarth, E. and Browne, J.A. (1971b), 'An item-factor-analysis of the 16PF', *Personality*, **2**, 117—39.

Isaka, H. (1990), 'Factor analysis of trait terms in everyday Japanese language', *Personality and Individual Differences*, **11**, 115—24.

Jackson, D.N. (1976), *JPI—Jackson Personality Inventory — Manual*, Goshen, NY: Research Psychologists Press.

Jackson, D.N. (1984), *Personality Research Form Manual* (3rd edn.), Goshen, NY: Research Psychologists Press.

John, O.P. (1982), 'German Adjective List' (GAL), unpublished assessment instrument, University of Bielefeld, Experimental and Applied Psychology Section, FRG.

John, O.P. (1990), 'The "Big-Five" factor taxonomy: dimensions of personality in the natural language and in questionnaires', in L.A. Pervin (ed.), *Handbook of Personality: Theory and Research*, New York, NY: Guilford Press, pp. 66—100.

John, O.P., Goldberg, L.R. and Angleitner, A. (1984), 'Better than the alphabet: taxonomies of personality-descriptive terms in English, Dutch and German', in H.C.J. Bonarius, G.L.M. Van Heck and N.G. Smid (eds.), *Personality Psychology in Europe. Theoretical and empirical developments*, Lisse, The Netherlands: Swets & Zeitlinger, vol. 1, pp. 83—100.

Johnson, J.H., Null, C., Butcher, J.N. and Johnson, K.N. (1984), 'Replicated item level factor analysis of the full MMPI', *Journal of Personality and Social Psychology*, **47**, 105—14.

Kline, P. and Barrett, P. (1983), 'The factors in personality questionnaires among normal subjects', *Advances in Behavioral Research and Therapy*, **5**, 141—202.

Krug, S.E. and Johns, E.F. (1986), 'A large scale cross-validation of second-order personality structure defined by the 16PF', *Psychological Reports*, **59**, 683—93.

McCormick, I.A., Green, D.E. and Walkey, F.H. (1991), 'A comparison between first, second, and third-order factor analysis in the multi-scale questionnaire — the Eysenck Personality Inventory', *Personality and Individual Differences*, **12**, 43—8.

McCrae, R.R. (1989), 'Why I advocate the five-factor model: joint factor analyses of the NEO-PI with other instruments', in D.M. Buss and N. Cantor (eds.), *Personality Psychology: Recent trends and emerging directions*, New York, NY: Springer, pp. 237—45.

McCrae, R.R. and Costa, P.T., Jr. (1985a), 'Updating Norman's adequate taxonomy: intelligence and personality dimensions in natural language and in questionnaires', *Journal of Personality and Social Psychology*, **49**, 710—21.

McCrae, R.R. and Costa, P.T., Jr. (1985b), 'Comparison of EPI and Psychoticism scales with measures of the five-factor model of personality', *Personality and Individual Differences*, **6**, 587—97.

McCrae, R.R. and Costa P.T., Jr. (1985c), 'Openness to experience', in R. Hogan and W.H. Jones (eds.), *Perspectives in Personality*, Greenwich, CT: JAI Press, vol. 1, pp. 145—72.

McCrae, R.R. and Costa, P.T., Jr. (1987), 'Validation of the five-factor model of personality across instruments and observers', *Journal of Personality and Social Psychology*, **52**, 81—90.

McCrae, R.R. and Costa, P.T., Jr. (1989a), 'Reinterpreting the Myers—Briggs Type Indicator from the perspective of the Five-Factor model of personality', *Journal of Personality*, **57**, 17—40.

McCrae, R.R. and Costa, P.T., Jr. (1989b), 'Rotation to maximize the construct validity of factors in the NEO Personality Inventory', *Multivariate Behavioral Research*, **24**, 107−24.

McCrae, R.R. and Costa, P.T., Jr. (in press), 'Conceptions and correlates of openness to experience', in S.R. Briggs, R. Hogan and W.H. Jones (eds.), *Handbook of Personality Psychology*, New York, NY: Academic Press.

McCrae, R.R., Costa, P.T., Jr. and Busch, C.M. (1986), 'Evaluating comprehensiveness in personality systems: the California Q-Set and the five-factor model', *Journal of Personality*, **54**, 430−46.

McKenzie, J. (1988), 'Three superfactors in the 16PF and their relations to Eysenck's P, E and N', *Personality and Individual Differences*, **9**, 843−50.

Matthews, G., Stanton, N., Graham, N.C. and Brimelow, C. (1990), 'A factor analysis of the scales of the occupational personality questionnaire', *Personality and Individual Differences*, **11**, 591−6.

Meehl, P.E., Lykken, D.T., Schofield, W. and Tellegen, A. (1971), 'Recaptured-Item Technique (RIT): a method for reducing somewhat the subjective element in factor naming', *Journal of Experimental Research in Personality*, **5**, 171−90.

Montag, I. and Comrey, A.L. (1990), 'Stability of major personality factors under changing motivational conditions, in J.W. Neuliep (ed.), *Handbook of Replication Research in the Behavioral and Social Sciences*, Special Issue, *Journal of Social Behavior and Personality*, **5**, 265−74.

Noller, P., Law, H. and Comrey, A.L. (1987), 'Cattell, Comrey, and Eysenck personality factors compared: more evidence for the five robust factors', *Journal of Personality and Social Psychology*, **53**, 775−82.

Norman, W.T. (1963), 'Toward an adequate taxonomy of personality attributes: replicated factor structure in peer nomination personality ratings', *Journal of Abnormal and Social Psychology*, **66**, 574−83.

Norman, W.T. (1967), '2800 personality trait descriptors: normative operating characteristics for a university population', Department of Psychology, University of Michigan.

Nunnally, J.C. (1978), *Psychometric Theory* (2nd edn.), New York, NY: McGraw-Hill.

Ostendorf, F. (1990), *Sprache und Persönlichkeitsstruktur. Zur Validität des Fünf-Faktoren-Modells der Persönlichkeit* [Language and Personality Structure: On the structural validity of the Five-Factor model of personality], Roderer, FRG: Regensburg.

Peabody, D. (1987), 'Selecting representative trait adjectives', *Journal of Personality and Social Psychology*, **52**, 59−71.

Peabody, D. and Goldberg, L.R. (1989), 'Some determinants of factor structures from personality-trait descriptors', *Journal of Personality and Social Psychology*, **57**, 552−67.

Piedmont, R.L., McCrae, R.R. and Costa, P.T., Jr. (1991), 'Adjective Check List scales and the five factor model', *Journal of Personality and Social Psychology*, **60**, 630−7.

Rushton, J.P. (1981), 'The altruistic personality', in J.P. Rushton and R.M. Sorrentino (eds.), *Altruism and Helping Behavior*, Hillsdale, NJ: Erlbaum, pp. 251−66.

Saville & Holdsworth, Ltd (1984), *Occupational Personality Questionnaires Manual*, Esher: Saville & Holdsworth, Ltd.

Schneewind, K.A. (1977), 'Entwicklung einer deutschsprachigen Version des 16 PF-Tests von Cattell' [Development of the German version of Cattell's 16 PF-test], *Diagnostika*, **23**, 188−91.

Schrueger, J.M. and Allen, L.C. (1986), 'Second-order factor structure common to five personality questionnaires', *Psychological Reports*, **58**, 119−26.

Sells, S.B., Demaree, R.G. and Will, D.P., Jr. (1970), 'Dimensions of personality: I. Conjoint factor structure of Guilford and Cattell trait markers', *Multivariate Behavioral Research*, **5**, 391−422.

Strelau, J. (1987), 'The concept of temperament in personality research', *European Journal of Personality,* **1**, 107—17.

Stumpf, H., Angleitner, A., Wieck, T., Jackson, D.N. and Beloch-Till, H. (1985), *Deutsche Personality Research Form (PRF)*, Göttingen, FRG: Hogrefe.

Vagg, P.R. and Hammond, S.B. (1976), 'The number and kind of invariant personality (Q) factors: a partial replication of Eysenck and Eysenck', *British Journal of Social and Clinical Psychology,* **15**, 121—9.

Wiggins, J.S. and Trapnell, P.D. (in press), 'Personality structure: the return of the Big Five', in S.R. Briggs, R. Hogan and W.H. Jones (eds.), *Handbook of Personality Psychology*, New York, NY: Academic Press.

Yang, K. and Bond, M.H. (1990), 'Exploring implicit personality theories with indigenous or imported constructs: the Chinese case', *Journal of Personality and Social Psychology,* **58**, 1087—95.

Zuckerman, M. (1979), *Sensation Seeking: Beyond the optimal level of arousal*, Hillsdale, NJ: Erlbaum.

Zuckerman, M., Kuhlman, D.M. and Camac, C. (1988), 'What lies beyond E and N?: an analysis of scales believed to measure basic dimensions of personality', *Journal of Personality and Social Psychology,* **54**, 96—107.

Zuckerman, M., Kuhlman, D.M., Thornquist, M. and Kiers, H. (1991), 'Five (or three) robust questionnaire scale factors of personality without culture', *Personality and Individual Differences,* **9**, 929—41.

PART III
The Psychodynamic
Approach

5/ Pychoanalysis as a theory of personality

Bert Westerlundh and Gudmund J.W. Smith
University of Lund, Sweden

Introduction

In his *The Foundations of Psychoanalysis: A philosophical critique*, Grünbaum (1984) concludes that there is as yet no empirical evidence for the principal psychoanalytic doctrines. An abridged version of the book was presented in *The Behavioral and Brain Sciences* (Grünbaum, 1986) followed by peer commentaries. For Grünbaum the possibility still seems to exist that empirical evidence can be obtained by means of well-designed extra-clinical studies. However, he says, these have for the most part not yet been attempted. In a concluding commentary the journal editor doubts the value of such an endeavour: 'Even if one grants that, in principle, some of Freud's claims can be reformulated in such a way as to be testable . . . , is there still a question as to whether or not it would be worthwhile to do so' (Harnad, 1986).

It is enlightening to observe how closely the criticism has been focused on Freud, an authorship the beginnings of which are more than a century old. This lends to the whole discussion a peculiarly anacronistic flavour. Where else in the realm of science would one criticize a person who died at an advanced age 50 years ago as if he were still a contemporary? Grünbaum himself has raised the question of what the post-Freudians may have contributed to the development of psychoanalysis, but does not seem to have found their undertakings worthy of serious comment. Even for other criticism, psychoanalysis has not only begun but also ended with Sigmund Freud himself. Why do we not, then, leave the whole discussion to the historians? Why are some people still so angry?

In his book *The Freudian Learning Hypotheses*, Hans Sjöbäck (1988) takes a very different view. Even if Sjöbäck, a scholar of distinction, was critical of many of the basic psychoanalytic tenets he is still basically sympathetic because, in contradistinction to much contemporary personality psychology, psychoanalysis has always tried to understand human beings in their complex entirety. To Sjöbäck it is very important not to confound psychoanalysis with Freudian assumptions alone. A very clear distinction should be made between Freudian psychoanalysis and later developments, the Freudian model, for all its originality, being hopelessly caught above all in outdated nineteenth-century thought. In other words, so much has

113

happened in the world of psychoanalysis that we would now prefer to use the term *psychodynamics* to cover the extent of the field (as can be seen in, for example, Reppen, 1985).

An interesting footnote to the question of whether psychoanalysis is solely Freud or much more than Freud was recently provided by Bettelheim (1988) in an article in the German periodical *Psychologie Heute*. According to Bettelheim, Freud has been corrupted by the translation of his texts to English. To quote:

> The main fault with the translations is that, by using abstractions, they remove the reader from what Freud tried to teach him about his inner life or, to take the consequences fully into consideration, remove him from himself. In its English version, psychoanalysis, being a system of intellectual constructions, becomes something that generally concerns others, but not the reader himself.

Bettelheim continues to discuss the aim of Freud's use of metaphor. The aim was to give true psychological insight by providing us with intellectual comprehension and emotional reaction at one and the same time. Perhaps the whole discussion about psychoanalysis would have taken another turn had we all been able to read Freud in the original. Possibly we would have been much more concerned with Freud the original observer of human conduct than with Freud the theorist.

Anyhow, a critical discussion has been raging for years. As Kline (1986) rightly pointed out, Grünbaum was far from the first critic. In spite of all attempts to nullify the importance of psychoanalysis, psychodynamic points of view have continued to make life complicated for its enemies and to deflect attention from what they consider to be worthier goals in life. Still more, the scientific language of the critics themselves is permeated by concepts originally derived from or stamped by psychoanalysis. Just think of the unconscious, preconscious processing, primary and secondary process characteristics, defence mechanisms, transference, complex, catharsis, introversion and extraversion, etc. We would not be able to communicate intelligibly about the experiential world, or discuss our understanding of ourselves and others, were it not for the rich vocabulary developed by psychoanalytically contaminated clinical practitioners.

Orthodox psychoanalysts have often been criticized — and rightly so — for their unwillingness to absorb negative commentaries directed at their basic assumptions. Some of them may have felt that the critics are usually unable to appreciate the psychoanalytic principles in their true context of a therapist—patient relation. Since most practising analysts have apparently found their basic postulates about human nature to be therapeutically fairly rewarding, they have seen no reason to relent. Why slaughter a cow that still yields milk, even if to some outsiders the milk may appear imaginary?

At the same time, many severe critics have tended to avoid a dialogue with their analytic adversaries. To some of them, often among puritanical cognitive psychologists, any inferences about non-conscious processing and similar matters are simply anathema. One of the main reasons why the issue of subliminal perception met with such vitriolic resistance may have been an 'unconscious' association between

no evidence 4 it but it
is still accepted

subliminality and the repugnant psychoanalytic unconscious. Some experimentalists, according to Dixon (1981), even rejected obvious experimental evidence. Today, however, cognitive psychologists in the front line of the field are ready to accept assumptions about preconscious processing, for instance, as preparatory stages in decision making which cannot be reached by means of conventional introspective methods.

As more and more psychologists move away from naive, pseudo-rationalistic notions about the mind (cf. Smith, 1987), it is time to ask whether psychodynamic psychologists can teach us anything about the unknown land we are approaching. For Freud and his followers this land was very different from the land of awareness, oblivious to the relations of space and time and the rules of logic. As has already been suggested, Freud should be regarded as part of the history of psychology rather than as a contemporary. Like all great scientists, he was not independent of the foibles of his time, particularly the mechanistic assumptions of the nineteenth century. (Observe the peculiar term defence *mechanism*.) At the same time, he may have made discoveries that cannot be wholly neglected by contemporary psychology. Still more important would be to bring the post-Freudians into the limelight and see what they could possibly contribute to present-day personality research.

We see this under the impression that personality psychology has not yet made the progress it should have made had it regarded the psychodynamic discoveries with an open yet critical mind, instead of rejecting them outright as false or irrelevant. Our field has remained static in many ways, unregarding of the fact that personality is not merely a bundle of traits, but a central organizing principle; that the present cannot be fully comprehended except in the context of past personal history; that what we can reveal about ourselves is only a fragment of our personal reality, and perhaps a very small fragment at that. This does not mean that the hidden reality must remain inaccessible to scientific inquiry. Freud gave us tools to lift the curtain. Experimental personality psychology has equipped us with other, perhaps more reliable tools. Not to try to use these tools is to condemn the study of personality to eternal dullness.

In short, then, the study of personality needs to open its field to the influence of psychodynamic insights. To open up is not to surrender but to use the observations and insights of generations of perceptive and empathic psychologists who have not all been biased, unscientific dopes.

It is our intention, after a critical scrutiny of some of the most essential tenets and research tools in psychoanalysis, old and contemporary, to try to estimate the value for a future theory of personality of what we have not seen fit to reject as old-fashioned or unproductive. Since a consummate scrutiny of psychoanalysis in its entirety would be a Herculean task, our account must be limited to a few central topics pertaining above all to *intrapsychic conflict*, *drive*, and *defence*. We have particularly avoided discussing psychoanalysis as a therapeutic technique or as a guideline for family relations, treatment of children (see, for example, Dazzi and De Coro, Chapter 6 in this volume) and the like.

The place of psychoanalytic theory among personality theories

Before beginning a more specific inquiry into psychoanalysis as a theory of personality we would like to define, in a general way, its position among competing personality theories. The prerequisite of such an inquiry is, however, that personality psychology should not be regarded as a special field besides other fields, like the psychologies of cognition or perception, but rather as a perspective integrating all these special fields, thus creating a theoretical hub for the study of the individual.

It should be admitted from the beginning that not all studies of personality refer to a theory, at least not an explicit one. Descriptive behaviourists and phenomenologists are often programmatically atheoretical; and theories in psychology, including personality theories, cannot stand up to a rigorous formal examination. Among the formal requirements usually brought to bear on scientific theories we would like to emphasize three in relation to personality. A close reading of them will make clear that few theories stand up well in the cold light of these requirements:

1. *Inner coherence*; that is, unequivocal relations between the substructures of the theory, and also between the substructures and the theoretical superstructure. This presupposes that the theory goes beyond naming the existence of relations and tries to analyse how they really function.
2. *Inclusiveness*. This term implies that assumptions within the frame of the theory should be sufficient for explaining data. Accessorial assumptions or additional constructions thus disclose lack of inclusiveness. An inclusive theory need not, of course, pretend to cover the entire field of personality, only to be inclusive within the bounds of its subject.
3. *Relevance* alludes to the closeness between the theory and its empirical referents. A psychological theory within the field of personality should have a clear relation to experiential reports and behavioural observations and thus be easily influenced by them.

The most efficient means to mark off psychoanalysis and related approaches from other theories of personality is, however, to bring out their explanatory modes. One important dividing line runs between mechanistic and dynamic explanations. The mechanistic explanations tend to be atomistic and to include reified concepts like dispositions. Personality is regarded as a collection of skills or traits, the visible manifestation of dispositions. Change is preferably described as quantitative; that is, as increments or decrements of performance levels.

In contrast, the dynamic explanations characteristic of psychoanalysis, but also of other theoretical trends in personality psychology, are apt to be holistic or field oriented. Instead of leaning on reified concepts they prefer functional ones. The central issue would thus be *how* change comes about. Since change is conceived not just as simple quantitative moderations, but as qualitative transformations, developmental discontinuities are regarded as the rule rather than as exceptions. Instead of a collection of traits, the dynamic orientations view personality as a system of interrelated structures.

Structure could be a risky concept in dynamic personality theory and could easily be confounded with dispositions if it were not explicitly related to growth and progress. Structure implies permanence, but only relative permanence. And structure, in its dynamic meaning, always refers to the life history of the individual. This has nothing to do with the perennial nature−nurture controversy, but should rather be seen as a declaration of a central aim of dynamic personality theory: to understand personality in the light of mental growth.

Using structure and development as orthogonal axes, we will now be able to define more accurately the position of psychoanalysis in relation to other personality theories. Among theories that do not employ structural concepts are the classical typologies and behaviouristically tinged theories. However, even statistically sophisticated factor theories (Cattell, Eysenck, etc.) should rather be termed dispositionalistic than structuralistic, at least when the statistical factors are handled like reified entities, an obvious temptation. Gordon Allport's personality psychology belongs to the same family, in spite of its explicitly humanistic gloss.

In the group of structuralistic theories only those should be included that regard structure as an intra-individual concept. A number of intra-structuralistic theories, moreover, are clearly agenetic; for instance, Kelly's cognitive version, Maslow's need hierarchy, the phenomenologists with their professed concentration on the here-and-now problems, and many existentialists. Stern and Goldstein are classics with a leaning towards dispositional concepts.

The remaining group embraces a developmental perspective, where development is seen as a series of qualitatively different stages. Besides classical psychoanalysis, apostates like Adler belong here; Erikson of course; and Angyal's holistic model. It is more difficult to place the revisionistic protesters, since their protests are seldom explicitly theoretical but rather diffusely ideological. As far as the basic structural-genetic characteristics are concerned, even new developments in psychoanalysis should be placed in the same pen as the classical versions.

As always, attempts at classifying psychological theories meet with difficulties. To make things still more complicated, psychoanalysis itself resists clear-cut classification. In all its attempts to be dynamic it lugs along a mechanistic inheritance from the last century and often yields to the temptation to reify its concepts; for example, defence mechanisms. In some of its versions, moreover, the developmental perspective is so radically foreshortened as to seem nearly non-existent. In Melanie Klein's model, for instance, children seem to reach a stage of adult comprehension surprisingly early (cf. the more general criticism below of many psychoanalysts' negligence of contemporary psychological knowledge). Still, in our view psycho-analysis is a scientific theory of personality, not a theory outside the range of rational critical inquiry. We certainly agree with Weinberger and Silverman (1990) that psychoanalytic theory and its constituent propositions are, in principle, testable. Thus, like Grünbaum (1984), we basically disagree with Popper's infamous dictum. We also hold that the reasoning of analysts, as seen in clinical contributions, is characterized by a *natural phenomenology*, where causal inferences play a major part. It is thus most properly understood within a natural scientific reconstruction of psychoanalysis, not a hermeneutical one. This should be clear from the methodological criteria for personality theories which we presented earlier.

Psychoanalytic theory: some developmental lines

Psychoanalysis started as a psychopathology, a theory of mental disturbances, but its claims to be a general psychology of personality were articulated quite early, and later emphasized by ego psychologists such as Hartmann and Rapaport. The justification for these claims can be found in the way of conceptualizing mental pathology: it is viewed in terms of structural (intra- and inter-systemic) conflicts, and these conflicts are always rooted in fixations, developmental disturbances. The genetic, structural, and motivational framework which we have stressed as fundamental to explanation in personality psychology was from the beginning central in psychoanalytic attempts to understand neuroses. These were thus seen not as aberrations or exceptions but as phenomena of the same qualitative order as 'normal' personality functioning.

Central to the explanation was the concept of intrapsychic conflict, what Horowitz (1988) has termed *psychodynamic configurations*. Such conflicts are motive constellations, usually involving a wish for a desired aim, a threat, and a defensive posture compromising the wish in order to evade the threat. The originally comparatively circumscribed and well-defined theory, which was paradigmatically formulated by Fenichel (1946), has changed extensively in recent decades. Some of these changes look 'top-down', initiated by leading theorists and sometimes with questionable impact on the analytic community at large, others 'bottom-up', reflecting the endeavours of analytical practitioners to explain and understand the changing aspects of mental malfunctioning, especially in the successively more important group of patients suffering from borderline pathology and narcissistic personality disturbance.

Superordinate models

Conflicts exist within and between the main intrapsychic systems. Different models of conceptualizing and classifying these systems have been proposed. The topographical model of (dynamically) unconscious, preconscious, and conscious contents is a theory of mental *locations*, varying in distance to consciousness and functioning according to different modes. It was in terms of this model that Freud originally described *how* the different systems work — whether they follow the rules of common sense or deviate more or less drastically from them. These formulations (for example, Freud, 1953) in terms of primary and secondary process, pleasure—unpleasure, and reality principle belong to Freud's basic contributions, introducing the irrational into normal personality functioning. Theorists like Sandler (for example,

Sandler *et al.*, 1978) have testified to the continuing usefulness of the model despite its limitations. In contrast to the latter, structural model, the topographical one is rather near to the language of experience. For example, it is possible within it to speak about a person's consciousness being overwhelmed by anxiety, in contrast to the structural formulation of his or her ego's being overwhelmed by unmanageable quantities of excitation.

The structural or tripartite model, introduced by Freud in 1923, divides the mental apparatus into the systems of id, ego, and superego. It is basically a model of systems characterized by specific motivations — the drive-ridden id, the moralistic superego, and the more or less realistic executive ego which tries to square the demands of the other systems with those of the outer world. Such a model of motivational systems in interaction is of course absolutely central to psychodynamic explanation, and as late as 1964 Arlow and Brenner proposed that it should be *the* psychoanalytic model replacing all others. However, in recent years this model has not fared so well. In a sense it invites reification, being characterized by some of the mechanistic and biologistic aspects of Freud's thinking. It is also a very general and abstract model of motivational levels, and there has been a growing preference for smaller functional entities. Among the ego psychologists, it was, for instance, fashionable to speak about different ego and superego functions. But there are other ways to move analysis to a more molecular level.

The structures mentioned here are of course constructs applied to mental contents and events. Certain contents, especially representations of the self and significant others, are extremely important in determining ideation and behaviour. This is the group of 'person schemata' and 'role relationship models', in the terminology of Horowitz (1988). Together they constitute the most important aspect of the representational world (Sandler and Rosenblatt, 1962). They were given strategic importance even in the classical definition of instinct, where the psychic representative of the instinct is a representation of the self in interaction with another person — the object of the instinct — in order to reach a specific type of satisfaction, the instinctual aim. They are the core of the concept of transference. They are also central to the concept of the superego, where representations of the idealized parents in particular form the basis of the ego ideal, and thus of the individual's values and moral system. This is of course a theme taken up later by self psychology. If the analysis is concentrated on representations of the self and significant others (at varying levels of development), the result is an object relations model. Certain concepts which were introduced quite early — for instance, narcissism and identification — can be treated in a much more precise way in this frame of reference.

In their influential book, Gedo and Goldberg (1973) try to integrate these models (together with the more primitive reflex arch model, which is an explanation of behaviour in unmediated stimulus-response terms) in a hierarchical framework. The reflex arch model is applied to traumatic states, a model of self and object nuclei to psychotic functioning, a self-and-object model to narcissistic personality disorders, the structural model to the true neuroses, and the topographical one to 'normal', expectable adult functioning. It is true that the topographic model has the best fit with current cognitive conceptions of the unconscious (Brody, 1987; Erdelyi, 1985). The different superordinate models are not necessarily mutually exclusive; in part, they are oriented toward different aspects of the subject matter. These different directions are reflected in psychoanalytic theorizing. Eagle (1984) finds three main clusters of theorists: those who retain a classical model, but stress the importance of self and object representations; those who freely use both models; and those who reject the classical framework in favour of object relations theory. The main trend as regards style of theorizing on this superordinate level has certainly been from high-level hypothetical constructs, inviting reification, to an emphasis on description of mental contents with a more limited use of explanatory terms.

Motivational constructs

Freud's main motivational construct, the instincts (*Triebe*), reflected a biological view of humankind, where they were seen as the most important precipitates of phylogenesis, created through the long development of the species and — as unchangeable biological (sexual) constitution — determining the individual's personality. In Freud's mature thinking, environmental influences on personality formation were quite limited (Sjöbäck, 1988; Sulloway, 1979). The construct also had a mechanistic bent, regarding satisfaction as the consequence of discharge of instinctual energy. A lot of discussion and dissent have taken place on all of the points touched upon here: the list of inborn motives, their immutability, the powerlessness of the environment, and the concept of psychic energy.

Many analytical theorists seem to avoid the concept of psychic energy today. It was a prime suspect in the great trial against metapsychology in the late sixties and early seventies, and not without reason. What had happened, especially in ego psychology, was that Freud's often metaphorical hypothetical constructs hardened into reifications. Further, these reified concepts of energy and structure were not treated as hypothetical entities intended to explain observable reality, but as a hidden reality *per se* which could be observed by the psychoanalytic method. Psychoanalytic discourse — case presentations, etc. — actually avoided the introduction of empirical referents and moved in a shadowland of constructs reified into spurious substantiality. This style was not effective even as a shorthand, and further tended to obscure aspects of the subject matter. The type of reification mentioned here has been a besetting sin of psychoanalysis and is, as Eagle (1984) points out, evident enough in later contributions like those of Mahler and Kohut.

The attack on metapsychology was thus well founded, and implied a demand for a theory closer to clinical reality and the experience of the individual. Instead of hypothetical drives one ought to speak about psychological wishes (Holt, 1976). Instead of substantive concepts, nouns, one should use an *action language* of verbs describing what the person was doing and trying to do psychologically (Schafer, 1976). Much of this was quite reasonable, but it tended to lead to a dogmatic exclusion of higher-level theoretical constructs. The main victim of this has been the concept of *psychic energy*.

Now, as academic psychologists we have little aversion to higher-order theoretical constructs as such. From this point of view, the remarks of Sjöbäck (1984a) seem well grounded. Following Rapaport (1960), he states that the concept of *mental energy* is intended to explain three aspects of motivation and behaviour: the experienced pressure to act; the emergence of 'spontaneous' behaviour unmotivated by external contingencies; and, finally, the transformation of drive aims, targets, etc. with preserved identity of the drive when direct expression is blocked. The rejection of any concept of psychic energy has led to a lessened interest in peremptory and spontaneous aspects of behaviour. Further, the lack of any such concept has left the issue of transformation in the air. 'As long as the concept of transmutation . . . is not discarded from psychoanalytic thinking, the problem of creating a convincing picture of the links between the different expressions of an impulse remains' (Sjöbäck, 1984a, p. 15). This quotation is intended to point to a problem in present-day theorizing, but certainly not to accept or excuse the traditional way of ascribing qualities to mental energies *per se*. Formulations such as 'aggressive energies are *per se* aggressive and are thus used in the process of defence' are certainly unacceptable, not only because they are question-begging but also because the massive reification here has unfortunate consequences for theory formulation.

Freud saw all behaviour as ultimately determined by the two immutable instinctual drives, sexuality and aggression. The ego psychologists added another ultimate motive, the primarily autonomous neutral energies of the ego. In recent years, psychoanalytic ideas about motivation have widened very much in scope and complexity. In abstract terms — if one speaks about a general need for self-assertion, for instance — it could seem as if psychoanalytic theory had discarded its biological fundament. But for an observer like Sjöbäck (1984a), it was not so. The new ideas rather concern biological instinctual and non-instinctual dispositions, evolving in interaction with the environment in accordance with a genetically determined, bionomic life plan. What supplants the classical form of drive determination is thus not environmentalism but a more complex interactionist standpoint. Two groups of motives are given an important position alongside the instinctual drives, namely developmental needs and unlearned responses (that is, the basic emotions).

For Freud, drive satisfaction was primary and an interest in and affective bonds to other people were derived from ('anaclitic upon') such satisfaction. A criticism of this position is central to Eagle's (1984) book. Loewald (1972, p. 242), in an often-quoted contribution, has summarized the new view: 'Instincts . . . are to be seen as relational phenomena from the beginning and not as autochtonous forces seeking discharge . . . Instinctual drives . . . are codetermined by the "environmental factors" which enter into their very organization as motivational forces.'

What this seems to imply is that the outer environment is given a much greater role than the classical one of suppression in personality development. An extreme example of this is of course the renewed interest in the infantile seduction theory of mental pathology, initiated by the provocative works of Miller and Masson (for example, Masson, 1984). A full presentation of the range of psychoanalytic assumptions concerning the role of outer reality is found in Sjöbäck (1988). The stress is moved from the abstract model of drive reduction to interactions of a much wider range taking place in the relationship between mother and child. This seems due to the increased importance given to the observations by child analysts of what actually happens in such relationships. The formulations of child analysis used to be lowly regarded, but today they are a main influence on theory construction, as can be seen in the influence of the work of Mahler (for example, Mahler *et al.*, 1975). Finally, to the instinctual drives are added other forms of biologically rooted motivations which are of a non-instinctual character, such as ego interests involving representations of self and others, and the need to exercise certain functions and skills. These assumptions reduce the special status accorded to sexual and aggressive instincts.

The list of other such motives which have been mentioned by psychoanalysts is quite long. The frustration of these needs is thought to produce permanent impairments of personality functioning and developmental deficits or arrests (Stolorow and Lachman, 1980), a concept to which we will have reason to return.

The emotions are clearly rooted in biological dispositions, but develop in interaction with the environment. During development they tend to change from somatopsychic to intrapsychic manifestations. In psychoanalysis, the emotions should be considered from three aspects: they are energetic discharge phenomena; they become cognitive signals, containing an evaluation of a situation; and they can function as relatively autonomous motivations in their own right (Rapaport, 1960, p. 32). However, this formulation is derived from Freud's second theory of anxiety (Freud, 1971b), which describes the development of anxiety from the primitive experience of panic, due to frustration of imperative needs, to cognitive signals of threatening danger situations, which in unfortunate cases create conflicts and serve as the proximal motive of defence mechanism activation. With the exception of guilt ('superego anxiety': Fenichel, 1946, p. 134), this type of theory of affects as patterns of anticipation, organized around the motivational core of a biologically given unlearned response, has rarely been seen in classical psychoanalytic discussions of the emotions. The energetic perspective has dominated; the cognitive evaluation and autonomous motivational ones have been played down. Object relations models are exceptions; here affective anticipatory schemata are of great importance and often introduced. However, such formulations, which are generally clinical, seldom contribute to a general psychodynamic theory of affect. But two theoretical developments should be mentioned.

The first concerns depressive affect. Classically, the root of depression was seen as the pathognomonic introjection of an ambivalently loved lost object, whereupon its bad qualities are seen as part of the self and so condemned (Fenichel, 1946, p. 396ff.). Today, this formula is limited to depressive illness, whereas depressive affect is considered a much more general phenomenon (see especially Bibring, 1953; Dorpat, 1977; Sandler and Joffe, 1965). Depression becomes an ordinary anticipatory emotion (concerned with the expectation of failure) with certain adaptive characteristics, which under special circumstances can turn maladaptive. Like anxiety, it has a complicated developmental history, and like anxiety it can serve as the motive of defensive operations. In fact, it takes its place alongside anxiety as a central component of intrapsychic conflict (Dorpat, 1977). In contrast to anxiety and guilt, the signal of depression is not concerned with threats following the transgression of some rule, but with those dangers which are a consequence of failure. This important dimension was earlier not conceptualized independently (Sjöbäck, 1988).

The second development concerns one of the primary unlearned responses, rage. There is a trend to see human aggression in terms other than those of an appetitive instinct. Sjöbäck (1984a) found this trend manifested in widely varying sources. Studies based on child observation (Parens, 1979), as well as theorizing in the realm of self psychology (Kohut, 1972, 1977), conclude that aggression is primarily an unlearned response to situations involving unpleasure. Kohut (1977, p. 123) further specifies this unpleasure as 'the faulty empathic response given by the self-object'. Other forms of aggression are seen as derived from this reactive type.

Those who suggest such a view have to explain how such early situation-bound manifestations are transformed into a permanent readiness for aggressive action. Hanley (1978) supplies an attractive answer: the unconscious persistence of infantile frustrated wishes, which have succumbed to primal repression and fixation, create a continuous motive for aggression. For Hanley, these inner stimuli are repressed Oedipal wishes, but 'there is no logical objection to extending it to other kinds of frustrated impulses, needs, or wishes' (Sjöbäck, 1984a, p. 30). Kohut's ideas of rage as a consequence of frustration of developmental needs of attention and empathy from the parent, which persists as later narcissistic rage, thus fit well enough into this framework.

Thus, the instinctual drives are no longer accorded a supreme place in human motivation. Sexuality retains a special place due to its unique flexibility, but the concept of instinct itself is changed to give a much more important role to the outer world. Aggression is sometimes regarded not as an instinct but as an unlearned response, and there are other indications of an increased interest in emotions as motives of human behaviour. Developmental needs of a non-instinctual type pertaining to self and object interactions have become important in discussions about personality development and pathogenesis.

Conflict and defence

Freud introduced the concept of *defence* quite early (1894; see *Complete Psychological Works*, 1962). With all types of defensive operations subsumed under the heading of repression, it continued to be of importance in the following period. However, with the introduction of the structural model and the second theory of anxiety, the idea of intrapsychic conflict took its typical form. Repression was seen as only one of the defence mechanisms of the ego, activated in danger situations by anxiety signals and turned against forbidden impulses emanating from the id. The formula for psychodynamic configurations thus became id impulse vs. ego defence. The theory got its classical formulation in Anna Freud's 1936 book (Freud, 1968).

The new ideas on motivation are of course reflected in current conceptualizations of psychological conflict and defence. Wallerstein (1985) gives a convenient summary. What characterizes the work of leading theorists is a broadening of concepts — defences can be conscious or unconscious, conflicts exist between wishes of one sort or another, the ego can use defensively whatever lies at hand. Such formulations have their strength in putting intrapsychic conflict into the context of psychic functioning in general. By applying a hierarchical perspective, they can, for instance, cover both pathogenic and adaptive uses of defences (Gill, 1963). However, they play down the fact that the classical defence mechanisms are automatic modes of functioning of primitive unconscious cognition, falling into classes with easily recognizable functional forms and often part of a general personality organization also characterized by specific impulses and types of anxiety.

This type of theorizing seems to be of limited importance to clinically oriented analytic practitioners. These seem rather to be interested in what new defences must be assumed in the context of analysis of borderline conditions and pathological narcissism. The classical list, as found in Anna Freud (1968) and Fenichel (1946), consisted of a number of neurotic defences such as repression, the varieties of isolation, reaction formation, neurotic denial, and intellectualization. To these were added a number of more primitive mechanisms thought to be characteristic of the perversions, impulse neuroses, and psychoses, such as identification, projection, psychotic denial of reality, and regression. Today, following Kernberg (for example, 1975), most analysts seem to keep the list of *high-level* defences but add a new group of *pre-neurotic* ones, such as splitting, projective identification, primitive idealization, primitive denial, grandiosity, and devaluation. The characteristics of the different mechanisms are much discussed.

The study of more severe personality disturbances has thus influenced conceptions of intrapsychic conflict. The construct itself has also come under debate. Kernberg (for example, 1975) stresses the causal role of primitive aggression — constitutional or reactive — in the development of narcissistic pathology. Thus, he retains the classical impulse-versus-defence (primarily splitting) model in his explanation of this type of pathogenesis. Kohut (1971, 1977) reached quite different conclusions from his observations of the same type of pathology. Among other things he stressed actual failure on the part of parental 'selfobjects' to meet the infant's developmental needs for empathy and mirroring as the most important pathogenic factor in narcissistic pathology, and by seeing developmental arrests and deficits as the prime pathological consequences of this failure, thus giving primitive aggression and conflicts around it a secondary role.

The stress on actual failure to meet developmental needs is well in line with the theoretical developments which have been discussed above, but to contrast this with an explanation in terms of conflict around aggression is not correct (cf. Eagle, 1984; Wallerstein, 1983). In Glassman's (1988) interesting extra-clinical study, the data rather speak for seeing Kohut's model as a special case of Kernberg's more general theory. The concept of *conflict* remains central, even in the study of primitive pathology. The description of the patient's subjective experience of personality deficit or actual lack is found already in, for instance, Balint (1968). This dimension is certainly interesting and seems central to this type of pathology. Sjöbäck (1984b) used it as a new image of the mentally suffering person: to the traditional one of the person plagued by anxiety and torn by inner conflicts is added the new one of the incomplete person, characterized by experiences of emptiness and feelings of deficits and lacks in his or her psychic functioning.

Psychoanalysis and personality psychology

Many of the changes which we observe in psychoanalytic theory seem — despite the differences between the fields — to parallel those in academic personality psychology. The stress on direct observation of children (with its implications of a true lifecycle perspective), the move from a simple drive reduction model of motivation, interactionism, the interest in the self-concept, and explicit formulations about cognitive and emotive aspects of personality functioning can all be found in front-line research within the latter field. Either we are looking at *Zeitgeist* phenomena or else the bulkheads between the fields are less watertight than we supposed. Yet, the criticism that psychoanalysts tend to disregard established knowledge in adjacent fields is not totally unwarranted. There are still analysts who will ascribe mature cognitive functioning to infants in the cradle, contrary to the findings of cognitive developmental psychology. However, leading theorists seem well aware of this danger.

We feel a lack of information about how new formulations become part of the more or less accepted body of psychoanalysis; metascientific studies in this area would certainly add to our understanding. Both academic psychology and psychoanalysis seem to deviate very much from a positivist ideal of continuous accumulation of knowledge. In both fields, fads and fashions are important. In analysis, a phenomenon may be described and put into an explanatory context in such a way as to make it seem important, a paradigmatic member of a strategically central class. This description and explanation are then taken up and extended to other fields by other investigators, sometimes successfully, sometimes less so, and the limits are decided by eventual consensus.

Winnicott's (1971) ideas about transitional objects and transitional phenomena are a case in point. The transitional objects are well known; security blankets and much-loved playthings of early childhood, which for a period seem to be of great importance to the child but are then simply forgotten. In Winnicott's description, these objects are made of mixed self and object representations and heavily flavoured with grandiosity. Their function is to aid the child in a situation where infantile omnipotence is dismantled. This description was brilliant: anybody reading it probably felt that this natural history of the teddy bear was in some sense true. The power of Winnicott's presentation was due to the fact that he anchored it in the central concepts of modern psychoanalysis. For a while, his conceptual framework was applied to most contents and events. Today, things are back to normal, but the constructs seem to have a secure, delimited place within psychoanalytic theory.

This seems much like what happens in academic psychology, but with the difference that the criteria involved are essentially soft, which has a number of unfortunate consequences. One is that different concepts will cover the same part of reality, and the same concept will have different meanings, for different analysts. They have notorious difficulties in agreeing about, for instance, what is meant by defences, what types of defence exist, and what characterizes the different ones. A typical example is the protean character of the concept of denial (Sjöbäck, 1973, Chapter 8). A basic agreement in the way of looking at reality is drowned in a sea of semantic confusion.

At a pinch one could live with this. The basic problems of science are not semantic but concern empirical validity. But here we come up against the next difficulty. The clinical situation is excellent for producing hypotheses, but not at all for testing them. This should be self-evident. Among others, Hardaway (1990) has listed some of the main reasons: according to analysts, the objectivation of the analytic situation necessary for scientific study will actually destroy it; the situation is highly reactive, probably producing self-fulfilling prophecies; the relationship between theoretical concepts and empirical referents is complex, as we said above, creating difficulties in data evaluation; and causal attributions are hardly possible. The result is a multiplication of competing hypotheses which, in the absence of predative validation techniques, will all survive as stunted small fry.

This is certainly a not-too-encouraging situation, but attempts are made to improve it. As regards the structure of the theory, one avenue is to study the 'logic in use', the actual use of constructs by practising analysts. The work of Elliott (1985), as supervised by Sandler, gives interesting information about this. She used multivariate techniques in order to study the conceptual structure of the construct of sublimation among a number of psychoanalytic practitioners. For those who believe in the hidden wisdom of clinicians, it should be noted that in this investigation, their ideas were badly articulated and not on a sophisticated theoretical level.

Another way is to strengthen the theory's reconstructed logic, to try to reconstruct it in a clear, parsimonious, and testable form. Many learned authors have tried to systematize the corpus of theoretical statements in different ways, including people such as Rapaport, Gill, Holt, Wallerstein, Sandler, and Sjöbäck — names which we have felt the need to call upon in the course of this essay. On a less extensive but more detailed level are the attempts to write computer simulation models of parts of the theory; for instance, the work of Moser and his colleagues (1968) on the theory of defensive processes.

As we have stated, the propositions of the theory are either structural/motivational, referring to present psychodynamics, or genetic, concerned with the role of the past in creating present-day functioning. As regards the genetic propositions, we have noted the much increased interest in child observation on the part of psychoanalysts, and its importance for present-day aetiological formulations. This is all to the good, but true psychoanalytically informed longitudinal studies, with all their attendant practical and methodological difficulties, need to be performed.

The dynamic here-and-now propositions invite different forms of research endeavour. First, let us refer again to Glassman's (1988) paper on Kernberg's and Kohut's theories of narcissism, which uses causal modelling in an attempt to evaluate the relative merit of the theories. But the classical research programme in this field is of course the work of Silverman (for example, Weinberger and Silverman, 1990). His dissatisfaction with the impossibility of testing alternative hypotheses in the analytic situation led to the formulation of the subliminal psychodynamic activation experimental paradigm, and the many studies performed according to this.

Here, increase or decrease in actual symptoms, or in behaviours structured as symptoms, are used as dependent variables, and subliminal presentations of psychodynamically relevant stimuli as independent ones. A lively debate on different aspects of Silverman's research has taken place. New studies using, for instance, meta-analytic techniques (Hardaway, 1990; Weinberger and Hardaway, 1990) seem to go a long way in meeting the methodological criticisms raised. The effects reported by Silverman and other researchers are real enough; we may, however, still have to wait for their ultimate explanation.

Another strategy is to create a controlled situation for the observation of psychodynamically important phenomena, a test situation which allows for the production not only of veridical reports but also of those subjective phenomena which are of interest in terms of psychoanalytic theory. In Lund (Sweden), the percept-genetic tradition has used iterated reports to initially subliminal (or nearly so) but successively prolonged presentations of visual stimuli with interpersonal themes as an approach to the psychoanalytic concept of defence. The theoretical background is twofold. The stimuli used refer to object relations conceptualizations of defensive processes, while the use of nearly subliminal stimuli relate to modern topographical ideas of perception as an act of construction, where the earlier stages of perceptual processing parallel those of drive derivative formation (Westerlundh, in press). These topographical ideas agree very well with the original microgenetic inspiration of percept-genesis. An evolutionary and hierarchical perspective is central in both contexts. An interesting development is that the same basic frame of reference has acquired prominence in clinical neuropsychology (cf. Brown, 1991). Percept-genesis has recently bridged the gap between psychodynamics and neuropsychology in personality research (Carlsson *et al.*, in press; Smith, in press).

The main advantage of the method is its ability to follow the development of perception from subjective stages to final intersubjective reports. Smith has been able to use a version of this approach, the Meta-Contrast Technique, with great success in extended studies concerned both with clinical validity (Smith *et al.*, 1989) and with descriptions of the development of anxiety and defensive strategies through childhood and adolescence (Smith and Danielsson, 1982).

Westerlundh (for example, Westerlundh and Sjöbäck, 1986) has combined the presentation method of the other well-known version of the technique, Kragh's Defense Mechanism Test (DMT: Kragh, 1985) with experimental operations. These include, for instance, sexual or aggressive themes introduced with Silverman's psychodynamic activation method as independent variables, while the percept-genetic reports serve as the dependent ones. In a long series of experiments, psychoanalytic generalizations, of the type that states that phallic sexual impulses tend to be countered by repression and aggressive impulses by isolation (Fenichel, 1946, pp. 149–50), have survived experimental scrutiny.

There are many more examples of extra-clinical, controlled research on psychodynamic propositions, but the field is still new. In our opinion, a nosey, inquisitive approach to this area is much more in the scientific spirit than the blanket condemnation of authors like Eysenck (for example, 1985) or Harnad (1986).

Concluding comments

This critical exposition of some of the most cherished psychoanalytic doctrines and methods of observation does not, in spite of all, convey the impression of a sickly and dying patient. On the contrary, the psychoanalytic kettle appears to be brimful with speculative activity as never before, always in close contact with basic human problems and inner conflicts. We cannot but draw the conclusion that psychoanalysis attracts so many creative minds because its soil is fundamentally sound and fertile. In this final section of our chapter we would, therefore, like to bring out some of its more promising features.

Comprehensiveness is probably one of the main attractions of psychoanalytic theory. It is meant to take care of all kinds of human experience even if they, at first glance, may seem difficult to handle theoretically. One case in point is the borderline condition, a touchstone of many persuasions of psychopathological theorizing. While it was often explained by means of accessorial assumptions in traditional branches of psychiatry, psychoanalytic theorizers made serious attempts to give it a niche within their model. And they seem to have succeeded fairly well, at least in describing the inner dynamics of that condition.

Basically, psychoanalysis has been a theory of *growth* and *development*. Whatever aspect of the theory one wants to actualize, development is always its explanatory core. As we pointed out in the introduction, development is conceived by psychoanalysts in terms of stages; that is, as a succession of qualitative transformations. In normal cases this succession is predictable, with the Oedipal phase as one of its key stages. The consequences of disturbances are dependent on the period in which they occur. This seems like an analogue of the developmental theorizing in ethology; it is no wonder that analysts like Bowlby were attracted by it. One earlier criticism against developmental thinking in psychoanalysis was that it did not take cognitive aspects into account. But this criticism does not seem entirely justified any more.

The growth of process perspectives makes possible a sophisticated concept of *structure*. Structure should not be confused with trait or disposition or any similar reified construct. Structure could be defined as process with a low rate of change.

Structure building really implies that one process limits the degrees of freedom of subsequent processes by forcing them to follow certain twists and turns, particularly in the beginning of their course (Smith, in press). The earlier the establishment of a structure, the greater is probably its binding influence on subsequent processes, so-called fixations being extreme cases. However, even if deep fixations can stamp the subject's personality for years to come, this does not, in principle, exclude the possibility of change because even a very dominant structure is, as defined, amenable to continued growth.

Structures are *hierarchically* organized. Early structure building corresponds to low levels in the hierarchy, and later structure building to higher, more differentiated levels. Development implies that primitive structures are superseded by more mature ones but remain to co-determine the perceptions and actions of the individual. Using a hierarchical model, it is easier to comprehend such phenomena as regressions or dreams, which in other models are either denied as not being presentable or relegated from the sphere of normal functioning to the abnormal one. The complications of human motivation are also easier to fathom within a hierarchically organized mind. To will several things at the same time, to say one thing but mean another, to be both good and bad, is just part and parcel of human existence, even the most normal and superficially equanimous one.

The special mark of psychoanalysis from its very beginning was the acknowledgement of *unconscious, irrational forces*. In the eyes of the analyst, we are not perfect, we easily fall victim to self-deception, we are at most pseudo-rational. But the fact that we are aware of our own limitations — much thanks to psychoanalysis — is in itself our basic strength. It is the naive belief in a rational human being, reflected in simple-minded personality theories, that is so deceptive.

The promising features brought out here make the task of submitting psychoanalysis to rigorous scientific testing all the more important. Contrary to Harnad (1986), we believe it worthwhile to do so. Preliminary attempts have brought hopeful results.

References

Arlow, J.A. and Brenner, C. (1964), *Psychoanalytic Concepts and the Structural Theory*, New York, NY: International Universities Press.

Balint, M. (1968), *The Basic Fault: Therapeutic aspects of regression*, London: Tavistock.

Bettelheim, B. (1988), 'Psychologie Heute', cited from *Svenska Dagbladet*, 6 June 1988.

Bibring, E. (1953), 'The mechanism of depression', in P. Greenacre (ed.), *Affective Disorders*, New York, NY: International Universities Press, pp. 13−47.

Brody, N. (ed.) (1987), 'The unconscious', *Personality and Social Psychology Bulletin*, (Special Issue), **13**, No. 3.

Brown, J.W. (in press), *Self and Process*, New York, NY: Springer.

Carlsson, I., Lilja, Å., Smith, G.J.W. and Johanson, A.M. (in press), 'Percept-genetic methodology in neuropsychology', in R.E. Hanlon (ed.), *Cognitive Microgenesis: A neuropsychological perspective*, New York, NY: Springer.

Dixon, N.F. (1981), *Preconscious Processing*, Chichester: Wiley.

Dorpat, T.L. (1977), 'Depressive affect', *The Psychoanalytic Study of the Child*, **32**, 3−27.

Eagle, M.N. (1984), *Recent Developments in Psychoanalysis*, New York, NY: McGraw-Hill.

Elliott, C.J. (1985), *Application of the Repertory Grid Model to the Study of the Psychoanalytic Concept of Sublimation*, Lund, Sweden: CWK Gleerup.

Erdelyi, M.H. (1985), *Psychoanalysis: Freud's cognitive psychology*, New York, NY: Freeman.

Eysenck, H.J. (1985), *The Decline and Fall of the Freudian Empire*, Harmondsworth: Penguin.

Fenichel, O. (1946), *The Psychoanalytic Theory of Neurosis*, London: Routledge & Kegan Paul.

Freud, A. (1968), *The Ego and the Mechanisms of Defence*, [translated from the German *Das Ich und die Abwehrmechanismen* by C. Bains], London: Hogarth Press. Revised edn.

Freud, S. (1953), 'The interpretation of dreams', in J. Strachey (ed. and trans.), *The Standard Edition of the Complete Psychological Works of Sigmund Freud*, London: Hogarth Press, vol. IV, pp. 1–338; vol. V, pp. 339–621.

Freud, S. (1962), 'The neuro-psychoses of defence', in J. Strachey (ed. and trans.), *The Standard Edition of the Complete Psychological Works of Sigmund Freud*, London: Hogarth Press, vol. III, pp. 43–61.

Freud, S. (1971a), 'The ego and the id', in J. Strachey (ed. and trans.), *The Standard Edition of the Complete Psychological Works of Sigmund Freud*, London: Hogarth Press, vol. XIX, pp. 3–68.

Freud, S. (1971b), 'Inhibitions, symptoms and anxiety', in J. Strachey (ed. and trans.), *The Standard Edition of the Complete Psychological Works of Sigmund Freud*, London: Hogarth Press, vol. XX, pp. 77–178.

Gedo, J.E. and Goldberg, A. (1973), *Models of the Mind: A psychoanalytic theory*, Chicago, IL: University of Chicago Press.

Gill, M.M. (1963), 'Topography and systems in psychoanalytic theory', *Psychological Issues*, Monograph **10**.

Glassman, M. (1988), 'Kernberg and Kohut: a test of competing psychoanalytic models of narcissism', *Journal of the American Psychoanalytic Association*, **36**, 597–625.

Grünbaum, A. (1984), *The Foundations of Psychoanalysis: A philosophical critique*, Berkeley, CA: University of California Press.

Grünbaum, A. (1986), 'Precis of the foundations of psychoanalysis: a philosophical critique', *The Behavioral and Brain Sciences*, **9**, 217–28.

Hanley, C. (1978), 'Instincts and hostile affects', *International Journal of Psychoanalysis*, **59**, 149–56.

Hardaway, R.A. (1990), 'Subliminally activated symbiotic fantasies: facts and artifacts', *Psychological Bulletin*, **107**, 177–95.

Harnad, S. (1986), 'Editorial commentary', *The Behavioral and Brain Sciences*, **9**, 266.

Holt, R.R. (1976), 'Drive or wish?: a reconsideration of the psychoanalytic theory of motivation', in M.M. Gill and P.S. Holzman (eds.), 'Psychology versus metapsychology: psychoanalytic essays in memory of George S. Klein', *Psychological Issues*, **9**, Monograph 36, 158–97.

Horowitz, M.J. (ed.) (1988), *Psychodynamics and Cognition*, Chicago, IL: University of Chicago Press.

Kernberg, O. (1975), *Borderline Conditions and Pathological Narcissism*, New York, NY: Aronson.

Kline, P. (1986), 'Grünbaum's philosophical critique of psychoanalysis: or what I don't know isn't knowledge', *The Behavioral and Brain Sciences*, **9**, 245–6.

Kohut, H. (1971), *The Analysis of the Self*, New York, NY: International Universities Press.

Kohut, H. (1972), 'Thoughts on narcissism and narcissistic rage', *The Psychoanalytic Study of the Child*, **27**, 360–400.

Kohut, H. (1977), *The Restoration of the Self*, New York, NY: International Universities Press.

Kragh, U. (1985), *DMT: Defense Mechanism Test Manual*, Stockholm: Persona.

Loewald, H.W. (1972), 'Freud's conception of the negative therapeutic reaction, with comments on instinct theory', *Journal of the American Psychoanalytic Association*, **20**, 235—45.

Mahler, M.S., Pine, F. and Bergman, A. (1975), *The Psychological Birth of the Human Infant*, New York, NY: Basic Books.

Masson, J.M. (1984), *Freud: The assault on truth. Freud's suppression of the seduction theory*, London: Faber & Faber.

Moser, U., von Zeppelin, I. and Schneider, W. (1968), 'Computer Simulation eines Modells neurotischer Abwehrmechanismen: Ein Versuch zur Formalisierung der psychoanalytischen Theorie (Klinischer Teil)' [Computer simulation of a model of neurotic defence mechanisms: an attempt to formalize the psychoanalytic theory (clinical part)], *Bulletin 2, Psychologisches Institut der Universität Zürich*, 1—78.

Parens, H. (1979), *The Development of Aggression in Early Childhood*, New York, NY: Aronson.

Rapaport, D. (1960), 'The structure of psychoanalytic theory: a systematizing attempt', *Psychological Issues*, Monograph, **6**.

Reppen, J. (ed.) (1985), *Beyond Freud: A study of modern psychoanalytic theorists*, Hillsdale, NJ: Analytical Press/Erlbaum.

Sandler, J. and Joffe, W.G. (1965), 'Notes on childhood depression', *International Journal of Psychoanalysis*, **46**, 88—96.

Sandler, J. and Rosenblatt, B. (1962), 'The concept of the representational world', *The Psychoanalytic Study of the Child*, **17**, 128—45.

Sandler, J., Dare, C. and Holder, A. (1978), 'Frames of reference in psychoanalytic psychology. XI: Limitations of the topographical model', *British Journal of Medical Psychology*, **51**, 61—5.

Schafer, R. (1976), *A New Language for Psychoanalysis*, New Haven, CT: Yale University Press.

Sjöbäck, H. (1973), *The Psychoanalytic Theory of Defensive Processes*, New York, NY: Wiley.

Sjöbäck, H. (1984a), 'The three basic biological assumptions of psychoanalysis', *Psychological Research Bulletin* (Lund, Sweden), **XXIV**, No. 6—8.

Sjöbäck, H. (1984b), *Psykoanalytisk Försvarsteori*, Lund, Sweden: Studentlitteratur.

Sjöbäck, H. (1988), *The Freudian Learning Hypotheses*, Lund, Sweden: Lund University Press.

Smith, G.J.W. (1987), 'Cognitive psychology on the decline', *Psychological Research Bulletin*, (Lund, Sweden), **XXVII**, No. 2.

Smith, G.J.W. (in press), 'Percept-genesis and neuropsychological research', in R.E. Hanlon (ed.), *Cognitive Microgenesis: A neuropsychological perspective*, New York, NY: Springer.

Smith, G.J.W. and Danielsson, A. (1982), 'Anxiety and defensive strategies in childhood and adolescence', *Psychological Issues*, Monograph 52.

Smith, G.J.W., Johnson, G. and Almgren, P.-E. (1988), *MCT: The Meta-Contrast Technique. Manual*. Stockholm: Psykologiförlaget.

Stolorow, R.D. and Lachman, F.M. (1980), *Psychoanalysis of Developmental Arrests*, New York, NY: International Universities Press.

Sulloway, F.J. (1979), *Freud, Biologist of the Mind*, New York, NY: Basic Books.

Wallerstein, R.S. (1983), 'Self psychology and "classical" psychoanalytic psychology: the nature of their relationship', *Psychoanalysis and Contemporary Thought*, **6**, 553—95.

Wallerstein, R.S. (1985), 'Defenses, defense mechanisms, and the structure of the mind', in H.P. Blum (ed.), *Defense and Resistance*, New York, NY: International Universities Press, pp. 201—25.

Weinberger, J. and Hardaway, R.A. (1990), 'Separating science from myth in subliminal psychodynamic activation', *Clinical Psychology Review*, **10**, 727—56.

Weinberger, J. and Silverman, L.H. (1990), 'Testability and empirical verification of psychoanalytic dynamic propositions through subliminal psychodynamic activation', *Psychoanalytic Psychology*, **7**, (Supplement), 299—339.

Westerlundh, B. (in press), 'Percept-genesis and the study of defensive processes', in U. Hentschel, G.J.W. Smith, W. Ehlers and J.W. Draguns (eds.), *The Concept of Defense in Contemporary Psychology*, New York, NY: Springer.

Westerlundh, B. and Sjöbäck, H. (1986), 'Activation of intrapsychic conflict and defense: the amauroscopic technique', in U. Hentschel, G.J.W. Smith and J.W. Draguns (eds.), *The Roots of Perception*, Amsterdam: North Holland, pp. 161–216.

Winnicott, D.W. (1971), *Playing and Reality*, London: Tavistock Publications.

6/ Psychoanalysis as a bipersonal psychology
Implications for a theory of personality

Nino Dazzi and **Alessandra De Coro**
University of Rome, 'La Sapienza', Italy

Introduction

To speak of psychoanalysis as a theory of personality could be inappropriate for at least three reasons, which we will briefly summarize.

First, from its origin psychoanalytic theory has been introduced as a model of the psychic functions, both normal and pathological. Despite the fact that once psyche was believed to be a totality, Freud's theory remains in fact, *atomistic* because it intends to study the *micro-anatomy* of the psychic phenomena and their causal relations which determine behaviour (Rapaport, 1960). Therefore, as far as we are concerned, classic psychoanalysis cannot be considered a theory of personality.

Freud very seldom mentions the term *personality* in his numerous writings. He essentially affirms that dreams, as well as the psychopathological phenomena of depersonalization and derealization, can be explained by assuming a 'splitting of the personality' founded on an intrapsychic conflict (Freud, 1953, p. 94; 1964b, pp. 478−9). We find this term again in the title of Lecture XXXI, but with a limited meaning: 'The dissection of the psychical personality'. The topic of this lecture is the development of his theoretical model, which has gradually transformed itself from a 'psychology of the neurosis' into a 'psychology of the ego' — where the ego is conceived as a unitary structure and yet differentiated — through continuous efforts to translate clinical data into theoretical acquisitions. The speculative aspects of such efforts do not go unnoticed by the author (Freud, 1964a, p. 170−90). Despite Freud's initial attempts to propose a classification of many psychopathological forms (Freud, 1962a, 1962b, 1962c) enlarged afterwards in an outline of 'characterology' founded on the theorization of libido development (Freud, 1957, 1959, 1961), we can state that his prominent interest was the formulation of explicative laws and not the description of phenomena and of psychic contents (Hartmann, 1927, 1950).

Therefore, psychoanalysis, according to the Freudian conception of unconscious conflict, has built an explicit theoretical model which accounts for the *dynamic structure* of the personality and the development of its *psychic organization*. It also simply suggests lines of research and proposes general concepts which have been useful as a point of reflection for the experimental research on personality (see, for example, Fraisse and Piaget, 1963).

Secondly, the method of psychoanalytic investigation is above all a method of treatment. Despite the prevailing focus on theoretical concerns in the majority of Freud's writings (Meltzer, 1978) and despite the convincing demonstration of Sulloway (1979) of his use of a hypothetical, deductive methodology founded on biological premises, psychoanalytic theory has still as its main objective the understanding of the types of symptom (the 'choice of neurosis') and of the psychic suffering; moreover, such understanding is primarily intended as the core of a technical intervention aimed at therapy and at psychological *change*. Gillespie (1989) expresses this in an attempt to indicate the legacy of Freud in contemporary psychoanalysis: 'the theory was not an armchair product but stemmed directly from observation of the behaviour of patients' (p. 43). The overlapping of the therapeutic method with the research method creates evident and serious problems for both the collecting and the validity of the empirical data on which the theory has been built, as has been noticed by many authors (see, for example, Bowlby, 1989; Westen, 1990; Westerlundh and Smith, Chapter 5 in this volume). In addition the introduction of an 'illusive' and fantastic dimension in the reconstruction of clinical stories and in the very essence of a treatment centred on transference makes empirical verification of the 'findings' obtained through the psychoanalytic method very difficult (Conte and Dazzi, 1988). In turn, the contemporary psychology of personality claims its contribution to a 'scientific psychology' by defining its objective as the following: 'to develop theories and conduct empirical research on the functioning of the individual as a totality' (Magnusson, 1990, p. 1).

Finally, it is very difficult today to give an unambiguous definition of modern psychoanalysis because of the schools' variety and because of the scattering of different theoretical and clinical viewpoints which still consider Freudian work as their common starting-point. The necessity, from time to time, to adjust the psychoanalytic method to new clinical demands (such as the application of psychoanalytic treatment to pathological forms and to institutional contexts different from the original ones) has produced multiple variations from Freud's recommended technique and, at the same time, the introduction of interpretive models of pathological behaviour and of psychic development often noticeably diverging among themselves (Farrell, 1981; Thomä and Kächele, 1985).

Moreover, the crisis of Freud's metapsychology, as far as it is concerned with the no-longer plausible scientific hypotheses of the nineteenth century, has contributed to marking a fundamental turn as concerns the recent developments of this discipline. A critical revision of theory has been solicited, through a distinction between an overstructural level of the conceptual system (which would require new terms to cope with the advancement of scientific findings) and a level closer to clinical experience. Such a distinction has forced influential theorists of psychoanalysis to answer the crucial question proposed by Klein (1976): 'two theories or one?'. Klein and other disciples of Rapaport's school (Gill, 1976; Rubinstein, 1976; Schafer,

1976; Wallerstein, 1976) have opened a vast debate, from which proposals and solutions at times opposing and at other times partially converging have originated. The result is a controversial scene: the most radical theorists, such as the followers of Ricoeur (1965), maintain that psychoanalysis needs a hermeneutics to deal with meanings and an energetics to deal with humankind instinctual life, while other authors get on with the job of extricating the clinical theory from metapsychology's dying clutches. Still others try to replace classical metapsychology with a new framework based on information processing and systems theory, which could explain the phenomena of body and mind, structure and meaning (see Holt, 1981).

Parallel to the demands for modification and revision, if not for a definitive abandoning of metapsychologic theory, the recent developments of psychoanalysis are characterized by the spread of a model of motivation and of psychic development centred on the concepts of 'objective relation'; such a model sees its origin in the interpersonal approach proposed by Sullivan (1953) and in the theoretical elaboration of authors of the English School (Greenberg and Mitchell, 1983) and has produced one more or less sharp contrast between the es—ego theory and the psychology of self, this latter connected to a more modern formulation of concepts of normal and pathological narcissism (Eagle, 1984; Holt, 1985). A major part of the present heterogeneity of psychoanalytic theory is in fact found in the way different authors and different schools interpret and integrate the relationship between objective internalized relations and interpersonal ones into their theoretical elaborations. Today, such a relationship is recognized worldwide as being of central importance in the construction of psychoanalytic hypotheses, in both clinical procedure and the development of the personality.

The above considerations justify our initial difficulty in treating (or considering) psychoanalysis as a theory of personality. This perplexity is somewhat reinforced by the specific criticism reported by Westerlundh and Smith (Chapter 5 in this volume). As they observe, there is no coherent model which could account for personality formation, and often the same terms are confusedly used in a metaphorical and explanatory way (see, for example, the terms referring to defence mechanism, etc.). It is true, however, that some psychoanalytic concepts are traditionally included in theoretical models which represent a dynamic conceptualization of personality (Fraisse and Piaget, 1963) and that even the most recent handbooks of personality psychology dedicate at least one chapter to the psychoanalytic approach (cf. Caprara and Gennaro, 1987; Pervin, 1990).

It seems timely, then, to take a survey of those lines of theoretical elaboration and of those developments of research in contemporary psychoanalysis which seem to offer useful points of reflection on the themes that are important for personality research. We will examine theoretical contributions which deal with the interpersonal dimension of the description of personality. This has promoted specific trends of research in both the clinical field and infant observation studies, in connection with other fields of psychological research (see, for example, empirical research in newborn psychology).

New trends in psychoanalytic theory: object relationships and self psychology

In the last twenty years, studies on personality have moved from the search for variables that show some constancy in intra-individual functioning to an approach which considers individual functioning 'as a process of continuous interaction among systems of psychological and biological factors in the individual and systems of psychical, social, and cultural factors in the environment' (Magnusson, 1990, p. 13). In other words, the prevailing of an *interactionist* paradigm has operated a shift in personality research towards an integration of the study of individual and idiosyncratic personality patterns with the investigation into those conditions of social cognitive learning which appear to foster the actualization of such patterns. Studies on personality in this perspective can be considered to fill a broader *transitional* area between developmental psychology and social psychology.

Likewise we can describe the recent developments in psychoanalytic theory as a result of a wider spread of interest towards those concepts relevant to the establishment of the *self* and of *object relationships*. These concepts involve new restatements of traditional hypotheses, often bringing about contradictions with respect to the central corpus of the classical theory (see Eagle, 1984). An interpersonal point of view has gradually become more important, tending to reduce, or even to eliminate, the focus on intrapsychic conflicts in the reading of clinical data. Present basic psychoanalytical trends of thought, in fact (with some differences in the different authors' positions), have integrated or replaced the classical instinctual theory of motivation[1] by an explanatory model which recognizes the origins of specific relational patterns in childhood interpersonal relationships. The individual's motivational structure is grounded on these patterns as on a kind of relational prototype, and is subject to a continuous process of remodelling in the course of life; however, repetitions and changes in the interaction with other people are constantly mediated by internalized object relationships (Greenberg and Mitchell, 1983).

Even though Freud never abandoned his search for a connection between his patients' *psychical reality* and their *real* life events, related to family interpersonal bonds, traditional psychoanalysis can easily be described as a 'one-person psychology', as long as it does now allow us to explain something occurring between two people otherwise than as 'an event in the mind of one person' (Modell, 1984, p. 11). Gradually, however, the focus on a new observational context — in connection with the study of pathological adaptation strategies and of early infant development — has required new explanations in terms of a 'two-persons psychology'.

The introduction of object-relations theory into the psychoanalytical literature of the thirties was obviously linked with an increase in available psychopathological data, as shown by Sullivan's (1931) research on schizophrenic patients, Klein's (1932) investigations into children's psychopathology and Fairbairn's (1940: see Fairbairn, 1952) studies on schizoid personality. In fact, these as well as other studies enhanced psychoanalysts' interest in basic clinical problems concerning therapy for serious personality disorders and early developmental breakdowns. New theoretical answers were required to such questions as these (Pine, 1988): To what degree are the old traumatizing relationships with the parents enacted in identification or repeated in action with others? How stable a sense of differentiated self-boundaries is present, and how do the differentiated boundaries stand up in relation to the stresses of living?

These three authors — Sullivan, Klein and Fairbairn — as pointed out by Greenberg and Mitchell (1983), are the first supporters of a relational standpoint in the history of psychoanalytic movement: noticeably, they indirectly share a common influence from Sandor Ferenczi, who was Klein's analyst and whose pupil Clara Thompson later became Sullivan's analyst. Ferenczi, still in the first psychoanalytic generation, wrote in 1909, in what is now considered a classic essay on *Introjection and Transference*: 'the neurotic is always seeking objects with which he can identify or onto which he can project his own feelings' (Ferenczi, 1950, p. 84). Ferenczi's basic orientation towards a more *active* technique in psychotherapy persuaded him to highlight the interpersonal relationship among the therapeutic factors of psychoanalysis; he suggested that analysts should adopt specific measures to realize the 'best-suited temperature' in the analytical relation, and should encourage patients to 'act out' their hidden emotions in front of the doctor (Ferenczi, 1969).

As Sandler points out in a recent survey on this subject, the controversial discussions in the British Psycho-Analytical Society of the forties originated from different standpoints in the interpretation of clinical data: here 'the viewing of psychological processes from the vantage point of object relations' began to contrast with 'the view stressing unconscious wish-fulfillment' (Sandler, 1989b, p. 66). Sandler (1989b) holds up as an example a short clinical report by John Rickman, one of Melanie Klein's collaborators who later greatly influenced Bion's and Lacan's thought: he interpreted a case of a wounded soldier affected by hysterical paralysis in terms of his mourning for a friend killed in action, and underlined the role of unconscious fantastic activity in maintaining a continuity between the relationships of his past and those of his present.

In Sandler's words: 'We can regard an object relationship as being a valued relationship between oneself and another person. Such relationships start early in life, and also exist in our wishful fantasy lives. We continually create new relationships that we value, but these new object relationships are often new editions of older relationships' (Sandler, 1989b, p. 70). He also draws our attention to the fact that psychoanalysis centres its focus on distinction as well as on the mutual interaction between external and internal worlds: such interaction is grounded in people's attempts 'to impose upon the other an *intrapsychic role relationship*' (Sandler, 1989b, p. 70). The heritage of Kleinian hypotheses about unconscious fantasy and internal objects is easily recognizable in these statements; despite the fact that she anchored her own theories on a Freudian instinctual model, and despite her questionable metaphorical usage of an extremely concrete language, it is undeniable that Klein's studies on children's emotional life have allowed her to deepen the understanding of psychical development's interactional processes, as is clearly shown by her latest writings (Klein, 1946, 1952, 1957).

Fairbairn, an English psychoanalyst who was certainly influenced by Klein's work, can be considered as the first to propose a revision of psychoanalytical psychopathology in terms of object relationships. Even though he was neither sufficiently appreciated nor integrated into the psychoanalytic movement, his radical assertions prove him to be an original thinker (cf. Greenberg and Mitchell, 1983). Fairbairn lays stress on the first individual's social relationship, as it is established between himself or herself and his or her mother: the core of this relationship being the suckling situation. Such a situation exerts a deep influence on the individuals' following relationships and on their social attitude in general (Fairbairn, 1952).

The starting point of the child's psychical development can be described as a situation in which the newborn baby is absolutely dependent on the person who takes care of him or her. So, Fairbairn suggests that seeking objects should be the basic motivational activity from early infancy. These objects are gradually interiorized, with different emotional qualities — such as 'good' and 'bad' — involved by actual affective experiences: the later development of ego structures seems to be intrinsically connected to the formation of such interiorized objects, which in certain conditions acquire 'a dynamic independence that cannot be overlooked' (Fairbairn, 1944, p. 63). The pathological personality's structuring can therefore be explained as the result of a process of incorporation of the relational objects and as a relative automatization of specific techniques of dealing with the incorporated objects (Fairbairn, 1941). Although his psychopathological typology again appears unsatisfactory and too schematic, it must be underlined that Fairbairn actually tries to define dynamic constants in the individual's behaviour in terms of recurrent relational patterns, which regulate interpersonal strategies.

At the same time, in the United States, Harry Stack Sullivan — who was part of that pragmatist school of American psychiatry focused on socio-cultural factors in the occurrence of mental disorders — attempted to revise the Freudian theory of psychopathological development in terms of social processes and interpersonal communication. Sullivan (1940) put forward the suggestion that psychiatry needed to study individual differences which are deep-rooted in non-genetic factors; first of all language, as well as other systems of 'human cultural transmission'. Actually, he thought that searching for invariants in the development of these systems could lead to the relating of pathological developments to deviated learning processes in interpersonal relationships.

Sullivan (1953) defined 'experience' as a set of interactional events which aim at adaptation; so, he conceptualized the 'ego-system' as a 'dynamism'; that is, a stable configuration of functional activities which recurrently characterizes the individual's interpersonal relationships. Such a system is produced by the child's manifold relational experiences: the resulting 'personification of the ego' should follow complex 'security' operations, directed at establishing a sufficient integration of interpersonal relationships. This integration aims to satisfy the primitive needs of tenderness and intimacy which are needed for the infant's survival and psychological growth.

The theoretical pattern which accounts for structure formation as a modulation of those adaptive interpersonal processes, following a complex developmental interaction between *external* and *internal* object relations, seems therefore to be closely linked with a focus on new psychopathological forms: the psychogenesis of early or severe personality disorders cannot simply be explained through intrapsychic conflicts, but rather can be referred to a structural *defect* or to developmental failures or *arrests*.[2] On the other hand, the need for a reformulation of psychoanalytic psychopathology in interactional terms has directed many psychoanalysts' interest towards topics such as these: How are boundaries between the external reality and the internal world built up? How do individuals learn about their self-image? What is the relation, if there is one, between the persistence of self-representation, the boundaries between self and others, and the phenomena of the personality's cohesion and fragmentation?

The premises for the use (and sometimes for the abuse) of the concept of *self*, which has become increasingly widespread in modern psychoanalysis (Eagle, 1984), can be found precisely in the attempts to answer these questions, in connection with the problems about the organization of identity and self-consciousness. Such attempts reflect the growing dissatisfaction with metapsychological concepts, on the basis of the clinical and epistemological considerations that we have mentioned previously.

In a clear and precise restatement of the manifold facets of the self conceptualization, Jervis (1989) points out two distinguishable trends in the often ambiguous definition of this term by contemporary psychoanalytic schools. The first can be related to the Jamesian meaning of the self as a preferential object of self-consciousness, and suggests an experiential interpretation of it as a representational centre of the sense of personal identity. On the other hand, the second trend can be brought back to a philosophical *spiritualistic* tradition, traceable in some of Jung's and Adler's theoretical elaborations: it gives a more substantialist interpretation of the self, by defining it as a real structure or rather as the structural matrix of the psychical activity and the unity/uniqueness of the individual personality. Winnicott and Kohut are put forward, respectively, as the most influential representatives of these two theorical orientations, though they both consider the origins of the self to be in the bipersonal field of mother—child relationships.

Donald W. Winnicott was one of the first to introduce the concept of *self* into psychoanalytic theory, by describing it as the mental representation of 'continuity of being': the experience of 'me' as differentiated from 'not me' should appear in the infant's mind as a result of the integration and personalization processes of the sensorial and emotional experiences, processes which are supported by suitable maternal care (Winnicott, 1958a). The function of a 'good enough mother' is precisely one of 'holding together' the infant's disintegrated experiences, therefore gradually allowing the 'location of self in one's own body' and the acquisition of a durable experience of oneself as differentiated from external reality (Winnicott, 1958b, 1958c).

Firstly, then, maternal care assures the progressive development of a 'personal pattern'; that is, the ability to perceive an inner reality (the infant's 'true self'); afterwards, the recognition of external reality and the development of a 'reality sense' is still made possible by sharing the mother's omnipotent control in the intermediate area of 'transitional phenomena' (Winnicott, 1960).[3] The self formation is therefore linked by Winnicott with the knowledge/construction of external reality through symbolic activity, which allows the child to distinguish 'between fantasy and fact, between inner objects and external objects, between primary creativity and perception' (Winnicott, 1958d, p. 233). If the environment fails to provide a harmonious sense of continuity of being, then the child's mental activity develops a 'false self' in order to safeguard the central self's stability. According to the level of the false self's rigidity, various psychopathological manifestations are derived, from inhibition of creativity, to a loss of reality-testing, up to experiences of self-mutilation (Winnicott, 1965).

Winnicott's clinical observation of psychosis, as well as his studies on infant's somatic and mental diseases, have led him to conceptualize the development of the self as closely related to sensorial and emotional exchanges within the mutual relationship between infants and their 'special object', the care-giver. It is interesting to notice that his theorical assumptions are in accordance with what is observed in recent longitudinal research on child development. We will discuss the results in detail in the next paragraph. Here, we just want to record what is pointed out by several researchers; that is, a fundamental connection between the sense of a subjective self and the experience of sharing affective states with the parents in infancy; such a connection denotes the acquisition of a mutual sense of 'us' as an essential requirement for an autonomous, motivated behaviour in new intersubjective contexts outside the family (Emde, 1988). So, the hypothesis that the quality of an individual's emotional responses takes quite a persistent configuration and character through the affective interactional pattern which is peculiar to the mother—baby dyad turns out to be confirmed by research using a direct observation method as well (Attili, 1990).[4]

Kohut's (1971) approach to the definition of self and its development instead arises out of his interest in the psychoanalytic treatment of the so-called 'narcissistic personality disorders'. These patients show serious oscillations in their self-assertion and self-esteem; the interpretation of their pathology should refer back to early developmental failures in the cohesion and persistency of the self. Kohut's self psychology, then, originates from his need to get new conceptual instruments, beyond classical metapsychology, in order to understand transference and the therapeutic factors in cases of narcissistic personalities better (Kohut, 1971). As a matter of fact, it seems unquestionable that Kohut's most important contribution to modern psychoanalysis is to be found in his views on the theory of cure in analysis, including his systematizations of transferences and their role in analytic cure (cf. Muslin, 1985).

What we want to examine here, however, is rather his theorization about specific self-needs and motivations which would aim at preserving the self's cohesion and regulating self-esteem. Such motivations, in turn, would become the ground on which a coherent affective modulation of interpersonal relationships could develop. Kohut follows George S. Klein's critique (1976) of the irrelevance of psychoanalytical metapsychology for clinical explanations, and works out the latter's interest for the self 'as the locus of experience'.

In Klein's opinion, a clinical theory of psychoanalysis should take into account the unconscious representations and symbolizations of interpersonal relationships. Therefore, he supposes the self to be a 'functional centre' of these representations and symbolizations, connected with the degree of ego organization and its experiences of self-identity. The self-schema, which would evolve from early differentiations between what is synchronous and what is dissonant with what one is, would imply an integration of sensorimotor and emotional experiences 'for the sake of achieving self-unity through extending the region of effective control consonant with self-identity' (1976, pp. 280−1). Moreover, Klein describes the 'self-syntonic values' as motivational objectives which characterize both the therapeutic process and artistic creativity. Both these activities, in fact, exploit identification with the purpose of bringing fractionated affective experiences and unconscious fantasies into syntonicity with the self-schema, aiming at a freshly organized symbolic experience.

In the Kohutian model, the fragmentation of the self is pointed out as a primary source of mental derangement, prior to the Oedipal conflict. The functions of mirroring and expressing the self need for firm ideals, calming, and guidance are highlighted in psychotherapy; such needs are realized in transference by means of idealization of the analyst as a 'selfobject' which can be internalized (Kohut, 1971; Muslin, 1985). In this kind of approach 'the interrelated processes of optimal frustrations and transmuting internalization . . . applied to both the theory of self development and the theory of the therapeutic action in the analysis of patients with developmental disturbances of the self' (Kohut, 1984, pp. 108−9). In Kohut's conceptions of the mode of cure, therefore, experiencing acquires a significant place besides interpretation, as far as the patient−analyst relationship can in part compensate for deficient experiences in the patient's childhood (Pine, 1988).

Kohut's latest theoretical elaborations, however, tend to give the self a structural priority, which means turning it into a metapsychological concept.[5] A 'virtual self' is advocated in the newborn child: it represents that geometric point in infinity at which two parallel lines meet each other (Kohut, 1977). The developmental course of motivations characterized by an endeavour for self-assertion is viewed as parallel to — that is, relatively independent from — the development of motivations related to object love. Though since actual relationships with other people are assumed to be built only when the self is sufficiently complete, affective attunement in early interpersonal relations turns out to be subordinate to self-needs which aim at survival and security.

This conception has aroused understandable perplexity in the psychoanalytic field, just because it appears to overlook the close dynamic connections existing between affective motivations (such as love and aggressiveness) and self-assertion. Among the critiques to Kohut's self psychology, Eagle's objectives seem of some relevance: on the one hand, concepts like those of 'self fragmentation' or 'idealization of selfobjects' recall a theoretically improper hypostatization of metaphorical terms which describe patients' subjective experience in clinical observation; on the other hand, the interpretation of clinical data appears itself to be forced into a Procrustean bed, as far as Kohut's metapsychological effort tries to safeguard the classical drive model alongside the 'modern' object-relations model (Eagle, 1984).

Lussier (1988) has pointed out a greater adherence to clinical observations in Jacobson's and Kernberg's theoretical proposals: object relationships are there considered as defensive organizations looking for adaptive solutions to basic emotional conflicts, in connection with the pleasure—frustration dimension. Jacobson (1964) and Kernberg (1976) try to integrate what is referred to as 'emotional block' or 'self defect' with the psychodynamic principle of intrapsychic conflictual motivation: in fact, they interpret the so-called 'character features' revealing structure formation's incompleteness and feebleness as the result of an adaptational defensive organization, which is linked with a specific developmental level of early affective conflicts.

An interesting mediation in these controversies has been proposed by Sandler. In order to clarify the links between unconscious wishes, on the one hand, and object relationships, on the other, Sandler (1989a) suggests finding out a new definition for the Freudian concept of *unconscious wish*; such a definition should account for its clinical meaning and theoretical implications, finally abandoning the old pattern of instinctual drives. Sandler (1983) states that the core question is not what psychoanalytic theory should be, but what should be emphasized within the whole compass of psychoanalytic thinking; he reminds us that what should be emphasized is that which relates to the (clinical) work we have to do.

Clinical investigation into mental wish representations shows that people have mental representations of wished-for interactions, which in turn encompass the wished-for or imagined response of the object as well as the subject's activity (Sandler and Sandler 1978). Then we can assume, from a developmental point of view, that conscious and unconscious wishes (whether cathected with pleasant or unpleasant affects) arise in the early interactions which are 'invested with a certain affective value cathexis of safety for the child' (Sandler, 1989a, p. 108). Even if he does distinguish an activity of 'well-being seeking' from an activity of 'pleasure seeking', Sandler shows how affective early interactions are characterized by both 'safety signals' and 'anxiety signals': the mental organization of all these experiences should later be the basis for a complex motivational structure underlying 'safety seeking' and 'pleasure seeking' behaviours.

It is important to note that individuals do not necessarily seek a replica of what they experienced in childhood. The need to obtain forms of actualization acceptable to the conscience, and to the person's developing sense of reality, leads them to disguise and distort the role relationships they want to impose upon others, and the needs of others force them to create and accept compromises. Nevertheless, unconscious wishes, whether they be sexual or aggressive or related to the preservation of self-esteem and safety, will profoundly affect relationships with others. These wishes and their fantasy elaborations are continually being revised and modified, even though they retain a central and enduring core that is highly specific to the person concerned (Sandler, 1989b, p. 81).

As we have tried to show, in conclusion, a relational approach leads us to prefer a representational self-concept, which can be considered both as a social construction and as a complex subjective modulation of the individual's emotional conflicts and motivations: either the intersubjective construction or the subjective modulation is constantly at work, and consequently produces possible fluctuations of the self. This kind of conceptualization accounts for dysfunctional aspects of the manifold versions of the self on a clinical level, while referring to an organizational context — which has precise *objective* implications in actual interpersonal relationships — on a developmental level.

The relevance of a developmental perspective and infant observation

From its origins, the psychoanalytic theory of mental functioning has taken an *ontogenetic* perspective, attributing to infant development the formation of psychoanalytic components and character traits that constitute the personality of an individual. The psychoanalytic theory of infant development began, as is well known, in the reconstructive hypotheses formulated by Freud concerning the origins of neurotic pathology during the infancy of his adult patients. Thanks to the work of psychoanalytic pioneers such as Anna Freud, Réné Spitz, Ernst Kris, Margareth Mahler, and others, however, the direct observation of infants, initially thought of simply as an auxiliary tool of research, gradually became recognized as an indispensable method for advancing psychoanalytic theory and clinical practice.

Recently, research results in this area have more often questioned basic assumptions of classical theory, among them the principle of reduction of tension (which supports the instinctual theory), the developmental model of erotogenic zones, the Freudian formulation of the concept of 'regression', and the plausibility of retrospective inference itself (Lichtenberg, 1983). The more recent research, in fact, evidences the presence of irregular jumps and sudden changes in emotional and behaviour growth; discontinuities, as pointed out by Silverman (1983), that highlight the need for great caution in defining the developing stages and attributing causal relations between one stage and another.

This is not the place to examine in detail the multiplicity of research conducted during the last 20 years on the behaviour of small children from the psychoanalytic standpoint. We will limit ourselves to indicating the impact that research data have had on a fundamental revision of the psychoanalytic theory of *affects*: the infant's affects can be described as an organized system of signals with a communicative function, in interaction with adults' behavioural schemes. The conceptual elaborations of the researchers, in fact, converge towards a hypothesis of an organized state within a human being from birth; the newborn, that is, seems endowed with integrated mechanisms at different levels (biological, neurophysiological, and behavioural), and each of these levels appear to be integrated simultaneously with the patterns and modality of the feedback from the surrounding environment, however it happens to be provided by the care-giver (Greenspan and Pollock, 1980).

We will devote the rest of this section to a deeper discussion of the theory of attachment proposed by Bowlby (1969, 1988) and the concept of self as elaborated by Stern (1985), since both seem to offer interesting ideas concerning the developing formation of relatively stable individual behavioural schemes, closely interdependent with the experience of interpersonal reality.

The research conducted by Bowlby (1969, 1973) in England and that of Ainsworth (1977) in Uganda and in the United States, using direct observations of mother—child interactions during the *first year of life*, led to the hypothesis that the natural exploratory behaviour of small children is encouraged to the extent that the mother gives the children a *secure base* from which they can depart to explore, and to which they can return whenever they are upset or scared. In contrast, when children experience separation or rejection from the mother during this crucial period of development, they will either escalate their requests for protection, or develop anger against their mother, and doubt the possibility of having a safe and loving relationship with anyone (Bowlby, 1988).

The bond between the child and the mother is defined by Bowlby (1969) as the result of a precise and, in part, pre-programmed system of behaviour patterns that has the result of maintaining the child in more or less close proximity to the mother. On the basis of ethological findings, Bowlby postulates that such behaviour fulfils the biological function of ensuring protection to the newborn, in particular protection from predators; he defines as 'ethological' his own approach to the *attachment behaviour* of the newborn, and brings out the compatibility of such an approach with theoretical models adopted by modern biology and neurophysiology.

This allows the reformulation, in less negative terms, of those child behaviours which were referred to traditionally as *dependency*, and has also allowed detailed analysis of such interactions. According to psychological data gathered using observational methods, and to biological postulates mentioned earlier, Bowlby (1988) lists a series of conditions that regulate the activation of attachment behaviours and shape relevant interpersonal interactions:

1. Attachment behaviour is *universal*, and can be activated in adolescence and adulthood too under conditions of stress and anxiety.
2. Attachment, at any age, is characterized by *very intense emotions*. The quality of these emotions depends on the quality of the relationships between the people involved.
3. Attachment behaviour has its origin in the mother—child interaction immediately after birth, and becomes *organized in the cybernetic sense* during the first year of the child's life (cf. Ainsworth *et al.*, 1978).
4. The *development* of attachment behaviour can be either facilitated or thwarted by specific circumstances *during or after birth*.
5. The *parents' own childhood experiences* and their mental organization of such experiences in childhood, that is, their peculiar 'styles of attachment' have a noticeable influence on the way in which they (mother and father) interact with

the attachment behaviour of their children (cf. De Lozier, 1982; Main and Hesse, 1990).

In conclusion, Bowlby's attachment theory highlights the primacy of the intimate emotional bonds that are considered to be independent of motivations tied to feeding or sex; such emotional bonds, modulated by specific complementary interactions between children and their parents, constitute the foundation of 'internal working models' of the self, of the figure of attachment, and of their relation with each other. Moreover, the relative persistence of these models or behaviour patterns presents, within a normal development and as time goes on, a noticeable plasticity in adapting to different interpersonal situations. On the other hand, a certain amount of rigidity of the working model in different situations seems to be connected with an anxiety level experienced in parental interaction, as it is prevailingly interiorized (Bowlby, 1979; Bretherton, 1987).

The study of attachment behaviours reinforces the need to abandon models of personality development that define, in relatively strict terms, progressive stages to which an individual could 'fix himself' or 'regress' (Bowlby, 1988). The most recent psychoanalytic psychopathology of children underscores the fact that manifestations of pathology can be different at various ages (cf. Novelletto, 1986; Sroufe and Rutter, 1984). Today it is believed that the most normal aspects of development can undergo noticeable transformations during one's lifetime; this evidences the presence of an uneven process within a progressive continuity (Hinde and Bateson, 1984).

Attachment theory, largely built on the methods and perspectives of developmental psychology, appears primarily centred, as we have seen, on an objective study of the mother–child dyad. Bowlby's approach has often been criticized by psychoanalysts as excessively behavioural, and has been accused of abandoning the psychoanalytic point of view, forgetting about the subjective experience of the infant. It is also true, however, that the concept of a 'model of the mother' working in the infant's mind introduces the subjective dimension of the experience; such a concept also allows us to construct predictive hypotheses about pathological developments of behaviour. Many recent studies try to develop this point of view, examining relationships between interpersonal experiences and different levels of mental representations of such experiences (Bretherton, 1985; Main *et al.*, 1985).

The operative concept of a developing formation of self proposed by Stern (1985) fulfils the need to give an account, through a stronger integration and theoretical elaboration of research data on children, of the complex mental operations that characterize psychological mediation between the internal world and external reality, between affective processes and cognitions, in the construction of prototypes and of *generalized* patterns of behaviour. Stern insists on the global nature of the infant's subjective experience. Research on development deals with perception, motor activity, affectivity, and states of consciousness as somewhat discrete or separable domains of experience; but, as he states, 'the commonalities are likely to be far greater than the differences' (Stern, 1985, p. 67). Infants

take sensations, perceptions, actions, cognitions, internal states of motivation, and states of consciousness and experience them directly in terms of intensities, shapes, temporal patterns, vitality affects, categorical affects, and hedonic tones. These are the basic elements of early subjective experience. Cognitions, actions, and perceptions, as such, do not exist. All experiences become recast as patterned constellations of all the infant's basic subjective elements combined ... And whenever any constellation is formed, the infant experiences the emergence of organization. (Stern, 1985, p. 67).

Such organization of the subjective experience operates outside of the conscience; it constitutes a type of experiential matrix from which, through the integration of interpersonal situations and the social interaction with an 'other regulator of self', a sense of 'core self' is born, around the second or third month of life. In contrast with the interpretation offered by Mahler, Pine, and Bergman (1975) of the psychological birth as a separation-individuation process, Stern's theory anticipates the differentiation of self from other people and asserts that 'the capacity to have merger- or fusion-like experiences as described in psychoanalysis is secondary to and dependent upon an already existing sense of self and other' (Stern, 1985, p. 70). According to Stern, therefore, infants get the experience *of being with another who helps them self-regulate*; that involves the experiencing of significant affective changes, mutually created by 'self with other', even recognizing an invariant core self and core other which act as a background to these events. Multiple specific pre-verbal memories of such episodes form 'Representations of Interactions that have been Generalized' (RIG): 'RIGs are flexible structures that average several actual instances and form a prototype to represent them all' (Stern, 1985, p. 110). Those memories are retrievable later whenever any of the attributes of the RIG is present. The reactivation of RIG involves the notion of an 'evoked companion'; that is, the recollection of 'being with an historical self-regulating other' (Stern, 1985, p. 111).

Such concepts as those of RIG and of an 'evoked companion' present some analogies with other concepts, such as 'internal working models' and 'selfobjects', coined to answer clinical demands that were not satisfied by the theory of internal object relations. On the other hand, some differences exist: (1) RIG is considered to be 'the basic building block from which working models are constructed'; (2) RIGs 'embody expectations about any and all interactions that can result in mutually created alterations in self-experience', not only those about regulation of security-attachment states; (3) the evoked companion does not share the abstract cognitive qualities of the self-object and of the working model, but rather 'is conceived in terms of episodic memory and lends itself better to the affective nature of being with others' (Stern, 1985, pp. 114–15).

Gradually, the subjective experience of interpersonal interactions is transferred from actions to internal feeling states that express themselves in behaviours; between the seventh and ninth month, according to Stern, another 'leap' occurs in the sense of self which permits the child to experiment with intersubjectivity as the possibility of perceiving communication (still not verbal) between two separate minds. This second system of interpreting interactive exchanges, which Stern defines as the 'sense of a subjective self', is founded on the experience of sharing affective states between his or her partners and himself or herself; it is only at this point that the child can show an intimate relationship with the care-giver, because now he or she is able to perceive the possibility of sharing, at least in part, moods, intentions, and motivations with another person. The next step in the development of self is the access to symbolic thought through the formation of 'the sense of a verbal self': 'a new organizing subjective perspective emerges and opens a new domain of relatedness' (Stern, 1985, p. 162). The exchange and sharing of emotional meaning with another takes place through speech between 15 and 18 months of age; at this age, children begin to see themselves 'objectively' and get what Stern calls a 'conceptual self', in distinction from the 'experiential self' described up to here.

It is important to note that Stern avoids terms such as 'developmental stages' but prefers to speak of 'sensitive periods' linked to specific 'domains of intersubjective relatedness'. The internal object originates, then, from early social relationships as far as it provides a clue to interpret interactions between himself or herself and others: at first, self and other are seen as separate, and later as communicating through 'sharing of experiences about events and things'. The definition of RIGs as prototype episodes retrievable in a here-and-now situation considers the continuity of developmental processes, but at the same time offers a plausible explanation of the adaptive modifications and irregularities of the psychological growth. A RIG represents, in fact a selection of actual memorized episodes and can be defined as *an active model of the event* (Lebovici, 1990).

On a clinical level, there are two main consequences deriving from Stern's theory of different senses of the self as related to major developmental changes in intersubjective patterns. In the first place, the relatively rigid categorizations of specific developmental stages connected to specific clinical problems (orality, dependency, etc.) are eliminated. Secondly, an accurate recollection and/or reconstruction of past experiences is needed to identify which domain of interpersonal relatedness could have created a limitation or deficiency in the development of the sense of self in the subjective experience of the patient.

From a psychoanalytic point of view, the question of the fantastic level of interaction remains unsolved, since Stern seems to employ the concept of 'unconscious' in a meaning closer to the cognitive than to the psychoanalytic conception of mental representations. Various authors have stated that Stern's 'observed infant' is still too far from the 'reconstructed child' of clinical psychoanalysis. For example, Lebovici (1990), among others, hopes that future research on infant observation can include new data on fantasy interaction and inter-generational transmission.

It cannot be denied, however, that the wide range of research through infant observation can offer new perspectives on the psychoanalytic cure. First of all, it appears to open new ways of investigation into past experiences. Stern concludes, at the end of his book: 'The view presented here is also intended to serve as a metaphor for clinical research . . . As the picture of the reconstructed past of a patient's life becomes altered, the therapist finds it necessary to think and act differently' (Stern,

1985, p. 276). In fact, changes in psychoanalytic views about infants and their development can allow analysts to create new *therapeutic narratives*, and consequently to bring out transformations in the technique and theory of therapeutics.

The interpersonal perspective in clinical research

The traditional ground on which to gather data and to test theoretical hypotheses in psychoanalysis has been and will continue to be clinical practice. As mentioned before, the multiple and relevant theory modifications of the last 50 years have often started with useful reflections about technical instruments and about the definition of therapeutic factors in the cure of psychoanalysis.

The interpersonal perspective, here synthetically presented with its effects on psychopathological conceptions, on developmental theory, and on psychoanalytic epistemology, has exercised an evident influence on the progress of technical theory and on the organization of clinical data (Eagle, 1984; Mitchell, 1991). On the other hand, it is interesting to note that Balint (1950) had already emphasized how a 'two-person' approach should prevail in psychoanalytic technique, while the study of pathological forms, on which theory was grounded, stressed the intrapsychic dimension and showed a 'physiological or biological' orientation.

The theoretical hypotheses which form the rationale for the psychoanalytic method of cure are themselves unsystematic and render problematic the very definition of testing the methodology of therapeutic results.[6] As Westerlundh and Smith write in Chapter 5 of this volume: 'The clinical situation is excellent for producing hypotheses, but not at all for testing them.'

Moreover, as we have already underlined, it is hard to identify a single coherent theory of psychoanalytic technique, if we consider the different points of view that loomed inside the psychoanalytic movement between the thirties and the sixties (Friedman, 1978). Eissler (1953), in proposing a sort of 'manifestor' of the classical technique, declared that he was aware of the abstract aspects of his formulation, stating that such technique in pure form had never been applied. The necessity to adjust, from time to time, the general rules of treatment to the specific needs of the single patient and/or to the personal equation of the single analyst has allowed a continuous oscillation between these two poles, that of 'internal and deep understanding' and that of 'emotional experience' (cf. Cremerius, 1985).

The proliferation of psychotherapies, which are recognized as deriving from a broader definition of psychodynamic principles, has further amplified the range of technical variations as well as the amount of subjectivity in the choice of technical instruments and of ways to assess therapeutic results. It is sufficient to consider, in addition to what has already been said about Kohut's self psychology, Kernberg's (1984) proposal to utilize new, differentiated forms of cure, such as expressive psychotherapy and support psychotherapy, in the cases of more severe personality disorders. These forms of psychoanalytic psychotherapy actually share some basic theoretical principles with classical psychoanalysis. Much the same can be said about the focused approach that is applied to 'brief dynamic psychotherapy' by the psychoanalytic group of Mount Zion in San Francisco (Silberschatz and Curtis, 1986; Weiss and Sampson, 1986).

On the other hand, the abandoning of clear-cut demarcations on the technical level, and the need to reconsider the theoretical assumptions of psychoanalysis in the light of their actual utilization in clinical practice, have rendered even more urgent a major systematization of the fundamental principles of the theory of psychoanalytic technique and a more organically structured methodology to test therapeutic results (Thomä and Kächele, 1985). A noticeable impulse to clinical research has come, without any doubt from George Klein's work: as we have already hinted before, he recommended a rereading of what happens in therapy in terms of more operational concepts. Klein confirmed, in fact, that the analytical situation is the only valid data laboratory, in spite of limits stemming from the conditions of clinical observation and of the therapeutic pact: 'This meaning-seeking orientation and the conceptual tools he uses for detecting purposeful dispositions enables the analyst to see regularities different from those other psychologists generally see when they look at the same behaviour' (1976, p. 51).

In the last 20 years, numerous trends of clinical research have arisen, focusing on an accurate survey of communication processes in the analytic bipersonal field, and of 'what the analysts do' and how their 'doing' is connected with the progress or regression of their patients. Such an approach reduces the gap between the criteria of therapeutic effectiveness and those of explanatory accuracy. This is in fact based on a 'technological' problem which inevitably refers to the investigation into the explanatory theoretical dimension. That is to say, the question of why certain technical advice is effective leads us to find out what connection there is between the condition set by the analyst (through his or her technical intervention) and the effect it has on the patient (Thomä and Kächele, 1985).

The dangerous tendencies to solve the problem of the effectiveness of interpretation by keeping inside the hermeneutic hypothesis are therefore frustrated.[7] The vicious circle of subjective self-confirmation of interpretation is interrupted by following Hirsch's proposal (1976). He suggests that we apply Piaget's concept of 'corrigible patterns' to the interpretation, seen as a 'constructive-corrective' process. Studies of linguistic processes, as well as studies of communicative exchanges in psychotherapeutic sessions, seem to show that the *understanding* process itself is actually a *validation* process.

According to this standpoint, the most recent trends in clinical research focus on the analyst's contribution to the therapeutic relationship as a *reality-stimulus*: recognizing that such a stimulus lets us understand the style of interpersonal interaction and that of fantastic elaboration which is produced by the analysand. In fact, almost all proposed methods of research rely on the transference assessment as the main reference point in order to test either interpretation or the therapeutic change (Dahl *et al.*, 1988). The patient's behaviour and fantasy transference reactions are released by and understandable in terms of what the therapist does or does not do in the analytical situation; both techical aspects and those aspects which are traditionally included in the counter-transference conception should obviously be taken into account (Gill, 1982).

Gill and Hoffman (1982a and 1982b) offered a very interesting method of reading records of psychoanalytic hours: patients' verbal communications are analysed by these authors in terms of expressed affective meanings and the associations' sequence and formal organization, based on the hypothesis that such communications can monitor the analyst–patient relationship from the patient's point of view.[8] The recorded sessions are therefore examined for those invariants in the patient's relation mental representations which can allow us to find the dominant cognitive-affective pattern in the transference relationship. The variations of such a pattern within a session or through subsequent sessions are examined in relation to the patient's awareness of his or her state of transference 'illusion'[9] and in relation to the analyst's actual interventions.

A somewhat similar method of data gathering is that proposed by Luborsky (1984) for supportive-expressive treatment. Luborsky's goal, through the experimental method of independent judges' evaluation, is to identify a 'core conflictual relational theme': he tries to find recurring characteristics of relational episodes in patients' free associations. In Luborsky's study, the core relational theme appears to be more detailed than in Gill and Hoffman's analysis of transference; though it is less dynamically interrelated with developments in the analytic relationship.

The efficiency of such relationships is, instead, at the centre of research conducted by Weiss and Sampson (1986) and their colleagues in San Francisco on recorded psychoanalytic and psychotherapeutic sessions. These authors suggest that we definitely abandon the 'explanation based on the automatic functioning hypotheses', which sees the patient seeking transference gratifications in the therapeutic relationship, and substitute it with an explanation 'based on the higher mental functioning hypothesis', which considers the patient's therapeutic work as a constant attempt at 'testing a frightening unconscious belief or expectation in relation to the therapist' (1986, p. 234). Such beliefs and expectations originate from previous meaningful interpersonal relationships, which caused anxiety, guilt, and frustration: the patient tries to re-experience such relational patterns during the sessions, where he or she feels a secure environment, in order to gain a better control of the negative emotions. The analyst's job should then consist primarily in inferring the patient's therapeutic plan, as well as the underlying pathogenic beliefs, so that he or she may be able to overcome the tests that, from time to time, the patient confronts him or her with.

Likewise, Gedo and Schaffer (1989) propose an empirical approach to the psychoanalytic process which is intended to codify the therapist's behaviour in its sequential context. The aim of this research, however, is defined in terms of the more traditional parameters of psychoanalytic technique: in fact, these authors investigate the sequential, complex relationship between the analyst's interpretations and the patient's transference insights, a relationship which appears to increase significantly with the therapeutic progress during analysis.

The analysis of transference is, then, still considered as the basic instrument which is peculiar to the psychoanalytic technique: 'What's unique about psychoanalysis, as opposed to other psychotherapies, is the focus on the patient—therapist relationship as the most immediate and experientially cogent arena in which to explore these patterns' (Basescu, 1988, p. 123). But the definition of what transference is has gradually undergone a progressive change towards a main stress on its *interpersonal* aspects: 'the therapeutic situation is a social one, in the sense that the experience of both participants is always contributed to by both participants ... and that the *patient's* contribution is best clarified, by carefully defining exactly what his experience is, including his experience of the *therapist's* contribution' (Gill, 1988, p. 268).

This trend of thought is shared today by the majority of psychoanalytic clinical literature, independently from the different methodological options about how to record and classify clinical observations. We can quote as an instance the recent book by Casement (1985), where the more traditional reports of clinical cases are programmatically assessed to point out how the patient, more or less consciously, tries to decipher the therapist's unconscious.

The prevailing approach to the study of clinical interactions in contemporary psychoanalysis can so easily be defined as a *social-constructivist* approach, since 'the constructivist paradigm actually demands taking account of both relatively social aspects of experience and relatively individual aspects' (Hoffman, 1991, p. 102). In clinical research, both these aspects appear to be complementary to each other: in fact, when one focuses on the interest that a patient has in communicating with the analyst as a person, the *two-person* aspect of motivation is placed in the foreground; when one, on the contrary, focuses on the interest that a patient has in ignoring the analyst as a desiring subject, the *one-person* dimension of experience is emphasized.

Some interesting theoretical remarks could derive from a comparison of this kind of psychoanalytic clinical study with the kind of personality research grounded on a constructivist or narratological approach. Empirical investigations on the different contexts in which the portrayal of personality is a central issue draw attention to clinical contexts as well as to the context of everyday talk about persons. The main theoretical issue of these studies is that the *scenarios* of everyday conversation presumably ground the ideas people form about each other: 'personality in this approach is primarily to be seen as the result of a process of negotiating the meaning of a person's action' (De Raad and Caljé, 1990, p. 20).

Focusing the attention on this process of negotiation leads unavoidably to considering the varying of narratological patterns in different relational contexts, and implies a dynamic approach to the definition of *personality* itself. We can find a similar approach in a recent article by Schafer on the 'narratives of the Self': he suggests that 'the experiential Self ... may be seen as a set of varied narratives that seem to be told *by* a cast of varied selves *to* and *about* a cast of varied selves' (1989, p. 157).

Clinical research in psychoanalysis is therefore likely to offer a promising contribution to further developments in personality research, as we have already noticed with regard to infant research. As we have observed, most modern psychodynamic research approaches are actually addressed to the investigation of individual invariants and differences in a multidimensional view: such a view, according also to empirical results in other psychological fields, above all aims to account for those psychological functions of adaptation which constantly interrelate (through memory, language, emotions, etc.) the *intrapsychical* meanings with the communicative patterns of *interpersonal* interactions.

Notes

1. By *Classical* theory we refer to the instinctual model, which is still the basis of the *structural* revision of both Freud's theory and the ego psychology. This model sees the instinctual drives and the intrapsychic structures derived from the latter as the causes for normal and pathological behaviour: instincts are, in such a view, the primary source of motivation, as well as the starting point of the infant's psychical development.
2. The psychoanalytic theory of conflict does not need necessarily to be abandoned, however, but can be usefully integrated with a bipersonal perspective, as Modell has recently shown (1984, chapters 7 and 8).
3. This is what Winnicott calls the 'area of illusion', because 'the transitional object is never under magical control like the internal object, nor is it outside control as the real mother is'; more exactly, then, we can say that 'the mother's main task (next to providing opportunity for illusion) is disillusionment' (Winnicott, 1958d, pp. 237—40).
4. The phrase 'direct observation' is meant to refer to that method which Anna Freud (1951) and Ernst Kris (1950) employed in the longitudinal study of the child; it is a 'participating' observation, hardly interfered with by experimental devices, which considers the infant's behaviour as a whole with its natural human environment.
5. As Modell (1984) puts it: 'This focus upon the self as opposed to the ego does introduce a new epistemological problem for psychoanalysis, as the self is primarily an endopsychic perception in contrast to the ego conceived as a structural organization, functioning in part automatically and unconsciously' (p. 126).
6. As an example, we can refer to hypotheses about the interpretation-reconstruction of unconscious subjective meanings of symptoms and fantasies, as well as to those about illusory conflict aspects of the relationship which develops between a patient and his or her analyst.
7. If psychoanalytic knowledge cannot derive from 'scientific' observation of facts, but can only rely on subjective interpretation, it matters no more what is 'true', but only what is 'effective'. The hypothesis that psychoanalysis should be considered a hermeneutic (or interpretive) discipline was first maintained by Ricoeur (1965) and receives its firmest support from the method of dream interpretation. But, as Modell suggests, the analogy with the hermeneutic method 'cannot be pushed too far, for the dream . . . provides the observer with a source of new, unexpected responses' (1984, p. 146).
8. A similar viewpoint is offered by Robert Langs's adaptational-interactional approach on his study of the 'bipersonal field' in the therapeutic situation (Langs, 1978, 1982). Langs's work is distinguished by an unjustified abuse of Kleinian poorly defined concepts, such as that of unconscious perception and projective identification; he also claims clearly to distinguish 'truth' from 'error' in the therapist's behaviours. In spite of the lack of methodological severity which characterizes Gill's work, some of Langs's elaborations, such as that of 'communicative styles', have been productive in clinical and theoretical developments (Raney, 1984).

9. We use the term 'illusion' not to underline the fantastic component of intrapsychic instances, but rather to show the existence of multiple levels of reality in the therapeutic relationship. As Modell writes, such levels include that of 'ordinary life' and that of 'therapeutic frame', but also those of the gratification and frustration of wishes. The analyst's ability to 'shift playfully from one level of reality to another' is what enables the patient to experience the therapeutic relationship as a 'paradoxical' experience. This allows each of the two participants to recognize in the other 'an individual in ordinary life' as well as 'someone transformed by the therapeutic process' (1991, p. 15).

References

Ainsworth, M.D.S. (1977), 'Social development in the first year of life: maternal influences on infant—mother attachment', in J.M. Tanner (ed.), *Developments in Psychiatric Research*, London: Tavistock Publications, pp. 49—67.

Ainsworth, M.D.S., Blehar, M.C., Waters, E. and Wall, S. (1978), *Patterns of Attachment: A psychological study of the strange situation*, Hillsdale, NJ: Erlbaum.

Attili, G. (1990), 'Gli affetti nello sviluppo: verso un costrutto organizzativo' [The development of affects: towards an organizational construct], in M. Ammaniti and N. Dazzi (eds.), *Affeti* [Affects], Bari, Italy: Laterza, pp. 177—89.

Balint, M. (1950), 'Changing therapeutical aims and techniques in psychoanalysis', *International Journal of Psychoanalysis*, **31**, 117—24.

Basescu, S. (1988), 'The therapeutic process', *Journal of Psychoanalytic Psychotherapy*, **1**, 119—25.

Bowlby, J. (1969), *Attachment and Loss. Vol. 1: Attachment*, London: Hogarth Press.

Bowlby, J. (1973), *Attachment and Loss. Vol. 2: Separation*, London: Hogarth Press.

Bowlby, J. (1979), *The Making and Breaking of Affectional Bonds*, London: Tavistock.

Bowlby, J. (1988), *A Secure Base*, London: Routledge & Kegan Paul.

Bowlby, J. (1989), 'Psychoanalysis as a natural science', in J. Sandler (ed.), *Dimensions of Psychoanalysis*, London: Karnac Books, pp. 99—121.

Bretherton, I. (1985), 'Attachment theory: retrospect and prospect', in I. Bretherton and E. Waters (eds.), 'Growing points of attachment theory and research', *Monographs of the Society for Research in Child Development*, **50**, 3—35.

Bretherton, I. (1987), 'New perspectives on attachment relations in infancy: security, communication and internal working models', in J.D. Osofsky (ed.), *Handbook of Infant Development*, New York, NY: Wiley, pp. 1061—99.

Caprara, G.-V. and Gennaro, A. (1987), *Psicologia della personalità e delle differenze individuali* [Personality Psychology and Individual Differences Psychology], Bologna, Italy: Il Mulino.

Casement, P. (1985), *On Learning from the Patient*, London: Paterson.

Conte, M. and Dazzi, N. (eds.) (1988), *La verifica empirica in psicoanalisi* [Empirical Verification in Psychoanalysis], Bologna, Italy: Il Mulino.

Cremerius, J. (1985), *Il mestiere dell'analista* [The Work of the Psychoanalyst], Turin, Italy: Boringhieri.

Dahl, H., Kächele, H. and Thomä, H. (eds.) (1988), *Psychoanalytic Process Research Strategies*, New York, NY: Springer.

De Lozier, P.P. (1982), 'Attachment theory and child abuse', in C.M. Parkes and J. Stevenson-Hinde (eds.), *The Place of Attachment in Human Behavior*, New York, NY: Basic Books, pp. 95—117.

De Raad, B. and Caljé, H. (1990), 'Personality in the context of conversation: person-talk scenarios replicated', *European Journal of Personality*, **4**, 19—36

Eagle, M.N. (1984), *Recent Developments in Psychoanalysis: A critical evaluation*, New York, NY: McGraw-Hill.

Eissler, K.R. (1953), 'The effect of the structure of the Ego on psychoanalytic technique', *Journal of the American Psychoanalytical Association*, **1**, 104–43.

Emde, R.N. (1988), 'Development: terminable and interminable', *International Journal of Psychoanalysis*, **69**, 154–76.

Fairbairn, W.R.D. (1941), 'A revised psychopathology of the psychoses and psychoneuroses', *The International Journal of Psycho-Analysis*, **22** (Parts 3 and 4). Also in W.R.D. Fairbairn (1952), *Psychoanalytic Studies of the Personality*, London: Tavistock Publications/ Routledge & Kegan Paul, pp. 28–58.

Fairbairn, W.R.D. (1944), 'Endopsychic structure considered in terms of object-relationship', *International Journal of Psychoanalysis*, **25** (Parts 1 and 2).

Fairbairn, W.R.D. (1952), 'Schizoid factors in the personality', in W.R.D. Fairbairn, *Psychoanalytic Studies of the Personality*, London: Tavistock, pp. 3–27.

Farrell, B.A. (1981), *The Standing of Psychoanalysis*, Oxford: Oxford University Press.

Ferenczi, S. (1950), 'Introjection and transference', in S. Ferenczi, *Contributions to Psychoanalysis*, London: Hogarth Press, pp. 35–93.

Ferenczi, S. (1969), 'The further development of an active therapy in psychoanalysis', in S. Ferenczi, *Further Contributions to the Theory and Technique of Psychoanalysis*, London: Hogarth Press, pp. 198–217.

Fraisse, P. and Piaget, J. (1963), *Traité de psychologie expérimentale. Vol. 5: Motivation, émotion et personnalité* [Experimental Psychology. Vol. 5: Motivation, Emotion, and Personality], Paris: P.U.F.

Freud, A. (1951), 'Observations on child development', *The Psychoanalytic Study of the Child*, **5**, 47–63.

Freud, S. (1953), 'The interpretation of dreams', in J. Strachey (ed. and trans.), *The Standard Edition of the Complete Psychological Works of Sigmund Freud*, London: Hogarth Press, vol. IV, pp. 1–338; vol. V, pp. 339–621.

Freud, S. (1957), 'Some character-types met with in psychoanalytic work', in J. Strachey (ed. and trans.), *The Standard Edition of the Complete Psychological Works of Sigmund Freud*, London: Hogarth Press, vol. XIV, pp. 311–33.

Freud, S. (1959), 'Character and anal erotism', in J. Strachey (ed. and trans.), *The Standard Edition of the Complete Psychological Works of Sigmund Freud*, London: Hogarth Press, vol. IX, pp. 169–75.

Freud, S. (1961), 'Libidinal types', in J. Strachey (ed. and trans.), *The Standard Edition of the Complete Psychological Works of Sigmund Freud*, London: Hogarth Press, vol. XXI, pp. 217–20.

Freud, S. (1962a), 'The neuro-psychoses of defence', in J. Strachey (ed. and trans.), *The Standard Edition of the Complete Psychological Works of Sigmund Freud*, London: Hogarth Press, vol. III, pp. 45–61.

Freud, S. (1962b), 'On the grounds for detaching a particular syndrome from neurasthenia under the description "Anxiety neurosis" ', in J. Strachey (ed. and trans.), *The Standard Edition of the Complete Psychological Works of Sigmund Freud*, London: Hogarth Press, vol. III, pp. 90–115.

Freud, S. (1962c), 'Further remarks on the neuro-psychoses of defence', in J. Strachey (ed. and trans.), *The Standard Edition of the Complete Psychological Works of Sigmund Freud*, London: Hogarth Press, vol. III, pp. 162–85.

Freud, S. (1964a), 'New introductory lectures on psychoanalysis', in J. Strachey (ed. and trans.), *The Standard Edition of the Complete Psychological Works of Sigmund Freud*, London: Hogarth Press, vol. XXII, pp. 1–182.

Freud, S. (1964b), 'A disturbance of memory on the Acropolis', in J. Strachey (ed. and trans.), *The Standard Edition of the Complete Psychological Works of Sigmund Freud*, London: Hogarth Press, vol. XXII, pp. 239–48.

Freud, S. (1985), *Übersicht der Übertragungsneurosen* [Overview of the Transference Neuroses] ed. I. Grubrich-Simitis, Frankfurt, FRG: Fischer Verlag.

Friedman, L. (1978), 'Trends in the psychoanalytic theory of treatment', *Psychoanalytic Quarterly,* **47**, 524—67.

Gedo, P.M. and Schaffer, N.D. (1989), 'An empirical approach to studying psychoanalytic process', *Psychoanalytic Psychology,* **6**, 277—91.

Gill, M.M. (1976), 'Metapsychology is not psychology', in M.M. Gill and P.S. Holzman (eds.), 'Psychology versus metapsychology: psychoanalytic essays in memory of George S. Klein', *Psychological Issues,* **9**, Monograph 36, 71—105.

Gill, M.M. (1982), 'Analysis of transference. Vol. 1: Theory and technique', *Psychology Issues,* Monograph 53.

Gill, M.M. (1988), 'Converting psychotherapy into psychoanalysis', *Journal of Psychoanalytic Psychotherapy,* **2**, 262—74.

Gill, M.M. and Hoffman, I.Z. (1982a), 'Analysis of transference. Vol. II: Studies of nine audio-recorded psychoanalytic sessions', *Psychological Issues,* Monograph 54.

Gill, M.M. and Hoffman, I.Z. (1982b), 'A method for studying the analysis of aspects of the patient's experience of the relationship in psychoanalysis and psychotherapy', *Journal of the American Psychoanalytic Association,* **30**, 137—67.

Gillespie, W. (1989), 'The legacy of Sigmund Freud', in J. Sandler (ed.), *Dimensions of Psychoanalysis,* London: Karnac Books, pp. 31—50.

Greenberg, J.R. and Mitchell, S.A. (1983), *Objects Relations in Psychoanalytic Theory,* Cambridge, MA: Harvard University Press.

Greenspan, S.I. and Pollock, G.H. (eds.) (1980), *The Course of Life: Psychoanalytic contributions toward understanding personality development. Vol. I: Infancy and early childhood,* Rockville: NIMH.

Hartmann, H. (1927), *Die Grundlagen per Psychoanalyse* [Fundamentals of Psychoanalysis], Leipzig, Germany: Thieme.

Hartmann, H. (1950), 'Psychoanalysis and developmental psychology', *The Psychoanalytic Study of the Child,* **5**, 7—17.

Hinde, R.A. and Bateson, P. (1984), 'Discontinuities versus continuities in behavioural development and the neglect of process', *International Journal of Behavioral Development,* **7**, 129—43.

Hirsch, E.D. (1976), *The Aims of Interpretation,* Chicago, IL: University of Chicago Press.

Hoffman, I.Z. (1991), 'Discussion: toward a social-constructivist view of the psychoanalytic situation', *Psychoanalytic Dialogues,* **1**, 74—105.

Holt, R.R. (1981), 'The death and transfiguration of metapsychology', *International Review of Psycho-Analysis,* **8**, 129—43.

Holt, R.R. (1985), 'The current status of psychoanalytic theory', *Psychoanalytic Psychology,* **2**, 289—315.

Jacobson, E. (1984), *The Self and the Object World,* New York, NY: International Universities Press.

Jervis, G. (1989), *La psicoanilisis come esercizio critico* [Psychoanalysis as a Critcial Exercise], Milan, Italy: Garzanti.

Kernberg, O.F. (1976), *Object-relations, Theory and Clinical Psychoanalysis,* New York, NY: Jason Aronson.

Kernberg, O.F. (1984), *Severe Personality Disorders: Psychotherapeutic strategies,* New Haven, CT: Yale University Press.

Klein, G.S. (1976), *Psychoanalytic Theory: An exploration of essentials,* New York, NY: International Universities Press.

Klein, M. (1932), *The Psychoanalysis of Children,* London: Hogarth Press (reprinted 1950).

Klein, M. (1946), 'Notes on some schizoid mechanisms', *International Journal of Psycho-Analysis,* **27**, 99—110.

Klein, M. (1952), 'Some theoretical conclusions regarding the emotional life of the infant', in M. Klein, P. Heimann, S. Isaacs and J. Riviere (eds.), *Developments in Psychoanalysis*, London: Hogarth Press, pp. 198—236.

Klein, M. (1957), *Envy and Gratitude: A study of unconscious sources*, New York, NY: Basic Books.

Kohut, H. (1971), *The Analysis of the Self*, London: Hogarth Press.

Kohut, H. (1977), *The Restoration of the Self*, New York, NY: International Universities Press.

Kohut, H. (1984), *How Does Analysis Cure?* (eds A. Goldberg and P. Stepansky), Chicago, IL: University of Chicago Press.

Kris, E. (1950), 'Notes on the development and on some current problems of psychoanalytic child psychology', *The Psychoanalytic Study of the Child*, **5**, 24—46.

Langs, R. (1978), *The Listening Process*, New York, NY: Aronson.

Langs, R. (1982), *Psychotherapy: A basic text*, New York, NY: Aronson.

Lebovici, S. (1990), 'Le psychanaliste et le développement des représentations mentales' [The psychoanalyst and the development of mental representations], *Psychiatrie de l'Enfant*, **33**, 325—84.

Lichtenberg, J.D. (1983), *Psychoanalysis and Infant Research*, Hillsdale, NJ: The Analytic Press.

Luborsky, L. (1984), *Principles of Psychoanalytic Psychotherapy*, New York, NY: Basic Books.

Lussier, A. (1988), 'The limitations of the object relations model', *The Psychoanalytic Quarterly*, **57**, 528—46.

Magnusson, D. (1990), 'Personality research: challenges for the future', *European Journal of Personality*, **4**, 1—17.

Mahler, M.S., Pine, F. and Bergman, A. (1975), *The Psychological Birth of the Human Infant: Symbiosis and individuation*, New York, NY: Basic Books.

Main, M. and Hesse, E. (1990), 'Parents' unresolved traumatic experiences are related to infant disorganized attachment status', in M.T. Greenberg, D. Cicchetti and E.M. Cummings (eds.), *Attachment in the Preschool Years: Theory, research and intervention*, Chicago, IL: University of Chicago Press, pp. 121—60.

Main, M., Kaplan, N. and Cassidy, J. (1985), 'Security in infancy, childhood, and adulthood: a move to the level of representation', in I. Bretherton and E. Waters (eds.), 'Growing points in attachment theory and research', *Monographs of the Society for Research in Child Development*, **50**, 66—104.

Meltzer, D. (1978), *The Kleinian Development. Vol. 1: Freud's Clinical Development*, Perth, Australia: Clunie.

Mitchell, S.A. (1991), 'Editorial philosophy', *Psychoanalytic Dialogues*, **1**, 1—7.

Modell, A.H. (1984), *Psychoanalysis in a New Context*, New York, NY: International Universities Press.

Modell, A.H. (1991), 'The therapeutic relationship as a paradoxical experience', *Psychoanalytic Dialogues*, **1**, 13—28.

Muslin, H.L. (1985), 'Heinz Kohut: beyond the pleasure principle', in J. Reppen (ed.), *Beyond Freud*, Hillsdale, NJ: The Analytic Press.

Novelletto, A. (1986), *Psichiatria psicoanalitica dell'adolescenza* [The Psychoanalytic Psychiatry of Adolescence], Rome: Borla.

Pervin, L.A. (ed.) (1990), *Handbook of Personality: Theory and research*, New York, NY: Guilford Press.

Pine, F. (1988), 'The four psychologies of psychoanalysis and their place in clinical work', *Journal of the American Psychoanalytic Association*, **3**, 571—95.

Raney, J. (ed.) (1984), *Listening and Interpreting: The challenge of the work of Robert Langs*, New York, NY: Aronson.

Rapaport, D. (1960), *The Structure of Psychoanalytic Theory*, New York, NY: International Universities Press.

Ricoeur, P. (1965), *De l'interprétation. Essai sur Freud* [On Interpretation: An essay on Freud], Paris: Seuil.

Rubinstein, B.B. (1976), 'On the possibility of a strictly clinical psychoanalytic theory: an essay on the philosophy of psychoanalysis', in M.M. Gill and P.S. Holzman (eds.), 'Psychology versus metapsychology: psychoanalytic essays in memory of George S. Klein', *Psychological Issues*, **9**, Monograph 36, 229–64.

Sandler, J. (1983), 'Reflections on some relations between psychoanalytic concepts and psychoanalytic practice', *International Journal of Psycho-Analysis*, **64**, 35–45.

Sandler, J. (1989a), 'Toward a reconsideration of the psychoanalytic theory of motivation', in A.M. Cooper, O.F. Kernberg and E.S. Person (eds.), *Psychoanalysis: Toward the second century*, New Haven, CT: Yale University Press, pp. 91–110.

Sandler, J. (1989b), 'Unconscious wishes and human relationships', in J. Sandler (ed.), *Dimensions of Psychoanalysis*, London: Karnac Books, pp. 65–81.

Sandler, J. and Sandler, A.M. (1978), 'On the development of object relations and affects', *International Journal of Psycho-Analysis*, **59**, 283–96.

Schafer, R. (1976), 'Emotion in the language of action', in M.M. Gill and P.S. Holzman (eds.), 'Psychology versus metapsychology: psychoanalytic essays in memory of George S. Klein', *Psychological Issues*, **9**, Monograph 36, 106–33.

Schafer, R. (1989), 'Narratives of the self', in A.M. Cooper, O.F. Kernberg and E.S. Person (eds.), *Psychoanalysis: Toward the second century*, New Haven, CT: Yale University Press, pp. 153–67.

Silberschatz, G. and Curtis, J.T. (1986), 'Clinical implications of research on brief dynamic psychotherapy: II. How the therapist helps or hinders therapeutic progress', *Psychoanalytic Psychology*, **3**, 27–37.

Silverman, D.K. (1983), 'Some proposed modifications of psychoanalytic theories of early childhood development', in J. Masling (ed.), *Empirical Studies of Psychoanalytic Theories*, Hillsdale, NJ: Analytic Press, vol. 2, pp. 49–72.

Sroufe, L.A. and Rutter, M. (1984), 'The domain of developmental psychopathology', *Child Development*, **55**, 17–29.

Stern, D.N. (1985), *The Interpersonal World of the Infant: A view from psychoanalysis and developmental psychology*, New York, NY: Basic Books.

Sullivan, H.S. (1931), 'The modified psychoanalytic treatment of schizophrenia', in H.S. Sullivan (ed.), *Schizophrenia as a Human Process*, New York, NY: Norton (reprinted 1962), pp. 261–84.

Sullivan, H.S. (1940), *Conceptions of Modern Psychiatry*, New York, NY: Norton.

Sullivan, H.S. (1953), *The Interpersonal Theory of Psychiatry*, New York, NY: Norton.

Sulloway, F.J. (1979), *Freud, Biologist of the Mind*, New York, NY: Basic Books.

Thomä, H. and Kächele, H. (1985), *Psychoanalytic Practice. Vol. 1: Principles*, Berlin: Springer-Verlag.

Wallerstein, R.S. (1976), 'Psychoanalysis as a science: its present status and its future tasks', in M.M. Gill and P.S. Holzman (eds.), 'Psychology and metapsychology: psychoanalytic essays in memory of George S. Klein', *Psychological Issues*, **9**, Monograph 36, 198–228.

Weiss, J. and Sampson, H. (1986), *The Psychoanalytic Process: Theory, clinical observation and empirical research*, New York, NY: Guilford Press,

Westen, D. (1990), 'Psychoanalytic approaches to personality', in L.A. Pervin (ed.), *Handbook of Personality: Theory and research*, New York, NY: Guilford Press, pp. 21–65.

Winnicott, D.W. (1958a), 'Primitive emotional development', in D.W. Winnicott, *Collected Papers*, London: Tavistock Publications, pp. 145–56.

Winnicott, D.W. (1958b), 'Paediatrics and psychiatry', in D.W. Winnicott, *Collected Papers*, London: Tavistock Publications, pp. 157–73.

Winnicott, D.W. (1958c), 'Mind and its relation to the psyche-soma', in D.W. Winnicott, *Collected Papers*, London, Tavistock Publications, pp. 243–54.

Winnicott, D.W. (1958d), 'Transitional objects and transitional phenomena', in D.W. Winnicott, *Collected Papers*, London: Tavistock Publications, pp. 229–42.

Winnicott, D.W. (1960), 'The theory of the infant–parent relationship', *International Journal of Psycho-Analysis,* **41**, 585–95.

Winnicott, D.W. (1965), *The Maturational Processes and the Facilitating Environment: Studies in the theory of emotional development*, London: Hogarth Press.

PART IV
The Behavioural – Cognitive Approach

7/   The psychological behaviourism theory of personality[1]

Arthur W. Staats
University of Hawaii at Manoa, USA

G. Leonard Burns
Washington State University, USA

Introduction

The present approach has been called *paradigmatic behaviourism*, a name that is being changed to psychological behaviourism — for reasons that will be indicated later on — and will be abbreviated as PB. This chapter has several purposes: to describe (1) the psychological behaviourism theory of personality; (2) the theoretical-empirical foundation of the theory, the fact that this foundation is different from those in other theories of personality, and that the difference has various effects; and (3) the new types of research that are deriving from the PB theory.

To begin with, the concept of the modern, disunified science has been advanced and psychology has been described as such a science (Staats, 1983, 1988). There are many dimensions of division for psychology — specific methodologies, general methodologies, problem areas, fields, concepts, theories, organizations, and so on. An important division involves the separation of mainstream psychology and behaviourism, and this division is based on various schismatic issues. One such issue is that involving personality. The traditional view is that personality is an internal process or structure that determines behaviour. This conception has given rise to a field intent on measuring personality.

Behaviourism has rejected these efforts and their products, beginning with Watson. He considered the concept as mentalistic and said, rather, that personality could only be considered as behaviour, the totality of the individual's behaviour. The traditional approach, thus, was to treat personality as an independent variable, a cause of behaviour. Watson, and radical behaviourism in general, considered personality solely as behaviour, a dependent variable that is determined by instrumental (operant) conditioning.

What resulted was one view that conceived of personality as a cause of behaviour, an independent variable, and another that conceived of personality simply as a name for behaviour, with behaviour considered as a dependent variable. This extreme divergence, which accepted no common ground, has resulted in a schism that has divided psychology in each of its fields of interest. Radical behaviourism and the larger field of traditional psychology have pretty much remained divided, to the detriment of both. Paradigmatic behaviourism has had a purpose in constructing a unifying approach to psychology generally. An essential tool for that purpose emerged with its development of a theory of personality, in which personality is seen to help determine behaviour, but where personality is specified as learned repertoires. The theory has behaviour principles as a foundation, but it employs empirical findings and conceptual developments that have arisen in the fields of personality and personality measurement. The theory is capable of resolving the behaviourism/ psychology schism. In its special area, however, the theory of personality provides many new avenues of research and theory development.

Paradigmatic behaviourism's basic conception of personality

Figure 7.1 provides a schematization of the paradigmatic behaviourism personality theory (see Staats, in press). The theory may be summarized as follows. The individual at birth begins to learn complex constellations of skills that may be called *basic behavioural repertoires* (or BBRs). They are learned in a cumulative-hierarchical way — where learning one repertoire is a prerequisite for learning another repertoire, in a continuing process across the lifespan. At first the repertoires are relatively simple. But they constitute the foundations for learning of a progressively more complex nature. This process eventually results in the individual acquiring very complex BBRs that affect the individual's *experience* of life situations, *the behaviour* the individual displays in those situations, and *learning* with respect to those situations (further development of the BBRs).

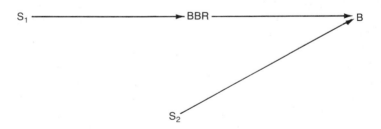

Figure 7.1 Model of the basic PB theory of personality

S_1 stands for the original learning conditions that produce the basic behavioural repertoires (BBRs) in a cumulative-hierarchical learning process. S_2 stands for the later environmental situations that elicit elements of the BBRs which result in the behaviour, B, that the individual displays in that situation.

The BBRs, although they are defined explicitly and objectively through research and theory, play the role of personality as it is considered by traditional psychology. Individuals with different BBRs will behave differently in the same situation. They will experience the same situation in different ways, and they will learn different things in the situation. Moreover, their different behaviours will have different effects on their environment, which in acting back on them will produce additional differences. So individuals, because of their different BBRs (personality), will progressively have a different learning history, a learning history which will also be increasingly determined by their BBRs across time.

This schematizes the theory of personality and may be compared to the traditional and the radical behaviouristic approaches. The individual's original learning experiences, up to the present life situation, are considered to produce his or her BBRs (personality). This fulfils the needs of behaviourism in that personality is composed of specifiable, learned behaviours, although the definition involves a new concept of the BBR. The conception also fulfils the needs of traditional approaches in that personality is considered as a cause of the individual's behaviour. The individual's personality, thus, can be considered to be a dependent variable in that original learning conditions determine personality. However, the personality repertoires are independent variables also since they, along with the current environment, determine the individual's behaviour, experience, and learning. This process involves a continuous, reciprocal, and cumulative interaction across the person's life. For example, the individual's behaviour affects the social and physical environment in ways that affect the individual's later experience, learning, and hence behaviour. PB's cumulative-hierarchical learning principles and other behavioural interactional principles are also important in the theory's analysis of the continuity of behaviour across time and the generality of behaviour across situations (Staats, 1980, 1986, p. 273), as will be indicated.

Resolution of the biological–behavioural schism

Another longstanding schism in psychology is that separating behavioural knowledge and biological knowledge (Staats, 1975, chapter 15). In various fields the two are not only separate, but antagonistic, as in the field of personality. Radical behaviourism has not bridged this schism. Some radical behaviourists have presented models that include an organic concept — models of the S-O-R type where the O stands for the organism (see, for example, Goldfried and Sprafkin, 1974). But the concept of the organism has been vague and unspecified in such treatments — consisting of individual differences that would ordinarily be considered as personality as well as biological differences — and has not been heuristic.

Paradigmatic behaviourism, in contrast, has a general characteristic of requiring specificity, and this has been carried into the present area of concern. PB's theory of personality (Staats, 1990) thus states that *organic conditions operate at various places and various times and that they have their effects on behaviour specifically through affecting behavioural processes*. Organic conditions have their effect within

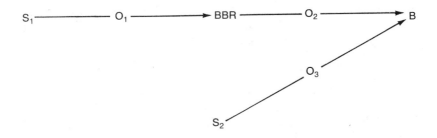

Figure 7.2 PB's triple-causation theory of biological variables in personality

The model has been expanded to indicate the several roles that organic conditions can play in affecting the individual's behaviour. Organic conditions can play a role in affecting the manner in which the original learning conditions, S_1, can affect the formation of the BBRs. This role is indicated by O_1. Organic conditions, however, can play a role after the BBRs have been learned, at O_2, by affecting the brain tissue in which the BBRs are stored. Organic conditions, O_3, can also affect the individual's sensory response to the S_2 environment and thereby affect behaviour, B.

each of the causal relationships depicted in Figure 7.1. The several roles of organic variables are depicted in the paradigmatic behaviourism model (see Staats, 1990, in press), as presented in Figure 7.2. As shown, biological (organic) variables, O_1, may affect the learning of the BBRs (personality); for example, in the case of Down's syndrome, phenylketonuria, microencephaly, early brain damage through mechanical trauma, and so on. In addition, organic conditions, O_2, may affect the individual's behaviour at a later time, *after* the individual has learned his or her BBRs (personality). The individual, for example, may suffer brain damage through accident, disease, drugs, and so on, that in effect knock out the BBRs the individual had previously learned. A drastic change in behaviour may then result, not through an environmental change, or through learning, but because the individual no longer has the BBRs he or she had before. Finally, there are biological conditions, O_3, that can interfere with the individual's sensory contact with the life environment, S_2. The individual may develop cataracts, have migraine headaches that distort vision, become blind, lose hearing, and so on, in such a manner that he or she is not able to respond to the environment in a manner that will elicit elements of the BBRs. This will affect the way the individual behaves in many of life's environments. As this model shows, organic conditions are important determinants of behaviour through affecting behavioural processes.

The inclusion of organic variables within PB's personality theory, with effects at different times, has many heuristic implications in the search for new biological-behavioural interactions. For example, the conception provides a framework for considering theoretically and empirically the phenomena within the fields of developmental psychology and developmental psychopathology. To illustrate, there are various effects of old age that may be considered to occur at O_1, O_2 and O_3. Thus, organic deterioration, which we may consider to occur at O_1, can affect learning. Organic deterioration at O_2 can also affect the extent to which the individual has retained the BBRs that were previously acquired. And organic deterioration at O_3 can affect the manner in which the individual can respond to the current environment too, as in losses in vision or hearing. Old age, of course, involves additional determinants at S_2 that are suggested by the model. To illustrate, the individual's environment changes — friends and loved ones die, jobs and earning power may be lost, and so on. The individual's overt behaviour changes as muscles weaken, and so on, which further affects the social environment. As this example shows, this framework, in its most general statement, provides a basis for integrating personality variables, organic variables, social environmental variables, and behaviour.

The development of the PB theory of personality and the resulting characteristics

The manner in which the PB theory of personality developed and the methodology involved are central to the nature of the theory, for they provide the theory with new conceptual, methodological, and empirical characteristics.

The development of the theory

The nature of a theory depends in important part upon the types of study that provide its foundation. Traditional theories of personality are not derived from principles established in some more basic area of study. Rather, they are based upon formal and informal observations of already formed human behaviours. The 'informal' observations usually occur in the clinical situation, as in the formation of psychoanalytic theory. The formal observations have been more closely associated with trait or psychometric approaches to personality (Cattell, 1990; John, 1990; Loevinger, 1987). Concepts and tests achieved in this type of research also generally have no connection to basic psychology; there is little experimental research that is done on what (for example, learning) produces personality differences.

In contrast, the PB theory of personality was constructed differently; it grew from below, out of the experimental study of actual complex human behaviour, in a long-term research-theoretical endeavour. The principles and concepts of the theory of personality evolved in the context of this work. To illustrate, the initial context for the work was that of studying how conditioning principles, derived from animal research, could be used to account for functional human behaviours — of which little evidence existed at the time. The research plan, begun in the 1950s, was to study, first, simple and basic forms of human behaviour, with the goal of progressively dealing with more and more complex human behaviour. Examination of the works of paradigmatic behaviourism will indicate that it has experimentally studied many types of human behaviour and made theoretical analyses of many more that pose empirical expectations.

The study of language may be used as an example. When this work began in the 1950s behaviourists had already studied certain principles — like mediated generalization, using word stimuli (see Cofer and Foley, 1942). But these were only incipient, partial efforts, did not include integrated understanding of both classical and instrumental (operant) conditioning, and involved no analyses or empirical studies of how language is learned and how it functions. By the early 1950s, PB included informal — but experimental — work on how behaviours could be conditioned to words, considered as stimuli, using a pet cat as a subject (see Staats, 1968a). This work revealed that both classical conditioning and instrumental conditioning could be used to produce simple language behaviours in a lower animal, and the findings provided the basis for formal experimentation. For example, one early experiment studied how affective word meaning, which is a major property of many words in every language, consists of an emotional response learned through classical conditioning (Staats and Staats, 1957; Staats, Staats and Crawford, 1962). Later studies showed the important functions that such words have in affecting human behaviour — as reinforcers (Finley and Staats, 1967; Harms and Staats, 1978) that will strengthen behaviours the words follow, and as directive (or incentive) stimuli that will elicit approach behaviour when the emotion elicited by the word is positive and avoidant behaviour when the emotion elicited is negative (see Staats and Warren, 1974). These studies also showed how deprivation/satiation manipulations could change the strength of the emotional response to words and thereby the strength of the reinforcer and directive functions are well (Harms and Staats, 1978; Staats and Hammond, 1972; Staats and Warren, 1974; Staats, Minke, Martin and Higa, 1972).

These studies resulted in the formulation of a new basic learning theory (Staats, 1970) with important differences from the basic learning theory of radical behaviourism (Skinner, 1938, 1975). PB's basic learning theory is referred to as 'three-function learning theory' to indicate that an emotional stimulus has three interrelated functions — an emotion-eliciting function, a reinforcer (reward or punishment) function, and a directive (incentive) stimulus function in the control of approach or avoidance behaviour. The PB theory of learning provides the basic principles by which to understand how human emotions can determine human behaviour, an effect that Skinner's radical behaviourism denies (see Skinner, 1975).

Advancing in complexity, another area of systematic experimental study of functional human behaviours dealt with reading, beginning in 1958. The first experiment introduced the first token-reinforcer or token-economy system for dealing with functional behaviour. This system was applied to children responding in a reading learning task. The child was given a token for imitating a word given by the experimenter, while looking at the printed word (see Staats and Butterfield, 1965; Staats, Staats, Schutz and Wolf, 1962; Staats, Finley, Minke and Wolf, 1964). Children who under ordinary classroom circumstances were very poor learners, including dyslexic children, could be turned into good learners using these procedures.

During this same period, work was commenced to study and produce learning in young children. While not having the formal properties that are necessary for journal publication, this study — called experimental-longitudinal research — was fundamental in allowing experimental work on a variety of basic types of learning, including early language-cognitive learning in young children. The research began with the detailed study of Staats's two children. Centrally, in the present context, beginning when the children were only a few months of age, various learning principles and procedures were employed to train them systematically in different language repertoires. They were trained to respond to verbal stimuli — using reinforcement procedures that had first been worked out in the research with the pet cat. Another type of training was devised to train the children in speech. The training involved different steps, and included classical conditioning as well as reinforcement procedures. In a later stage of this process, when the child had developed a vocal sound that was like the name of a common object — as in saying 'Da-da-da-da-da', in what is commonly called babbling — a procedure was commenced where the child would be prompted to make the sound in the presence of the object, and then was reinforced. For example, when the first child could say 'Bah', procedures were arranged to have her say this in the presence of a ball, followed by the reinforcement of playing with the ball. She soon named and requested the object spontaneously. Following such procedures the child had a 13-word labelling repertoire by the time she was 9 months old.

The child was trained in number concepts beginning when she was only 18 months old, and she could count unarranged objects up to 12 before she was 2 years old, although Piaget has said that this is a performance that does not occur before 6 or 7 years of age and cannot be hastened by training. In addition, in contrast to what is usually thought appropriate, reading training was commenced with this child at the age of 2, using the token-reinforcement procedures. Various repertoires of which reading is composed were produced in the child through this training. She was also trained in writing the letters of the alphabet as well as in writing words and names. This child (at the age of 6, let me add) scored at the 99+ percentile on a standard test of reading administered at school. All of the training was voluntary, based upon positive reinforcement principles. While this research could not be employed in journal articles, it was described in books (see Staats, 1963, 1968a, 1971). Moreover, the systematic study was buttressed by traditional types of study, by the formalization of the experimental-longitudinal methods, and through the combination of these methods with more traditional research methods. For example, formal experimental-longitudinal methods were employed in detailed studies of children learning repertoires in reading, writing, and number concept skills, conducted with groups of children in a special experimental classroom constructed at the University of Wisconsin and later at the University of Hawaii (see Staats, 1968a; Staats, Brewer and Gross, 1970). Every stimulus presented to the child was recorded as well as every response made and every reinforcer given — essential to the experimental-longitudinal method. These records then provided a detailed picture of the child's learning, in a manner that has not been available elsewhere, as well as indicating new learning principles. It is important to note that psychometric tests also provided data in this study. It is also central to note that the PB theory of personality is developmental in nature and utilizes and extends methods for the study of child development.

Cumulative-hierarchical learning, the concept of the basic behavioural repertoire, and the language-cognitive repertoire

This PB programme of research thus advanced in the direction of dealing with more and more complex types of human behaviour, always within explicit principles and explicit analyses of the behaviour, and in conjunction with empirical study — formal and informal. The programme used various existing research methodologies, along with conceptual analyses to justify their use. The programme also devised new methods of research for the new problems treated.

In the process of this advance, theories of aspects of human behaviour that were considered important were formulated. The first of these was almost coincident with the beginning of the research programme, the theory of language. PB study began in the context of language phenomena, with the idea that language was central to human behaviour. Thus, in addition to the studies already mentioned, PB made analyses of problem solving, reasoning, communication (and vicarious learning through communication), the defence mechanisms of psychoanalytic theory, the self-concept, and so on (see Staats, 1963, 1968a).

The important thing that should be indicated in the present context, however, is that this long-term research programme began to build upon itself in a manner that opened new discoveries, conceptual as well as methodological and empirical. Importantly, the study of language from its simple beginnings in infants to more advanced skills such as reading revealed what were called the cumulative-hierarchical principles of human learning. The child first learns certain repertoires which provide a basis for learning later repertoires, which provide the foundation for learning yet later repertoires. For example, the child's development of a verbal labelling repertoire (speech) is hastened by, and depends in large part on, previously having acquired a verbal imitation repertoire. Moreover, to continue, learning to read depends upon having a verbal labelling repertoire (as well as the other language repertoires). Still later, the reading repertoire is basic to learning various advanced repertoires in particular subject matters. Human learning and human behaviour cannot be understood without knowledge of the cumulative-hierarchical learning of repertoires. Moreover, this developmental study, through learning, also revealed another concept; that is, that a repertoire could have *functions* for the individual.

The language-cognitive repertoire

It was in the context of such work that the concept of the basic behavioural repertoire emerged. The term 'repertoire' is in our common language and has been used many times in the behavioural literature. But paradigmatic behaviourism's study gave the concept of the BBR a new and scientific definition whose meaning is central in constructing the personality theory, as will be seen. The whole definition cannot be detailed here (see also Burns, 1990, p. 104; Staats, 1975, chapters 4, 5 and 6, in press). Let it be said, however, that not all repertoires of responses are basic behavioural repertoires. To illustrate the distinction, most of us have a repertoire of phone numbers. We can say our own business and home numbers, those of close friends, of some colleagues, and so on. This is not a BBR, however — for one thing, the phone number repertoire is not basic to other learning. There are many such repertoires, useful, but not basic behavioural repertoires. BBRs, for one thing, are involved in cumulative-hierarchical learning and thus are determinants for the individual's experience and behaviour. Other aspects of the definition of the BBR will be made clear in introducing the concept of personality.

Here, in the context of the study of language, it is important to indicate that the human ordinarily learns an exceedingly complex repertoire which we call the language-cognitive repertoire. This repertoire is central to the individual's behaviour. The individual thinks, plans, reasons, images, solves problems, communicates, interacts socially, and learns via this repertoire. The individual who has this repertoire is capable of learning and behaving in all manner of ways that a person without the repertoire is not. The individual will experience life's situations, respond in life's situations, and learn in life's situations in ways that are dependent upon his or her language-cognitive repertoire. That is why this huge repertoire is termed a BBR.

The emotional-motivational repertoire

There are two other major BBRs that should be mentioned here, the first being the emotional-motivational repertoire. As in the case with the language-cognitive repertoire, the theory of the emotional-motivational BBR emerged in basic research. The studies that isolated how words come to be emotion-eliciting stimuli revealed an important basic behavioural repertoire. That is, a person who has learned many emotion-eliciting words is prepared to learn new emotional responses to any stimulus with which such words are paired, and there are many emotional words in every language (Osgood and Suci, 1955). PB theory states that this constitutes one of the unique human characteristics. Humans learn emotional responses to a vast number of stimuli because those stimuli are paired with emotion-eliciting words. This applies to all types of object and event — social stimuli, work stimuli, recreational stimuli, material possessions stimuli, religious stimuli, and so on, as well as a huge number of single words and combinations of words (ideas, values, beliefs, opinions). Not all of the learning depends upon language conditioning. There are other types of vicarious and primary learning that operate as well (see Staats, 1963, 1975), but language plays an important role.

This research and the resulting theory of emotions (see Staats, 1975, chapter 4; Staats and Eifert, 1990) provided the basis for the concept of the emotional-motivational BBR. This BBR may be considered to consist of all of the stimuli that elicit an emotional response in the individual. Each individual has a unique learning experience and thereby acquires a unique emotional-motivational repertoire, although similarities also result from shared experiences. Centrally, differences in individuals' emotional-motivational repertoires will determine importantly what different individuals experience in later situations, what they will learn, and what their behaviours will be.

The importance of these principles for understanding human behaviour is vastly increased when they are elaborated within the context of PB's basic learning theory (which is different from Skinner's: see Staats, 1975). This theory states that any stimulus that elicits an emotional response will as a consequence be capable of serving as a reinforcing stimulus (reward or punishment) and also as a directive (incentive) stimulus for the individual. Directive stimuli, in the three-function learning theory, elicit approach behaviour in the positive case and escape and avoidance behaviour in the negative case. It has been shown that positive and negative emotional words will function as positive and negative reinforcers (Finley and Staats, 1967). Moreover, it has been shown that subjects will approach positive emotional words (Staats and Warren, 1974). The principles of motivation — deprivation and satiation — have been demonstrated with the three functions of emotional stimuli. When subjects are deprived of food, for example, they will salivate more copiously to food words (Staats and Hammond, 1972), they will be reinforced more by food words (Harms and Staats, 1978), and they will approach food words more strongly (Staats and Warren, 1974).

The specification of this repertoire is of the utmost importance for understanding human behaviour, including personality, abnormal behaviour (such as depression and anxiety), and psychological measurement, as will be indicated. For it is this BBR that determines the infinitely varied motivational characteristics that different people have and hence, to a large extent, their infinitely varied behaviour. Radical behaviourists (see, for example, Zettle and Hayes, 1982) have begun to adopt some of the basic principles involved, but within the context of the radical behaviourism theory framework, where there is no evidence to support them, and where the principles do not fit. Nevertheless, this constitutes recognition that Skinner's (1938, 1975) learning theory, which states that emotions do not affect behaviour, is not tenable.

The sensory-motor repertoire

Paradigmatic behaviourism very early also began conducting studies on the learning of sensory-motor repertoires. For example, in beginning this work, the same cat already mentioned was trained to various sensory-motor behaviours under the control of word stimuli, through the use of reinforcement. For example, she was trained to approach when her name was called, to sit on command, and so on. In 1953 there were no studies that took reinforcement principles out of the laboratory and into the naturalistic situation. Using the training skills gained in such endeavours, reinforcement principles and procedures were later used in the development of experimental-longitudinal methods for training children to toilet skills (see Staats, 1963, pp. 377–9), to walk (see Staats, 1963, pp. 369–73), to swim, and so on.

The toilet training methods were later expanded into a formal programme (see Foxx and Azrin, 1973). A systematic project was conducted on the child's first learning of writing (see Staats, 1968a; Staats and Burns, 1981; Staats, Brewer and Gross, 1979); and it yielded a programme for very generally training children in this complex sensory-motor repertoire.

The general principles being advanced here also apply to this area; that is, humans learn a very large and complex repertoire of sensory-motor skills. Whether the individual is considered aggressive, active or passive, competent or not, masculine or feminine, a good or poor lover, and so on, will be in part a function of the sensory-motor behaviours he or she displays, and this repertoire is an important part of personality. There are great individual differences in the nature of different humans' experience in this respect and thus each individual learns a unique repertoire. The differences between people's repertoires will vary depending upon family, school, gender, cultural, professional, recreational, and other experiences. What the individual experiences and learns and how he or she behaves in the situations that life presents will depend in part on his or her sensory-motor repertoire.

BBR interaction and overlap

Although the three general BBRs may be described separately, they are not actually separate and independent. I have already referred to cases of overlap — for example, the sub-repertoire of emotion-eliciting words, which could be considered part of both the language-cognitive and emotional-motivational repertoires. As another example, it is also the case that humans learn a large verbal-motor repertoire, where a particular word (for example, a verb like 'sit', 'run', or 'give') controls a particular response. This repertoire may be considered an element in the language-cognitive as well as the sensory-motor repertoire.

There is also interaction between the BBRs. For example, if the stimuli of engaging in sports — exerting effort, sweating, getting exhausted, winning, and so on — elicit a positive emotional response (and hence constitute positive reinforcers), the individual will participate in such activities, for the behaviour will be reinforced. As a consequence the individual will additionally develop elements of the sensory-motor repertoire involved in sports. As a further consequence, the skill of the individual will gain success (positive emotional stimuli), which will result in further positive emotional conditioning to sports activities. The interacting BBRs in this case will culminate in characteristics of the emotional-motivational, sensory-motor, and language-cognitive repertoires that will differentiate this individual from others where the interactions have been different.

Behaviour as an independent variable: a psychological concept

Very importantly, the extensive study summarized began to recognize the significance of the fact that behaviour (and repertoires) could be an independent variable, as well as a dependent variable. Many studies have shown that one response can elicit another response, of course. But a new concept of causation is provided by the recognition that having acquired one repertoire can determine the individual's behaviour widely; for example, by determining whether another repertoire can be learned. The concept of repertoires, thus, through this extended series of studies, began to take a new form. A repertoire could be seen to be a basic *cause*. Thus, children could be seen to be different in their learning ability, not because of some quality of mind or of nervous system or maturity, or because of different contemporary learning conditions, but because they differed with respect to having previously acquired certain necessary BBRs. The concept of the basic behavioural repertoire came to have new and different meanings, in a way that attributed psychological characteristics to the concept.

The BBRs, personality, and personality structure

While recognition of the significance of these developments for a theory of personality was not yet complete, by the time of paradigmatic behaviourism's first general statement (Staats, 1963), analyses were made of personality concepts and personality tests in terms of the repertoires that were being studied. For example, one experiment published in 1962 (Staats, Staats, Heard and Finley) demonstrated experimentally that responses to items composing a personality trait factor (for example, *sociability*) functioned as a class, in that reinforcement of one response increased the probability of responding the same way to other items. Moreover, the analysis of the repertoires began to be applied to the analysis of personality tests as will be indicated.

Intelligence test items

One of these analyses concerned intelligence. In it intelligence tests were not considered as signs of an unspecified internal mental or personality quality; rather, test items were considered as measures of whether or not the individual had learned certain elements of the BBRs. Those BBR elements were necessary for solution of the items. Only examples can be given here. As one, there are various items that measure the child's verbal labelling repertoire. Thus, the child shown pictures of common objects and asked 'What's this? What do you call it? (Terman and Merrill, 1937, p. 77) can only respond successfully if he or she has the necessary labelling repertoire. Other items at the lower age levels measure the child's word association repertoire. For example, there are various items that require the child to repeat complex statements the examiner makes — and this depends on having previously acquired a repertoire of word associations (phrases). The child's verbal imitation repertoire — such as in repeating numbers the examiner has said — is tested on other items. Also, what PB has called the verbal-motor repertoire — that is, the child's ability to make specific motor responses to particular words — is measured on many items. For example, at the three-and-a-half-year level the child is asked to 'Give me the kitty' (Terman and Merrill, 1937, p. 83), and other such items, and the child passes the item if the words elicit the appropriate sensory-motor response. (The verbal labelling repertoire is also involved on such items.)

Various items on intelligence tests were analysed *in terms of the repertoires composing the PB theory of language* (Staats, 1963, pp. 407–11; 1968a, pp. 388–91; 1971a). Those repertoires were described not only in terms of the principles by which they were learned, but also by the types of *condition* of learning involved. That is, the conditions by which the parents could train their children to have the repertoires were indicated (see Staats, 1971a). The theory said intelligence 'in general is learned behaviour, largely of a verbal nature' (Staats, 1963, p. 411). Radical behaviourism never included such analyses of personality tests (Skinner, 1957).

The same type of analysis was made of constituents of other personality concepts, such as interests and values, and the self-concept. The following characterizes the analysis made with respect to the concept of the individual's 'reinforcer system', which was the original name used for the concept of the emotional-motivational repertoire. The concept is applied to interest tests.

> Perhaps the function of certain types of tests used by the applied psychologist is at least in part to assess the reinforcers that are effective for the individual or a group . . . For example, more than half the items on the Strong Vocational Interest Blank (1952) ask the subject to state whether he likes, dislikes, or is indifferent to various occupations, school subjects, amusements, activities, and characteristics of people. This may be considered to involve a simple listing of reinforcers for the individual. (Staats, 1963, p. 305)

A few years later this analysis of the reinforcer (emotional-motivational) system was given a further behavioural assessment definition with the development of the *Pleasant Events Schedule* (MacPhillamy and Lewinsohn, 1971). This instrument was considered to assess the individual's positive reinforcers. In the paradigmatic behaviourism view, tests of interests, attitudes, values, preferences, and so on were considered to measure the emotional and directive value of stimuli, as well as the reinforcing value.

The point is that analysis of these particular tests of personality in terms of elements of the BBRs that were being stipulated and studied empirically began to suggest there was a basis for constructing a general theory of personality. Even at this stage of development, this represented a sharp break with traditional behaviourism as well as with traditional psychology. For the first time, personality tests were being analysed in a specific and detailed way with conceptual elements based on an extension of behavioural principles. The implications, however, needed much further development.

The tripartite theory of personality

The theory continued to grow. By the time of the second general statement of paradigmatic behaviourism (Staats, 1975), the concept of the basic behavioural repertoires and cumulative-hierarchical learning were formally developed (see also Staats, 1968a, 1971). Basic behavioural repertoires were considered to be relevant to many situations in life, to provide response elements called out in different configurations by the combinations of stimuli in those life situations. Configurations resulted that were original, to the extent that the combinations of situational stimuli were novel. The BBRs, especially, were seen to be causes that affected learning and behaviour in life situations. In addition, the analysis of personality concepts and especially personality tests underwent the same type of development through empirical studies, as will be indicated. With this progress, the identification of personality and personality testing with the basic behavioural repertoires became more and more close and detailed, and allowed the approach to deal with typically human characteristics such as originality and purpose (see Staats, 1975, chapter 14).

In summarizing the resulting theory, the central structure is composed of three general BBRs, or areas of personality — the language-cognitive, the emotional-motivational, and the sensory-motor. The theory states that the descriptions of personality that psychology has isolated — whether through clinical or naturalistic observations, or through psychometric techniques — actually are descriptions of aspects of the BBRs. Intelligence tests, thus, are primarily measurements of the language-cognitive repertoire, especially, and the sensory-motor repertoire (Staats, 1963, 1968a, 1971a, 1975; Staats and Burns, 1981). Readiness tests have been considered in a similar framework. Reading achievement tests are seen to measure more specific aspects of the language-cognitive repertoire that deal especially with reading. Interests and values and personal preference tests, on the other hand, have been analysed as measures of life stimuli that elicit a positive or negative emotional response in the individual and thus will serve as reinforcers and incentives for that individual (Staats, 1963, 1968b, 1975). Attitude tests and motivation tests (see Staats, 1963, pp. 293–312) also measure aspects of this large repertoire of emotion-reinforcing-incentive stimuli. Anxiety tests and tests for detecting phobias deal with specific aspects of this same repertoire — involving stimuli that elicit a negative emotional response and hence are negative reinforcers and negative incentives (see Staats, 1989).

It is important to indicate that the BBRs are considered to be more basic than the traditional concepts of personality. To illustrate, research has shown that a particular basic behaviour repertoire may underlie personality processes that are traditionally considered to be different. For example, it was established (see Staats and Burns, 1981) that the same letter-writing repertoire is important for performance on *two different* sub-tests of the Wechsler Preschool and Primary Scale of Intelligence (WPPSI: Wechsler, 1967), thought to measure two independent aspects of intelligence. As another example, the emotional-motivational repertoire is involved in depression (Staats and Heiby, 1985), interests (Staats, Gross, Guay and Coulson, 1973), attitudes (Staats and Staats, 1958), values (Staats and Burns, 1982), anxiety and phobias (Staats, 1989), and so on. In this and the other examples, knowledge of the BBRs better explains the phenomena of personality than the concepts developed in the field of psychometrics itself.

New characteristics in the personality theory

We can see the character of the PB theory of personality by contrasting it with traditional theories of personality. Although personality tests measure 'personality', they do not say what it is, how it comes about, how it functions, if it can be changed, or (if it can) how to do so. Moreover, they do not have programmes or methodologies by which to establish those necessary specifications. The field of personality and its measurement has not linked itself with the substance or method of general psychology. Personality theories arise either within naturalistic study — as in psychotherapy — or in the construction of psychometric instruments.

There are weaknesses also in the traditional behaviouristic approach to personality, beginning with Watson but carried forward in Skinner's radical behaviourism. The approach is really not a theory; it is largely nihilistic. It rejects the traditional concept of personality, but offers nothing in its place. Behaviourism has not seriously confronted and dealt with the legitimate phenomena that give rise to the concept of personality — such as the fact that people confronted with the same environment behave differently. Behaviourism makes reference to the concept of differing learning histories, but never specifies what they are, as paradigmatic behaviourism has indicated. This weakness is finally being more generally recognized (Wanchisen, 1990). Likewise, behaviourism has not analysed why individual differences in behaviour generalize across time and situations. Rather, the attempt has been to deny such phenomena (Mischel, 1968). Behaviourism has never accounted for the success of psychological tests in predicting behaviour. The implicit message in this approach is that personality does not have to be studied specially, that the fields devoted to this study can be dispensed with and ignored, without systematic analysis, along with their methods of study. Such a programme is unlikely to gain supporters in the fields of personality and personality measurement. Moreover, these are not characteristics of a strong and useful theory that should be given much consideration; after all, no guides are provided for studying the important phenomena of concern to these fields.

Paradigmatic behaviourism has characteristics that differ from both approaches. It demands specification of the principles by which the BBRs, in conjunction with the present environmental situation, produce the individual's behaviour. Paradigmatic behaviourism takes the approach that this is a multilevel and *multimethod* endeavour. Research of a general-experimental nature is demanded; for example, in the study of the language repertoires. Research of an applied nature is demanded, as in studies to stipulate how children can be trained to language, including reading and other educationally relevant skills. Research in personality theory and personality measurement is demanded, in a manner that analyses personality concepts and tests in terms of the BBRs, and that uses the findings in advancing the study of personality concepts and tests.

This theory body has, it is suggested, an immense heuristic potential that has not been exploited. Let me give an example of a heuristic implication. Theoretical analysis has said that items on intelligence tests measure the extent to which the child has acquired stipulated language repertoires. Research in paradigmatic behaviourism has also shown that pre-school children who learned repertoires in reading, writing, and number concepts increased in measured intelligence by about 12 IQ points. But just how the learning affected the intelligence needed further specification. What specifically were the repertoires that boosted the performance, and which items were affected? Would training in certain BBRs produce correct responding to the items in certain areas of intelligence testing, and could this be shown in experimental studies that manipulated the BBRs? Staats and Burns (1981) conducted three studies to test such possibilities. In one study one group of children was trained in writing letters and another was not. The writing training had been analysed in terms of the BBR that it produced — including the skills of holding a pencil, where to begin writing a line to make a particular figure, how to scrutinize small stimuli, how to imitate (copy) lines, and the like. Analysis of the WPPSI had indicated that two of its ten sub-tests — geometric design and mazes — required that same BBR for solution. Therefore training children to write letters of the alphabet should have raised their IQ scores on these two sub-tests but not on other sub-tests of the intelligence scale. That is exactly what happened — the study thus showed that intelligence in this case was composed of a repertoire that could be taught. It should be noted that, traditionally, geometric design and mazes tests are considered to measure different kinds of intelligence, which are also different from letter-writing ability. Analysis of the BBRs involved showed the three involve much the same elements — the BBR concept was basic to the several *kinds* of intelligence. The Staats and Burns (1981) study made similar theoretical-experimental analyses of two additional types of intelligence. In the three studies, children were never trained to respond to intelligence test items. They learned *repertoires*, disconnected from any concern with intelligence, that would generalize to various situations. The test items, however, constituted stimulus situations to which the BBRs were relevant. We need additional PB analyses of various aspects of intelligence towards the goal of providing a complete theory of intelligence, what it is, how it is learned, how it has its effects, and how it can be produced (see Staats, 1989, 1990).

The same type of theory, analysis, and experimentation has been extended into the emotional-motivational area of personality. That is, tests such as the strong interest inventory were said to measure aspects of the individual's emotional-motivational system (composed of the stimuli that elicit emotional responses in the individual). When that analysis is made in specific terms it should be heuristic and produce empirical implications. For example, the analysis specifically says that the items on the strong inventory elicit a positive emotional response in people to differing degrees. People in certain occupations, for example, have learned a positive emotional response to certain occupationally relevant stimuli, whereas other people have not. The test differentiates and classifies people in those terms. A series of studies have been conducted to test these expectations and to stipulate in addition how differences in measured interests affect differences in individuals' behaviours (see Staats, Gross, Guay and Carlson, 1973; Staats, Minke, Martin and Higa, 1972). One study showed that interest test items do indeed differentially elicit emotional responses in individuals, and serve as reinforcing and incentive stimuli. These studies provide a foundation for the theory that humans learn emotional responses, through classical conditioning principles, to a very large number of different stimuli — social, recreational, occupational, religious, sexual, and so on. This emotional-motivational repertoire then determines, among other things, what things in life will serve as reinforcers for them and what stimuli will attract or repel them — thus having a very important effect on their behaviour. This work suggests much additional research be conducted in order to provide a complete account of the emotional-motivational repertoire, what its elements are, how they are learned and can be changed, and how the repertoire functions in affecting the individual's behaviour.

The result of this long-term programme of study is a new type of personality theory; new because it arises in basic, empirically specified principles, because it makes specific and detailed analyses appropriate for cause-and-effect studies, and because it projects heuristic possibilities that other theories do not. For the first time, studies have been done of an experimental — that is, manipulative — type, in which personality (intelligence) is specifically changed. The fact is that the value of a theory and its models rests upon the nature of the theory; how detailed the theory is in an analytic sense, how internally consistent, how closely the theory is tied to its realm of empirical events, the extent to which it states the various variables that are involved in the phenomena of its interest, how comprehensive the theory is, and so on. Such things will determine the various types of heuristic value the theory may have. PB's theory of personality should be compared with traditional theory as well as radical (and cognitive) behaviourism theory in these respects. The subsequent sections will further extend the PB theory.

Paradigmatic behaviourism's abnormal psychology theory

One of the approach's implications is that the new personality theory can serve as the foundation for a new approach to abnormal behaviour. There have been general theories of abnormal psychology of a psychoanalytic nature (Arieti, 1955; Cameron, 1963). Such theories are not generally considered or used by radical behaviourists. Behavioural approaches, on the other hand, have not produced a theory of abnormal behaviour. A general abnormal psychology book written from a radical behaviourism view, for example, employed traditional descriptions of psychopathology along with behavioural research involving treating behaviour problems (Ullman and Krasner, 1969), but did not involve interweaving behavioural knowledge and traditional knowledge of abnormal psychology into a unified theory. Moreover, behaviour accounts have generally rejected the goals of a theory of abnormal behaviour; that is, explanation of what psychopathologies are or how they come about, or how they have their effects. This can be exemplified by reference to the work that is done in behaviour therapy that uses a token-reinforcement system to strengthen certain behaviours (like self-care, attendance at meals, and so on) in schizophrenics. Such research was valuable as a beginning step, but did not go on to study what schizophrenia is, what its learning aetiological factors are, or, indeed, how to change a person from being schizophrenic. Although patients treated by behavioural token-economy methods may exhibit better self-care behaviour, and the like, they remain schizophrenics. Because these studies adopted the radical behaviourist approach — a concern only with specific, overt behaviours — the approach never progressed past the use of reinforcement with such behaviour.

PB, in contrast, although providing important parts of the framework that underlay the token-economy studies, did not stop with analysing specific behaviour problems in terms of reinforcement principles. With its progress in analysing complex human behaviour, even the first general paradigmatic behaviourism account included an incipient theory of abnormal behaviour (see Staats, 1963, chapter 11). Eysenck (1960) had considered abnormal behaviour in terms of deficient and surplus behaviours. The dimension was considerably advanced in the paradigmatic behaviourism treatment, even in its first effort, in the process of introducing various new elements of analysis. Abnormal behaviour was first considered to involve deficits in needed behaviours (as in mental retardation) and the presence of inappropriate behaviours (as in the bizarre sensory-motor behaviours of catatonia). In addition, it was said that behaviour could be abnormal because of deficit stimulus control (as in the autistic child's lack of response to verbal stimuli) or inappropriate stimulus control (as in phobias where the individual responds with fear to an innocuous stimulus). Abnormal behaviour could also involve deficit reinforcement (emotional-motivational) systems (as in the flat affectivity of schizophrenia) or inappropriate reinforcement systems (as in the inappropriate sexual emotional responses in the paraphilias). (This theory was adopted, essentially, by Bandura, 1968, and called a social learning theory of psychopathology.) By the second general paradigmatic behaviourism theoretical statement, and on the basis of having clarified and specified the concept of personality as the BBRs, it was possible to outline a more advanced framework for a paradigmatic behaviourism abnormal psychology (Staats, 1975, chapter 8). This work and other paradigmatic behaviourism works have included thumbnail sketches of different psychodiagnostic categories such as learning disabilities (Staats, 1971, 1975), mental retardation (see Staats, 1963, 1971; Staats and Burns, 1981), schizophrenia (Staats, 1963, 1975), childhood autism (Staats, 1971, 1975), and so on. The general theory, entitled 'personality and abnormal behaviour' (Staats, 1975), was intended to serve as the basis for specialized works that would make detailed theories of the psychodiagnostic categories, within the context of the conceptual framework.

This work has continued, and the general model of paradigmatic behaviourism (see Figure 7.1) was elaborated in the context of the theory of abnormal behaviour. This model is presented in Figure 7.3. The individual's original environment can be deficit or inappropriate and hence produce deficit or inappropriate BBRs, in any of the three areas, and the BBRs can in turn produce behaviours that are deficit or inappropriate and hence abnormal. However, the individual's current life environment can also be deficit or inappropriate and itself directly produce behaviour that is deficit or inappropriate. Or the current life environment can produce abnormal behaviour through *interaction* with the personality (BBRs) of the individual. The model shown

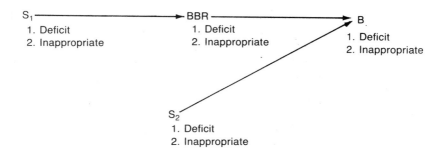

Figure 7.3 Model of the basic PB theory of abnormal behaviour

Deficit or inappropriate original learning conditions, S_1, will produce deficit or inappropriate BBRs that, in interaction with the current environmental conditions, S_2, will produce deficit or inappropriate (that is, abnormal) behaviour.

in Figure 7.3 has been in progressive elaboration since its first presentation (see Staats, 1977, 1979).

As has been indicated, the PB theory and model of abnormal behaviour has had various implications; for example, it takes the position that aetiology is important — something that had been denied in behaviour therapy (Eysenck, 1960) and radical behaviourist approaches (Lovaas, 1966). The PB model says that there is a personality, that it is learned in a cumulative-hierarchical manner, and that it can be abnormal and thus produce abnormal behaviour. Moreover, the theoretical model says that the environment has to be considered in a more refined way: there is (1) the current or maintaining environment, as well as (2) the past or original environment, and both have independent effects. The latter is responsible for producing the individual's abnormal (deficit or inappropriate) BBRs. The former interacts with the BBRs to produce the individual's abnormal behaviour.

'Finally, it is suggested that this paradigm of social (paradigmatic) behaviourism will serve as the basis for a new abnormal psychology that represents a more basic level of *description* and *explanation* of abnormal behaviour than the approach of traditional abnormal psychology' (Staats, 1979, p. 36). This included the plan of making specialized analyses of the behaviour disorders within the theory, such as the paradigmatic behaviourism theory of depression (Staats and Heiby, 1985). In this theory the aetiology of depression is seen to lie at the sites described in Figure 7.3. For example, depression can result from an environmental loss, coupled with a deficit in the personality repertoires. To illustrate, other things being equal, a woman whose emotional-motivational repertoire is deficit (lacking positive emotions for friends, recreations, marital relations, and career goals, and so on) will experience the loss of an only child — her singularly central source of positive emotions — more gravely than a woman with a rich emotional-motivational repertoire and access to the stimuli involved. As Rose and Staats (1988) indicate, the extent to which the individual has a full or sparse emotional-motivational repertoire is important, as well as whether or not the individual's present life circumstances provide access to the positive social objects and events (stimuli) in that repertoire. As another example, it would also be expected that the social skill of the individual (another BBR) would be important in determining the extent to which the individual can obtain those things that are elements in the individual's emotional-motivational system, and Heiby (1986) has provided evidence that helps validate this expectation. It may be added that the Staats—Heiby theory of depression grows out of research on more basic levels of study. The theory is heuristic and suggests important variables to be studied at each of the sites of causation illustrated in the model. The theory is serving as the foundation for a number of more specialized works (see Heiby, 1986; Rose and Staats, 1988) toward further construction of a detailed, empirically based theory of depression.

Work on the more general theory of psychopathology also continues. Several years ago, for example, the theory added the role of biological factors in the aetiology of abnormal behaviour (see Staats, 1989, 1990). This more complete model (see Figure 7.4) shows the various sites of behavioural causation that have already been described. In addition, however, the Os in the model indicate that each of the three processes involved can be affected by biological conditions. To summarize the model, the individual's original learning, S_1, may be deficit or inappropriate and produce deficit or inappropriate BBRs. However, although learning conditions may be normal, the individual's biological nature, O_1, may be deficit or inappropriate, and produce deficit or inappropriate BBRs. The child, for example, might not learn normal language repertoires because of Down's syndrome or brain injury. To continue, however, even though normal BBRs have been learned, they may be made deficit or inappropriate later on by abnormal biological conditions. Let us say that the individual sustains brain damage through disease, accident, or drug use so that

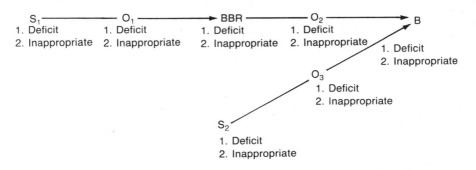

Figure 7.4 PB's triple-causation theory of biological variables in abnormal personality and abnormal behaviour

Deficit or inappropriate original learning conditions (S_1), or organic conditions at O_1 or O_2 or O_3, can produce deficit or inappropriate BBRs. Those BBRs in interaction with deficit or inappropriate environmental conditions — or perception of them, due to O_3 — will produce deficit or inappropriate behaviour.

already-learned BBRs are destroyed or put in disarray; in this way, organic conditions at O_2 can also have the effect of producing abnormal behaviour. To continue describing the model, the individual's current life situation, S_2, may also be deficit or inappropriate. But even when that is normal, abnormal behaviour may be produced by the deficit or inappropriate biological conditions at O_3 that affect responsivity to the current life situation. For example, because of drug use the individual may misperceive social circumstances and consequently behave in a paranoid manner.

There have been behavioural models that include the organism — for example, there are variations of the S-O-R model where O stands for organism. However, in those accounts just what O consists of has been left unspecified — usually it is considered to be a combination of individual difference variables, regardless of source. The PB approach calls for specification: systematic knowledge of organic causation must specify how organic conditions can affect the *behavioural* processes depicted in the model. In doing so, the model requires that the behavioural and biological principles can be interconnected — setting forth a new agenda for considering organic causes. Just as it is important to realize that the environment acts upon the individual's behaviour at different sites (times), the approach recognizes that biological conditions can affect the acquisition of the BBRs and the function of the BBRs, as well as the individual's sensory response to the environment in a manner that affects the functioning of the BBRs.

A major work is now available that presents theories of additional behaviour disorders (Fernandez-Ballesteros and Staats, 1992). As an example, a theory of the anxiety disorders has been formulated that deals with both the commonalities (that is, generalized anxiety) and differences (such as the compulsions of OCD — obsessive—compulsive disorder) among the disorders. This theory has been disseminated and is already being used heuristically by other paradigmatic behaviourists in research studies on the anxiety disorders (see Eifert *et al.*, 1990; Sternberger and Burns, 1991). The point to be made here is that the models shown in Figures 7.3 and 7.4, and the larger theory of paradigmatic behaviourism's abnormal psychology, aim to be general, in the way that psychoanalytic theory was once generally employed (see Arieti, 1955; Cameron, 1963). This new approach says that it is the variation of the specific events at the different sites of causation that have been described herein that give rise to the various psychological disorders (see Staats, 1975, chapter 8, for an early summary). In a later section, the heuristic value of the paradigmatic behaviourism theory of abnormal behaviour will be further specified.

Paradigmatic behaviourism's personality measurement theory

This multilevel theory — advancing in levels from the basic learning theory, to a theory of human learning (of language, emotions, and sensory-motor skills), of personality, and of abnormal behaviour — also has a psychological measurement level. Moreover, because of its unification characteristics, this level has implications for bringing together the presently separated fields of traditional measurement and behavioural assessment. The traditional field, by and large, aims to measure *psychological traits* in order to understand and deal with behaviour and problems of behaviour. Weaknesses of the traditional approach lie in lack of contact with the study of the determinants of its inferred traits, as well as with how the traits have their effects. As a consequence, although traditional psychology has tests of traits which *predict* performance (behaviour), the field cannot say what traits are, how they come to be, how they affect behaviour, or how to produce or change them. Traditional psychological tests provide little information on what to do about problems of behaviour. Moreover, because the field is essentially based upon common-sense conceptions of many different traits, there are hundreds of tests, but little in the way of a theory that relates them in the process of producing an integrated conception of personality.

The contemporary field of behavioural assessment, on the other hand, having taken on primary characteristics from radical behaviourism, rejects the concept of personality, the methodology of psychometrics, and psychological testing instruments (in theory, if not in practice). Behavioural assessment, however, has not itself provided a generally useful framework that can replace the traditional approach, as it once intended. Haynes and O'Brien (1990) give evidence of the weakness of the field of behavioural assessment, showing that even behaviour therapists use behavioural assessment instruments or methods much less than they use traditional psychological tests. Moreover, the general field of psychological assessment or measurement is divided and weakened by having two incompatible approaches.

Paradigmatic behaviourism's first theory of abnormal behaviour (see Staats, 1963, chapter 11) provided conceptual materials on which behaviour assessment was founded (see Bandura, 1968; Goldfried, 1976. Goldfried and Sprafkin, 1974). However, the addition of the full personality theory to the approach provided a more advanced framework with which to bridge the traditional/behavioural schism (Staats, 1975, chapter 13). (Additional works are elaborating the framework: see Burns, 1980, 1990; Fernandez-Ballesteros and Staats, 1992; Staats, 1986.) Moreover, the framework is heuristic in ways that will enhance both the psychological measurement and behaviour assessment approaches. In this effort, psychological tests are given behavioural content by analysing them in terms of the BBRs, as described above with respect to the original research. Such analyses establish what personality traits are, how they are learned, and how they function in the process of producing the individual's behaviour. Moreover, the PB framework theory asks for the use of behavioural methods in the study of new things that have not concerned orthodox behavioural assessment (see Fernandez-Ballesteros and Staats, 1992).

This can be done because of the multilevel theory development, which develops a theory of personality and then a theory of abnormal behaviour based upon the personality theory. Central in this approach is that if one is interested in understanding, predicting, and affecting human behaviour, then each of the sites of interest specified in the paradigmatic behaviourism model must be observed (measured) in the necessary detail — S_1, O_1, BBR, O_2, S_2, O_3, and B. Neither the traditional nor the behavioural assessment approach has indicated recognition of the complexity of this task. Thus neither has studied the various sites of interest depicted in the original PB model (Staats, 1979, 1986) or the PB model that includes the organic variables (Staats, 1990, in press) and called for the study of how the various events are related.

It is easy to see how the three models — traditional, standard behavioural, and paradigmatic behavioural — differ, but deep exploration is necessary to realize the many implications that lie behind the differences. To illustrate, traditional psychological measurement and behavioural assessment have focused on existing personality characteristics, or *existing* problem behaviours. Since S_1 lies in the past and can no longer be manipulated, it is ignored in each framework. This has left concern with S_1 to other fields of psychology, like developmental psychology (which, unfortunately, is also not focally concerned with child learning). Thus, as an example, while the field of psychological measurement constructs tests of intelligence, it does very little to study how intelligence might be learned; and other fields of psychology do little too. A concern with S_1, thus, falls through the cracks in psychology, and as a consequence intelligence tests (and tests in general) have, at best, vague implications for prevention or treatment concerns. Paradigmatic behaviourism study (see Leduc, 1988a,b; Staats, 1971; Staats and Burns, 1981) has shown how paradigmatic behaviourism's concern with S_1 can be used in specifying treatment, as an example of the new directions that paradigmatic behaviourism gives to the study of original learning.

An another example, PB has shown that personality tests are valuable *because* they measure individual differences in the BBRs (Staats and Burns, 1981, 1982; Staats, Gross, Guay and Carlson, 1973). On the one hand, these studies provide behavioural stipulation for what personality is, how personality is learned, how it affects the behaviour of the individual, and how it can be measured. On the other hand, they utilize the knowledge of personality provided by psychological tests as a means of enlarging the understanding of human behaviour in ways not available to standard behaviourism. The studies thus contribute to the field of traditional psychological measurement, but they also demonstrate how behavioural principles and a behavioural approach to research can be combined with traditional psychometric knowledge — yielding a framework that can be heuristic for test construction as well as for behaviour change. These efforts may be considered only as prototypical, since there are multitudes of personality measures to be analysed in behavioural terms. At this point, however, in addition to the studies on intelligence, paradigmatic behaviourism has theory-research definitions of interests, values, and attitudes, showing how these aspects of personality constitute parts of the emotional-motivational BBR and how they affect behaviour. There are also studies to understand better the measurement of depression (Rose and Staats, 1988), and research on measuring the negative emotional state of dysphoria is under way. Research is needed to analyse the various psychometric instruments in terms of the BBRs they measure, to establish how the BBRs are learned, and to stipulate experimentally how these BBRs affect individual differences in behaviour of the type that the tests predict.

It is suggested that the paradigmatic behaviourism analysis of psychopathology (see Staats, 1989) will give additional stipulation to the paradigmatic behaviourism framework in a manner that will have additional heuristic value for psychological measurement.

As a final example, the PB model, in saying that the environment enters into the determination of behaviour at two different times, has implications for psychological measurement. The environment is important in terms of producing learning of the BBRs, at S_1. The environment is also important later on, as it varies for different individuals at a later time, S_2, where it helps determine what behaviour the individual will display. At this later time, the environment selects which elements will be elicited from the individual's BBRs. (Learning will also result at the later time, of course, which must be considered separately elsewhere.) It is important to distinguish these two roles of the environment. Lack of that distinction in behavioural assessment models causes confusion. For example, intervention (treatment) involves an S_1-type process, where learning processes of various types can be applied, and it demands S_1-type knowledge as well as knowledge of the BBRs. That is, after establishing the deficits or inappropriate BBRs involved in a problem, it is necessary to know how they can be changed or manipulated to affect treatment — and this is where knowledge of original learning is necessary. However, since the problem may stem from deficits or inappropriate aspects of the present environment, S_2, it is necessary to be able to assess this possibility. The distinction is one of the things that defines the PB concerns of assessment and treatment and is heuristic in research (see Fernandez-Ballesteros and Staats, 1992, for a more complete treatment).

Current research in the PB theory of personality

It has been said that the PB theory of personality has grown within a different conceptual and methodological framework and that this gives the theory different characteristics. This can be seen in the types of research that have been described. It can also be seen in the heuristic value of the framework for the research and theory it is now stimulating, as will be indicated.

To begin with, there is a group of leading paradigmatic behaviourists — including Aimee Leduc, Karl Minke, Rocio Fernandez-Ballesteros, Leonard Burns, Elaine Heiby, Hamid Hekmat, Ian Evans, Georg Eifert and Warren Tryon — who are leading programmes of research and extending the theory on a variety of topics. Much of this work concerns the more basic levels of PB (see Burns, 1980, 1988, 1990; Burns and Staats, in press; Lohr and Hamberger, 1990; Minke, 1987, 1990; Rosenbaum, 1990; Tryon and Brionnes, 1985). Minke, for example, beginning as an undergraduate assistant, has been a contributor to the PB research programme since the late 1950s, has led a research programme of his own in basic questions in PB that has trained various PhDs in the approach, and has produced important works in PB's methodology and philosophy of science (see Minke, 1980, 1986, 1987, 1990).

As another illustration, Leduc leads a large group of researchers centred in various universities in Quebec who are generally advancing paradigmatic behaviourism (see Cicchetti, 1992; Dussault, 1992; Leduc, 1984; Roy, 1992). However, a number of the studies in personality are focused at the abnormal personality, measurement, and therapy levels of the theory, as this final section will briefly note.

Reading repertoires and developmental reading disorder

Learning disorders in general and developmental reading disorder (dyslexia) in particular represent significant problems for many children and their parents as well as the school (Heaton, 1988). Other problems such as attention deficit-hyperactivity disorder, conduct disorders, low self-esteem and poor motivation are also associated with developmental reading disorder (Chapman, 1988; Kistner and Torgesen 1987; Taylor, 1988, 1989). This disorder thus represents 'a serious educational, economic, and social issue' (Treiber and Lahey, 1985, p. 744), as would be expected from the PB conception of reading as a BBR necessary in our society for normal experience, learning, and behaviour.

PB has formulated a theory of reading that describes the development of the reading repertoires from the beginning stages of individual letter discrimination to more complex comprehension skills (Staats, 1968a, pp. 470−529; 1975, chapter 11). Reading is considered a BBR acquired in a cumulative-hierarchical learning process, on the basis of previously learned language repertoires. The theory was composed in the context of the work already described and in work with children with reading deficits (Collette-Harris and Minke, 1978; Ryback and Staats, 1970; Staats and Butterfield, 1965; Staats, Minke and Butts, 1970).

Currently, one group of researchers at Université Laval (Leduc, 1991) and another at Washington State University (Burns and Kondrick, 1992) are using the theory to guide their research on developmental reading disorder. Since the theory assumes developmental reading disorder is due to deficits in specific BBRs, it should be theoretically possible to 'cure' the disorder. These researchers are attempting to determine whether this is possible and, if so, how many hours of therapy are required. A secondary goal is to attempt to synthesize the current work in cognitive psychology on the role of language deficits in reading (for example, Mann and Brady, 1988) with the PB analysis of the role of deficit language-cognitive BBRs (Leduc, 1991).

The first study in the Burns programme of research examined whether parents could administer the PB reading therapy programme five days per week for 70 thirty-minute sessions (that is, 35 hours of therapy) in the treatment of their children's dyslexia. The ten second-to-fourth-grade children had been identified by the school as having significant delays in reading prior to their involvement in the study. All of the ten parents successfully administered the programme for 35 hours, with the children reading an average of approximately 60,000 words during the therapy. The children were very positive in regard to their participation (for example, they were told at the start of the study that they were free to stop at any time). Experimental-longitudinal research methods were employed, in which records were kept of every reading stimulus presented, every reading response, and every reinforcer during the therapy, something that the parents were able to accomplish with minor supervision, in order to allow a detailed study of the learning process (see Burns and Kondrick, 1992).

While this information is too voluminous to present here, some of the pre-post-change data can be noted. For example, the ten children were administered the Gray Oral Reading Tests-Revised (Wiederholt and Bryant, 1986), a measure of reading accuracy and comprehension, using a pre-test (Form A of the Gray) and a post-test (Form B). These measures yield an oral reading quotient, which is similar to an IQ score, with a mean of 100 and a standard deviation of 15. The ten children obtained a pre-test oral reading quotient of 79.30 (SD = 14.03) and a post-test oral reading quotient of 106.30 (SD = 13.30), t (9) = 9.67, p < 0.0001. This dramatic result represents a change of nearly two standard deviations from approximately the 8th percentile to the 66th percentile. A significant change, though not as large, also occurred on the Woodcock Reading Mastery Tests — Revised (Woodcock, 1987). Finally, the children showed a significant improvement in reading *self-concept* as measured by the Perceived Competence Scale for Children (Harter, 1982), an example of the interaction of the BBRs (personality repertoires) as a consequence of learning.

While the study did not include a control group and the therapy only lasted 35 hours, the strong results, plus what is known of the types of child involved, may be considered solid evidence. Moreover, Burns and his group are currently beginning the process of examining the impact of longer interventions as well as designing data-collection procedures which will allow a more detailed focus on certain of the BBRs relevant to phonological skills. Similar studies are also currently under way at Université Laval by Robert David and Aimee Leduc, as well as research which is dealing with the analysis and treatment of more global language-cognitive, emotional-motivational, and sensory-motor delays (Leduc, 1988a, 1988b). An important aspect of both of these research programmes is that they include analytic, basic research on the cognitive abilities involved, at the same time as they are being conducted for therapeutic purposes.

The theory has also made detailed analyses of several other of the diagnostic categories for children and adolescents. For example, Staats (1989b) has treated the categories of autistic disorder, mental retardation, and attention-deficit hyperactivity disorder. While detailed programmatic research has yet to begin from these analyses, the heuristic value of detailed analysis of problems of BBR development has been shown with the extensive work in the treatment of dyslexia (see also Moreau, 1992).

In this context, the research programme of Ian Evans is so extensive that it cannot be described here. He has researched many years in the area of developmental disabilities and his creativity has been expressed in important works with various types of children. He has, centrally, employed the concept of the BBRs (functional competencies), in dealing with various types of problems in children, for example, aggression (see Evans and Scheuer, 1987), especially in treating severe deficits in the BBRs as in mental retardation (Evans, 1989; Evans and Meyer, 1985; Evans and Scotti, 1989), in a manner that provides an important basis for PB theory. In addition, Evans' work has extended into other areas that can be only mentioned. He has made substantial contributions to the field of behavioural assessment, as will be further indicated, elaborating the field with paradigmatic behaviourism developments. He has likewise addressed topics in child behaviour therapy (see Evans, Meyer, Kurkjian and Kishi, 1988). He has also done basic research in paradigmatic behaviourism (Evans and Weiss, 1978), and he has made a variety of theoretical contributions (see Eifert and Evans, 1990; Evans, 1986; Evans and Wilson, 1983). His thematic body of works make him one of the leaders in the field of psychological behaviourism.

Anxiety disorders

As noted earlier in the chapter, Staats (1989b) has expanded the PB theory of abnormal psychology to provide an analysis of the anxiety disorders. 'The two major principles in the theory are that: (a) a central emotional response is at the core of anxiety problems ... and (b) this emotional response can be acquired directly through aversive classical conditioning or indirectly through language experiences' (Staats and Eifert, 1990, p. 560). In addition, the theory introduces the concept of the negative emotional state, in contrast to the negative emotional response, as part of this analysis (Staats, 1989b). The emotional state was defined in precise terms in the context of the paradigmatic behaviourism theory of depression.

> That is, single stimuli can elicit specific emotional responses. However, *it is ordinarily multiples of negative emotional stimuli, multiple or very strong deficits of positive emotional stimuli, and combinations of these conditions that as a conglomerate produce a negative emotional state ... that is, a state that is deep, of some duration, and that itself produces further behavioral symptoms.* (Rose and Staats, 1988, p. 490)

PB's introduction of the distinction between the emotional response and emotional state in conjunction with the general model of psychopathology shown in Figure 7.4, provides the basis for the analysis of the various anxiety disorders in a very detailed manner. One outcome of this analysis has been the development of a framework for understanding the relation of the various anxiety disorders to each other. For example, generalized anxiety is considered to be basic to most of the anxiety disorders (Staats, 1989). In this analysis, disorders such as obsessive-compulsive disorder are seen to include symptoms in addition to the anxiety in generalized anxiety disorder. An implication of this analysis is that generalized anxiety disorder (GAD) should be a prerequisite disorder for obsessive-compulsive disorder (OCD). An individual with OCD should thus meet criteria for GAD at a much higher frequency than that at which an individual with GAD meets criteria for OCD.

Keortge and Burns (1992) have hypothesized on the basis of this analysis that there should be a developmental progression from GAD to OCD. They tested their hypothesis, employing a sample of 885 individuals. The results provided clear support for the prediction. Of individuals who met criteria for OCD, 63 per cent also met criteria for GAD. The OCD individuals who did not meet criteria for GAD were close to doing so. There is thus good evidence that obsessive-compulsive individuals have general anxiety disorder. In contrast, of individuals who met criteria for GAD, only 25 per cent also met criteria for OCD. That is, most individuals who have GAD do not have OCD. Keortge and Burns are currently repeating this study with a second sample of 800 individuals. In addition, these studies are investigating the role of deficit and inappropriate aspects of the language-cognitive repertoire system in the distinction between the worry of GAD and the obsessions of OCD (see Turner *et al.*, 1992, for a review of this issue). New avenues of knowledge concerning abnormal personality are being opened in this work.

While bulimia is not considered as anxiety disorder, several individuals have recently suggested process similarities between OCD and bulimia (Fahy, 1991; Rothenberg, 1990). Another project in the Burns research programme (Formea and Burns, 1992) is using the PB analysis of anxiety disorders to examine more closely the commonalities of these two disorders in terms of the emotional-motivational and language-cognitive repertoire systems. This analysis and the projected study aim to expand further PB's specific theory of anxiety disorders as well as PB's more general theory of abnormal psychology.

Other individuals are also using the PB theory of anxiety disorders in their research programmes. Eifert is using and extending the theory in his analysis of cardiac phobia and agoraphobia as well as more general issues on the relation between emotion, cognition, and behaviour (Eifert, 1990, in press; Eifert and Craill, 1989; Eifert, Craill, Carey and O'Connor, 1988; Eifert *et al.*, 1990; Eifert and Wilson, 1991). Eifert has a very active programme of research, with various publications of an empirical and theoretical nature that make him the leading paradigmatic behaviourist specializing in the fields of the anxiety disorders. Of those who have come to be paradigmatic behaviourists, Hekmat has had the longest programme of research in this theoretical framework, adopting the principles in the 1960s and beginning basic research in the conditioning of emotions through language. Having clinical interests, he was the first in applying the PB principles and methods to the study of phobias, studying what phobias are, how they are learned, and how they can be treated (Hekmat, 1972, 1973, 1987a, 1990, 1992; Hekmat and Vanian, 1971). Hekmat's work has thus constituted one of the earliest and most complete experimentally based theories of phobic disorders involving conditioning principles. More recently, Hekmat has applied PB theory to the analysis and management of human pain (Hekmat, 1987b; Hekmat and Schwieger, 1988; Hekmat and Hertel, 1991). In doing so he has created a paradigmatic behaviourism theory of pain (Hekmat, 1992) in a manner which has much heuristic value for additional research and for the growing theory of abnormal personality. Hekmat's research programme has been a fundamental pillar of PB and it continues to add to that structure.

Mood disorders

The model depicted in Figure 7.4 has also been used in constructing the paradigmatic behaviourism theory of depression already mentioned (Heiby and Staats, 1990, and Staats and Heiby, 1985). Heiby, a central figure in this area, leads a programme of theoretical and empirical research in depression and has completed a number of important studies in this programme (Heiby, 1983a,b, 1986, 1989, 1992; Heiby, Campos, Remick and Keller, 1987), one of which can be exemplified. That is, one of the characteristics of the PB theory is that depression can have different types of aetiology. One possibility is that the individual may become depressed in the face of some environmental deficit because deficits in aspects of the personality repertoires make it difficult for the person to replace (or gain) that which is absent. In the study, following the analysis, Heiby used depressed subjects with either deficits in social skills or deficits in self-reinforcement skills. First she gave therapy to the former subjects in self-reinforcement skills and the latter in social skills — that is, therapy not suited to their BBR deficit. A test of depression revealed no improvement. However, when she reversed the therapy conditions — giving therapy to repair the deficits of the subjects — they became significantly less depressed (Heiby, 1986). The study showed the value of the PB conception of different aetiologies for depression, the importance of assessing the BBRs, and the importance of treatment suited to the BBR problem. Heiby, besides specializing in depression, has projected PB in other areas, for example, in creating the first PB theory of compliance (Heiby, Gefarian and McCann, 1989).

As an example of another study in the area of mood disorders stimulated by the PB theory, Rose and Staats (1988) provided an analysis of the MacPhillamy and Lewinsohn (1971) Pleasant Events Schedule, a test that predicts for depression. The Pleasant Events Schedule asks individuals to indicate the frequency of occurrence of 49 events (called reinforcers) as well as their degree (strength) of pleasantness. MacPhillamy and Lewinsohn, on the basis of their radical behaviourism analysis, combine the frequency and strength measures into a single score. The PB analysis, however, indicated that frequency and strength should be considered to measure different things with respect to depression. The frequence of occurrence of pleasant events is primarily an environmental circumstance, part of S_2 (the current situation in Figure 7.4), while the strength of the pleasant events (that is, the degree to which such events elicit a positive emotional response) measures part of the person's emotional-motivational repertoire. Use of a combined score would classify as the same people who are actually quite different. For example, people who do not care about the events on the scale but have access to those events would get a low score, as would people who did care about the events but had no access to them. However, the same score would mean different things about the two types of person — stated simply, the first group have a personality (BBR) problem and the second have an environmental problem. These differences require different types of treatment. Rose and Staats's (1988) study supported the analysis. Other studies by Heiby (1989; Heiby *et al.*, 1987) also support the PB view that there are sub-types of depression.

Personality measurement and basic studies in personality

Fernandez-Ballesteros (1979, 1980, 1981a; Fernandez-Ballesteros and Vizcarro, 1985) contributed various important developments to the behavioural assessment field, within an orientation compatible with that of paradigmatic behaviourism. Recognizing this compatibility, Fernandez-Ballesteros visited the University of Hawaii during a summer in 1986, beginning a collaboration between the two research traditions. The first product of the collaboration was an analysis that justified in behavioural terms the use of verbal reports in psychological testing (Staats and Fernandez-Ballesteros, 1987). The collaboration since has produced a general paradigmatic behavioural assessment approach which has been drafted in book form (Staats and Fernandez-Ballesteros, in press; and summarized in a recent article see Fernandez-Ballesteros and Staats, 1992). This publication indicates more fully the problems of the radical behaviourism approach to assessment, outlines the most developed PB analysis of psychological measurement, and indicates directions for the development of the PB approach. A number of studies are called for in exploiting the heuristic value of the theory in the field of psychological measurement and behavioural assessment. Fernandez-Ballesteros, as the leading paradigmatic behaviourist in the area of measurement, continues her programme of research methodologically, theoretically, and in research in elaborating these research directions (Fernandez-Ballesteros and Silva, 1990). She is presently using the paradigmatic behavioural theory of personality, with its specification of the several roles of biological variables, in the gerontological study of changes that take place with age.

In addition, Evans and his associates have done a number of works within the PB framework in the context of psychological measurement. One analysis utilizes the tripartite structure — language-cognitive, emotional-motivational, and sensory-motor — in considering behaviour assessment (Evans, 1986). Another paper deals with the role of the assessment of BBRs as a basis for considering programmes of treatment for children with disabilities (Evans *et al.*, 1987).

Finally, it may be added that one of the foci of interest of Leduc's Canadian group has been the analysis of personality in terms of the BBRs. For example, Leduc (see 1980b) has conducted a group of studies of attitudes. She has also studied the self-concept as part of the emotional-motivational system (Leduc, 1980b). And her experimental-longitudinal efforts to create a normal language-cognitive repertoire in remediating a 'wild child' leads the way in demonstrating the length and detail of analysis that is necessary for the study of major personality reconstruction (see Leduc, 1988a,b). Various studies in this programme are advancing the PB theory of personality (see Leduc, 1984).

Psychological behaviourism

Tryon (1990) has made an important contribution to the present development in his statement that paradigmatic behaviourism should be retitled *psychological behaviourism*. He bases this conclusion on his analysis that PB is behavioural but also psychological, and aims to deal with phenomena in psychology. He argues that PB has a theory of personality and deals with psychological testing. Tryon also makes the point that this change is needed. That is, because the present name refers to behaviourism without indicating the theory's psychological interests, non-behaviouristic psychologists avoid considering the theory. The present name leads to this rejection, because behaviourism in its opposition to traditional psychology has been irrelevant to the interests of traditional psychology. Tryon thus suggests retitlement of the theory to indicate that paradigmatic behaviourism has been constructed to deal with the traditional concerns of psychology, especially in terms of personality.

In conclusion, while it has not been possible here to make more than a suggestive presentation, PB is a comprehensive framework theory, a blueprint for the development of behavioural psychology in a manner that brings it back to Watson's original goal — that of providing a general approach to psychology. That goal can only be achieved within an approach that recognizes and incorporates the productive elements of traditional psychology. Rejecting most of psychology, as radical behaviourism has done, only creates a split that leaves behaviourism weak and alone (see Epstein, 1984; Fraley and Vargas, 1986, for the lengths to which this can be carried). Radical behaviourism has been unable to make sense of most of the important knowledge elements of non-behavioural psychology. That should be recognized as a central problem, not paraded as a virtue. The fact is, alienation of most of psychology cannot produce a unified, articulated discipline.

The multilevel theory construction strategy of paradigmatic behaviourism, in contrast, has the aim of progressively developing its set of behavioural principles in a level-by-level manner to *include* the central aspects of psychology. This goal has involved a long development, and it must continue for a long time and involve many theorists, methodologists, researchers, and applied researchers. This development has now reached the point where its aims and heuristic potentialities have become clear, and its new directions are progressively more within reach of those who work within the framework. The framework has much potential for the various parts of behavioural psychology and for non-behavioural psychology as well, making the name of *psychological behaviourism* very apt indeed. That potential will not be realized in a behavioural psychology that devotes itself primarily to the basic theory of radical behaviourism, on the one hand, or to the eclecticism of cognitive behavioural approaches (see Minke, 1987), on the other.

Notes

1. This chapter is based on the first author's most recent presentation of his psychological behaviourism theory of personality (Staats, in press). The second author's contribution to the chapter has been in writing the section on current research in the theory.

References

Arieti, S. (1955), *Interpretation of Schizophrenia*, New York, NY: Bruner.
Bandura, A. (1968), 'A social learning interpretation of psychological dysfunctions', in P.

London and D. Rosenhan (eds.), *Foundations of Abnormal Psychology*, New York, NY: Holt, Rinehart & Winston, pp. 293−344.

Bijou, S.W. (1957), 'Methodology for an experimental analysis of child behavior', *Psychological Reports,* **3**, 243−50.

Burns, G.L. (1980), 'Indirect measurement and behavioral assessment: a case for social behaviorism psychometrics', *Behavioral Assessment,* **2**, 197−206.

Burns, G.L. (1988), 'Radical and paradigmatic behaviorism: alternative theory construction methodologies', *Behavior Analysis,* **23**, 66−72.

Burns, G.L. (1990), 'Affective-cognitive-behavioral assessment: the integration of personality and behavioral assessment', in G.H. Eifert and I.M. Evans (eds.), *Unifying Behavior Therapy: Contributions of paradigmatic behaviorism*, New York, NY: Springer, pp. 98−125.

Burns, G.L. and Kondrick, P.A. (1992), 'Analysis and treatment of developmental reading disorder (dyslexia)', symposium paper presented at the 18th annual meeting of the Association for Behavior Analysis, San Francisco.

Burns, G.L. and Staats, A.W. (in press), 'Rule-governed behavior: unifying radical and paradigmatic behaviorism', *Analysis of Verbal Behavior,* **9**, 129−43.

Cadieux, A. (1992), 'Relationship between the school self-concept and approach and avoidance behaviors in the school situation', symposium paper presented at the 18th annual meeting of the Association for Behavior Analysis, San Francisco.

Cameron, N. (1963), *Personality Development and Psychopathology: A dynamic approach*, Boston, MA: Houghton Mifflin.

Cattell, R.B. (1990), 'Advances in Cattellian personality theory', in L.A. Pervin (ed.), *Handbook of Personality: Theory and research*, New York, NY: Guilford Press, pp. 101−10.

Chapman, J.W. (1988), 'Cognitive-motivational characteristics and academic achievement of learning disabled children: a longitudinal study', *Journal of Educational Psychology,* **80**, 357−65.

Cicchetti, A. (1992), 'Classical conditioning and acquisition, by the stimulus, of the conditioned, reinforcing and directive functions', symposium paper presented at the 18th annual meeting of the Association for Behavior Analysis, San Francisco.

Clark, L.A. and Watson, D. (1991), 'Tripartite model of anxiety and depression: psychometric evidence and taxonomic implications', *Journal of Abnormal Psychology,* **100**, 316−36.

Cofer, C.N. and Foley, J.P. (1942), 'Mediated generalization and the interpretation of verbal behavior: I. Prolegomena', *Psychological Review,* **49**, 513−40.

Collette-Harris, M.A. and Minke, K.A. (1978), 'A behavioral experimental analysis of dyslexia', *Behavior Research and Therapy,* **16**, 291−5.

Dussault, M. (1992), 'Effects of the supervisor's verbal behavior on his subordinate's attitudes toward him', symposium paper presented at the 18th annual meeting of the Association for Behavior Analysis, San Francisco.

Eifert, G.H. (1987), 'Language conditioning: clinical issues and applications in behavior therapy', in H.J. Eysenck and I.M. Martin (eds.), *Theoretical Issues in Behavior Therapy*, London: Pergamon, pp. 167−93.

Eifert, G.H. (1990), 'The acquisition and treatment of phobic anxiety: a paradigmatic behavioral perspective', in G.H. Eifert and I.M. Evans (eds.), *Unifying Behavior Therapy: Contributions of paradigmatic behaviorism*, New York, NY: Springer, pp. 173−200.

Eifert, G.H. (in press), 'Cardiac phobia: a subtype of panic disorder or a "different" anxiety disorder?', *Behaviour Change*.

Eifert, G.H. and Craill, L. (1989), 'The relationship between affect, behaviour, and cognition in behavioural and cognitive treatments of depression and phobic anxiety', *Behaviour Change*, **6**, 96−103.

Eifert, G.H. and Evans, I.M. (eds.) (1990), *Unifying Behavior Therapy: Contributions of paradigmatic behaviorism*, New York, NY: Springer, pp. 81−97.

Eifert, G.H. and Wilson, P.H. (1991), 'The triple response approach to assessment: a conceptual and methodological reappraisal', *Behaviour Research and Therapy*, **29**, 283−92.

Eifert, G.H., Evans, I.M. and McKendrick, V.G. (1990), 'Matching treatments to client problems not diagnostic labels: a case for paradigmatic behavior therapy', *Journal of Behavior Therapy and Experimental Psychiatry*, **21**, 163−72.

Eifert, G.H., Craill, L., Carey, E. and O'Connor, C. (1988), 'Affect modification through evaluative conditioning with music', *Behaviour Research and Therapy*, **26**, 321−30.

Evans, I.M. (1986), 'Response structures and the triple response mode concept in behavioral assessment', in R.O. Nelson and S.C. Hayes (eds.), *Conceptual Foundations of Behavioral Assessment*, New York, NY: Guilford Press, pp. 131−55.

Evans, I.M. (1989), 'A multi-dimensional model for conceptualizing the design of child behavior therapy', *Behavioral Psychotherapy*, **17**, 237−51.

Evans, I.M. and Meyer, L.M. (1985), *An Educative Approach to Behavior Problems: A practical decision model for intervention with severely handicapped learners*, Baltimore, MD: Paul H. Brookes.

Evans, I.M. and Scheuer, A.D. (1987), 'Analyzing response relationships in childhood aggression: the clinical perspective', in D.C. Crowell, I.M. Evans and C.R. O'Donnell (eds.), *Childhood Aggression and Violence: Sources of influence, prevention and control*, New York, NY: Plenum Press, pp. 75−94.

Evans, I.M. and Scotti, J.R. (1989), 'Defining meaningful outcomes for persons with profound disabilities', in F. Brown and D. Lehr (eds.), *Persons with Profound Disabilities: Issues and practices*, Baltimore, MD: Paul H. Brookes, pp. 83−107.

Evans, I.M. and Weiss, A.R. (1979), 'Process studies in language conditioning: II. The role of semantic relevance, in conditioning negative emotional responses', *Journal of Behavior Therapy and Experimental Psychiatry*, **9**, 121−4.

Evans, I.M. and Wilson, F.E. (1983), 'Behavioral assessment as decision making: a theoretical analysis', in M. Rosenbaum, C.M. Franks and Y. Jaffe (eds.), *Perspectives on Behavior Therapy in the Eighties*, New York, NY: Springer, pp. 35−53.

Evans, I.M., Meyer, L.M., Kurkjian, J.A. and Kishi, G.S. (1988), 'An evaluation of behavioral interrelationships in child behavior therapy', in J.C. Witt, S.N. Elliott and F.N. Gresham (eds.), *Handbook of Behavior Therapy in Education*, New York, NY: Plenum Press, pp. 189−215.

Evans, I.M., Brown, F.A., Weed, K.A., Spry, K.M. and Owen, V. (1987), 'The assessment of functional competencies: a behavioral approach to the evaluation of programs for children with disabilities', in R.J. Prinz (ed.), *Advances in Behavioral Assessment of Children and Families*, Greenwich, CT: JAI Press, vol. 3, pp. 195−239.

Epstein, R. (1984), 'The case for praxis', *The Behavior Analyst*, **7**, 101−19.

Eysenck, H.J. (1960), *Behavior Therapy and the Neuroses*, New York, NY: Pergamon.

Fahy, T.A. (1991), 'Obsessive-compulsive symptoms in eating disorders', *Behavior Research and Therapy*, **19**, 113−16.

Fernandez-Ballesteros, R. (1979), *Los metodos en evaluacion conductual* [The Methods of Behavioral Assessment], Madrid: Pablo del Rio.

Fernandez-Ballesteros, R. (1981), 'Comparaciones entre la evaluacion tradicional y la evaluacion condutual' [Comparisons between traditional assessment and behavioral assessment], in R. Fernandez-Ballesteros and J.A.I. Carrobles (eds.), *Evaluacion conductual* [Behavioral Assessment], Madrid: Editorial Piramide, pp. 63−89.

Fernandez-Ballesteros, R. and Silva, F. (1990), 'Evaluacion psicologica: aportaciones para una crisis' [Psychological assessment: contributions to a crisis], *Evalucion Psicologica/Psychological Assessment,* **5**, 119−34.

Fernandez-Ballesteros, R. and Staats, A.W. (1992), 'Paradigmatic behavioral assessment, treatment, and evaluation: answering the crisis in behavioral assessment', *Advances in Behaviour Research and Therapy,* **14**, 1−28.

Fernandez-Ballesteros, R. and Vizcarro, A. (1985), 'Problemas metodologicos en el analisis funcional de la conducta' [Methodological problems in the functional analysis of behavior], *Anales del I Congreso de Psicologos* [Annals of the First Congress of Psychology], Madrid: COP, pp. 44−57.

Finley, J.R. and Staats, A.W. (1967), 'Evaluative meaning words as reinforcing stimuli', *Journal of Verbal Learning and Verbal Behavior,* **6**, 193−7.

Formea, G.M. and Burns, G.L. (1992), 'Bulimia and obsessive compulsive disorder: symptomatology and process', manuscript in preparation.

Foxx, R.M. and Azrin, N.H. (1973), *Toilet Training the Retarded: A rapid program for day and nighttime independent toileting,* Champaign, IL: Research Press.

Fraley, L.E. and Vargas, E.A. (1986), 'Separate disciplines: the study of behavior and the study of the psyche', *The Behavior Analyst,* **9**, 47−59.

Goldfried, M.R. (1976), 'Behavioral assessment', in I. Weiner (ed.), *Clinical Methods in Psychology,* New York, NY: Wiley, pp. 212−14.

Goldfried, M.R. and Sprafkin, J. (1974), *Behavioral Personality Assessment: Behavioral approaches to therapy,* Morristown, NJ: General Learning Press.

Harms, J.Y. and Staats, A.W. (1978), 'Food deprivation and conditioned reinforcing value of food words: interaction of Pavlovian and instrumental conditioning', *Bulletin of the Psychonomic Society,* **12**, 294−6.

Harter, S. (1982), 'The perceived competence scale for children', *Child Development,* **53**, 87−9.

Harter, S. (1986), 'Processes underlying construction, maintenance, and enhancement of the self concept in children', in J. Suls and A.G. Greenwald (eds.), *Psychological Perspectives on the Self,* Hillsdale, NJ: Erlbaum, pp. 137−81.

Haynes, S.N. and O'Brien, W.H. (1990), 'Functional analysis in behavior therapy', *Clinical Psychology Review,* **10**, 649−68.

Heaton, R.K. (1988), 'Introduction to the special series', *Journal of Consulting and Clinical Psychology,* **56**, 787−8.

Heiby, E.M. (1983a), 'Depression as a function of the interaction of self and environmentally controlled reinforcement', *Behavior Therapy,* **14**, 430−3.

Heiby, E.M. (1983b), 'Toward the prediction of mood change', *Behavior Therapy,* **14**, 110−15.

Heiby, E.M. (1986), 'Social and self-reinforcement deficits in four cases of depression', *Behavior Therapy,* **17**, 158−69.

Heiby, E.M. (1989), 'Multiple skill deficits in depression', *Behaviour Change,* **6**, 76−84.

Heiby, E.M. (1991), 'Implications of chaos theory for the study of depression, symposium paper presented at the 99th annual meeting of the American Psychological Association, San Francisco.

Heiby, E.M. (1992), 'Suggestions from chaos theory for the behavioral assessment of depression', in P. McGuffin (chair), *Advances from Paradigmatic Behaviorism: New directions in clinical research,* symposium presented at the 18th annual meeting of the Association for Behavior Analysis, San Francisco.

Heiby, E.M. and Staats, A.W. (1990), 'Depression: classification, explanation, and treatment', in G.H. Eifert and I.M. Evans (eds.), *Unifying Behavior Therapy: Contributions of paradigmatic behaviorism,* New York, NY: Springer, pp. 220−46.

Heiby, E.M., Campos, P.E., Remick, R.A. and Keller, F.D. (1987), 'Dexamethasone suppression and self-reinforcement correlates of clinical depression', *Journal of Abnormal Psychology*, **96**, 70–2.

Heiby, E.M., Gefarian, G.T. and McCann, S.C. (1989), 'Situational and behavioral correlates of compliance to a regimen', *Journal of Compliance in Health Care*, **4**, 101–16.

Hekmat, H. (1972), 'The role of imagination in semantic desensitization', *Behavior Therapy*, **3**, 223–31.

Hekmat, H. (1973), 'Systematic versus semantic desensitization and implosive therapy', *Journal of Consulting and Clinical Psychology*, **40**, 202–9.

Hekmat, H. (1987a), 'Origins and development of human fear reactions', *Journal of Anxiety Disorders*, **1**, 197–218.

Hekmat, H. (1987b), 'Semantic relaxation: an intervention program for pain control', paper presented at the 21st annual meeting of the Association for the Advancement of Behavior Therapy in Boston, MA.

Hekmat, H. (1990), 'Semantic behavior therapy of anxiety disorders', in G.H. Eifert and I.M. Evans (eds.), *Unifying Behavior Therapy: Contributions of paradigmatic behaviorism*, New York, NY: Springer, pp. 201–46.

Hekmat, H. (1992), 'Paradigmatic behaviorism's theory and management of human pain reactions: integrative behavioral perspectives', symposium paper presented at the 18th annual meeting of the Association for Behavior Analysis, San Francisco.

Hekmat, H. and Hertel, J. (1991), 'Pain attenuating effects of affective distractors', paper presented at the 12th Annual Scientific Session of the Society of Behavioral Medicine.

Hekmat, H. and Schwieger, P. (1988), 'Paradigmatic behavior therapy and chronic pain: gerontological perspectives', symposium paper presented at the 96th Convention of the American Psychological Association in Atlanta, GA.

Hekmat, H. and Vanian, D. (1971), 'Behavior modification through covert semantic desensitization', *Journal of Consulting and Clinical Psychology*, **36**, 248–51.

Herry, M. (1984), 'Le principe du conditionnement instrumental d'ordre superieur' [The principle of higher-order instrumental conditioning], in A. Leduc (ed.), *Recherches sur le behaviorisme paradigmatique ou social* [Research in Paradigmatic or Social Behaviorism], Brossard, Quebec: Editions Behaviora Inc., pp. 31–42.

Hishinuma, E.S. (1989), 'The future of radical behaviorism: brief comments on Glenn's editorial and Drash's "On Terms" ', *The Behavior Analyst*, **12**, 93–5.

Keortge, S. and Burns, G.L. (1992), 'Relation between worry, intrusive thoughts, generalized anxiety disorder, and obsessive compulsive disorder, manuscript in preparation.

Kistner, J.A. and Torgesen, J.K. (1987), 'Motivational and cognitive aspects of learning disabilities', in B.B. Lahey and A.E. Kazdin (eds.), *Advances in Clinical Child Psychology*, New York, NY: Plenum Press, vol. 10, pp. 289–333.

John, O.P. (1990), 'The "big five" factor taxonomy: dimensions of personality in the natural language and in questionnaires', in L.A Pervin (ed.), *Handbook of Personality: Theory and research*, New York, NY: Guilford Press, pp. 66–100.

Leduc, A. (1980a), 'L'apprentissage et le changement des attitudes: l'approche interactioniste de Staats' [The learning and change of attitudes: the interactionist approach of Staats], *Revue canadienne de l'education*, **5**, 15–53.

Leduc, A. (1980b), 'L'apprentissage et le changement des attitudes envers soi-meme: le concept de soi' [The learning and change of the attitudes towards the self: the concept of self], *Revue canadienne de l'education*, **5**, 91–101.

Leduc, A. (1984), *Recherches sur le behaviorisme paradigmatique ou social* [Research in Paradigmatic or Social Behaviorism], Brossard, Quebec: Editions Behaviora.

Leduc, A. (1988a), 'A paradigmatic behavioral approach to the treatment of a "wild" child', *Child and Family Behavior Therapy*, **9**, 1–16.

Leduc, A. (1988b), *L'histoire d'apprentissage d'une enfant 'sauvage': Si toutes et tous les Dominques avaient la chance d'apprendre!* [The History of Learning of a 'Feral' Child:

If everyone and all Dominiques would have a chance to learn], Brossard, Quebec: Editions Behaviora.

Leduc, A. (1991), 'Une tentative de rapprochement entre les conceptions des troubles d'apprentissage' [A tentative rapprochement among the conceptions of learning problems], *Comportement Humain*, **5**, 41−54.

Lindsley, O.R. (1956), 'Operant conditioning methods applied to research in chronic schizophrenia', *Psychiatric Research Reports*, **5**, 118−53.

Loevinger, J. (1987), *Paradigms of Personality*, New York, NY: W.H. Freeman.

Lohr, J.M. and Hamberger, L.K. (1990), 'Verbal, emotional, and imagery repertoires in the regulation of dysfunctional behavior: an integrative conceptual framework for cognitive-behavioral disorders and interventions', in G.H. Eifert and I.M. Evans (eds.), *Unifying Behavior Therapy: Contributions of paradigmatic behaviorism*, New York, NY: Springer, pp. 153−72.

Lovaas, O.I. (1967), 'A behavior therapy approach to the treatment of childhood schizophrenia', in J.P. Hill (ed.), *Minnesota Symposium on Child Psychology*, Minneapolis, MN: University of Minnesota Press, vol. 1, pp. 108−59.

MacPhillamy, D. and Lewinsohn, P. (1971), *The Pleasant Events Schedule*, Eugene, OR: University of Oregon.

Mann, V.A. and Brady, S. (1988), 'Reading disability: the role of language deficiencies', *Journal of Consulting and Clinical Psychology*, **56**, 811−16.

Minke, K.A. (1980), 'Behavioral engineering', in L.P. Ince (ed.), *Behavioral Psychology in Rehabilitation Medicine*, Baltimore, MD: Williams and Wilkins, pp. 3−22.

Minke, K.A. (1986), 'Toward a general theory of behaviour: two-level vs. multilevel theory methodology', *International Newsletter of Social Behaviorism*, 3−8.

Minke, K.A. (1987), 'A comparative analysis of the general theories of modern behaviorism: unification through generational advance', in A.W. Staats and L.P. Moos (eds.), *Annals of Theoretical Psychology*, New York, NY: Plenum Press, vol. 5, pp. 315−44.

Minke, K.A. (1990), 'Research foundations of a developing paradigm: implications for behavioral engineering', in G. Eifert and I.M. Evans (eds.), *Unifying Behavior Therapy: Contributions of paradigmatic behaviorism*, New York, NY: Springer, pp. 57−80.

Mischel, W. (1968), *Personality and Assessment*, New York, NY: Wiley.

Moreau, C.A. (1992), 'Effects of social contact from multiple peers on social skills in a mentally retarded child' symposium paper presented at the 18th annual meeting of the Association for Behavior Analysis, San Francisco.

Osgood, C.E. and Suci, G.J. (1955), 'Factor analysis of meaning', *Journal of Experimental Psychology*, **50**, 325−38.

Rose, G.D. and Staats, A.W. (1988), 'Depression and the frequency and strength of pleasant events: exploration of the Staats−Heiby theory', *Behavior Research and Therapy*, **26**, 489−94.

Rosenbaum, M. (1990), 'A model for research on self-regulation: reducing the schism between behaviorism and general psychology', in G. Eifert and I.M. Evans (eds.), *Unifying Behavior Therapy: Contributions of paradigmatic behaviorism*, New York, NY: Springer, pp. 126−49.

Rothenberg, A. (1990), 'Adolescence and eating disorder: the obsessive compulsive syndrome', *Psychiatric Clinics of North American*, **13**, 469−88.

Roy, S. (1992), 'Learning mental images', symposium paper presented at the 18th annual meeting of the Association for Behavior Analysis, San Francisco.

Ryback, D. and Staats, A.W. (1970), 'Parents as behavior therapy technicians in treating reading deficits (dyslexia)', *Journal of Behavior Therapy and Experimental Psychiatry*, **1**, 109−19.

Skinner, B.F. (1938), *The Behavior of Organisms*, New York, NY: Appleton.

Skinner, B.F. (1957), *Verbal Behavior*, New York, NY: Appleton-Century Crofts.

Skinner, B.F. (1975), 'The steep and thorny way to a science of behavior', *American Psychologist*, **30**, 42−9.

Sternberger, L.G. and Burns, G.L. (1991), 'Obsessions and compulsions in a college sample: distinction between symptoms and diagnosis', *Behavior Therapy*, **22**, 569−76.

Staats, A.W. (1957), 'Learning theory and "opposite speech" ', *Journal of Abnormal and Social Psychology*, **55**, 268−9.

Staats, A.W. (with contributions by C.K. Staats) (1963), *Complex Human Behavior*, New York, NY: Holt, Rinehart & Winston.

Staats, A.W. (ed.) (1964), *Human Learning*, New York, NY: Holt, Rinehart & Winston.

Staats, A.W. (1968a), *Learning, Language and Cognition*, New York, NY: Holt, Rinehart & Winston.

Staats, A.W. (1968b), 'Social behaviorism and human motivation: principles of the attitude-reinforcer-discriminative system', in A.G. Greenwald, T.C. Brock and T.N. Ostrom (eds.), *Psychological Foundations of Attitudes*, New York, NY: Academic Press, pp. 33−66.

Staats, A.W. (1970), 'A learning-behavior theory: a basis for unity in behavioral-social science', in A.R. Gilgen (ed.), *Contemporary Scientific Psychology*, New York, NY: Academic Press, pp. 183−239.

Staats, A.W. (1971), *Child Learning, Intelligence and Personality*, New York, NY: Harper & Row.

Staats, A.W. (1972), 'Language behavior therapy: a derivative of social behaviorism', *Behavior Therapy*, **3**, 165−92.

Staats, A.W. (1975), *Social Behaviorism*, Homewood, IL: Dorsey.

Staats, A.W. (1977), 'Experimental-longitudinal methods in assessment, research, and treatment', *Journal of Abnormal Child Psychology*, **5**, 323−33.

Staats, A.W. (1979), 'El conductismo social: un fundamento de la modificacion del comportamiento' [Social behaviorism: a foundation for behavior modification], *Revista Latinoamericana de Psicologia*, **11**, 9−46.

Staats, A.W. (1980), 'Behavioral interaction, and interactional psychology theories of personality: similarities, differences, and the need for unification', *British Journal of Psychology*, **71**, 205−20.

Staats, A.W. (1983), *Psychology's Crisis of Disunity: Philosophy and method for a unified science*, New York, NY: Praeger.

Staats, A.W. (1986), 'Behaviorism with a personality: the paradigmatic behavioral assessment approach', in R.O. Nelson and S.C. Hayes (eds.), *Conceptual Foundations of Behavioral Assessment*, New York, NY: Guilford Press, pp. 242−96.

Staats, A.W. (1988), 'Paradigmatic behaviorism, unified positivism, and paradigmatic behavior therapy', in D.B. Fishman, F. Rotgers and C. Franks (eds.), *Paradigms in Behavior Therapy: Present and promise*, New York, NY: Springer, pp. 211−53.

Staats, A.W. (1989), *Personality and Abnormal Behavior: A psychological behaviorism approach*, New York, NY: Pergamon, in press.

Staats, A.W. (1990), 'Paradigmatic behaviorism and intelligence: task analysis? technical plan? or theory?', *Psicothema*, **2**, 7−24.

Staats, A.W. (1991), 'Unified positivism and unification psychology: fad or new field?', *American Psychologist*, **46**, 899−912.

Staats, A.W. (in press), 'Personality theory, abnormal psychology, and psychological measurement: a psychological behaviorism', *Behavior Modification*.

Staats, A.W. and Burns, G.L. (1981), 'Intelligence and child development: what intelligence is and how it is learned and functions', *Genetic Psychology Monographs*, **104**, 237−301.

Staats, A.W. and Burns, G.L. (1982), 'Emotional personality repertoire as cause of behavior: specification of personality and interaction principles', *Journal of Personality and Social Psychology*, **43**, 873−81.

Staats, A.W. and Burns, G.L. (1989), 'Stimulus equivalence: principle or functioning of learned

S-R mechanisms?', symposium paper presented at the 97th annual meeting of the American Psychological Association, New Orleans.

Staats, A.W. and Butterfield, W.H. (1965), 'Treatment of reading in a culturally-deprived juvenile delinquent: an application of reinforcement principles', *Child Development*, **36**, 925–42.

Staats, A.W. and Eifert, G.H. (1990), 'The paradigmatic behaviorism theory of emotions: basis for unification', *Clinical Psychology Review*, **10**, 539–66.

Staats, A.W. and Fernandez-Ballesteros, R. (1987), 'The self-report in personality measurement: a paradigmatic behaviorism approach to psychodiagnostics', *Evaluacion Psicologica-Psychological Assessment*, **3**, 151–90.

Staats, A.W. and Fernandez-Ballesteros, R. (in press), *Evaluacion socioconductual* [Social Behavioral Assessment], Barcelona: Editorial Martinez Roca.

Staats, A.W. and Hammond, W.W. (1972), 'Natural words as physiological conditioned stimuli: food-word elicited salivation and deprivation effects', *Journal of Experimental Psychology*, **96**, 206–8.

Staats, A.W. and Heiby, E. (1985), 'Paradigmatic behaviorism's theory of depression: unified, explanatory, and heuristic', in S. Reiss and R. Bootzin (eds.), *Theoretical issues in behavior therapy*, New York, NY: Academic Press, pp. 279–330.

Staats, A.W. and Staats, C.K. (1958), 'Attitudes established by classical conditioning', *Journal of Abnormal Social Psychology*, **57**, 37–40.

Staats, A.W. and Warren, D.R. (1974), 'Motivation and three-function learning: deprivation-satiation and approach-avoidance to food words', *Journal of Experimental Psychology*, **103**, 1191–9.

Staats, A.W., Brewer, B.A. and Gross, M.C. (1970), 'Learning and cognitive development: representative samples, cumulative-hierarchical learning, and experimental-longitudinal methods', *Monographs of the Society for Research in Child Development*, **35**, (8, whole no. 141).

Staats, A.W., Minke, K.A. and Ban, P. (1984), 'L'apprentissage d'un repertoire langagier et al recherche experimentale longitudinale: l'apprentissage de l'imitation de la parole par un enfant non verbal' [The learning of a language repertoire and experimental–longitudinal research: learning verbal imitations by a non-verbal child], translation: A. Leduc, *Revue de modification du comportement*, **14**, 51–65.

Staats, A.W., Minke, K.A. and Butts, P. (1970), 'A token-reinforcement remedial reading program administered by black instructional technicians to backward black children', *Behavior Therapy*, **1**, 331–53.

Staats, A.W., Staats, C.K. and Crawford, H.L. (1962), 'First-order conditioning of a GSR', *Journal of General Psychology*, **67**, 159–67.

Staats, A.W., Finley, J.R., Minke, K.A. and Wolf, M.M. (1964), 'Reinforcement variables in the control of unit reading responses', *Journal of the Experimental Analysis of Behavior*, **7**, 139–49.

Staats, A.W., Gross, M.C., Guay, P.F. and Carlson, C.C. (1973), 'Personality and social systems and attitude-reinforcer-discriminative theory: interest (attitude) formation, function, and measurement', *Journal of Personality and Social Psychology*, **26**, 251–61.

Staats, A.W., Minke, K.A., Martin, C.H. and Higa, W.P. (1972), 'Deprivation-satiation and strength of attitude conditioning: a test of attitude-reinforcer-discriminative theory', *Journal of Personality and Social Psychology*, **24**, 178–85.

Staats, A.W., Staats, C.K., Schutz, R.E. and Wolf, M.M. (1962), 'The conditioning of reading responses using "extrinsic" reinforcers', *Journal of the Experimental Analysis of Behavior*, **5**, 33–40.

Staats, A.W., Staats, C.K., Heard, W.G. and Finley, J.R. (1962), 'Operant conditioning of factor analytic personality traits', *Journal of General Psychology*, **66**, 101–14.

Staats, C.K. and Staats, A.W. (1957), 'Meaning established by classical conditioning', *Journal of Experimental Psychology*, **54**, 74–80.

Sternberger, L.G. and Burns, G.L. (1991), 'Obsessions and compulsions in a college sample: distinctions between symptoms and diagnosis', *Behavior Therapy*, **22**, 569–76.

Taylor, H.G. (1988), 'Learning disabilities', in E.J. Mash and L.G. Terdal (eds.), *Behavioral Assessment of Childhood Disorders* (second edition), New York, NY: Guilford Press, pp. 402–50.

Taylor, H.G. (1989), 'Learning disabilities', in E.J. Mash and R.A. Barkely (eds.), *Treatment of Childhood Disorders*, New York, NY: Guilford Press, pp. 347–80.

Terman, L.M. and Merrill, M.A. (1937), *Measuring Intelligence*, Boston, MA: Houghton Mifflin.

Thorndike, R.L., Hagen, E.P. and Sattler, J.M. (1986), *Guide for Administering and Scoring the Stanford-Binet Intelligence Scale* (fourth edition), Chicago, IL: Riverside Publishing.

Treiber, F.A. and Lahey, B.B. (1985), 'A behavioral model of academic remediation with learning disabled children', in P.H. Bornstein and A.E. Kazdin (eds.), *Handbook of Clinical Behavior Therapy with Children*, Homewood, IL: Dorsey Press, pp. 742–71.

Tryon, W.W. (1990), 'Why paradigmatic behaviorism should be retitled psychological behaviorism', *The Behavior Therapist*, **13**, 127–8.

Tryon, W.W. and Briones, R.G. (1985), 'Higher-order semantic counterconditioning of Filipino women's evaluation of heterosexual behaviors', *Journal of Behavior Therapy and Experimental Psychiatry*, **16**, 125–31.

Turner, S.M., Beidel, D.C. and Stanley, M.A. (1992), 'Are obsessional thoughts and worry different cognitive phenomena?', *Clinical Psychology Review*, **12**, 257–70.

Ullman, L.P. and Krasner, L. (1969), *A Psychological Approach to Abnormal Behavior*, New York, NY: Prentice Hall.

Wanchisen, B.A. (1990), 'Forgetting the lessons of history', *The Behavior Analyst*, **13**, 31–8.

Watson, J.B. (1930), *Behaviorism*, rev. ed., Chicago, IL: University of Chicago Press.

Wechsler, D. (1967), *Wechsler Preschool and Primary Scale of Intelligence*, New York, NY: Psychological Corporation.

Wiederholt, J.L. and Bryant, B.R. (1986), *Gray Oral Reading Tests — Revised*, Los Angeles, CA: Western Psychological Services.

Woodcock, R.W. (1987), *Woodcock Reading Mastery Tests — Revised*, Circle Pines, MN: American Guidance Service.

Zettle, R.D. and Hayes, S.C. (1982), 'Rule-governed behavior: a potential theoretical framework for cognitive-behavior therapy', in P.C. Kendall (ed.), *Advances in Cognitive-behavioral Research and Therapy*, New York, NY: Academic Press.

8/ Social cognitive theory and personality

Daniel Cervone
University of Illinois at Chicago, USA

S. Lloyd Williams
Lehigh University, USA

Introduction

Social cognitive theory has evolved. Although its roots are found in behaviourism, it has developed far from its learning theory past. Contemporary social cognitive theory (Bandura, 1986) is founded on two key principles: (1) that human functioning is best understood in terms of reciprocal interactions among the environment, behaviour, and personal factors (including cognitive, affective, and physiological processes); (2) that within this model of reciprocal influences, the nature of persons is best understood in terms of a number of basic human capabilities; in particular, cognitive capabilities that enable people to learn about their environment, develop skills and competencies, reflect upon themselves, and evaluate, guide, and motivate their own behaviour. These principles do not merely differentiate the theory from behavioural approaches (for example, Skinner, 1953), they give it an entirely different focus. Although social cognitive theory addresses the influence of the environment on behaviour, it equally highlights personal determinants of action, the mechanisms through which individuals exert influence over their own lives and personal development.

In this chapter, we first describe the causal model that underlies social cognitive theory analyses and the nature and functioning of personality processes within this model. We then explore three recent areas of research that, we feel, constitute important developments in the social cognitive approach: the study of perceived self-efficacy in psychotherapeutic behaviour change, self-referent cognitive processes in goal-directed behaviour, and the causal impact of self-efficacy judgment on action. Finally, we examine social cognitive theory as a theory of personality. We consider relations between the social cognitive approach and some of the traditional theories and issues of personality psychology.

Reciprocal determinism

The natural starting place for any discussion of social cognitive theory is the principle of reciprocal determinism (Bandura, 1978b). Many theorists stress that personal and situational factors interact to determine behaviour (for example, Bowers, 1973; Magnusson and Endler, 1977; see Hettema and Kenrick, Chapter 15 in this volume). Although such conceptions have considerable virtue, any theoretical scheme that merely depicts social behaviour as being a function of personal and situational factors may overlook a number of important facts. First, personal and situational factors interact not merely in a predictive, statistical sense, but dynamically. Person factors influence the situations in which people find themselves. People select and avoid situations according to personal preferences and beliefs (Betz and Hackett, 1981; Emmons *et al.*, 1986; Snyder, 1981). Conversely, situational factors influence personality processes. Contextual factors partially govern the accessibility of personal beliefs (Higgins, 1987, 1990) and the activation of self-regulatory processes (Bandura and Cervone, 1983, 1986; Cervone *et al.*, 1991).

A second limitation of such formulations is their failure to acknowledge that social behaviour not only is affected by personal and situational factors, but also is a determinant of those factors. People's views of themselves are partly based on observations of their own behaviour (Bem, 1972). Actions evoke reactions in others, and thereby shape the environment (Buss, 1991; Snyder and Ickes, 1985). Thus, personal factors, situational influences, and social behaviour are best viewed as reciprocal determinants of one another. This principle of triadic reciprocal determinism serves as the guiding model of causality in social cognitive theory.

Although psychological factors influence each other reciprocally, they do not do so simultaneously. Influences exert their effects sequentially, over time. This makes possible empirical investigations of the sequential reciprocal relations among personal, environmental, and behaviour factors (for example, Cervone *et al.*, 1991; Wood and Bandura, 1989). The principle of reciprocal determinism, however, does not imply that all psychological research must investigate such complex, reciprocal relations. Much progress can be made by decomposing reciprocal influences; in other words, isolating and investigating particular segments of the larger universe of reciprocal determinants. This strategy is adopted in most of the research we will review in this chapter. Indeed, as a number of commentators have noted (Kihlstrom and Harackiewicz, 1990; Lerner, 1990), relatively few investigations have fully examined reciprocal interactions among personal, behavioural, and situational factors. The sheer complexity of assessing reciprocal relations among a diverse set of influences impedes such investigations. However, methodologies specifically designed to analyse dynamic reciprocal processes (for example, Thomas and Malone, 1979) may aid such research.

Basic human capabilities

From the perspective of personality psychology, the key questions that arise in this model of reciprocal determinism concern nature of the 'person factors'. How can one best conceptualize personality variables? What basic units of study have greatest utility in furthering our understanding of human functioning? Such relatively abstract theoretical questions have important implications. Basic theoretical conceptions shape empirical inquiries, interventions for personal and social problems, and, ultimately, the type of knowledge about human nature that one acquires.

Social cognitive theory analyses personality by examining the psychological processes through which people learn about themselves and the environment and orchestrate courses of action. The basic units of study in this analysis are the cognitive and affective processes that, in interaction with the environment, determine social behaviour. The theoretical goal, then, is to identify and characterize these personal determinants of action.

It should be noted that this focus on personal determinants of action differentiates social cognitive theory from trait or dispositional approaches (for example, Buss and Craik, 1983; John, 1989; McCrae and Costa, 1990; see Bandura, 1991; Cervone, 1991). Trait theories primarily are concerned with identifying broad dispositional tendencies and discovering a taxonomy of dispositions that is adequate to describe individual differences in the population (John, 1990). Charting broad dispositional tendencies can provide informative descriptive data about human conduct. However, it also can leave questions about the determinants of action unanswered (Buss and Craik, 1983). The social cognitive analysis shifts the focus 'from inferences about what broad traits a person *has*, to focus instead on what the person *does* [behaviourally, cognitively, and affectively] in particular conditions in the coping process' (Mischel, 1990, p. 116). This shift reflects the belief that investigating the cognitive and affective processes that function as personal determinants of action holds the greatest utility for improving our understanding of persons and our technologies for dealing with personal and social problems. We discuss distinctions between social cognitive theory and dispositional approach in greater detail later in this chapter.

People's ability to acquire knowledge and direct their behaviour rests on a set of basic human capabilities. These capabilities are the core elements of the social cognitive analysis of personality. They are the basic tools with which people address the requirements and tasks of social life. From a personality theory perspective, these capabilities encompass both the 'process' and the 'structure' aspects (Pervin, 1989b) of social cognitive theory. In other words, they include motivational processes that mediate social behaviour as well as cognitive structures that form the basis of enduring human competencies, values, preferences, and rules of conduct.

Symbolizing capability

The most basic of human capabilities is people's ability to use mental symbols. Thanks to their cognitive capabilities, people do not merely respond to the environment in a reflexive manner. Rather, people acquire and draw on symbolic representations that allow them to deal flexibly and adaptively with environmental demands. Knowledge of past errors and symbolic representations of optimal performance allow one to modify behaviour to meet situational requirements. The ability to use symbols enables people not only to adapt to a given environment, but also to envision alternative environments for themselves. Creative solutions to personal problems arise from the ability to envision alternatives and consider the consequences of potential courses of action.

Human language is perhaps the most complex and most pervasive example of people's ability to use symbols. Much of our cognitive activity involves linguistic symbols through which we assign meaning to events. Since these symbols are shared throughout a given culture, language enables people to communicate with others to learn whether their own interpretation of events is idiosyncratic or commonplace. The particular linguistic units a culture uses partly shape the nature of thought (Hunt and Agnoli, 1991).

The ability to store and draw upon symbolic representations of the world has important consequences not only for human learning, but also for motivation. Representations of future goals and possibilities for oneself can serve as incentives that motivate current behaviour. In their discussion of 'possible selves', Markus and Nurius (1986) argue that people's representations of their personal goals, hopes, and fears are cognitive factors that motivate and guide behaviour. People pursue courses of action in part based on the consequences of these behaviours for their future desired or undesired selves.

Symbolic representations of the environment are also critical to people's ability to overcome aversive situations. Mischel's programme of research on delay of gratification (Mischel *et al.*, 1989) vividly illustrates the behavioural consequences of alternative mental representations. When attempting to attain an attractive food reward, children who think about the consummatory properties of the reward are relatively unable to delay gratification. Alternative cognitions greatly facilitate delay behaviour. Dwelling on the physical features of the reward (Mischel and Baker, 1975) or mentally transforming it into an imagined picture of the object (Moore *et al.*, 1976) significantly facilitates delay behaviour. Thus, the nature of one's subjective, symbolic representation of the environment can powerfully influence the effectiveness of one's behaviour.

Symbolic representations of themselves engaging in adaptive coping actions can help people to master taxing situations and overcome severe distress reactions, as in various imagery-based therapies for maladaptive fears and inhibitions. In systematic desensitization (Wolpe, 1958), anxious clients imagine themselves attempting a graduated sequence of progressively more scary activities. In implosion (Stamfl and Levis, 1967), clients imagine themselves rapidly confronting their worst fears. In covert modelling (Kazdin, 1984), they envision someone else coping with the phobic stressor. A vast body of research reveals that such imagery benefits anxious individuals, lowering their fear and increasing their ability to cope with former threats (Bandura, 1969; Kazdin, 1984). Symbolic representations of action thus can continue to lasting changes in personality functioning by reducing self-defeating inhibitions and needless vulnerability to distress.

Social cognitive theory and cognitive psychology

The social cognitive theory analysis of symbolizing capabilities (Bandura, 1986), is, of course, highly influenced and informed by developments in cognitive science. Many cognitive psychologists see the ability to input, store, modify, and draw upon symbolic information as the defining characteristic of intelligent action (for example, Newell and Simon, 1976). From this perspective, 'the human brain is (at least) a physical symbol system' (Simon, 1990, p. 3).

Although social cognitive theory analyses are congruent with an information-processing perspective, it should be noted that social cognitive theory and mainstream cognitive science tend to focus on different aspects of human thinking. Social cognitive theory is deeply concerned with subjectively experienced cognitive states and the ways in which these cognitions serve as the basis for human agency. Through conscious reflection upon themselves and the environment, people are seen as causally contributing to their own motivation and achievement (Bandura, 1989). In contrast, these aspects of human thought have been seen to be relatively neglected in contemporary cognitive psychology (Bruner, 1990). Bruner laments that the development of computational models of cognition has led cognitive scientists to devote little attention to subjectively experienced mental states. He further argues that cognitive science remains cautious about considering intentional states to be causes of action, suggesting that the field 'is still chary of a concept of agency' (Bruner, 1990, p. 8).

A second difference in emphasis is that social cognitive theory highlights the mechanisms through which knowledge is translated into the execution of response patterns. Much research in cognitive psychology has investigated the representation of knowledge and the performance of cognitive skills, such as problem solving, decision making, or language (for example, Anderson, 1983). Somwhat less attention has been devoted to the performance of motor skills and social skills (for example, riding a bicycle, giving a public speech). Even when cognitive scientists have addressed such topics, they have devoted little consideration to the self-referent thinking processes that can enhance or impair the execution of response patterns. In contrast, social cognitive theory places great emphasis on self-referent cognitions thay may intervene between knowledge and action.

The ability to use and draw upon symbols is basic to each of the other distinct capabilities that are the focus of social cognitive theory.

Vicarious capability

We acquire much of our knowledge of the world through observation. The ability to encode and draw upon symbolic representations of observed events enables people to learn about the attractions, hazards, and behavioural requirements of social situations without experiencing them directly. In contrast to behavioural theories that emphasized learning through direct experience of rewarding and punishing consequences, social cognitive theory argues that vicarious processes are central to most human learning.

The proliferation of electronic media heightens the importance of vicarious processes in human affairs. Thanks to cable TV channels and instructional videos, people can learn from expert models who enact skilled performance in a diverse array of activities. Media displays not only aid in the development of skills. They also shape people's interests and values (Liebert and Sprafkin, 1988). Indeed, vicarious processes play a significant role in learning, motivation, and emotion.

Observational learning

The ability to acquire knowledge and skills through the observation of informative social cues is central to human learning. This capacity for observational learning often enables people to bypass tedious trial-and-error learning experiences. In novel situations, people do not need to start 'from scratch', relying on response consequences to shape behaviour gradually. Rather, by observing others, one can develop basic competencies prior to entering a new environment. This vicarious capability is not a mere convenience. Due to the costs of mis-steps, many situations utterly require such a competency. One cannot afford to learn to drive by testing out, in trial-and-error fashion, the effects of turning the wheel in various directions. Instead, one must have the capacity to execute correctly many components of the behaviour sequence the very first time.

Perhaps the most pervasive and important of cues for observational learning is the behaviour of other people. Through their actions, psychological models convey much of the information that one needs to function in society. Social skills are naturally developed and can be further enhanced by the observation of peers who display skilled performance (Ladd and Mize, 1983). It is important to recognize that such observational learning does not involve the mere mimicry of others' actions. Rather, observers abstract general strategies for dealing with problems (Rosenthal and Zimmerman, 1978). Research on aggression, for example, provides numerous examples in which modelling conveys generalized aggressive tactics and strategies (Bandura, 1973). For example, longitudinal studies reveal that observing large amounts of televised aggression at age 8 increases the level of aggression displayed at age 19 (Eron *et al.*, 1972). Clearly, teenagers are not continually enacting the same aggressive sequences they originally saw on TV crime shows and westerns in their childhood. Rather, children abstract generalized problem-solving styles from observing aggressive episodes (Eron, 1987). Cognitive representations of these aggressive strategies endure into adulthood. Social cues related to aggression can automatically activate these cognitive structures, thereby triggering aggressive responses (Huesmann, 1988).

Bandura (1986) provides a multiprocess analysis of observational learning. Observational learning is viewed as an information-processing activity that can be analysed in terms of a number of distinct stages, each of which is necessary for the acquisition of novel response patterns. The first stage involves attentional processes. For observational learning to succeed, one must attend to important aspects of the behaviour of a relevant model. Numerous factors influence the degree to which observers attend to a given modelled performance. People devote greater attention to modelled sequences that are vivid and easily discriminable, have proven functional value, contain attractive affective cues, and are enacted by individuals who are similar to themselves (Bandura, 1986; Rosenthal and Zimmerman, 1978). When encoding social information, individuals generally devote greater attention to people on whom they are dependent for valued outcomes (Neuberg and Fiske, 1987) or who are salient due to their having unique or 'solo' status in a group (Taylor and Fiske, 1978). The role of attentional factors in observational learning is most clearly revealed by detailed analyses of the direction of learners' visual attention during a modelling sequence. Yussen (1974) found that both vicarious rewards and vicarious punishments increased the frequency and duration of attention to a model. Measures of attention, in turn, predicted subsequent recall of the modelled actions.

The second stage in observational learning involves retention processes. Retaining accessible knowledge of the modelled sequence is, of course, necessary for future execution of the behaviour. Various mnemonic aids can enhance observers' retention of modelled sequences. Retention and later performance of complex motor responses is maximized when observers create verbal labels that summarize various aspects of the response (Gerst, 1971). Learning is also significantly enhanced by rehearsing vivid mental images of the modelled sequence or forming verbal descriptions of particular sequences (Gerst, 1971). Causal analyses provide evidence that the effects of verbal coding on reproduction accuracy are mediated by changes in the accuracy of cognitive representations of the behavioural sequence (Carroll and Bandura, 1990). After much task experience, individuals do not have to rely on such consciously recalled declarative information. With practice, performance becomes automatic; declarative knowledge is 'compiled' (Anderson, 1983), facilitating quick, efficient performance (see also Fitts, 1964).

Successfully executing a complex sequence of behaviours requires more than simply a mental representation of what needs to be done. Perfecting a skill requires practice. One must attempt the behaviour, attend to errors, and gradually refine one's efforts. The third stage of learning by observation thus involves production processes, through which individuals attempt to convert mental representations into appropriate behaviours. Carroll and Bandura (1982, 1985, 1987) describe the refinement of skills as a 'conception-matching' process. They suggest that individuals compare ongoing performance to a mental conception of desired performance and, when mismatches are detected, make adjustments to achieve a progressively closer match between conception and action. It is sometimes difficult if not impossible to detect such mismatches. On many activities, aspects of one's own performances are only partly observable. For example, when learning a sport such as golf or tennis, many critical aspects of the motor activity lie outside of one's field of vision. The learning of an action pattern can be greatly accelerated by providing learners with visual feedback (for example, through the use of video) after they first have formed an adequate mental representation of the desired behaviour (Carroll and Bandura, 1982).

Vicarious motivators

Vicarious processes not only play a role in the acquisition of knowledge and skills, they also influence the motivation and regulation of responses that already have been learned. Vicarious factors influence a number of distinct motivational processes. People's expectations about the outcomes that will follow a given response are partly based on the rewards and punishments they see others receive (Bandura *et al.*, 1963). Conceptions of one's own capabilities are affected by the performance of others who are similar to oneself (Brown and Inouye, 1978). When evaluating their own behaviour, people often adopt the standards that are used by others (Bandura and Kupers, 1964; Lepper *et al.*, 1975). Indeed, vicarious factors importantly influence each of the motivational processes that we will discuss throughout this chapter.

Particularly interesting are those instances in which a model's behaviours and verbal pronouncements conflict. Parents, for example, convey performance standards to their children through both action and instruction. Children are more likely to internalize stringent standards when practising and preaching coincide than when adults preach stringency but behave self-indulgently (Rosenhan *et al.*, 1968).

Vicarious processes in affective arousal and emotion

Vicarious processes are also heavily involved in the acquisition of emotional responses. Modelled emotions serve as cues that can readily elicit similar emotions in viewers. Theatre-goers respond to displays of mirth, sorrow, fear, or anger with similar reactions. Emotions can be 'contagious' in social gatherings. Of particular theoretical interest is the vicarious acquisition of stable emotional responses to formerly neutral cues. In vicarious affective learning, neutral stimuli become emotion arousing when an observer sees other people aroused by the stimuli (Berger, 1962).

Vicarious acquisition of phobic responses illustrates well the possibility that powerful enduring emotional and behavioural reactions can be acquired largely by vicarious means. Many snake phobics have never personally seen a snake, and virtually none has been bitten or otherwise traumatized by a snake (Bandura *et al.*, 1969). Their extreme distress and disability at even the thought of a snake appears often to have been acquired from observing fearful models (Murray and Foote, 1979; cf. Merckelbach *et al.*, 1991). It is likely that human fears are acquired by various pathways, including direct and vicarious experiences, verbally transmitted information, and genetic influences (Rachman, 1977). Retrospective studies with phobic individuals cannot easily disentangle the contributing factors. However, powerful experimental evidence has emerged that modelling alone can produce persistent, severe fears. Laboratory-reared rhesus monkeys, which initially display no fear towards snakes, quickly became intensely fearful upon observing wild-reared monkeys behaving fearfully towards snakes. The intense fear reactions were undiminished three months later (Cook *et al.*, 1985; Mineka *et al.*, 1984). Modelling can also serve to reduce a wide variety of fears and other negative emotional reactions (Rosenthal and Bandura, 1978), as we discuss in detail below.

Forethought and prediction

A central premise of social cognitive theory is that people regulate their behaviour on the basis of forethought. People anticipate what upcoming situations will be like, how they will react to those situations, and the consequences that are likely to follow from alternative action. This capability for forethought is based on people's ability not only to store information about past experiences, but to reason about that information, using acquired knowledge to predict what the future may be like.

Accurate prediction rests in large part on the ability to detect covariations among events. The ability to determine whether a given stimulus covaries with, and thereby signals, the occurrence of other stimuli has long been of interest in the conditioning literature. Increasingly, conditioning has come to be viewed as an information-processing activity (Brewin, 1988, 1989). Alloy and Tabachnik (1984) argue that, in both humans and animals, covariation detection involves an interaction of prior expectations with current stimulus information. When people have strong expectations about whether two events covary, their ability to detect stimulus information that is discrepant with their expectations is very poor (Nisbett and Ross, 1980). When people do not have strong expectations, they detect relations more accurately.

Prediction strategies and biases

In recent years, considerable progress has been made in understanding the processes through which people make judgments and predictions. One must often predict outcomes in contexts that involve great complexity and uncertainty. Predicting whether a client will respond to a therapeutic procedure, a job applicant will be a good employee, or a friend can be trusted with personal information are difficult judgment tasks. The relevant outcomes are affected by numerous factors, many of which cannot be known with certainty. Although there exist formal processes for optimizing judgments and decisions (DeGroot, 1970), it is generally impossible for the intuitive decision maker to engage in mental operations that resemble these optimizing procedures. Due to the limited capacity of information processing, people cannot accurately weigh and integrate large numbers of factors (Simon, 1983). In addition, time constraints may militate against a careful analysis of all relevant aspects of a problem.

People often based their predictions on relatively simple strategies, or judgmental heuristics (Tversky and Kahneman, 1974), that reduce complex inferential tasks to simple cognitive operations. For example, predictions may be based on the similarity between the information one has and the outcome under consideration (Kahneman and Tversky, 1972), or the subjective ease with which information suggestive of an outcome comes to mind (Schwarz *et al.*, 1991; Tversky and Kahneman, 1973). These simple strategies are quite functional; in general, they efficiently produce adequate judgments. However, reliance on simplifying heuristics can leave judgment open to systematic errors and biases that can have serious personal consequences (Nisbett and Ross, 1980). When motivated to do so, individuals are capable of engaging in more careful, self-critical thinking that can partially overcome these judgmental biases (Showers and Cantor, 1985). Knowing that one will be held accountable for one's judgments increases the complexity of cognitive processing and the accuracy of person prediction (Tetlock and Kim, 1987). Instruction in statistical reasoning can improve the quality of inferences (Nisbett *et al.*, 1987).

Rewards and punishments

The effects of rewards and punishments on social behaviour are largely mediated by forethought. The consequences that follow a response serve an informative function, influencing the expectancies people held regarding rewards and punishments that are likely in the future. Social cognitive theory recognizes the profound influence of rewards and punishments on social behaviour. However, this influence is best understood not as a simple conditioning process, but as a cognitive activity in which people's expectations about environmental contingencies mediate the effects of rewards and punishments on behaviour.

Expectations about environmental consequences can be more influential than the contingencies that are actually in effect. Kaufman, Baron and Kopp (1966) informed individuals that they would be rewarded on either a variable-interval, variable-ratio, or fixed-interval basis for performing a manual response. Although all subjects were actually rewarded on a fixed-interval schedule, their rates of performance strongly reflected the schedule they anticipated. Those who expected a variable-ratio schedule performed substantially more responses than subjects in the other groups.

Self-reflection

People do not just react to the environment. They see themselves acting in it. They consider the meaning and consequences of events for their well-being. They organize their actions in an attempt to attain a coherent, stable, and positive sense of self. These self-reflective processes give meaning to life. Baumeister (1989) suggests that people have basic 'needs for meaning'; in other words, ways in which they need their lives to make sense. These basic needs for meaning involve different aspects of self-reflective thought. People need to be able to justify their own actions, maintain a sense of esteem and self-worth, and develop feelings of personal efficacy (Baumeister, 1989).

Perceived self-efficacy

Of the various aspects of self-referent thought, perhaps none is more important to personality functioning than judgments of one's capability to do what is needed to cope effectively with life's demands and challenges. People must continually make decisions about what courses of action to follow and how long to pursue those they have undertaken. Perceptions of self-efficacy (Bandura, 1977), people's judgments of the level or type of performance they are capable of achieving in a given setting, play a critical role in such decisions. Relatively accurate appraisal of one's mental and physical capabilities is necessary for adaptive functioning. Believing that one can manage a task that lies far beyond one's abilities fosters action that is futile or even dangerous. Judging oneself unable to perform potentially rewarding activities needlessly limits opportunities for personal growth and gain.

Although it is maladaptive to be markedly unrealistic in appraising one's self-efficacy, it is sometimes adaptive to slightly overestimate what one can manage. Slight overoptimism can motivate efforts toward enriching self-development that more realistic efficacy judgments would prevent. Overestimating self-efficacy may actually promote mental health by insulating people from depressing awareness of their own limitations (Bandura, 1990; Bjorklund and Green 1992; Taylor and Brown, 1988).

In social cognitive theory, self-efficacy judgments influence not only choice behaviour, but also the effort people expend, and how much they persist in the face of difficulties, failures, and aversive experiences (Bandura and Cervone, 1983, 1986; Schunk, 1984; Weinberg *et al.*, 1979). People who have greater confidence in their performance capabilities display greater effort and persistence in facing challenges and difficulties (Brown and Inouye, 1978; Cervone, 1989; Cervone and Peake, 1986; Peake and Cervone, 1989; Stock and Cervone, 1990) and in tolerating aversiveness (Bandura *et al.*, 1987; Williams and Kinney, 1991). They more readily enter into challenging environments (Betz and Hackett, 1986).

The sense of self-efficacy also affects thought patterns and emotional reactions. Self-doubt in the face of potential dangers gives rise to anticipated calamities, feelings of fear, and physiological distress (Bandura *et al.*, 1977, 1982, 1985, 1988; Williams and Watson, 1985; Williams *et al.*, 1984, 1985). Threat is not a fixed property of events or circumstances, but rather a perception resulting from weighing the relation between potential dangers in the environment and one's ability to manage them. A view down a steep snowy slope can be either terrifying or delightful, depending upon one's self-perceived skiing capabilities. In the social cognitive analysis, anxiety results not only from inefficacy for coping behaviourally with perceived threat, but also from inefficacy for controlling scary trains of thought (Bandura, 1988). It is not the sheer frequency of distressing thoughts, but the perceived ability to turn them off, that bears more directly on fear arousal (Kent, 1987; Kent and Gibbons, 1987; Salkovskis and Harrison, 1984).

Depression and despondency, on the other hand, are partly the result of doubts about being able to do what is necessary to achieve valued personal goals. Such inefficacy leads people to be preoccupied with their deficiencies, feel down on themselves, and become depressed (Beck *et al.*, 1979; Cutrona and Troutman, 1986; Holahan and Holahan, 1987; Kanfer and Zeiss, 1983; Seligman, 1975; Stanley and Maddux, 1986).

Self-efficacy judgments and outcome expectations

Many theories of motivation and personality emphasize the role of outcome expectations; that is, people's thoughts regarding the consequences or outcomes that are likely to follow a given action (Atkinson, 1964; Bolles, 1975; Rotter, 1966; Seligman, 1975; Tolman, 1932). Self-efficacy judgments are conceptually distinct from outcome expectations. Self-efficacy judgments refer to beliefs about whether one can execute a particular course of action, as opposed to expectations about what outcomes might accrue if that action were to be performed. I can judge myself quite capable of doing something that I think would produce undesirable outcomes (for example, park illegally in Manhattan), and judge myself quite *un*able to do something that I think would produce desirable outcomes (for example, compose lovely music).

Outcome expectations are a powerful source of motivation. Environmental consequences influence behaviour largely by creating and altering expectations about action—outcomes relationships. Outcome expectations can affect behaviour independently of efficacy judgments. Other things being equal, people are most likely to do what they expect to be rewarding than what they expect to be unrewarding, aversive, or harmful. On the other hand, efficacy judgments also comprise an independent source of motivation. However marvellous the outcomes of an action might seem, people will not attempt it or persist at it if they profoundly disbelieve they can execute it. Students may be sure that earning a medical degree will result in a lucrative career, but if they believe themselves incapable of managing the mathematics and physical science requirements, they will not choose pre-medical training. Resolute effective action requires both positive outcome expectations and positive self-efficacy judgments.

Although self-efficacy judgments and outcome expectations are conceptually distinct constructs, empirically they are often strongly related. In many circumstances, the outcomes one experiences are a function of how well one executes antecedent actions. Inept social approach fosters rejection, whereas adept approach fosters welcoming acceptance. Academic honours are contingent on the successful demonstration of intellectual skills. When actions and outcomes are strongly linked, outcome expectations will be partly a function of one's level of self-efficacy. Conversely, efficacy judgments and outcome expectations may be unrelated when powerful social forces intervene between actions and outcomes. Victims of social prejudice learn that the quality of their performances and their professional advancement are unrelated. Thus, their efficacy beliefs and outcomes expectations are quite distinct.

Generality and specificity of self-efficacy perceptions

Self-efficacy judgments are not conceived as broad response dispositions, but as domain-specific judgments of whether one can manage particular kinds of activity. People almost always have a high sense of efficacy for some activities but low self-efficacy for others. It is difficult to be competent — or incompetent — in every possible human endeavour. Even within a general domain, efficacy judgments might vary dramatically as a function of seemingly subtle situational differences. The introductory psychology instructor may lecture confidently on theories of personality, but be filled with dread at the prospect of delivering a lecture on the nervous system.

This is not to say that efficacy perceptions are entirely bound to specific activities. People may have a generalized sense of efficacy across a range of activities they see as functionally related. Successes can produce relatively generalized gains in self-efficacy; indeed, self-efficacy theory arose from the observation that phobics who mastered their dread of snakes often reported, at follow-up evaluations, that they had gained the confidence to tackle other, quite distinct inhibitions and anxieties (Bandura *et al.*, 1977). A recent analysis of therapeutic change revealed both the generality and specificity of perceptions of self-efficacy (Williams *et al.*, 1989). People with agoraphobia (multiple phobias of activities away from home such as driving, shopping, crossing bridges, and ascending heights) each received performance mastery treatment for some phobic areas, while other phobic areas were left untreated. In the treated areas, subjects displayed large gains in self-efficacy and coping behaviour. In their transfer phobias, subjects showed highly variable and idiosyncratically patterned degrees of change. For example, if two individuals were successfully treated for driving phobia, one might show a large gain in self-efficacy for ascending heights but no gains for shopping, whereas the other might show the reverse pattern. Thus, the findings reveal specificity in that transfer phobias improved only about half as much as treated ones. They reveal generality in that transfer phobias of treated subjects improved significantly as compared to the phobias of subjects who received no treatment. We return to the issue of the contextual definition and assessment of efficacy judgments below.

Sources of efficacy information

Social cognitive theory addresses not only the consequences of self-efficacy judgment but also the personal and environmental influences that create feelings of efficacy or inefficacy. Bandura (1977, 1986) outlines four principal sources of information for judging one's self-efficacy: performance accomplishments, vicarious experiences, verbal persuasion, and physiological arousal.

Performance accomplishments are the most potent source of efficacy information because they are based on first-hand experience of success and mastery. Self-efficacy and accomplishments are linked reciprocally. Successes tend to increase efficacy perceptions, which in turn promote further success. However, the effect of attainments on efficacy judgments is not automatic. Self-efficacy perceptions are a product of cognitive processing in which individuals access, interpret, and integrate information. Those who focus on difficult aspects of an activity (Cervone, 1989), attribute success to external, unstable factors (Weiner, 1985), or are in a negative mood-state that biases information processing (Kavanagh and Bower, 1985; Salovey and Birnbaum, 1989) may judge themselves relatively inefficacious in the absence of corresponding negative performances. Thus, similar attainments can differentially affect the efficacy perceptions of different people (Bandura *et al.*, 1982). Idiosyncratic cognitive processing of attainments contributes to the generality and specificity of treatment gains (Williams *et al.*, 1989).

People partly base self-efficacy judgments on vicarious experiences, the observed or imagined actions of others. Vicarious influences are apt to be especially potent when people have relatively few first-hand experiences from which to judge, or when those experiences contain mixed or ambiguous information about their functional capabilities. Because vicarious sources are less trustworthy, in that their personal relevance is more open to question than that of first-hand experiences, they are a less potent means of enhancing self-efficacy (Bandura and Adams, 1977; Bandura *et al.*, 1977, 1980, 1982). One interesting technique for enhancing the perceived relevance of an observed performance is self-modelling, in which individuals observe themselves on videotapes that are edited to display desired target behaviours (Dowrick, 1983). Self-modelling has been applied successfully in diverse settings, such as the training of individuals with physical handicaps (Dowrick and Hood, 1981) and the enhancement of skilled athletic performance (Dowrick, 1989).

Verbal persuasion — trying to convince someone by conversation that they can function effectively — is a common but relatively weak mode of instating efficacy beliefs (Biran and Wilson, 1981). Persuasion can, however, have some value if combined with more potent sources. For example, encouragement to try tasks, given with assurance that the person might well do better than they expect, can facilitate attempts at mastery. Enduring changes in efficacy perceptions, however, generally result from the performance itself. If persuasory messages unrealistically inflate self-efficacy perceptions, disconfirming negative experiences will quickly erase the temporary boosts in self-perceptions. Persuasion probably has more potency in undermining self-efficacy than enhancing it, since those who are persuaded they cannot succeed will not attempt an endeavour, thereby validating their self-doubts.

Physiological states provide another source of efficacy information. People may interpret perceived autonomic arousal as a sign of impending inability to cope, or lack of arousal as a sign that they can handle a situation. In athletic activities, people judge their efficacy partly by how tired, winded, or sore they feel. Autonomic reactions are generally a weak source of information because people know from experience that how their viscera feel tells them relatively little about what they can do. People are notoriously poor at estimating their autonomic arousal (for example, Mandler, 1962), thus making it a treacherous guide in any case. Moreover, even if they could accurately perceive their visceral stirrings, they would be badly misled because of the empirically poor relationship between physiological arousal and coping capabilities (Bandura, 1986; Lang, 1971; Williams, 1987). A pounding heart can mean 'fired up' or 'exhilarated' for one person, but 'terrified' for another. It is the interpretation more than the arousal *per se* that will determine the effects on self-efficacy.

Self-regulation: personal standards and self-evaluation

People's cognitive abilities enable them to direct and regulate their own behaviour. Rather than merely responding to rewards and punishments in the immediate environment, people plan courses of action that are directed toward distal aims. They judge whether their ongoing behaviour is succeeding or failing in meeting those aims. They adjust their efforts in response to discrepancies between attainments and standards (Bandura, 1978a,b; Carver and Scheier, 1981).

In social cognitive theory, personal standards and self-evaluative reactions serve as central mechanisms in the self-regulation of behaviour. Standards are criteria used to evaluate the acceptability or quality of outcomes (Higgins, 1990). Personal performance standards, then, are the criteria people use in evaluating their own actions. On valued tasks, individuals generally develop clear criteria for evaluating their own performance. These criteria may be based on one's own prior accomplishments, the achievements of others, and one's personal desires for success on the task. In the course of performing an activity, people will frequently judge the relation between the outcomes they achieve and these standards.

The comparison of outcomes to personal standards is not a 'cold' cognitive process. Rather, discrepancies between outcomes and standards generate strong affective reactions. People experience pride and self-satisfaction upon meeting challenging aims. Outcomes judged as sub-standard foster dissatisfaction and self-criticism. Appraising an event as being either congruent or incongruent with one's goals largely determines whether one's resulting emotions are positive or negative (Lazarus, 1991). Different types of standard foster different classes of emotion in reaction to negative events. When standards represent ideals that one would like to possess, sub-standard performances generate feelings of dejection. When standards represent demands people feel they ought to achieve, inadequate performances generate anxiety and agitation (Higgins, 1987; Higgins *et al.*, 1986). Chronic negative evaluations that stem from excessively high standards may predispose one to depression (Ahrens, 1987; Rehm, 1977).

Self-evaluative reactions serve an important motivational function. People can motivate their own behaviour by making self-satisfaction contingent upon achieving desired outcomes. When performances fall short of standards, self-dissatisfaction spurs individuals to take corrective action. Those who are highly dissatisfied with sub-standard performances exert great effort to change, whereas individuals who react to the same performances in a complacent manner show little improvement (Bandura and Cervone, 1983, 1986). Through self-evaluative processes, people can motivate themselves to work toward challenging standards of achievement even in the relative absence of external constraints or rewards for behaviour. The achievements of artists, writers, and athletes in solitary training provide vivid testimony to this human capacity for self-direction. We consider the role of self-evaluative processes in self-directed motivation in detail below.

Perceived self-efficacy and psychological treatment

Self-efficacy-based psychological treatment

Theories of personality must be judged in part by their capacity to generate effective methods of helping people overcome personality problems. Identifying effective means of helping people change has long been a focus of social cognitive theory (Bandura, 1969); indeed, self-efficacy theory was originally proposed as a step 'toward a unifying theory of behavioural change' (Bandura, 1977). Self-efficacy theory generally prescribes performance-based mastery experiences as central elements in treatment programmes because such experiences are the most potent source of information for building a strong sense of efficacy (Bandura, 1977). It has become increasingly clear over the past two decades that performance-based models of treatment are among the most effective for a variety of problems, such as phobias (Bandura *et al.*, 1969; Leitenberg, 1976), compulsions (Roper *et al.*, 1975), sexual dysfunctions (Masters and Johnson, 1970; Wolpe and Lazarus, 1966), eating problems (Wilson *et al.*, 1986), and depression (Beck *et al.*, 1979; Lewinsohn *et al.*, 1982).

Interpretations of performance treatment of phobias often heavily emphasize the non-cognitive concept of 'exposure' to phobic stimuli (Marks, 1978). This likens treatment to a classical extinction procedure. Performance purportedly functions simply to bring clients into proximity to scary stimuli, until a mechanistic deconditioning of anxiety occurs. The exposure principle not only has serious conceptual failings (Williams, 1987, 1988, 1990), but it gives therapists little guidance as to optimal procedures to follow, beyond the generalized suggestion somehow to bring clients into some kind of prolonged commerce with phobic stimuli. The exposure perspective emphasizes neither active performance accomplishments, nor how therapists might assist clients in tackling difficult tasks, nor the quality of clients' performance of scary tasks. All that seems to matter (both in theory and in procedural accounts) is urging clients to place themselves for prolonged periods in proximity to scary stimuli, usually on their own between therapy sessions (Williams, 1987). The high rate of failure and limited improvement with such exposure therapies (Barlow and Wolfe, 1981) called for development of a more specific technology of performance-based treatment.

In treatment based on self-efficacy theory, or *guided mastery therapy* (Williams, 1990), the emphasis is not on mere stimulus exposure, but on the quality and amount of information people gain about what they can manage, and the sense of effectiveness they thereby develop. Time and fear arousal are incidental, since what counts is rapid mastery irrespective of initial fear levels. During therapeutic performance, people are not passively absorbing stimuli, but actively mastering a challenge. Therapists, too, play an active role. Severe phobics generally require more than mere urging to expose themselves to the most terrifying situations for prolonged periods. Such a prescription is more easily given than filled. The therapist must assist people to tackle tasks that otherwise would be too difficult, and thereby create an interim increase in self-efficacy, which will enable the person to tackle yet more challenging tasks, continuing in an ascending spiral of therapeutic change. The mastery therapist also helps clients do tasks more proficiently, free of embedded defensiveness and self-restrictions that limit the sense of accomplishment. Once the person's progress and proficient performance are restored, the therapist withdraws the assistance, and arranges for people to have varied and independent success experiences so their sense of mastery will be unconditional. In the exposure view, in contrast, such active therapist assistance could be construed as *reducing* exposure because it might reduce anxiety and the threat value of the stimuli.

Guided mastery treatment has been applied successfully to a wide range of phobias, including agoraphobia and mixed multiphobic conditions (Williams *et al.*, 1984; Williams and Zane, 1989), social phobias (Mattick and Peters, 1988), and specific phobias (for example, Bandura *et al.*, 1969, 1974, 1977, 1985; Ost *et al.*, 1991; Williams *et al.*, 1985). The most exacting and direct test of guided mastery is to compare it to the same or longer duration of 'pure' stimulus exposure. Seven studies have compared one group of phobic subjects who received a varied repertoire of guided mastery aids during therapeutic performance to a comparison group receiving strong encouragement to remain fully exposed to the same scary stimuli, but few specific mastery aids (Bandura *et al.*, 1974; Bourque and Ladouceur, 1980; O'Brien and Kelley, 1980; Ost *et al.*, 1991; Williams *et al.*, 1984, 1985; Williams and Zane, 1989). Six of the seven (excluding only the Bourque and Ladouceur study) found therapist-guided mastery to be substantially superior to mere exposure. These findings illustrate that self-efficacy theory is a powerful guide for structuring treatments to achieve maximal therapeutic impact.

We have discussed the application of self-efficacy theory to phobic problems at some length in part because phobia was the first area to which self-efficacy theory was applied, and partly because of our own interest in phobias. However, self-efficacy theory has been successfully applied to domains such as health behaviour (O'Leary, 1985), pain (Bandura *et al.*, 1987; Williams and Kinney, 1991), sports performance (Weinberg *et al.*, 1979), organizational management (Wood and Bandura, 1989), addictive behaviour (DiClemente, 1986), career development (Betz and Hackett, 1986), and others. These areas of investigation lie beyond the scope of the present chapter, but the diversity of domains of applicability provide eloquent testimony to the explanatory breadth and generality of self-efficacy theory.

Self-efficacy, control and stress

Personality psychologists have increasingly recognized the importance of feelings of efficacy and personal control for psychological well-being and physical health (Abramson *et al.*, 1978; Lazarus and Folkman, 1984; Miller, 1979a,b; Mineka and Kelly, 1989; O'Leary, 1985). The perceived ability to prevent, control, or mitigate aversive events has benefits beyond merely being able to predict the events. Individuals who can influence the rate, intensity, or pattern of aversive events will be less distressed and vulnerable to depression or fear than others who do not exercise influence, even when the actual aversive events experienced are identical (Miller, 1989; Seligman, 1975). Exposure to stressors without control impairs components of the immune system, whereas the same stressors with control have no adverse physiological impact (Maier *et al.*, 1985). The benefits of perceived control are evident even when one does not make any controlling responses; the mere belief that they can potentially exercise control shields people from distress (Miller, 1989; Mineka, 1985; Sanderson *et al.*, 1989).

The causal link between perceptions of self-efficacy and physiological stress and immune reactions has been established in research with phobic subjects whose initial low self-efficacy for coping with phobic stressors produces high levels of autonomic arousal and plasma catecholamine release. These individuals quickly gain a sense of self-efficacy when given performance mastery experiences, which rapidly eliminate their stress reactions toward the phobic object (Bandura *et al.*, 1982, 1985). Interestingly, exposure to stressors while rapidly acquiring a sense of mastery over them enhances immune functioning, but when the gains in self-efficacy are slow, exposure to stressors tends to suppress the immune system (Wiedenfeld *et al.*, 1990).

Self-referent cognitions in goal-based motivation and performance

Psychologists working from a variety of theoretical perspectives have analysed people's personal standards and goals for performance. Level of aspiration research (Lewin *et al.*, 1944), control theory models (Campion and Lord, 1982; Carver and Scheier, 1981, 1990; Miller *et al.*, 1960), and theories of achievement motivation (for example, Heckhausen, 1967) accord prominent status to people's standards for behaviour and reactions to performance feedback. Clinical programmes foster self-regulated behaviour change by teaching clients to monitor their behaviour in relation to well-specified behaviour-change goals (Thoresen and Mahoney, 1974; Watson and Tharp, 1977). A number of sub-processes are seen as important to successful self-regulation, including monitoring one's performance, evaluating attainments, and self-rewarding desirable outcomes (Kanfer, 1980).

Recent years have witnessed a resurgence of interest in goal concepts in personality psychology. Many investigators suggest that personality is best characterized in terms of the aims, aspirations, and goals toward which individuals are working at various points in their lives (see Buss and Cantor, 1989; Pervin, 1989a). Identifying individuals' personal goals and aims can enable one to understand why they adopt particular courses of action, and how different actions relate to one another in serving a larger purpose.

Perhaps the most extensive body of empirical research on goal setting, motivation, and performance is found not in mainstream personality or social psychology, but in organizational psychology. Locke's (1968; Locke and Latham, 1990) goal theory proposes that performance goals, aims one is trying to achieve on an activity, serve as immediate regulators of action. Goal theory identifies a number of dimensions along which goals can differ. One dimension is goal difficulty: people's aims can vary in the level or quality of performance they require. As long as individuals accept and remain committed to their goals, more difficult goals foster superior achievement (Mento *et al.*, 1987; Tubbs, 1986; Wood *et al.*, 1987). A second dimension is goal specificity. A student could decide to 'get as much reading done as I can' in an evening or, alternatively, could set a specific goal of trying to read *X* pages. More than 90 per cent of studies comparing specific and non-specific goals demonstrate the clear superiority of specific goal setting (Locke *et al.*, 1981). Finally, goals can differ in proximity. Although 'graduating in four years with a 3.5 GPA' and 'getting a 3.5 GPA this semester' may be equally difficult and specific ideals, their considerable difference in proximity can have important implications. Motivation is most reliably enhanced by proximal goals that give immediate direction to one's action and, when achieved, provide salient markers of progress (Bandura and Schunk, 1981; Stock and Cervone, 1990).

In order for goals to have a strong motivational impact, individuals must receive feedback on their ongoing performance. Lasting motivational effects result not merely from having a challenging aim in mind, but from being able to monitor one's progress toward that aim. The superiority of a combination of goals and feedback over either factor alone has been demonstrated in a variety of domains (Bandura and Cervone, 1983; Becker, 1978; Kazdin, 1974; Stevenson *et al.*, 1984). Feedback facilitates the effects of both assigned and self-set goals (Erez, 1977), and most strongly affects performance when attainments fall markedly short of one's standard (Matsui *et al.*, 1983).

One important qualification to these goal effects involves task complexity. Until recently, most goal-setting research has involved relatively simple activities for which subjects already possessed the rudimentary knowledge and skills necessary to succeed (Mento *et al.*, 1987; Wood *et al.*, 1987). Although useful, such tasks may not tap processes critical to performance on cognitively complex activities, such as the development of task strategies (Christensen-Szalanski, 1980; Locke *et al.*, 1984). Goal effects are weaker on cognitively complex tasks (Wood *et al.*, 1987), on which successful performance requires the development and testing of strategic knowledge.

This extensive body of findings on the effects of goal setting naturally raises the question of how goals enhance achievement. Why do individuals with concrete, challenging, proximal goals (such as 'reduce food intake to 1,400 calories a day') so frequently outperform those with ambiguous, value, or long-range aims ('drop some of this darned weight')? There are two senses in which one can answer this question. The first addresses behavioural mechanisms through which goals enhance achievement. The second concerns the psychological processes through which goals affect these behaviours.

Goals affect achievement through a number of behavioural mechanisms (Locke and Latham, 1990). Commitment to challenging goals enhances effort. People exert greater physical effort (Bandura and Cervone, 1983; Earley *et al.*, 1987) and work at higher rates of performance (Sales, 1970) under challenging goal conditions. A related mechanism is task persistence. Success often requires 'sticking to' a task. Challenging, proximal goals can enhance persistence in diverse domains (Huber and Neale, 1987; LaPorte and Nath, 1976; Stock and Cervone, 1990). Thirdly, goals serve a directional function, directing effort and attention to important aspects of a task (Rothkopf and Billington, 1975, 1979) and guiding information processing so that individuals more thoroughly process goal-relevant information (Cohen and Ebbesen, 1979; Hoffman *et al.*, 1981).

Self-referent processes in goal motivation

Social cognitive theory addresses not only these behavioural mechanisms, but also the cognitive processes through which goals and feedback affect the behaviours. From a social cognitive theory perspective, the motivational power of goal setting derives not from the goals themselves, but from the influence of a set of self-referent thinking processes, or self-regulatory processes. When people work towards a specific goal or standard, they will periodically gauge the relation between this standard and their actual attainments. This comparison of goals and attainments can generate a number of different types of reaction to one's performance. Three classes of self-reaction are seen as central to the regulation of goal-directed action: self-evaluative reactions to one's performance, judgments of self-efficacy, and personal goal setting.

Affective, self-evaluative reactions to one's performance serve as an important source of self-motivation. Self-criticism of one's inadequate attainments can spur people to greater effort. People can motivate themselves over long periods of time by making self-satisfaction contingent on reaching an internalized performance standard (Bandura, 1989).

Superior attainments generally foster more positive self-evaluations. However, factors other than sheer positivity and negativity of outcome influence people's reactions. Those who view a performance standard as internally generated experience different reactions to failure from those whose standards are externally imposed (Higgins, 1987). Level of attainment and self-evaluation are more strongly linked when individuals highly value an activity (Simon, 1979). Satisfaction is related not only to the magnitude of outcomes, but to the rate at which outcomes change over time (Hsee and Abelson, 1991; Hsee *et al.*, 1991).

A second motivational process involves perceptions of self-efficacy. Successfully regulating one's goal-directed performance requires a sense that one is capable of reaching the standard. As noted elsewhere in this chapter, much work documents the impact of self-efficacy judgment on the behaviours that are responsible for the performance effects of goal setting.

Self-efficacy judgments can influence behaviour both directly and through their effect on a third self-regulatory mechanism: personal standards, or self-set goals for performance. In the course of performing an activity, individuals may redefine or reinterpret their aims, raising or lowering their personal performance goals (Campion and Lord, 1982). Commitment to these adjusted standards can strongly influence subsequent efforts.

Various social and personal factors influence the standards that people adopt. Those who view models displaying high performance standards adopt stringent standards for themselves (Bandura and Kupers, 1964; Bandura *et al.*, 1967; Lepper *et al.*, 1975). Individuals with a stronger sense of self-efficacy set higher personal goals (Bandura and Cervone, 1986; Wood *et al.*, 1990) and remain more committed to achieving them (Locke *et al.*, 1984). When goals are externally assigned, more authoritative figures foster greater goal commitment (Locke and Latham, 1990).

Differential engagement of self-regulatory influences

Self-regulatory influences are not static motivational forces, but dynamic psychological processes that are differentially activated, or engaged, by different performance environments. Different settings, in other words, affect the degree to which individuals engage in self-referent thinking, and the degree to which self-referent processes contribute to performance.

Of particular interest is the role of alternative goal and feedback systems in activating self-regulatory processes. Individuals may often lack clear goals for performance or specific feedback on their efforts. Indeed, many behaviour-change efforts must begin by teaching people to translate vague aims into specific goals and to monitor their progress explicitly (Watson and Tharp, 1977). Social systems may fail to provide explicit goals and feedback. For example, graduate students may complain justifiably that it is impossible for them to tell 'how they're doing' because of a lack of explicit feedback from faculty.

The presence or absence of specific goals and feedback should moderate the strength of relations between self-regulatory processes and performance. The reason for this is that appraisals and evaluations of one's performance are based largely on the comparison of goals to ongoing efforts. In the absence of relatively specific performance feedback, one cannot make such comparisons. In the absence of clear performance standards, such comparisons are inherently ambiguous. Under either of these conditions, outcomes are unlikely to elicit strong self-reactions, and performance, in turn, should be only weakly affected by self-referent thinking. The hypothesis that varying goal and feedback conditions moderate the impact of self-regulatory processes has been tested in two very different domains: effortful physical performance (Bandura and Cervone, 1983, 1986), and complex decision making (Cervone *et al.*, 1991; Cervone and Wood, 1991).

Bandura and Cervone (1983) investigated the role of self-regulatory processes in performance of an effortful aerobic task. Subjects performed the task for three sessions under conditions that factorially manipulated the presence/absence of challenging assigned goals, and the presence/absence of performance feedback. After the first session, half the subjects were assigned the goal of improving their initial performance by 40 per cent. After the second session, subjects receiving feedback were told that their performance had improved by 24 per cent. Thus, when goals are combined with feedback, subjects faced a marked negative discrepancy between attainments and goals. Self-regulatory processes were assessed via direct self-report during a break period between the second and third sessions.

As shown in Figure 8.1, left panel, the combination of challenging goals and clear feedback substantially boosted performance, with subjects increasing by an average of more than 50 per cent — a particularly notable increase in the third session of a highly fatiguing task. The other three conditions were, in terms of mean output,

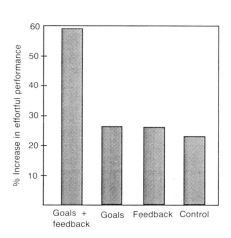
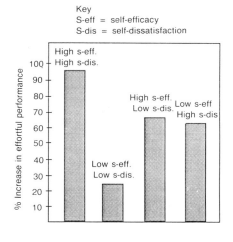

Figure 8.1 Mean percentage increase in effortful performance (Source: Bandura and Cervone, 1983)

The left panel displays mean change in performance in experimental conditions combining goals with feedback, providing goals alone, feedback alone, or neither of these factors. The right panel displays performance within the condition combining goals and feedback, as a function of differential combinations of self-dissatisfaction with performance and perceived self-efficacy for goal attainment.

equivalent and substantially below the goal + feedback group. Neither goals in the absence of performance feedback, nor knowledge of one's performance in the absence of challenging goals, increased motivation in this session.

Although, in general, the combination of challenging goals and feedback markedly increased performance, there were substantial individual differences in performance *within* this experimental condition. When faced with a discrepancy between goals and attainments, some subjects were highly dissatisfied with themselves, whereas others reacted with relative complacency. Some remained confident of their capabilities, whereas others suffered from a low sense of efficacy. These differential reactions strongly predicted variations in performance within this condition (Figure 8.1, right panel). Subjects who retained a high sense of efficacy and were highly dissatisfied with sub-standard attainments nearly doubled their output. Those who were satisfied with their performance and lacked a strong sense of efficacy improved only marginally. As predicted, these relations between performance and both self-evaluation and perceived self-efficacy held only within the condition combining assigned goals with feedback. In the other conditions, the relations were variable and substantially weaker.

The type and magnitude of discrepancy between goals and feedback also affects the degree to which self-processes regulate effort expenditure. Falling far short of a valued goal generates a qualitatively different set of cognitive and affective reactions from coming close to meeting the standard. Subsequent research employing the same aerobic task (Bandura and Cervone, 1986) again found that when attainments fall markedly short of one's goal, higher perceptions of efficacy and greater dissatisfaction with one's performance spur individuals to greater effort. However, when subjects learned that their performance fell just slightly short of their goal, the determinants of motivation were strikingly different. Under this condition, some subjects remained committed to their assigned performance goal. Others responded to their near miss by setting higher goals for themselves. Still others apparently become discouraged by their near miss and abandoned the assigned goal, setting lower personal goals for themselves. These variations in self-set goals were highly predictive of changes in performance, accounting for nearly two-thirds of the variance in performance change (Bandura and Cervone, 1986). Interestingly, under this circumstance, subjects' self-set goals were unrelated to their perceptions of self-efficacy or self-evaluative reactions, neither of which contributed to changes in performance. Such 'near-miss' conditions are deserving of further study. People's reactions may depend, in part, on whether they can easily envision alternative actions that would have brought success (Kahneman and Tversky, 1982).

Research by Podsakoff and Farh (1989) provides additional evidence of the differential engagement of self-efficacy processes. Self-efficacy judgments strongly predicted increments in performance on an object-listing task when subjects received negative feedback, but were unrelated to performance in a positive feedback condition. On tasks that are not physically taxing, performances generally are easily replicable. Success feedback will quell people's doubts about their capabilities, whereas failure feedback causes people to dwell on their capabilities for future action.

Self-regulatory influences on complex performance

Recent work has investigated a cognitive complex setting, dynamic decision making (Wood and Bailey, 1985). Decision making in complex, dynamic settings requires considerable self-directed effort. One must attend to multiple cues, monitor the effects of decision options, and develop and test task strategies. Success results not from the sheer application of effort but from the systematic development and application of knowledge about the task. Self-reactions to performance are particularly important because, although systematically testing strategic options is necessary for success, novel task strategies occasionally do fail. One's reactions to setbacks can influence decision efforts and the eventual quality of performance (Wood and Locke, 1990). A series of studies by Wood and Bandura (Bandura and Jourdan, 1991; Bandura and Wood, 1989; Wood and Bandura, 1989; Wood et al., 1990) demonstrates that self-efficacy perceptions influence the quality of analytic thinking and complex decision making. Individuals with a strong sense of self-efficacy develop more effective strategies, learn more from feedback, respond more adaptively to the decision environment, and, over time, are better able to translate their learning into improved performance.

The effect of self-referent thinking on complex performance has been investigated using a computer-based simulation of business decision making (Wood and Bailey, 1985). Subjects manage a simulated small business organization. They make a series of decisions about a set of employees, and receive numerical feedback on the performance of each employee after each set of decisions. By using this feedback to vary and test decision options systematically over a series of trials, one can discover relations between decision options and organizational performance and thereby increase the organization's efficiency (Wood and Bailey, 1985).

According to the social cognitive theory model of self-referent thinking and performance, different goal conditions should moderate the degree to which self-regulatory processes affect complex decision making. Cervone *et al.* (1991) got subjects to perform the decision-making task under conditions that involved either no specific goal or a specific, challenging standard. Subjects received feedback on their performance after each trial. Findings revealed that self-regulatory processes and decision performance are strongly reciprocally related when subjects work toward a specific goal (Table 8.1). Higher attainments predicted greater self-satisfaction, enhanced efficacy perceptions, and more challenging personal goal levels. These self-processes, in turn, significantly predicted subsequent performance. Those who were highly efficacious, satisfied with their performance, and adhered to challenging personal goals greatly improved. In contrast, in the absence of a specific goal for performance, attainments and self-reactions were unrelated (Table 8.1). Even when controlling for initial performance, the interaction of goal condition and both self-evaluative processes and self-efficacy perceptions significantly predicted future performance.

The findings on this complex task differ from earlier results using simple activities in two important and potentially interrelated respects. First, goal assignment only weakly affected mean levels of performance (Cervone *et al.*, 1991), a result consistent

Table 8.1 Correlations between decision performance and self-reactive processes

	Goal condition	
	No goal	Specific goal
Block 1 performance with subsequent assessments		
Self-efficacy	−0.014	0.353*
Self-evaluation	0.108	0.363*
Self-set goal	0.226	0.631**
Assessments after Block 1 with subsequent performance		
Self-efficacy	−0.231	0.424*
Self-evaluation	0.088	0.400*
Self-set goal	0.285	0.657**

Notes
* $p < 0.05$
** $p < 0.01$

Source: From Cervone *et al.*, 1991.

with recent reviews documenting the relatively weak effects of goal assignment on cognitively complex activities (Wood *et al.*, 1987). Second, the impact of self-evaluation on performance was *the opposite of* that found previously. On simple activities, dissatisfaction with one's efforts fosters superior effort and performance (Bandura and Cervone, 1983, 1986). On the decision task, subjects who became dissatisfied with their progress toward a performance goal performed more poorly (Cervone *et al.*, 1991; see also Bandura and Jourdan, 1991).

This detrimental impact of negative self-evaluations provides some insight into a central question in the goal-setting literature: why are goal effects weaker on complex tasks? On both simple and complex activities, a commitment to challenging goals fosters dissatisfaction with sub-standard performance. On simple activities, this dissatisfaction enhances effort and thereby contributes to the power of goal setting (Bandura and Cervone, 1983). On complex tasks, the same self-reaction impairs performance, attenuating the effects of challenging goals. Negative discrepancies between attainments and standards have the same effect on self-evaluations on simple and complex tasks, but self-evaluative processes have an opposite effect on performance.

Two processes may contribute to the detrimental effect of self-criticism and negative self-evaluation on complex tasks. Negative affect resulting from self-evaluations can undermine performance by deleteriously affecting the required short-term memory functions (Humphreys and Revelle, 1984), biasing recall of previously encoded information (Isen, 1987; Isen *et al.*, 1978), or diverting attention from task-relevant thoughts (Sarason, 1975; Sarason *et al.*, 1990). Negative self-evaluations which lead to private ruminations about oneself may divert essential attentional resources away from task execution, thereby undermining performance. Second, people who become dissatisfied with their attainments tend to make many changes in their task strategies in an effort to improve. On highly complex tasks, making many changes from trial to trial can be a mistake. Keeping track of the many changes, and their effects, may simply overwhelm the capacity of short-term memory. Analyses of subjects' strategies on the decision task reveal that those who become dissatisfied with their performance make many trial-to-trial changes — so many that they create for themselves a decision environment in which they are incapable of succeeding due to 'information overload' (Cervone *et al.*, 1991).

Factors in addition to the presence or absence of a specific performance goal can moderate the impact of self-regulatory processes on decision performance. As with simple activities, clear performance feedback is necessary to activate self-referent processes. Efficacy perceptions, self-evaluations, and personal goals contribute to decision performance when subjects receive specific feedback on the success or failure of their decisions, but do not affect performance when such feedback is lacking (Cervone and Wood, 1991). When one's goal is to learn about a task, as opposed to maximizing one's current level of performance, self-evaluative reactions have less of an impact on decision performance (Cervone and Kopp, 1991). This latter result is consistent with a body of literature suggesting that different types of aim and goal may be associated with qualitatively different affective reactions and self-referent cognitions (Ames, 1986; Dweck and Leggett, 1988; Elliott and Dweck, 1988; Nicholls, 1984).

The social cognitive theory model of self-regulatory processes, goal setting, and performance (Bandura, 1989; Cervone, 1992) addresses a former criticism of the social cognitive approach. Control theory researchers had argued that social cognitive theory fails to recognize that different contexts differentially activate self-regulatory processes (Carver *et al.*, 1979). Our model predicts, and our results (Bandura and Cervone, 1983, 1986. Cervone *et al.*, 1991; Cervone and Wood, 1991) clearly reveal that variations in goals, feedback, and goal—feedback discrepancies govern the activation of multiple aspects of self-referent thinking.

Causal analysis of thought and action

An issue of central importance to any cognitively based theory of personality and social behaviour is the question of causality. Are the cognitive components of one's theory truly *determinants* of behaviour? Do people's thoughts about themselves, others, and the environment truly function as *causal* factors?

To the layperson, speaking of mental events as causes of action is not controversial. People commonly explain others' behaviour in terms of their expectations, plans, or feelings about various courses of action. Despite the intuitive appeal of this reasoning, many psychologists have viewed such explanations as fundamentally flawed. The behaviourist would argue that cognitions are not causes of action, but are themselves 'behaviour' that may accompany an overt action of interest. Both overt actions and the behaviours of thinking and feeling would need to be explained in terms of environmental factors that have acted upon the person (Skinner, 1953, 1974).

The causal status of cognitive states is not merely a question for philosophical inquiry. Empirical data can bear on the question of whether a cognitive state functions as a proximal determinant of behaviour. In social cognitive theory, this issue has been most fully explored with respect to the potential causal of role of self-efficacy judgment. We consider two domains in which this issue has been addressed: the effect of self-efficacy perceptions on phobic behaviour change, and the motivational impact of self-efficacy judgments that are biased by subtle situational cues.

Self-efficacy judgment and phobic behaviour

Much research has explored the causal relation between self-efficacy and phobic behaviour. The most basic criterion is to establish that efficacy judgments are strongly correlated with phobic avoidance. In the standard methodology, before and after treatment, phobic people rate their self-efficacy for doing a graduated series of phobia-related tasks, and then attempt the tasks (Williams, 1985). Studies with diverse phobic conditions, employing vicarious, imaginal, and performance-based treatments, reveal extremely close correspondences between the level to which self-efficacy is raised by treatment and the level of actual functional capabilities instated (Bandura and Adams, 1977; Bandura *et al.*, 1977, 1980, 1982, 1985; Biran and Wilson, 1981; Bourque and Ladouceur, 1980; Emmelkamp and Felten, 1985; Ladouceur, 1983; Southworth and Kirsch, 1988; Williams *et al.*, 1984, 1985, 1989; Williams and Rappoport, 1983; Williams and Watson, 1985). Despite these results, some have criticized the conclusion that efficacy judgments truly affect behaviour; indeed, more than simple correlational data are required to conclude that efficacy judgments play a causal role. We will consider these arguments briefly here; more detailed discussion can be found elsewhere (for example, Bandura, 1978a, 1982, 1984; Rachman, 1978).

One argument is that relations between self-efficacy judgment and behaviour reflect social pressures. Subjects may feel pressure to make their performances and their self-rating match. Although such pressures could occur in some contexts, the possibility that they influence results in phobia research is remote. The experimental methodologies minimize such social pressure. Subjects complete the self-efficacy scales in relative or complete privacy. The scales are commonly embedded among other rating forms. When these steps are not taken, the correspondence between efficacy ratings and behaviour is lowered because subjects report conservative underestimates of their capabilities (Telch *et al.*, 1982). The psychological context of behavioural tests with phobic subjects also renders the efficacy-matching hypothesis implausible. People come for treatment of a serious personal problem. They have a strong stake in performing as well as they can. They are confronted with real phobic threats, which cause considerable distress. In this context, social pressures for congruence between behaviour and questionnaire responses made many minutes, hours, or sometimes days earlier are trivial. Numerous studies corroborate that the mere act of rating self-efficacy has no bearing on subsequent coping behaviour, unless the experimenter deliberately introduces distorting factors (Bandura, 1982; Gauthier and Ladouceur, 1981).

Analyses of discrepancies that do occur between efficacy judgments and behaviour also support this conclusion. If subjects were motivated to match self-ratings and accomplishments, the distribution of discrepancies would be asymmetric. Subjects would infrequently do more than they judged, because once their behaviour reached the level of their judgment, they would stop, so as to produce an exact match. In fact, analyses from many hundreds of behavioural tests with diverse phobias reveal that coping behaviour tends to *surpass* the previous efficacy judgment (Williams and Bauchiess, 1992).

Another argument is that self-efficacy is merely a 'reflection' of behavioural change, not a cause of it (Borkovec, 1978). This conclusion can be rejected on several grounds. Efficacy judgments and behaviour are strongly related following treatments with vicarious or imaginal methods that involve no actual coping with phobic activities or objects, and that therefore provide no behavioural basis for judging one's self-efficacy (Bandura and Adams, 1977; Bandura *et al.*, 1977, 1980, 1982). When agoraphobics receive performance-based treatment for one phobia (such as, driving), while another phobia (such as grocery shopping) is left untreated, generalized improvement in the untreated phobias is accurately predicted by self-efficacy perceptions for those phobias, despite subjects having no behavioural experience during treatment with those activities (Williams *et al.*, 1989). Further, when treatments do consist of overt performance, post-treatment coping behaviour generally is predicted more accurately by self-efficacy perceptions than by the level of behavioural accomplishment achieved during treatment (for example, Bandura *et al.*, 1977, 1980; Williams *et al.*, 1984, 1989). This finding holds not only when predicting aggregate levels of performance, but also at a 'microanalytic' level, in which self-efficacy measures are used to predict behaviour at the level of individual tasks (Bandura *et al.*, 1977; Cervone, 1985; Williams *et al.*, 1984). This type of finding has been obtained in other domains. For example, self-efficacy perceptions add to the prediction of dynamic decision-making performance even after controlling for the effects of past decision outcomes (Cervone *et al.*, 1991; Wood and Bandura, 1989).

Perhaps the most common criticism is that correlations between self-efficacy and coping behaviour are due to the operation of some third variable, such as conditioned autonomic anxiety (Eysenck, 1978; Wolpe, 1978). Although anxiety arousal has long been argued to be the main determinant of phobic behaviour (for example, Mowrer, 1960; Wolpe, 1958), this notion suffers from serious explanatory weaknesses (Bandura, 1969, 1988; Lang, 1971; Mineka, 1979; Rachman, 1976; Schwartz, 1984; Seligman and Johnston, 1973; Williams 1987, 1988). Particularly telling are data indicating that arousal and treatment gains are often uncorrelated (for example, Leitenberg *et al.*, 1971), which logically eliminates a causal role for arousal. Fear arousal is better conceived as part of the problem to be solved than as the mechanism underlying changes in phobic behaviour.

Cognitively oriented critics have proposed that phobic behaviour and distress are caused by anticipated negative outcomes, such as personal or psycho-social harm, or anticipated high distress (for example, Beck, 1976; Beck *et al.*, 1985; Goldstein and Chambless, 1978). The most direct test of these competing hypotheses is to determine which variables contribute independently to a prediction of the target behaviour. A series of studies with severely phobic subjects (Arnow *et al.*, 1985; Telch *et al.*, 1985; Williams, 1991; Williams *et al.*, 1984, 1985, 1989; Williams and Rappoport, 1983; Williams and Watson, 1985) each measured perceived self-efficacy, subjective fear, and at least one kind of anticipated negative consequence prior to assessing subjects' coping behaviour. Subjects rated the various expected negative outcomes for each task of the behavioural test. Perceived danger was measured in four studies as the likelihood of a harmful consequence, anticipated anxiety in seven studies as the anxiety subjects thought they would experience, and anticipated panic in three studies as the likelihood of having a panic attack. The cognitive and behavioural measures were gathered before and after treatment.

Results showed that self-efficacy was a consistently accurate predictor of post-treatment approach behaviour (*r* averaging about 0.80). Anticipated anxiety and anticipated panic also consistently predicted behaviour (*r* for both averaging about −0.70). In contrast, both subjective anxiety and perceived danger predicted at modest and relatively inconsistent levels (*r* averaging, respectively, about −0.45 and −0.25).

Partial correlation analyses (summarized in Bandura, 1989, and Williams, 1992) revealed that self-efficacy consistently remained a strong predictor of behaviour when the various outcome expectations were held constant, whereas the outcome expectations consistently lost their capacity to predict behaviour when self-efficacy was held constant. Subjective fear during the behavioural test was only moderately correlated with behaviour. Anxiety lost most or all predictive accuracy with self-efficacy held constant.

These data support the view that perceptions of self-efficacy are primary, and that self-efficacy theory cannot be dismissed by simply assuming the primacy of some other kind of cognitive or emotional process. Given the growing body of evidence showing self-efficacy perceptions to be more accurate than a number of proposed alternative mediators, the burden grows increasingly heavy on advocates of 'third factor' interpretations.

An even stronger strategy for examining the potential causal role of self-efficacy judgment would involve not merely statistical controls, but the manipulation of self-efficacy perceptions while other relevant variables — such as prior experience and information about an activity — were held constant. Research on judgmental heuristics and biases in judgment under uncertainty has provided insight into ways of accomplishing this goal.

Self-efficacy judgment under uncertainty

When judging their self-efficacy on an activity, individuals are considering the relation between two sets of factors: their own skills, motivation, and abilities; and the difficulties and demands of the prospective situation. There may be many relevant personal and situational factors, and much uncertainty associated with them. One may not be sure of the exact circumstances that may arise, the knowledge and skills that will be required, and one's capability of executing actions at a given time. In natural interactions, there may be little time to dwell on these self-assessments. Such considerations led us (Cervone, 1989; Cervone and Peake, 1986) to propose that self-efficacy judgments may be products of systematic judgmental strategies of the sort uncovered in research on human judgment (Kahneman *et al.*, 1982; Nisbett and Ross, 1980).

As noted earlier, people rely on simplifying judgmental heuristics to make judgments and predictions in complex settings (Tversky and Kahneman, 1974). One highly pervasive heuristic is the process of 'anchoring and adjustment' (Tversky and Kahneman, 1974). This heuristic applies when people make estimates by considering an initial value, and subsequently adjust this value to yield a final estimate. Initial values may come from a variety of sources: the answer to a similar problem, a relevant piece of information, a 'wild guess'. For example, a student considering her potential performance on an SAT exam may begin by considering the level of performance achieved by a friend who has taken the test. Final estimates are often 'biased' in the direction of the initially considered values, or 'anchor' values (Tversky and Kahneman, 1974). In general, such a result is not surprising; many situations contain important cues that serve as viable and valid 'anchors' in making estimates. However, anchoring biases result even when the anchors are normatively irrelevant, random cues (Tversky and Kahneman, 1974).

This impact of random cues that are devoid of any informational value suggested a novel strategy for manipulating perceived self-efficacy, and assessing the behavioural impact of self-efficacy judgments (Cervone and Peake, 1986). Affecting self-efficacy judgment through random, informationless cues can create groups of individuals with differential levels of perceived self-efficacy, yet with equivalent exposure to, experience on, and information about a given activity. Despite these groups being equivalent in these many ways, social cognitive theory predicts that the differential levels of perceived self-efficacy will affect future performance.

The potential impact of anchoring biases was investigated by introducing anchoring cues prior to subjects' performance on a challenging cognitive task, and examining the impact of anchors on self-efficacy judgment and task persistence (Cervone and Peake, 1986). Subjects completed a pre-experimental questionnaire in which they were asked to consider whether they could successfully complete 'more or less than X' items of the task, where X appeared to be a random number. (A pseudo-randomization procedure was employed to ensure that this anchor value appeared to have been randomly generated.) After answering 'more' or 'less', subjects indicated their exact level of self-efficacy, the exact number of items they judged they were capable of solving. In a control condition, no anchor value was presented. Subjects then worked on the task. Anchoring biases powerfully affected self-efficacy judgments (Figure 8.2). Subjects exposed to a high anchor judged they could solve approximately 50 per cent more of items than did low-anchor subjects — despite the fact that the

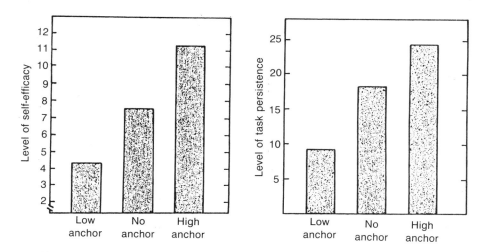

Figure 8.2 Mean levels of perceived self-efficacy (left panel) and task persistence (right panel) as a function of exposure to apparently random high and low anchor values (Source: Cervone and Peake, 1986)

low and high anchor values appeared to be random numbers. These differences in perceived self-efficacy generated corresponding differences in task persistence (Figure 8.2). Regression analyses indicated that self-efficacy perceptions fully mediated the effect of anchoring cues on behaviour.

One might argue that the presentation of a single high or low anchor value — even a random one — presents a subtle social demand for high or low levels of performance. In part to address this alternative explanation, subsequent research explored the possibility that anchoring biases would result from considering a given set or sequence of possible outcomes in different orders (Peake and Cervone, 1989). In a pre-experimental questionnaire, subjects rated their confidence in attaining five different performance levels, ranging from very low to very high levels of performance. Subjects made these ratings in either an ascending order, first considering whether they would reach a low performance level, or a descending sequence, with high performance levels considered first. Subjects in the descending sequence condition displayed higher levels of perceived self-efficacy and greater subsequent persistence on the task (Peake and Cervone, 1989). Sequence anchoring biases were found to be a general phenomenon. Across a variety of factual judgments, the order in which subjects considered various possibilities strongly affected their estimates, with judgments biased in the direction of whatever value was presented first (Peake and Cervone, 1989).

In many respects, the behavioural impact of anchor-biased self-efficacy judgments is quite surprising. Anchoring cues were presented, and perceived self-efficacy assessed, before subjects had ever attempted the task. They subsequently experienced numerous performance trials, with equivalent rates of success and failure in all experimental conditions. Given the general power of first-hand performance feedback, one might have expected this performance information quickly to eliminate any initial group differences in perceived self-efficacy. However, the results — substantial group differences in task persistence over a large number of trials — suggest that initial efficacy judgments may have been highly perseverant; that is, the groups may have had differing efficacy perceptions even after much equivalent experience, with these differences in self-efficacy sustaining the differences in behaviour. Recent findings provide evidence of this (Cervone and Palmer, 1990). Even after numerous trials with controlled, equivalent rates of success, subjects exposed to a low anchor value judge themselves less efficacious than high-anchor subjects (Cervone and Palmer, 1990). Thus, judgmental biases have an enduring behavioural impact, in part because people's initial perceptions of their capabilities are themselves highly persistent. In general, personal and social beliefs are often surprisingly resistant to change. Beliefs can withstand even the complete discrediting of the evidence on which they are based (Anderson *et al.*, 1980; Ross *et al.*, 1975).

Anchoring biases represent a specific type of judgmental influence that arises when people begin an inferential task by considering a specific potential outcome. More generally, judgmental biases occur because it is impossible fully to consider and integrate all of the information that might be pertinent to making a complex judgment. Instead, judgments must be based on a quick assessment of information that happens to come to mind. Self-efficacy judgments, then, may be a product of the relative ease with which a small bit of self-knowledge, autobiographical memory, or situational information comes to mind — in other words, the extent to which such information is cognitively available (Schwarz *et al.*, 1991; Tversky and Kahneman, 1973).

The most cognitively available factors may often be the most important ones to consider. One's vivid memory of tumbling down a slope may indeed be quite pertinent when judging which run to attempt on one's next ski trip. However, factors other than normative importance can affect availability. An arbitrary factor or experience may lead one to focus on a specific feature of the environment, or a personal strength or weakness, and thereby unduly influence efficacy judgments and behaviour. Research reveals that focusing on upcoming factors that might impair or facilitate performance (Cervone, 1989) or past events that worked out poorly or favourably (Sarason *et al.*, 1986) affects persistence on challenging tasks. Variations in perceived self-efficacy mediate such behavioural effects (Cervone, 1989).

The influence of judgmental strategies and biases in self-efficacy judgment may provide insight into diverse phenomena. One's own past performance may commonly serve as an anchor in self-judgment; if so, anchoring-and-adjustment processes may be at least partly responsible for the considerable temporal stability often found in both self-perceptions and behaviour (for example, Mischel and Peake, 1982). Anchoring processes also may be at work in social situations that involve subtle indicants of ability. Performance can be impaired by subtle interpersonal factors such as the assignment of a social label that connotes inferiority (Langer and Benevento, 1978). Such influences may arise, at least in part, through the inferior labels functioning as a low anchor in self-assessments. Availability processes may be partly responsible for the effects of therapeutic interventions such as cognitive modelling (for example, Hersen *et al.*, 1979). Envisioning personal success may raise the cognitive availability of manageable aspects of a task or one's own coping skills.

Social cognitive theory and personality psychology

In recent years, social cognitive theory has become a predominant perspective in personality psychology. Pervin describes the social cognitive approach as a 'favorite among academic personality psychologists, and a good number of clinicians' (1989b, p. 420). Bower and Hilgard suggest that social cognitive theory 'may provide a basis of consensus' (1981, p. 472) for research on learning and cognition. Loevinger remarks that the general social-cognitive perspective is 'the predominant school of personality psychology today' (1987, p. 136).

Despite this acclaim, social cognitive theory is not without its critics. Often, criticism centres not on the contributions the approach has made, but on the apparent failure of social cognitive theory to address a number of issues that have traditionally been of concern in personality psychology (for example, Hogan, 1982). In this concluding section, we consider some of these issues, and the manner in which social cognitive theory does, or can, address them. First, we briefly consider the theoretical domain of social cognitive theory and related approaches.

Social cognitive theory and the family of social-cognitive theories

Throughout this chapter, we have presented a theoretical perspective that has been immeasurably influenced by the social cognitive theory of Albert Bandura. We feel that Bandura's writings, particularly his *Social Foundations of Thought and Action* (1986), provide a singularly broad and integrative perspective on cognitive and social factors in personality functioning.

Social cognitive theory has not, however, evolved in isolation. It can be understood as part of a family of theoretical perspectives that are concerned with cognitive processes and structures in personality functioning, and the social contexts in which these cognitions develop. Indeed, recent years have witnessed a highly encouraging convergence of social-cognitive theorizing and research. Rather than working in isolation or competition, numerous investigators are beginning to provide complementary knowledge about personality (Cervone, 1991). As Mischel suggests, 'what appears to be evolving is . . . a general shared perspective . . . a framework for the analysis and clarification of more specific issues and concerns basic for personality psychology about the processes and consequences of social-cognitive development in the person' (1990, p. 116). Cervone (1991) outlined three themes that characterize this perspective: a concern with cognitive processes and structures related to the self, the role of social contexts in activating these self-related cognitions, and the reciprocal interactions among environments, persons, and their behaviour. These themes are found in the work of numerous investigators, some of whom explicitly adopt a 'social-cognitive' label for their work, and others of whom do not (Cantor and Kihlstrom, 1987, 1989a,b; Dweck and Leggett, 1988; Higgins, 1990; Markus and Wurf, 1987; Wright and Mischel, 1987). In the following discussion, we draw on both social cognitive theory and these related social-cognitive approaches.

Social-cognitive and trait/dispositional units of analysis

It is important to consider how this evolving social-cognitive perspective differs from traditional trait or dispositional approaches to personality. The difference lies not simply in alternative terminology or methodology, but in the basic units of analysis used to conceptualize personality (Cervone, 1991). Social-cognitive and trait/disposition units differ in a number of ways. Personality traits or dispositions are generally not defined contextually; in other words, the units of analysis are tendencies to act in a certain manner, without specification of the situations in which one acts. If one views these constructs not merely as statistical summaries of act tendencies (Buss and Craik, 1983), but as determinants of behaviour (Funder, 1991), then they are internal structures that generate a given class of behaviour across situations.[1] The Big Five personality factors (Norman, 1963; see also Hofstee and

DeRaad, Chapter 3 in this volume; Ostendorf and Angleitner, Chapter 4 in this volume) are prototypical of such personality units. Each factor is a context-free personality dimension. For example, 'conscientiousness' refers to a disposition to achieve and to act in a highly 'directed' manner (Digman, 1990; McCrae and Costa, 1987), a disposition that is defined independently of the situations in which, or the reasons for which, one acts conscientiously.

In contrast, social-cognitive units are generally person-in-context variables. People's competencies, goals and standards for performance, and appraisals of the environment and their personal capabilities are conceptualized and assessed with regard to the contexts in which, and life tasks on which, people must bring their knowledge to bear (Cantor and Kihlstrom, 1987). Social-cognitivists reject context-free units for a number of reasons. People's personal and social knowledge and skills for coping with the environment develop in and inherently pertain to specific life contexts. Indeed, a variety of cognitive architectures concur in emphasizing the domain-specificity of knowledge and skills (Linville and Clark, 1989). Adopting context-free units, such as generalized expectations, overall social IQ, or global personality dispositions sacrifices much important information. Such global units obscure the processes that enable people to adapt their behaviour in a flexible manner to meet varying situational requirements.

A second reason for rejecting non-contextual trait units is empirical. A sizable body of data indicates that behaviour is often far more variable across situations than broad, context-free personality units imply. The degree to which social behaviour is consistent across situations has been the focus of much attention, debate, and controversy (Epstein, 1979; Forgas and Van Heck, Chapter 16 in this volume; Hettema and Kenrick, Chapter 15 in this volume; Kenrick and Funder, 1988; Mischel, 1968; Mischel and Peake, 1982). Although opinions and interpretations may differ, the empirical data clearly reveal that one cannot accurately predict specific behaviours without carefully attending to context. Relatively accurate disposition-based predictions can be made when one specifies particular environmental conditions under which a disposition is most relevant (Wright and Mischel, 1987) or narrows down a broad dispositional construct psychometrically, identifying a specific cluster of behaviours that intercorrelate (Jackson and Paunonen, 1985; Mischel, 1983). Without such contextual fine-tuning, cross-situational predictions are generally weak (Mischel and Peake, 1982).

The social cognitivist chooses to adopt units of analysis that neither assume nor necessarily imply that individuals will act in a consistent manner across diverse contexts. From the social-cognitive perspective, the degree of consistency in social behaviour across situations is an empirical question (Cantor and Kihlstrom, 1989b), one whose answer is likely to depend on the particular persons, situations, and behaviours under consideration. When people perceive situations as similar (Champagne and Pervin, 1987; Lord, 1982) or acquire coping skills that can be applied in diverse contexts (Smith, 1989) they may behave in a relatively 'consistent' manner. The social-cognitivist does not deny such consistency, but does choose to adopt units of analysis and associated assessment strategies that are sensitive to the possibility that individuals will discriminate between seemingly similar situations, and will differ from one another in the discriminations they make.

Betz and Hackett's (1981) research on perceived self-efficacy and career decision making illustrates this conceptual and methodological strategy. Rather than adopting a global, non-contextual unit (such as generalized feelings of self-confidence), Betz and Hackett assessed students' perceived self-efficacy for completing the education and training required for each of a series of specific occupations. They found that males had a relatively generalized sense of efficacy; they judged themselves capable of completing the requirements of occupations that have traditionally been dominated by men (engineering, sales manager), as well as those traditionally dominated by women (dental hygienist, secretary). In contrast, women sharply differentiated between these contexts, judging themselves efficacious for traditionally female occupations but relatively inefficacious for traditionally male jobs. Perceptions of self-efficacy predicted the range of career options individuals considered for themselves (Betz and Hackett, 1981). This pattern of results would have been obscured by the use of global assessments that disregard the specific contexts in which students appraised their capabilities.

A more fundamental distinction between social-cognitive and trait/dispositional units concerns one's basis for inferring these constructs, and the theoretical functions they serve. Trait approaches — at least, of the Allportian variety (Allport, 1937; Funder, 1991) — begin with the observation of patterns of behaviour (for example, 'friendly' or 'generous' acts). They then infer constructs ('friendliness', 'generosity') that summarize the behaviour and are taken as an explanation of it (Funder, 1991). Alternatively, trait approaches may begin with the set of natural language personality adjectives that one finds in a dictionary, terms that presumably evolved through the culture's observation of patterns of behaviour. Cluster- and factor-analytic procedures are used to pare down this large list of person descriptors into a simple framework (Cattell, 1943; Goldberg, 1981). Again, the resulting units summarize types of behaviour (for example, 'agreeable', 'conscientious', or 'cultured' acts; Norman, 1963) and may be taken to refer to underlying causal entities.

Social-cognitive approaches adopt a significantly different strategy. The 'conceptual starting point' for the social-cognitive approach is the analysis of person variables that derive from psychology's knowledge of cognition, affect, and social learning (Mischel, 1973). The units of analysis, then, are not summaries of different types of action. Rather, they are psychological processes and structures that generate behaviour and simultaneously characterize the individual. Indeed, at the heart of the social-cognitive enterprise is the argument that a personality theory should (1) *explain* behaviour by identifying the specific psychological structures and processes through which people learn about the world and themselves, and regulate their behaviour; and (2) *describe* personality in terms of this same class of variables. The manner in which these variables influence specific categories or patterns of social behaviour is then an empirical question.

Dweck and colleagues' (Dweck and Leggett, 1988) analysis of personality and motivation illustrates this social-cognitive strategy. Differential patterns of achievement behaviour are explained in terms of goal structures and self-perceptions. Variations in self-perceived capability affect achievement behaviour when individuals have the goal of documenting their level of competence (Elliot and Dweck, 1988). Individual differences in achievement behaviour are described not using summary disposition labels, but in the terms of the explanatory theory: some individuals hold implicit theories of intelligence that lead them chronically to interpret situations as involving the documentation of competence. Their implicit theories, in other words, foster the goal orientations that, in combination with low perceptions of competence, generate maladaptive patterns of behaviour (Dweck and Leggett, 1988). Once one understands (1) the processes that underlie different patterns of achievement, and (2) the enduring knowledge structures that generate individual differences in this behaviour, global disposition terms are not necessary for explaining behaviour or describing the individual in this achievement context. Trait or dispositional units, from this perspective, are merely summary labels that observers may use to describe patterns of behaviour (Mischel, 1973). An observer may conclude that some children appear to be 'helpless' in achievement contexts. The psychologist, however, need not explain their behaviour by postulating a trait of 'helplessness'. Other theoretical perspectives, such as Read and Miller's (1989) interpersonalism approach, similarly suggest that goal-based units can serve as a common language for analysing the dynamics of behaviour and describing individual differences.

Although we reject disposition terms as core elements of a personality theory, we do not wish to argue that there is no utility to studying such variables. The analysis of dispositional units can illuminate many important issues: the structure of individual difference terms in our culture and others (for example, Goldberg, 1981), the way these terms are used in natural discourse (Wright and Mischel, 1988), and the relation between personality inferences and social behaviour (Mischel and Peake, 1982). Trait structures such as the Big Five have the advantage of yielding a simple framework for what otherwise might be a confusing mass of trait terms (McCrae and Costa, 1986). Understanding the structure of natural-language disposition terms is a valuable goal. However, one simply cannot assume that a taxonomy of the layperson's intuitive, natural-language disposition terms is adequate to describe the personality of any and all individuals (Cervone, 1991).

Comprehensiveness in personality description

One of the functions a personality theory should serve is personality description. A theory should provide some method of describing individuals, and should provide or at least suggest a methodology for assessment. Social-cognitive theories have achieved notable success in personality description and assessment. Work on perceived self-efficacy (Bandura, 1989), person variables in self-control and delay of gratification (Mischel *et al.*, 1989), and the structure of individuals' social and self-knowledge and strategies for dealing with life tasks (Cantor and Kihlstrom, 1987, 1989a) illustrate the social-cognitive approach.

One criterion on which to evaluate a personality theory is *comprehensiveness*. A theory should provide a relatively broad, comprehensive picture of human personality. In many respects, social cognitive theory is admirably comprehensive. Its set of basic capabilities (Bandura, 1986) encompasses many if not most of the mechanisms underlying adaptive and maladaptive behaviour. Bandura (1986) has documented the role of these capabilities in a remarkably diverse array of individual and social phenomena.

However, combining the goal of description with the criterion of comprehensiveness reveals a limitation to current social-cognitive theories. The social-cognitive approach does not provide an assessment strategy that yields a comprehensive description of an individual's personality. If asked to provide a relatively comprehensive social-cognitive description of an individual, one finds there is no simple algorithm to follow.

In many respects, the lack of a simple yet comprehensive assessment technology is quite appropriate on theoretical grounds. Social cognitive theory clearly rejects any universal 'taxonomy of persons' in which a fixed set of categories or dimensions is used to characterize individuals. Indeed, the goal of social-cognitive assessment is not to categorize a person as being of a certain 'type'. Instead, the goal is to characterize the cognitive processes and structures that are particularly important to the individual's personal experience and social functioning. Such assessment must consider the domains, or contexts, in which these cognitions come into play. The social-cognitivist generally 'doubt[s] that assessments of personality in the abstract, without regard for context, are of much practical or theoretical use' (Cantor and Kihlstrom, 1989b, p. 207).

One promising assessment strategy is to identify the social contexts that are especially important to a given individual, and the cognitive processes and structures that determine the adaptiveness of his or her behaviour in these domains. Such a strategy is seen in the field's recent attention to 'middle-level' units of analysis (Cantor and Zirkel, 1990). Numerous investigators argue that personality and purposive behaviour are best understood by identifying the relatively enduring goals that organize individuals' behaviour at a given point in their life, and the associated beliefs that influence the effectiveness of their goal-directed efforts. These constructs are referred to as 'middle-level' units because they refer neither to highly specific task goals nor to highly abstract motives. Rather, they pertain to those self-defined life tasks ('finding a mate', 'getting a better job', 'getting into medical school', 'becoming a better parent') that organize and give meaning to a significant pattern of activities over an extended period of time.

Numerous research programmes have adopted middle-level constructs. Little (1989) focuses on the 'personal projects' to which individuals commit themselves. Klinger's (1975) work on 'current concerns' analyses the way people's goals direct their action and conscious experience. Cantor and her colleagues investigate the 'life tasks' towards which individuals are working (Cantor and Kihlstrom, 1987). They focus on life tasks during periods of transition, such as the transition from high school to college. Their research reveals that students adopt varying strategies for dealing with stressful achievement tasks, strategies that often involve 'optimistic' versus 'pessimistic' ways of confronting task-related anxieties (Cantor *et al.*, 1987). In the social domain, some students appraise the task of establishing new friendships in a negative manner, which leads them to adopt relatively maladaptive strategies of social interaction (Langston and Cantor, 1989). Finally, Emmons's (1989) 'personal strivings' approach is designed to capture a somewhat broader, higher-level aspect of goal-directed action. Personal strivings are seen are superordinate aims that make a cluster of goals functionally equivalent for an individual. For example, the striving 'make life easier for my parents' might organize various financial, independent, and family harmony goals (Emmons, 1989).

The identification of an individual's central life goals, as well as the person's associated knowledge, strategies, appraisals of self-efficacy, and self-evaluations of their goal-directed efforts, promises to expand the social-cognitive analysis and assessment of personality (Cervone, 1990). Despite this promise, numerous conceptual challenges remain. The goals and aims that organize behaviour may not be fully available to awareness (Pervin, 1989c); thus, an analysis based on self-described tasks and goals may be incomplete. Important aspects of personality that differ from 'tasks' or 'strivings' may be overlooked in goal-based assessments. For example, people hold enduring ethical and moral standards that direct much of their experience and action. However, they may not describe adherence to these standards as a 'goal' towards which they are working.

An additional challenge involves the comparison of individuals to one another. Individual difference comparisons are difficult because life tasks, goals, and strivings may be highly idiosyncratic. Rather than trying to identify a universal set of aims and goals that can serve as the basis of individual difference analyses, it may be desirable to assess middle-level goals idiographically. An idiographic approach does not, however, preclude the identification of some nomothetic principles that would have general utility in assessment. The goal-setting literature (Locke and Latham, 1990) is suggestive in this regard. Whether a person's goals involve professional achievement, romantic success, or the development of deeper self-understanding, it may be informative to analyse the degree to which his or her goals are clearly articulated or ambiguous, involve only distal aims or combine distal goals with proximal plans and sub-goals, and whether the person is able to assess their progress meaningfully in meeting his or her aims.

Biological, affect-based dispositions

An aspect of personality that has received relatively little attention from social-cognitive theorists is affect-based dispositions and temperament. Research on childhood personality indicates significant genetic influences on broad temperament factors such as levels of emotionality and activity (Goldsmith, 1983). Of course, inherent biological predispositions tell only part of the story; environmental influences on such personality factors are generally at least as large as genetic effects (Plomin and Daniels, 1987; Plomin *et al.*, 1990). Whatever the sources of differences between individuals, biologically based temperament factors have yet to be fully incorporated into social-cognitive models.

In considering biologically based factors, the social-cognitivist would generally reject conceptual models such as Eysenck's (1990), in which broad personality types (such as extraversion) are seen as integrating diverse types of social behaviour (such as carefree and dominant acts). Rather, the social-cognitivist would view emotional temperament as simply one of a number of factors that feeds into the interaction of contextual influences and cognitive factors. Contrada, Leventhal, and O'Leary (1990) present a process model of hostile behaviour that illustrates such an approach. Hostility arises from a system of interrelated beliefs, self-regulatory processes, and cognitive appraisals. Constitutional factors such as emotional temperament can intensify the negative emotions and physiological responses that stem from appraising the environment as hostile and threatening. Emotional temperament can also influence the cognitive appraisal process (Contrada *et al.*, 1990), a suggestion similar to Bandura's (1977) proposal that affective and physiological reactions serve as a source of information in self-efficacy appraisal.

Personality strategies: top-down and bottom-up

Some personality theories have developed via a 'top-down' strategy. Theory construction begins with a search for a set of broad variables that — in theory — can provide a comprehensive description of personality. Factor theories (Sells and Murphy, 1984) have generally adopted such a strategy. The initial theoretical task is to identify a set of factors, or dimensions, that can provide a comprehensive description of all persons (Cattell, 1943, 1965). The limitation to a top-down approach is that one may have little understanding of the mechanisms that underlie one's central theoretical variables. For example, despite a relatively long history of study of the Big Five factor structure (Goldberg, 1981; McCrae and Costa, 1990; Norman, 1963), which itself derived from the earlier work of Cattell (Cattell, 1943; Fiske, 1949; Tupes and Christal, 1961), a recent review (John, 1990) recognizes that the Big Five dimensions 'provide only a list of descriptive contents at the highest level' (p. 94) of a personality taxonomy, and that 'the structures and processes underlying them remain to be explicated' (p. 95).

In contrast, social cognitive theory has evolved from the bottom up. The social cognitive theorist did not begin by postulating an array of variables explicitly designed to capture all aspects of personality. Instead, research has explicated each of a series of personal determinants of behaviour and experience, and explored the social contexts in which they develop and the phenomena they help to explain. The scope of social cognitive theory thus has expanded gradually over the years, as our knowledge of social learning, cognition, affect, and self-regulation has increased. We feel there is great virtue to such a 'bottom-up' strategy. Its shortcomings are greatly offset by the detailed understanding of the determinants and mechanisms of personality functioning that it yields. We look forward to the further evolution of social cognitive theory.

Authors' note

Our thanks to J.T. Ptacek for his comments on the manuscript.

Note

1. We do not wish to imply that trait approaches completely overlook social influences. Our point is that their basic units of analysis are generally defined and assessed without regard to context.

References

Abramson, L.Y., Seligman, M.E.P. and Teasdale, J.D. (1978), 'Learned helplessness in humans: critique and reformulation', *Journal of Abnormal Psychology*, **87**, 49–74.
Ahrens, A.H. (1987), 'Theories of depression: the role of goals and the self-evaluation process', *Cognitive Therapy and Research*, **11**, 665–80.
Alloy, L.B. and Tabachnik, N. (1984), 'Assessment of covariation by humans and animals: the joint influence of prior expectations and current situational information', *Psychological Review*, **91**, 112–49.
Allport, G.W. (1937), *Personality: A psychological interpretation*, New York, NY: Holt.
Allport, G.W. (1966), 'Trait revisited', *American Psychologist*, **21**, 1–10.
Ames, C.A. (1986), 'Conceptions of motivation within competitive and noncompetitive goal structures', in R. Schwarzer (ed.), *Self-related Cognitions in Anxiety and Motivation*, Hillsdale, NJ: Erlbaum, pp. 229–45.
Anderson, C.A., Lepper, M.R. and Ross, L. (1980), 'Perseverance of social theories: the role of explanation in the persistence of discredited information', *Journal of Personality and Social Psychology*, **39**, 1037–49.
Anderson, J.R. (1983), *The Architecture of Cognition*, Cambridge, MA: Harvard University Press.
Arnow, B.A., Taylor, C.B., Agras, W.S. and Telch, M.J. (1985), 'Enhancing agoraphobia treatment outcome by changing couple communication patterns', *Behavior Therapy*, **16**, 452–67.
Atkinson, J.W. (1964), *An Introduction to Motivation*, Princeton, NJ: Van Nostrand.
Bandura, A. (1969), *Principles of Behavior Modification*, New York, NY: Holt, Rinehart & Winston.
Bandura, A. (1973), *Aggression: A social learning analysis*, Englewood Cliffs, NJ: Prentice Hall.
Bandura, A. (1977), 'Self-efficacy: toward a unifying theory of change', *Psychological Review*, **84**, 191–215.
Bandura, A. (1978a), 'Reflections on self-efficacy', *Advances in Behaviour Research and Therapy*, **1**, 237–69.
Bandura, A. (1978b), 'The self system in reciprocal determinism', *American Psychologist*, **33**, 344–58.
Bandura, A. (1982), 'The assessment and predictive generality of self-percepts of efficacy', *Journal of Behavior Therapy and Experimental Psychiatry*, **13**, 195–9.
Bandura, A. (1984), 'Recycling misconceptions of perceived self-efficacy', *Cognitive Therapy and Research*, **8**, 231–55.
Bandura, A. (1986), *Social Foundations of Thought and Action: A social cognitive theory*, Englewood Cliffs, NJ: Prentice Hall.
Bandura, A. (1988), 'Self-efficacy conception of anxiety', *Anxiety Research*, **1**, 77–98.
Bandura, A. (1989), 'Self-regulation of motivation and action through internal standards and goal systems', in L.A. Pervin (ed.), *Goal Concepts in Personality and Social Psychology*, Hillsdale, NJ: Erlbaum, pp. 19–85.
Bandura, A. (1990), 'Conclusion: reflections on nonability determinants of competence', in J. Kolligan and R.J. Sternberg (eds.), *Competence Considered: Perceptions of competence and incompetence across the lifespan*, New Haven, CT: Yale University Press, pp. 315–62.

Bandura, A. (1991), 'The changing icons of personality psychology', in J.H. Cantor (ed.), *Psychology at Iowa: Centennial essays*, Hillsdale, NJ: Erlbaum, pp. 117−39.

Bandura, A. and Adams, N.E. (1977), 'Analysis of self-efficacy theory of behavioral change', *Cognitive Therapy and Research*, **1**, 287−308.

Bandura, A. and Cervone, D. (1983), 'Self-evaluative and self-efficacy mechanisms governing the motivational effects of goal systems', *Journal of Personality and Social Psychology*, **45**, 1017−28.

Bandura, A. and Cervone, D. (1986), 'Differential engagement of self-reactive influences in cognitive motivation', *Organizational Behavior and Human Decision Processes*, **38**, 92−113.

Bandura, A. and Jourdan, F.J. (1991), 'Self-regulatory mechanisms governing the impact of social comparison on complex decision making', *Journal of Personality and Social Psychology*, **60**, 941−51.

Bandura, A. and Kupers, C.J. (1964), 'The transmission of patterns of self-reinforcement through modeling', *Journal of Abnormal and Social Psychology*, **69**, 1−9.

Bandura, A. and Schunk, D.H. (1981), 'Cultivating competence, self-efficacy and intrinsic interest through proximal self-motivation', *Journal of Personality and Social Psychology*, **41**, 586−98.

Bandura, A. and Wood, R. (1989), 'Effect of perceived controllability and performance standards on self-regulation of complex decision-making', *Journal of Personality and Social Psychology*, **56**, 805−14.

Bandura, A., Adams, N.E. and Beyer, J. (1977), 'Cognitive processes mediating behavior change', *Journal of Personality and Social Psychology*, **35**, 125−39.

Bandura, A., Blanchard, E.B. and Ritter, B. (1969), 'Relative efficacy of desensitization and modeling approaches for inducing behavioral, affective, and attitudinal changes', *Journal of Personality and Social Psychology*, **13**, 173−99.

Bandura, A., Grusec, J.E. and Menlove, F.L. (1967), 'Some social determinants of self-monitoring reinforcement systems', *Journal of Personality and Social Psychology*, **5**, 449−55.

Bandura, A., Jeffrey, R.W. and Wright, C.L. (1974), 'Efficacy of participant modeling as a function of response induction aids', *Journal of Abnormal Psychology*, **83**, 35−64.

Bandura, A., Reese, L. and Adams, N.E. (1982), 'Microanalysis of action and fear arousal as a function of differential levels of perceived self-efficacy', *Journal of Personality and Social Psychology*, **43**, 5−21.

Bandura, A., Ross, D. and Ross, S.A. (1963), 'Imitation of film-mediated aggressive models', *Journal of Abnormal and Social Psychology*, **66**, 3−11.

Bandura, A., Adams, N.E., Hardy, A. and Howells, G. (1980), 'Tests of the generality of self-efficacy theory', *Cognitive Therapy and Research*, **4**, 39−66.

Bandura, A., Cioffi, D., Taylor, C.B. and Brouillard, M.E. (1988), 'Perceived self-efficacy in coping with cognitive stressors and opioid activation', *Journal of Personality and Social Psychology*, **55**, 479−88.

Bandura, A., O'Leary, A., Taylor, C.B., Gossard, D. and Gauthier, J. (1987), 'Perceived self-efficacy and pain control: opioid and nonopioid mechanisms', *Journal of Personality and Social Psychology*, **55**, 479−88.

Bandura, A., Taylor, C.B., Williams, S.L., Meffort, I.N. and Barchas, J.D. (1985), 'Catecholamine secretion as a function of perceived coping self-efficacy', *Journal of Consulting and Clinical Psychology*, **53**, 406−14.

Barlow, D.H. and Wolfe, B.E. (1981), 'Behavioral approaches to the anxiety disorders: a report of the NIMH-SUNY, Albany, research conference', *Journal of Consulting and Clinical Psychology*, **49**, 448−54.

Baumeister, R. (1989), 'The problem of life's meaning', in D.M. Buss and N. Cantor (eds.), *Personality Psychology: Recent trends and emerging directions*, New York, NY: Springer-Verlag, pp. 138−48.

Beck, A.T. (1976), *Cognitive Therapy and the Emotional Disorders*, New York, NY: International Universities Press.

Beck, A.T., Emery, G. and Greenberg, R.L. (1985), *Anxiety Disorders and Phobias: A cognitive perspective*, New York, NY: Basic Books.

Beck, A.T., Rush, A.J., Shaw, B.F. and Emery, G. (1979), *Cognitive Therapy of Depression*, New York, NY: Guilford Press.

Becker, L.J. (1978), 'Joint effect of feedback and goal setting on performance: a field study of residential energy conservation', *Journal of Applied Psychology*, **63**, 428–33.

Bem, D.J. (1972), 'Self-perception theory', in L. Berkowitz (ed.), *Advances in Experimental Social Psychology*, New York, NY: Academic Press, vol. 6, pp. 1–62.

Berger, S.M. (1962), 'Conditioning through vicarious instigation', *Psychological Review*, **69**, 450–66.

Betz, N.E. and Hackett, G. (1981), 'The relationship of career-related self-efficacy expectations to perceived career options in college men and women', *Journal of Counseling Psychology*, **28**, 399–410.

Betz, N.E. and Hackett, G. (1986), 'Applications of self-efficacy theory to understanding career choice behavior', *Journal of Social and Clinical Psychology*, **4**, 279–89.

Biran, M. and Wilson, G.T. (1981), 'Treatment of phobic disorders using cognitive and exposure methods: a self-efficacy analysis', *Journal of Consulting and Clinical Psychology*, **49**, 886–99.

Bjorklund, D.F. and Green B.L. (1992), 'The adaptive nature of cognitive immaturity', *American Psychologist*, **47**, 46–54.

Bolles, R.C. (1975), *Learning Theory*, New York, NY: Holt, Rinehart & Winston.

Borkovec, T.D. (1978), 'Self-efficacy: cause or reflection of behavioral change?', in S. Rachman (ed.), *Advances in Behaviour Research and Therapy*, Oxford: Pergamon, vol. 1, pp. 163–70.

Bourque, P. and Ladouceur, R. (1980), 'An investigation of various performance-based treatments with agoraphobics', *Behaviour Research and Therapy*, **18**, 161–70.

Bower, G.H. and Hilgard, E.R. (1981), *Theories of Learning* (fifth edition), Englewood Cliffs, NJ: Prentice Hall.

Bowers, K.S. (1973), 'Situationism in psychology: an analysis and critique', *Psychological Review*, **80**, 307–36.

Brewin, C.R. (1988), *Cognitive Foundations of Clinical Psychology*, Hillsdale, NJ: Erlbaum.

Brewin, C.R. (1989), 'Cognitive change processes in psychotherapy', *Psychological Review*, **96**, 379–94.

Brown, I., Jr. and Inouye, D.K. (1978), 'Learned helplessness through modeling: the role of perceived similarity in competence', *Journal of Personality and Social Psychology*, **36**, 900–8.

Bruner, J. (1990), *Acts of Meaning*, Cambridge, MA: Harvard University Press.

Buss, D.M. (1991), 'Evolutionary personality psychology', *Annual Review of Psychology*, **42**, 459–91.

Buss, D.M. and Cantor, N. (eds.) (1989), *Personality Psychology: Recent trends and emerging directions*, New York, NY: Springer-Verlag.

Buss, D.M. and Craik, K.H. (1983), 'The act frequency approach to personality', *Psychological Review*, **90**, 105–26.

Campion, M.A. and Lord, R.G. (1982), 'A control systems conceptualization of the goal-setting and changing process', *Organization Behavior and Human Performance*, **30**, 265–87.

Cantor, N. and Kihlstrom, J.F. (1987), *Personality and Social Intelligence*, Englewood Cliffs, NJ: Prentice Hall.

Cantor, N. and Kihlstrom, J.F. (1989a), 'Social intelligence and cognitive assessments of personality', in R.S. Wyer, Jr. and T.K. Srull (eds.), *Advances in Social Cognition*, Hillsdale, NJ: Erlbaum, vol. 2, pp. 1–60.

Cantor, N. and Kihlstrom, J.F. (1989b), 'Social intelligence and personality: there's room for growth', in R.S. Wyer, Jr. and T.K. Srull (eds.), *Advances in Social Cognition*, Hillsdale, NJ: Erlbaum, vol. 2, pp. 197—214.

Cantor, N. and Zirkel, S. (1990), 'Personality, cognition, and purposive behavior', in L.A. Pervin (ed.), *Handbook of Personality: Theory and research*, New York, NY: Guilford Press, pp. 135—64.

Cantor, N., Norem, J.K., Niedenthal, P.M., Langston, C.A. and Brower, A.M. (1987), 'Life tasks, self-concept ideals, and cognitive strategies in a life transition', *Journal of Personality and Social Psychology*, **53**, 1178—91.

Carroll, W.R. and Bandura, A. (1982), 'The role of visual monitoring in observational learning of action patterns: making the unobservable observable', *Journal of Motor Behavior*, **14**, 153—67.

Carroll, W.R. and Bandura, A. (1985), 'Role of timing of visual monitoring and motor rehearsal in observational learning of action patterns', *Journal of Motor Behavior*, **17**, 269—81.

Carroll, W.R. and Bandura, A. (1987), 'Translating cognition into action: the role of visual guidance in observational learning', *Journal of Motor Behavior*, **19**, 385—98.

Carroll, W.R. and Bandura, A. (1990), 'Representational guidance of action production in observational learning: a causal analysis', *Journal of Motor Behavior*, **22**, 85—97.

Carver, C.S. and Scheier, M.F. (1981), *Attention and Self-regulation: A control theory approach to human behavior*, New York, NY: Springer-Verlag.

Carver, C.S. and Scheier, M.F. (1990), 'Principles of self-regulation: action and emotion', in E.T. Higgins and R.M. Sorrentino (eds.), *Motivation and Cognition: Foundations of social behavior*, New York, NY: Guilford Press, vol. 2, pp. 527—61.

Carver, C.S., Blaney, P.H. and Scheier, M.F. (1979), 'Reassertion and giving up: the interactive role of self-directed attention and outcome expectancy', *Journal of Personality and Social Psychology*, **37**, 1859—70.

Cattell, R.B. (1943), 'The description of personality: basic traits resolved into clusters', *Journal of Abnormal and Social Psychology*, **38**, 476—506.

Cattell, R.B. (1965), *The Scientific Analysis of Personality*, Baltimore, MD: Penguin Books.

Cervone, D. (1985), 'Randomization tests to determine significance levels for microanalytic congruences between self-efficacy and behavior', *Cognitive Therapy and Research*, **9**, 357—65.

Cervone, D. (1989), 'Effects of envisioning future activities on self-efficacy judgments and motivation: an availability heuristic interpretation', *Cognitive Therapy and Research*, **13**, 247—61.

Cervone, D. (1990), 'A review of Cantor and Kihlstrom's *Personality and Social Intelligence*', *American Journal on Mental Retardation*, **94**, 456—9.

Cervone, D. (1991), 'The two disciplines of personality psychology', *Psychological Science*, **2**, 371—7.

Cervone, D. (1992), 'The role of self-referent cognitions in goal setting, motivation, and performance', in M. Rabinowitz (ed.), *Applied Cognition*, Norwood, NJ: Ablex.

Cervone, D. and Kopp, D.A. (1991), 'Learning goals, performance goals and the differential influence of self-regulatory processes on complex decision making', unpublished manuscript, University of Illinois at Chicago.

Cervone, D. and Palmer, B.W. (1990), 'Anchoring biases and the perseverance of self-efficacy beliefs', *Cognitive Therapy and Research*, **14**, 401—16.

Cervone, D. and Peake, P.K. (1986), 'Anchoring, efficacy, and action: the influence of judgmental heuristics on self-efficacy judgments and behavior', *Journal of Personality and Social Psychology*, **50**, 492—501.

Cervone, D. and Wood, R. (1991), 'Goals, feedback, and the differential influence of self-regulatory processes on a complex decision task', unpublished manuscript, University of Illinois at Chicago.

Cervone, D., Jiwani, N. and Wood, R. (1991), 'Goal-setting and the differential influence of self-regulatory processes on complex decision-making performance', *Journal of Personality and Social Psychology,* **61**, 257–66.

Champagne, B. and Pervin, L.A. (1987), 'The relation of perceived situation similarity to perceived behavior similarity: implications for social learning theory', *European Journal of Personality,* **1**, 79–92.

Christensen-Szalanski, J.J.J. (1980), 'A further examination of the selection of problem-solving strategies: the effects of deadlines and analytic aptitudes', *Organizational Behavior and Human Performance,* **25**, 107–22.

Cohen, C.E. and Ebbesen, E.B. (1979), 'Observational goals and schema activation: a theoretical framework for behavior perception', *Journal of Experimental Social Psychology,* **15**, 305–29.

Contrada, R.J., Leventhal, H. and O'Leary, A. (1990), 'Personality and health', in L.A. Pervin (ed.), *Handbook of Personality: Theory and research,* New York, NY: Guilford Press, pp. 576–608.

Cook, M., Mineka, S., Wolkenstein, B. and Laitsch, K. (1985), 'Observational conditioning of snake fear in unrelated rhesus monkeys', *Journal of Abnormal Psychology,* **94**, 591–610.

Cutrona, C.E. and Troutman, B.R. (1986), 'Social support, infant temperament, and parenting self-efficacy: a mediational model of postpartum depression', *Child Development,* **57**, 1507–18.

DeGroot, M.H. (1970), *Optimal Statistical Decisions,* New York, NY: McGraw-Hill.

DiClemente, C.C. (1986), 'Self-efficacy and the addictive behaviors', *Journal of Social and Clinical Psychology,* **4**, 302–15.

Digman, J.M. (1990), 'Personality structure: emergence of the five-factor model', *Annual Review of Psychology,* **41**, 417–40.

Dowrick, P.W. (1983), 'Self-modeling', in P.W. Dowrick and S.J. Biggs (eds.), *Using Video: Psychological and social applications,* New York, NY: Wiley, pp. 105–24.

Dowrick, P.W. (1989), 'Videotraining strategies for beginners, champions, and injured athletes', in A.A. Turner (ed.), *Arctic Sports Medicine: Proceedings of the first Alaska regional chapter of the American College of Sports Medicine,* Anchorage, AL: American College of Sports Medicine, pp. 1–9.

Dowrick, P.W. and Hood, M. (1981), 'Comparison of self-modeling and small cash incentives in a sheltered workshop', *Journal of Applied Psychology,* **66**, 394–7.

Dweck, C.S. and Leggett, E.L. (1988), 'A social-cognitive approach to motivation and personality', *Psychological Review,* **95**, 256–73.

Earley, P.C., Wojnaroski, P. and Prest, W. (1987), 'Task planning and energy expended: exploration of how goals influence performance', *Journal of Applied Psychology,* **72**, 107–14.

Elliott, E.S. and Dweck, C.S. (1988), 'Goals, an approach to motivation and achievement', *Journal of Personality and Social Psychology,* **54**, 5–12.

Emmelkamp, P.M.G. and Felten, M. (1985), 'The process of exposure *in vivo*: cognitive and psychological changes during treatment of acrophobia', *Behaviour Research and Therapy,* **23**, 219–23.

Emmons, R.A. (1989), 'The personal striving approach to personality', in L.A. Pervin (ed.), *Goal Concepts in Personality and Social Psychology,* Hillsdale, NJ: Erlbaum, pp. 87–126.

Emmons, R.A., Diener, E. and Larsen, R.J. (1986), 'Choice and avoidance of everyday situations and affect congruence: two models of reciprocal interactionism', *Journal of Personality and Social Psychology,* **51**, 815–26.

Epstein, S. (1979), 'The stability of behavior: on predicting most of the people much of the time', *Journal of Personality and Social Psychology,* **37**, 1097–126.

Erez, M. (1977), 'Feedback: a necessary condition for the goal setting–performance relationship', *Journal of Applied Psychology,* **62**, 624–7.

Eron, L.D. (1987), 'The development of aggressive behavior from the perspective of a developing behaviorism', *American Psychologist*, **42**, 435–42.

Eron, L.D., Huesmann, L.R., Lefkowitz, M.M. and Walder, L.O. (1972), 'Does television violence cause aggression?', *American Psychologist*, **27**, 253–63.

Eysenck, H.J. (1978), 'Expectations as causal elements in behavioural change', *Advances in Behaviour Research and Therapy*, **1**, 171–5.

Eysenck, H.J. (1990), 'Biological dimensions of personality', in L.A. Pervin (ed.), *Handbook of Personality: Theory and research*, New York, NY: Guilford Press, pp. 244–76.

Fiske, D.W. (1949), 'Consistency of the factorial structure of personality ratings from different sources', *Journal of Abnormal and Social Psychology*, **44**, 329–44.

Fitts, P.M. (1964), 'Perceptual-motor skill learning', in A.W. Melton (ed.), *Categories of Human Learning*, New York, NY: Academic Press, pp. 243–85.

Funder, D.C. (1991), 'Global traits: a neo-Allportian approach to personality', *Psychological Science*, **2**, 31–9.

Garber, J. and Seligman, M.E.P. (1980), *Human Helplessness: Theory and application*, New York, NY: Academic Press.

Gauthier, J. and Ladouceur, R. (1981), 'The influence of self-efficacy reports on performance', *Behavior Therapy*, **12**, 436–9.

Gerst, M.S. (1971), 'Symbolic coding processes in observational learning', *Journal of Personality and Social Psychology*, **19**, 7–17.

Goldberg, L. (1981), 'Language and individual differences: the search for universals in personality lexicons', in L. Wheeler (ed.), *Review of Personality and Social Psychology*, Beverly Hills, CA: Sage, vol. 2, pp. 141–65.

Goldsmith, H.H. (1983), 'Genetic influences on personality from infancy to adulthood', *Child Development*, **54**, 331–55.

Goldstein, A.J. and Chambless, D.L. (1978), 'A reanalysis of agoraphobia', *Behavior Therapy*, **9**, 47–59.

Heckhausen, H. (1967), *The Anatomy of Achievement Motivation*, New York, NY: Academic Press.

Hersen, M., Kazdin, A.E., Bellack, A.S. and Turner, S.M. (1979), 'Effects of live modeling, covert modeling, and rehearsal on assertiveness in psychiatric patients', *Behaviour Research and Therapy*, **17**, 369–77.

Higgins, E.T. (1987), 'Self-discrepancy: a theory relating self and affect', *Psychological Review*, **94**, 319–40.

Higgins, E.T. (1990), 'Personality, social psychology, as person–situation relations: standards and knowledge activation as a common language', in L.A. Pervin (ed.), *Handbook of Personality: Theory and research*, New York, NY: Guilford Press, pp. 301–38.

Higgins, E.T., Bond, R.N. and Straumann, T. (1986), 'Self-discrepancies and emotional vulnerability: how magnitude, accessibility and type of discrepancy influence effect', *Journal of Personality and Social Psychology*, **51**, 5–15.

Hoffman, C., Mischel, W. and Mazze, K. (1981), 'The role of purpose in the organization of information about behavior: trait-based versus goal-based categories in person cognition', *Journal of Personality and Social Psychology*, **40**, 211–25.

Hogan, R. (1982), 'On adding apples and oranges in personality psychology', *Contemporary Psychology*, **27**, 851–2.

Holahan, C.K. and Holahan, C.J. (1987), 'Life stress, hassles, and self-efficacy in aging: a replication and extension', *Journal of Applied Social Psychology*, **17**, 574–92.

Hsee, C.K. and Abelson, R.P. (1991), 'Velocity relation: satisfaction as a function of the first derivative of outcome over time', *Journal of Personality and Social Psychology*, **60**, 341–7.

Hsee, C.K., Abelson, R.P. and Salovey, P. (1991), 'The relative weighting of position and velocity in satisfaction', *Psychological Science*, **2**, 263–6.

Huber, V.L. and Neale, M.A. (1987), 'Effects of self- and competitor goals in performance in an interdependent bargaining task', *Journal of Applied Psychology*, **72**, 197–203.

Huesmann, L.R. (1988), 'An information processing model for the development of aggression', *Aggressive Behavior*, **14**, 13–24.

Humphreys, M.S. and Revelle, W. (1984), 'Personality, motivation, and performance: a theory of the relationship between individual differences and information processing', *Psychological Review*, **91**, 153–84.

Hunt, E. and Agnoli, F. (1991), 'The Whorfian hypothesis: a cognitive psychology perspective', *Psychological Review*, **98**, 377–89.

Isen, A.M. (1987), 'Positive affect, cognitive processes, and social behavior', in L. Berkowitz (ed.), *Advances in Experimental Social Psychology*, San Diego, CA: Academic Press, vol. 20, pp. 203–53.

Isen, A.M., Shalker, T.E., Clark, M. and Karp, L. (1978), 'Affect, accessibility of material in memory, and behavior: a cognitive loop?', *Journal of Personality and Social Psychology*, **36**, 1–12.

Jackson, D.N. and Paunonen, S.V. (1985), 'Construct validity and the predictability of behavior', *Journal of Personality and Social Psychology*, **49**, 554–70.

John, O.P. (1989), 'Towards a taxonomy of personality descriptors', in D.M. Buss and N. Cantor (eds.), *Personality Psychology: Recent trends and emerging directions*, New York, NY: Springer-Verlag, pp. 261–71.

John, O.P. (1990), 'The "Big Five" factor taxonomy: dimensions of personality in the natural language and in questionnaires', in L.A. Pervin (ed.), *Handbook of Personality: Theory and research*, New York, NY: Guilford Press, pp. 66–100.

Kahneman, D. and Tversky, A. (1972), 'Subjective probability: a judgment of representativeness', *Cognitive Psychology*, **3**, 430–54.

Kahneman, D. and Tversky, A. (1982), 'The simulation heuristic', in D. Kahneman, P. Slovic and A. Tversky (eds.), *Judgment under Uncertainty: Heuristics and biases*, Cambridge: Cambridge University Press, pp. 201–8.

Kahneman, D., Slovic, P. and Tversky, A. (1982), *Judgment under Uncertainty: Heuristics and biases*, Cambridge: Cambridge University Press.

Kanfer, F.H. (1980), 'Self-management methods', in F.H. Kanfer and A.P. Goldstein (eds.), *Helping People Change* (second edition), New York, NY: Pergamon, pp. 334–89.

Kanfer, R. and Zeiss, A.M. (1983), 'Depression, interpersonal standard-setting, and judgments of self-efficacy', *Journal of Abnormal Psychology*, **92**, 319–29.

Kaufman, A., Baron, A. and Kopp, R.E. (1966), 'Some effects of instructions on human operant behavior', *Psychonomic Monograph Supplements*, **1**, 243–50.

Kavanagh, D.J. and Bower, G.H. (1985), 'Mood and self-efficacy: impact of joy and sadness on perceived capabilities', *Cognitive Therapy and Research*, **9**, 507–25.

Kazdin, A.E. (1974), 'Reactive self-monitoring: the effects of response desirability, goal setting, and feedback', *Journal of Consulting and Clinical Psychology*, **42**, 704–16.

Kazdin, A.E. (1984), 'Covert modeling', *Advances in Cognitive-behavioral Research and Therapy*, **3**, 103–29.

Kenrick, D.T. and Funder, D.C. (1988), 'Profiting from controversy: lessons from the person–situation debate', *American Psychologist*, **43**, 23–34.

Kent, G. (1987), 'Self-efficacious control over reported physiological, cognitive and behavioural symptoms of dental anxiety', *Behaviour Research and Therapy*, **25**, 341–7.

Kent, G. and Gibbons, R. (1987), 'Self-efficacy and the control of anxious cognitions', *Journal of Behavior Therapy and Experimental Psychiatry*, **18**, 33–40.

Kihlstrom, J.F. and Harackiewicz, J.M. (1990), 'An evolutionary milestone in the psychology of personality: book review essay on Bandura's *Social Foundations of Thought and Action*', *Psychological Inquiry*, **1**, 86–92.

Klinger, E. (1975), 'Consequences of commitment to and disengagement from incentives', *Psychological Review*, **82**, 1–25.

Ladd, G.W. and Mize, J. (1983), 'A cognitive-social learning model of social-skill training', *Psychological Review*, **90**, 127–57.

Ladouceur, R. (1983), 'Participant modeling with or without cognitive treatment of phobias', *Journal of Consulting and Clinical Psychology*, **51**, 942–4.

Lang, P.J. (1971), 'The application of psychophysiological methods to the study of psychotherapy and behavior modification', in A.E. Bergin and S.L. Garfield (eds.), *Handbook of Psychotherapy and Behavior Change*, New York, NY: Wiley, pp. 75–125.

Langer, E. and Benevento, A. (1978), 'Self-induced dependence', *Journal of Personality and Social Psychology*, **36**, 886–93.

Langston, C. and Cantor, N. (1989), 'Social anxiety and social constraint: when "making friends" is hard', *Journal of Personality and Social Psychology*, **56**, 649–61.

LaPorte, R.E. and Nath, R. (1976), 'Role of performance goals in prose learning', *Journal of Educational Psychology*, **68**, 260–4.

Lazarus, R.S. (1991), *Emotion and Adaptation*, New York, NY: Oxford University Press.

Lazarus, R.S. and Folkman, S. (1984), *Stress, Appraisal, and Coping*, New York, NY: Springer.

Leitenberg, H. (1976), 'Behavioral approaches to treatment of neuroses', in H. Leitenberg (ed.), *Handbook of Behavior Modification and Behavior Therapy*, Englewood Cliffs, NJ: Prentice Hall, pp. 124–67.

Leitenberg, H., Agras, S., Butz, R. and Wincze, J. (1971), 'Relationship between heart rate and behavioral change during the treatment of phobias', *Journal of Abnormal Psychology*, **78**, 59–68.

Lepper, M.R., Sagotsky, J. and Mailer, J. (1975), 'Generalization and persistence of effects of exposure to self-reinforcement models', *Child Development*, **46**, 618–30.

Lerner, R.M. (1990), 'Weaving development into the fabric of personality and social psychology — on the significance of Bandura's *Social Foundations of Thought and Action*', *Psychological Inquiry*, **1**, 92–6.

Lewin, K., Dembo, T., Festinger, L. and Sears, P.S. (1944), 'Level of aspiration', in J.M. Hunt (ed.), *Personality and the Behavior Disorders*, New York, NY: Ronald Press, vol. 1, pp. 333–78.

Lewinsohn, P.M., Sullivan, J.M. and Grosscup, S.J. (1982), 'Behavioral therapy: clinical applications', in A.J. Rush (ed.), *Short-term Psychotherapies for Depression: Behavior, interpersonal, cognitive, and psychodynamic approaches*, Chichester: Wiley/New York: Guilford Press, pp. 50–87.

Liebert, R.M. and Sprafkin, J. (1988), *The Early Window: Effects of television on children and youth*, New York, NY: Pergamon.

Linville, P.W. and Clark, L.F. (1989), 'Production systems and social problem solving: specificity, flexibility, and expertise', in R.S. Wyer and T.K. Srull (eds.), *Advances in Social Cognition*, Hillsdale, NJ: Erlbaum, vol. 2, pp. 123–30.

Little, B.R. (1989), 'Personal projects analysis: trivial pursuits, magnificent obsessions, and the search for coherence', in D.M. Buss and N. Cantor (eds.), *Personality Psychology: Recent trends and emerging directions*, New York, NY: Springer-Verlag, pp. 15–31.

Locke, E.A. (1968), 'Toward a theory of task motivation and incentives', *Organizational Behavior and Human Performance*, **3**, 157–89.

Locke, E.A. and Latham, G.P. (1990), *A Theory of Goal Setting and Task Performance*, Englewood Cliffs, NJ: Prentice Hall.

Locke, E.A., Frederick, E., Lee, C. and Bobko, P. (1984), 'Effect of self-efficacy, goals, and task strategies on task performance', *Journal of Applied Psychology*, **69**, 241–51.

Locke, E.A., Shaw, K.N., Saari, L.M. and Latham, G.P. (1981), 'Goal setting and task performance: 1969–1980', *Psychological Bulletin*, **90**, 125–52.

Loevinger, J. (1987), *Paradigms of Personality*, New York, NY: Freeman.

Lord, C.G. (1982), 'Predicting behavioral consistency from an individual's perception of situational similarities', *Journal of Personality and Social Psychology*, **42**, 1076–88.

McCrae, R.R. and Costa, P.T. Jr. (1986), 'Clinical assessment can benefit from recent advances in personality psychology', *American Psychologist*, **41**, 1001–3.

McCrae, R.R. and Costa, P.T. Jr. (1987), 'Validation of the five-factor model of personality across instruments and observers', *Journal of Personality and Social Psychology*, **52**, 81–90.

McCrae, R.R. and Costa, P.T. Jr. (1990), *Personality in Adulthood*, New York, NY; Guilford Press.

Magnusson, D. and Endler, N.S. (eds.) (1977), *Personality at the Crossroads: Current issues in interactional psychology*, Hillsdale, NJ: Erlbaum.

Maier, S.F., Laudenslager, M.L. and Ryan, S.M. (1985), 'Stressor controllability, immune function, and endogenous opiates', in F.R. Brush and J.B. Overmier (eds.), *Affect, Conditioning, and Cognition: Essays on the determinants of behavior*, Hillsdale, NJ: Erlbaum, pp. 183–201.

Mandler, G. (1962), 'Emotion', in R. Brown, E. Galanter, E. Hess and G. Mandler (eds.), *New Directions in Psychology I*, New York, NY: Holt, Rinehart & Winston, pp. 269–343.

Marks, I.M. (1978), 'Behavioral psychotherapy of adult neurosis', in S.L. Garfield and A.E. Bergin (eds.), *Handbook of Psychotherapy and Behavior Change*, New York, NY: Wiley, pp. 493–547.

Markus, H. and Nurius, P. (1986), 'Possible selves', *American Psychologist*, **41**, 954–69.

Markus, H. and Wurf, E. (1987), 'The dynamic self-concept: a social psychological perspective', *Annual Review of Psychology*, **38**, 299–337.

Masters, W.H. and Johnson, V. (1979), *Human Sexual Inadequacy*, Boston, MA: Little, Brown.

Matsui, T., Okada, A. and Inoshita, O. (1983), 'Mechanism of feedback affecting task performance', *Organizational Behavior and Human Performance*, **31**, 114–22.

Mattick, R.P. and Peters, L. (1988), 'Treatment of severe social phobia: effects of guided exposure with and without cognitive restructuring', *Journal of Consulting and Clinical Psychology*, **56**, 251–60.

Merckelbach, H., Arntz, A. and De Jong, P. (1991), 'Conditioning experiences in spider phobics', *Behaviour Research and Therapy*, **29**, 333–5.

Mento, A.J., Steel, R.P. and Karren, R.J. (1987), 'A meta-analytic study of the effects of goal setting on task performance: 1966–1984', *Organizational Behavior and Human Decision Processes*, **39**, 52–83.

Miller, G.A., Galanter, E. and Pribram, K.H. (1960), *Plans and the Structure of Behavior*, New York, NY: Holt, Rinehart & Winston.

Miller, S.M. (1979a), 'Controllability and human stress: method, evidence, and theory', *Behaviour Research and Therapy*, **17**, 287–304.

Miller, S.M. (1979b), 'Why having control reduces stress: if I can stop the rollercoaster I don't want to get off', in J. Garber and M.E.P. Seligman (eds.), *Human Helplessness: Theory and research*, New York, NY: Academic Press, pp. 71–95.

Miller, S.M. (1989), 'Cognitive informational styles in the process of coping with threat and frustration', special issue, 'the role of individual differences in stress and stress management', *Advances in Behaviour Research and Therapy*, **11**, 223–4.

Mineka, S. (1979), 'The role of fear in theories of avoidance learning, flooding, and extinction', *Psychological Bulletin*, **86**, 985–1010.

Mineka, S. (1985), 'The frightful complexity of the origins of fears', in F. Brush and J. Overmier (eds.), *Affect, Conditioning, and Cognition: Essays on the determinants of behavior*, Hillsdale, NJ: Erlbaum, pp. 55–73.

Mineka, S. and Kelly, K.A. (1989), 'The relationship between anxiety, lack of control and loss of control', in A. Steptoe and A. Appels (eds.), *Stress, Personal Control and Health*, New York, NY: Wiley, pp. 163−91.

Mineka, S., Davidson, M., Cook, M. and Keir, R. (1984), 'Observational conditioning of snake fear in rhesus monkeys', *Journal of Abnormal Psychology, 93*, 355−72.

Mischel, W. (1968), *Personality and Assessment*, New York, NY: Wiley.

Mischel, W. (1973), 'Toward a cognitive social learning reconceptualization of personality', *Psychological Review, 80*, 252−83.

Mischel, W. (1983), 'Alternatives in the pursuit of the predictability and consistency of persons: stable data that yield unstable interpretations', *Journal of Personality, 51*, 578−604.

Mischel, W. (1990), 'Personality dispositions revisited and revised: a view after three decades', in L.A. Pervin (ed.), *Handbook of Personality: Theory and research*, New York, NY: Guilford Press, pp. 111−64.

Mischel, W. and Baker, N. (1975), 'Cognitive transformations of reward objects through instructions', *Journal of Personality and Social Psychology, 31*, 254−61.

Mischel, W. and Peake, P.K. (1982), 'Beyond déjà-vu in the search for cross-situational consistency', *Psychological Review, 89*, 730−55.

Mischel, W., Shoda, Y. and Rodriguez, M. (1989), 'Delay of gratification in children', *Science, 244*, 933−8.

Moore, B., Mischel, W. and Zeiss, A.R. (1976), 'Comparative effects of the reward stimulus and its cognitive representation in voluntary delay', *Journal of Personality and Social Psychology, 34*, 419−24.

Mowrer, O.H. (1960), *Learning Theory and Behavior*, New York, NY: Wiley.

Murray, E.J. and Foote, F. (1979), 'The origins of fear of snakes', *Behaviour Research and Therapy, 17*, 489−93.

Neuberg, S.L. and Fiske, S.T. (1987), 'Motivational influences on impression formation: outcome dependency, accuracy-driven attention, and individuating processes', *Journal of Personality and Social Psychology, 53*, 431−44.

Newell, A. and Simon, H.A. (1976), 'Computer science as empirical inquiry: symbols and search', *Communications of the ACM, 19*, 113−26.

Nicholls, J.G. (1984), 'Achievement motivation: conceptions of ability, subjective experience, task choice, and performance', *Psychological Review, 91*, 328−46.

Nisbett, R. and Ross, L. (1980), *Human Inference: Strategies and shortcomings of social judgment*, Englewood Cliffs, NJ: Prentice Hall.

Nisbett, R.E., Fong, G.T., Lehman, D.R. and Cheng, P.W. (1987), 'Teaching reasoning', *Science, 238*, 625−31.

Norman, W.T. (1963), 'Toward an adequate taxonomy of personality attributes: replicated factor structure in peer nomination personality ratings', *Journal of Abnormal and Social Psychology, 66*, 574−83.

O'Brien, T. and Kelley, J. (1980), 'A comparison of self-directed and therapist-directed practice for fear reduction', *Behaviour Research and Therapy, 18*, 573−9.

O'Leary, A. (1985), 'Self-efficacy and health', *Behaviour Research and Therapy, 23*, 437−51.

Ost, L., Salkovskis, P.M. and Hellstrom, K. (1991), 'One-session therapist-directed exposure vs. self-exposure in the treatment of spider phobia', *Behavior Therapy, 22*, 407−22.

Peake, P.K. and Cervone, D. (1989), 'Sequence anchoring and self-efficacy: primacy effects in the consideration of possibilities', *Social Cognition, 7*, 31−50.

Pervin, L.A. (ed.) (1989a), *Goal Concepts in Personality and Social Psychology*, Hillsdale, NJ: Erlbaum.

Pervin, L.A. (1989b), *Personality: Theory and research* (fifth edition), New York, NY: Wiley.

Pervin, L.A. (1989c), 'Psychodynamic-systems reflections on a social-intelligence model of personality', in R.S. Wyer, Jr. and T.K. Srull (eds.), *Advances in Social Cognition*, Hillsdale, NJ: Erlbaum, vol. 2, pp. 153−61.

Plomin, R. and Daniels, D. (1987), 'Why are children in the same family so different from one another?', *Behavioral and Brain Sciences,* **10**, 1−16.

Plomin, R., Chipuer, H.M. and Loehlin, J.C. (1990) 'Behavioral genetics and personality', in L.A. Pervin (ed.), *Handbook of Personality: Theory and research,* New York, NY: Guilford Press, pp. 225−43.

Podsakoff, P.M. and Farh, J. (1989), 'Effects of feedback sign and credibility on goal setting and task performance', *Organizational Behavior and Human Decision Processes,* **44**, 45−67.

Rachman, S. (1976), 'The passing of the two-stage theory of fear and avoidance: fresh possibilities', *Behaviour Research and Therapy,* **14**, 125−31.

Rachman, S. (1977), 'The conditioning theory of fear-acquisition: a critical reexamination', *Behaviour Research and Therapy,* **15**, 375−87.

Rachman, S. (ed.) (1978), 'Perceived self-efficacy: analyses of Bandura's theory of behavioural change', special issue, *Advances in Behaviour Research and Therapy,* **1**(2).

Read, S.J. and Miller, L.C. (1989), 'Inter-personalism: toward a goal-based theory of persons in relationships', in L.A. Pervin (ed.), *Goal Concepts in Personality and Social Psychology,* Hillsdale, NJ: Erlbaum, pp. 413−72.

Rehm, L.P. (1977), 'A self-control model of depression', *Behavior Therapy,* **8**, 787−804.

Roper, G., Rachman, S. and Marks, I. (1975), 'Passive and participant modelling in exposure treatment of obsessive-compulsive neurotics', *Behaviour Research and Therapy,* **13**, 271−9.

Rosenhan, D., Frederick, F. and Burrowes, A. (1968), 'Preaching and practicing: effects of channel discrepancy on norm internalization', *Child Development,* **39**, 291−301.

Rosenthal, T.L. and Bandura, A. (1978), 'Psychological modeling: theory and practice', in S.L. Garfield and A.E. Bergin (eds.), *Handbook of Psychotherapy and Behaviour Change* (second edition), New York, NY: Wiley, pp. 621−58.

Rosenthal, T.L. and Zimmerman, B.J. (1978), *Social Learning and Cognition,* New York, NY: Academic Press.

Ross, L., Lepper, M.R. and Hubbard, M. (1975), 'Perseverance in self-perception and social perception: biased attributional processes in the debriefing paradigm', *Journal of Personality and Social Psychology,* **32**, 880−92.

Rothkopf, E.Z. and Billington, M.J. (1975), 'A two-factor model of the effect of goal descriptive directions on learning from text', *Journal of Educational Psychology,* **67**, 692−704.

Rothkopf, E.Z. and Billington, M.J. (1979), 'Goal-guided learning from text: inferring a descriptive processing model from inspection times and eye movements', *Journal of Educational Psychology,* **71**, 310−27.

Rotter, J.B. (1966), 'Generalized expectancies for internal versus external control of reinforcement', *Psychological Monographs,* **80** (1, whole no. 609).

Sales, S.M. (1970), 'Some effects of role overload and role underload', *Organizational Behavior and Human Performance,* **5**, 592−608.

Salkovskis, P.M. and Harrison, J. (1984), 'Abnormal and normal obsessions — a replication', *Behaviour Research and Therapy,* **22**, 549−52.

Salovey, P. and Birnbaum, D. (1989), 'Influence of mood on health-relevant cognitions', *Journal of Personality and Social Psychology,* **57**, 539−51.

Sanderson, W.C., Rapee, R.M. and Barlow, D.H. (1989), 'The influence of an illusion of control on panic attacks induced via inhalation of 5.5% carbon-dioxide enriched air', *Archives of General Psychiatry,* **46**, 157−62.

Sarason, I.G. (1975), 'Anxiety and self-preoccupation', in I.G. Sarason and D.C. Spielberger (eds.), *Stress and Anxiety,* Washington, DC: Hemisphere, vol. 2, pp. 27−44.

Sarason, I.G., Potter, E.H., III and Sarason, B.R. (1986), 'Recording and recall of personal events: effects on cognitions and behavior', *Journal of Personality and Social Psychology,* **51**, 347−56.

Sarason, I.G., Sarason, B.R. and Pierce, G.R. (1990), 'Anxiety, cognitive interference, and performance', *Journal of Social Behavior and Personality*, **5**, 1–18.

Schunk, D.H. (1984), 'Self-efficacy perspective on achievement behavior', *Educational Psychologist*, **19**, 48–58.

Schwartz, B. (1984), *Psychology of Learning and Behavior*, New York, NY: Norton.

Schwarz, N., Bless, H., Strack, F., Klumpp, G., Rittenauer-Schatka, H. and Simons, A. (1991), 'Ease of retrieval as information: another look at the availability heuristic', *Journal of Personality and Social Psychology*, **61**, 195–202.

Seligman, M.E.P. (1975), *Helplessness: On depression, development, and death*, San Francisco, CA: Freeman.

Seligman, M.E.P. and Johnston, J.C. (1973), 'A cognitive theory of avoidance learning', in F.J. McGuigan and D.B. Lumsden (eds.), *Contemporary Approaches to Conditioning and Learning*, Washington, DC: Winston & Sons, pp. 69–110.

Sells, S.B. and Murphy, D. (1984), 'Factor theories of personality', in N.S. Endler and J.M. Hunt (eds.), *Personality and the Behavioral Disorders*, New York, NY: Wiley, pp. 39–72.

Showers, C. and Cantor, N. (1985), 'Social cognition: a look at motivated strategies', *Annual Review of Psychology*, **36**, 275–306.

Simon, H.A. (1983), *Reason and Human Affairs*, Stanford, CA: Stanford University Press.

Simon, H.A. (1990), 'Invariants of human behavior', *Annual Review of Psychology*, **41**, 1–19.

Simon, K.M. (1979), 'Self-evaluative reactions: the role of personal valuation of the activity', *Cognitive Therapy and Research*, **3**, 111–16.

Skinner, B.F. (1953), *Science and Human Behavior*, New York, NY: Macmillan.

Skinner, B.F. (1974), *About Behaviorism*, New York, NY: Random House.

Smith, R.E. (1989), 'Effects of coping skills training on generalized self-efficacy and locus of control', *Journal of Personality and Social Psychology*, **56**, 228–33.

Snyder, M. (1981), 'On the influence of individuals on situations', in N. Cantor and J.F. Kihlstrom (eds.), *Personality, Cognition, and Social Interaction*, Hillsdale, NJ: Erlbaum, pp. 309–29.

Snyder, M. and Ickes, W. (1985), 'Personality and social behavior', in G. Lindzey and E. Aronson (eds.), *Handbook of Social Psychology*, New York, NY: Random House, pp. 883–947.

Southworth, S. and Kirsch, I. (1988), 'The role of expectancy in exposure-generated fear reduction in agoraphobia', *Behaviour Research and Therapy*, **26**, 113–20.

Stamfl, T.G. and Levis, D.J. (1967), 'Essentials of implosive therapy', *Journal of Abnormal Psychology*, **72**, 270–6.

Stanley, M.A. and Maddux, J.E. (1986), 'Self-efficacy theory: potential contributions to understanding cognitions in depression', *Journal of Social and Clinical Psychology*, **4**, 268–78.

Stevenson, M.K., Kanfer, F.H. and Higgins, J.M. (1984), 'Effects of goal specificity and time cues on pain tolerance', *Cognitive Therapy and Research*, **8**, 415–26.

Stock, J. and Cervone, D. (1990), 'Proximal goal-setting and self-regulatory processes', *Cognitive Therapy and Research*, **14**, 483–9.

Taylor, S.E. and Brown, J.D. (1988), 'Illusion and well-being: a social psychological perspective on mental health', *Psychological Bulletin*, **103**, 193–210.

Taylor, S.E. and Fiske, S.T. (1978), 'Salience, attention, and attribution: top of the head phenomena', in L. Berkowitz (ed.), *Advances in Experimental Social Psychology*, New York, NY: Academic Press, vol. 11, pp. 249–88.

Telch, M.J., Agras, W.S., Taylor, C.B., Roth, W.T. and Gallen, C.C. (1985), 'Combined pharmacological and behavioral treatment for agoraphobia', *Behaviour Research and Therapy*, **23**, 325–35.

Telch, M.J., Bandura, A., Vinciguerra, P., Agras, A. and Stout, A.L. (1982), 'Social demand for consistency and congruence between self-efficacy and performance', *Behavior Therapy*, **13**, 694–701.

Tetlock, P.E. and Kim, J.I. (1987), 'Accountability and judgment processes in a personality prediction task', *Journal of Personality and Social Psychology*, **52**, 700–9.

Thomas, E.A.C. and Malone, T.W. (1979), 'On the dynamics of two-person interactions', *Psychological Review*, **86**, 331–60.

Thoresen, C.E. and Mahoney, M.J. (1974), *Behavioral Self-control*, New York, NY: Holt, Rinehart & Winston.

Tolman, E.C. (1932), *Purposive Behavior in Animals and Men*, New York, NY: Century.

Tubbs, M.E. (1986), 'Goal setting: a meta-analytic examination of the empirical evidence', *Journal of Applied Psychology*, **71**, 474–83.

Tupes, E.C. and Christal, R.C. (1961), *Recurrent Personality Factors Based on Trait Ratings* (Tech. Rep. No. ASD-TR-61-97), Lackland Air Force Base, TX: US Air Force.

Tversky, A. and Kahneman, D. (1973), 'Availability: a heuristic for judging frequency and probability', *Cognitive Psychology*, **5**, 207–32.

Tversky, A. and Kahneman, D. (1974), 'Judgment under uncertainty: heuristics and biases', *Science*, **185**, 1123–31.

Watson, D.L. and Tharp, R.G. (1977), *Self-directed Behavior: Self-modification for personal adjustment* (second edition), Monterey, CA: Brooks/Cole.

Weinberg, R.S., Gould, D. and Jackson, A. (1979), 'Expectations and performance: an empirical test of Bandura's self-efficacy theory', *Journal of Sport Psychology*, **1**, 320–31.

Weiner, B. (1985), 'An attributional theory of achievement motivation and emotion', *Psychological Review*, **92**, 548–73.

Wiedenfeld, S.A., O'Leary, A., Bandura, A., Brown, S., Levine, S. and Raska, K. (1990), 'Impact of perceived self-efficacy in coping with stressors on components of the immune system', *Journal of Personality and Social Psychology*, **59**, 1082–94.

Williams, S.L. (1985), 'On the nature and measurement of agoraphobia', *Progress in Behavior Modification*, **19**, 109–44.

Williams, S.L. (1987), 'On anxiety and phobia', *Journal of Anxiety Disorders*, **1**, 161–80.

Williams, S.L. (1988), 'Addressing misconceptions about phobia, anxiety, and self-efficacy: a reply to Marks's, *Journal of Anxiety Disorders*, **2**, 277–89.

Williams, S.L. (1990), 'Guided mastery treatment of agoraphobia: beyond stimulus exposure', *Progress in Behavior Modification*, **26**, 89–121.

Williams, S.L. (1992), 'Perceived self-efficacy and phobic disability', in R. Schwarzer (ed.), *Self-efficacy: Thought control of action*, New York, NY: Hemisphere, pp. 149–76.

Williams, S.L. and Bauchiess, R. (1992), 'Cognitive factors influencing the persistence of agoraphobic avoidance and the rapidity of change during treatment', unpublished manuscript, Lehigh University.

Williams, S.L. and Kinney, P.J. (1991), 'Performance and nonperformance strategies for coping with acute pain: the role of perceived self-efficacy, expected outcomes, and attention', *Cognitive Therapy and Research*, **15**, 1–19.

Williams, S.L. and Rappoport, A. (1983), 'Cognitive treatment in the natural environment for agoraphobics', *Behavior Therapy*, **14**, 299–313.

Williams, S.L. and Watson, N. (1985), 'Perceived danger and perceived self-efficacy as cognitive determinants of acrophobic behavior', *Behavior Therapy*, **16**, 237–47.

Williams, S.L. and Zane, G. (1988), 'Guided mastery and stimulus exposure treatments for severe performance anxiety in agoraphobics', *Behaviour Reseach and Therapy*, **27**, 237–47.

Williams, S.L., Dooseman, G. and Kleifield, E. (1984), 'Comparative effectiveness of guided mastery and exposure treatments for intractable phobias', *Journal of Consulting and Clinical Psychology*, **52**, 505–18.

Williams, S.L., Kinney, P.J. and Falbo, J. (1989), 'Generalization of therapeutic changes in agoraphobia: the role of perceived self-efficacy', *Journal of Consulting and Clinical Psychology,* **57**, 436–42.

Williams, S.L., Turner, S.M. and Peer, D.F. (1985), 'Guided mastery and performance desensitization treatments for severe acrophobia', *Journal of Consulting and Clinical Psychology,* **53**, 237–47.

Wilson, G.T., Rossiter, E., Kleifield, E.I. and Lindholm, L. (1986), 'Cognitive-behavioral treatment of bulimia nervosa: a controlled evaluation', *Behaviour Research and Therapy,* **24**, 277–88.

Wolpe, J. (1958), *Psychotherapy by Reciprocal Inhibition,* Stanford, CA: Stanford University Press.

Wolpe, J. (1978), 'Self-efficacy theory and psychotherapeutic change: a square peg for a round hole', *Advances in Behaviour Research and Therapy,* **1**, 231–6.

Wolpe, J. and Lazarus, A.A. (1966), *Behavior Therapy Techniques,* New York, NY: Pergamon.

Wood, R. and Bailey, T. (1985), 'Some unanswered questions about goal effects: a recommended change in research methods', *Australian Journal of Management,* **10**, 61–73.

Wood, R.E. and Bandura, A. (1989), 'Impact of conceptions of ability on self-regulatory mechanisms and complex decision making', *Journal of Personality and Social Psychology,* **56**, 407–15.

Wood, R.E. and Locke, E.A. (1990), 'Goal setting and strategy effects on complex tasks', in E.A. Locke and G.P. Latham, *A Theory of Goal Setting and Task Performance,* Englewood Cliffs, NJ: Prentice Hall.

Wood, R.E., Bandura, A. and Bailey, T. (1990), 'Mechanisms governing organizational productivity in complex decision-making environments', *Organizational Behavior and Human Decision Processes,* **46**, 181–201.

Wood, R.E., Mento, A.J. and Locke, E.A. (1987), 'Task complexity as a moderator of goal effects: a meta-analysis', *Journal of Applied Psychology,* **72**, 416–25.

Wright, J.C. and Mischel, W. (1987), 'A conditional analysis of dispositional constructs: the local predictability of social behavior', *Journal of Personality and Social Psychology,* **53**, 1159–77.

Wright, J.C. and Mischel, W. (1988), 'Conditional hedges and the intuitive psychology of traits', *Journal of Personality and Social Psychology,* **55**, 454–69.

Yussen, S.R. (1974), 'Determinants of attention and visual recall in observational learning by preschoolers and second graders', *Developmental Psychology,* **10**, 93–100.

PART V
The Cognitive Approach

9/ The cognitive view of personality
The approaches of meaning and cognitive orientation

Shulamith Kreitler and Hans Kreitler

University of Tel Aviv, Israel

Introduction

The domain of personality has characteristically focused on the individual as a whole. Yet, within the framework of this emphasis on totality two issues remain focal in the past and present efforts at understanding the human being. Not surprisingly, these issues are also of importance for the layperson's conduct of his or her continuous interactions with human beings. One concerns the individual's *nature* and underlies questions such as these: What kind of person is he or she?; What is this person really like?; What kind of personality does he or she have?; Which personality characteristics does he or she have?; What is unique about this individual's personality?; How is personality acquired and developed?; What are the determinants of personality characteristics?; How can personality features be modified? The other issue concerns the individual's *behaviour* and underlies questions such as these: How will this person behave or react?; Why did he or she react as he or she did?; What are the determinants of behaviour?; What is unique about this person's behaviour?; How are behaviours acquired and developed?; How can behaviour be modified?

The variation in the form of the questions concerning each issue reflects differences in theoretical and methodological approaches. Thus, questions about the determinants of personality or behaviour reflect concern for causality, motivation, and understanding, whereas questions about specific characteristics of personality or expected behaviour reflect concern for assessment and prediction of traits and behaviours. The former are generally more theoretically oriented, the latter more applicational. Further, concerning each issue some questions refer to general laws or to characteristics shared by many or most individuals, whereas others refer to unique features of a specific individual. The former are generally of the nomothetic type, the latter of the ideographic class. These are, however, merely examples of differences in approach characterizing attempts to resolve one or both of the basic issues about human nature and human behaviour.

It is noteworthy also that all the major controversies characteristic of the field of personality in recent decades refer to one or another of the problems mentioned. Thus, one of the controversies clearly concerns the nature of the individual. More precisely, it refers to traits — one of the most basic constructs in personality — their nature, number, and functioning. A recent summary of the major viewpoints in this domain lists seven hypotheses about traits, none of which has been supported by data (Kenrick and Funder, 1988). These include claims that traits are unitary configurations in behaviour (Cattell, 1965) or units in individual consistency in behaviour (Allport, 1931), idiosyncratic constructs in the eye of the beholder (Gergen, 1968; Schank and Abelson, 1977), reputations of individuals shared by observers (Funder, 1980), or interpersonally shared linguistic labels (Bourne, 1977).

Other problems that have formed the core for controversies in recent years refer more clearly to behaviour. One of these is the problem of inconsistency of behaviour across situations (see Schmitt and Borkenau, Chapter 2 in this volume). The findings disconfirmed the assumption about stable characteristic individual tendencies that constitute the basis for personality (Kenrick and Funder, 1988) and supported rather the rival assumption about the impact of the external situation on behaviour. This problem is sometimes called the person—situation controversy. Attempts to resolve it include the different variants of interactionism (Endler and Edwards, 1978; Pervin, 1978; Staub, 1978; see also Forgas and Van Heck, Chapter 16 in this volume; Hettema and Kenrick, Chapter 15 in this volume). So far they have produced a large body of research demonstrating that behaviour is indeed co-determined by both personal and situational variables.

The trait—behaviour problem also refers to behaviour and its determinants. Traits have commonly been assumed to be related to behaviour, initiating and guiding it, as claimed by the strong version of this thesis (for example, Allport, 1966) or indicating some expected frequency of the behaviour corresponding to the trait or at least a tendency towards it, as claimed by the weak version of the thesis, sometimes known as the 'summary view' (Mischel, 1968; Shweder, 1975; Wiggins, 1973) or 'dispositional view' (Alston, 1975; Hirschberg, 1978), respectively. Yet, empirical evidence has contrasted with all three positions, showing that trait measures do not correlate with overt molar behaviours (Argyle and Little, 1972; Geis, 1978; Kendon and Cook, 1970; Mann 1959; Porter *et al.*, 1970). Some attempts to resolve this problem have focused on interactionism, which allocates a role to situations in shaping human tendencies (Berkowitz, 1967; Bowers, 1973; Endler, 1981; Hettema and Kenrick, Chapter 15 in this volume; Magnusson 1981; Magnusson and Endler, 1977). Other resolution attempts are based on adopting a critical approach to traits or research methodology, attributing the low relations of traits to behaviour to factors such as low reliability (Block, 1964) or low observability of the assessed traits (Kenrick and Stringfield, 1980), or to the procedure of correlating traits with single specific behaviours rather than with combinations of behaviours, global measures of behaviour (Argyle and Little, 1972), or extended samples of behaviour (Epstein, 1983).

Traits and behaviour, separately and in interrelation, seem to be the major foci of interest in the theory of personality. Thus, any new approach to personality is expected to provide new answers on these issues. The answers may be regarded as cornerstones for the structure of a new theory of personality. Our chapter will deal with these issues separately and then in their interrelation.

The major theoretical and methodological elements we apply are derived from *cognitive psychology*. Cognition is not a newcomer in the domain of personality. Previous applications, however, have characteristically focused on selected issues, such as consciousness (Kihlstrom, 1990), emotion (Ortony *et al.*, 1988; Weiner, 1985), or the self (Epstein, 1990). The exceptions, such as the attempts by George Kelly (1955) and Forgus and Shulman (1979) to present more complete theories of personality, do not yet address the issues that are of major concern on the modern scene of personality. In contrast, our approach is both comprehensive and addresses these major issues. We adopted the cognitive approach mainly because it provides the possibility of coping with the problems of personality on the level of underlying psychological processes. This possibility is important, especially because the controversial issues in personality present rifts between theoretical tenets and empirical data of the kind which, in other sciences, has frequently been resolved by proceeding beyond the given level of theorizing to a deeper and more basic level of conceptualization.

The psychosemantic theory of personality traits

Personality traits are a major construct representing a common psychological conceptualization in the domain of human nature. The underlying level to which we proceeded in our attempt to resolve some of the difficulties plaguing this construct is the psychosemantic level, defined by the statics and dynamics of meaning. Our theoretical and empirical explorations on the psychosemantic level have resulted in a new conception of traits. It is based on over 20 studies in which 115 of the commonly used personality traits were examined (Kreitler and Kreitler, 1984b, 1990a), allows for new solutions to some of the old problems about the nature, functioning, and manifestations of traits, and provides for the assessment of over 100 traits by means of one relatively simple test, namely, the Meaning Test. It may be summarized in the form of a definition. According to this psychosemantic conception, a trait is defined as a *unique pattern of meaning assignment tendencies*; these tendencies are within a limited numerical range, represent specific kinds of meaning variable, are applied by the individual partly frequently and partly infrequently, constitute together a specific structure, and reflect a characteristic grouping of perceptual, cognitive, emotional, and attitudinal manifestations.

The major element in this definition is the concept of meaning. Hence, understanding the definition, its operation, and its theoretical and practical advantages requires a presentation of the meaning system (Kreitler and Kreitler, 1976, 1982).

The system of meaning

The system of meaning provides for the characterization and assessment of human meanings of different kinds (for example, Kreitler and Kreitler, 1982, 1985a, 1985b, 1986a, 1986b, 1990a, 1990b, 1990c). It was designed to be broader in coverage and to have higher validity than the available measures of meaning (Kreitler and Kreitler, 1976, Chapter 2). In the present context, we will describe only those aspects of this psychosemantic system which are necessary for understanding our findings in regard to personality traits.

The major assumptions underlying the new system are that meaning is a complex phenomenon with a multiplicity of aspects, that it is essentially communicable, that it may be expressed through verbal and different non-verbal means, and that it comes in two varieties — the lexical, interpersonally shared meaning and the subjective, personal one. These assumptions have made possible the collecting and coding of a great number of empirical data. The standard situation for meaning assessment consists in asking a subject to communicate the meaning of given stimuli to an imaginary other person. Meaning communications given in response to a great variety of stimuli were obtained from thousands of subjects, differing in age, education, social status, gender, and cultural background. In view of theoretical considerations and the empirical data, *meaning was defined as a referent-centred pattern of cognitive contents*. In this definition, the *referent* is the input, the carrier of meaning, anything to which meaning can be assigned, including objects, words, concepts, events, situations, images, etc. The cognitive contents — for example, the responses of an individual — can be expressed verbally or non-verbally and may differ in veridicality and interpersonal sharedness. When cognitive contents function for expressing and/or communicating the meaning of a referent, they are called *meaning values*. For example, if the referent is 'desk', responses such as 'bought in a department store', 'is made of wood', 'is placed in offices' would be three meaning values. The referent and the meaning value form together a *meaning unit*; for instance 'desk — is made of wood'.

Four sets of variables were defined and tested empirically for characterizing different aspects of the meaning unit (see Table 9.1): (1) *meaning dimensions*, which characterize the contents of the meaning value from the point of view of the specific information communicated about the referent, such as the referent's sensory qualities (for example, sun — yellow), or feelings and emotions (for example, death — grief); (2) *types of relation*, which characterize the immediacy of the relation between the meaning value and the referent; for example, attributive (such as: pants — is a garment), comparative (such as: swimming pool — a little like a pond but different from the ocean), or exemplifying-illustrative (such as: country — Great Britain); (3) *forms of relation*, which characterize the formal-logical aspect of the relation between the meaning value and the referent, which may be positive (for example, sun — is bright), negative (for example, sun — is not green), conjunctive (for example, sun — is both round and yellow), etc.; and (4) *referent shifts*, which characterize the relations between the referents in the chain of responses constituting meaning assignment to some referent; for example, the referent to which meaning is assigned may deviate from the original input or previous referents and may be one of the formerly used meaning values, or a part of the initial referent, its superordinate category, its opposite, or even just an association to it. Thus, if the referent is 'road', the response 'is a place where cars drive', includes two meaning values: (a) 'is a place' and (b) 'where cars drive', whereby the first meaning value serves as a referent for the second.

Together the four sets of variables constitute the system of meaning. When analysing material, usually verbal, in terms of the meaning system, the material is first divided into meaning units, each of which is then coded in line with the four sets of meaning variables; that is, it is assigned one meaning dimension, one type of relation, one form of relation, and one referent shift variable. For example, the response 'brown' given to the stimulus 'hair', is coded on the meaning dimension sensory qualities, on the exemplifying-illustrative type of relation, on the positive form of relation, and on the referent shift variable of referent identical to the presented input. Summing the codings of all the separate meaning units results in a profile of the frequencies with which each meaning variable was used across all meaning units. The reliability of the codings is usually in the range of 0.89 to 0.97 for two independent coders.

The Meaning Test

The test consists of a standardized list of 11 stimuli (to create, street, life, bicycle, feeling, to murder, to take, friendship, art, ocean, telephone) designed to stimulate all of the subject's meaning potentials. The instructions call for communicating to an imaginary other person the interpersonally shared and personal meaning of each stimulus, using any verbal or non-verbal means of communication considered by the subject as adequate. The test may be administered orally or in writing, individually or in group sessions. The subjects' responses are coded in terms of the four sets of meaning variables. Summing all the codings of the meaning units in the responses of a particular subject across the 11 stimuli produces the subject's meaning profile. The profile consists of the frequencies of the subject's responses in each of the meaning variables, reflecting the individual's meaning potentials.

Different manifestations of meaning variables

Since meaning is fundamentally a cognitive construct, cognition was the first domain in which we sought manifestations of meaning variables. The cognitive manifestations of the meaning variables were studied mostly by correlating the meaning profiles of individuals with their performance on cognitive tasks, and then affecting the performance in the desired direction by modifying systematically the task-relevant meaning variables. The findings showed that each meaning variable denotes a specific complex of cognitive processes and domain of operation that define it. For example, subjects who frequently use a meaning dimension such as locational qualities (Dim.

Table 9.1 Major variables of the meaning system

Number	Variable
Meaning dimensions	
Dim. 1	Contextual allocation
Dim. 2	Range of inclusion (2a: sub-classes of referent; 2b: parts of referent)
Dim. 3	Function, purpose, and role
Dim. 4	Actions and potentialities for action (4a: by referent; 4b: to/with referent)
Dim. 5	Manner of occurrence or operation
Dim. 6	Antecedents and causes
Dim. 7	Consequences and results
Dim. 8	Domain of application (8a: referent as subject; 8b: referent as object)
Dim. 9	Material
Dim. 10	Structure
Dim. 11	State and possible changes in state
Dim. 12	Weight and mass
Dim. 13	Size and dimensionality
Dim. 14	Quantity and number
Dim. 15	Locational qualities
Dim. 16	Temporal qualities
Dim. 17	Possessions (17a) and belongingness (17b)
Dim. 18	Development
Dim. 19	Sensory qualities (19a: of referent; 19b: by referent)
Dim. 20	Feelings and emotions (20a: evoked by referent; 20b: felt by referent)
Dim. 21	Judgments and evaluations (21a: about referent; 21b: by referent)
Dim. 22	Cognitive qualities (22a: evoked by referent; 22b: of referent)
Types of relation	
TR 1	Attributive
	1a Qualities to substance
	1b Actions to agent
TR 2	Comparative
	2a Similarity
	2b Difference
	2c Complementariness
	2d Relationality
TR 3	Exemplifying-illustrative

cont.

15) as compared with those who use it infrequently notice perceptual cues relevant for location sooner, have more associations concerning locations, recall items that refer to location better, orient themselves better in line with a map, solve problems like mazes that involve locational aspects more quickly, and so on (Arnon and Kreitler, 1984; Haidu, 1988; Kreitler and Kreitler, 1985a, 1988b). Similarly, the frequent application of the comparative types of relation (TR 2a−d) promotes the various processes of matching and comparison that play a role, for example, in analogical thinking (Kreitler and Kreitler, 1990a); the frequent application of the meaning variable function, purpose, and role (Dim. 3) underlies the processes and contents relevant for grasping and manipulating functionality and purposefulness; and so on. A large body of research showed the role of meaning variables in the

Table 9.1 *cont.*

Number	Variable
TR 4	3a Exemplifying instance 3b Exemplifying situation 3c Exemplifying scene Metaphoric-symbolic 4a Interpretation 4b Conventional metaphor 4c Original metaphor 4d Symbol

Modes of meaning
Lexical mode: TR 1 + TR 2
Personal mode: TR 3 + TR 4

Forms of relation
FR 1	Positive
FR 2	Negative
FR 3	Mixed positive and negative
FR 4	Conjunctive
FR 5	Disjunctive
FR 6	Combined positive and negative
FR 7	Double negative
FR 8	Obligatory
FR 9	Question

Shifts of referent
SR 1	Identical
SR 2	Opposite
SR 3	Partial
SR 4	Modified by adding a meaning value
SR 5	Previous meaning value
SR 6	Associative
SR 7	Unrelated
SR 8	Grammatical variation
SR 9	Linguistic label
SR 10	Several previous meaning values combined
SR 11	Higher-level referent

different domains of cognitive functioning, such as perception, comprehension, problem solving, creativity, planning, narration, communication, answering questions (Arnon and Kreitler, 1984; Kreitler and Kreitler, 1984a, 1985b, 1986a, 1986b, 1987a, 1988a, 1988b, 1990b, 1990c), and even understanding jokes (Kreitler *et al.*, 1988) and responding to the Rorschach test (Kreitler *et al.*, 1987–8).

The close correspondence of meaning variables to cognitive functions justifies defining cognition as a meaning-processing system; that is, a system that produces, assigns, stores, transforms, and elaborates meanings. Accordingly, the four types of meaning variable are not only aspects of cognitive contents or means for its characterization (the *static* view of meaning) but also active agents for the retrieval and assignment of particular meanings (the *dynamic* view of meaning). The dynamic approach to meaning variables indicates that they may be considered as meaning assignment tendencies. Thus, meaning dimensions are strategies for the retrieval and assignment of specific types of content, such as feelings and emotions, or judgments and evaluations; types of relation represent tendencies for relating the contents to the referents in specific ways or in line with particular rules, such as attribution or exemplification; forms of relation regulate the relating of the contents to the referent in line with formal and logical rules, such as assertion or negation; and shifts of referent are strategies for modifying referents and for proceeding from one referent to another, resulting in the enrichment of meaning assignment and sometimes in mind-wandering and confabulations.

However, very soon it became evident that meaning variables also have manifestations in domains other than cognition, such as emotions and attitudes, which are of consequence for personality. For example, a study on anxiety showed that there is a pattern of meaning variables that corresponds to each of seven standard anxiety scales (Kreitler and Kreitler, 1985a). The pattern includes, for example, high frequencies of the meaning dimensions feelings and emotions, judgments and evaluations, and the metaphoric type of relation, and low frequencies on the meaning dimension actions and the attributive type of relation. The pattern specifies the meaning assignment tendencies which mediate the occurrence and maintenance of anxiety. Modifying this pattern of meaning assignment tendencies in a systematic manner produced decreases in anxiety and its effects (Kreitler and Kreitler, 1987b, 1988c). Other studies revealed that meaning variables also had manifestations in the domain of attitudes (Kreitler and Kreitler, 1990a). For example, individuals whose meaning profiles showed high frequencies of the meaning dimension feelings and emotions had more beliefs in regard to emotions than individuals with low frequencies of this dimension, although the beliefs were not necessarily all supportive of emotions. Findings of this kind have served as impetus for exploring the relations between traits and meaning variables.

Studies on personality traits and meaning

Over 25 studies were carried out in order to explore the relations of traits to meaning variables. Most of the studies focused on analysing the relations between the scores on standard tests of traits and the meaning profiles of subjects. The analyses were statistical as well as in terms of the wealth of findings available in the literature about each of the better-known traits. We used a great variety of samples and selected a broad range of different traits; for example, social traits like Machiavellianism, temperamental traits like extraversion, cognitive style traits like intolerance of ambiguity or external—internal control, traits of attitudes like dogmatism, Freudian traits like anality, Jungian traits like those assessed by the Myers-Briggs Type Indicator, traits that form part of multitrait instruments such as the California Psychological Inventory, the Sixteen Personality Factors, the Personality Research Form or the Minnesota Multiphasic Personality Inventory, and so on.

The main finding was that each of the studied traits corresponded to a pattern of

Table 9.2 Patterns of meaning variables corresponding to extraversion and Machiavellianism

The trait	The pattern of meaning variables
Extraversion	*Positive constituents*: Meaning dimensions — contextual allocation, actions (active), size and dimensionality, possessions and belongingness, development, sensory qualities (especially form and shape, auditory, taste, temperature, smell); types of relation— attributive, and exemplifying-illustrative (scene); shifts in referent — to referents related merely by association or unrelated in any obvious way, and total number of different shifts in referent. *Negative constituents*: Meaning dimensions — range of inclusion (classes), results, locational qualities, temporal qualities, sensations (especially temperature and internal), judgments and evaluations, and total number of different meaning dimensions; types of relation — metaphoric (conventional); shifts of referent — to referents that are a whole or a part of a previous one.
Machiavellianism	*Positive constituents*: Meaning dimensions — function, purpose and role, state, quantity and number, locational qualities, possessions and belongingness; type of relation — attributive. *Negative constituents*: Meaning dimensions — causes, results.

Note: The patterns have been reduced to listings of constituents and the correlation coefficients have been deleted. The pattern of extraversion is based on Kreitler and Kreitler, 1990a, Table 6, p. 138, and that of Machiavellianism on Table 11, p. 171, and Table 12, p. 176. Extraversion was assessed by the EPI (Eysenck and Eysenck, 1964), and Machiavellianism by the Mach IV (Christie and Geis, 1970).

meaning variables, some of high frequency in the subjects' meaning profiles, some of low. Special methodological analyses were made in order to ensure that the patterns are not subject to biases *pro* or *contra* particular meaning variables, reflecting the structure of the meaning system or any specific groupings of meaning variables (Kreitler and Kreitler, 1990a, Chapter 6). Further, we showed that the patterns are correlated neither with the meaning that subjects assign directly to the trait or its label, nor with the manifest content of the questionnaire commonly used for assessing the trait (Kreitler and Kreitler, 1990a, Part 2, Studies 10 and 15). Table 9.2 presents two examples of the observed patterns.

The pattern reveals the meaning assignment tendencies of the individuals scoring high on the trait; namely, the manner in which they characteristically process external and internal inputs. Hence, the pattern provides information about the kinds of cue these individuals notice or overlook, the kinds of content they consider, their tendencies to specific opinions, attitudes, beliefs, moods, emotions, etc.

Analysis of the meaning variables in the patterns showed that they had a broad range of manifestations reflecting the operation, functioning, and expression of the traits in different spheres. Some of the manifestations were expected in view of previous findings about the traits. For example, the pattern of extraversion included the positive constituents of action and possessions and the negative ones of judgments and evaluations and of results (see Table 9.2; Kreitler and Kreitler, 1990a, Part 2, Study 1). These findings indicate the tendencies of extraverts to focus on dynamic activities and on material goods and to disregard values and expected results, in conformity with the claims about their relatively weak superego and low constraints in general. Notably, the latter two findings suggest the mechanisms underlying the impulsivity of extraverts. Similarly, the finding that hypochondriacs focus on internal sensations explicates one mechanism about how hypochondriasis functions (Kreitler and Kreitler, 1990a, Part 2, Study 10). Again, the findings that high scores on order (Personality Research Form; Kreitler and Kreitler, 1990a, Chapter 11, p. 312) frequently use the meaning dimensions function and locational qualities and the comparative type of relation indicate how these individuals actually implement their tendency for order; namely, by focusing on the functions and locations of objects and on their similarities and differences from other objects rather than, say, by classifying them into abstract categories or focusing on structure.

In some cases analysis of the patterns provided insights into controversial issues concerning traits. For example, the approval motive has often been assumed to assess a special concern about and craving for positive evaluation by others. But observations were far from consistent with this. The meaning pattern of the approval motive clarifies the reason for this: it includes the meaning dimension of feelings and emotions, especially those evoked in others (positive constituent), but does not include the meaning dimension judgments and evaluations. Hence, the pattern accords with the observations that high scorers on the approval motive are concerned about evoking in others positive emotions rather than merely positive evaluations (Kreitler and Kreitler, 1990a, Part 2, Study 8). Another example concerns extraversion. It seemed theoretically justified to assume that extraverts have a particularly high tolerance for pain. However, research carried out with common electrodermal and thermal stimuli yielded inconsistent results. The pattern for extraversion includes thermal sensations (negative constituent) but not kinaesthetic or dermal ones. Hence, extraverts may be expected to evidence higher tolerance of pain when the stimuli are thermal than when they are electrodermal, as indeed they do (Kreitler and Kreitler, 1990a, Part 2, Study 1).

Analysis of the patterns of the 115 studied personality traits yielded a set of seven characteristics of the patterns corresponding to traits. These are as follows:

1. *Specificity*: Each pattern is a unique combination of meaning assignment variables. Patterns that correspond to scores on different scales assessing allegedly the same trait share a more or less extensive set of meaning variables that constitute the unique pattern of that trait.
2. *Two levels of generality*: The manifestations of the meaning variables in the pattern are partly of a more general kind and partly more specific and bound to particular contexts.
3. *Structure*: Through interactions within and among the meaning assignment variables constituting the pattern, the pattern gets oversummative characteristics that account for its structure. Further, some patterns include particular groupings of meaning variables, such as the two sub-clusters of internality in the pattern of internal control, one focused on considering actions and the involvement of people, the other focused on considering more impersonal features of situations.

4. *Different kinds of meaning variable*: The patterns include representatives of the four kinds of meaning variable, and in specific proportions; namely 54.7 per cent meaning dimensions, 25.7 per cent types of relation, 12.6 per cent shifts of referent, and 5.9 per cent forms of relation.

5. *Positive and negative components*: The patterns include both positive and negative components; namely, meaning variables that are used frequently by the high scorers on the traits and those that are used infrequently, respectively. Characteristically, there are more positive than negative elements (the proportion of the negative is 0.38).

6. *The number of meaning variables in the pattern*: The pattern includes a mean of 13.8 meaning variables ($SD = 6.5$).

7. *Coherence*: The patterns are characterized by different degrees of cohesion, reflecting not only how clear the role is that each meaning variable fulfilled in the pattern, but also the manner in which the pattern's meaning variables were related to each other as well as to the overall characteristics of the trait indexed by the pattern.

Theoretical and practical advantages of the new psychosemantic approach to traits

According to the psychosemantic approach to traits described above, traits are patterns of preferred (frequently used) and non-preferred (infrequently used) meaning assignment tendencies. This new definition indicates a specific level of operation for traits, which is that of meaning assignment. This implies that manifestations of traits are most likely to occur in those spheres in which meaning variables have their most pronounced manifestations — namely, perception, cognitive functioning, beliefs, attitudes, and emotions. One implication thereof is that the sphere of operation of traits includes a broader range of phenomena that those commonly identified with personality. The manifestations of traits also include purely cognitive and perceptual aspects, side by side with emotional and attitudinal ones that correspond more closely to the traditional approach to traits. This may contribute to resolving the issue of the relations between personality traits and other individual characteristics, as in cognition and perception.

Another implication is that a trait may potentially be evoked in a wide variety of situations, because the trait pattern includes a great number of meaning assignment tendencies. Hence the broad-range applicability of traits.

The new definition of traits also sheds light on the manner in which traits function. It has made it possible to show that not all of the pattern's constituents are activated whenever the trait is elicited, and thus to study the determinants of the selection and differential activation. These include mainly processes of meaning assignment, interactions within and among meaning assignment tendencies, and the formation of sub-clusters within the patterns.

Analysing the functioning of traits in terms of meaning variables suggests that the stronger a trait is, the stronger or at least more dominant it tends to become over time. The mechanism whereby this takes place has been clarified by our microgenetic studies of input identification and interpretations (Kreitler and Kreitler, 1984a, 1986c). One of the findings was that subjects tend to apply one of their more preferred meaning variables, especially types of relation and forms of relation, even in the very initial stage of input identification. After initial input identification and when exposure conditions are greatly improved, subjects interpret the input by applying their most preferred meaning dimensions, which are obviously increasingly in line with their salient traits. This amounts in fact to a spiral effect. The more trait-dominated input identification and interpretation are, the more task-relevant beliefs are developed or acquired; this in turn increases the tendency to attend to particular aspects of the human and physical environment, which increases the trait-adequate meaning values and belief arousal. Thus, the miser will eventually have more meaning values and beliefs in the meaning dimension possessions that is preferred by misers than, say, an introvert, who may preferentially regard his or her surroundings in terms of judgments and evaluations, and cultivate meaning values and beliefs in these domains.

The new approach to traits also has a contribution to validation, especially construct validation. The common procedures for construct validation consists in looking for domains in which there might be correlates of the trait. The search is guided by theoretical considerations and is usually subject to intuition and trial and error. The absence of a systematic and reliable method of identifying manifestations of traits has led to a plethora of unintegrated findings, which often accumulate without promoting any advance in theory or understanding. However, the pattern of meaning assignment tendencies corresponding to a trait constitutes the set of systematic principles that is required to detect the trait's manifestations. Thus, the pattern provides clear and straightforward directives about the domains in which manifestations of the trait can be detected. The manifestations are found in domains of content and processes defined by the meaning variables included in the pattern corresponding to the trait. *Validation by meaning* is the title we suggest for the method of testing the validity of a trait construct following the guidelines of the pattern of meaning variables corresponding to the trait. It is a systematic procedure, grounded in our theory about the trait's nature and dynamics and resulting in a set of findings that is comprehensive, coherent, and meaningful (Kreitler and Kreitler, 1990a, Chapter 13).

The psychosemantic approach to traits has also inspired new approaches to trait classification based on the formal characteristics of the trait patterns, such as the relative proportions of the meaning variables of different kinds. Alternatively, it is also possible by these means to test the validity of existing trait classifications. For instance, we found that patterns corresponding to mental health traits had a higher proportion of meaning dimensions (revealing concern with specific contents) than the patterns corresponding to cognitive traits which had a higher proportion of forms of relation (revealing concern with stylistic aspects). Similar procedures are applied for characterizing general or specific classes of traits or factors that result from factor analyses, as well as for comparing traits, such as two similar traits assessed by two different scales or two different traits from the same conceptual sphere. Further, the seven characteristics of trait patterns allow for checking to what extent different personality constructs (assessing emotions, personality dispositions, cognitive styles, etc.) resemble personality traits. Thus, we found that the patterns of meaning assignment tendencies corresponding to anxiety scales greatly resemble those that correspond to personality traits, but are not identical to them in all seven characteristics. Hence, it is justified to conclude that anxiety scales assess a construct that, though similar to traits, is not a full-fledged trait (Kreitler and Kreitler, 1985a). The same procedure for identifying traits has also served for suggesting patterns for new personality traits.

On the applicational level, the meaning test may well prove to be the most efficient and, we hope, the most prominent contributions because it allows for assessing by means of *one* test — the meaning test — all the 120 traits whose meaning patterns have been identified up to now, as well as additional ones whose patterns will doubtless be identified in the future. The method consists in administering and scoring the meaning test (that is, setting up the individual's meaning profile); identifying in the profile the patterns of the different personality traits, which provides the scores of the traits; and looking up in a manual the manifestations of the different patterns and their constituents. All three stages may be performed at present by following detailed instructions and with the help of tables and manuals (presented in Kreitler and Kreitler, 1990a) and will soon be available in a computerized form. The advantages of using the meaning-based test scores are evident. Administering one test for all traits instead of one test for each trait results in a gain in time, resources, and reliability (the last of which decreases when many questionnaires are administered to one subject). Moreover, even in regard to one single trait, meaning-based trait scores provide more information than the regular scale, because in addition to the total score one gets not only a specification of the meaning assignment tendencies constituting the trait pattern but also lists of the manifestations of these tendencies in the diverse fields of personality and cognition, as well as of their interactions. The information is also more personalized, because one gets a precise listing of the positive and negative constituents of the trait in the case of the particular individual. This precise indication allows a much finer-grained evaluation of the individual's tendencies than the more global scale-based trait diagnosis. Further, the fact that the meaning test provides scores for a great number of traits in the same quantitative terms provides information not only about the strength of different traits in a certain individual but also about the strength of each trait relative to other traits of that individual. This provides insight into the overall structure of the personality and into the role and status of each trait within this structure.

No conception of traits can be complete if it does not deal with the relation of traits to behaviour. One major implication of the psychosemantic conception of traits is that behaviour is not a regular and characteristic manifestation of traits. In other words, traits are not related to behaviour directly. In the best case, the relation could only be indirect. The patterns of meaning assignment tendencies corresponding to traits or some of the patterns' constituents could affect to some extent cognitive processes and contents that could participate in the determination of behaviour; for example, the meanings assigned to inputs or beliefs. In order to understand the relation of traits to behaviour it is necessary to describe, however briefly, the *theory of cognitive orientation* (CO) (Kreitler and Kreitler, 1976, 1982) which provides a cognitively based account of the determinants of behaviour. Thus, it will also enable us to deal with the second major issue in personality: human behaviour.

The CO theory of human behaviour

The CO theory

The main tenet of the CO theory is that cognitive contents — namely, meanings, beliefs, and behavioural programmes — guide human behaviour, so that information about the predictive constructs provides reliable predictions of human molar behaviour, and moreover constitutes the basis for eventual behaviour modification. The predictive power of the CO theory has been tested in more than 40 studies that provided successful predictions of overt behavioural performance in a variety of domains; for example, coming on time, reactions to success and failure, curiosity, achievement, planning, overeating, undergoing tests for the early detection of breast cancer, assertiveness, conformity, self-disclosure, reactions to threat (fear control or danger control), pain tolerance, smoking, or the cessation of smoking (Breier, 1980; Kreitler and Chemerinski, 1988; Kreitler and Kreitler, 1976, 1982, 1987a; Kreitler *et al.*, 1976, 1987; Lobel, 1982; Tipton and Riebsame, 1987; Westhoff and Halbach-Suarez, 1989). The predictions also refer to phenomena that have not commonly been assumed to be controlled by cognitions, such as menstrual disorders, vaginal infections, sexual dysfunctions, chronic pain, and other medical symptoms (Kreitler and Kreitler, 1990d, 1991; Kreitler *et al.*, 1987, in press). The CO theory has also made possible successful modifications of behaviour, such as rigidity, impulsivity, and curiosity (Kreitler and Kreitler, 1988d, in press — a; Zakay *et al.*, 1984). The predictions and modifications were obtained in a variety of samples, including normal adults, children, retarded individuals, and schizophrenics.

CO is a cognitive model of behaviour, but contrary to other models (such as Ajzen and Fishbein, 1980) it does not confound cognition with rationality and voluntary control, and does not assume that behaviour is the product of rational decision or carefully reasoned weighting of benefits and losses. Instead, it specifies the underlying cognitive dynamics and shows how behaviour proceeds from meanings and clustered orientative beliefs. The detailed descriptions the theory provides of the processes intervening between input and output can be grouped into four stages, each characterized in terms of metaphorical questions and answers. The first stage is initiated by an external or internal input and is focused on the following implied question: What is it? It consists in assigning meaning to the input (since it is limited and primary we call it 'initial meaning') and may result in identifying the input as follows: (1) as a signal for defensive, adaptive, or conditioned response; (2) as a signal for molar action; (3) as irrelevant in the present situation; or (4) as new or particularly significant and hence as a signal for an orienting response.

The second stage is focused on the following implied question: What does it mean in general and what does it mean to me and for me? It is initiated when the input has not been identified sufficiently to inhibit the orienting response, or by a meaning signalling the need to consider molar action, or by feedback indicating failure of the conditioned or unconditioned responses to cope with the situation. By means of enriched meaning generation, it leads to a specification of whether action is required or not.

A positive answer initiates the third stage which is focused on the following implied question: What will I do? The answer is sought by means of relevant beliefs of the following four types: (1) *Beliefs about goals*, which express actions or states desired or undesired by the individual; for instance, 'I want to be respected by others', 'I want to be very lean'; (2) *Beliefs about rules and norms*, which express ethical, aesthetic, social, and other rules and standards; for instance, 'One should be assertive', 'One should not comply with all medical instructions'; (3) *Beliefs about self*, which express information about oneself, such as one's habits, actions, feelings, abilities, etc.; for instance, 'I often get very excited', 'I like going to parties', 'As a child I was often punished by my parents'; and (4) *General beliefs* that express information concerning others and the environment; for instance, 'Most people try to get the better of you', 'In life there is more happiness than unhappiness.'

The meaning elaboration involves matchings and interactions between beliefs ('belief clustering'), based on clarifying the orientativeness of the beliefs (namely, the extent to which they support or do not support the indicated course of action). If the majority of beliefs of a certain type support the action, that belief type is considered as positively oriented in regard to that action. Alternately, it may be negatively oriented, or may lack orientativeness. If all four belief types point in the direction of the same behaviour, or when three belief types support it whereas the fourth is neutral, a cluster of beliefs (called a CO cluster) orienting toward a particular act will result. Thus, a unified tendency orienting toward the performance of the action is formed. It is called behavioural intent and may answer the question: 'What will I do?' In other cases, when two belief types point in one direction and two in another, the resulting conflict may induce the formation of two CO clusters and two behavioural intents (called *intent conflicts*). There are still further alternatives to the formation of a full-fledged CO cluster. These include the retrieval of an almost complete CO cluster that has been formed in the past owing to a series of similar recurrent situations (for example, a CO cluster orienting towards achievement) and has merely to be completed and slightly adapted to a current situation; the emergence of an incomplete CO cluster due, for example, to the paucity of beliefs in one of the belief types; or the formation of an inoperable cluster due, for example, to the inclusion of 'as if' beliefs in one or more belief types, which may orient toward daydreaming.

The fourth stage is focused on the following question: 'How will I do it?' The answer is in the form of a programme; namely, a hierarchically structured sequence of instructions governing the performance of some act. Often it may be analysed profitably in terms of two kinds of level: that of the more general instructions or *strategy* (called the *programme scheme*) and that of the more specific instructions or *tactics* (called the *operational programme*).

Different programmes are involved in executing an overt molar act (performance programmes), in a merely daydreamed act, in resolving a conflict, etc. It is convenient to classify programmes into the following four kinds in line with their origin: (1) innately determined programmes, such as those controlling reflexes or tropisms; (2) programmes determined both innately and through learning, such as those controlling instinctive sequences or linguistic behaviour; (3) programmes acquired through learning or imitation, such as those controlling culturally shaped behaviours (for example, running political elections) and personally formed habits (for example, modes of preparing for an exam, taking revenge or relaxing); and (4) programmes constructed by the individual *ad hoc*. Implementing a behavioural intent by a programme requires selecting a programme, retrieving it, and often adapting it to prevailing circumstances before it can be set into operation. Sometimes the need arises to resolve a conflict between two different programmes that appear to be equally adequate for implementing the same behavioural intent, or between two programmes of which one cannot be set in operation because another programme is still being enacted (called *programme conflict*). Some of these programme conflicts are trivial, others may be indicative of an obsessional neurosis.

Predicting and changing human behaviour

As mentioned above, there is a large body of research demonstrating the predictions and modifications of behaviour based on the CO theory (for example, Kreitler and Kreitler, 1976, 1982, in press — a). The brief account of the CO theory indicates that the major constructs to be considered in studies of predicting and changing behaviour are the meaning assigned by the subject to the situation, the CO cluster concerning the particular act, and the availability of an adequate programme for performing the act. In order to obtain the most accurate prediction or change of behaviour, all three factors are to be assessed or changed, though in practice one may often focus on the CO cluster while taking the chance of drawing conclusions from pre-test subjects about the meaning likely to be assigned to the situation, or of assuming the availability of common programmes. Since in many cases the meaning likely to be assigned to the situation and the availability of the programme can be assumed with high probability, one may predict that an individual will show the expected behaviour if there are enough relevant beliefs orienting toward that behaviour in all four belief types, or in three if the fourth does not point in a contrary direction. Beliefs are identified as relevant for a certain behaviour if they represent important aspects of the meaning of that behaviour. The CO theory has generated a systematic procedure for exploring and determining the meanings of a behaviour (Kreitler and Kreitler, 1982).

In principle, this procedure consists in requesting the subject to communicate the personal meaning, first of key constructs relating to the behaviour in question and its context or situation, and then of the meaning values the individual has used in his or her communications of meaning. The recurrent meaning values in the last stage are selected as themes for beliefs of the four kinds. For example, for predicting overeating the beliefs of the CO questionnaire of obesity refer to themes such as rejection of limitations or avoidance of overt expressions of hostility (Kreitler and Chemerinksi, 1988). Notably, the beliefs of the questionnaire refer to themes of this kind and not to eating, dieting, or other terms referring directly to the behaviours in question. For each behaviour type, a CO questionnaire specific to that behaviour has to be constructed. Yet, different behaviours may share some themes. Over 50 questionnaires are already available. Again, the procedures for modifying behaviour also focus on changing the beliefs related to the themes and not those that refer directly to the behaviour in question.

Trait—CO interactions

As may be expected, there are various interactions between traits and the constructs of the CO theory. These vary in line with the four stages of the CO theory. The stage of initial input identification, characterized by the metaphoric question 'What is it?', is probably the one that is least influenced by traits. One or two of the individual's preferred meaning variables may perhaps be applied at this stage, but as a rule this does not suffice for qualifying as a particular trait impact. Exceptions have been observed in pathological cases, such as of hallucinating schizophrenics or patients suffering from anxiety neurosis, who may use the yet unidentified input as a trigger for presenting their hallucinations or fears (Kreitler and Kreitler, 1986c).

The second stage of input elaboration provides an almost unrestricted opportunity for bringing trait-related meaning preferences into play. For mentally normal individuals, the only restrictions are input characteristics already established in the first stage. However, the metaphoric questions characterizing this stage, 'What does it mean in general and what does it mean to me and for me?', require eliciting not only meaning values but also an increasing number of beliefs. The emphasis is on beliefs that are both trait-related as well as situation adequate. As noted, individuals have far more beliefs in domains corresponding to preferred meaning variables than in those corresponding to non-preferred ones. Thus, the miser can be expected to retrieve or produce a great number of beliefs about possessions (for example, transfer of belongings) and quantities (for example, degrees of gain and loss), whereas the introvert would have many beliefs about sensory experiences, say internal sensations, and results of actions, such as the likely reactions of others to some act (Kreitler and Kreitler, 1990a, Studies 1 and 10).

The third stage, characterized by the metaphoric question 'What am I to do?', is dominated by belief retrieval for the sake of CO cluster formation, and therefore it is only indirectly influenced by trait-related meaning preferences. Even an extreme introvert is likely to have some norm beliefs indicating that at a friendly gathering one should actively contribute to the conversation. Were it otherwise, strong traits would produce obsessions which in turn would blur reality testing and thus eventually frustrate the success of trait-guided behaviour. Hence, though it is likely that the majority of CO clusters, the retrieved as well as *ad hoc* formed ones, are in line with dominant traits, this would certainly not hold in regard to all CO clusters.

The fourth and last stage, characterized by the metaphoric question 'How will I do it?', poses a problem that is often overlooked by dynamically oriented psychotherapists. It is not enough (as an individual) to have a behavioural intent or (as a therapist) to be able to account for it. In order for behaviour to occur, it is necessary to implement the behavioural intent by means of a behavioural programme that is retrieved or *ad-hoc* formed. Every adult individual disposes of a great number of programmes, of different degrees of elaboration — some more schematic, others highly detailed — and of different degrees of flexibility — some still open to adjustments, others rigid and encapsulated. It is likely that individuals with dominant personality traits have many trait-adequate behavioural programmes. But it is unlikely that these programmes are particularly rigid, because the scope of application of a rigid programme is highly limited and hence restricts the variety of trait-satisfying performance. Thus, the above-mentioned miser, for example, may have a great many behavioural programmes for avoiding loss of possessions or for minimizing expenses — at any rate, many more than the introvert is likely to have. But the miser can likewise be expected to have some behavioural programmes for spending a lot of money in order eventually to increase his or her possessions.

Answers to some questions

The two approaches outlined, the one to traits (based on the theory of meaning), the other to behaviour (based on the theory of CO), will now be applied to answering some of the more basic problems that recur in the domain of personality. However briefly presented, the answers may serve to provide the blueprints for a cognitive theory of personality.

The relation of traits to behaviour

Traits, as assessed by almost all current assessment instruments, are patterns of preferred and non-preferred meaning assignment tendencies. In line with the theory of meaning, behaviours do not constitute a common manifestation of meaning assignment tendencies. Moreover, in line with the CO theory it is evident that patterns of meaning variables do not suffice for eliciting overt molar behaviours. However, these patterns may affect to some extent factors that do play an important role in eliciting behaviour, mainly the meaning assigned to the input, CO cluster, and the behaviour programme. Analysis of these effects (see the section above on trait–CO interactions) shows that traits are only one of the determinants shaping these factors, and often not even the major one. Hence, traits should not as a rule be expected to be indicative of molar behaviour. The impact of traits on factors that determine behaviour is of a nature and strength that makes the relation unreliable. In other words, it may happen that a trait is related to a behaviour, but the trait—behaviour relation is too tenuous for traits to be useful in the diagnosis or prediction of behaviour. These conclusions, however, refer to actually observed overt behaviour and not, for example, to self-reports about behaviour, which are often used as measures of behaviour but in fact reflect beliefs about self, which may be expected to be related to behaviour more closely.

The inconsistency of behaviour

Of the various possible kinds of inconsistency, the kind that has seemed to be most bothersome from a theoretical point of view is based on the variation in the behaviour of the same individual in the same situation on two different occasions. The reason is that it apparently contradicts the assumption of trait-consistent behaviour. In line with the cognitive approach the description 'same situation on two different occasions' is to be replaced by 'a situation to which the *same meaning* has been assigned by the individual on two different occasions'. Hence, if that which seems to an outside observer — including the experimenter — to be the same situation is assigned different meanings by the individual on two occasions, the situation may no longer be classified as the same. Accordingly, even a staunch supporter of the classical trait conception should not expect the same behaviour from the individual under these circumstances.

However, according to our cognitive approach, more than the meaning of the situation is involved in eliciting behaviour. The CO theory alerts us to the need to consider in addition the CO cluster, with the behavioural intent it generates and the behavioural programme. Indeed, the situation meaning may often be expected to remain similar on two occasions, at least in regard to the applied meaning variables, because the individual's meaning assignment is based on applying the salient ('preferred') meaning variables in the individual's meaning profile. But even then, there are variations in some or all of the constituent meaning values, due to the dynamics of perception and meaning assignment (Kreitler and Kreitler, 1981, 1984c, 1985b). These variations may bring about changes in beliefs, reflected in turn in changes in behavioural intents and even programmes. Hence, the cognitive approach suggests that behaviour would be at least as often inconsistent as it would be consistent in the same (and different) situations (Kreitler and Kreitler, 1983, 1984b).

Trait—situation interactions

Describing the dynamics of interaction is one of the major difficulties of the emergent paradigm that assumes the co-determination of behaviour by both traits (and other personality tendencies) and situations (Higgins, 1990; Magnusson, 1990). The basic contribution of the cognitive approach to this issue is that the interaction occurs by means and by force of the elements common to the interacting entities, which are meanings — meaning values and meaning variables. In other words, situations are perceived and elaborated according to the dominant (that is, preferred) meaning variables of the individual. Traits correspond to preferred and non-preferred meaning variables that also affect beliefs, which are in fact complex structures of meaning values. Studies (Kreitler and Kreitler, 1990a) have shown that a person has more meaning values in preferred than in non-preferred meaning variables. Thus, all interactions — between traits and situations as well as between traits and behaviour tendencies — are interactions of meaning with meaning. They proceed in terms of strategies based on common elements (viz. meaning values or meaning variables), structural completions, inferences, or orientative relations (Kreitler and Kreitler, 1985b, 1990a).

Constant and shifting manifestations of personality

Theorists of personality share with the layperson the conviction that, beyond the variation in responses, there is a stable core that represents relatively more constant factors responsible for recurrent regularities in behaviour. For the purpose of identifying these factors, it would be advisable to distinguish the following three levels: (1) a *primary level* that consists of meaning assignment tendencies and meaning values; (2) a *second level* that consists of initial and comprehensive meanings, CO clusters, behavioural intents, and behavioural programmes; and (3) a *third level* that consists of actual molar behaviours (see Table 9.3). The first level contains what we consider to be the cognitive foundations of the variables in the second level, shaping their contents and structure and affecting the conditions under which they are elicited. In turn, the variables on the second level can be considered as giving rise to and guiding the behavioural manifestations on the third level. From the viewpoint of overt molar behaviour, the three levels form a kind of continuum in terms of depth of operation and relative proximity to observable effects. Hence, if the variables of the first level are regarded as the underlying core, the third level may be considered as the manifestations on the surface. Thus, if the major concern is predicting behaviour, it is the variables on the second level that would be most appropriate, while if the long-range shaping of the predictors of behaviour is of concern, the variables on the primary level also have to be considered. Accordingly, the names we suggest for the levels are the *foundational level*, the *operative level*, and the *manifestational level*, respectively.

Table 9.3 Schematic presentation of the three conceptual personality levels

Level	Included constructs	Suggested title
First	Meaning assignment tendencies Meaning values	Foundational level
Second	Initial meanings Comprehensive meanings CO clusters Behavioural intents Behavioural programmes	Operative level
Third	Actual molar behaviours	Manifestational level

The more constant factors of personality may be expected to be detected on the foundational and operative levels. These are the factors that can be assumed to promote regularities on the manifestational level of behaviours. On the foundational level, the factors corresponding to personality include the following: (1) *the individual's preferred meaning assignment tendencies in patterns (viz. traits) and singly*; and (2) the *reservoir of meaning values* available to the individual. On the operative level the factors corresponding to personality are as follows:

1. *Particular meaning values* used recurrently by the individual, which may shape input identification in the framework of initial meaning (for example, an individual may use a meaning value like 'danger' or 'dirt' or 'sexual temptation' for identifying a broad range of situations).
2. *Specific groupings of meaning values.*
3. *Particular individually shaped schemes for meaning assignment* to specific referents or classes of referents, which are applied recurrently by the individual and may play a role in shaping comprehensive meaning (for example, an individual may tend to assign meaning to interpersonal situations in terms of specific meaning dimensions — say, feelings and emotions, and judgments and evaluations — reflecting concern with the emotional and evaluative reactions of others to him or her).
4. *Specific beliefs, beliefs of a particular kind and belief groupings* in respect to specific referents or situations or classes of referents or situations, which are often evoked or expressed by the individual and may play a role in the formation of the CO cluster, either as beliefs that enter directly into the cluster or more often indirectly by affecting the formation of other beliefs (for example, concerning him or herself a person may often express the belief that he or she has been very lucky or successful; concerning the economy one may often express beliefs about rules and norms).
5. *Stored CO clusters* of the individual, orienting towards particular actions or classes of actions (for example, achievement, travelling, curiosity), which may form the basis for *ad-hoc* produced CO clusters.
6. *Stored behavioural intents* of the individual, which may be retrieved by a wide range of *ad-hoc* formed CO clusters (for example, an intent like 'I will increase my material possessions', which may be elicited in a broad range of situations including work, interpersonal relations, family, etc.).
7. *Stored behavioural programmes* of the individual, which may be bound to a particular situation, a class of situations, or a broad range of situations, and may be used in the production of further programmes (for example, programmes for relaxing, forming, or maintaining interpersonal relations, working, habitual movements and postures, etc.).

The personality factors listed differ in their contents, structure, and function. The factors on the foundational level may be considered as broad range dispositions, with manifestations in domains beyond personality proper too (for example, problem solving), whereas those on the operative level affect the individual's actual behaviours more directly. Common to the factors on both levels is the fact that they exert their impact primarily through selectivity. For example, patterns of preferred meaning assignment tendencies (viz. traits) narrow down the range of situational cues that the person notices, whereas stored CO clusters narrow down the clusters likely to generate the intent that would actually be implemented in action. The selectivity exerted through personality factors results in increased regularities of behaviour on the manifestational level, which in turn strengthen the personality factors themselves.

Some of the personality factors listed resemble constructs identified in other theoretical frameworks; for example, constant beliefs about the self form at least part of the self-concept as conceived by Epstein (1990), Gergen (1968), and others (for example, Markus and Wurf, 1987; McGuire and McGuire, 1988); the stored CO clusters and behavioural intents represent response dispositions (Mischel, 1990); beliefs correspond to values, expectancies (Bandura, 1986; Mischel, 1969), and characteristic goals (Pervin, 1989); and stored behavioural programmes correspond to habits, life style, action routines, instrumental traits, etc. (Mischel, 1990).

The factors listed are subject to individual differences in terms of their number, strength, completeness, generality, complexity, operability, flexibility, and boundedness to specific situations or referents. These characteristics can help in identifying and defining particular types of individual.

The approach outlined rests on identifying personality factors that correspond to general and specific determinants of recurrent and salient behaviours of the individual. The advantages of this approach are obvious:

1. It specifies personality factors whose relation to the level of behavioural manifestations is known, so that it is possible to apply them in research, and applications dealing with the prediction and modification of behaviour.

2. It includes factors on the foundational as well as the operative level of conceptualization, related in a predictable way to the third level of behavioural manifestations, so that the approach is sufficiently complex to do justice to the conception of personality as a multilevelled system.

3. It lists factors that represent relatively stable configurations of contents and processes, which, however, enter into specific interactions with elements representing the prevailing situation in order to elicit particular acts in particular situations, so that it takes account both of the more constant and the more variable aspects of the individual's behaviour.

4. It specifies personality factors that are types of content closely bound to processes, so that it is in accord with the conception of personality as a system of both static and dynamic constituents.

5. It specifies personality factors that represent general variables shared by all individuals, yet allows for specifying unique characteristics of groups and specific individuals by means of particular values along these variables.

6. Though rooted in the particular theories of meaning and cognitive orientation, it provides coverage of a sufficiently large and variegated set of variables to do justice to the richness of human personality, and makes it possible to integrate

other, different approaches to personality, focused, for example, on values, habits, motives, etc.

7. It lists personality factors which, when activated, stand in need of completion by contents and processes representing the prevailing situations, so that it turns development into an integral aspect of personality.

The major shortcoming of the approach described is that at present it represents an orientation still focused primarily on molar behaviour. The reason is that up to now we have devoted the bulk of our research to this domain, because of its importance both in psychology in general and for personality in particular. Work under progress indicates that extending the outlined methodology and paradigm to other domains — such as emotions and fantasy — yields results that in principle correspond closely to those valid for overt behaviour. Yet, the variations and deviations would have to be considered for the purpose of presenting the new, emergent definition of personality. This definition would specify lawfully related and structurally integrated personality factors, which represent major kinds of content and process involved in the determination of responses in the varied spheres of human functioning. Some of the factors would be broad-range predispositions on the foundational level, while others would be factors on the operative level related as determinants to specific responses on the manifestational level.

The hallmark of this new image of individuals is its *cognitive nature*. This is hardly avoidable if we consider that the psychological impact of any input must be mediated through the meaning assigned to it by the individual. The view that cognition is a meaning-processing system introduces cognition into the very core of human personality, operating not in addition to other factors but as a medium that enables the other factors to exert an impact on the psychological level.

However, a cognitive image of man or woman does not imply that man or woman is essentially rational, moving around in the world as a scientist (Kelly, 1955), or irrational, moving around in the world as a hopeless victim of cognitive biases (Kahneman *et al.*, 1982). Indeed, both alternatives are possible and predictable in terms of variables such as meaning assignment tendencies and CO clusters, but they are no more characteristic than other potential developments, such as controlling emotions or drives or being dominated by them, being active or passive, exerting a modicum of free will or letting circumstances dictate one's fate. These as well as other dichotomies common in theorizing about human beings are resolvable within the context of a cognitive image of man or woman.

References

Ajzen, I. and Fishbein, M. (1980), *Understanding Attitudes and Predicting Social Behavior*, Englewood Cliffs, NJ: Prentice Hall.

Allport, G.W. (1931), 'What is a trait of personality?' *Journal of Abnormal and Social Psychology*, **25**, 368—72.

Allport, G.W. (1966), 'Traits revisited', *American Psychologist*, **21**, 1–10.

Alston, W.P. (1975), 'Traits, consistency and conceptual alternatives for personality theory', *Journal for the Theory of Social Behaviour*, **5**, 17–47.

Argyle, M. and Little, B.R. (1972), 'Do personality traits apply to social behaviour?', *Journal for the Theory of Social Behaviour*, **2**, 1–35.

Arnon, R. and Kreitler, S. (1984), 'Effects of meaning training on overcoming functional fixedness', *Current Psychological Research and Review*, **3**, 11–24.

Bandura, A. (1986), *Social Foundations of Thought and Action*, Englewood Cliffs, NJ: Prentice Hall.

Berkowitz, L. (1967), 'Stimulus qualities of the target of aggression: a further study', *Journal of Personality and Social Psychology*, **5**, 364–8.

Block, J. (1964), 'Recognizing attenuation effects in the strategy of research', *Psychological Bulletin*, **62**, 214–16.

Bourne, E. (1977), 'Can we describe an individual's personality?: agreement on stereotype versus individual attributes', *Journal of Personality and Social Psychology*, **35**, 863–72.

Bowers, K.S. (1973), 'Situationism in psychology: an analysis and critique', *Psychological Review*, **80**, 307–36.

Breier, G. (1980), 'Effects of cognitive orientation on behavior under threat', Master's thesis, Tel Aviv University, Israel (summarized in Kreitler and Kreitler, 1982).

Cattell, R.B. (1965), *The Scientific Analysis of Personality*, Harmondsworth, UK: Penguin Books.

Christie, R. and Geis, F.L. (1970), *Studies in Machiavellianism*, New York, NY: Academic Press.

Endler, N.S. (1981), 'Persons, situations and their interactions', in A.I. Rabin, J. Aronoff, A.M. Barclay and R.A. Zucker (eds.), *Further Explorations in Personality*, New York, NY: Wiley, pp. 114–51.

Endler, N.S. and Edwards, J. (1978), 'Person by treatment interactions in personality research', in L.A. Pervin and M. Lewis (eds.), *Perspectives in Interactional Psychology*, New York, NY: Plenum Press, pp. 141–70.

Epstein, S. (1983), 'Traits are alive and well', in D. Magnusson and N.S. Endler (eds.), *Personality at the Crossroads: Current issues in interactional psychology*, Hillsdale, NJ: Erlbaum, pp. 83–98.

Epstein, S. (1990), 'Cognitive-experiential self-theory', in L.A. Pervin (ed.), *Handbook of Personality: Theory and research*, New York, NY: Guilford Press, pp. 165–92.

Eysenck, H.J. and Eysenck, S.B.G. (1964), *Manual of the Eysenck Personality Inventory*, London: London University Press.

Forgus, R. and Shulman, B.H. (1979), *Personality: A cognitive view*, Englewood Cliffs, NJ: Prentice Hall.

Funder, D.C. (1980), 'On seeing ourselves as others see us: self–other agreement and discrepancy in personality ratings', *Journal of Personality*, **48**, 473–93.

Geis, F.L. (1978), 'The psychological situation and personality traits in behavior', in H. London (ed.), *Personality: A new look at metatheories*, New York, NY: Hemisphere, pp. 123–52.

Gergen, K.J. (1968), 'Personal consistency and the presentation of self', in C. Gordon and K.J. Gergen (eds.), *The Self in Social Interaction*, New York, NY: Wiley, pp. 299–308.

Haidu, G. (1988), 'The meaning variables corresponding to territorial orientation and navigation', unpublished seminar paper, Department of Psychology, Tel Aviv University, Israel.

Higgins, E.T. (1990), 'Personality, social psychology, and person–situation relations: standards and knowledge activation as a common language', in L.A. Pervin (ed.), *Handbook of Personality: Theory and research*, New York, NY: Guilford Press, pp. 303–38.

Hirschberg, N. (1978), 'A correct treatment of traits', in H. London (ed.), *Personality: A new look at metatheories*, New York, NY: Hemisphere, pp. 45–68.

Kahneman, D., Slovic, P. and Tversky, A. (eds.) (1982), *Judgment under Uncertainty: Heuristics and Biases*, New York, NY: Cambridge University Press.

Kelly, G.A. (1955), *A Theory of Personality: The psychology of personal constructs*, New York, NY: Norton, vols. 1 and 2.

Kendon, A. and Cook, M. (1970), 'The consistency of gaze patterns in social interaction', *British Journal of Psychology*, **60**, 481—94.

Kenrick, D.T. and Funder, D.C. (1988), 'Profiting from controversy: lessons from the person—situation debate', *American Psychologist*, **43**, 23—34.

Kenrick, D.T. and Stringfield, D.O. (1980), 'Personality traits and the eye of the beholder: crossing some traditional philosophical boundaries in the search of consistency in all of the people', *Psychological Review*, **87**, 88—104.

Kihlstrom, J.F. (1990), 'The psychological unconscious', in L.A. Pervin (ed.), *Handbook of Personality: Theory and research*, New York, NY: Guilford Press, pp. 445—64.

Kreitler, H. and Kreitler, S. (1976), *Cognitive Orientation and Behavior*, New York, NY: Springer.

Kreitler, H. and Kreitler, S. (1982), 'The theory of cognitive orientation: widening the scope of behavior prediction', in B. Maher and W.B. Maher (eds.), *Progress in Experimental Personality Research*, New York, NY: Academic Press, vol. 11, pp. 101—69.

Kreitler, S. and Chemerinski, A. (1988), 'The cognitive orientation of obesity', *International Journal of Obesity*, **12**, 403—12.

Kreitler, S. and Kreitler, H. (1981), 'Item content: does it matter?', *Educational and Psychological Measurement*, **41**, 635—41.

Kreitler, S. and Kreitler, H. (1983), 'The consistency of behavioral inconsistencies', *Archives of Psychology*, **135**, 199—218.

Kreitler, S. and Kreitler, H. (1984a), 'Meaning assignment in perception', in W.D. Froehlich, G.J.W. Smith, J.G. Draguns and U. Hentschel (eds.), *Psychological Processes in Cognition and Personality*, Washington, DC: Hemisphere, pp. 173—91.

Kreitler, S. and Kreitler, H. (1984b), 'Traits and situations: a semantic reconciliation in the research of personality and behavior', in H. Bonarius, G.L. Van Heck and N. Smid (eds.), *Personality Psychology in Europe: Theoretical and empirical developments*, Lisse, The Netherlands: Swets & Zeitlinger, pp. 233—51.

Kreitler, S. and Kreitler, H. (1984c), 'Test item content versus response style', *Australian Journal of Psychology*, **36**, 255—66.

Kreitler, S. and Kreitler, H. (1985a), 'The psychosemantic determinants of anxiety: a cognitive approach', in H. Van Der Ploeg, R. Schwarzer and C.D. Spielberger (eds.), *Advances in Test Anxiety Research*, Lisse, The Netherlands: Swets & Zeitlinger, vol. 4, pp. 117—35.

Kreitler, S. and Kreitler, H. (1985b), 'The psychosemantic foundations of comprehension', *Theoretical Linguistics*, **12**, 185—95.

Kreitler, S. and Kreitler, H. (1986a), 'Individuality in planning: meaning patterns of planning styles', *International Journal of Psychology*, **21**, 565—87.

Kreitler, S. and Kreitler, H. (1986b), 'The psychosemantic structure of narrative', *Semiotica*, **58**, 217—43.

Kreitler, S. and Kreitler, H. (1986c), 'Schizophrenic perception and its psychopathological implications', in U. Hentschel, G.J.W. Smith and J.G. Draguns (eds.), *The Roots of Perception*, Amsterdam: North-Holland, pp. 301—30.

Kreitler, S. and Kreitler, H. (1987a), 'The motivational and cognitive determinants of individual planning', *Genetic, Social & General Psychology Monographs*, **113**, 81—107.

Kreitler, S. and Kreitler, H. (1987b), 'Modifying anxiety by cognitive means', in R. Schwarzer, H.M. Van Der Ploeg and C.D. Spielberger (eds.), *Advances in Test Anxiety Research*, Lisse, The Netherlands: Swets & Zeitlinger, vol. 5, pp. 195—206.

Kreitler, S. and Kreitler, H. (1988a), 'Meanings, culture, and communication', *Journal of Pragmatics*, **12**, 135—52.

Kreitler, S. and Kreitler, H. (1988b), 'Horizontal decalage: a problem and its resolution', *Cognitive Development,* **4**, 89—119.

Kreitler, S. and Kreitler, H. (1988c), 'Trauma and anxiety: the cognitive approach', *Journal of Traumatic Stress,* **1**, 35—56.

Kreitler, S. and Kreitler, H. (1988d), 'The cognitive approach to motivation in retarded individuals', in N.W. Bray (ed.), *International Review of Research in Mental Retardation,* San Diego, CA: Academic Press, vol. 15, pp. 81—123.

Kreitler, S. and Kreitler, H. (1990a), *The Cognitive Foundations of Personality Traits,* New York, NY: Plenum Press.

Kreitler, S. and Kreitler, H. (1990b), 'The psychosemantics of responses to questions', in K.J. Gilhooly, M. Keane, R. Logie and G. Erdos (eds.), *Lines of Thought: Reflections on the psychology of thinking,* Chichester, UK: Wiley, vol. 1, pp. 15—28.

Kreitler, S. and Kreitler, H. (1990c), 'Psychosemantic foundations of creativity', in K.J. Gilhooly, M. Keane, R. Logie and G. Erdos (eds.), *Lines of Thought: Reflections on the psychology of thinking,* Chichester, UK: Wiley, vol. 2, pp. 191—201.

Kreitler, S. and Kreitler, H. (1990d), 'Cognitive orientation and sexual dysfunctions in women', *Annals of Sex Research,* **3**, 75—104.

Kreitler, S. and Kreitler, H. (1991), 'Cognitive orientation and physical disease or health', *European Journal of Personality,* **5**, 109—29.

Kreitler, S. and Kreitler, H. (in press —a), 'Motivational and cognitive determinants of exploration', in H. Keller and K. Schneider (eds.), *Curiosity and Exploration: Theoretical perspectives, research fields, and applications,* New York, NY: Springer-Verlag.

Kreitler, S. and Kreitler, H. (in press — b), 'Cognitive orientation and disorders of the menstrual cycle', *Archives of Psychology.*

Kreitler, S., Drechsler, I. and Kreitler, H. (1988), 'How to kill jokes cognitively: the meaning structure of jokes', *Semiotica,* **68**, 297—319.

Kreitler, S., Kreitler, H. and Carasso, R. (1987), 'Cognitive orientation as predictor of pain relief following acupuncture', *Pain,* **28**, 323—41.

Kreitler, S., Kreitler, H. and Schwartz, R. (in press), 'Cognitive orientation and genital infections in young women', *Women and Health.*

Kreitler, S., Kreitler, H. and Wanounou, V. (1987—8), 'Cognitive modification of test performance in schizophrenics and normals', *Imagination, Cognition, and Personality,* **7**, 227—49.

Kreitler, S., Schwartz, R. and Kreitler, H. (1987), 'The cognitive orientation of expressive communicability in schizophrenics and normals', *Journal of Communication Disorders,* **24**, 73—91.

Kreitler, S., Shahar, A. and Kreitler, H. (1976), 'Cognitive orientation, type of smoker and behavior therapy of smoking', *British Journal of Medical Psychology,* **49**, 167—75.

Lobel, T. (1982), 'The prediction of behavior from different types of beliefs', *Journal of Social Psychology,* **118**, 213—33.

McGuire, W.J. and McGuire, C.V. (1988), 'Content and process in the experience of self', in L. Berkowitz (ed.), *Advances in Experimental Social Psychology,* San Diego, CA: Academic Press, vol. 21, pp. 97—144.

Magnusson, D. (ed.) (1981), *Toward a Psychology of Situations: An interactional perspective,* Hillsdale, NJ: Erlbaum.

Magnusson, D. (1990), 'Personality development from an interactional viewpoint', in L.A. Pervin (ed.), *Handbook of Personality: Theory and research,* New York, NY: Guilford Press, pp. 193—222.

Magnusson, D. and Endler, N.S. (eds.) (1977), *Personality at the Crossroads: Current issues in interactional psychology,* Hillsdale, NJ: Erlbaum.

Mann, R.D. (1959), 'A review of the relationships between personality and performance in small groups', *Psychological Bulletin,* **56**, 241—70.

Markus, H. and Wurf, E. (1987), 'The dynamic self concept: a social psychological perspective', *Annual Review of Psychology*, **38**, 299–337.

Mischel, W. (1968), *Personality and Assessment*, New York, NY: Wiley.

Mischel, W. (1969), 'Continuity and change in personality', *American Psychologist*, **24**, 1012–18.

Mischel, W. (1990), 'Personality dispositions revisited and revised: a view after three decades', in L.A. Pervin (ed.), *Handbook of Personality: Theory and research*, New York, NY: Guilford Press, pp. 111–34.

Ortony, A., Clore, G.L. and Collins, A. (1988), *The Cognitive Structure of Emotions*, New York, NY: Cambridge University Press.

Pervin, L.A. (1978), 'Theoretical approaches to the analysis of individual–environment interaction', in L.A. Pervin and M. Lewis (eds.), *Perspectives in Interactional Psychology*, New York, NY: Plenum Press, pp. 67–86.

Pervin, L.A. (ed.) (1989), *Goal Concepts in Personality and Social Psychology*, Hillsdale, NJ: Erlbaum.

Porter, E.R., Argyle, M. and Saltern, V. (1970), 'What is signalled by proximity?', *Perceptual and Motor Skills*, **30**, 39–42.

Schank, R.C. and Abelson, R.P. (1977), *Scripts, Plans, Goals, and Understanding*, Hillsdale, NJ: Erlbaum.

Shweder, R.A. (1975), 'How relevant is an individual difference theory of personality?', *Journal of Personality*, **43**, 455–84.

Staub, E. (1978), 'Predicting prosocial behavior: a model for specifying the nature of personality–situation interaction', in L.A. Pervin and M. Lewis (eds.), *Perspectives in Interactional Psychology*, New York, NY: Plenum Press, pp. 87–110.

Tipton, R.M. and Riebsame, W.E. (1987), 'Beliefs about smoking and health: their measurement and relationship to smoking behavior', *Addictive Behaviors*, **12**, 217–23.

Weiner, B. (1985), 'An attributional theory of achievement motivation and emotion', *Psychological Review*, **92**, 548–73.

Westhoff, K. and Halbach-Suarez, C. (1989), 'Cognitive orientation and the prediction of decisions in a medical examination context', *European Journal of Personality*, **3**, 61–71.

Wiggins, J.S. (1973), *Personality and Prediction: Principles of personality assessment*, Reading, MA: Addison-Wesley.

Zakay, D., Bar-El, Z. and Kreitler, S. (1984), 'Cognitive orientation and changing the impulsivity of children', *British Journal of Educational Psychology*, **54**, 40–50.

10/ Personality and language

Gün R. Semin
Free University of Amsterdam, The Netherlands

Barbara Krahé
Free University of Berlin, Germany

Introduction

The relationship between personality and language can be conceptualized in many ways, and even the way in which the two words *language* and *personality* are juxtaposed in a title or a question may channel the different approaches and answers to how the two are related to each other or what is regarded as influencing what: does language influence personality, or, vice versa, is it personality that influences language? Is language and its use an index of personality, or can one regard language merely as a 'treasure house' where the secrets of personality are buried?

What literature there is on the subject is not particularly consistent and, somewhat surprisingly, the question has not evoked any systematic of longstanding interest in psychology. Although there are some reviews on personality and language (such as Brown and Bradshaw, 1985; Furnham, 1990a; Scherer, 1979), these predominantly address specific aspects of this interface rather than raising broader questions or advancing a more general framework within which the relationship between language and personality can be considered.

To an overview of the work on language and personality, one should add the fact that there exist a number of systematic research traditions in personality which can be regarded as intimately tied up with language. Interestingly, this is not the perspective from which the researchers in these fields necessarily present their work, and attempts to inject a language-based perspective are sometimes regarded as intrusive, unconstructive, and 'de-psychologizing' the phenomena under examination. An example of one such systematic research domain is the work on taxonomic models of personality, which has addressed the question of how best to represent the underlying structure of trait terms (cf. Semin, 1990). Another broad domain to be found in social psychology serves as a further example of research which is on language but not identified as such; namely, the work to do with what are identified as 'structural differences among traits' (Schneider, 1991, p. 548ff). The research work in this social psychological framework is concerned with identifying systematic differences between traits (adjectives) in terms of the different types of cognitive inference they mediate. Such traditions, the former more directly anchored in the domain of personality and the latter in social cognition, can be regarded as work concerned with a systematic analysis of the properties of terms used in everyday language in the description and commentary on persons; in other words, what one may, broadly speaking, refer to as 'personality language'. The aim of this chapter is to furnish one possible analytic framework to chart questions that have been addressed on the subject of personality and language, as well as questions that have as yet not been systematically addressed. The main part uses this framework and provides examples of the type of research conducted to date. The conclusions provide an outline of a potential research agenda in this domain, listing, among other things, research items that remain open.

Towards a framework for personality and language

There are a number of different ways in which personality and language have been regarded as the subject of research, but to our knowledge, there has not been a systematic framework that has been used to examine the different facets of the relationship between language and personality. One such possible framework is provided below with the intention of bringing some order into this field.

The very first question that one can start with is about where and in which form language makes provisions for the 'person'. It is undoubtedly the case that the category of the person is marked in language at the first and most basic level, in terms of personal pronouns, and with different indices to distinguish *between* persons as entities (although this may not necessarily be a universal — see below). Such markers can be seen as indices which reflect the category of the person as such. The next set of markers in language consists of those linguistic indices or terms that give colour and shape to this category. Thus, there are a large number of verbs that are available to describe the actions of a person as distinct from other actions as well as a number of verbs to describe the cognitive, emotional states that people experience in relation to each other. These verbs can be referred to as interpersonal terms and they constitute an integral part of what can be regarded as personality language. Another set of terms, describing persons in a less contextualized manner than verbs, are adjectives, to the extent that they abstract from the here and now of the person by identifying a person's 'enduring' qualities. Adjectives (also known more popularly in personality as dispositions or traits) have been the bread and butter of a considerable amount of personality work (some of which is described below), generally with a view to examining the semantic properties of adjectives.

These particular linguistic categories (pronouns, interpersonal verbs, adjectives) have generally been examined without any focused concern about specific linguistic features that may systematically distinguish between and within such categories. Such features may actually contribute to an improved understanding of the regularities that one observes in studies examining the semantic properties of these terms, and the attempts to apply such categories as psychologically meaningful properties or dimensions capturing 'constitutive' features of persons. The same criticism applies to work that is concerned with the cognitive, representational properties of adjectives (for example, Hampson *et al.*, 1986; John *et al.*, 1991, *inter alia*). There is some recent work, however, that attempts to introduce a more systematic understanding of the linguistic properties of these terms independent of the psychological implications that they may carry (for example, Semin and Fiedler, 1991).

A different type of analysis that one can identify in this domain is at a more descriptive level. This work consists of approaches that attempt to identify lay or everyday theories of personality as they are expressed and found in ordinary language. Examples of this type of research can be found in studies on, for instance, everyday conceptions or ordinary language theories of the genotypic and phenotypic bases of extraversion—introversion (cf. Semin and Krahé, 1987). These descriptive approaches generally pursue the objective of contrasting everyday conceptions of personality as they are found or manifested in ordinary language with 'scientific' theories of personality. The interesting question that such descriptive research poses is whether scientific theories in personality constitute anything more than the descriptive theories that one encounters in ordinary language. Here, the concern is with the content of representations that are socially shared (possibly in Moscovici's, 1984, sense) rather than with language in the narrower sense, as in the type of emphasis on personality and language noted earlier, which is concerned with linguistic markers of persons, their actions, states, and personality.

The final range of research in this field treats language as a diagnostic instrument (from both a lay and a scientific perspective) in order to identify whether and how language use (for example, in speech) can be taken as an index of systematic differences in personality. Thus, language is used in this context as practice (or *parole*), and the interest is certainly not in distinct properties of language as such in marking persons and personality, but in individual differences in speech. This threefold distinction (see Table 10.1) characterizes the possible range of research in the domain of personality and language.

Table 10.1 Possible domains of personality language

Aspect of language examined	Examples of properties	Information yield
Linguistic categories	Personal pronouns, action and state verbs, adjectives	Psychological implications for the representation of persons and information processing
World knowledge as sedimented in language	Ordinary language theories of personality	Analysis of distinctive individual difference models
Speech	Accent, speed, vocabulary, etc.	Diagnostic tool for individual differences

Personality and language

Language and markers of persons

There are a number of different ways in which persons and their features are marked in language. A variety of approaches within social psychology, cross-cultural psychology, anthropological psychology, and personality have addressed different facets of specific linguistic categories. One instance is work concerned with the cross-cultural implications of the availability of personal pronouns for the cultural constitution of the category of the person (for example, Heelas and Lock, 1981).

Personal pronouns

Indeed, one of the fundamental ways in which persons are marked in language is by personal pronouns. A very important one is the linguistic marking of 'self' with the personal pronoun 'I' as distinct from non-self (cf. Hallowell, 1971, p. 90). Mauss (1938/1985), for instance, suggests that all linguistic communities (cultures) must have the personal pronoun 'I' and other related *personal pronouns, or positional suffixes* dealing with relationships that exist between a speaker and the object that is being spoken about. It is by no means clearly established (despite what Mauss and Hallowell maintain) that personal pronouns and the use of 'I' are a universally established and distinct category. For instance, Best writes (in relation to the earlier Maori) that 'it is well to bear in mind that a native so thoroughly identifies with his tribe that he is ever employing the first personal pronoun [when referring to his tribe]' (1924, vol. 1, p. 397; cf. also Johanson, 1954, pp. 35–9).

Personal pronouns constitute one of the categories that can be seen in Table 10.2. Aside from personal pronouns and positional or possessional suffixes, there are distinct categories in language (*interpersonal terms*) which refer to persons, their doings, and their feelings as well as their qualities or properties. The distinct devices that are meant are: *interpersonal verbs*, which refer to actions (such as, help, cheat, kiss, phone, etc.) and states (such as, love, hate, despise, etc.) and *adjectives*, which are essentially devices that are used to describe properties of persons — traits or dispositions (such as, charismatic, friendly, lovable, introverted) (cf. Semin and Fiedler, 1988, 1991). These linguistic devices mark different features of personality, ranging from behaviours, to states, to traits or dispositions. There are a number

Table 10.2 Linguistic categories with implications for personality

Linguistic category	Psychological implications/referent
Personal pronouns	Category of person
Verbs of action	Behaviour
Verbs of state	Affective/cognitive relations
Adjectives	Dispositions/traits

of research traditions within social psychology and personality that focus on interpersonal verbs and adjectives with different theoretical and empirical strategies. In the following, brief overviews of these approaches are provided.

Adjectives as dispositional markers

One of the longest-standing traditions in personality language is research which has addressed the features of adjectives with a view to providing taxonomic representations of personality. The idea is to examine how personality characteristics have been coded in language. Thus, one has approached this problem in this tradition by investigating trait terms and other personality descriptive terms. The guiding view was provided by Cattell:

> The position we shall adopt is a very direct one ... making only the one assumption that all aspects of human personality which are or have been of importance, interest or utility have already been recorded in the substance of language. For, throughout history, the most fascinating subject of general discourse, and also that in which it has been most vitally necessary to have adequate, representative symbols, has been human behavior. Necessity could not possibly have been barren where so little apparatus is required to permit the birth of invention. (1943, p. 483)

This so-called 'sedimentation' or 'lexical hypothesis' (Goldberg, 1981) has provided a general intellectual framework for much research focusing on examinations of how to represent interrelationships between trait terms (adjectives) (see Hofstee and De Raad, Chapter 3 in this volume; Ostendorf and Angleitner, Chapter 4 in this volume and Krahé, 1992, Chapter 3). As some (such as, Goldberg, 1989) point out, the origins of this hypothesis may be even older (Galton, 1984). The current work focuses on what may be regarded as a mainly methodological entry (essentially factor analytic) to find the dimensions by which one may have the best possible representation of the trait terms. This essentially consists of finding properties common to a variety of trait terms that allow a simpler representation of the enormous variety that one can find in a dictionary (for example, Allport and Odbert, 1936, extracted approximately 18,000 terms descriptive of personality).

The active research line on this theme which finds its modern origins in the early sixties (Norman, 1963; Tupes and Christal, 1961) employing different data collection methods with different subjects and conditions, yielded a consistent and stable factorial structure. The precise labelling of these factors is a matter of debate. One consensus presented by Goldberg and his colleagues (for example, Peabody and Goldberg, 1989) suggest the following descriptive labels for these factors: I surgency (bold—timid). II agreeableness (warm—cold). III conscientiousness (thorough—careless); IV emotional stability (relaxed—tense); and V culture (intelligent—unintelligent). More recently, this work has provided an interesting advance by combining factorial with circumplex models (for example, Hofstee *et al.*, 1992). The interesting and problematic issue in this context is what these representations of adjectives in fact mean (cf. Mulaik, 1964). Earlier work oscillated between ascribing the stable patterns to properties of language and properties of personality (for example, five meaning concepts that are fundamental to the person domain versus five robust factors of personality). The latter view has gained some acceptance in recent years (cf. Digman and Takemoto-Chock, 1981; Peabody, 1987, *inter alia*).

The more radical views have argued that the systematic pattern that emerges in the diverse analyses is merely one mediated by the semantic relationships between the trait terms under examination (for example, D'Andrade, 1965; Mulaik, 1964; Shweder, 1982). This argument focuses on the view that language conventions mediate the judgments that subjects provide, and that the interrelationships between trait terms have to do with conceptual associations rather than being reflective either of personality or properties of personality.

Irrespective of which side of the argument one takes, it is undoubtedly the case that what is being examined is the semantics of adjectives, and that these display some regular and stable properties that are uncovered by factor-analytic approaches. The questions that have not been addressed are whether the semantic factorial solutions: (1) have any linguistic features that distinguish one from another — this would allow one to anchor the systematic relationships that are found in some distinctive and objective properties of language; (2) correspond to any psychological reality in terms of either behaviour or language use (descriptions of persons in everyday life); or (3) have any psychological reality for the make-up of persons. Essentially, this work can be regarded as a concern with the *semantics of linguistic devices in the domain of personality* (for more detail see Semin, 1990).

Cognitive properties of trait terms

There is a very extensive tradition of research which is mainly located in the social cognition tradition (for example, Reeder and Brewer, 1979. Rothbart and Park, 1986) and which examines systematic differences between trait terms (adjectives) with respect to the differential inferential processes that they mediate. An example is Rothbart and Park's (1986) suggestion that there are systematic differences between adjectives in terms of the ease or difficulty with which their presence or absence in a person can be confirmed or disconfirmed. Generally, adjectives with negative connotations are easy to acquire and hard to get rid of. The reverse is found to apply for traits with positive connotations. For instance, one observation of dishonest behaviour is sufficient to identify the presence of a property (dishonesty), but you need a large number of disconfirmations of dishonesty or a large number of confirmatory instances to infer that the person is honest. This work, which has in part been confirmed (cf. Funder and Dobroth, 1987), is derived from earlier work by Reeder and his colleagues (for example, Reeder, 1979; Reeder and Brewer, 1979). This work shows that morality-related behaviours with negative connotations have a higher diagnostic value than behaviours with positive connotations in the same domain. A contrasting pattern is observed for ability-related behaviours, where positive evidence is regarded as more diagnostic than negative evidence.

A further related field is concerned with the representational properties of adjectives, and this work, conducted by Hampson, Goldberg, and their colleagues (for example, Hampson *et al.*, 1986, 1987; John *et al.*, 1991) is based on the argument that traits exist in hierarchical structures, with broad traits subsuming narrower traits in the same behavioural domain. Trait (or adjective) breadth is defined in terms of the number of behaviours that a trait encompasses. A broad trait encompasses a large number of behaviours and a narrow one only a sub-set of those subsumed in a broad-trait category. A typical instance they use to illustrate this argument is the relation between 'reliable' and 'punctual'. The former refers to a range of behaviours across a number of situations and occasions, whereas the latter refers to only a sub-set of the same or related behaviours. One of the types of question that arise in this type of work is how choice of narrow or broad terms is influenced in descriptions of others (for example, Hamilton *et al.*, 1992; John *et al.*, 1991).

The main problem with this type of work is the inevitable impression of circularity of hierarchical relations or inferential properties. To the extent that there are no independent and external anchors in language by which differences between adjectives can be identified, research and theory on, for instance, trait hierarchy relations will always arouse the possible critique of circularity: if I choose broad and narrow traits on *a priori* empirical grounds than I shall always prove my theory! Although this work is highly informative it still requires some conceptual advance.

Finally, there are the beginnings of some work which is more linguistically anchored, suggesting different morphological origins for specific personality referent terminology. This finds its origins in early personality work, such as activity, state, and trait terms. The first category can be shown to be derived from verbs of action (help—helpful), the middle category derives from verbs of state (like—likeable), and the last category consists of adjectives which do not have a verb stem (such as, friendly, extraverted, etc.). This argument, developed by Semin and Fiedler (1991), also extends to differential influence implications of interpersonal verbs for personality, where it is shown that verbs of action in description of interpersonal relations give rise to strong dispositional inferences, in contrast with verbs of state (Semin and Marsman, 1991).

Everyday language and personality

Another concern that has enjoyed a growing interest is the relationship between theories of personality as they are represented in everyday language and so-called 'scientific' theories of personality (cf. Furnham, 1990b; Semin, 1987, 1990). Here the notion of language is used with a broader reference to common-sense theories of personality as they are represented in language as the repository of world knowledge.

The counterpart to examinations of how personality is represented in language (at different levels of analysis of language) is the question of how these terms, categories, concepts, or theories are employed and deployed in discourse. How do we explain our own and other people's behaviours? Which types of personality theory do we bring to bear upon certain types of behaviour that we witness, in order to make them meaningful? When do we utilize personality theories and when not? In a sense, these are all questions that have enjoyed a long research history in social psychology, particularly under the rubric of 'attribution theory' (for a recent review and synthesis, see Hewstone, 1989). More recently, there has been a re-emphasis of the role played by communication and language use in how such attributional inferences are mediated (cf. Fiedler and Semin, 1992). The more specific question addressed by the research in this rubric is about the types of systematic everyday theory about personality that one finds in ordinary language and the status of such everyday theories. It is to this that we now turn.

With ordinary language, the reference is to knowledge that is stored in language as the product of cultural evolution and passed on in socialization (cf. Berger, 1966). Obviously, there are diverse facets of knowledge that are found in ordinary language, also termed 'common-sense knowledge'. The aspect that is relevant in the context of this chapter is the representation of persons and personality. The particular research tradition that has examined 'common-sense knowledge' with respect to how personality is represented has grown chiefly with the aim of empirically contrasting the similarities and differences between 'scientific' knowledge and 'everyday knowledge' (cf. Semin, 1987, 1990). The general argument guiding this work is the following: 'psychological realities must always refer to the corresponding cultural and historical background upon which they are predicated' (Semin, 1990, p. 164). To that extent, the appropriateness of 'scientific' theories depends upon the degree to which they accurately reflect socially shared theories (namely, common-sense knowledge). There is a substantial amount of evidence which comes from empirical investigations of diverse facets of the person, ranging from different features of personality to aspects of intelligence, that suggests considerable overlap between conceptions developed within a 'scientific tradition' and common-sense knowledge. These studies demonstrate that lay conceptions of intelligence and creativity (for example, Sternberg, 1985), extraversion−introversion (for a review, see Semin, 1987), common-sense abilities to discriminate the different facets of multiphasic personality inventories (cf. Krahé, 1989; Semin, 1990), lay conceptions of neuroticism (Furnham, 1984, 1990b), and genotypic assumptions about the basis of extraversion−introversion (Semin and Krahé, 1987) are no different from 'scientific conceptions'. Indeed, the conclusion of these diverse studies is that the diverse methodologies employed in personality under the term 'scientific method' have essentially reproduced systematic knowledge that is available in ordinary language or in common sense.

The most interesting aspect of this work is probably the fascinating multitude of conceptions that exist simultaneously in everyday language, whereby the scientific work focuses on slices of these conceptions as and when scientific interest is raised on a specific feature of psychological reality. What has attracted little interest is how people use these theories about personality and different facets of the person in everyday discourse and how such use effects self- and other-perception, as well as the functions of such theories of personality in terms of predictive and retrodictive explanations or accounts in ordinary discourse.

Speech and personality

Another way of looking at personality and language is to examine the differences in speech as a function of the dispositions of speakers, or alternatively to examine how adopting distinct speech habits may influence personality. The question that has been addressed is more specifically the following: how do distinct personality types use language and can one use language as a diagnostic tool to discriminate between different types of personality? This question about how personality influences speech can be examined by showing the relationship between individual differences and systematic differences in language use, such as linguistic code in use (for example, elaborated or restricted), grammar, vocabulary, accent, and speed, among other observable linguistic phenomena. Indeed, most previous reviews of the personality and language domain (for example, Brown and Bradshaw, 1985; Furnham, 1990a; Scherer, 1979) have considered this specific focus as the locus of the personality—language domain at the expense of other considerations.

The review that Scherer (1979) provided of the existence of personality markers in speech still remains valid. He argues that 'It is not sheer scientific curiosity which stimulates further inquiry into the origins, functions and mechanisms of personality marking. It has become painfully clear in the course of this review that most research done in this area has been carried out in the spirit of a drag-net fishing expedition' (p. 194). In general, he identified four aspects of speech in their relation to personality. The first is the *frequency, intensity*, and *quality of voice* as a function of dispositional characteristics. The evidence of an association between, for example extraversion and voice intensity, or higher frequency and competence and dominance, remain tendentious findings. The second aspect is *fluency*, namely the presence or absence of pauses and speech rate. Extraverts, for instance, appear to show a higher speech rate than introverts and fewer pauses. The third aspect refers to *morphological* and *syntactical properties* in their relation to personality. One could, for instance, speculate that cognitively more complex people would be more likely to generate more complex sentence structures. Again, the research in this field, as Scherer (1979) presents it, seems to be inconclusive. Finally, *conversational behaviour* constitutes the fourth factor. The seemingly consistent finding here is the high correlation between large amount of verbal output and extraversion.

Overall, the research in this field is relatively inconclusive and unsystematic. There is, of course, the other side of the coin, which is concerned with what the types of personality inference are that people make on the basis of specific speech styles. This work has already been extensively reviewed (cf. Brown and Bradshaw, 1985; Scherer, 1979).

Conclusions and directions

Characteristically, the research on personality and language in its diverse facets described above takes a non-dynamic and synchronic approach. Its other shortcoming is the decontextualized focus on language, as in the case of studies on the semantic properties of the adjectival (trait) domain. This is not to undervalue this work, but to draw attention to the *ecological* conditions of the interface between language and personality. It is in conversation that we use personality language to describe ourselves, our friends, or our enemies. It is within such dynamic contexts that we strategically employ different interpersonal terms, depending on the demands of the situation and our interlocutors. Other types of situation involving personality language include those in which we form impressions about others, and there is substantial research in social cognition about how people use category membership, for instance, to form impressions (for example, Allport, 1954; Fiske and Neuberg, 1990; Tajfel, 1981). There is precious little on how we use language in mediating personality impressions and how such impressions are shaped in the course of social interaction.

If one were to employ the distinction between 'langue' and 'parole' advanced by Saussure, then one would locate the majority of the work to date on the subject on the side of 'langue', because this research has little to report on interaction and communication as a dialogical, processual, and negotiated activity in which central aspects of personality language are manifested. This includes, in our case, the use of the knowledge about persons, as manifested in studies on ordinary language analyses of personality, and theories guiding the inferences people make about personality from speech in discourse about persons. The idealized knowledge we have about language and personality, represented in Table 10.1, refers to work on world knowledge as sedimented in language with particular reference to personality, on the one hand. On the other, it refers to linguistic categories such as personal pronouns, interpersonal verbs, and adjectives. Finally, it refers to speech, which has been examined as a diagnostic tool. But none of this research examines personality language in the sense of how world knowledge that is sedimented in language is deployed in discourse, through the strategic use of specific, personality-referent linguistic categories. The examination of *how* and *when* people apply person terms is an important question, which follows from the distinctions introduced in this chapter. Such analyses of personality language in dialogue would help to elucidate the processes involved in the interpretation of actions and the negotiation of interpretations. Thus, the direction of research that is regarded as a field in need of examination is the analysis of how person terms are used in ordinary discourse, where they feature naturally, and of how they influence the reception and manifestation of personality.

References

Allport, G.W. (1954), *The Nature of Prejudice*, Reading, MA: Addison-Wesley.
Allport, G.W. and Odbert, H.S. (1936), 'Trait names: a psycholexical study', *Psychological Monographs*, **47** (1, whole no. 211).
Berger, P. (1966), 'Identity as a problem in the sociology of knowledge', *Archives Européennes de Sociologie*, **7**, 105–15.

Best, E. (1924), *The Maori*, 2 vols, Wellington, NZ: Polynesian Society Memoir Tombs.

Brown, B. and Bradshaw, J. (1985), 'Towards a social psychology of voice variations', in H. Giles and R. St Clair (eds.), *Recent Advances in Language, Communication, and Social Psychology*, London: Erlbaum, pp. 144−81.

Cattell, R.B. (1943), 'The description of personality: basic traits revolved into clusters', *Journal of Abnormal and Social Psychology*, **38**, 476−506.

D'Andrade, R.G. (1965), 'Trait psychology and componential analysis', *American Anthropologist*, **67**, 215−28.

Digman, J.M. and Takemoto-Chock, N.K. (1981), 'Factors in the natural language of personality: re-analysis, comparison, and interpretation of six major studies', *Multivariate Behavioral Research*, **13**, 475−82.

Fiedler, K. and Semin, G.R. (1992), 'Language as a socio-cognitive ecology', in G.R. Semin and K. Fiedler (eds.), *Language, Interaction and Social Cognition*, London and Newbury Park, CA: Sage, pp. 79−101.

Fiske, S.T. and Neuberg, S.L. (1990), 'A continuum of impression formation from category based to individuating processes: influences of information and motivation on attention and interpretation', in M.P. Zanna (ed.), *Advances in Experimental Social Psychology*, San Diego, CA: Academic Press, vol. 23, pp. 23−48.

Funder, D.C. and Dobroth, K.M. (1987), 'Differences between traits: properties associated with interjudge agreement', *Journal of Personality and Social Psychology*, **52**, 409−18.

Furnham, A. (1984), 'Lay theories of neuroticism', *Personality and Individual Differences*, **5**, 95−103.

Furnham, A. (1990a), 'Language and personality', in H. Giles and W.P. Robinson (eds.), *Handbook of Language and Social Psychology*, Chichester, UK: Wiley, pp. 73−98.

Furnham, A. (1990b), 'Commonsense theories of personality', in G.R. Semin and K.J. Gergen (eds.), *Everyday Understanding: Social and scientific implications*, London and Newbury Park, CA: Sage, pp. 176−203.

Galton, F. (1884), 'Measurement of character', *Fortnightly Review*, **36**, 179−85.

Goldberg, L.R. (1981), 'Language and individual differences: the search for universals in personality lexicons', in L. Wheeler (ed.), *Review of Personality and Social Psychology*, Beverly Hills, CA: Sage, vol. 2, pp. 141−65.

Goldberg, L.R. (1989), 'Standard markers of the Big Five factor structure', paper presented at the Workshop on Personality Language, University of Groningen, Groningen, The Netherlands.

Hallowell, A.I. (1971), *Culture and Experience* (second edition), Philadelphia, PA: University of Pennsylvania Press.

Hamilton, D.L., Gibbons, P.A., Stroessner, S.J. and Sherman, J.W. (1992), 'Stereotypes and language use', in G.R. Semin and K. Fiedler (eds.), *Language, Interaction and Social Cognition*, London and Newbury Park, CA: Sage, pp. 108−28.

Hampson, S.E., John, O.P. and Goldberg, L.R. (1986), 'Category breadth and hierarchical structure in personality: studies of asymmetries in judgments of trait implications', *Journal of Personality and Social Psychology*, **51**, 37−54.

Heelas, P. and Lock, A. (1981), *Indigenous Psychologies*, London: Academic Press.

Hewstone, M. (1989), *Causal Attribution*, Oxford: Blackwell.

Hofstee, W.K.B., DeRaad, B. and Goldberg, L.R. (1992), 'Integration of the big five and circumplex approaches to trait structure', *Journal of Personality and Social Psychology*, **63**, 146−63.

Johanson, J.P. (1954), *The Maori and his Religion in its Non-ritualistic Aspects*, Copenhagen: Munksgaard.

John, O.P., Hampson, S.E. and Goldberg, L.R. (1991), 'The basic level in personality-trait hierarchies: studies of trait use and accessibility in different contexts', *Journal of Personality and Social Psychology*, **69**, 348−61.

Krahé, B. (1989), 'Faking personality profiles on a standard personality inventory', *Personality and Individual Differences*, **10**, 437—43.

Krahé, B. (1992), *Personality and Social Psychology: Towards a synthesis*, London and Newbury Park, CA: Sage.

Mauss, M. (1938/1985), 'A category of the human mind: the notion of person; the notion of self', in M. Carrithers, S. Collins and S. Lukes (eds.), *The Category of the Person*, Cambridge: Cambridge University Press, pp. 1—25.

Moscovici, S. (1984), 'The phenomenon of social representations', in R.M. Farr and S. Moscovici (eds.), *Social Representations*, Cambridge: Cambridge University Press, pp. 3—70.

Mulaik, S.A. (1964), 'Are personality factors raters' conceptual factors?', *Journal of Consulting Psychology*, **28**, 506—11.

Norman, W.T. (1963), 'Toward an adequate taxonomy of personality attributes: replicated factor structure in peer nomination personality ratings', *Journal of Abnormal and Social Psychology*, **66**, 574—83.

Peabody, D. (1987), 'Selecting representative trait adjectives', *Journal of Personality and Social Psychology*, **52**, 59—71.

Peabody, D. and Goldberg, L.R. (1989), 'Some determinants of factor structures from personality trait descriptors', *Journal of Personality and Social Psychology*, **57**, 552—67.

Reeder, G.D. (1979), 'Context effects for attributions of ability', *Personality and Social Psychology Bulletin*, **5**, 65—8.

Reeder, G.D. and Brewer, M. (1979), 'A schematic model of dispositions attribution in interpersonal perception', *Psychological Review*, **86**, 61—79.

Rothbart, M. and Park, B. (1986), 'On the confirmability and disconfirmability of trait concepts', *Journal of Personality and Social Psychology*, **50**, 131—42.

Scherer, K. (1979), 'Personality markers in speech', in K. Scherer and H. Giles (eds.), *Social Markers in Speech*, Cambridge: Cambridge University Press, pp. 147—210.

Schneider, D. (1991), 'Social cognition', *Annual Review of Psychology*, **42**, 527—61.

Semin, G.R. (1987), 'On the relationship between theories in ordinary language and psychology', in W. Doise and S. Moscovici (eds.), *Current Issues in European Social Psychology*, Cambridge: Cambridge University Press, vol. 2, pp. 307—48.

Semin, G.R. (1989), 'Impressions of personality revisited: the contribution of linguistic factors to attribute inferences', *European Journal of Social Psychology*, **19**, 85—101.

Semin, G.R. (1990), 'Everyday assumptions, language, and psychology', in G.R. Semin and K.J. Gergen (eds.), *Everyday Understanding: Social and scientific implications*, London and Newbury Park, CA: Sage, pp. 151—75.

Semin, G.R. (1992), 'The linguistic category model and personality language', in J. Siegfried (ed.), *The Status of Common Sense in Psychology*, New York, NY: Plenum Press.

Semin, G.R. and Fiedler, K. (1988), 'The cognitive functions of linguistic categories in describing persons: social cognition and language', *Journal of Personality and Social Psychology*, **54**, 558—67.

Semin, G.R. and Fiedler, K. (1991), 'The linguistic category model, its bases, applications and range', in W. Stroebe and M. Hewstone (eds.), *European Review of Social Psychology*, Chichester, UK: Wiley, vol. 2, pp. 1—30.

Semin, G.R. and Fiedler, K. (1992), 'The configuration of social interaction in interpersonal terms', in G.R. Semin and K. Fiedler (eds.), *Language, Interaction and Social Cognition*, London and Beverly Hills, CA: Sage.

Semin, G.R. and Krahé, B. (1987), 'Lay conceptions of personality: eliciting tiers of a scientific conception of personality', *European Journal of Social Psychology*, **17**, 199—209.

Semin, G.R. and Marsman, G. (1991), 'Taal en cognitie' [Language and cognition], in N.K. De Vries and J. Van der Pligt (eds.), *Cognitieve Sociale Psychologie* [Cognitive Social Psychology], Meppel, The Netherlands: Boom, pp. 237—54.

Semin, G.R. and Rubini, M. (1990), 'Unfolding the category of person by verbal abuse', *European Journal of Social Psychology*, **20**, 463—74.

Shweder, R.A. (1982), 'Fact and artifact in trait perception: the systematic distortion hypothesis', in B.A. Maher and W.B. Maher (eds.), *Progress in Experimental Personality Research*, New York, NY: Academic Press, vol. 2, pp. 65–100.

Sternberg, R.J. (1985), 'Implicit theories of intelligence, creativity, and wisdom', *Journal of Personality and Social Psychology*, **49**, 607–27.

Tajfel, H. (1981), *Human Groups and Social Categories*, Cambridge: Cambridge University Press.

Tupes, E.C. and Christal, E.E. (1961), *Recurrent Personality Factors Based on Trait Ratings*, Tech. Rep. ASD-TR-61-97. Lackland Air Force Base, TX: US Air Force. Reprinted in *Journal of Personality*, 1992, **60**, 225–51.

11/ Attribution and attributional processes in personality

Craig Anderson
University of Missouri, USA

Bernard Weiner
University of California, USA

Introduction

Everyday interactions with other people and environments consist of a complex mix of thoughts, feelings, and behaviours. How one responds to various events, be they work-related successes (such as promotion to district manager), interpersonal failures (such as an argument with a close friend), or personal tragedies (such as the death of a spouse), largely depends on one's interpretations and understandings of the events. Well-functioning adults have developed a useful understanding of both the non-social and the social worlds around them. They have beliefs about how the world works, about their role in it, and about their relationships with others. These beliefs are, to a large extent, causal beliefs. With these beliefs people can predict, explain, and to a great extent control their life situations.

Attribution theory is concerned with causal inferences, or the perceived reason(s) why an event has occurred. Thus, attribution theorists attempt to resolve how individuals answer questions like: 'Why has Mary rejected my proposal?' 'Has Bill intentionally harmed me?' and so forth. The originator of this conceptual approach, Fritz Heider, and subsequent key contributors, including Edward Jones and Harold Kelley, are social psychologists. However, causal issues are as much a concern to personality psychologists as to social psychologists. For instance, answers to a question such as 'Why have I failed?' can surely affect self-esteem (consider the consequences of the answer: 'I am dumb'). In addition, self-esteem is likely to influence the answer to that question. The importance of the social/personality interface is nowhere more apparent than the mutual interest in and contributions of attribution theory.

Our main goal in this chapter is to describe the basic processes and consequences of explaining everyday events. To accomplish this, it is helpful to employ a time-honoured distinction called upon by Kelley and Michela (1980) in their review of the attributional literature. They state that the linkage between antecedents and causal inferences, a stimulus—organism (S—O) connection, should be labelled 'the attribution process,' while the relation between causal inferences and the organism's responses to those constructions (O—R) should be called 'the attributional process.' The attribution process pertains to how causal inferences are reached; that is, how one knows. As such, the attribution process relates to epistemology. Attributional processes, on the other hand, refer to 'so what?'; that is, given a causal inference, what are its implications for future thought and action? Attributional processes thus relate to function. Attribution theory, which includes both attribution and attributional processes, may therefore be considered a cognitive functionalism.

The attribution process: explaining events

Early models

An early issue of concern to attribution theorists was whether the perception of people obeys the same rules as the perception of objects. Heider (1958), for example, contended that: 'Many of the principles underlying social perception have parallels in the field of nonsocial or thing perception' (p. 21). However, he and others certainly acknowledged some differences in perceptual rules. Important differences include the fact that people but not objects are interactive with the perceiver, evaluate the perceiver, and express emotions. In a similar vein, questions were raised about the similarity of the rules of other-perception and self-perception. And again there was recognition of differences but also of congruence.

The most influential and enduring conceptual approach to the formation of causal ascriptions was offered by Kelley (1967, 1971). As a social psychologist, he was more concerned with general rules rather than possible differences when judging the self as opposed to judging others. Kelley, like others before him, presumes that covariation is the foundation of the attribution process and likens the ascription of causality to the more formal statistical procedures employed by scientists. Assume, he writes, that an individual enjoys a movie. A question then raised is whether the enjoyment is to be attributed to the person (for example, he or she is easily pleased) or to the perceived properties of the entity (it is a good movie). Kelley (1967) reasons that the responsible factor is primarily determined by examining the covariation of the effect and the causal factors over (1) entities (movies), (2) persons (other viewers of the movie), and (3) time (the same person on repeated exposures). Attribution of enjoyment to the entity rather than to the person (or self) is more likely if the individual responds differentially to movies, if the response to this movie is consistent over time, and if the response agrees with the social consensus of others. Thus, the probability of attribution to the movie is maximized when the individual enjoys only that movie, he or she enjoys it on repeated occasions, and others also like the movie. On the other hand, if the individual likes all movies (that is, his or her response to the entity is not distinctive), and if no one else likes this particular movie (that is, there is low consensus), then the person or others would ascribe the enjoyment to attributes of the viewer (for example a movie cultist). In other words, in the multiple instance case (that is where there are multiple data points available), causality is attributed to the factor that covaries with the effect. In these multiple instance cases, then, the attributor acts (according to Kelley) much like an intuitive statistician.

There are times, however, when attributions are made for an event in which the primary data come from a single instance. For example, we might witness a person shoplifting. If we do not know the person, then we cannot do the covariance analysis to test whether this person shoplifts a lot or seldom, whether he or she does so only in this particular store, or in others, and so on. In such cases, the attibutor acts much more like an intuitive psychologist (Ross and Anderson, 1982), using prior beliefs and knowledge about various factors that influence behaviour to make an inference. Two key principles in this process are the discounting principle and the augmentation principle. The discounting principle is stated as follows: 'The role of a given cause in producing a given effect is discounted if other plausible causes are also present' (Kelley, 1973, p. 113). Thus, a shoplifter who appears destitute and hungry is less likely to receive a dispositional attribution for stealing a can of food than is a well-dressed shoplifter stealing the same can of food. The 'other plausible cause' of the shoplifting behaviour, specifically poverty-induced hunger, dilutes the dispositional attribution 'he or she is a kleptomaniac'.

The discounting principle comes into play when the additional external cause appears to facilitate the target behaviour (for example poverty facilitates stealing). The augmenting principle comes into play when the additional external cause appears to inhibit the target behaviour. Specifically, 'the augmentation principle refers to the familiar idea that when there are known to be constraints, costs, sacrifices, or risks involved in taking an action, the action once taken is attributed more to the actor than it would be otherwise' (Kelley, 1973, p. 114). For example, a shoplifter would receive a more dispositional attribution if the act was done in a store where surveillance was obviously high than if done in a store with no apparent protection against shoplifting.

Other early attribution researchers focused more specifically on the conditions which foster dispositional attributions. *Correspondent inference theory* (Jones and Davis, 1965; Jones and McGillis, 1976) identified a number of variables that influence the extent to which a particular action is attributed to dispositional characteristics of the actor. For example, the attributor must believe that the actor: (1) knew the likely consequences of the action, (2) had the necessary abilities, knowledge and/or means to control the action, (3) had other possible courses of action available which would not have produced the same outcome. If a child knocks another one down the slide at school, resulting in a broken arm, the attribution that the transgressor is an aggressive person is less likely if the attributor believes that the child did not know the likely consequences of pushing the victim on the slide, or that the child could not avoid bumping into the victim, or that the child was unaware of other courses of action that would be less dangerous.

These various logic-based predictions have been confirmed under many circumstances (see Kelley and Michela, 1980). However, complex issues remain to be resolved (see, for example, Hewstone and Jaspers, 1987; Hilton and Slugoski, 1986; Pruitt and Insko, 1980). A continuing problem in this area is that these models have little to say about how attributions are actually made (cf. Hansen, 1985). That is, there is little process to these process models. A second problem is that the attributions people make often depart significantly from these logic-based predictions (cf. Nisbett and Ross, 1980).

Recent advances

A number of researchers have, in recent years, proposed more detailed process models of how people make attributions. The specific details and particular domains of application vary considerably, but several common features are emerging. We will mention some of these in this section, primarily because they bear on other issues of interest to personality theorists.

One increasingly agreed-upon feature is that attributions are frequently made quickly, spontaneously, with little or no effort, sometimes even without awareness (for example, Gilbert *et al.*, 1988; Uleman, 1987; Wong and Weiner, 1981). It is almost as if the process of characterizing an action or event automatically ties the actor to the action or event. Such spontaneous correspondent inferences about the actor can be modified by other situational cues, but this correction process requires additional cognitive capacity (Gilbert *et al.*, 1988). So, observing a person behaving anxiously may immediately lead to the attribution that this is an anxious person. The additional (discounting) information that the person is discussing anxiety-inducing topics (for example, sexual fantasies) has the predicted discounting effect on attributions only if the attributor is not otherwise cognitively busy.

A second emerging feature is that the attribution process is a multi-stage one (for example, Anderson, 1983 a, b, 1985; Anderson and Slusher, 1986; Gilbert *et al.*, 1988; Trope, 1986). Different processes are carried out at a different stages. The earliest task, mentioned above, is characterizing (that is, perceiving and interpreting) the event. Such characterizations depend upon the event, but also upon the contextual features of the situation, the relatively enduring categorization schemes of the attributor, and the expectancies of the attributor. Contextual features can lead the same interpersonal bump to be characterized as either an intentional shove or an unintentional jostle. The attributor's typical or easily accessible categorical schemata may also play a role. For example, some people see personal affronts everywhere, whereas others characterize even blatant personal attacks as constructive criticism. Finally, prior expectancies about the actor can lead the same slap on the back to be characterized as a friendly gesture or an aggressive act.

Other stages certainly include some type of problem formulation stage, where the basic attribution question is framed and relevant data are brought to mind, and some type of information integration or problem resolution stage, where the salient data are analysed for fit with various attributional possibilities (cf. Anderson and Slusher, 1986; Kruglanski, 1980). These stages too are of interest to personality researchers. How attribution questions are framed presumably depends a great deal on the individual's past experiences. That is, people may differ a great deal in the kinds of cause seen as potentially relevant to the present situation, and in the kinds of information that they retrieve from memory or seek in the situation to address the attribution question. When making self-attributions, for instance, self-schemata would seem to provide a common jumping-off point for the analysis. Thus, self-esteem issues are relevant, as are any personality variables that influence self-beliefs, memories, or images (see Brown, 1988).

Indeed, variables such as self-esteem may influence the attribution process at any and all of the three stages. In characterizing the event of being turned down for a date, a high self-esteem male may characterize it as a promise of a future acceptance (for example, 'She is going to go out with me when I ask her again and she is not already committed to something else'), whereas a low self-esteem male may characterize the same turn-down as a clear rejection. In formulating the attribution question after being turned down for a date, a high self-esteem male would be likely to consider a variety of relatively adaptive causal candidates (such as 'Did I make some behavioural mistake, or was she previously committed'), and would recruit from memory fairly positive instances and self-beliefs (such as 'I remember a couple of good dates last month, I am pretty good at getting along with women'). Low self-esteem males would typically consider less adaptive causal candidates (such as 'Maybe I am not attractive') and negative instances and self-beliefs (such as 'I remember getting turned down last month, I don't know how to get along with women'). At the problem resolution stage, then, these quite different information sets produced by high versus low self-esteem individuals can produce very different outcomes. The high self-esteem one will tend to be very optimistic, whereas the low self-esteem one will tend to be very pessimistic.

Note that the latter two cognitive stages may also be carried out fairly quickly and outside of awareness, though they presumably require relatively more cognitive resources than simple characterization (cf. Gilbert *et al.*, 1988). Figure 11.1 displays this rough sequence of events in the attribution process.

Still another common feature of the newer approaches to the attribution process, apparent in some of the previous examples, is an increasing reliance upon the beliefs, memories, and styles brought to the attribution situation by the attributor. That is, unlike those following early models of the attribution process, we now know that attributions are not made in a historical or cultural vacuum. This is a particularly

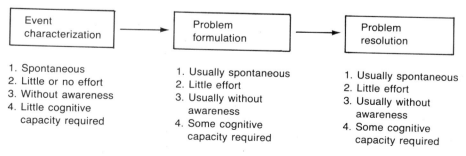

Figure 11.1 The attribution process

important contribution from personality theorists (or from social types who think like personality theorists). This contribution not only gives us better insight into how attributions are made, but also provides a major locus for individual difference effects.

Key phenomena related to the attribution process

Several key phenomena discovered by attribution researchers have provided fertile ground for the development and testing of attribution models. These phenomena also prove to be highly relevant to the understanding of personality. We will focus on three such phenomena: the hedonic bias, the actor—observer effect, and process-related individual differences.

The hedonic bias

The hedonic bias (or error) is also known as the self-serving attribution bias, ego-enhancement, ego-defensiveness, and beneffectance. The concept refers to people's tendency to take more credit for success than responsibility for failure. It is presumed that this pattern of ascriptions maximizes the pleasure linked with success and minimizes the pain generated by failure. Hence, the hedonic bias is one manifestation of the underlying pleasure—pain principle of personality and motivation, most often associated with Freudian thinking and philosophers such as Bentham. Other hedonic attribution patterns are also possible, such as ascribing success to permanent (stable) factors and failure to temporary or unstable causes. However, differences in the perceived locus of causality (internal or external to the actor) have been the focus of attention when examining hedonic or motivational influences on perceived causality. In our view, the key to understanding this phenomena is to distinguish clearly between the potential functional consequences of such 'self-serving' biases and the causal processes involved. Throughout this debate there has been a strong tendency to reason teleologically—to assume that because the functional consquences of a self-serving pattern of attributions is motivationally relevant the causal process must be motivationally driven. Such reasoning is faulty, though motivational factors may play a role.

Many personality theorists have contended that we are motivated to see ourselves in a positive light. But Heider (1958) first applied this principle to the formation of causal ascriptions, suggesting that the perceived reasons for an event or outcome tend to 'fit the wishes' of the person. In opposition to the cognitive antecedents outlined by Kelley and the presumed rationality of the attribution process, the hedonic bias intimates that causal beliefs are also determined by 'irrational' forces, or by rationalization as well as rationality. Dynamically oriented psychologists embraced the idea of a self-serving bias, and a large experimental literature emerged examining this phenomenon. Three questions can be raised with regard to hedonic biasing: (1) Is it true?, (2) What accounts for such biases?, and (3) What effects might this have on personality functioning?

The existence of a self-serving attributional pattern has been amply demonstrated in a variety of settings (see reviews by Bradley, 1978; Miller and Ross, 1975; Tetlock and Levi, 1982; Zuckerman, 1979). For example, prototypical studies in achievement-related contexts have revealed that: in athletic settings, players in a competitive game attribute their wins to skill and effort and their losses to bad luck (Snyder *et al.*, 1976; see review in Mullen and Riordan, 1988); in school environments, teachers ascribe improved performance of students to good teaching, but lack of improvement to students' low ability and/or effort (Beckman, 1970; Johnson *et al.*, 1964); and in gambling situations, following a loss but not a win, gamblers search for possible external reasons (Gilovich, 1983). Similar findings have also been observed in the political arena. For example, politicians ascribe victories to personal characteristics but losses to party label (Kingdon, 1967).

Three mechanisms have been proposed to account for the observed hedonic biasing of causal attributions. The most obvious possible mechanism underlying self-serving biases is that the individual wants to 'appear good'. That is, attributions are conscious devices used to make the individual appear favourably in the eyes of others. There are obvious motivational reasons for a homicide suspect denying responsibility for a shooting death, especially when in front of a jury. There are obvious motivational reasons for a politician claiming credit for an improved national economy, especially to voters. Although impression management processes are in themselves interesting, they are mostly irrelevant to understanding how people come to make attributions that they believe to be accurate. For this reason, most research of self-serving biases has attempted to assess people's true beliefs. Inasmuch as experimental investigations of biasing have taken place in the presence of others, though, impression management could account for some of the self-serving ascriptions. It could also account for the occasional reversal of the self-serving pattern (for example, Ross *et al.*, 1974), if one assumes that the attributor believes that his or her public will think better of someone who accepts personal blame for failure or who is endearingly modest with success. Because the main theoretical and empirical focus of this debate has been on attributions that people presumably believe to be true, we will not discuss the impression management position further.

A second postulated mechanism has already been introduced — hedonic biasing is in service of the pleasure—pain principle. It is ego-enhancing to take credit for success rather than to ascribe success externally, and it is ego-defensive to place fault externally rather than on the self. Such a motivational interpretation of self-serving ascriptions assumes that attributions influence emotions (see review in Weiner, 1986). That is, internal ascriptions for success enhance self-esteem more than external ascriptions, while external ascriptions for failure maintain self-worth relative to internal ascriptions. The fact that this assumption is well supported by research does not confirm that self-serving biases are *caused* by motivational factors, though. The ego-defensive consequences of self-serving biases provide no evidence that a desire or need to defend one's ego produces the biases, just as the lung-cancer consequences of smoking provide no evidence that a desire to die produces smoking behaviour.

A third mechanism proposed to account for hedonic biasing relies on principles of rational inference making (see Miller and Ross, 1975). It has been suggested that most individuals (and particularly the oft-tested college students) have had general success in life and expect further success. If success is anticipated, then actual success will tend to result in an internal ascription, inasmuch as the behaviour is consistent with the past. On the other hand, failure is inconsistent with prior outcomes and thus promotes an entity (external) attribution. In sum, the self-serving bias can be explained by using principles of attribution proposed by Kelley (1967) without postulating 'irrational forces'.

A related argument of the cognitivists is that some errors in causal ascription may result from ignorance or misuse of information. Specifically, success is congruent with our intentions and efforts, whereas failure occurs in spite of them. Thus, success seems to covary with what we are trying to do, whereas failure does not.

In sum, there are two major positions on what produces the self-serving pattern of attributions so often seen in the laboratory and in everyday interactions. The main strength of the motivational position is that it is so intuitively appealing. The main weakness is that it actually provides no mechanism for its operation. The main strength of the cognitive position is that proposed mechanisms (such as the effects of prior expectations on perceptions of covariation) have been successfully tested.

Recently, one of us has attempted to integrate the two positions by showing how motivational variables (such as ego-involvement) can have their impact on attributions via purely cognitive mechanisms operating at the latter two stages depicted in Figure 11.1 (Anderson and Slusher, 1986). Specifically, the expectancies, prior beliefs, and relevant information brought to bear on a particular attribution question (at the problem formulation stage) are influenced by motivational features via a feature-matching process. For example, if the current situation is perceived as being a very important interpersonal one, the attributor accesses past occasions in which he or she had to perform in important interpersonal situations (that is, matching the features *important* and *interpersonal*). The attribution selected during the problem-resolution stage depends on the information collected at this earlier stage.

To be more concrete, consider a person making an attribution for an interpersonal failure that is either highly ego-involving or not at all ego-involving. To be highly ego-involving means that the situation is seen by the person as relevant to many aspects of his or her life. Thus, much information about past performances and abilities in that domain will be brought to bear on the current attribution question. If the person has been successful in the past (for example, has normal to high self-esteem), then the current failure will be seen as fairly atypical, and attributed to unstable or external factors. However, if ego-involvement is low, that means that the person sees the situation as relatively unrelated to other aspects of his or her life, past or present. Thus, little information about past performances and related abilities will come to mind, and the attribution analysis will result in the person taking relatively more responsibility for the failure. (See Anderson and Slusher, 1986.)

This same type of analysis accounts for the occasional finding that self-attributions display a stronger 'self-serving' pattern than do attributions to others. Basically, motivational variables seem to have their impact on attributions via their effects on what information or beliefs are salient or brought to mind.

The self-serving bias and the proposed underlying processes have several implications for personality. The functional outcome of such a bias is the maintenance of a positive affective state for the individual. It is generally accepted that a positive view of the self and positive mood state are necessary for adaptation and for persistence toward goals. Thus, this is a very central ego mechanism, deserving more study within the larger framework of other possible self-enhancing and self-protective mechanisms. The absence of such a systematic bias, or a reversed bias, in which responsibility is denied for success but accepted for failure, may cause considerable disruption in daily functioning, and presumably underlies some depression problems (Kuiper, 1978).

The self-serving pattern can also exact a price. Most obviously, sometimes the pattern will allow people to hold positive beliefs about themselves that simply are not true. Some of those beliefs may be self-defeating. An untalented student may incur considerable financial and emotional costs in pursuing an impossible career goal kept active by self-serving attributions. Further, Jones and Berglas (1978) have uncovered a phenomenon in which people create situations so that failure is non-diagnostic of their ability. For example, a student may party the night before an important exam, so that poor performance on the exam tells nothing about actual ability. Jones and Berglas (1978) also reason that self-destructive behaviours such as alcoholism may in some instances be instigated by a self-handicapping strategy. Although it is not well-documented, and one wonders about the pervasiveness of this phenomenon (after all, most individuals prefer success to failure), the analysis by Jones and Berglas could provide novel insights into some apparently dysfunctional behaviours (see Arkin and Baumgardner, 1985; Berglas, 1989).

The actor–observer perspective

The notion that the causal perceptions of actors and observers may systematically differ is also traceable to an insight of Heider (1958). He stated: 'The person tends to attribute his own reactions to the object world, and [the reactions] of another . . . to personal characteristics [of that other]' (p. 157). This assumption was elaborated and formalized by Jones and Nisbett (1971). Their frequently cited contention is that: 'There is a pervasive tendency for actors to attribute their actions to situational requirements whereas observers tend to attribute the action to stable dispositions' (p. 80). Both the actor and the observer are therefore presumed to be engaged in the same attributional endeavour — attempting to explain some observed behaviour. The answers to the 'why' question, however, are assumed to differ as a function of the perspective of the perceiver: actors see the situation as causal (for example, 'I did it because I was provoked') whereas observers perceive the person as causal (for example, 'He did it because he is aggressive'). Here again three questions can be addressed regarding the hypothesized effects of viewer perspective on attributions: (1) Is is true?, (2) If true, then why?, and (3) What are the implications of this disparity for personality?

Following the Jones and Nisbett publication (1971), a plethora of studies was conducted to attempt to verify the suggested actor—observer attributional disparity (see review in Monson and Snyder, 1977). Typical among the types of investigation was a series of studies conducted by Nisbett, Caputo, Legant, and Maracek (1973). They asked subjects to consider why they had chosen their girlfriend, as opposed to the reasons for an acquaintance's choice of a girlfriend. More trait attributions were made in the latter than in the former judgment (for example, 'He is the kind of person who likes . . .).

Unfortunately, such results are not always replicable. Monson and Snyder (1977) conclude that 'in a variety of circumstances, actors attribute to themselves more responsibility for their own behaviors and the consequences of their actions than do observers' (p. 92). Furthermore, at times it is difficult to distinguish a person from a situation attribution, so that some reported findings regarding actor—observer differences are ambiguous. For example, choosing a girlfriend because she is tall implies a situation (entity) attribution, yet this is perhaps indistinguishable from an ascription 'I like tall girls', which is a person attribution. In their review, Monson and Snyder (1977) agree that the attributions of actors and observers differ. However, they argue instead that actors are more accurate in their causal inferences than are observers.

Clean tests of the general versions of either the situational or the accuracy hypothesis are impossible. To show that people generally make relatively more situational attributions for their own behaviour and relatively more person attributions for the behaviour of others would require an adequate definition of the universe of self and other behaviours, a random sample from that universe, and generated attributions for the sample. The same problems exist in testing the general proposition that actors are more accurate in their attributions than are observers. An appropriate universe of behaviours must be randomly sampled, we would have to assess the attributions of actors and observers, and we would then have to assess the accuracy of those attributions. The impossibility of even creating the appropriate universe of behaviours, coupled with the extant research, leads us to conclude that actors frequently make more situational attributions than do observers, but not always, and that actors frequently make more accurate attributions than do observers, but not always.

Two main hypotheses have been advanced to account for the suggested attribution disparities between actors and observers. First, actors know more about themselves and their personal histories than do observers. Similarly, it is argued that they have monitored themselves in a variety of situations and therefore recognize the variety of responses that they have displayed in these environments. Conversely, because observers repeatedly interact with actors in the same restricted settings, where high behavioural consistency is likely, they have less information about behavioural variability across situations. This account fits in well with the attribution process sketched in Figure 11.1. These differences between actors and observers would certainly produce difference formulations of the attribution problem and may even influence the characterization process.

A second explanation for the hypothesized differences between actors and observers, also first mentioned by Heider (1958), relates to focus of attention. There is a great deal of evidence that behaviour is attributed to what is visually salient (see Taylor and Fiske, 1978). As actors, people typically focus on the situational cues around them; that is, the situational constraints. For the observer, though, the actor is focal. Hence, there is differential salience of potential causal factors between actors and observers. In one early study supporting this line of reasoning, Storms (1973) videotaped and replayed a conversation so that actors viewed themselves as respondents, while observers viewed the environment from the perspective of the actor. Given these conditions, the 'usual' actor−observer difference in causal inference was reversed. Similarly, Eisen (1979) showed that observers given the information available to the typical actor subjects produce the typical 'self-serving' pattern of attributions. She also showed that actor subjects given the information available to typical observers produce the same typical non-self-serving pattern of attributions.

Note that the source of both phenomena lies in the information cognitively available to the attributor at the time the attributions are being made. Once again this fits in well with the attribution process in Figure 11.1. Only information activated in the problem-formulation stage can influence the attribution. What becomes available in that stage varies as a function of perspective, motivational features of the situation, and a variety of cognitive factors.

What consequences do these actor−observer differences have for personal functioning and for issues germane to personality psychology? For one thing, if actors perceived their behaviour to be situationally determined, then they would tend to expect others to display the same behaviours when in the same situations. Personal behaviour would therefore be perceived as normative. This has implications for under-recognition of personal pathology and the uniqueness and distinctiveness of the self. Evidence supporting this deduction emerges from work related to the so-called 'false consensus effect'. For example, Ross, Greene, and House (1977) report that students overestimate the commonness of their own responses; that is, they perceive that their own behaviour is relatively more typical of what other students think and do than is actually the case (see Marks and Miller, 1987; Mullen *et al.*, 1985).

Another consequence of the actor−observer differences described is that if observers perceive that behaviour is person-determined, then the situational determinants of others' behaviours are discounted. The tendency to overattribute behaviour to the person and underestimate the influence of the environment is captured by 'the fundamental attribution error' (Ross and Anderson, 1982), or the 'correspondence bias' (Jones and Davis, 1965). For example, it has been reported that even if individuals are forced to write an essay from a particular vantage point, the writer is thought to have the opinion expressed in the essay (Jones and Harris, 1967; but see Wright and Wells, 1988). Failure to recognize the situational constraints on others' behaviours may result in a host of maladaptive judgments and actions, with various social prejudices against disadvantaged groups being a societal-level example.

In sum, actor−observer attribution differences imply that actors generally subscribe to a theory of personality akin to that espoused by contingency-reinforcement theorists, whereas observers generally entertain naive theories of personality that are more consistent with the beliefs of 'pure' trait theorists. These perspective differences have been suggested to be one reason why personality psychologists have pursued the discovery of traits.

The comparison of the naive psychology of actors and observers with the formal psychology of social and personality psychologists can be carried further. An important distinction made by personality psychologists, perhaps most fully examined in the study of anxiety, contrasts traits and states. This distinction has been justified on a variety of empirical criteria employed in test assessment. For example, measures of traits are expected to have higher test-retest reliability than measures of states. In addition, state indicators should change more in different situations than those of traits (see Chaplin *et al.*, 1988). Indeed, Chaplin *et al.* (1988) have demonstrated that perceptions of stability, consistency, and internal causality are linked with traits, whereas instability, inconsistency, and external causality are associated with states. As already discussed, consistency over time and lack of distinctiveness have been identified by Kelley (1967) as criteria for personal causality. On the other hand, inconsistency over time and distinctive responding are criteria for entity causality. In sum, the trait—state distinction finds correspondence in the analysis of causal attributions, and particularly in the distinction between internal and external causality.

Chaplin *et al.* (1988) also discuss the function or utility of the trait—state distinction. They reason:

> We have suggested that traits and states serve people's needs to predict, explain, and control social behavior. The easiest way to accomplish this would be to have only two kinds of person characteristics. The first kind would include those that enable people to predict behavior reliably over time and situations and thus lead to social actions based on the person (e.g., to seek out or to avoid people with that characteristic). The second kind of characteristic, being unstable over time, cannot be predicted from past experience with the person, but may be controlled by manipulating the situation.' (p. 555)

They conclude that the trait—state distinction therefore 'organized the layperson's understanding of human action' (p. 555). This statement certainly is in accord with the presumptions of attribution theorists.

Process-related individual differences

Most research on individual differences in causal perception has been concerned with attributional rather than attribution processes. However, the search for reliable individual differences and their impact on a variety of outcome variables (such as affect or persuasibility or expectancy change) has the potential for producing insights into the attribution process itself.

For example, Cacioppo and Petty (1982) developed a 'need for cognition' scale assessing the need to explain events in the world and the tendency to enjoy this type of cognitive activity. In a similar manner, Fletcher, Danilovics, Fernandez, Peterson, and Reeder (1986) advanced an attributional complexity scale that is designed to predict the complexity of causal ascriptions that are made for behavioural events.

They also present evidence that scores on this scale are only weakly related to the need for cognition.

The instruments of Cacioppo and Petty (1982) and Fletcher *et al.* (1986) relate to the process, rather than to the content, of causal thinking. That is, they focus on the likelihood of making attributions and how many will be called forth, as opposed to what specific causal ascriptions will be made. These individual difference measures have only recently been proposed and have not (yet) spawned a large supporting literature.

The more dominant individual difference approach in attribution theory pertains to the content of causal ascriptions, or the tendency to perceive that particular causes or types of cause will have or have had an effect. A wide variety of such attributional style scales have been developed and have proved useful in a variety of contexts (Anderson *et al.*, 1988; Feather and Tiggemann, 1984; Peterson *et al.*, 1982; Rotter, 1966). However, to date the study of individual differences in attributional style has produced little advance in understanding how attributions are made. None the less, any adequate model of the attribution process must be able to account for the reliable individual differences found in attributional style. The most likely location of such effects would be in the problem formulations stage. Do people with different attributional styles think of different causal candidates when first formulating the attribution question? Do they bring different information to bear on the question? Research in which attributional style is treated as the result of the attribution process — that is, as the dependent measure — will greatly enhance both the social and the personality theorists' understanding of attribution issues.

The attributional process: the results of explanations

The structure of causes

To understand the effects of attributions on the dynamics of behaviour, one must understand the content and structure of attributions. One may think of the structure of attributions in terms of types or in terms of dimensions (Anderson, 1983b; 1989). By types we mean sets of causes that share key properties, just as different types of furniture share key features. For example, 'tried hard', 'worked hard', and 'much effort' may be thought of as constituting a type of cause having to do with effort. People seem to think spontaneously in terms of causal types, and may draw their inferences directly from them (Anderson, 1989). Although both typological and dimensional approaches warrant the close attention of attribution scholars, we focus on dimensional work because it is by far the most highly developed at this time.

By dimensions we mean certain second-order concepts that can be used to distinguish among causes (and causal types). Certainly two, and perhaps as many as four, properties of causes have been identified in addition to locus (see Weiner, 1985, 1986). Consider, for example, the two causal ascriptions of aptitude and effort, which are reported to be salient causes of achievement success and failure. These two are similar in that both causes are internal to the actor. However, effort is thought

of as more fluctuating over time than is aptitude. The causes therefore differ in what
is called 'stability'. Furthermore, effort is subject to volitional change, but aptitude
is not. That is, causes also vary in perceived controllability. Controllability and locus
are conceptually independent of causal stability. Some investigators also distinguish
between stability over time and stability over situations (or what is called 'globality').
In addition, others distinguish between controllability and intentionality (consider
the difference between manslaughter and murder). For empirical reasons and the
sake of brevity, our subsequent discussion of causal consequences largely ignores
the properties of globality and intentionality.

Expectancy of success

It is evident that some themes throughout the study of personality dynamics are
considered more important or central than others and constantly reappear. One such
focus is goal expectancy. A number of major theorists, including Atkinson, Lewin,
and Rotter include the expectancy of success among the determinants of aspiration
level (goal selection). In criticizing the approach of psychoanalytic theory to goal
seeking, Rotter and Hochreich (1975) stated:

> Simply knowing how much an individual wants to reach a certain goal is not sufficient
> information for predicting his behavior. A student may want very badly to finish school
> and qualify himself for a well paying job. But his past experiences may have led him to
> believe that no amount of studying will result in a passing grade ... A fellow student
> may share the same strong goals and, as a result of a different set of past experiences
> in school, will have a high expectancy that studying will lead to academic success ...
> The goals in these two cases are identical, but the expectancies differ, and as a result,
> the behavior of the two students is likely to differ. (p. 95)

There have been numerous approaches to and theories about expectancy of success
and expectancy change. One influential conception associated with Rotter and his
colleagues has linked perceived locus of control to expectancy. It is known, for
example, that following failure at a chance task (external causality), expectancies
tend not to shift downwards and may actually increase. On the other hand, following
failure at a skill task (internal causality) there are downward shifts in expectation
of future success.

In contrast to this 'focus on locus', a second attributional position contends that
the stability of a cause determines expectancy shifts. If conditions (the presence or
absence of causes) are expected to remain the same, then the outcomes experienced
on past occasions will be expected to recur. A success under these circumstances
would produce relatively large increments in the anticipation of future success, and
a failure would strengthen the belief that there will be subsequent failures (as in
skill tasks). On the other hand, if the causal conditions are perceived as likely to
change, then the present outcome may not be expected to be repeated in the future,
or there may be uncertainty about subsequent outcomes. A success would therefore
yield relatively small increments, if any, and perhaps decrements in the expectancy
of subsequent success, whereas a failure need not necessarily intensify the belief

that there will be future failures (as in chance tasks). This connection of causal stability with future expectancy is in accord with the logic of cause—effect associations and has received extensive empirical support (see review in Weiner, 1986).

It has been proposed that the stability of attributions for negative outcomes influence future expectancies which, in turn, affect persistence in the face of failure. Anderson (1983a) and Anderson and Jennings (1980) documented that there are both dispositional and situational determinants of causal stability ascriptions that affect persistence at an achievement-related task (see also Anderson *et al.*, 1988). In one study (Anderson, 1983a), subjects engaged in telephone solicitations to donate blood to the Red Cross. The first call, however, was to a confederate who refused to donate. Prior to this rejection, the subjects' attributional styles were assessed. Some subjects' style focused on ability and trait attributions for interpersonal failures (characterological blame); others focused on lack of effort and strategic behavioural mistakes for interpersonal failures (behavioural blame). In addition, an experimental manipulation varied the perceived cause of the rejection. The instruction eliciting stable attributions stated that success was determined by a stable personality trait ('some guys have it, some don't'); the instruction evoking unstable attributions indicated that strategy was the main outcome determinant ('use different tactics . . . until finding one that works'). Other studies in the series used similar dispositional and situational independent variables.

In these studies, it was found that both the dispositional tendency and the attributional manipulation influenced subjects' motivation levels (for example, how many subsequent phone calls were made after the initial failure). Given no experimental manipulation, those high in behavioural blame persisted longer than subjects classified as high in characterological blame. But in the experimental conditions, the instructions overrode the individual difference tendencies, with subjects given instructions that elicited unstable ascriptions making more phone calls than those ascribing rejection to a personality trait.

There is a bi-directional relation between causal ascriptions and expectancy of success; that is, just as causal ascriptions influence subsequent expectancy, expectancy of success also has an effect on causal attributions. The logic of this argument is similar to that offered in the cognitive explanation of the self-serving bias. Specifically, if expectancy of success is high, then failure is non-confirmatory and elicits an unstable ascription (such as bad luck). But if expectancy of success is low, then failure is consistent with the prior belief and elicits a stable attribution (such as low ability). Likewise, high expectancy followed by success results in a stable attribution (such as high ability), while low expectancy followed by success evokes an unstable ascription (such as good luck). Thus, low expectancies of success are difficult to alter and a self-perpetuating cycle of pessimism is established.

Self-maintaining, dysfunctional belief systems have been identified for many groups and vulnerable individuals, including psychiatric rehabilitees, lonely, and depressed persons, the retarded, and those low in self-esteem. In addition, when failing at male-defined tasks, females exhibit this same pattern of expectations (see review in Weiner, 1986). We will explore several of these findings in the last section of this chapter.

Emotion

Certainly the study of personality and personality processes must include an analysis of emotion. The initial attributional theory of emotion was proposed by Schachter and Singer (1962). Their conception was in part responsible for the revival of the study of affective states in psychology. The concept of arousal, which refers to the intensity or state of activation of an individual, plays a central role in the Schachter and Singer (1962) conception. They specify two different ways an emotion can be generated, one being the usual, everyday experience; the second more atypical but responsible for a number of oft-cited research studies. In everyday emotional states, according to Schachter and Singer, external cues trigger physiological processes and serve as the label to which feelings are attached. For example, someone takes out a gun, this is appraised and interpreted as a threat, arousal increases, the arousal is linked with (attributed to) the gun, and an emotion is experienced. The second way an emotional state can be initiated is with the perception of 'unexplained' arousal. In an experimental setting, this can be created by having the subjects unknowingly ingest an activating drug. The arousal theoretically generates a search to determine the source of the arousal, given that an instigating source is not immediately evident. Again arousal plus the attribution or inference about the arousal source then produce an emotional state.

Perhaps the most influential research growing from this conception involved a 'misattribution' paradigm. In these investigations, subjects may be provided with a false reason for an event, or they may experience arousal but misattribute its source. For example, in what is known as a transfer excitation paradigm, subjects might exercise or hear a loud noise at Time 1. They then experience another source of arousal at Time 2, such as an attractive member of the opposite sex. It has been reported that many emotional states (such as sexual excitement) and actions (such as aggression) are enhanced when the total arousal is a composite of the events experienced at Time 1 and Time 2, given that activation is attributed to only the Time 2 experience (see review in Reisenzein, 1983).

The Schachter and Singer formulation 'has . . . become the most influential cognitive approach to emotions' (Reisenzein, 1983, p. 239). However, in the past few years this theory has met with many criticisms and its influence has been greatly reduced. There is evidence, for example, that unexplained arousal is in itself a negative affective state; that individuals do not necessarily search the environment for the source of their arousal; and that arousal is not necessary for an emotional experience. That is, 'the role of arousal in emotion has been overstated' (Reisenzein, 1983, p. 239).

Weiner, Russell, and Lerman (1978, 1979) also proposed an attributional framework for the study of emotions. Further, in that framework it is also assumed that cognitions of increasing complexity enter into the emotion process to refine and differentiate affective experience further. It was proposed that following the outcome of an event, there is initially a generally positive or negative reaction (a 'primitive' emotion) based on the perceived success or failure of that outcome (the 'primary'

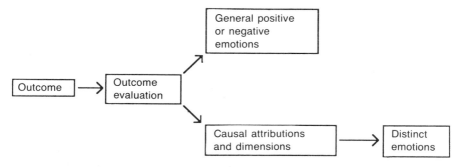

Figure 11.2 The cognition—emotion process (Source: Weiner *et al.*, 1978, 1979)

appraisal). For example, after receiving an A in a course, hitting a home run in a baseball game, or being accepted for a date the individual will feel 'happy'. In a similar manner, after receiving an F in a course, failing to get a hit, or being rejected the person will experience sadness. These emotions are labelled 'outcome dependent-attribution independent', for they are determined primarily by the attainment or non-attainment of a desired goal, and not by the cause of that outcome.

Following the appraisal of the outcome, a causal ascription is sought. A different set of emotions is then generated by the chosen attribution(s). Each dimension of the ascription is uniquely related to a set of feelings. The cognition—emotion sequence proposed is depicted in Figure 11.2.

Causal locus and self-esteem (pride)

Locus of causality, the dimension of ascription first introduced by Rotter and initially thought to be linked with expectancy of success, influences self-esteem and self-worth. More specifically, successful outcomes that are ascribed to the self (such as personality, ability, effort) result in greater self-esteem (pride) than success that is externally attributed (such as task ease, good luck). As Isenberg (1980) stated: 'The definition of pride, then, has three parts. There is (1) a quality which (2) is approved and (3) is judged to belong to oneself' (p. 357). This quality is exemplified in self-statements such as : 'I succeeded because I (am smart; worked hard; etc.).'

The relation between self-ascription and pride is directly relevant to the hedonic bias, examined in an earlier section of this chapter. Indeed, the basic premise of hedonic bias research is that internal attributions for goal attainment, and external attributions for non-attainment of a goal, enhance and protect self-esteem. Thus, the documentation of the self-serving attributional bias can also be considered as evidence supporting the relation between locus of causality and self-esteem. In addition, a variety of excuses, rationalization, self-handicapping strategies, etc., document clearly that self-esteem is a function of causal locus (see review by Snyder and Higgins, 1988).

Causal controllability and social emotions

A variety of salient emotions are associated with the concept of controllability, or whether one 'could have done otherwise'. These include anger, pity, guilt, and shame (see reviews in Weiner, 1986).

Anger is elicited by the violation of an 'ought' or 'should'. Thus, anger is an attribution of blame (see Averill, 1983). Most instances of anger in everyday life involve a voluntary and unjustified act, such as telling a lie, or a potentially avoidable accident.

In contrast to the linkage between controllability and anger, uncontrollable causes are associated with *pity* and *sympathy*. Thus, another's loss of a loved one because of an accident or illness, or failure by another because of a physical handicap, are prevalent situations that elicit pity.

In their review of the *guilt* literature, Wicker, Payne, and Morgan (1983) concluded: 'In general, guilt is said to follow from acts that violate ethical norms . . . or moral values. Guilt is accompanied by feelings of personal responsibility' (p. 26). Thus, if guilt is experienced, then perceived self-responsibility seems to be a necessary antecedent (Hoffman, 1975).

Shame is often indistinguishable from guilt in that both 'involve negative self-evaluations that are painful, tense, agitating, real, present, and depressing' (Wicker *et al.*, 1983, p. 33). However, shame and the related affect of humiliation seems to arise from uncontrollable causes, such as lack of aptitude. This contrasts with guilt, which is particularly elicited by lack of effort in achievement contexts.

The four affects examined above are interrelated in complex ways. Anger, for example, serves as a cue to others that a moral wrong has been committed. Hence, if it is accepted, the targetted individual will experience guilt. Pity, on the other hand, conveys that the person 'could not have done otherwise' and is 'fundamentally different'. Hence, if accepted from others, pity is a stimulus for feelings of shame and humiliation.

Causal stability and time-related emotions

Thus far, outcome-dependent emotions of happiness and sadness have been examined, as well as the attribution-dependent emotions of pride, anger, pity, guilt, and shame. The dimension-affect association yet to be discussed involves causal stability. Recall that causal stability in part determines future expectancy of success and failure. Thus, emotions such as hope and fear, which are influenced by future anticipations are guided by perceived causal stability (see review in Weiner, 1986).

In sum, attribution theorists have been concerned with both the emotional process and specific emotions. Two processes have been proposed, one focusing on the concept of arousal, the other eschewing the need for arousal and assuming that cognitions are sufficient antecedents of emotional states. Both theories are able to address very prevalent human emotions that lie at the very essence of personality.

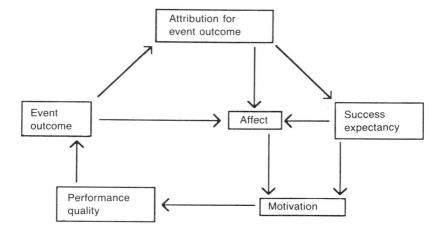

Figure 11.3   The attributional process

Behaviour

Personality and motivational theorists including Lewin, Rotter, and Atkinson presume that behaviour is a function of the likelihood of attaining a desired goal (the subjective expectancy of success) and the affective or incentive value associated with that goal. The essence of expectancy-value theory, which they espouse, is that behaviour is governed by hedonic concerns and there is an attempt to maximize expected utility. Inasmuch as causal ascriptions influence both expectancy of success and affect, attributional analyses have provided a theoretical vehicle to interpret the dynamics of action. Figure 11.3 presents an obviously simplified model of the attributional process. Note that between event occurrence and attribution are all the attribution processes discussed in the first part of this chapter.

Because the model is circular, one can begin at any point. It makes most sense to enter after some event has occurred. Attribution processes (event characterization, problem formulation, problem resolution) lead to a particular causal understanding. This, in turn, influences expectancy and affective reactions, both of which influence what might generically be called motivation. Motivation, of course, includes both strength of approach or avoidance (that is, an energizing component), and also the particular way the action is carried out (that is, a directing component). This results in some particular performance, which may produce the intended outcome or may fail to do so.

One final point to consider concerns the directional cues of the affects that have been examined. For example, anger tends to evoke retaliation or, in the words of Karen Horney (1937), going against others; guilt and pity tend to elicit 'restitution', or going toward tasks or others (see Trivers, 1971). Shame tends to produce withdrawal and retreat. Again using the vocabulary of Horney, a person who feels shame is inclined to go away from others. Note, then, that each of these affects brings with it a programme for action. Thus, affects summarize the past, providing an overall evaluation for what has occurred, and they also prescribe for the future. Hence, they seem to provide the glue between thinking and acting, or between attributions and behaviour.

One question that arises from these considerations concerns the role of expectancies in motivation. Should we expect a fairly direct effect of success expectancies on motivation, as shown in Figure 11.3, or are expectancy effects on motivation entirely mediated by their effects on emotion? Because there is no clear answer and we see no easy way to tease these effects apart, we decided to maintain the somewhat inelegant representation shown in Figure 11.3.

Applications of the attributional model

The attributional model outlined in Figure 11.3 (or some version of it) has been usefully applied to understand, and in some cases treat, a wide range of personality-related problems. Included in this list are problems related to achievement strivings (for example, Dweck and Goetz, 1977), various everyday problems in living such as depression, loneliness, and shyness (for example, Anderson and Arnoult, 1985 a, b), Type-A behaviour pattern (for example, Rhodewalt *et al.*, 1988), marital distress (for example, Baucom *et al.*, 1989), self-esteem (for example, Tennen and Herzberger, 1987), aggression (for example, Zillmann, 1978), and even long-term health (for example, Peterson *et al.*, 1988). The most extensive work has been done with achievement and with various problems in living (especially depression), so we turn now to those problems.

Achievement strivings

The key question in most of this research has been how people respond to failure outcomes. According to the attributional formulation, response to failure depends to a great extent upon the attribution made for the failure. The person will probably experience the outcome-related affects of frustration and sadness. If the failure is attributed to a lack of effort or preparation, then we may expect a fairly positive response to the failure. Because the causes are unstable and controllable, the person can maintain a strong expectation of success in the future, and therefore may feel hopeful. Because the causes are internal and controllable, the person may experience guilt and may perceive anger on the part of, say, parents and teacher. High expectations of future success, along with hopefulness and guilt, often result in an increase in motivation. On the other hand, consider the sequence if the initial failure is attributed to lack of ability, which is internal, stable, and uncontrollable. The initial outcome-related affects of sadness and frustration will be present, of course. The ability attribution adds to those negative affects by lowering self-esteem, producing low future expectancies or hopelessness, and generating feelings of shame and humiliation. If parents and teachers, say, accept this ability attribution (or foster it) they will be likely to communicate it via their pity or sorrow. These various thoughts and affects decrease achievement strivings, and often result in withdrawal (actual and psychological) from the achievement setting.

Various aspects of these scenarios have been confirmed in several research settings with subject populations ranging from elementary students with arithmetic problems to college students failing a mid-term exam (for example, Andrews and Debus, 1978; Chapin and Dyck, 1976; Dweck and Goetz, 1977; Wilson and Linville, 1982). Covington and Omelich (1984), for example, examined the attributions, affects, and subsequent performance of students who described their mid-term exam as a failure. Lack of effort ascriptions were most highly correlated with guilt, whereas low ability attributions were most positively correlated with shame. In addition, guilt and high expectancy were positively related to performance on the next exam, whereas humiliation was negatively related with subsequent school grade.

Evidence from these and other studies of achievement (see Weiner, 1986, for a review) demonstrate that many achievement problems are related to a maladaptive achievement attributional style. Similarly, much work reveals that short-term interventions can reduce or eliminate the observed problems. Systematic intervention research is lacking, however. More work is needed on how to effect long-term change in achievement attributions. For many achievement problems, effective intervention will certainly require assessment of and training in the skills necessary for successful performance in conjunction with attribution training designed to keep motivation levels appropriately high. Another topic needing investigation concerns the possible negative impact of maintaining high motivation levels in domains in which the person truly does lack the requisite abilities.

Depression, loneliness, and shyness

Most research has been done on the relation between attributional style (AS) and depression (see Sweeney *et al.*, 1986, for a meta-analytic review). The logic and findings for loneliness and shyness have been essentially the same, with the exception that, as expected, the latter two problems are more uniquely linked to attributional styles for interpersonal situations (for example, Anderson *et al.*, 1988).

Most of the published studies on attributional style and depression have been associated with the learned helplessness model espoused by Abramson, Seligman, and Teasdale (1978), though conceptually the research is more closely related to traditional attribution theory than to the original learned helplessness paradigm. The Abramson *et al.*, (1978) version stresses the importance of attributions along the internality, stability, and globality dimensions. Others, particularly Anderson (Anderson and Arnoult, 1985b; Anderson and Riger, 1991), have stressed the importance of internality, stability, and especially controllability.

A formidable number of research studies on the AS−depression relation have been conducted. In the past few years numerous reviews of these topics have appeared (for example, Anderson and Arnoult, 1985a; Anderson *et al.*, 1988; Brewin, 1985;

Coyne and Gotlib, 1983; Peterson and Seligman, 1984; Robins, 1988; Sweeney *et al.*, 1986). The reviews vary considerably in the range of studies covered; Sweeney *et al.*, analysed the results of over 100 studies of the Attributional Style Questionnaire developed by the Seligman group (Peterson *et al.*, 1982), whereas Anderson *et al.* (1988) examined the results of the four studies that had used the Attributional Style Assessment Test.

Although the specifics of the theories and the scales used to measure them differ somewhat, the basic attributional model in Figure 11.3 is common to all. Depression (and within more specific domains, loneliness and shyness) is the end result of a series of failures or negative outcomes attributed maladaptively. Depressed people see the failures as being their fault (internal), due to causes that they cannot change (uncontrollable), that are not likely to change on their own (stable), and that apply to many situations (global).

The question posed by most research has been, simply: is there a relation between AS and depression? Although some rather selective reviews have denied that there is evidence, the more complete reviews unequivocally demonstrate that there is a consistent relation between AS and depression (and loneliness and shyness, also). This holds true almost regardless of how one assesses AS or depression (see Sweeney *et al.*, 1986).

A related question concerns how general or situationally specific are attributional styles, and their relations to various kinds of problem. The early and dominant view was that AS was general across diverse situations. Most research never examined this assumption, but recent research that did look into the problem called into question the cross-situational consistency of AS (for example, Cutrona *et al.*, 1985). In discussing this issue, Anderson *et al.* (1988) proposed that attributional style has a 'moderate level of specificity'. That is, scores may be:

> cross-situationally consistent only across situations that are similar in psychologically meaningful ways, but not across very divergent types of situations. This view maintains that within situation types (e.g. interpersonal failure) the relative standing of individuals will remain fairly constant from one situation to another, but that between different situation types (e.g., interpersonal failure vs. noninterpersonal success) there will be little correspondence. (p. 980)

The data support this view.

A number of important issues are simply not addressed by this rough model of depression and similar problems in living. Some have received enough attention to deserve being called controversies; others have for the most part been ignored. A most obvious question concerns whether or not each causal dimension uniquely contributes to the prediction of depression. For instance, does a person's globality AS predict concurrent depression after controllability has been partialled out? Similarly, do both success and failure attributional styles contribute uniquely to the prediction of depression? These questions have received scant attention, but the research that does exist suggests that controllability is the most important dimension, but that stability and locus both contribute uniquely as well; both success and failure

ASs contribute to the prediction of depression (Anderson and Arnoult, 1985b; Anderson and Riger, 1990).

A related, though less obvious question, concerns how various dimensions of AS might combine to predict depression (cf. Carver, 1989). Various writings suggest that an interactive combination may be most maladaptive. For example, attributing failure to a cause that is uncontrollable *and* stable *and* internal may be particularly damaging to one's success expectancies, self-esteem, pride, and so on. Yet, we know of only one major attempt to test such interactive models of AS (Anderson and Riger, 1990). That research strongly supports the idea that the interactive combination of AS dimensions is important. Specifically, for failure situations, the relation between controllability AS and the depression/loneliness composite used in this study was quite strong when the AS was also relatively stable. People who habitually made more uncontrollable attributions suffered more depression and loneliness than those who made more controllable attributions. For success situations, a three-way interaction emerged. The controllability relation to depression/loneliness was quite strongly negative in all cases except when the AS was both relatively unstable and internal. Under those specific conditions the relation between controllability AS and depression/loneliness was not significantly different from zero.

A third question receiving little attention to date concerns the specific relation of AS dimensions to different effects. The basic model suggests that the locus dimension should be primarily related to self-esteem, the stability dimension should be related to success expectancies, and controllability should be related to several specific social emotions. One problem in testing these various more specific predictions is that in naturalistically generated populations of causes, the attribution dimensions correlate with each other quite highly (for example, Anderson, 1985). Thus, data showing that the locus of attributions is correlated with self-esteem are almost always confounded with other causal dimensions, such as controllability. This confounding problem occurs both in research of individual differences in attributional style, and in most experimental research. In the latter case, most researchers have simply manipulated attributions along one dimension without carefully checking to see whether other dimensions might have inadvertently been manipulated as well.

Perhaps the most important question lacking a clear answer concerns the causal status of attributional style. We know from many experimental studies that attributions are causal agents in success expectancies, affect, motivation, and performance quality. But does AS play a causal role in depression and related problems in living? If so, in what way? Brewin (1985) and others (Anderson and Arnoult, 1985a) have pointed out a number of ways that AS may be related to depression. AS may be a predisposing cause, or a vulnerability. This seems to be the crux of the 'diathesis-stress' version emphasized by Metalsky, Abramson, Seligman, Semmel, and Peterson (1982). That is, a maladaptive attributional style produces depression when a sufficiently high level of stress (negative outcomes) is experienced and maladaptively interpreted. Alternatively, AS may be a maintaining cause. In this case, the maladaptive AS may not even develop until a series of events produces depression. Once developed, though, the AS then serves to maintain or even intensify the depression (cf. Brewin's,

1985, recovery model). Several other models are also possible, including the possibility that AS is merely a correlate of depression, playing no causal role whatsoever. Testing these models is extremely difficult, and consequently rare. At this point in time, the fairest conclusion is that there is some support for viewing AS as a predisposing and as a maintaining cause, but that considerably better methodologies are needed to test the models adequately.

Attributional therapy

In conjunction with the growth of an attributional approach to personality dynamics, there has been a growing field of attributional therapy (see Forsterling, 1985, 1986). Attributional therapies are guided by the fundamental principle that thoughts (in this case, causal ascriptions) guide behaviour. It then follows that a change in thinking should produce a change in action. The goal of attributional therapies has therefore been to substitute adaptive causal ascriptions for those that are dysfunctional, with the anticipation that this alteration will produce changes in behaviour.

Attributional therapies have been, for the most part, confined to achievement-related contexts, though numerous authors have suggested attribution-related therapies for a variety of clinical problems. Within the achievement domain, researchers (change agents) have assumed that dysfunctional attributions have greater impact in situations of failure than of success, and that the most maladaptive causal ascription for achievement failure is lack of ability. This logically follows inasmuch as lack of ability is conceived as an internal, stable, and uncontrollable cause. In the majority of experimental reports, the adaptive cause that the therapist or researcher has sought to substitute is lack of effort. Lack of effort is considered an internal cause, just as is low ability. However, effort is conceived of as unstable and controllable. Less frequently, the designated causal attribution for achievement failure in the published literature has been bad luck or an overly difficult task. Because these are external causes for failure, self-esteem is maintained. Luck and task difficulty ascriptions do differ, however, in other respects. Luck is perceived as more unstable than is task difficulty, so that expectancies for success should be higher given luck rather than a difficulty ascription. It should be noted, therefore, that lack of effort as against bad luck as against an overly difficult task are all specified to improve motivation and coping relative to a low ability ascription for failure. However, the variables mediating the hypothesized improvement are not identical for the three causal ascriptions. Effort attributions theoretically maintain expectancy and induce guilt (positive motivators), while still lowering self-esteem (a performance inhibitor); luck attributions theoretically maintain expectancy of success as well as self-esteem; and task difficulty attributions only maintain positive self-esteem, while lowering expectancy estimates. (See Weiner, 1988, for fuller discussion of attributional therapy.)

In more clinical contexts, attribution theory advances have been applied to problems ranging from mild phobias to general depression (for example, Brewin and Antaki, 1982; Layden, 1982). Rehm (1982) has explicitly incorporated attributional components in his self-management approach to the treatment of depression. Unfortunately, there has been relatively little therapy outcome research specifically designed to test the unique effects of attributional components.

We should also point out that most popular cognitive-behavioural intervention approaches (for example, the work of Bandura, 1977; Beck, 1967; Ellis, 1977; Meichenbaum, 1977) include many features that would warm the heart of any good attribution theorist. For example, many of the negative thoughts that clients are taught to identify and change are basically maladaptive self-attributions. Also, many of the skills acquistion tasks are structured in such a way as to maximize the client's self-attributions for success. Thus, the effectiveness of supposedly non-attributional therapies may often be due, to a great extent, to the attributional changes wrought by the therapies.

Summary and conclusions

The centrality of attribution theory to both social and personality psychologists has been documented throughout this chapter, which has examined: attributions as defence mechanisms; attributions as determinants of trait inferences; individual differences in causal ascriptions; and attributional determinants of expectancy of success, affective experience, and the dynamics of behaviour and behavioural change. One cannot ask for a broader range of relevance from any extant theoretical system.

We believe that the future of attribution theory is very bright indeed, unlike many popular paradigms which dominate for a brief period, only to disappear as quickly as they arose. We are optimistic for several reasons. The belief in the importance of conscious experience and the ascendance of cognitive psychology have not waned. In addition, attribution theory continues to incorporate new concepts. Attribution theory is now becoming an established part of psychotherapy (see Brewin, 1988; Forsterling, 1988); it is being applied to areas ranging from sports psychology to consumer behaviour (see Graham and Folkes, 1990); it has successfully addressed issues related to reactions to the stigmatized, excuse-giving, consequences of perceived responsibility (see review in Weiner, 1986); it is established in motivational and educational psychology; and on and on.

Despite the success of attribution theory in such an array of domains, much basic research remains to be done. The attribution process, as laid out in the first part of this chapter, needs considerable refinement and testing. A better understanding of what kinds of information are used in attribution analyses and how that information becomes salient and relevant to the attributor will certainly influence the development of attributional interventions. Much remains to be done in development and testing of attributional interventions, either as 'stand-alone' therapies or, more likely, as components of large behaviour-change programmes. Certainly personality psychology, with the ever-increasing interest in self-perception, affective experience, and construals of the environment, will remain at the core of attributional concerns.

References

Abramson, L.Y., Seligman, M.E.P., and Teasdale, J. (1978), 'Learned helplessness in humans: critique and reformulation,' *Journal of Abnormal Psychology*, **87**, 49–74.

Anderson, C.A. (1983a) 'Motivational and performance deficits in interpersonal settings: the effects of attributional style', *Journal of Personality and Social Psychology*, **45**, 1136–47.

Anderson, C.A. (1983b), 'The causal structure of situations: the generation of plausible causal attributions as a function of type of event situation', *Journal of Experimental Social Psychology*, **19**, 185–203.

Anderson, C.A. (1985), 'Actor and observer attributions for different types of situations: causal structure effects, individual differences, and the dimensionality of causes,' *Social Cognition*, **3**, 323–340.

Anderson, C.A. (1989), 'How people think about causes: examination of the typical phenomenal organization of attributions', paper presented at the Nags Head Conference on Social Cognition, Kill Devil Hills, NC, 11–16 June 1989.

Anderson, C.A., and Arnoult, L.H. (1985a), 'Attributional models of depression, loneliness, and shyness,' in J. Harvey and G. Weary (eds.), *Attribution: Basic issues and applications*, New York, NY: Academic Press, pp. 235–79.

Anderson, C.A. and Arnoult, L.H. (1985b), 'Attributional style and everyday problems in living: depression, loneliness, and shyness', *Social Cognition*, **3**, 16–35.

Anderson, C.A., and Jennings, D.L. (1980), 'When experiences of failure promote expectations of success: the impact of attributing failure to ineffective strategies', *Journal of Personality*, **48**, 393–407.

Anderson, C.A. and Riger, A.L. (1991), 'A controllability attribution model of problems in living: dimensional and situational interactions in the prediction of depression and loneliness', *Social Cognition*, **9**, 149–81.

Anderson, C.A., and Slusher, M.P. (1986), 'Relocating motivational effect: a synthesis of cognitive and motivational effects on attributions for success and failure', *Social Cognition*, **4**, 270–92.

Anderson, C.A., Jennings, D.L., and Arnoult, L.H. (1988), 'Validity and utility of the attributional style construct at a moderate level of specificity,' *Journal of Personality and Social Psychology*, **55**, 979–90.

Andrews, G.R., and Debus, R.L. (1978), 'Persistence and causal perception of failure: modifying cognitive attributions', *Journal of Educational Psychology*, **70**, 154–166.

Arkin, R.M., and Baumgardner, A.H. (1985), 'Self-handicapping', in J.H. Harvey and G. Weary (eds.), *Attribution: Basic issues and applications*, New York, NY: Academic Press, pp. 169–202.

Averill, J.R. (1983), 'Studies on anger and aggression', *American Psychologist*, **38**, 1145–60.

Bandura, A. (1977), *Social Learning Theory*, Englewood Cliffs, NJ: Prentice Hall.

Baucom, D., Sayers, S.L., and Duhe, A. (1989), 'Attributional style and attributional patterns among married couples', *Journal of Personality and Social Psychology*, **56**, 596–607.

Beck, A.T. (1967), *The Diagnosis and Management of Depression*, Philadelphia, PA: University of Pennsylvania Press.

Beckman, L. (1970), 'Effects of students' performance on teachers' and observers' attributions of causality', *Journal of Educational Psychology*, **61**, 76–82.

Berglas, S. (1989), 'Self-handicapping behavior and the self-defeating personality disorder: toward a refined clinical perspective', in R. Curtis (ed.), *Self-defeating Behaviors: Experimental research, clinical impressions, and practical implications*, New York, NY: Plenum Press, pp. 261–88.

Bradley, G.W. (1978), 'Self-serving biases in the attribution process: a reexamination of the fact or fiction question', *Journal of Personality and Social Psychology*, **36**, 56–71.

Brewin, C.R. (1985), 'Depression and causal attributions: what is their relation?', *Psychological Bulletin*, **98**, 297–309.

Brewin, C.R. (1988), *Cognitive Foundations of Clinical Psychology*, Hillsdale, NJ: Erlbaum.

Brewin, C., and Antaki, C. (1982), 'The role of attributions in psychological treatment', in C. Antaki and C. Brewin (eds.), *Attributions and Psychological Change*, New York, NY: Academic Press, pp. 23–44.

Brown, J.D. (1988), 'Self-directed attention, self-esteem, and causal attributions for balanced outcomes', *Personality and Social Psychology Bulletin*, **14**, 252–63.

Cacioppo, J.T., and Petty, R.E. (1982), 'The need for cognition', *Journal of Personality and Social Psychology*, **42**, 116–31.

Carver, Charles S. (1989), 'How should multifaceted personality constructs be tested? issues illustrated by self-monitoring, attributional style, and hardiness', *Journal of Personality and Social Psychology*, **56**, 577–85.

Chapin, M., and Dyck, D.G. (1976), 'Persistence in children's reading behaviors as a function of N length and attribution retraining', *Journal of Abnormal Psychology*, **85**, 511–15.

Chaplin, W.F., John, O.P., and Goldberg, L.R. (1988), 'Conceptions of traits and states: dimensional attributes with ideals as prototypes', *Journal of Personality and Social Psychology*, **54**, 541–57.

Covington, M.V., and Omelich, C.L. (1984), 'An empirical examination of Weiner's critique of attributional research', *Journal of Educational Psychology*, **76**, 1214–25.

Coyne, J.C., and Gotlib, I.H. (1983), 'The role of cognition in depression: a critical appraisal', *Psychological Bulletin*, **94**, 472–505.

Cutrona, C.E., Russell, D., and Jones, R.D. (1985), 'Cross-situational consistency in causal attributions: does attributional style exist?', *Journal of Personality and Social Psychology*, **47**, 1043–58.

Dweck, C.S., and Goetz, T.E. (1977), 'Attributions and learned helplessness', in J.H. Harvey, W.J. Ickes, and R.F. Kidd (eds.), *New Directions in Attribution Research*, New York, NY: Erlbaum, vol. 2, pp. 157–79.

Eisen, V. (1979), 'Actor–observer differences in information inference and causal attribution', *Journal of Personality and Social Psychology*, **37**, 261–72.

Ellis, A. (1977), 'The basic clinical theory of rational-emotive therapy', in A. Ellis and R. Grieger (eds.), *Handbook of Rational-emotive Therapy*, New York, NY: Springer, pp. 3–34.

Feather, N.T., and Tiggemann, M. (1984), 'A balanced measure of attributional style', *Australian Journal of Psychology*, **36**, 267–83.

Fletcher, G.J.O., Danilovics, P., Fernandez, G., Peterson, D., and Reeder, G.D. (1986), 'Attributional complexity: an individual difference measure', *Journal of Personality and Social Psychology*, **51**, 857–84.

Forsterling, F. (1985), 'Attributional training: a review', *Psychological Bulletin*, **98**, 495–512.

Forsterling, F. (1986), 'Attributional conceptions in clinical psychology', *American Psychologist*, **41**, 275–85.

Forsterling, F. (1988), *Attribution Theory in Clinical Psychology*, New York, NY: Wiley.

Frieze, I.H., and Weiner, B. (1971), 'Cue utilization and attributional judgments for success and failure, *Journal of Personality*, **39**, 591–606.

Gilbert, D.T., Pelham, B.W., and Krull, D.S. (1988), 'On cognitive busyness: when person perceivers meet persons perceived', *Journal of Personality and Social Psychology*, **54**, 733–40.

Gilovich, T. (1983), 'Biased evaluation and persistence in gambling', *Journal of Personality and Social Psychology*, **44**, 1110–26.

Graham, S. and Folkes, V.S. (eds) (1990), *Attribution Theory: Applications to achievement, mental health, and interpersonal conflict*, Hillsdale: NJ: Erlbaum.

Hansen, R.D. (1985), 'Cognitive economy and commonsense attribution processing', in J.

Harvey and G. Weary (eds.), *Attribution: Basic issues and applications*, New York, NY: Academic Press, pp. 65—85.

Heider, F. (1958), *The Psychology of Interpersonal Relations*, New York: Wiley.

Hewstone, M., and Jaspars, J. (1987), 'Covariation and causal attribution: a logical model of the intuitive analysis of variance', *Journal of Personality and Social Psychology*, **53**, 663—72.

Hilton, D.J., and Slugoski, B.R. (1986), 'Knowledge based causal attribution: the abnormal conditions focus model', *Psychological Review*, **93**, 75—88.

Hoffman, M.L. (1975), 'Developmental synthesis of affect and cognition and its implications for altruistic motivation', *Developmental Psychology*, **11**, 607—22.

Horney, K. (1937), *Neurotic Personality of Our Times*, New York: Norton.

Isenberg, A. (1980), 'Natural pride and natural shame', in A.O. Rorty (ed.), *Explaining Emotions*, Berkeley, CA: University of California Press, pp. 355—84.

Johnson, T.J., Feigenbaum, R., and Weiby, M. (1964), 'Some determinants and consequences of the teacher's perception of causation', *Journal of Educational Psychology*, **55**, 237—46.

Jones, E.E., and Berglas, S. (1978), 'Control of attributions about the self through self-handicapping strategies: the appeal of alcohol and the role of underachievement', *Personality and Social Psychology Bulletin*, **4**, 200—6.

Jones, E.E., and Davis, K.W. (1965), 'From acts to dispositions: the attribution process in person perception', in L. Berkowitz (eds.), *Advances in Experimental Social Psychology*, New York, NY: Academic Press, vol. 2, pp. 219—66.

Jones, E.E., and Harris, V.A. (1967), 'The attribution of attitudes, *Journal of Experimental Social Psychology*, **3**, 1—24.

Jones, E.E., and McGillis, D. (1976), 'Correspondent inferences and the attribution cube: a comparative reappraisal', in J. Harvey, W.J. Ickes, and R.F. Kidd (eds.), *New Directions in Attribution Research*, Hillsdale, NJ: Erlbaum, vol. 1, pp. 389—420.

Jones, E.E., and Nisbett, R.E. (1971), 'The actor and the observer: divergent perceptions of the causes of behavior', in E.E. Jones, D.E. Kanouse, H.H. Kelley, R.E. Nisbett, S. Valins, and B. Weiner (eds.), *Attribution: Perceiving the causes of behavior*, Morristown, NJ: General Learning Press, pp. 79—94.

Kelley, H.H. (1967), 'Attribution theory in social psychology', in D. Levine (ed.), *Nebraska Symposium on Motivation*, Lincoln, NE: University of Nebraska Press, vol. 15, pp. 192—238.

Kelley, H.H. (1971), 'Causal schemata and the attribution process', in E.E. Jones, D.E. Kanouse, H.H. Kelley, R.E. Nisbett, S. Valins, and B. Weiner (eds.), *Attribution: Perceiving the causes of behavior*, Morristown, NJ: General Learning Press, pp. 151—74.

Kelley, H.H. (1973), 'The process of causal attribution', *American Psychologist*, **28**, 107—28.

Kelley, H.H., and Michela, J.L. (1980), 'Attribution theory and research', *Annual Review of Psychology*, **31**, 457—501.

Kingdon, J.W. (1967), 'Politicians' beliefs about voters', *American Political Science Review*, **14**, 137—45.

Kruglanski, A.W. (1980), 'Lay epistemo-logic — process and contents: another look at attribution theory', *Psychology Review*, **87**, 70—87.

Kuiper, N.A. (1978), 'Depression and causal attributions for success and failure', *Journal of Personality and Social Psychology*, **36**, 236—46.

Layden, M.A. (1982), 'Attributional style therapy', in C. Antaki and C. Brewin (eds.), *Attributions and Psychological Change*, New York, NY: Academic Press, pp. 63—82.

Marks, G., and Miller, N. (1987), 'Ten years of research on the false-consensus effect: an empirical and theoretical review', *Psychological Bulletin*, **102**, 72—90.

Meichenbaum, D. (1977), *Cognitive-behavior Modification*, New York, NY: Plenum Press.

Metalsky, G.I., Abramson, L.Y., Seligman, M.E.P., Semmel, A., and Peterson, C. (1982), 'Attributional styles and life events in the classroom: vulnerability and invulnerability to depressive mood reactions', *Journal of Personality and Social Psychology*, **43**, 612—17.

Miller, D.T., and Ross, M. (1975), 'Self-serving biases in the attribution of causality: fact or fiction?', *Psychological Bulletin*, **82**, 213−25.

Monson, T.C., and Snyder, M. (1977), 'Actors, observers, and the attribution process: toward a reconceptualization', *Journal of Experimental Social Psychology*, **13**, 89−111.

Mullen, B., and Riordan, C.A. (1988), 'Self-serving attributions for performance in naturalistic settings: a meta-analytic review', *Journal of Applied Social Psychology*, **18**, 3−22.

Mullen, B., Atkins, J.L., Champion, D.S., Edwards, C., Hardy, D., Story, J.E., and Vanderklok, M. (1985), 'The false consensus effects: a meta analysis of 115 hypothesis tests', *Journal of Experimental Social Psychology*, **21**, 262−83.

Nisbett, R.E., and Ross, L. (1980), *Human Inference: Strategies and shortcomings*, Englewood Cliffs, NJ: Prentice Hall.

Nisbett, R.E., Caputo, C., Legant, P., and Marecek, J. (1973), 'Behavior as seen by the actor and as seen by the observer', *Journal of Personality and Social Psychology*, **27**, 154−65.

Peterson, C., and Seligman, M.E.P. (1984), 'Causal explanations as a risk factor for depression: theory and evidence', *Psychological Review*, **91**, 347−74.

Peterson, C., Seligman, M.E.P., and Vaillant, G. (1988), 'Pessimistic explanatory style is a risk factor for physical illness: a thirty-five year longitudinal study', *Journal of Personality and Social Psychology*, **55**, 23−7.

Peterson, C., Semmel, A., von Baeyer, C., Abramson, L.Y., Metalsky, G.I., and Seligman, M.E.P. (1982), 'The Attributional Style Questionnaire', *Cognitive Therapy and Research*, **6**, 287−99.

Pruitt, D.J., and Insko, C.A. (1980), 'Extension of the Kelley attribution model: the role of comparison object consensus, target object consensus, distinctiveness and consistency', *Journal of Personality and Social psychology*, **39**, 39−58.

Rehm, L.P. (1982), 'Self-management in depression', in P. Karoly and F.H. Kanfer (eds.), *The Psychology of Self-management: From theory to practice*, New York, NY: Pergamon, pp. 522−70

Reisenzein, R. (1983), 'The Schachter theory of emotions: two decades later', *Psychological Bulletin*, **94**, 239−64.

Reisenzein, R. (1986), 'A structural equation analysis of Weiner's attribution-affect model of helping behavior', *Journal of Personality and Social Psychology*, **50**, 1123−33.

Rhodewalt, F., Strube, M.J., Hill, C.A., and Sansone, C. (1988), 'Strategic self-attribution and Type A behavior', *Journal of Research in Personality*, **22**, 60−74.

Robins, C.J. (1988), 'Attributions and depression: why is the literature so inconsistent?', *Journal of Personality and Social Psychology*, **54**, 880−9.

Ross, L. and Anderson, C.A. (1982), 'Shortcomings in the attribution process: on the origins and maintenance of erroneous social assessments', in D. Kahneman, P. Slovic, and A. Tversky (eds.), *Judgement under Uncertainty: Heuristics and biases*, New York, NY: Cambridge University Press, pp. 129−52.

Ross, L., Bierbrauer, G., and Polly, S. (1974), 'Attribution of educational outcomes by professional and nonprofessional instructors', *Journal of Personality and Social Psychology*, **29**, 609−18.

Ross, L., Greene, D., and House, P. (1977), 'The "false consensus effect": an egocentric bias in social perception and attribution processes', *Journal of Experimental Social Psychology*, **13**, 279−301.

Rotter, J.B. (1966), 'Generalized expectancies for internal versus external control of reinforcement', *Psychological Monographs*, **80**, whole no. 609.

Rotter, J.B., and Hochreich, D.J. (1975), *Personality*, Glenview, IL: Scott Foresman.

Schachter, S., and Singer, J.E. (1962), 'Cognition, social and physiological determinants of emotional state', *Psychological Review*, **69**, 379−99.

Seligman, M.E.P., Abramson, L.Y., Semmel, A., and von Baeyer, C. (1979), 'Depressive attributional style', *Journal of Abnormal Psychology*, **88**, 242−7.

Snyder, C.R., and Higgins, R.L. (1988), 'Excuses: their effective role in the negotiation of reality', *Psychological Bulletin*, **104**, 23–35.

Snyder, M.L., Stephan, W.G., and Rosenfield, D. (1976), 'Egotism and attribution', *Journal of Personality and Social Psychology*, **33**, 435–41.

Storms, M.D. (1973), 'Videotape and the attribution process: reversing actors' and observers' point of view'. *Journal of Personality and Social Psychology*, **27**, 165–75.

Sweeney, P., Anderson, K., and Bailey, S. (1986), 'Attributional style in depression: a meta-analytic review', *Journal of Personality and Social Psychology*, **50**, 974–91.

Taylor, S.E., and Fiske, S.T. (1978), 'Salience, attention, and attribution: top of the head phenomena', in L. Berkowitz (ed.), *Advances in Experimental Social Psychology*, New York, NY: Academic Press, vol. 11, pp. 249–88.

Tennen, H., and Herzberger, S. (1987), 'Depression, self-esteem, and the absence of self-protective attributional biases', *Journal of Personality and Social Psychology*, **52**, 72–80.

Tetlock, P.E., and Levi, A. (1982), 'Attribution bias: on the inconclusiveness of the cognition-motivation debate', *Journal of Experimental Social Psychology*, **18**, 68–88.

Trivers, R.L. (1971), 'The evolution of reciprocal altruism', *Quarterly Review of Biology*, **46**, 35–57.

Trope, Y. (1986), 'Identification and inferential processes in dispositional attribution', *Psychological Review*, **93**, 239–57.

Uleman, J.S. (1987), 'Consciousness and control: the case of spontaneous trait inferences', *Personality and Social Psychology Bulletin*, **13**, 337–54.

Weiner, B. (1985), 'Attributional theory of achievement motivation and emotion', *Psychological Review*, **92**, 548–73.

Weiner, B. (1986), *An Attributional Theory of Motivation and Emotion*, New York, NY: Springer-Verlag.

Weiner, B. (1988), 'Attribution theory and attributional therapy: some theoretical observations and suggestions', *British Journal of Clinical Psychology*, **27**, 93–104.

Weiner, B., Russell, D., and Lerman, D. (1978), 'Affective consequences of causal ascriptions', in J.H. Harvey, W.J. Ickes and R.F. Kidd (eds.), *New Directions in Attribution Research*, Hillsdale, NJ: Erlbaum, vol. 2, pp. 59–88.

Weiner, B., Russell, D., and Lerman, D. (1979), 'The cognition-emotion process in achievement-related contexts', *Journal of Personality and Social Psychology*, **37**, 1211–20.

Wicker, W.F., Payne, G.C., and Morgan, R.D. (1983), 'Participant descriptions of guilt and shame', *Motivation and Emotion*, **7**, 25–39.

Wilson, T.D., and Linville, P.W. (1982), 'Improving the academic performance of college freshmen: attribution therapy revisited', *Journal of Personality and Social Psychology*, **42**, 367–76.

Wright, E.F., and Wells, G.L. (1988), 'Is the attitude-attribution paradigm suitable for investigating the dispositional bias?', *Personality and Social Psychology Bulletin*, **14**, 183–90.

Wong, P.T.P., and Weiner, B. (1981), 'When people ask "why" questions, and the heuristics of attributional search', *Journal of Personality and Social Psychology*, **40**, 650–63.

Zillmann, D. (1978), 'Attribution and misattribution of excitatory reactions', in J. Harvey, W.J. Ickes, and R. Kidd (eds.), *New Directions in Attribution Research*, Hillsdale, NJ: Erlbaum, vol. 2, pp. 335–68.

Zuckerman, M. (1979), 'Attribution of success and failure revisited, or: the motivational bias is alive and well in attribution theory', *Journal of Personality*, **47**, 245–287.

PART VI
The Biological Approach

12/ A tale of two theories of temperament

Jan Strelau
University of Warsaw, Poland

Robert Plomin
Pennsylvania State University, USA

Introduction

In keeping with the spirit of this volume, this chapter will describe and contrast our two approaches to temperament with the hope that a synthesis will emerge from this dialectic that transcends our specific theories. We begin with a description of Buss and Plomin's (1984) EAS theory and then consider the approach of the Warsaw group (Strelau, 1983, 1989a). The third section compares the two approaches and attempts to extract themes of general relevance for the study of temperament. As has been pointed out (for example, Strelau, 1985a, 1991), it is surprising that so many theories of temperament have developed independently during the past two decades and that there has been so little communication among them despite some obvious points of overlap (Goldsmith *et al.*, 1987). The differences are not just between the East and the West but, within the West, there is little communication among the three major research orientations for which temperament theories have emerged: clinical (for example, Thomas and Chess, 1977, 1986), infancy (for example, Goldsmith and Campos, 1986; Rothbart, 1989), and personality, which is the origin of Buss and Plomin's (1975, 1984) approach. This lack of communication makes us especially appreciative for this opportunity to take a small step towards increasing interaction, at least between our two approaches to the study of temperament.

Emotionality/activity/sociability (EAS)

Unlike several theories of temperament that are based on neurological constructs, Buss and Plomin's focus is on personality with no attempt to specify neural phenomena associated with personality. The key element in their approach is the selection of the most heritable dimensions of personality:

> A major distinction between our theory and other approaches to temperament is that
> we specify a genetic origin, whereas other theorists tend to be vague about the
> origins of temperament. We have been impressed during the past decade with the
> extent to which behavioral genetic data — often obtained by researchers with
> perspectives quite different from ours — support our major contention that
> emotionality, activity, and sociability are among the most heritable aspects of
> personality in early childhood. (Buss and Plomin, 1984, pp. 156–7)

Their theory identifies emotionality, activity, and sociability (EAS) as personality traits that appear early in life and show the greatest genetic influence (Buss and Plomin, 1975, 1984). *Traits* are individual differences that are relatively enduring across time and situations. *Personality* is meant to exclude other traits such as physical and physiological characteristics and, by convention, intelligence. Emotionality refers to distress, the tendency to become upset easily and intensely. It is assumed to differentiate into fear and anger during the first year of life and appears to be the foundation of adult neuroticism, with neuroticism's cognitive component of anxiety not yet developed in childhood. EAS emotionality focuses on the high-arousal negative emotions rather than low-arousal positive affects — the latter show less evidence for genetic influence (Buss and Plomin, 1984). Activity includes tempo and vigour. Sociability refers to gregariousness or the preference for being with other people. It is the key component of extraversion in infancy, when the impulsivity facet of adult extraversion is not very important. Shyness, responses to interactions with strangers, tends to be assessed in infancy rather than sociability.

Criteria

The EAS criteria for distinguishing temperament from other personality dimensions are meant to make the theory testable:

> In describing our theory, we have tried to be specific and to outline ways of testing
> it. We propose that emotionality, activity, and sociability are the major dimensions of
> personality in infancy and early childhood; if not, the theory is wrong. We propose
> that these three traits are heritable; if not, the theory is wrong. If other early-
> appearing personality traits are shown to be heritable and not derivable from our
> three temperaments, the theory must be amended. If there are better ways to slice
> the personality pie early in life, the theory may have to be discarded. (Buss and
> Plomin, 1984, p. 156)

Two points should be made concerning the criterion of heritability. First, the heritability criterion is clear and testable, which contrasts with other theories of temperament, for which it is difficult to explain why certain traits have been selected as temperament from the diverse array of personality traits. Other theories of temperament are much less explicit concerning the origins of temperament, although they all agree that 'biological underpinnings' are part of the definition of temperament (Goldsmith *et al.*, 1987, p. 507; see also Strelau, 1987a). Second, the EAS traits are central to nearly all theories of temperament (Goldsmith *et al.*, 1987; Plomin and Dunn, 1986), perhaps because the heritability of the EAS traits makes them more distinct factorially, more stable, and less modifiable than other personality traits. None the less, the EAS focus on the most heritable personality traits in childhood is not meant to denigrate the study of other personality traits.

It is important to emphasize that the criterion of heritability does not mean that the EAS temperaments are completely heritable, stable, or immutable — the issue is their *relative* heritability, stability, and modifiability as compared to other personality traits. Heritability only means that the differences in temperament observed among children are due in part to genetic differences among them given the genetic and environmental differences that exist in the populations sampled (Plomin, DeFries and McClearn, 1990). Although the EAS temperaments show appreciable genetic influence, most of the variance in these traits appears to be non-genetic in origin. Moreover, heritability *per se* does not necessarily imply stability: genetic factors contribute to change as well as to continuity during development, as discussed later.

Evidence for heritability and stability of the EAS temperaments

The basic element of the theory, that the EAS traits are among the most heritable dimensions of personality, has been largely confirmed:

> The major conclusion to emerge from the research reviewed in this chapter is that support for the heritability of the EAS traits has broadened since the publication of our 1975 book. There are now twin and family studies using a diverse array of measures, all converging on the conclusion that the EAS traits are heritable. (Buss and Plomin, 1984, p. 139)

A review of behavioural genetic research on the EAS traits from a developmental perspective shows that the EAS traits are consistently among the most heritable personality traits throughout infancy, childhood, adolescence, and adulthood and, surprisingly, that heritability for the EAS traits tends to increase rather than decrease during development (Plomin, 1986). A recent study in the last half of the lifespan using the powerful design of twins reared apart and matched twins reared together has also shown significant genetic influence on the EAS traits (Plomin, Pederson *et al.*, 1988). Other relevant reviews show substantial genetic influence on the fearfulness component of emotionality (Plomin and Stocker, 1990) and on shyness (Plomin and Daniels, 1986), both of which are relevant to Kagan's (for example, 1989) dimension of behavioural inhibition. Evidence for genetic influence on other traits — aggressiveness, for example, (Plomin, Nitz and Rowe, 1990) — is less consistent.

One problem with the conclusion that the EAS traits are the most heritable personality traits in childhood is that so many personality traits show some genetic influence. This makes it difficult to prove that the EAS traits are significantly more heritable than other personality traits. Part of the difficulty in demonstrating differential heritability is lack of statistical power. Given the usual identical and fraternal twin correlations of 0.50 and 0.30, respectively, for self-report questionnaires, it will be difficult to demonstrate significant differences in heritability. For example, with 100 pairs of each type of twin, a heritability of 0.40 based on an identical twin correlation of 0.50 and a fraternal twin correlation of 0.30 has a standard error of $+/-0.24$. This means that the typical personality heritability of 0.40 cannot be reliably discriminated from another trait whose heritability is zero. With 1,000 pairs of each type of twin, researchers can detect heritability differences on the order of 0.40 vs. 0.00, but still cannot reliably discriminate the usual heritability of 0.40 from a more modest heritability of 0.20. However, replication of results across studies cuts down on these odds; moreover, some recent questionnaires studies of adults include thousands of pairs of twins, and these find evidence for differential heritability with EAS traits generally showing the greatest heritabilities.

A second problem is that fraternal twins correlations tend to be too low relative to identical twin correlations, especially when parental ratings are employed (Buss and Plomin, 1984; Plomin, Chipuer and Loehlin, 1990). A possible genetic explanation is non-additive genetic variance (Plomin, DeFries and McClearn, 1990). When we say that the coefficient of genetic relationship for first-degree relatives is 0.50, this refers only to additive genetic variance, genetic influences that sum linearly in their effect on the phenotype and thus breed true from parent to offspring. However, parents and their offspring do not resemble each other if genetic effects are non-additive, due to interactions between alleles at a locus (dominance) or across loci (epistasis). Siblings share a quarter of the genetic variance due to dominance and very little genetic variance due to higher-order epistatic interactions that involve nonlinear effects of several genes. In contrast, identical twins share all genetic effects whether additive or non-additive. Thus, if non-additive genetic variance is important, identical twins will be more than twice as similar as fraternal twins.

Non-additive genetic variance could also explain why adoption studies of first-degree relatives suggest less genetic influence than twin studies. Twin studies of infants and young children indicate substantial genetic influence for parental ratings of the EAS temperaments, but adoption data have only recently been reported at these ages from the longitudinal Colorado Adoption Project (Plomin, DeFries and Fulker, 1988). In contrast with twin results, little evidence is found for genetic influence in parent—offspring comparisons, as well as in the first comparisons between adoptive and non-adoptive siblings when each child was 1, 2, 3, and 4 years of age (Plomin, Coon *et al.*, in press). It was concluded that the difference between the twin and adoption results may be due to non-additive genetic variance. If non-additive genetic variance is important, twin studies are needed to detect it.

The phenomenon of identical twin correlations that are more than twice as large as fraternal twin correlations can also be explained *post hoc* by violations of the equal environments assumption of the twin method, namely, contrast effects that exaggerate fraternal-twin differences (Buss and Plomin, 1984) and assimilation effects that inflate identical-twin resemblance. Recent work along these lines suggests that both non-additive genetic variance and assimilation effects are important (Plomin, Chipuer and Loehlin, 1990).

Buss and Plomin (1984) also review evidence for the stability of the EAS traits and conclude: 'In summary, though heritable personality traits present in early childhood need not be stable, the EAS temperaments appear to be among the most stable personality traits in childhood' (p. 146).

Extraversion and neuroticism

Not previously discussed is the support for the EAS theory that comes from behavioural genetic research on extraversion and neuroticism in adults. Most temperament theorists pay little attention to adult personality. In research on adult personality, attention in recent years in the West has turned to the so-called 'Big Five' (Digman, 1990; Digman and Inouye, 1986; Norman, 1963). Although there is confusion concerning the definitions of these five traits, the biggest two of these are clearly extraversion and neuroticism. In the behavioural genetics literature, there is general agreement that extraversion and neuroticism are among the most heritable personality traits (for example, Henderson, 1982; Loehlin, 1989). Indeed, Loehlin (1989) has argued that the lack of evidence for differential heritability of self-report personality questionnaires may be due to the pervasiveness of these two super-traits. That is, genetic influence on extraversion and neuroticism might mask the differential heritability of other traits. In support of this hypothesis, Loehlin created scales that were orthogonal to extraversion and neuroticism and found that several of these — such as masculinity, tolerance of ambiguity, and persistence — yielded much lower heritability estimates. A recent study using the powerful design of twins reared apart and twins reared together is the first behavioural genetic study to focus specifically on the 'Little Three' of the 'Big Five' personality traits (Bergeman *et al.*, in press). The study found that one of these dimensions, agreeableness, showed little genetic influence, whereas the same sample showed substantial genetic influence on extraversion and neuroticism (Pedersen *et al.*, 1988).

These data are relevant to the EAS theory. In children, the essence of extraversion is sociability, and emotionality is at the core of neuroticism stripped of its anxiety features. Thus, if extraversion and neuroticism are the most heritable aspects of personality, these findings provide at least indirect evidence that sociability and emotionality in childhood may be highly heritable as well.

What about activity? By historical happenstance, few adult self-report questionnaires include a dimension of activity or energy level. In contrast, few systems of temperament in childhood have neglected activity level (Goldsmith *et al.*, 1987). Twin studies consistently show genetic influence for activity after the first year of life (Plomin, 1986).

It is interesting that nearly all temperament theories include emotionality and most include activity level, but sociability is seldom considered. Kagan's dimension of behavioural inhibition involves shyness, as does the New York Longitudinal Study (NYLS) approach—withdrawal. However, shyness is not the same as low sociability (Buss and Plomin, 1984; Plomin and Daniels, 1986). This omission is interesting because sociability is a major component of extraversion. Although sociability is neglected, temperament theories that derive from Pavlov's (1927) distinction between strong and weak nervous systems, including theories such as Strelau's that emphasize optimal levels of arousal, are known in the West in relation to Eysenck's (1967) theory of extraversion.

Future directions for EAS research

We will not concern ourselves with the philosophical intricacies of the word 'theory'. The term obviously means different things to different psychologists, as illustrated by formal differences among the best-known theories in psychology, such as learning theories, theories of personality, and Piagetian theory. None the less, from the pragmatic view of a behavioural researcher, theories should clarify our thinking by describing, predicting, and explaining behaviour. At the very least, theories should be descriptive, organizing and condensing existing facts in a reasonable, internally consistent manner. The contribution of the EAS theory is its identification of emotionality, activity, and sociability as the most heritable among the welter of personality dimensions that have been studied. At their best, theories explain phenomena as well as describe them. Because it rests on the foundation of quantitative genetic theory and its powerful methods, the EAS theory is able to explain temperament in terms of its genetic and environmental origins.

Beyond organizing and explaining existing facts, theories should also make predictions concerning phenomena not yet investigated and allow clear tests of these predictions. Because it identifies the most heritable dimensions of personality in childhood, the EAS theory predicts that these temperaments will be among the most stable and least modifiable personality traits. (As emphasized above, this does not mean that the EAS traits are completely heritable, stable, or unmodifiable.) Its quantitative genetic foundation leads the EAS theory to other genetic predictions. For example, because no single gene has been shown to account for a detectable amount of variance in the normal range of individual differences in behaviour (Plomin, DeFries and McClearn, 1990), it is predicted that the genetic origins of the EAS traits are polygenic, involving small effects of many genes. It should be noted that recent reports of single-gene linkage for manic depression and for schizophrenia are limited to isolated pedigrees and do not indicate a single major gene in the population; moreover, these reported linkages have not replicated (Plomin, Rende and Rutter, in press).

A new development in quantitative genetics is to consider genetic contributions to change as well as to continuity during development (Plomin, 1986). So far, it appears that: (1) when the heritability of personality changes during infancy and childhood, it increases; and (2) genetic factors contribute substantially to personality change from year to year during childhood but not in adulthood (Plomin and Nesselroade, 1990). In contrast, although heritability increases for IQ during infancy and childhood (Fulker *et al.*, 1988), genetics almost exclusively contributes to continuity from age-to-age for IQ (DeFries *et al.*, 1987). Thus, the EAS theory makes the counterintuitive prediction that if heritability changes for the EAS temperaments it will increase, and that genetics contributes to age-to-age change as well as continuity for the EAS temperaments. These issues will be addressed by a collaborative longitudinal twin study that began in 1982 and includes more than 300 same-sex pairs of twins tested in the home and laboratory at 14, 20, 24, and 36 months of age, in order to explore genetic and environmental contributions to change and continuity in temperament, emotion, and cognition (Plomin, Campos *et al.*, 1990).

A third example of a genetic prediction involves the increasing evidence for the importance of non-additive genetic variance, especially for extraversion (Plomin, Chipuer and Loehlin, 1990). This leads to the prediction that some of the genetic variance for sociability will be non-additive, which can only be detected via twin studies because only identical twins are identical for all genetic effects, whether additive or non-additive.

The quantitative genetic foundation of the EAS theory also leads to several predictions concerning environmental influences and the interface between nature and nurture. For example, given that quantitative genetic analyses of many behavioural traits yield few examples of heritabilities greater than 50 per cent, it is safe to predict that at least half of the variance of the EAS traits is non-genetic in origin. The most dramatic finding from human behavioural genetics research on personality is that this environmental influence operates to make children in the same family as different from one another as pairs of children picked at random from the population (Dunn and Plomin, 1990; Plomin and Daniels, 1987). That is, growing up together in the same family does not make siblings similar in personality. For example, a direct test of the extent to which shared experiences make children in the same family similar is provided by adoptive siblings, genetically unrelated children adopted into the same families early in life. Because these siblings are not genetically related, their similarity can be caused only by shared family environment. The average correlation for adoptive siblings is only 0.05 for personality, suggesting that growing up in the same family accounts for a negligible amount of the variance of personality traits. Recent studies of twins reared apart also indicate that they are not more dissimilar in personality than twins reared together (Plomin, in press).

The convergence of evidence on this conclusion leads to the prediction that similar results will be found for the EAS traits. This topic, referred to as non-shared environment, opens the door to a new area of environmental research that attempts to identify differential experiences of siblings that account for differences in their personality. The key question is why children in the same family are so different, and the answer to this question will come from studying more than one child per family and the experiences specific to each child. That is, instead of thinking about environmental influences on a family-by-family basis, we need to think on an individual-by-individual basis.

A second example of a prediction that involves nurture rather than nature is the topic of genotype–environment (GE) correlation. GE correlation literally refers to a correlation between genetic deviations and environmental deviations as they affect a particular trait. In other words, it describes the extent to which individuals are exposed to environments as a function of their genetic propensities. Three types of genotype-environment correlation have been described (Plomin, DeFries and Loehlin,

1977). *Passive* GE correlation occurs because children share heredity as well as environmental influences with members of their family and can thus passively inherit environments correlated with their genetic propensities. *Reactive* or evocative GE correlation refers to experiences of the child that derive from other people's reactions to the child's genetic predispositions. *Active* GE correlation occurs when, for example, children actively select or even create environments that are correlated with their genetic propensities. This has been called 'niche picking' or 'niche building' (Scarr and McCartney, 1983). Adoption studies make it possible to explore these types of GE correlation. Because the EAS temperaments are the most heritable dimensions of personality in childhood, they are the best candidates for analyses of this type. Buss and Plomin (1984) detail ways in which the EAS temperaments are expected to modify the impact of the environment, affect social environments, and select environments.

A related prediction concerns a new area of research in developmental genetics that finds substantial genetic influence on measures of environment, including children's and parent's perceptions of the family environment (Plomin and Bergeman, 1991), observations of parent−child interaction (Plomin, 1986), and even measures of life events (Plomin, Lichtenstein *et al.*, 1990). Because EAS temperaments are the most heritable personality dimensions in childhood, it is predicted that the EAS temperaments contribute genetic variance to children's perceptions of their experience as well as to parents' treatment of children.

A final example of the predictive value of the quantitative genetic underpinnings of the EAS theory involves recent advances in understanding genetic and environmental links between the normal and abnormal (DeFries and Fulker, 1985; Plomin, Rende and Rutter, in press; Plomin, in press). The societal impact of temperament research lies in the extremes of its normal distributions — for example, in the highly emotional, highly active, and low sociable children. These new techniques make it possible to address what may be the most important question in psychiatric genetics: the extent to which genetic influences on disorders represent the extremes of genetic influences on the normal range of variability in behaviour. That is, to what extent are psychosocial disorders the result of the co-occurrence of many of the same genetic factors that are responsible for variability in the normal range? The few studies utilizing these new techniques suggest that disorders may be, aetiologically speaking, the extremes of normal distributions of variability. This work leads to the prediction that the EAS temperaments are related genetically to disorders in the domain of developmental psychopathology. Specifically, genetic influences on high emotionality and activity may contribute to genetic influence on externalizing diagnoses, and genetic influence on low sociability may contribute to genetic influence on internalizing diagnoses. Stock in temperament research will increase in value if it can be shown that some facets of psychopathology are indeed aetiologically the extreme of normal personality dimensions.

No single approach to temperament can suffice, for each approach yields insights not perceived by others. The contribution of the EAS approach is its identification of emotionality, activity, and sociability as the most heritable personality traits in childhood. It may not be coincidental that these are the traits studied by other temperament researchers and that the EAS traits also appear to be among the most stable traits from childhood to adulthood.

The regulative theory of temperament (RTT)

The roots of the RTT

The Regulative Theory of Temperament (RTT) is a result of Strelau's (1983) and his co-workers' studies which have their beginning in the late 1950s. During more than a dozen years Strelau (1958, 1969, 1974) conducted many experiments aimed at examining the essence of the Pavlovian central nervous system (CNS) properties — strength of excitation, strength of inhibition, and mobility of CNS. Configurations of these properties constitute, according to Pavlov (1951−2), types of higher nervous activity considered as the physiological bases of temperament or treated as synonyms of temperament (see Nebylitsyn, 1972; Teplov, 1964). Studies conducted by Pavlov (1951−2) and his successors (Krasnogorsky, 1954; Merlin, 1973; Nebylitsyn, 1972; Teplov, 1964), as well as by Strelau (1969), have shown that the CNS properties play an important role in human adaptation. Strength of excitation manifests itself in the individual's ability to endure intense and/or long-lasting stimulation. Strength of inhibition reveals itself in the ability to maintain a state of conditioned inhibition, such as extinction, differentiation, and delay. The essence of mobility of the CNS processes consists in the ability to respond adequately as soon as possible to changes in the surroundings.

Another approach which influenced the development of the regulative theory of temperament stems from the Russian tradition according to which actions are treated as the core of human behaviour (Leontev, 1978; Rubinstein, 1946). This conceptualization, thoroughly modified by Tomaszewski (1978), facilitated investigation of temperament features from the point of view of reciprocal relations between humans and their environment, where human activity plays the most important role in regulating these relations.

Gray's (1964) interpretation of strength of excitation in terms of arousal and arousability helped us to move beyond the Pavlovian tradition in temperament research (Strelau, 1983). Important for developing our theory was Hebb's (1955) concept of *optimal level of arousal* regarded as the standard of regulation of stimulation (Eliasz, 1981; Strelau, 1983).

The East−West influences mentioned above, and especially studies which have been conducted for 30 years by the Warsaw group at the Department of Psychology, University of Warsaw, are the main roots of the RTT.

The concept of temperament

There is no agreement among psychologists as regards the understanding of temperament. The round-table discussion conducted by American experts in the field of temperament reflects this view (Goldsmith *et al.*, 1987). However, the same discussion has also shown that at least some common denominators in the understanding of temperament may be found (for example, the biological background of temperament).

According to the RTT, temperament refers to relatively stable characteristics of behaviour. This means, among other things, that temperament traits are more stable or less prone to undergo changes than other behaviour characteristics. However, long-lasting influences of the environment, like noise, nutrition, temperature, etc., when causing some alterations in the biological mechanisms underlying temperament, lead to changes in temperament. Data supporting the hypothesis regarding changes under chronic stimulation have been collected in the Warsaw laboratory by Eliasz (1980). The relative stability of temperamental traits does not contradict developmental changes in temperament (Strelau, 1984).

The RTT implies that temperament is above all a result of biological evolution (Strelau, 1983, 1987a). The interpretation of this general statement says that: (1) primarily, temperament has a biological basis; (2) temperamental traits are present in the individual beginning early in childhood; (3) temperamental characteristics may be found not only in humans but also in animals, and (4) temperament refers first of all to the formal characteristics and not to the content of behaviour. A short explanation of these attributes is needed.

Whatever the theory of temperament is, the biological backgrounds of temperament traits are far from being discovered. This also means that the considerations regarding the biological bases of temperament have in the RTT a hypothetical status.

> An individual at birth has a given temperament which is determined by the physiological mechanism shaped during prenatal life on the basis of a particular genetic endowment. This inborn physiological mechanism forms the initial basis of the individual's temperament, which is in turn subjected during ontogenesis to changes due to maturation and environmental influences. (Strelau, 1983, pp. 173–4)

In the RTT, the biological basis of temperament is regarded as a *neuro-endocrine individuality* (Strelau, 1983, 1985b). By this is meant that temperament is determined by an individual-specific configuration of neurological (central and autonomous) and endocrine mechanisms regulating, among other things, the level of arousal. There exist intra- and inter-individual differences in the functioning of the separate mechanisms. Individuals also differ in configurations of these mechanisms. Temperament characteristics revealed in behaviour are the outcome of the interaction between all neuro-endocrine mechanisms included into the individual-specific configuration. This explains to a given extent the lack of a point-to-point relationship between the functioning of a separate physiological mechanism and a given temperament trait.

We do not have data collected within the RTT approach supporting the statement that temperament is present from early childhood. The East European tradition shows that whereas temperament in animals was often in the centre of study (for example, Fedorov, 1962; Pavlov, 1951–2; Matysiak, 1985), infants were almost never subject to investigation (Strelau, 1984, 1991). The physiological mechanisms underlying temperament are present from birth. If so, one of the consequences of the assumption that temperament has a biological background is that temperament is already present in early infancy. The many studies conducted by American temperament experts support this view (Bates, 1987; Buss and Plomin, 1975, 1984; Matheny *et al.*, 1985; Ross, 1987).

One of the peculiarities of the RTT, also to be met with in the neo-pavlovian approach to temperament (Merlin, 1973; Teplov, 1964), is to treat this phenomenon in terms of formal characteristics of behaviour. They are expressed in energetic and temporal features. These formal characteristics are present in all kinds of reaction and behaviour. Emotions and cognitive functioning as well as motor reactions have their energetic aspects. All types of behaviour and reaction, whether simple or complex, also have their temporal characteristics.

> As far as the temporal and energetic characteristics of behavior may be regarded as more or less stable, I consider these aspects of behavior as temperament. Temperament, of course, does not exist as such; it is a type of a theoretical construct, referring to existing phenomena, just like the theoretical construct of intelligence. Temperament is something like an attribute of all types of behavior. (Strelau, 1986, p. 62)

Temperament, being a result of biological evolution and a phenomenon that comprises above all formal characteristics of behaviour, is regarded in the RTT as one of the components of personality. This statement holds true if personality is considered as a concept that refers to individual differences in traits. If, however, the concept of personality is understood as a product of the historically determined social environment or as a result of social learning, as many neo-behaviourists, cognitive- or psychoanalytic-oriented personality psychologists assume, then temperament has not much in common with personality. To put it broadly, such a concept of personality refers mainly to the *content* of behaviour, expressed, among other things, in characteristics reflecting the individual's relation to him or herself, to others, and towards the world.

The discussion regarding the understanding of the concept of temperament may be summarized by the following definition of temperament:

> In our theory temperament is defined as a set of relatively stable features of the organism that reveal themselves in such formal traits of behavior as energetic level and temporal characteristics. Being primarily determined by inborn physiological mechanisms, temperament is subjected to slow changes caused by maturation and by some environmental factors. (Strelau, 1989a, p. 38)

The structure of temperament

The number of traits comprised by the notion of temperament varies from theory to theory. The question of what kinds of trait belong to the domain of temperament is also highly influenced by theoretical conceptualizations. According to the RTT, these traits should be included in the structure of temperament which refers to the formal aspect of behaviour expressed in energetic and temporal characteristics.

In the RTT, the structure of temperament comprises eight traits, two of which belong to the energetic characteristics of behaviour (reactivity and activity) and six to the temporal features (persistence, recurrence, mobility, regularity, speed, and tempo). Much attention has been paid in our theory to traits referring to the energetic components of behaviour which are significant for human adaptation, especially in situations and for actions characterized by extreme stimulation.

Reactivity reveals itself in the intensity (magnitude) of reactions to acting stimuli. This temperament trait co-determines the individual's sensitivity (sensory and emotional) and endurance (capacity to work). Endurance expresses itself in the ability to react adequately to strong and/or long-lasting stimulation. Reactivity resembles the Pavlovian concept of strength of excitation. According to Pavlov (1951–2), the appearance of protective inhibition expressed in a decrease or disappearance of reaction (behaviour) under intense or continuing stimulation was the most valid measure of strength of excitation.

Teplov and Nebylitsyn (1963) have given some evidence which allows us to assume that there exists a relatively stable opposite relationship between sensitivity and endurance. Individuals who occupy a place close to the pole characterized by high sensitivity and low endurance on the dimension of reactivity are labelled as high reactives. Low-reactive individuals, who occupy the opposite pole of the reactivity dimension, have low sensitivity and high endurance. The physiological mechanisms underlying reactivity are responsible for individual differences in modulating the intensity of stimulation. In high-reactive individuals, this physiological mechanism augments stimulation. Using Gray's (1964) terminology, these individuals are characterized by high arousability. In low-reactive individuals, the physiological mechanism reduces stimulation, this being true also for low arousability. A detailed description of reactivity and its physiological bases may be found elsewhere (Strelau, 1983, 1985b).

Activity, which is the second trait assigned to the energetic characteristic of behaviour, has in the RTT a specific meaning. '*Activity* is a temperament trait which reveals itself in the amount and range of undertaken actions (goal-directed behaviors) of a given stimulative value' (Strelau, 1989a, p. 40). By means of activity the individual regulates the stimulative value of behaviour and/or situations in such a way as to satisfy his or her need for stimulation (Eliasz, 1985; Strelau, 1983). The latter is co-determined by the individual's level of reactivity. The need to maintain or attain an optimal level of arousal is regarded in the RTT as a standard of regulation of stimulation (Eliasz, 1981, 1985).

The stimulative value of activity consists in the fact that activity by itself is a source of stimulation. The more complex and difficult the activity, the higher the stimulation being generated. One of the most efficient generators of stimulation is the emotional connotation of activity. Risk-taking or threatening actions are good examples of highly stimulative activity. By means of activity the individual may also modify the stimulative value of the environment. Activity aimed at approaching or avoiding stimulation stemming from the surroundings exemplifies this idea. It is important to emphasize that any kind of human activity, at any period of life, has a given stimulative value. When characterizing activity as a temperament trait in terms of being high or low, the kind of activity does not count. The criterion is the energetic characteristic; that is, the stimulative value of activity.

There exists a relationship between reactivity and activity. High-reactive individuals, characterized by low need for stimulation (because of their high sensitivity and low endurance) in order to attain or maintain an optimal level of arousal, prefer activity of low stimulative value. In our terminology they are characterized by low activity. Low-reactive individuals, who are known as having high need for stimulation (low sensitivity and high endurance), prefer activity of high stimulative value, thus implying high activity.

Since activity develops in ontogenesis under the influence of social environment and educational treatment, it happens that the stimulative value of the individual's activity does not correspond with his or her biologically determined level of reactivity. As has been shown in our studies (Strelau, 1983, 1988) a long-lasting discrepancy between level of reactivity and level of activity may lead to disturbances in behaviour. A high and persistent discrepancy between those temperament traits is regarded as a temperament risk factor (Strelau, 1989b).

Factor analysis of the six temperament traits referring to the temporal characteristics of behaviour has shown that they can be grouped into two factors (Gorynska and Strelau, 1979).

Factor I has the highest loadings in persistence and recurrence of reaction. Since both traits refer to a kind of rigidity in behaviour, this factor may be identified as *perseverance*. It is similar to Heymans and Wiersma's (1906−9) secondary function, also known as perseveration and treated in terms of durability of reactions. According to these authors, perseveration is one of the three basic temperament dimensions (besides activity and emotionality).

Tempo and speed have the highest loading scores in Factor II. In the RTT, tempo is expressed in the number of homogeneous reactions performed in a given period of time, whereas speed is defined by time required to generate reactions to given stimuli or situations (Gorynska and Strelau, 1979). Taking these characteristics into account, we labelled Factor II as *liveliness*.

It is worth noting that mobility, understood as the ability to switch behaviour in response to changes in the surroundings, shares its loadings with both factors (I and II). This suggests that mobility of behaviour is a secondary trait. The physiological mechanism underlying this trait may be very complex. On the one hand, it has something to do with speed of generating nervous processes (this mechanism probably co-determines temperament speed and tempo). On the other hand, mobility might be co-regulated by the speed of disappearance of nervous processes, the latter being probably responsible for perseverance. Several studies (Strelau, 1983, 1984) suggest that mobility plays an important role in human adaptation and that this temperament trait allows us to search for links between temperament and abilities (Strelau, 1977).

Regularity, which seems to be a trait having not much in common with the remaining five temporal characteristics, was mostly beyond our interests in temperament research.

Empirical evidence supporting the RTT

As mentioned above, Strelau and his co-workers did not collect behaviour genetics data and did not search for psycho-neuro-physiological mechanisms that speak directly in favour of the RTT. The statements regarding the biological (and to some extent genetic) backgrounds of temperament, as understood in the RTT theory, have the status of hypotheses. Probably the strongest side of the RTT is the arguments which show the benefit of this theory when applied to behaviour in real-life situations, or in laboratory settings simulating such behaviours.

It has been mentioned several times (Strelau, 1983, 1988, 1989b) that temperament traits are strongly expressed in behaviour, when the individual is confronted with extreme tasks or situations. Taking as a point of departure the reactivity dimension, several studies have been conducted which show that in situations of high stimulative value (such as time pressure, high responsibility in task performance, competition, risk-taking behaviour, noise), the level of performance of low-reactive individuals is higher than that of high-reactive subjects. The performance of the latter under high-stimulating situations is also lower than their performance under less stimulating situations (so-called 'normal situations'). There also exists an opposite relationship between level of performance and level of reactivity, when situations of low stimulative value are considered, as, for example, deprivation or monotony. In these situations the performance of high-reactive individuals is higher than the performance of low-reactives. Evidence supporting these statements has been reported in many publications (see, for example, Eliasz, 1981; Klonowicz, 1987a, 1987b; Strelau, 1969, 1983, 1988).

Strelau and his co-workers have also collected data in their laboratory which show that some individuals, differing in level of reactivity, may not express differences in performance level when confronted with highly stimulating tasks or situations. The differences between high- and low-reactive individuals are, however, still present. They occur in the shape of psycho-physiological costs an individual pays during the performance of highly stimulating tasks, or in highly stimulating situations in which tasks are performed. The psycho-physiological costs are expressed in changes in level of arousal, in state anxiety, or in reaction time (RT) parameters. The results show that high-reactive individuals pay higher psycho-physiological costs for efficient performance under highly stimulating conditions than do low-reactive individuals. The relationship between costs to be paid and level of reactivity is reversed when task performance takes place in deprivation or monotony conditions (see Eliasz, 1981; Klonowicz, 1974, 1987b; Strelau, 1983, 1988). Recently, Eliasz and Wrzesniewski (1989) were able to show that Type A behaviour pattern, when found in low-reactive students, is accompanied by low levels of anxiety, whereas when present in high-reactive individuals, it goes together with high levels of anxiety. The latter study was conducted using a sample of more than 1,000 high-school students. If one considers that Type A is an extreme example of the price an individual pays to maintain a given performance level (cf. Friedman and Rosenman, 1974), then the finding by Eliasz and Wrzesniewski is understandable. High-reactive individuals pay higher psycho-physiological costs (expressed here in terms of level of anxiety) for behaviour characterized by high competition, high level of achievement, activity under time pressure, etc.; that is, behaviours typical of Type A.

There are several other aspects of the RTT which demonstrate the benefit of this temperament theory. They refer to such issues as temperament and stress (Strelau, 1988), temperament risk factors (Strelau, 1989b), and temperamental traits and style of action (Strelau, 1983). Because of space limitation, they cannot be discussed in this chapter.

Future directions for RTT research

Probably the best way to draw the perspective of further research on temperament within the RTT is to concentrate on the weakest parts of the RTT. A theory has a chance to survive only when methods (tools, diagnostic procedures), by means of which the basic statements and principles can be empirically verified, are incorporated into the theory.

As mentioned before, according to the RTT, the structure of temperament comprises two traits which refer to the energetic level of behaviour, and six traits related to the temporal characteristics. The way Strelau arrived at the structure of temperament, as proposed by the RTT, was partly theoretical and partly empirical. Reactivity is somewhat similar to the concept of strength of excitation, whereas mobility is reminiscent of the concept of mobility of nervous processes (see Strelau, 1983; Strelau, Angleitner and Ruch, 1990). The main difference consists in giving the Pavlovian concepts a psychological interpretation. The concept of activity has its basis in the theory of action, according to which any activity has important regulatory functions. As regards the temporal traits mentioned before, they are distinguished on an empirical basis, for which the definition of temperament, which stresses that this phenomenon comprises *formal* traits of behaviour, was the starting point. This retrospection regarding the origins of temperament traits offered by the RTT was needed to understand the unsatisfactory state of affairs when diagnostic methods are considered within our theory.

Until 1990, there was no psychometric tool which allowed one to diagnose the *whole* range of temperament traits comprised by the RTT. Since the beginning of the 1970s, the Strelau Temperament Inventory (STI), originally aimed at measuring the Pavlovian CNS properties, has also been used for measuring reactivity and mobility in adults and adolescents (Strelau, 1972, 1983). Another method for measuring reactivity is the Reactivity Rating Scale (Friedensberg, 1982; Strelau, 1983), which has been constructed in three versions, allowing the measurement of this temperament trait in pre-school, primary-school, and secondary-school children. For assessing the whole range of temporal temperament traits, the Temporal Traits

Inventory (TTI: Gorynska and Strelau, 1979; Strelau, 1983) is used. The last method is assigned for adolescents and adults. The estimation of activity (understood as a temperament trait) was limited to measures based on field studies or to behaviours scored in laboratory settings (see Strelau, 1983).

Only recently was a satisfactory inventory constructed for measuring the whole range of temperament traits incorporated in the RTT. This is the Regulative Theory of Temperament Inventory (RTTI), constructed by Zawadzki and Strelau (1991). The research regarding the construction of the RTTI, conducted on over 2,000 subjects of both sexes (from 15 to 85 years), permitted a revision of the structure of temperament. In fact, the number of temperament traits referring to the energetic characteristics has changed from two to the following three: *sensory sensitivity* (expressed in behaviour that depends on the sensory threshold in different modalities), *endurance* (upper threshold of reactivity), and *activity*. The temporal characteristic has expanded from one trait — mobility — to the following three: *mobility, perseverance*, and *liveliness* (speed and tempo). An important factor emerged which refers to the formal characteristics of emotional behaviour. Preliminarily, we have given this trait the label *emotional reactivity*. It is hardly possible to speak about temperament without referring directly to the emotional aspects of human behaviour (Strelau, 1987b). Therefore, the lack of a trait that refers to emotions was one of the weakest points of the RTT.

The Pavlovian construct of temperament, which was the starting point of the RTT, still seems to be highly significant, for researchers interested in studying other dimensions of temperament also. To give a few examples, Eysenck's (1970) extraversion, Zuckerman's (1979) sensation seeking, or Petrie's (1967), as well as Buchsbaum's (1978), concept of augmenting/reducing may be mentioned here. The only inventory aimed at measuring the Pavlovian CNS properties was the STI. A series of studies (see Strelau, Angleitner and Ruch, 1990) has demonstrated unsatisfactory psychometric characteristics of this tool. Taking this critique as a starting point, Strelau, Angleitner, Bantelmann and Ruch (1990) have constructed a revised version of the STI (STI-R). The STI-R, which is essentially different from the original inventory, has sufficient validity characteristics (Ruch *et al.*, 1991), and has already been developed in many language versions (including, among others, English, German and Polish). Since the STI, especially in its revised version, is one of the crucial diagnostic tools by means of which validity of our RTTI can be estimated, it was also important for the RTT to develop studies aimed at improving the original Strelau Temperament Inventory. It has to be added that the STI-R, in spite of its label, does not correspond with the RTT. It is assumed that this tool allows one to measure, by means of a psychometric technique, the Pavlovian nervous system properties. To avoid confusions and misunderstandings, the senior authors of the STI-R inventory have decided to rename it the Pavlovian Temperament Survey (PTS: see Strelau and Angleitner, 1992).

One of the main directions in Strelau's studies on temperament is the search for links between the RTT and the many other concepts of temperament that are popular in both hemispheres. If temperament has a strong biological background — a statement accepted by most temperament researchers — then it is highly probable that the structure of temperament is more or less universal. In order to prove this hypothesis, intensive as well as extensive cross-cultural studies must be conducted, and this is one of the tasks Strelau and Angleitner have undertaken recently (see Strelau, Angleitner, Bantelmann and Ruch, 1990; Ruch *et al.*, 1991), by developing an international project on cross-cultural studies on temperament.

EAS and RTT: similarities and differences

The presentation of the two theories of temperament may serve as a good example of the diversities to be met with in this field of study. In fact, the differences among other temperament theories are even stronger (see Strelau and Angleitner, 1991). In spite of the differences between the EAS theory and the RTT, which we will summarize later, there also exist several links and similarities. If cumulation of data and integration in theories of temperament is expected, then the emphasis on similarities seems to be of special importance. A thorough comparison between the EAS and RTT approaches to temperament needs to go beyond the information presented in this chapter. As a frame of reference, the monographs of Buss and Plomin (1984) and Strelau (1983) may serve.

Similarities

In both theories, the biological background of temperament is a definitional component of this phenomenon. Whereas Plomin and Buss take heritability as a crucial criterion for distinguishing temperament traits from other personality traits, Strelau weakens this criterion by saying that temperament is a result of biological evolution. The statement that there exist biological mechanisms underlying temperament stresses that non-heritable prenatal influences, as well as postnatal changes in biological mechanisms, should be regarded as co-determinants of temperament. This does not contradict the EAS theory, because such traits could none the less be highly heritable.

It is emphasized in both theories that temperament is present from early childhood. Buss and Plomin (1984) provide evidence supporting this view. Additionally, Strelau (1983) writes that temperament may also be met with in animals. Buss and Plomin provide some evidence that the EAS traits 'are also found in other primates and even in nonprimate mammals' (1984, p. 10); in their earlier book, presence in animals was emphasized as one of the criteria for temperament (Buss and Plomin, 1975).

For Buss and Plomin, temperament is the part of personality that is inherited and present from early childhood. Strelau too considers temperament as a part of personality, but only if personality is understood as a composition of traits in which individuals differ. It has to be stressed that the trait-oriented understanding of personality is not obvious among researchers in this field of study. To exemplify this statement, psychoanalytic or cognitive-oriented personality theories may be mentioned, where not traits but such constructs as id, ego, self, cognitive maps, scripts, etc. are in the centre of interests.

In both theories, temperament, as compared with other psychological traits and characteristics, is regarded as relatively stable. None the less, developmental changes in temperament occur, and slow changes due to environmental influences are possible. As shown by Plomin (1986), a genetic influence on behavioural characteristics does not necessarily imply their stability or immutability.

Authors of both theories do not pretend to identify or specify the neurophysiological mechanisms underlying temperament. However, in both theories reference is made to the concept of arousal. In the EAS approach arousal is used as a theoretical construct for a better understanding of the traits emotionality and activity. In the RTT, the concept of arousal serves for interpreting individual differences in such temperament characteristics as reactivity and activity.

The EAS and RTT approaches are open to other theories of temperament. This means, among other things, that the authors of the two theories investigate how their temperament traits relate to other conceptualizations of temperament. At first glance, it seems to be obvious that researchers ask such questions. In practice, however, this is often not the case in the area of temperament (see Strelau, 1991).[1] The temperament characteristics to which both theories refer are first of all the Eysenckian dimensions of extraversion and neuroticism. Extraversion seems to correlate with EAS-sociability, whereas neuroticism correlates with EAS-emotionality. As regards the RTT traits, it has been shown many times that reactivity is negatively related to extraversion and positively to neuroticism. Mobility correlates positively with extraversion. In a study conducted by Ruch, Angleitner and Strelau (1991) on 85 subjects (both sexes, ages ranging from 18 to 86 years), the EASI temperaments (emotionality, activity, sociability and impulsivity) were correlated with three STI-R scales — strength of excitation (the reverse of reactivity), strength of inhibition and mobility. Reactivity correlated positively with emotionality (0.42; $p < 0.001$) and negatively with activity (-0.43; $p < 0.001$). Mobility showed negative correlations with emotionality (-0.46; $p < 0.001$) and positive correlations with both activity (0.42; $p < 0.001$) and sociability (0.33; $p < 0.01$).

To conclude, it might be stated that both theories (EAS and RTT) regard temperament as biologically determined, present from early childhood, and relatively stable. According to EAS and the RTT, temperament is not a synonym of personality, but a part of it, assuming that personality is understood as a composition of traits. Both theories refer to the concept of arousal, but at the same time they do not strive to identify the neuro-physiological mechanisms underlying temperament characteristics. The EAS theory and the RTT are theories open to other approaches in temperament.

Differences

In some ways, the differences between the two theories emerge from differences in the original questions asked by the theorists. Buss and Plomin began with a method, behavioural genetics, that makes it possible to distinguish personality traits on the basis of their heritability. In contrast, the origin of the RTT theory lies in an attempt to encompass the formal energetic and temporal properties of neural systems and behaviour, beginning with the Pavlovian concepts of nervous system properties. Given these vast differences in the original perspectives of the two approaches, the convergences that we have seen are more remarkable than their differences.

If essential differences between the EAS theory and the RTT were missing, there would be no reason to treat the two conceptualizations as two distinct approaches to temperament. It is impossible here to draw attention to all the aspects in which EAS theory and the RTT differ. We will limit our review to some essential distinctions between EAS and RTT, which can be deduced from the definitions of temperament both theories offer. Answers to the question concerning differences between the two sets of traits lead to better understanding of the specificity of both theories.

According to the EAS theory, personality traits are considered as temperament if they are: (1) inherited, and (2) present from early childhood. The definition of RTT says that temperament traits: (1) are biologically determined, and (2) refer to the formal aspects of behaviour.

These criteria resulted in the selection of two different sets of temperament traits: emotionality, activity, and sociability in the case of the EAS theory, and reactivity, activity, and mobility[2] within the RTT. Some of the differences that ensue from their different definitions are given below.

1. Whereas all three EAS traits have a genetic determination, there is no information at our disposal concerning heritability of the RTT traits.
2. In spite of the same number of traits, their names, except activity, differ, as do their definitions; this also implies differences in their conceptualization.
3. The RTT traits refer to the formal aspects of behaviour — energetic and time characteristics. The EAS traits should be regarded as a combination of formal and content characteristics. The definition of sociability, 'the tendency to prefer the presence of others to being alone' (Buss and Plomin, 1984, p. 63), refers to the content of behaviour. In contrast, activity, viewed in the EAS theory as the energy output expressed in the tempo and vigour of motor behaviour is primarily a formal characteristic of behaviour. Emotionality involves both content and the formal properties or reactivity.
4. The EAS temperament traits refer separately to three different components of behaviour — emotionality to emotions, activity to motor behaviour, and sociability to social behaviour. Each of the three RTT traits may be met in all kinds of behaviour, because every behaviour has its energetic and temporal characteristics.
5. In spite of the similarity in names, activity as a temperament trait has different meanings in both theories. In the EAS theory, activity, which has two components — vigour and tempo — 'is equivalent to movement: the person who moves more is called more active' (Buss and Plomin, 1975, p. 32). According to the RTT, activity is expressed not only in motor reactions, but in all kinds of behaviour. Activity as a goal-directed behaviour 'serves as a source and regulator of stimulation need and ensures the optimal level of activation' (Strelau, 1983, p. 191).

6. The statement in the EAS definition of temperament which says that the traits under discussion have a strong genetic determination indicates at the same time one of the main directions in research undertaken by the authors. In studying the roots of temperament traits they often use the behaviour genetics approach, a method almost lacking in investigating temperament within the RTT.
7. The definitional criterion saying that temperament is present from early childhood stresses that the centre of gravity in the EAS theory consists in studying temperament in children. This is not the case within the RTT, where most of the research has been conducted on adults, partly also on animals (rats).
8. The author of the RTT pays much attention to the role that temperament traits play in human adjustment, especially when confronted with extreme demands and/or environments. The main concern of the EAS authors consists of studying the origins of temperaments.

Final remarks

The similarities and differences between both temperament theories under discussion show whether bridges can be built, and if so of what kind between the EAS theory and the RTT. The conclusions regarding some common elements to be met in both approaches are rather optimistic concerning further integration of the theories. In turn, the awareness of distinctions between the EAS theory and the RTT allows us to avoid simplification and misunderstandings when trials for synthesis in research on temperament are undertaken. It is our impression that the tale of the two theories of temperament presented in this chapter can be regarded as an example of efforts to be undertaken for better understanding and communication among temperament researchers representing different approaches in this field of study.

Authors' notes

Preparation of the part of the chapter written by Strelau was supported by the Minister of National Education (Grant RPBP III.25).

Notes

1   Rothbart (1989), whose developmental theory of temperament has much in common with the RTT in that she also stresses the regulative functions of temperament characteristics (reactivity and self-regulation), is in her theorizing also open to other conceptualizations in temperament.
2   The RTT proposes six temporal traits. It has been shown, however, that they can be reduced to one more general factor — mobility.

References

Bates, J.E. (1987), 'Temperament in infancy', in J.D. Osofsky (ed.), *Handbook in Infant Development* (second edition), New York, NY: Wiley, pp. 1101−49.

Bergeman, C.S., Chipuer, H.M., Plomin, R., Pedersen, N.L., McClearn, G.E., Nesselroade, J.R., Costa, P.T., Jr. and McCrae, R.R. (in press), 'Genetic and environmental effects of openness to experience, agreeableness, and conscientiousness: an adoption/twin study', *Journal of Personality.*

Buchsbaum, M.S. (1978), 'Neurophysiological studies of reduction and augmentation', in A. Petrie (ed.), *Individuality and Pain and Suffering* (second edition), Chicago, IL: Chicago University Press, pp. 141−57.

Buss, A.H. and Plomin, R. (1975), *A Temperament Theory of Personality Development*, New York, NY: Wiley.

Buss, A.H. and Plomin, R. (1984), *Temperament: Early-developing personality traits*, Hillsdale, NJ: Erlbaum.

DeFries, J.C. and Fulker, D.W. (1985), 'Multiple regression of twin data', *Behavior Genetics,* **15**, 467−73.

DeFries, J.C., Plomin, R. and LaBuda, M.C. (1987), 'Genetic stability of cognitive development from childhood to adulthood', *Developmental Psychology,* **23**, 4−12.

Digman, J.M. (1990), 'Personality structure: emergence of the five-factor model', *Annual Review of Psychology,* **41**, 417−40.

Digman, J.M. and Inouye, J. (1986), 'Further specification of the five robust factors of personality', *Journal of Personality and Social Psychology,* **50**, 116−23.

Dunn, J. and Plomin, R. (1990), *Separate Lives: Why siblings are so different*, New York, NY: Basic Books.

Eliasz, A. (1980), 'Temperament and transsituational stability of behavior in the physical and social environment', *Polish Psychological Bulletin,* **11**, 143−53.

Eliasz, A. (1981), *Temperament a system regulacji stymulacji* [Temperament and System of Regulation of Stimulation], Warsaw: Panstwowe Wydawnictwo Naukowe.

Eliasz, A. (1985), 'Transactional model of temperament', in J. Strelau (ed.), *Temperamental Bases of Behavior: Warsaw studies on individual differences*, Lisse, The Netherlands: Swets & Zeitlinger, pp. 41−78.

Eliasz, A. and Wrzesniewski, K. (1989), *Ryzyko chorob psychosomataycznych: Srodowisko i temperament a Wzor Zachowania A* [Psychosomatic Disease Risk: Environment, temperament, and Type A behaviour], Wroclaw, Poland: Ossolineum.

Eysenck, H.J. (1967), *The Biological Basis of Personality*, Springfield, IL: Charles C. Thomas.

Eysenck, H.J. (1970), *The Structure of Human Personality* (third edition), London: Methuen.

Fedorov, V.K. (1962), 'Some results of investigation of typological features of higher nervous activity in animals', *Doklady Akademii Nauk SSSR,* **142**, 1432−5 (in Russian).

Friedensberg, E. (1982), 'Skala ocen jako narzedzie do pomiaru reaktywnosci' [The rating scale as a device for the measurement of reactivity], in J. Strelau (ed.), *Regulacyjne funkcje temperamentu* [The Regulating Functions of Temperament], Wroclaw, Poland: Ossolineum, pp. 237−57.

Friedman, M. and Rosenman, R.H. (1974), *Type A Behavior and Your Heart*, New York, NY: Knopf.

Fulker, D.W., DeFries, J.C. and Plomin, R. (1988), 'Genetic influence on general mental ability increases in infancy and middle childhood', *Nature,* **336**, 767−9.

Goldsmith, H.H. and Campos, J.J. (1986), 'Fundamental issues in the study of early temperament: the Denver Twin Temperament Study', in M.E. Lamb, A.L. Brown and B. Rogoff (eds.), *Advances in Developmental Psychology*, Hillsdale, NJ: Erlbaum, vol. 4, pp. 231−83.

Goldsmith, H.H., Buss, A.H., Plomin, R., Rothbart, M.K., Thomas, A., Chess, S., Hinde, R.A. and McCall, R.B. (1987), 'Roundtable: what is temperament? Four approaches', *Child Development*, **58**, 505−29.

Gorynska, E. and Strelau, J. (1979), 'Basic traits of the temporal characteristics of behavior and their measurement by an inventory technique', *Polish Psychological Bulletin*, **10**, 199−207.

Gray, J.A. (ed.) (1964), *Pavlov's Typology*, Oxford: Pergamon.

Hebb, D.O. (1955), 'Drives and the C.N.S. (conceptual nervous system)', *Psychological Review*, **62**, 243−59.

Henderson, N.D. (1982), 'Human behavior genetics', *Annual Review of Psychology*, **33**, 403−40.

Heymans, G. and Wiersma, E.D. (1906−9), 'Beitrage zur speziellen Psychologie auf Grund einer Massenuntersuchung' [Contribution to special psychology based on a large-scale investigation], *Zeitschrift für Psychologie*, **42**, 81−127; **43**, 321−73; **45**, 1−42; **46**, 321−33; **49**, 414−39; **51**, 1−72.

Kagan, J. (1989), 'Temperament contributions to social behavior', *American Psychologist*, **44**, 668−74.

Klonowicz, T. (1974), 'Reactivity and fitness for the occupation of operator', *Polish Psychological Bulletin*, **5**, 129−36.

Klonowicz, T. (1987a), 'Reactivity and the control of arousal', in J. Strelau and H.J. Eysenck (eds.), *Personality Dimensions and Arousal*, New York, NY: Plenum Press, pp. 183−96.

Klonowicz, T. (1987b), *Reactivity, Experience, and Capacity: Experiments with stimulation load*, Warsaw: Warsaw University Press.

Krasnogorsky, N.I. (1954), *Studies on Higher Nervous Activity of Man and Animals*, vol. 1, Leningrad: Medgiz (in Russian).

Leontev, A.N. (1978), *Activity, Consciousness, and Personality*, Englewood Cliffs, NJ: Prentice Hall.

Loehlin, J.C. (1986), 'Are CPI scales differentially heritable?', *Behavior Genetics*, **12**, 412−28.

Loehlin, J.C. (1989), 'Partitioning environmental and genetic contributions to behavioral development', *American Psychologist*, **44**, 1285−92.

Matheny, A.P., Jr., Riese, M.L. and Wilson, R.S. (1985), 'Rudiments of infant temperament: newborn to 9 months', *Developmental Psychology*, **21**, 486−94.

Matysiak, J. (1985), 'Need for sensory stimulation: effects on activity', in J. Strelau (ed.), *Temperamental Bases of Behavior: Warsaw studies on individual differences*, Lisse, The Netherlands: Swets & Zeitlinger, pp. 141−80.

Merlin, V.S. (1973), *Outline of the Theory of Temperament* (second edition), Perm, USSR: Permskoye Knizhnoye Izdatelstvo.

Nebylitsyn, V.D. (1972), *Fundamental Properties of the Human Nervous System*, New York, NY: Plenum Press.

Norman, W.T. (1963), 'Toward an adequate taxonomy of personality attributes: replicated factor structure in peer nomination personality ratings', *Journal of Abnormal and Social Psychology*, **66**, 574−83.

Pavlov, I.P. (1927), *Conditioned Reflexes: An investigation of the physiological activity of the cerebral cortex*, trans. and ed. G.V. Anrep, Oxford: Oxford University Press.

Pavlov, I.P. (1951−2), *Complete Works* (second edition), Moscow and Leningrad: SSSR Academy of Sciences (in Russian).

Pedersen, N.L., Plomin, R., McClearn, G.E. and Friberg, L. (1988), 'Neuroticism, extraversion, and related traits in adult twins reared apart and reared together', *Journal of Personality and Social Psychology*, **55**, 950−7.

Petrie, A. (1967), *Individuality in Pain and Suffering*, Chicago, IL: University of Chicago Press.

Plomin, R. (1986), *Development, Genetics, and Psychology*, Hillsdale, NJ: Erlbaum.

Plomin, R. (1991), 'Genetic risk and psychosocial disorders: links between the normal and abnormal', in M. Rutter and P. Casaer (eds.), *Biological Risk Factors for Psychosocial Disorders*, Cambridge, Cambridge University Press, pp. 101–38.

Plomin, R. (in press), 'Behavioral genetic evidence for the importance of nonshared environment', in E.M. Hetherington, D. Reiss and R. Plomin (eds.), *Nonshared Environment*, Hillsdale, NJ: Erlbaum.

Plomin, R. and Bergeman, C.S. (1991), 'The nature of nurture: genetic influence on environmental measures', *Behavior and Brain Sciences*, **14**, 313–427.

Plomin, R. and Daniels, D. (1986), 'Developmental behavioral genetics and shyness', in W.H. Jones, J.M. Cheek and S.R. Briggs (eds.), *Shyness: Perspectives on research and treatment*, New York, NY: Plenum Press, pp. 63–80.

Plomin, R. and Daniels, D. (1987), 'Why are children in the same family so different from each other?', *The Behavioral and Brain Sciences*, **10**, 1–16.

Plomin, R. and Dunn, J. (eds.) (1986), *The Study of Temperament: Changes, continuities, and challenges*, Hillsdale, NJ: Erlbaum.

Plomin, R. and Nesselroade, J.R. (1990), 'Behavioral genetics and personality change', *Journal of Personality*, **58**, 191–220.

Plomin, R. and Stocker, C. (1990), 'Behavioral genetics and emotionality', in J.S. Reznick (ed.), *Perspectives on Behavioral Inhibition*, Chicago, IL: University of Chicago Press, pp. 219–40.

Plomin, R., Chipuer, H. and Loehlin, J.C. (1990), 'Behavioral genetics and personality', in L.A. Pervin (ed.), *Handbook of Personality: Theory and Research*, New York, NY: Guilford Press, pp. 225–43.

Plomin, R., DeFries, J.C. and Fulker, D.W. (1988), *Nature and Nurture during Infancy and Early Childhood*, New York, NY: Cambridge University Press.

Plomin, R., DeFries, J.C. and Loehlin, J.C. (1977), 'Genotype–environment interaction and correlation in the analysis of human behavior', *Psychological Bulletin*, **84**, 309–22.

Plomin, R., DeFries, J.C. and McClearn, G.E. (1990), *Behavioral Genetics: A primer* (second edition), New York, NY: W.H. Freeman.

Plomin, R., Nitz, K. and Rowe, D.C. (1990), 'Behavioral genetics and aggressive behavior in childhood', in M. Lewis and S.M. Miller (eds.), *Handbook of Developmental Psychopathology*, New York, NY: Plenum Press, pp. 119–33.

Plomin, R., Rende, R. and Rutter, M. (in press), 'Quantitative genetics and developmental psychopathology', in D. Cicchetti (ed.), *Rochester Symposium on Developmental Psychopathology*, Hillsdale, NJ: Erlbaum.

Plomin, R., Coon, H., Carey, G., DeFries, J.C. and Fulker, D.W. (in press), 'Parent–offspring and sibling adoption analyses of parental ratings of temperament in infancy and early childhood', *Journal of Personality*.

Plomin, R., Lichtenstein, P., Pedersen, N., McClearn, G.E. and Nesselroade, J.R. (1990), 'Genetic influence on life events', *Psychology and Aging*, **5**, 25–30.

Plomin, R., Pedersen, N.L., McClearn, G.E., Nesselroade, J.R. and Bergeman, C.S. (1988), 'EAS temperaments during the last half of the life span: twins reared apart and twins reared together', *Psychology and Aging*, **3**, 43–50.

Plomin, R., Campos, J., Corley, R., Emde, R.N., Fulker, D.W., Kagan, J., Reznick, J.S., Robinson, J., Zahn-Waxler, C. and DeFries, J.C. (1990), 'Individual differences during the second year of life: the MacArthur Longitudinal Twin Study', in J. Colombo and J. Fagen (eds.), *Individual Differences in Infancy: Reliability, stability and predictability*, Hillsdale, NJ: Erlbaum, pp. 431–55.

Ross, G. (1987), 'Temperament of preterm infants: its relationship to perinatal factors and one-year outcome', *Journal of Developmental and Behavioral Pediatrics*, **8**, 106–10.

Rothbart, M.K. (1989), 'Temperament in childhood: a framework', in G.A. Kohnstamm,

J.A. Bates and M.K. Rothbart (eds.), *Temperament in Childhood*, Chichester: Wiley, pp. 59−73.

Rubinstein, S.L. (1946), *Fundamentals of Psychology* (second edition), Moscow: Institute of Philosophy of SSSR Academy of Sciences (in Russian).

Ruch, W., Angleitner, A. and Strelau, J. (1991), 'The Strelau Temperament Inventory-Revised (STI-R): validity studies', *European Journal of Personality*, **5**, 287−308.

Scarr, S. and McCartney, K. (1983), 'How people make their own environments: a theory of genotype-environment effects', *Child Development*, **54**, 424−35.

Strelau, J. (1958), 'Problem parcjalnych typow wyzszej czynnosci nerwowej' [The problem of partial types of higher nervous activity], *Psychologia Wychowawcza*, **1**, 244−51.

Strelau, J. (1969), *Temperament i typ ukladu nerwowego* [Temperament and Type of Nervous System], Warsaw: Panstwowe Wydawnictwo Naukowe.

Strelau, J. (1972), 'A diagnosis of temperament by nonexperimental techniques', *Polish Psychological Bulletin*, **3**, 97−105.

Strelau, J. (1974), 'Temperament as an expression of energy level and temporal features of behavior', *Polish Psychological Bulletin*, **5**, 119−27.

Strelau, J. (1977), 'Behavioral mobility versus flexibility and fluency of thinking: an empirical test of the relationship between temperament and abilities', *Polish Psychological Bulletin*, **8**, 75−82.

Strelau, J. (1983), *Temperament — Personality — Activity*, London: Academic Press.

Strelau, J. (1984), *Das Temperament in der psychischen Entwicklung* [Temperament in Mental Development], Berlin: Volk und Wissen Volkseigener Verlag.

Strelau, J. (ed.) (1985a), *Temperamental Bases of Behavior: Warsaw studies on Individual differences*, Lisse, The Netherlands: Swets & Zeitlinger.

Strelau, J. (1985b), 'Pavlov's typology and the regulative theory of temperament', in J. Strelau (ed.), *Temperamental Bases of Behavior: Warsaw studies on individual differences*, Lisse, The Netherlands: Swets & Zeitlinger.

Strelau, J. (1986), 'Stability does not mean stability', in G.A. Kohnstamm (ed.), *Temperament Discussed: Temperament and development in infancy and childhood*, Lisse, The Netherlands: Swets & Zeitlinger, pp. 59−62.

Strelau, J. (1987a), 'The concept of temperament in personality research', *European Journal of Personality*, **1**, 107−17.

Strelau, J. (1987b), 'Emotion as a key concept in temperament research', *Journal of Research in Personality*, **21**, 510−28.

Strelau, J. (1988), 'Temperament dimensions as co-determinants of resistance to stress', in M.P. Janisse (ed.), *Individual Differences, Stress, and Health Psychology*, New York, NY: Springer, pp. 146−69.

Strelau, J. (1989a), 'The regulative theory of temperament as a result of East−West influences', in G.A. Kohnstamm, J.A. Bates and M.K. Rothbart (eds.), *Temperament in Childhood*, Chichester: Wiley, pp. 35−48.

Strelau, J. (1989b), 'Temperament risk factors in children and adolescents as studied in Eastern Europe', in W.B. Carey and S.C. McDevitt (eds.), *Clinical and Educational Applications of Temperament Research*, Lisse, The Netherlands: Swets & Zeitlinger, pp. 65−77.

Strelau, J. (1991), 'Renaissance in research on temperament: where to?', in J. Strelau and A. Angleitner (eds.), *Explorations in Temperament: International perspectives on theory and measurement*, New York, NY: Plenum Press, pp. 337−58.

Strelau, J. and Angleitner, A. (eds.), (1991), *Explorations in Temperament: International perspectives on theory and measurement*, New York, NY: Plenum Press.

Strelau, J. and Angleitner, A. (1992), 'Cross-cultural studies on temperament: theoretical considerations and empirical studies based on the Pavlovian Temperament Survey (PTS)', unpublished manuscript, University of Warsaw and University of Bielefeld, Warsaw-Bielefeld.

Strelau, J., Angleitner, A. and Ruch, W. (1990), 'Strelau Temperament Inventory (STI): general review and studies based on German samples', in J.N. Butcher and C.D. Spielberger (eds.), *Advances in Personality Assessment*, Hillsdale, NJ: Erlbaum, vol. 8, pp. 187−241.

Strelau, J., Angleitner, A., Bantelmann, J. and Ruch, W. (1990), 'The Strelau Temperament Inventory — Revised (STI-R): theoretical considerations and scale development', *European Journal of Personality*, **4**, 209−35.

Teplov, B.M. (1964), 'Problems in the study of general types of higher nervous activity in man and animals', in J.A. Gray (ed.), *Pavlov's Typology*, Oxford: Pergamon, pp. 3−153.

Teplov, B.M. and Nebylitsyn, V.D. (1963), 'The study of the basic properties of the nervous system and their significance in the psychology of individual differences', *Voprosy Psikhologii*, **9**, 38−47 (in Russian).

Thomas, A. and Chess, S. (1977), *Temperament and Development*, New York, NY: Brunner/Mazel.

Thomas, A. and Chess, S. (1986), 'The New York Longitudinal Study: from infancy to early adult life', in R. Plomin and J.F. Dunn (eds.), *The Study of Temperament: Changes, continuities and challenges*, Hillsdale, NJ: Erlbaum, pp. 39−52.

Tomaszewski, T. (1978), *Tätigkeit und Bewusstsein* [Action and Consciousness], Weinheim-Basel, Switzerland: Beltz Verlag.

Zawadzki, B. and Strelau, Jan (1991, September), 'The Regulative Theory of Temperament Inventory (RTTI): preliminary information concerning the strategy of a tool construction and properties of measurement', Paper presented at the International Workshop on Cross-Cultural Studies on Temperament, Nieborów, Poland.

Zuckerman, M. (1979), *Sensation Seeking: Beyond the optimal level of arousal*, Hillsdale, NJ: Erlbaum.

13/ Genes, environment, and personality

John C. Loehlin
University of Texas, USA

David C. Rowe
The University of Arizona, USA

Introduction

The genes influence human personality in two ways. In part, the genotype shapes the pattern of development that all humans share; in part, it accounts for variations on that common pattern. The traditional methods of human behaviour genetics — twin and adoption studies — have primarily focused on the second of these two roles: the allocation of personality variation to genetic and environmental sources. The first part of the chapter surveys some of this work. Next, we consider some relations between genetic and environmental influences: that they may be correlated, that they may interact, and that one may sometimes masquerade as the other. Finally, we return to the topic of the shared human genetic heritage — our common human nature — as we consider personality and its biological evolution.

Heredity—environment analysis of personality traits

People differ in personality (and other) traits, and these individual differences may be assignable to genetic sources, to environmental sources, and to various sub-categories and combinations of these. It is important to be clear that this apportionment concerns *differences* among individuals. The development of the behaviour of any individual involves both genes and environment, intertwined in almost inconceivably complex ways. One can fully grant this, however, and still have a simple theory of the origins of individual differences. One might, for example, believe such differences to be almost entirely due to environmental variation, which results in the common human genotype developing in different directions. Or one might hold that environments merely impose random surface variation on a number of underlying gene-based personality types. Or one might conceive of broad, genetically based dimensions of personality variation that are enhanced or damped to varying degrees by the systematic influences of the family environments within which humans are reared. Or one could hold other beliefs: that environments, though not family environments, are important; that the genes contribute to personality variation early in life and the environment chiefly has its effects later; or that the reverse is true — early environmental effects and later genetic ones, as a gene-based personality structure gradually asserts itself through environmental noise.

In the limited space available, we cannot go into all of these possibilities in detail. However, we will look at the evidence bearing on one of them. Specifically, we will examine the relative genetic and environmental contributions to individual variation along the broad dimensions of personality known as the 'Big Five' personality factors (see Digman, 1990, or John, 1990, for reviews). We will begin by focusing on two of the five: Factor 1, described variously as surgency or extraversion, and Factor 4, emotional stability, often identified by its opposite pole of neuroticism or anxiety. The remaining three dimensions — Factor 2, agreeableness; Factor 3, conscientiousness; and Factor 5, intellectual openness — will subsequently be considered briefly.

Tables 13.1−13.4 present correlations of extraversion and emotional stability for four of the major research designs used in human behaviour genetics: (1) the comparison of the resemblance of identical (monozygotic, MZ) twins with that of same-sex fraternal (dizygotic, DZ) twins; (2) the comparison of adoptive and

Table 13.1 Correlations for two personality traits in five large twin studies

Correlation between	Location of study	Extraversion		Emotional stability	
		r	Pairs	r	Pairs
Male MZ twins	Britain	0.65	70	0.51	70
	USA	0.57	197	0.58	197
	Sweden	0.47	2274	0.46	2279
	Australia	0.50	566	0.46	566
	Finland	0.46	1027	0.33	1027
Female MZ twins	Britain	0.46	233	0.45	233
	USA	0.62	284	0.48	284
	Sweden	0.54	2713	0.54	2720
	Australia	0.53	1233	0.52	1233
	Finland	0.49	1293	0.43	1293
Male DZ twins	Britain	0.25	47	0.02	47
	USA	0.20	122	0.26	122
	Sweden	0.20	3660	0.21	3670
	Australia	0.13	351	0.18	351
	Finland	0.15	2304	0.12	2304
Female DZ twins	Britain	0.18	125	0.09	125
	USA	0.28	190	0.23	190
	Sweden	0.21	4130	0.25	4143
	Australia	0.19	751	0.26	751
	Finland	0.14	2520	0.18	2520

Sources: Britain: Eaves *et al.*, 1989; USA: Loehlin and Nichols, 1976; Sweden: Floderus-Myrhed *et al.*, 1980; Australia: Martin and Jardine, 1986; Finland: Rose *et al.*, 1988.

biological parent—child and sibling resemblances; (3) the comparison of various relationships in the families of MZ twin pairs; and (4) the comparison of the resemblance of twins reared together and apart. Many of these correlations are based on versions of Eysenck's extraversion and neuroticism scales; others are based on similar scales and factors from other personality inventories. The particular studies included in these tables were brought together in Loehlin (1992), and further details concerning scales and populations can be found there or in the original sources cited.

A good deal can be learned simply by inspection of the tables, keeping in mind that considerable fluctuation in correlations is to be expected simply from sampling error, especially when *Ns* are small, as some of these are. In the case of Table 13.1, the correlations for MZ twins, in the top half of the table, are decidedly higher than the correlations for DZ twins, in the bottom half, suggesting genetic influence on these traits. Indeed, almost without exception, the MZ correlations in particular studies are more than twice the corresponding DZ correlations, suggesting either that the genetic influences on these traits are at least partly non-additive or that the 'equal environments' assumption often made in interpreting twin studies — the assumption that MZ and DZ twins have equally similar environments — is incorrect.

Non-additive genetic influences refer to such factors as genetic dominance and epistasis, which depend on the configuration of genes present, and not just the summed effects of individual genes. Resemblances between identical twins fully reflect both additive and non-additive genetic factors, since MZ twins, having identical genotypes, share gene configurations as well as genes. Genetic resemblances between other relatives depend mostly (siblings) or entirely (parents and offspring) on the additive effects of genes.

The adoption studies in Table 13.2 have smaller samples and consequently less consistency in correlations than the twin studies; nevertheless, at least for extraversion, appreciable correlation for most of the biological relationships combined with near-zero correlations for the adoptive relationships suggests some genetic contribution to individual variation and little if any resemblance due purely to shared family environments. In fact, genetically unrelated individuals growing up in the same family show practically no resemblance at all in extraversion. The picture is less clear for emotional stability; here there are both more small correlations among biological relatives and more appreciable correlations among adoptive ones.

Perhaps the point of chief interest in the twin-family studies (Table 13.3) is the comparison between the MZ twin and his own and his twin's child: the two are equally similar to him genetically, but one has grown up in a different family. For extraversion the two correlations are similar; for emotional stability, there appears to be a greater resemblance to the own child.

Finally, there is the interesting combination of twin and adoption study, the comparison of twins reared together and apart (Table 13.4). The evidence here is not entirely unequivocal, no doubt due in part to the small samples, but on the whole it appears that MZ twins who were reared apart in childhood tend to be less alike than those who were reared together (which is evidence of some effect of a shared family environment), yet remain more similar than DZ twins or other relatives who were reared together (which is evidence of a larger effect of the genes).

Table 13.2 Correlations for two personality traits in three adoption studies

Correlation between	Location of study	Extraversion		Emotional stability	
		r	Pairs	r	Pairs
Biological:					
Mother and child	Britain	0.21	309	0.13	309
	Minnesota	0.04	255	0.21	255
	Texas	−0.03	57	0.01	57
Father and child	Britain	0.21	236	0.10	236
	Minnesota	0.21	255	0.14	255
	Texas	0.20	56	−0.13	56
Siblings	Britain	0.25	418	0.04	418
	Minnesota	0.06	135	0.28	135
	Texas	0.13	17	−0.12	17
Adoptive:					
Mother and child	Britain	−0.02	127	−0.03	127
	Minnesota	−0.03	187	0.12	187
	Texas	0.00	257	−0.03	257
Father and child	Britain	−0.03	93	0.21	93
	Minnesota	0.05	182	−0.09	182
	Texas	0.03	247	0.16	247
Siblings	Britain	−0.11	58	0.23	58
	Minnesota	0.07	75	0.05	75
	Texas	−0.13	125	0.09	125

Note: Some Minnesota *N*s approximate.
Sources: Britain: Eaves *et al.*, 1989; Minnesota: Scarr *et al.*, 1981, and unpublished appendix, courtesy the author; Texas: Loehlin *et al.*, 1985, data from Loehlin, 1992.

Table 13.3 Correlations for two personality traits in two twin-family studies

Correlation between	Location of study	Extraversion		Emotional stability	
		r	Pairs	r	Pairs
MZ twins	Sweden	0.49	72	0.45	72
	USA	0.34	44	0.51	44
Offspring	Sweden	0.33	75	0.21	75
	USA	0.15	102	0.01	102
Twin, own child	Sweden	0.25	264	0.20	264
	USA	0.18	149	0.10	149
Twin, twin's child	Sweden	0.15	71	0.06	71
	USA	0.24	121	0.02	121
Cousins via MZs	Sweden	0.13	54	0.16	54
	USA	0.18	84	−0.02	84

Note: Offspring refers to siblings among children of a twin. Cousins via MZs are half-siblings genetically.
Sources: Sweden: Price *et al.*, 1982; USA: see Loehlin, 1986.

These impressions can be quantified by a procedure increasingly becoming standard in behaviour-genetic practice: the fitting of models to the combined data sets (Eaves *et al.*, 1989; Loehlin, 1979, 1989). This procedure provides the advantages of: (1) an overall summary of all the data at once, (2) tests of the fit of particular heredity—environment models to the data, (3) statistical comparisons of alternative models

Table 13.4 Correlations for two personality traits in four studies of twins reared together and apart

Correlation between	Location of study	Extraversion		Emotional stability	
		r	Pairs	r	Pairs
MZ twins, together	Finland	0.33	47	0.32	47
	Sweden	0.54	150	0.41	151
	USA	0.63	217	0.54	217
	Britain	0.42	43	0.38	43
MZ twins, apart	Finland	0.38	30	0.25	30
	Sweden	0.30	95	0.25	95
	USA	0.34	44	0.61	44
	Britain	0.61	42	0.53	42
DZ twins, together	Finland	0.13	135	0.10	135
	Sweden	0.06	204	0.24	204
	USA	0.18	114	0.41	114
DZ twins, apart	Finland	0.12	95	0.11	95
	Sweden	0.04	220	0.28	218
	USA	−0.07	27	0.29	27

Sources: Finland: Langinvainio *et al.*, 1984; Sweden; Pedersen *et al.*, 1988; USA: Tellegen *et al.*, 1988; Britain: Shields, 1962.

Table 13.5 Equations for relationships in Tables 13.1−13.4, and tests of homogeneity of observed correlations

Relationship	Equation	Test of homogeneity		
		df	p_e	p_s
MZ twins, reared together	$h^2 + i^2 + c^2$	15	<0.001	<0.001
MZ twins, reared apart	$h^2 + i^2$	3	>0.20	>0.05
DZ twins or sibs, reared together	$1/2\ h^2 + c^2$	17	>0.05	<0.001
DZ twins, reared apart	$1/2\ h^2$	2	>0.50	>0.30
Parent and biological child	$1/2\ rh^2 + pc$	7	>0.20	>0.30
Parent and MZ twin's child	$1/2\ rh^2$	1	>0.50	>0.70
Parent and adopted child	pc	5	>0.95	<0.05
Adoptive siblings	c^2	2	>0.30	>0.50
Cousins via MZ twins	$1/4h^2$	1	>0.70	>0.30

Notes: Symbols in equations: h = additive genetic effect, i = non-additive genetic effect (assumed due to multiple-gene epistasis), c = shared environmental effect, r = correlation between child and adult genes, p = influence of parental phenotype on child shared environment. Subscripts: e = extraversion, s = emotional stability. The *p*-values are based on chi-square tests of the homogeneity of correlations in the given category.

having more or fewer genetic or environmental parameters, and (4) estimates of the values of the genetic and environmental parameters in the best-fitting models.

Table 13.5 gives the model, in the form of equations for the nine different relationships found in Tables 13.1−13.4. Each observed correlation is expressed as a function of five parameters: an additive genetic effect h. a shared environmental effect c, a non-additive genetic effect i, a correlation r between the parent's genotype at the time of the study and what it had been at the child's age, and an effect p of the parent's trait on the child's environment with respect to the trait.

The equations as given assume: (1) that spouses are uncorrelated for extraversion and emotional stability; (2) that the degree of shared relevant environment is comparable for both kinds of twins and for twins and siblings; (3) that the children were not selectively placed in adoption with regard to these traits; and (4) that the non-additive genetic variance is in the form of epistasis involving many genes. Probably none of these assumptions is exactly true, but, empirically, departures from the first and third appear to be minimal. The second, the equal environments assumption, is more controversial; we comment on it and the fourth later.

Table 13.5 shows at the right the results of chi-square tests of the homogeneity of the observed correlations within each of the nine categories (the number of observed correlations in each category is one greater than the *df* shown). Probability values of less than 0.05 may be taken as evidence of significant heterogeneity of the correlations within a category. Most appear to be satisfactorily homogeneous. Exceptions include MZ twins reared together, for both traits, and DZ twins and adoptive parent−child correlations for emotional stability. The significant MZ twin heterogeneity is presumably a result of the power to detect modest but real differences provided by the large samples in the five twin studies. Analyses reported elsewhere indicate both significant but small gender differences and a difference between the Finnish and the other twin studies (Loehlin, 1989, 1992).

Table 13.6 summarizes the fitting of several models to the combined data. The first row is the heterogeneity analysis just described: the chi-squares and *df*s are simply the sums of those in the nine separate relationships in Table 13.5 (this summing represents an approximation, because not all the groups are strictly independent). The significant heterogeneity is indicated by the probability values of <0.01 and <0.001 for extraversion and emotional stability, respectively. Line 2 shows the fits of the model equations to the data on extraversion and emotional stability. The chi-squares are not notably higher than those for the heterogeneity tests, considering that only five rather than nine unknowns are being fitted. That is, most of the lack of fit lies within sets of correlations assumed to be equivalent, rather than in an inability of the model to account for differences between relationships. Heterogeneity

Table 13.6 Model fitting to combined data sets for two personality traits

Unknowns in model	Difference from	*df*	Extraversion		Emotional stability	
			χ^2	p	χ^2	p
1. homogeneity		53	84.90	<0.01	163.00	<0.001
2. *h,i,c,p,r*		57	93.18	<0.01	167.27	<0.001
3. *h,i,c*	line 2	2	2.50	>0.20	4.47	>0.10
4. *h,i*	line 3	1	1.35	>0.20	10.71	<0.01
5. *h,c*	line 3	1	84.01	<0.001	41.30	<0.001
6. *i,c*	line 3	1	69.13	<0.001	47.96	<0.001

Note: In line 3 and after, $p = 0$ and $r = 1.0$, and χ^2s shown are for differences from the indicated line. For details, see text.

of given correlations across studies is far from surprising: different questionnaires were used, samples were differently selected, the studies were carried out in different parts of the world, and so on.

Line 3 of the table asks whether the parameters p and r can be dispensed with; that is, by assuming no effect of the parent's trait on the child's trait-relevant environment, and setting the genetic correlation across ages to 1.0. The non-significant chi-squares for the test of differences from line 2 suggest that such simplifications may be made. Line 4 indicates that eliminating the shared environment parameter c has a negligible effect for extraversion, but not so for emotional stability — dropping it in the latter case leads to a significant increase in chi-square. Lines 5 and 6 say that neither the additive nor the non-additive genetic parameter h or i can be dropped for either trait — in each case a highly significant increase in chi-square results.

Table 13.7 shows the estimates of the additive genetic contribution h^2, the non-additive genetic contribution i^2, and the shared environmental contribution c^2, from the preceding analyses when h, i, and c are solved for (with p and r fixed). Also shown is the variance u^2 unaccounted for by these three, a component which gathers together the effects of unshared environmental factors, errors of measurement, and genotype–environment interactions (these last will be discussed later in the chapter). Estimates are given for extraversion and emotional stability, along with estimates of the same quantities for the other three of the 'Big Five' dimensions. The latter are based on similar analyses carried out with the somewhat less extensive twin, adoption, and family data available for these traits (Loehlin, 1992).

The story told by Table 13.7 is fairly straightforward. The largest of the four components of variance is always the last — the residual due to measurement error, unshared environment, genotype–environment interaction, etc. Next comes the first component, the additive effects of genes. Then, except for Factor 5, come non-additive genetic effects. And finally, there is a small but consistent contribution of shared family environment. Somewhere between 40 per cent and 50 per cent of the Big Five traits is genetic, according to this analysis, and between 50 per cent and 60 per cent is due to environment, plus error and interaction. The environmental effects are mostly non-familial, but there is a small component due to shared environment. For four of the Big Five dimensions the genetic variance contains an

Table 13.7 Estimates of h^2, i^2, and c^2 for the 'Big Five' personality dimensions

Dimension	h^2	i^2	c^2	u^2
I. Surgency (extraversion)	0.32	0.17	0.02	0.49
II. Agreeableness	0.29	0.10	0.09	0.52
III. Conscientiousness	0.22	0.18	0.05	0.55
IV. Emotional stability	0.27	0.14	0.07	0.52
V. Intellectual openness	0.43	0.02	0.06	0.49

Notes: Estimates for dimensions I and IV from analyses in Table 13.6, line 3; others from Lochlin (1992). u^2 is obtained as a residual.

appreciable non-additive component. For the fifth, intellectual openness, the genetic effect is almost entirely additive.

Are such trait-to-trait differences as occur in Table 13.7 dependable? For extraversion and emotional stability, a direct test is available by attempting to fit the same values for h, i, and c to both traits in the data of Tables 13.1–13.4. The result is a chi-square of 280.83, compared to the combined chi-square of 267.42 when separate values are allowed for the two traits. The chi-square increase of 23.41 for 3 degrees of freedom ($p < 0.001$) suggests that the differences between the estimates for these two traits are real. Can we localize the difference to h, i, or c? No. In further analyses (not shown) we can require any one of these to be the same for the two traits without leading to a significant increase in chi-square, provided that the other two are left free. Thus we can conclude that there are differences across the traits, but not that the difference lies in any particular component.

The models we have fitted involve certain assumptions; for example, that MZ and DZ environments are equal in similarity, and that the non-additive genetic variation is due to epistasis rather than dominance. These assumptions are not carved in stone. What would happen if we made them otherwise?

Assuming that the non-additive genetic variance is entirely due to genetic dominance rather than epistasis does not affect the estimates in Table 13.7 very much. Typically, it shifts a little more of the genetic variance from additive to non-additive. (The only difference in the equations is that one-quarter of the dominance variance gets added to the sibling/DZ equation.)

An alternative model which eliminates non-additive genetic variance altogether, and instead explains the high MZ correlations by postulating a special environmental resemblance unique to MZ twins, can also give a reasonably good account of the data. The changes required in the Table 13.5 equations are to substitute a special MZ environment parameter c_m for c in the first equation, and delete i^2 in the first and second. The three-parameter fits (h, c_m, c) are expressed by chi-squares of 92.62 for extraversion and 174.14 for emotional stability — not very different from the 95.68 and 171.74, respectively, yielded by the three-parameter model h, i, c.

The parameter estimates are shown in Table 13.8. In general, h^2 and c^2 do not change much — h^2 goes up a little, c^2 down a little; the special c_m parameter pretty

Table 13.8 An alternative model: estimates of h^2, c_m^2, *and* c^2 for the 'Big Five' personality dimensions

Dimension	h^2	c_m^2	c^2	u^2
I. Surgency (extraversion)	0.36	0.15	0.00	0.64
II. Agreeableness	0.32	0.16	0.07	0.61
III. Conscientiousness	0.29	0.16	0.02	0.69
IV. Emotional stability	0.31	0.17	0.05	0.64
V. Intellectual openness	0.47	0.04	0.05	0.48

Note: Data and models are the same as for Table 13.7, except that c_m replaces c for MZ twins reared together, and i is dropped from MZs together and apart.

much accounts for the variance previously attributed to genetic non-additivity. The estimates of the effect of unshared environment go up, because they are now obtained as $1 - h^2 - c^2$, and the estimates of the total effect of the genes drop down to the 30–45 per cent rather than the 40–50 per cent range.

Given enough cases of MZ twins reared apart, these two models can be distinguished: the latter model predicts a greater drop-off in correlation for twins reared apart, who no longer share environments but still share non-additive genes. The presently available data are not compelling either way, and, clearly, intermediate hypotheses involving both kinds of factor could also fit the data. One can advance some arguments in favour of the first, genetic model. For example, is it plausible that shared environment should count for so much in the case of MZ twins when it apparently counts for so little in the case of DZ twins and ordinary siblings? Also, there are direct studies that tend to support the equal environments assumption (for example, Matheny *et al.*, 1976; Morris-Yates *et al.*, 1990; Plomin *et al.*, 1976; Rowe *et al.*, 1987). Nevertheless, large, well-matched samples of MZ twins reared apart and together would probably be the most effective way of deciding the issue.

The presence of non-additive genetic variance on a trait is of some theoretical interest. The application of natural or artificial selection tends to reduce additive genetic variation more rapidly than non-additive genetic variation. Thus if a trait has a relatively high proportion of non-additive genetic variance, this may be evidence that the trait has been subject to natural selection during the course of human evolution. We will return to the topic of evolution in the final section of this chapter.

In the next two sections of the chapter we consider two ways in which genetic and environmental influences impinging on personality may be related. First, there may be an interaction between the two. Second, they may be correlated.

Genotype–environment (GE) interaction

The concept of interaction is used by psychologists in a variety of senses. One arises from experimental studies in which two or more treatments are manipulated. An interaction is present when the outcome in a particular cell is not an additive combination of the treatment effects. This is the sense in which behaviour geneticists use the term 'GE interaction', referring to a non-additive combined effect of genotype and environment. In contrast, 'interaction' is often used by psychologists to describe transactions between the organism and the environment in which the two reciprocally influence each other. Behaviour geneticists tend to treat this kind of interaction as a variety of genotype–environment correlation. In this chapter, we use 'interaction' only in the first sense above, for an outcome that is a non-additive function of genetic and environmental effects. An ability of a 'maze–bright' strain of rats to do well in both poor and enriched environments, whereas a 'maze-dull' strain does well only in the enriched ones, would be a hypothetical example.

Interaction effects typically contribute to the residual component of variation, u^2, because any effect of unique experiences impacting on unique genotypes winds up here. However, completely idiosyncratic interactions are probably not going to aid us much in understanding the causes of personality development. Of greater potential interest would be interactions holding over categories of environmental conditions and individuals. For example, if hypothetical genes disposing towards criminality were expressed in a lower but not in an upper social class context, then such an interaction effect would provide a potential means to reduce crime by changing social environments. Many behavioural scientists assume — without much evidence — that systematic GE interactions are a major contributor to variation in personality.

The earlier model-fitting analyses of the Big Five personality traits would argue against a major role of interactions of this sort in the personality domain, at least in so far as major social stratifications such as social class provide the environmental categories. Families are typically nested within such categories, and thus interactions of this sort would tend to contribute to familial correlations. And for personality traits, family correlations are low.

Few studies have taken the difficult but direct approach of screening for GE interaction effects by using a full adoption research design. In this design, genotypes can be represented by characteristics of the biological parents who relinquished the adoptee; environments by characteristics of the adoptive parents; and interactions by non-additive effects of the two backgrounds (Plomin *et al.*, 1977).

An occasional interpretable interaction effect has been reported in the behaviour genetic literature. Figure 13.1 provides an example. Delinquent behaviour in adolescent adoptees was conditional on *both* the characteristics of their biological parents (mostly antisocial personality or alchoholism), *and* the presence of adverse home environments. The presence of adverse home environments plus adverse genotypes nearly quadrupled the adoptees' delinquency rates (Cadoret *et al.*, 1983). This result, however, is not completely unambiguous because the home environmental measures — divorce and problem behaviour in adoptive parents or siblings — could conceivably sometimes be a consequence rather than a cause of the adoptee's behaviour.

Plomin (1986) undertook a far-ranging search for interaction effects on infant temperament and behaviour problems using data from the Colorado Adoption Project. Child outcome measures were predicted from measures of the biological parents' temperaments and behaviour problems. Interactions were represented by product terms (biological parent measure × adoptive parent measure) which were tested in a hierarchical regression analysis for contributions beyond those of the adoptive and biological parent measures alone. The main result was an almost total lack of interaction effects — of 30 genotype–environment analyses on infant behaviour problems, only four produced significant interactions; and of 80 analyses in the temperament domain, only two were statistically significant (fewer than chance).

In summary, the evidence for systematic GE interaction effects in personality is weaker than one may have supposed, but data on this question are difficult to gather and the issue is by no means closed.

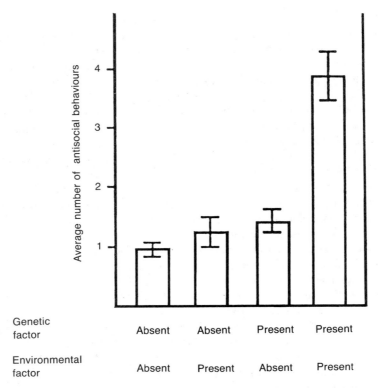

Figure 13.1 Genotype–environment interaction for antisocial behaviour (Source: Cadoret *et al.*, 1983)

Genotype–environment (GE) correlations

The beaver's building a dam is as much a part of its genetic destiny as its genes' construction of its eye or tail. As Dawkins (1982) observes, genes may reach beyond the immediate cellular environment and can affect an 'extended phenotype' of constructions in the physical environment and instinctive social responses (such as the beaver's dam, a cricket's mating song). In behaviour genetics, these innumerable transactions between genes and their usual environments, both physical and social, both at the microscopic level of the cytoplasm and at the molar level of the organism, most often count as part of the *genetic* variation. GE correlations represent a restricted set of gene–environment transactions, a subset defined by a statistical association between environmental and genetic effects. When there is a tendency for an individual with an above-average genotype to be exposed to an above-average environment, and vice versa, a GE correlation is present.

GE correlations may take one of several forms (Plomin *et al.*, 1977). A *passive* GE correlation may result from genes shared by parent and child. When these genes lead to a particular parental phenotype (such as high IQ, sociability) and to a similar phenotype in the child, the parental phenotype may act via the environment to reinforce the child's genetic dispositions. For instance, parental sociability might reinforce the matching genetic tendency in children because sociable parents may provide opportunities for meeting playmates and friends. A *reactive* GE correlation refers to the social environment's responding to genetic dispositions in an individual (for example, a child with emotional problems is provided with special help). Lastly, an *active* GE correlation refers to an individual's picking environmental opportunities that reinforce his or her inherited personality dispositions. Examples would include the tendency to marry a spouse or select as friends individuals similar to oneself in personality (Buss, 1985, Rushton *et al.*, 1984).

Estimating passive, reactive, and active components of variation is difficult because they are weaker effects than the main effects of environmental and genetic deviations — this is by definition, because no GE correlation can exist unless G and E effects exist to be correlated. Applying a path analytic model to data from adoptive and non-adoptive families in the Colorado Adoption Project, Plomin and his colleagues concluded that passive GE correlation played a negligible role for their measures of infant and child temperament (Plomin and DeFries, 1985; Plomin *et al.*, 1988). Another approach to GE correlation is to see whether the family environment in adoptive homes can be predicted from the characteristics of the adoptees' biological parents. Using this approach, Plomin (1986, p. 123) discovered that some traits of biological parent were correlated with measures of adoptees' home environments, suggesting the possibility of a reactive correlation whereby adoptive parents were responding to the adoptees' genotypes.

An intriguing type of *active* GE correlation may be the extent of relatives' social contacts. Twins who have frequent contact with one another tend to be more similar in personality than twins who have infrequent contacts. For example, frequency of adult social contact predicted twins' personality similarity on a group of 157 MMPI items (Rose *et al.*, 1990). This result held after controlling statistically for the twins' childhood separation ages — thus the effect was more one of the current adult social environment than one of the childhood environment (that is, duration of living in the same home as children). Accordingly, we may interpret this result as the twins' actively seeking out each other as environments, and thus reinforcing their mutual personality dispositions, a social process tending to make them more alike in behaviour. In ordinary model-fitting, this type of GE correlation effect is analysed as shared environmental variation. It does not so much reduce estimates of heritability as shift some of the environmental variation from the unshared to the shared category.

The nature of nurture

The familiar interpretation of an environmental measure is that it represents variation in the social context which may mould behavioural traits. The environment is regarded as fixed and external, while attention is directed toward the exposed individual. This view of the environment ignores the possible influence of genetic factors on environmental measures in two ways. First, 'environment' often reflects the behaviour of other individuals (parents, peers) and thus may be regarded as an aspect of their phenotypes potentially influenced by genes. For example, 'books in the home' do not appear by magic, but must be acquired by parents, and so reflect their interests and ambitions. Second, associations among environmental measures and child outcomes may be mediated indirectly through the heredity shared by parent and child instead of representing a social influence of one on the other.

Socio-economic status (SES) is a classic example of an environmental variable which has been related in many ways to behaviour. Table 13.9 presents estimates of variance components for socio-economic status based on an American twin study and a Danish adoption study, both using large, national samples. The American study included about 1,000 adult male twin pairs of each type, from a registry of World War 2 veterans. In the Danish study, male adoptees (then adults) were located in a comprehensive and nationwide system of records, which allowed identification of their occupations about 40 years after the adoptions had occurred. Occupational titles were rated for prestige. In the US twin study, data on income and educational attainment were obtained. For the studies in both countries, variance components — estimated from the equations in Table 13.5 — fell into the same rank order: heredity explained the largest portion of the SES variance, followed by unshared environment, and then shared family environment. The heritabilities from all comparisons were about 40 per cent. These data bring into question the common-sense view that SES is mainly a measure of 'environment': rather, substantial SES variation was genetically based.

Another frequently discussed environmental factor is parents' child-rearing styles. Child-rearing styles can be categorized along two broad dimensions — warmth and control — and viewed from the perspective of either the parent (origin) or child (recipient). In two studies (Rowe, 1981, 1983), adolescent twins' reports of their

Table 13.9 Variance components of socio-economic status (SES)

SES measure	Pairs	Correlations		Components
Occupational prestige	2467	$r_{BF.AC}$	= 0.20	$h^2 = 0.40$
	1137	$r_{AF.AC}$	= 0.22	$pc = 0.22$
				$u^2 = 0.38$
Income	1019	r_{MZ}	= 0.54	$h^2 = 0.48$
	907	r_{DZ}	= 0.30	$c^2 = 0.06$
				$u^2 = 0.46$
Years of schooling	1019	r_{MZ}	= 0.76	$h^2 = 0.44$
	907	r_{DZ}	= 0.54	$c^2 = 0.32$
				$u^2 = 0.24$

Notes: Components obtained using Table 13.5 equations; symbols as in Table 13.5. All subjects adult males. Occupational prestige — Danish data from Teasdale, 1979, Tables VI and VII. BF = biological father, AF = adoptive father, AC = adopted child. Income (= log income) and years of schooling — US veterans' data from Taubman, 1976, Table 2. MZ = monozygotic twins, DZ = dizygotic twins.

Table 13.10 Twin correlations for family environment: monozygotic twins reared apart and together

Family environment scale	Reared apart	Reared together
Cohesion	0.10	0.30
Expressiveness	0.37	0.22
Conflict	0.16	0.27
Achievement	0.16	0.23
Cultural	0.45	0.37
Active	0.12	0.37
Organization	0.30	0.31
Control	0.36	0.18
Mean	0.25	0.24

Note: *N* pairs: reared apart, 40–50; reared together, 82–92.
Source: Plomin *et al.*, 1989.

parents' child-rearing styles were obtained and correlated. Perceived warmth showed heritability in both studies but perceived control did not.

Different results may obtain for parents' reports of their styles of rearing their children. In a Swedish study of adult twins in their fifties and sixties, reporting retrospectively on the families they had reared, most aspects of parenting showed genetic influence, as indicated by the comparison of MZ and DZ twins reared apart and together (Plomin *et al.*, 1989). Table 13.10 shows these correlations for the MZ twins. The greater differences in childhood experience of those MZ twins who had been reared in different families did not result in greater differences in the way they reared their own children (mean correlations of 0.25 and 0.24, respectively).

If there is a substantial genetic component in child-rearing and parental SES measures, their association with child outcome variables in ordinary families may be genetically mediated. For IQ, this inference is supported by adoption studies from the 1920s to the present, in that correlations between SES and child IQ are greater in biological families than in adoptive families (Bouchard and Segal, 1985). In the Colorado Adoption Project, similar results were obtained for child-rearing styles and child temperament and problem behaviours (Plomin *et al.*, 1985). For example, the mean correlation of child-rearing style and temperament measures was 0.06 in adoptive families (*N*s 139–80 versus 0.20 in biological families (*N*s 130–63). The lack of social-causal effects of child-rearing on temperament is consistent with the earlier analysis of the Big Five personality traits that showed no significant parent-child environmental transmission of personality dispositions (that is, the parameter *p* could be omitted without worsening the fit to the data).

Personality and biological evolution

Evolutionary theorists and behaviour geneticists look at personality as though through opposite ends of a telescope. The former survey the broad sweep of human evolutionary history and make cross-species comparisons of behaviour patterns in order to ascertain the origin of adaptive traits that represent modal responses to encountered environments. The evolutionary psychologist asks, 'how has a trait evolved?' and 'what adaptive function does it serve?' The behaviour geneticist typically picks traits not because of their evolutionary significance but because of their social significance or convenience of measurement. The focus is on how people differ from each other, and hence on existing genetic variance in a population. For the evolutionary theorist's understanding of an adaptive trait, within-population genetic variance is not necessary: the relevant genes may have 'gone to fixation' through biological selection and be present in all individuals in a species. Thus, ironically, a highly genetic, adaptive trait may be 'invisible' to behaviour genetic analysis precisely because genetic variation has been exhausted. For example, having two eyes is adaptive for humans, but not genetically variable.

Genetic variation in a trait may also serve no evolutionary purpose. According to the 'neutralist' theory of biological selection (Kimura, 1983), much existing genetic variation is a byproduct of the accumulation of mutations that have little positive or negative effect on biological fitness (reproductive success). Heritable variation in personality traits could result from these neutral mutations, variation that would be purposeless from an adaptive, functionalist standpoint. Or the variation could be an inadvertent consequence of evolutionary selection for non-behavioural traits, such as disease resistance, where genes selected for the non-behavioural trait also happen to affect behaviour.

Neither of these possibilities is as theoretically attractive to most evolutionists as the one that heritable personality variation serves some strategic, adaptive function. There are some conditions under which heritable trait variation can serve adaptive functions in the long term. These conditions include: (1) heritable alternative strategies, and (2) heritable calibration of physiological mechanisms (Buss, 1991). The former condition refers to a variety of histories of biological selection that preserve genetic variation, including frequency-dependent selection, where rare traits accrue greater fitness but lose their advantage as they become more common. The second condition refers to selection within alternative niches. This involves historical variation in the optimal threshold for trait expression, a process that prevents alleles from going to fixation.

Neither of these conditions is easily demonstrable with existing data, because long-term information on the relative fitness of different traits is lacking. Buss offered Zuckerman's (1990) trait of sensation seeking as possibly representing selection for different thresholds of expression, because high sensation seeking may provide greater reproductive opportunities, but it also carries with it greater survival costs, and these relative costs and benefits may be changed by environmental fluctuations in the availability of resources.

Evolutionary theorists now debate the relative value of information on current reproductive success and of reconstructions of reproductive success during the long Pleistocene existence of our species. Theorists on one side maintain that environmental conditions have changed so drastically since the period of major human evolution that modern reproductive efforts are probably disconnected from their earlier psychological and adaptive functions; the other side argues that humans can evolve in periods as short as 300—1,000 years and that current reproductive behaviour reflects evolved psychological adaptations.

Whichever side is more correct, there is currently a dearth of information on the genetics of human reproduction — even the basic question of whether fitness is heritable in modern populations is largely unanswered. Moreover, little work has been done linking personality with reproductive success. One exception is a recent paper by Eaves and his colleagues, who studied the traits of extraversion and neuroticism (emotional instability). They found an interaction, in that stable introverts and unstable extraverts had fewer than average children, whereas unstable introverts and stable extraverts had an excess (Eaves *et al.*, 1990). If the dimension running from stable introversion to unstable extraversion is taken to represent impulsivity, this would imply a selection against the extremes and in favour of intermediate levels of this trait, which seems plausible. The apparent selection in favour of both extremes on the orthogonal trait is more puzzling. The one extreme, the favouring of stable extraversion, is readily interpretable, but the other extreme, the favouring of unstable introversion, would seem to present something of a challenge to the sociobiologically inclined theorist. Clearly, further research is needed into the possible adaptive functions of individual differences in personality, and conversation among sociobiologists, behaviour geneticists, and personality theorists is to be encouraged.

Summary and conclusions

Personality traits are to some degree heritable — this message sounds clearly through the variety of research approaches to the genetics of behaviour. The degree of heritability is moderate — about 30 per cent for additive genetic variation in the Big Five personality traits; somewhat greater if non-additive genetic variation is included. Although this idea once encountered much resistance from social scientists, opposition seems to be lessening as more is learned about how the physiology of the brain relates to psychiatric illness and normal behaviour. Few now take issue with the possibility that the genes influence the structure and physiology of the brain, just as they do for non-behavioural organ systems.

As Loehlin and Nichols (1976) observed in their report on the National Merit Twin Study, the real surprise has been the near-absence of systematic, shared environmental influences on personality. In practical terms, child-rearing styles and social class appear to affect personality development weakly, or not at all; this conclusion may extend to intellectual traits as well (Rowe, 1990). This result is sure to engender opposition — because it indicates that changing family environments in which a child is reared (if one excludes pathological extremes) probably will not affect personality trait distributions much, if at all. And in a way, it threatens the livelihood of social scientists. On the whole, they are in business as social-environmental specialists, who interpret nearly every parent—child and sibling behavioural similarity in terms of one social influence process or another, and who seem wedded to research designs that confound environmental with genetic influences. But there is another possible response to these results, and that is a paradigm shift — a revolution in our thinking about the causes of development and the best ways in which to study them. To lay out the details of these changes is beyond the scope of this chapter — but it is a task that should challenge young scholars interested in understanding the transmission and maintenance of behavioural traits in human populations.

References

Bouchard, T.J., Jr., and Segal, N.L. (1985), 'Environment and IQ', in B.J. Wolman (ed.), *Handbook of intelligence: Theories, measurements, and applications*, New York, NY: Wiley, pp. 391—464.

Buss, D.M. (1985), 'Human mate selection', *American Scientist*, **73**, 47—51.

Buss, D.M. (1991), 'Evolutionary personality psychology', *Annual Review of Psychology*, **42**, 459—91.

Cadoret, R.J., Cain, C.A., and Crowe, R.R. (1983), 'Evidence for gene—environment interaction in the development of adolescent antisocial behavior', *Behavior Genetics*, **13**, 301—10.

Dawkins, R. (1982), *The Extended Phenotype: The gene as the unit of selection*, Oxford: Freeman.

Digman, J.M. (1990), 'Personality structure: emergence of the five-factor model', *Annual Review of Psychology*, **41**, 417—40.

Eaves, L.J., Eysenck, H.J., and Martin, N.G. (1989), *Genes, Culture and Personality*, London: Academic Press.

Eaves, L.J., Martin, N.G., Health, A.C., Hewitt, J.K., and Neale, M.C. (1990), 'Personality and reproductive fitness', *Behavior Genetics*, **20**, 563—8.

Floderus-Myrhed, B., Pedersen, N., and Rasmuson, I. (1980), 'Assessment of heritability for personality, based on a short-form of the Eysenck Personality Inventory', *Behavior Genetics*, **10**, 153—62.

John, O.P. (1990), 'The "Big Five" factor taxonomy: dimensions of personality in the natural language and in questionnaires', in L.A. Pervin, (ed.), *Handbook of Personality: Theory and research*, New York, NY: Guilford Press, pp. 66—100.

Kimura, M. (1983), *The Neutral Theory of Molecular Evolution*, Cambridge: Cambridge University Press.

Langinvainio, H., Kaprio, J., Koskenvuo, M., and Lönnqvist, J. (1984), 'Finnish twins reared apart III: Personality factors', *Acta Geneticae Medicae et Gemellologiae*, **33**, 259—64.

Loehlin, J.C. (1979), 'Combining data from different groups in human behavior genetics', in J.R. Royce and L.P. Moos (eds.), *Theoretical Advances in Human Behavior Genetics*, Alphen aan de Rijn, The Netherlands: Sijthoff & Noordhoff, pp. 303—34.

Loehlin, J.C. (1986), 'Heredity, environment, and the Thurstone Temperament Schedule', *Behavior Genetics*, **16**, 61—73.

Loehlin, J.C. (1989), 'Partitioning environmental and genetic contributions to behavioral development', *American Psychologist*, **44**, 1285—92.

Loehlin, J.C. (1992), *Genes and Environment in Personality Development*, Newbury Park, CA: Sage.

Loehlin, J.C., and DeFries, J.C. (1987), 'Genotype—environment correlation and IQ', *Behavior Genetics*, **17**, 263—77.

Loehlin, J.C. and Nichols, R.C. (1976), *Heredity, Environment and Personality*, Austin, TX: University of Texas Press.

Loehlin, J.C., Willerman, L., and Horn, J.M. (1985), 'Personality resemblances in adoptive families when the children are late-adolescent or adult', *Journal of Personality and Social Psychology*, **48**, 376–92.

Martin, N., and Jardine, R. (1986), 'Eysenck's contributions to behaviour genetics', in S. Modgil and C. Modgil (eds.), *Hans Eysenck: Consensus and controversy*, Philadelphia, PA: Falmer Press, pp. 13–47.

Matheny, A.P., Jr., Wilson, R.S., and Dolan, A.B. (1976), 'Relations between twins' similarity of appearance and behavioral similarity', *Behavior Genetics*, **6**, 343–51.

Morris-Yates, A., Andrews, G., Howie, P., and Henderson, S. (1990), 'Twins: a test of the equal environments assumption', *Acta Psychiatrica Scandinavica*, **81**, 322–6.

Pedersen, N.L., Plomin, R., McClearn, G.E., and Friberg, L. (1988), 'Neuroticism, extraversion, and related traits in adult twins reared apart and reared together', *Journal of Personality and Social Psychology*, **55**, 950–7.

Plomin, R. (1986), *Development, Genetics, and Psychology*, Hillsdale, NJ: Erlbaum.

Plomin, R., and DeFries, J.C. (1985), *Origins of Individual Differences in Infancy: The Colorado Adoption Project*, Orlando, FL: Academic Press.

Plomin, R., DeFries, J.C., and Fulker, D.W. (1988), *Nature and Nurture during Infancy and Early Childhood*, Cambridge: Cambridge University Press.

Plomin, R., DeFries, J.C., and Loehlin, J.C. (1977), 'Genotype–environment interaction and correlation in the analysis of human behavior', *Psychological Bulletin*, **84**, 309–22.

Plomin, R., Loehlin, J.C., and DeFries, J.C. (1985), 'Genetic and environmental components of "environmental" influences', *Developmental Psychology*, **21**, 391–402.

Plomin, R., Willerman, L., and Loehlin, J.C. (1976), 'Resemblance in appearance and the equal environments assumption in twin studies of personality traits', *Behavior Genetics*, **6**, 43–52.

Plomin, R., McClearn, G.E., Pedersen, N.L., Nesselroade, J.R., and Bergeman, C.S. (1989), 'Genetic influence on adults' ratings of their current family environment', *Journal of Marriage and the Family*, **51** 791–803.

Price, R.A., Vandenberg, S.G., Iyer, H., and Williams, J.S. (1982), 'Components of variation in normal personality', *Journal of Personality and Social Psychology*, **43**, 328–40.

Rose, R.J., Kaprio, J., Williams, C.J., Viken, R., and Obremski, K. (1990), 'Social contact and sibling similarity: facts, issues and red herrings', *Behavior Genetics*, **20**, 763–78.

Rose, R.J., Koskenvuo, M., Kaprio, J., Sarna, S., and Langinvainio, H. (1988), 'Shared genes, shared experiences, and similarity of personality', *Journal of Personality and Social Psychology*, **54**, 161–71.

Rowe, D.C. (1981), 'Environmental and genetic influences on dimensions of perceived parenting: a twin study', *Developmental Psychology*, **17**, 203–8.

Rowe, D.C. (1983), 'A biometrical analysis of perceptions of family environment: a study of twin and singleton kinships', *Child Development*, **54**, 416–23.

Rowe, D.C. (1990), 'As the twig is bent?: the myth of child-rearing influence on personality development', *Journal of Counseling and Development*, **68**, 606–11.

Rowe, D.C., Clapp, M., and Wallis, J. (1987), 'Physical attractiveness and the personality resemblance of identical twins', *Behavior Genetics*, **17**, 191–201.

Rushton, J.P., Russell, R.J.H., and Wells, P.A. (1984), 'Genetic similarity theory: beyond kin selection', *Behavior Genetics*, **14**, 179–93.

Scarr, S., Webber, P.L., Weinberg, R.A., and Wittig, M.A. (1981), 'Personality resemblance among adolescents and their parents in biologically related and adoptive families', *Journal of Personality and Social Psychology*, **40**, 885–98.

Shields, J. (1962), *Monozygotic Twins: Brought up apart and brought up together*, London: Oxford University Press.

Taubman, P. (1976), 'The determinants of earnings: genetics, family and other environments: a study of white male twins', *American Economic Review*, **66**, 858–70.

Teasdale, T.W. (1979), 'Social class correlations among adoptees and their biological and adoptive parents', *Behavior Genetics*, **9**, 103–14.

Tellegen, A., Lykken, D.T., Bouchard, T.J., Jr., Wilcox, K.J., Segal, N.L., and Rich, S. (1988), 'Personality similarity in twins reared apart and together', *Journal of Personality and Social Psychology*, **54**, 1031–9.

Zuckerman, M. (1990), 'The psychophysiology of sensation seeking', *Journal of Personality*, **58**, 313–45.

14/ Brain, behaviour, and personality

John H. Gruzelier
Charing Cross Hospital Medical School, England

Luciano Mecacci
University of Rome 'La Sapienza', Italy

Introduction

From a historical perspective, research on the physiological bases of personality has been gradually shifting from the autonomic nervous system (ANS) and the functions of subcortical structures to the central nervous system (CNS) and functions of cortical structures, especially the two cerebral hemispheres. These two levels were apparently based on the differentiation — introduced since the beginning of the century — between *energy* and *content* of behaviour; the former related to what was called 'activation' and 'arousal' and the latter to what was labelled 'performance'.

Around the 1950s, a large literature referred to the physiological bases of personality almost exclusively in terms of the energetic or arousal dimension, giving minor emphasis to the content or performance aspect. Research on the reticular formation (Lindsley, 1960; Magoun, 1963; Moruzzi and Magoun, 1949) played an important role in providing a fundamental physiological substrate for the arousal dimension. After initial work by Eysenck (1947), the many conceptual and empirical contributions published in the 1950s and 1960s (Berlyne, 1960; Duffy, 1951, 1962; Gray, 1964; Hebb, 1955; Lacey, 1967; Malmo, 1959) and important new work by Eysenck (1967) on the biological bases of personality, the question became inextricably one of an arousal–personality relationship.

Several monographs have been published on this relationship and related topics such as temperament and personality disorders (chronologically: Claridge, 1967; Fahrenberg, 1967; Nebylitsyn and Gray, 1972; Zuckerman, 1979; Gray, 1982; Mangan, 1982; Strelau, 1983; Zuckerman, 1983; Myrtek, 1984; Eysenck and Eysenck, 1985; Strelau *et al.*, 1985–6; Strelau and Eysenck, 1987).

Between the 1970s and the 1980s, research on the physiological bases of personality was growing because of new trends in neuropsychology, particularly on the functional specialization of the two cerebral hemispheres, and due to the influential approaches of information processing and cognitive psychology. New attention was and continues to be devoted to the role of cortical structures, especially the two hemispheres, anterior–posterior relationships, and cognitive activity in the structure of personality.

This cognitive-oriented line of research characterized, for instance, the monograph by Michael Eysenck (1982), linking arousal, attention, cognition, and performance. Furthermore, relationships of the two hemispheres with personality, both normal and pathological, was systematically investigated in the edited collection by Gruzelier and Flor-Henry (1980).

Pavlovian theory of higher nervous activity may be implicitly or explicitly seen to be the theoretical background of all research on the physiological bases of personality, at least until the more recent contributions of the past decade. Pavlov's heritage provided first a model of brain functions, more conceptually based (a *conceptual nervous system*, as Skinner, 1938, described it) than empirically and physiologically investigated; second, an integrated view of brain functioning in opposition to the reductionist and molecular approach dominant at the end of the last century; third, a strict relationship between general properties of brain functions and individual differences in behaviour (typology of higher nervous activity); fourth, the search for a psychopathology and psychiatry founded on a global view of the cerebral bases of behaviour (see Mecacci, 1979). Of course, a particular relevance was assigned to the typology of higher nervous activity, with the notion of *properties of the nervous system* and the idea of four types of nervous system. In the original Pavlovian typology, the properties were related to general characteristics of the nervous system, such as the strength of excitation and the inhibition of nerve cells.

In the new formulation carried out by Nebylitsyn (1972a, 1972b), these properties were more directly linked to the functions of specific brain structures. Nebylitsyn distinguished between general and unitary neurophysiological dimensions of properties of the brain as a whole, and partial properties related to functions of various cortical sub-regions. The energetic dimension, the tone of behaviour, was supposed to be regulated by the anterior regions (frontal lobes) of the brain in association with the sub-cortical regions specifically involved in changes in activation level. Individual differences in the functioning of this set of brain structures would be responsible for general individual differences in the modulation of behavioural tone (according to the terminology of Luria, 1973). Nebylitsyn continued relating directly the functioning of these cerebral structures involved in arousal to personality. Because of this cerebral system, 'the process of general control over actions and states of the organism takes place, and it is its structures that carry out the synthesis of integral, adaptive, and in Man, reasonable and creative behaviour as an indispensable attribute of personality' (Nebylitsyn, 1972b, p. 411). On the other hand, the partial properties were related to individual differences in the processing of different modalities of information, multimodal integration, and memory. Since information processing was thought to be the main function of posterior regions (occipital, temporal, and parietal lobes), individual differences in cognitive performance should, it was thought, depend on the functioning of these cortical areas. For Nebylitsyn, personality (general properties) and cognition (partial properties) remained two separate dimensions of behaviour.

A further step in the revision of Pavlovian typology was made by one of Nebylitsyn's students, Rusalov (1979, 1989). He referred to the theory of functional systems of Anochin, and focused on temperament as a sub-system of human psychological individuality to be distinguished from personality. Also in the perspective by Strelau (1983; see also Strelau and Plomin, Chapter 12 in this volume), an authoritative scholar who has renewed Pavlovian typology, temperament has to be differentiated from personality. Temperament is related to the formal characteristics of behaviour and is biologically grounded; personality is related to the content of behaviour and is influenced by social factors (see also Endler, 1989).

As was pointed out by Gale (1987), reviewing different approaches to the topic of biological bases of personality, a systemic conception of behaviour should prevent research falling into the common error of considering personality as an isolated and monolithic system with its own biological ground. Behaviour should be considered as a complex set of interacting sub-systems, such as temperament, personality, and cognition, whose biological bases are represented by the integrated activity of the nervous system, central and autonomic, in general, and of the brain structures, cortical and sub-cortical, in particular.

Individual differences in arousal, personality, and cognition

According to Eysenck's theory, arousal represents a bridge between personality and cognition. On the one hand, arousal is inversely related to the level of extraversion (extraverts are less aroused and introverts more aroused) and, on the other hand, performance (sensory, motor, and cognitive) has a curvilinear relationship with arousal level. Moreover, this link between arousal, personality, and performance depends on the arousability value of environmental conditions and external stimuli; performance will be better in introverts than in extraverts for low-arousing conditions (non-stressful tasks, above-threshold stimuli), and it will be better in extraverts than in introverts for high-arousing conditions (stressful tasks; near threshold stimuli relatively high doses of caffeine). This complex pattern of interaction between the personality and arousal characteristics of the individual and the environmental conditions has been tested in many experiments on different types of performance from classical conditioning (Eysenck and Levey, 1972) to verbal ability (Revelle *et al.*, 1976).

Another relevant interacting variable emerged from work by Revelle, Humphreys, Simon, and Gilliland (1980). These authors confirmed that an extraversion sub-scale, EPI-impulsivity (Eysenck and Eysenck, 1964), had a relationship with performance as a function of the arousing effect of caffeine, but that this relationship also varied according to the time of day when subjects were tested. In the morning the performance of impulsives (extraverts) was improved by caffeine, whereas the performance of non-impulsives (introverts) was hindered; in the evening the non-impulsives (introverts) were facilitated in performance by caffeine, whereas the impulsives (extraverts) were hindered. A relationship between arousal and time of day has already been shown by Blake (1967, 1971): body temperature (an index of arousal) varied over the day with a different phase in introverts and extraverts (higher values in the morning for introverts than for extraverts, and higher values in the late afternoon for extraverts than introverts).

The effects of time of day on performance might be expected on the basis of the arousal model. As activation level changes throughout the day, according to a circadian sleep—wake cycle (Kleitman, 1963), daily variations in performance relating to arousal might also be postulated. Moreover, because remarkable individual differences were known to exist in circadian cycles, individual differences in performance related to daily variations of arousal might also be expected.

In the mid 1970s, a large number of empirical data began to be collected in the field of individual differences in the circadian system and their relevance to arousal theories of personality. Early research on the human sleep—wake cycle (Kleitman, 1963) has suggested that two main types exist (morning and evening types, with an intermediate type between the two extremes. Differences in physiological variables (such as body temperature) and behavioural variables (such as accuracy in attention tasks) were described, and morning types were found to usually have the peak earlier than the evening types. Using the Morningness—Eveningness Questionnaire (MEQ), developed by Horne and Östberg (1976), many comparisons were made between morningness—eveningness and introversion—extraversion continuums. Generally it was found that evening types tend to have higher extraversion scores than morning types (for a review see Kerkhof, 1985). Also, relationships with the other scales of the Eysenck Personality Questionnaire (EPQ; Eysenck and Eysenck, 1976) were described by Mecacci, Zani, Rocchetti, and Lucioli (1986): morning types were found to have higher neuroticism scores, and evening types higher psychoticism scores (this latter result was confirmed by Matthews, 1988). Nevertheless, caution should be exercised in studying circadian typology in relation to personality profiles by means of the MEQ. A set of studies has recently shown that significant differences in the distribution of MEQ scores are found when samples different for age and profession are compared: (1) a significant shift toward a morningness typology with age and the disappearance of eveningness (Mecacci *et al.*, 1986); (2) a shift toward morningness in workers with a regular morning work schedule (Meccaci and Zani, 1983); and (3) morningness and eveningness preferences in athletes practising disciplines normally performed at different times of day (Zani *et al.*, 1984).

Since on the whole, circadian typology turns out to be affected by at least two main factors (age and daily habitual activity), investigation of the relationships between circadian typology, personality, and performance should firstly consider that diurnal variation differentiates both within a single sample and between samples that are different for age and habitual activity. In stressful conditions, such as in shift work, these variables interact significantly and morning and evening types, probably because of their different personality, show different coping mechanisms (Colquhoun and Folkard, 1978). Another subject variable is sex, which has never been found to be significantly related to either circadian or introversion—extraversion typology (Kerkhof, 1985). However, in recent work Mecacci, Scaglione, and Vitrano (1991) have shown that sex effects may emerge when morning and evening types are compared in both their diurnal and monthly variations, probably in relation to the physiological and behavioural variations linked to the menstrual cycle in females.

Finally, the relationships between arousal, personality, and cognition is further complicated by task variables. While previously reference was made to the arousing or stressful effects of external stimuli in terms of their physical properties (such as intensity), we now have to consider the kind of information processing which is involved in the task. This question was clearly elucidated by Humphreys and Revelle (1984) on the basis of a set of results showing that performance in tasks which required rapid and sustained information transfer was facilitated by arousal, whereas the performance in tasks which required storage or retrieval of information in memory was hindered by arousal (Folkard, 1975, 1990). Since arousal effects vary throughout the day, it is evident that the interaction arousal—time of day—task might be found (Craig *et al.*, 1987; Revelle *et al.*, 1987). It is evident that this interaction should be further related to the circadian typology of subjects, as was shown in several studies (such as Adan, 1991; Horne *et al.*, 1980; Kerkhof, 1985; Wilson, 1990).

Individuals' performance is hence the interactive output of different factors, both internal and external to the individual. Internal factors are represented by: (1) the arousability of the subject, a general property of his or her nervous system which has a strong biological foundation and is reflected in temperament more than in personality (Rusalov, 1979; Strelau, 1983; see also Strelau and Plomin, Chapter 12 in this volume); and (2) the cognitive architecture of his or her mind, which is less biologically founded and which depends partly on information exchange between the mind and the environment. From a physiological point of view, temperament and cognitive architecture involve the activity of different, integrated sub-systems of the brain, which on the whole develop its functioning in relation to the demands of the natural and, in particular, the socio-cultural environment (Mecacci, 1984).

Brain activity and personality

As was mentioned above, research on brain activity and personality was carried out later than research on autonomic functions. In the 1950s and 1960s, the psychophysiology of emotions and affective dimensions of behaviour stressed the role of autonomic nervous system in both normal and pathological conditions. Brain activity, as might be detected by means of electroencephalographic (EEG) procedures, was considered less relevant. Some studies focused on the relationship between EEG rhythms, especially the alpha rhythm, and personality profiles. The main objective in this kind of research was the attempt at finding a direct link between the EEG data and the personality profile. This was attempted without having a clear and systematic hypothesis as to the physiological bases (here electrical output) to be considered as involved in personality structure. New perspectives emerged at the end of the 1960s with the growth of computerized electrophysiology, in particular of event-related potentials (ERP). The advantage of ERP techinques was the possibility of correlating personality parameters with different components, each linked to different stages of information processing. In this way, links between personality and cognition might be searched for on a more founded physiological basis. New trends of investigation seem to be bound to develop with the recent introduction in psychophysiology of other techniques such as Positron Emission Tomography (Haier _et al._, 1987), the measurement of regional cerebral flood (Rosadini _et al._, 1991). and dynamic brain mapping (Itil _et al._, 1991).

A first set of results concerns the correlation between the amplitude of auditory ERP and introversion—extraversion. Larger amplitudes were often found in introverts than extraverts and the interpretation was given in terms of higher levels of cortical excitation in the former (Stelmack and Michaud-Achorn, 1985; Stelmack _et al._, 1977). This finding is akin to the difference in ERP amplitude described for other typological dimensions on a number of sensory modalities. Larger amplitudes were found in augmenters than reducers (Buchsbaum and Pfefferbaum, 1971; Buchsbaum _et al._, 1983); in sensation seekers than sensation avoiders (Zuckerman, 1987); in weak than in strong types (Rusalov, 1979; and in high-impulsive than low-impulsive subjects (Barratt and Patton, 1983). Since it has been found that these dimensions correlated with each other and with the introversion—extraversion dimension, ERP results would show a general and common trend to differentiate physiologically between two main types of subject in correlation with their personality or temperament characteristics. Moreover, as differences in amplitude are found specifically for the early components related to the first stages of sensory input processing, and this processing is affected by activation levels, ERP results may indeed give physiological support to the arousal model of personality. According to the model of extraversion developed by Brebner and Cooper (1974, 1978, 1985), central processes concerned with the analysis of stimuli have to be differentiated from those involved in response organization. Extreme introverts are supposed to be characterized by the deriving of excitation from stimulus analysis and inhibition from response organization, whereas extreme extraverts are supposed to be inhibited by stimulus analysis and excited by response organization. In this perspective, differences in ERP amplitudes would be associated with stimulus analysis and the results of larger amplitude in introverts (and related types) would be coherent with the hypothesis of their higher level of arousal.

Another important direction of research regards the morphological characteristics of ERPs in psychopathological disorders. Two disorders have been particularly investigated: infantile autism and schizophrenia.

In autistic children ERPs were found to have morphological abnormalities related to deficits in information filtering and processing, and in sustained and selective attention (Courchesne _et al._, 1984; Courchesne _et al._, 1985; Niwa _et al._, 1983; Oades _et al._, 1988, 1990; Ornitz, 1985; Pritchard, 1986; Pritchard _et al._, 1987).

Similar findings were obtained in schizophrenic subjects: (1) reduction of ERP amplitude (according to these results, schizophrenic subjects should be reducers, as Schooler _et al._, 1976, confirm; but see the critical remarks by Prescott _et al._, 1984); (2) reduced selective attention, associated with smaller amplitudes of N100 or Nd components (Baribeau-Braun _et al._, 1983); (3) delay in evaluating operations of stimulus sequences associated with abnormalities in the amplitude of the P300 component and other late components (Raine and Venables, 1988; Roth _et al._, 1980); (4) different topographic distributions of ERP values in normal and schizophrenic subjects, the latter having a 'focal cortical arousal' in the left hemisphere (Morihisa and Duffy, 1986; Shagass and Roemer, 1991); (5) abnormalities of hemispheric lateralization of ERPs during cognitive tasks (Kemali *et al.*, 1991). According to Raine (1989a), psychopaths might be differentiated from schizophrenics on the basis of ERP data, showing that the former have patterns typical of augmenters and schizophrenics have patterns typical of reducers (see the remarks by Howard, 1989; Jutai, 1989; Raine, 1989b). On the whole, ERP results in psychiatric patients show abnormalities particularly in the early stages of information processing and in attention control, in strict independence of the arousal modulation and hemispheric functional specialization (see further a more detailed model of physiological bases of psychiatric disorders).

Although the above-mentioned ERP research presents many relevant data which permit one to go deeper into the relation between personality and cognition from a physiological point of view, some reservations should be made. First, in this kind of psychophysiology of personality, ERP data are considered a hard and sound index in comparison to the weakness of personality data, just because they are brain-based physiological responses coming out from the brain. Usually, more methodological attention is given to the definition of psychological and psychometric instruments than to the methodological accuracy of ERP techniques. This point was made by Connolly and Gruzelier (1986) in relation to the differences in ERP amplitude between augmenters and reducers, showing relevant methodological flaws in currently used methodology. The most serious flaw is found when a small range of values of some physical parameters of the stimulus (such as intensity) is used and the comparison between subjects is limited to this restricted range. A more fruitful and less equivocal approach consists in a within- or mixed-subject design with a large range of values to be tested in the same individual, and in the comparison between the individual trends of electrophysiological responses.

Second, individual differences in ERP amplitude and latency might depend on physiological parameters which are not necessarily related to the individual personality. To illustrate this point, a hint will suffice at the daily variation in ERP amplitude and latency, and at their individual differences. When ERPs are recorded throughout the day, a decrease in amplitude is generally recorded, faster for the morning than for the evening types (Kerkhof, 1985). Also short-term variations (cycle periods shorter than 20-minute periods) were observed in our research (Mecacci, unpublished data) and appear to be linked to time of day and individual circadian typology. For this reason, some between-subject differences might depend on the time of day at which subjects are tested and to what extent their circadian typology accommodates, more than on a substantial physiological organization permanently fixed throughout the day and constantly correlated with personality dimensions.

Finally, it is worth noting that all the results on the relationship between ERP and personality are generally based on groups of subjects chosen according to their extreme positions on a personality dimension evaluated by means of psychometric instruments (for example, introverts vs. extraverts according to the EPQ). Then, ERP data of the two extreme groups are compared to substantiate their personality differences physiologically. However, an opposite way of subject sampling might be chosen: two extreme groups might be represented by those who have, for instance, ERP amplitude at least two standard deviations below and above the whole sample mean, or two different trends of ERP amplitude over the day; then their personality scores should be compared. A similar type of approach is examined in the next section with regard to autonomic parameters. As we have observed in Mecacci's preliminary research, the correspondence between the results obtained through the two ways of subject sampling is not substantial.

These remarks concerning ERP research lead to the general conclusion that the physiological and psychometric approaches to individual differences in personality are not mutually complementary and that psychophysiological correlations should be cautiously interpreted as evidence of a common causal substrate. If the individual personality emerges from a set of different factors (physiological, cognitive, and social), it is more likely that physiological correlates may be significantly found for different and separate sub-systems than for the personality system as a whole.

Autonomic activity, habituation, arousal and anxiety

Turning to the autonomic nervous system, *habituation* has been one of the more widely investigated indices. Habituation is relevant to theories of extraversion—introversion, where in the case of Eysenck (1967) the dimension was posited to reflect a cortical excitation—inhibition dimension, and, as conceptualized earlier (Eysenck, 1957; Martin, 1960), extraverts generate more reactive inhibition and habituate or learn to stop responding more quickly than introverts. Habituation is also relevant to theories that link arousal to sub-cortical relationships; for example, the association of anxiety with high tonic arousal of sub-cortical systems (Claridge, 1967).

O'Gorman (1977) has provided a thorough review of relationships between habituation and normal personality, and concluded that extraversion provided the stronger relationship with habituation, so that extraverts habituate more quickly than introverts. These conclusions were based on personality measures such as the Taylor Manifest Anxiety Scale or similar scales, and with habituation measured by electrodermal activity, which has been the preferred measure in so far as it records sympathetic activity and is not so susceptible to contamination by parasympathetic activity as are cardiovascular measures. While relationships with anxiety and habituation have often been reported, these have not been as consistent as the relationship with extraversion. Nevertheless, clinical anxiety is frequently associated with retarded habituation (Lader and Wing, 1966).

Subsequently, brain lateralization has been included in considerations of central mechanisms and personality as well as habituation. Rate of habituation of electrodermal orienting responses in three experiments ($N = 109$) correlated with lateral asymmetries in the amplitude of the responses; a relationship was also found between the number of non-specific responses occurring in the inter-stimulus intervals and their lateral response amplitude asymmetries (Gruzelier *et al.*, 1981). The direction of the relationship was such that with fast habituation, responses were larger on the left hand than the right; as habituation became slower, responses were symmetrical; while at the slowest rates of habituation, the asymmetry reversed. Scatterplots indicated that there were many individuals who did not obey the relationship; consideration of these disclosed important individual differences. Female subjects and sinistrals, both of whom are thought to show more equipotentiality of hemispheric function, were among the outliers. Anxiety was another factor, and is considered below.

Consideration of whether the direction of the correlations between rate of habituation and unilateral response amplitudes was positive or negative could shed light on the question of whether hemispheric influences on habituation were reciprocal, so that when tipped one way habituation was fast and when tipped the other habituation was slow, or alternatively whether control over habituation resided in one hemisphere. This analysis disclosed negative correlations with the left hand and positive correlations with the right hand, in support of a reciprocal control or imbalance model.

In view of evidence in support of the predominance of contralateral inhibitory influences on electrodermal responses in the passive state, the reciprocal hemispheric influences on rate of habituation were such that fast habituation was associated with left-hemisphere control and slow habituation with right-hemisphere control. As the orienting response represents a psychophysiological index of the focusing of attention on the source of stimulation, to what extent was the model consistent with evidence relating hemispheric specialization to modes of attention? Focused, selective attention has been associated with the left hemisphere as a requirement of sequential processing, while broad, vigilant attention is associated with the parallel-processing capabilities of the right hemisphere (Dimond, 1970; Dimond and Beaumont, 1973). The model relating rate of habituation and lateral asymmetries in electrodermal responses is therefore consistent with theories of cerebral laterality. It is also consistent with evidence relating electrodermal responsiveness to selective attention and vigilance (Crider and Augenbraun, 1975; Stern, 1966; Waters *et al.*, 1977).

Classical evidence has shown that relations between attention and performance may be disrupted through anxiety, taking the form of the inverted-U relationship between arousal/anxiety and performance. The possible effect of anxiety was examined in our data by sub-dividing the larger sample ($N = 62$) into those who were fast or moderate habituators and those who were slow habituators (Gruzelier, 1987). Anxiety scores on the IPAT and the STAI, as well as EPI neuroticism, were higher in slow habituators, but of greater interest was the sub-division of slow habituators into two groups with opposite lateral asymmetries. Those with larger left-hand responses — namely, the anomalous group with asymmetries the same as fast habituators — had higher levels of anxiety than those slow habituators with the opposite asymmetry on IPAT sub-scales of frustration—tension whose descriptors included 'tense, frustrated, driven, overwrought', but differed most of all on the apprehension sub-scale with descriptors like 'apprehensive, self-reproaching, insecure, worrying and troubled'. We would argue that these sub-scales indicate

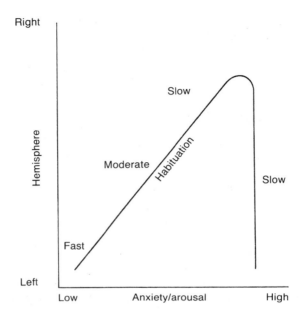

Figure 14.1 Habituation and electrodermal reactivity as a function of hemispheric activation and anxiety/arousal

a verbal cognitive component to anxiety in keeping with the direction of asymmetry in the electrodermal responses. No relationships were found with non-specific forms of anxiety such as those measured with the IPAT scales of emotional instability or low self-control.

The relationship between lateral asymmetry in electrodermal activity, rate of habituation, and individual differences in anxiety have the following implications for functional lateralization, shown schematically in Figure 14.1. Fast habituation and low anxiety reflect a dominance of left-hemispheric inhibition. The shift in excitation−inhibition balance seen in decreasing rates of habituation reflects a reversal in hemispheric influences, resulting in a dominance of right-hemispheric activation. Under states of high anxiety, control may revert to the left hemisphere without influencing the exitation−inhibition balance, which remains in a state of excitation, as reflected in slow habituation. The dominance of excitation, a state out of keeping with left-sided inhibition, may overload the capacity of left-hemispheric structural processes. The schema in Figure 14.1 is the familiar inverted-U relationship between arousal/anxiety and performance, mapped on to brain lateralization. The behavioural disorganization which characterizes over-arousal and the down-swing of the inverted-U is depicted as a consequence of the shift in hemispheric control to the left hemisphere that occurs with high states of arousal−excitation. Predictions follow as to individual differences in the quality of anxiety according to the asymmetry in activational dominance. A left-hemisphere dominance underlies cognitive, ruminative forms of anxiety, whereas a right-hemispheric dominance will underlie generalized, free-floating forms of anxiety.

This model was applied to results obtained with DSM III anxiety patients (Kopp and Gruzelier, 1989). Patients and controls were classified as low, medium or high in electrodermal reactivity, measured unilaterally. Functional lateralization was measured with bilateral auditory thresholds, Low-reactive patients exhibited right ear−left hemispheric activational dominance, as did the low-reactive normals. Patients with medium levels of reactivity showed the opposite, right-hemispheric activational dominance, as did reactive controls. However, reactive patients showed the same left-hemispheric activational dominance as the low reactives — in accordance with the schema in Figure 14.1.

There is growing evidence for the importance of cerebral functional lateralization in individual differences in anxiety. Tucker, Stenislie, and Barnhardt (1978) obtained evidence in high-trait anxious students which they interpreted as exemplifying a processing load on the left hemisphere; they exhibited a right-ear advantage in loudness judgments, indicative of greater left-hemispheric activation, whereas low-anxious subjects showed the opposite asymmetry. The effect in the high-anxious group coincided with poorer processing in the left than right hemisphere in divided visual-field tachistoscope tasks. Gruzelier and Phelan (1991) showed complementary effects as a result of state anxiety in students before an exam. Students were examined twice in a counterbalanced design, once before an exam and once four weeks before or after, on a less stressful occasion. Frustration−tension scores on the IPAT were raised before the exam and electrodermal activity showed slower habituation and more non-specific responses before the exam. In addition, the expected left-hemisphere advantage in verbal processing in the divided visual-field task which was found in the non-stressful condition before the exam was replaced by a right-hemisphere advantage. Studies of brain bloodflow in normals and patients have shown that raised levels of metabolism in right frontal and parahippocampal regions are associated with anxiety (Reiman *et al.*, 1984; Reivich *et al.*, 1983).

Functional cerebral laterality and psychotic syndromes

Imbalances in hemispheric activity have also been found relevant to individual differences in the expression of psychotic symptoms. Undrugged schizophrenic patients were classified into two groups on the basis of lateral asymmetries in electrodermal orienting responses (Gruzelier and Manchanda, 1982). Those with an asymmetry indicative of left-hemispheric activation were characterized on psychiatric ratings by positive symptoms such as delusions, cognitive acceleration, positive affect, and behavioural overactivity, while those with an imbalance indicative of raised right-hemispheric activation and lowered left-hemispheric activation were characterized by negative symptoms such as social and emotional withdrawal, blunted affect, motor retardation, and poverty of speech. The two syndromes appeared at opposite poles of an arousal dimension. Other psychotic symptoms, such as auditory hallucinations and passivity experiences, did not distinguish the groups, and thereby comprised a third syndrome independent of the other two. Liddle (1987; see also Liddle and Barnes, 1990, Liddle *et al.*, 1989), on the basis of a factor analysis of mostly chronic patients, has also described three syndromes with a somewhat similar character, notably the negative syndrome, to the above model.

Other measures of functional cerebral laterality have produced evidence in support of opposite states of hemispheric imbalance in two schizophrenic syndromes having close affinities with those delineated with the electrodermal measure. These included measures of EEG power, the contingent negative variation, cortical evoked potentials, the recovery curve of the Hoffman reflex to somatosensory stimulation, lateral eye movements, dichotic listening, visual search, auditory thresholds, brain metabolism and bloodflow, and a number of neuropsychological tests (see Gruzelier, 1983, 1984, 1985, 1989). Further work has shown that losses of cognitive function, as on tests of recognition memory, reside largely in the less-activated hemisphere: the right in the active syndrome characterized by delusions and positive symptoms, the left, in the withdrawn syndrome. Important in the context of this chapter is the fact that consideration of the nature of the symptoms delineated by the lateral asymmetries, in the light of contemporary neuropsychology, may not only provide validation of the syndromes, but offer an exemplar for further work in the area.

There is much evidence to support the link between polarity of mood states and the laterality of frontolimbic systems (Sackheim *et al.*, 1982) with the expression of positive affect arising from left-sided systems and the expression of negative affect from right-sided systems. Here the raised mood of the active syndrome is consistent with this evidence, as is the negative, blunted affect of the withdrawn syndrome. Similarly, pressure of speech and increased rate of cognitive activity, associated with the active syndrome, are consistent with raised activity in left-hemispheric linguistic and speech-production systems, whereas the converse is true of poverty of speech, a component of the withdrawn syndrome. Finally, raised levels of behavioural activity contrasted with motor retardation and withdrawal, the behavioural dimension giving rise to the labels *active* and *withdrawn*, are in keeping with the theory of hemispheric specialization which posits that the left hemisphere controls approach behaviour while the right is receptive and passive, and controls withdrawal (Tucker and Williamson, 1984).

Research on personality differences and temporal lobe epilepsy also exemplifies this neuropsychological strategy. Bear and Fedio (1977) suggest that in seizure disorders like temporal-lobe epilepsy, hyperconnections develop over time between limbic and cortical regions, and accentuate neuropsychological functions. They found that patients with left-sided seizures display exaggerated intellectualization and hyper-religiosity, and tend to be ideational rather than emotional. Patients with right-sided seizures, in contrast, were emotionally labile.

Hemispheric imbalance, arousal, and syndromes of schizotypy

Evidence for a genetic component to the aetiology of schizophrenia has contributed to a dimensional view that posits a continuity between the disorder and a sub-clinical predisposition in the normal population, a predisposition that may provide markers of the disorder (Claridge, 1985, 1987). Factor analytic studies have disclosed three-factor solutions of schizotypy scales (Bentall *et al.*, 1989). We investigated possible affinities between the three-syndrome model of schizophrenia and the three-factor structure of schizotypy (Gruzelier *et al.*, in press). An affinity seemed probable on the basis of a review of the literature, which also covered evidence of cerebral asymmetries of function in schizotypy (Gruzelier, 1990). The Raine Schizotypy scale was chosen because it comprehensively covers all nine of the components of DSM-III-R schizotypy: ideas of reference, odd beliefs, unusual perceptual experiences, eccentricity, odd speech, suspiciousness, social anxiety, no close friends, and inappropriate/constricted affect (Raine, in press). The Thayer (1967) Activation–Deactivation checklist was included, as activation appears as an underlying dimension of the active and withdrawn schizophrenic syndromes. Cerebral asymmetries of function were examined with a recognition memory test of words and faces which had shown in schizophrenic syndromes poorer word–left-hemisphere than faces–right-hemisphere memory in the withdrawn syndrome and the opposite effect in the active syndrome (Gruzelier, 1990).

The investigation showed that there was a three-factor structure to schizotypy, and that the three factors had a strong affinity with both the three-factor schizotypical personality structure obtained by Bentall, Claridge, and Slade (1989) and the three-syndrome model of schizophrenia. The first factor included the scales of no close friends, social anxiety, and inappropriate/constricted affect, in keeping with the withdrawn syndrome in schizophrenia. The other two were positive syndrome factors, one consisting of odd speech and eccentricity and the other of unusual perceptual experiences, odd beliefs, ideas of reference, and suspiciousness. Sub-division of dextral subjects on the basis of word–face recognition memory discrepancy scores resulted in evidence of withdrawn syndrome features in those with a faces memory advantage, whereas those with a word advantage had active syndrome features. Results with the Activation–Deactivation checklist were also consistent with the model. High activation was associated with both active syndrome features and word-memory advantages, while general deactivation was associated with the withdrawn syndrome and faces-memory advantages. Additional validation was provided through a single case study of a student who presented with an extreme face–word discrepancy score and subsequently became schizophrenic, presenting with the withdrawn and non-lateralized clinical syndromes.

Thus, evidence was provided for considering the importance of schizotypal personality as syndromal rather than as a homogeneous construct, and close parallels were found between syndromes in schizotypal personality and syndromes in schizophrenia. Relationships were demonstrated between both arousal and imbalances in hemispheric function, and specific syndromes of schizotypal personality, predicted on the basis of hemisphere-imbalance/syndrome relationships in schizophrenia.

Conclusion

These are preliminary steps in seeking relationships between brain function and personality. When Powell (1979) wrote his monograph on *Brain and Personality*, he commented on the neglect of this field, in saying that Luria (1966), for one, did not mention the term, yet Hecaen (1964) reported that at least 21 per cent of cerebral tumour cases suffer some kind of personality change, while Lishman (1968) found that 87 per cent of penetration injuries coexisted with some degree of personality impairment. Currently, the interrelationships between mood and cognition are coming to the fore, through evidence of the importance of these relationships in neuropsychological investigations of HIV infection. Perhaps one small benefit of this catastrophic illness will be to awaken interest in this still neglected field.

References

Adan, A. (1991), 'Influence of morningness—eveningness preference in the relationship between body temperature and performance: a diurnal study', *Personality and Individual Differences*, **12**, 1159–61.

Baribeau-Braun, J., Picton, T.W., and Gosselin, J. (1983), 'Schizophrenia: a neurophysiological evaluation of abnormal information processing', *Science*, **219**, 874–6.

Barratt, E.S., and Patton, J.H. (1983), 'Impulsivity: cognitive, behavioural, and psychophysiological correlates', in M. Zuckerman (ed.), *Biological Basis of Sensation Seeking, Impulsivity and Anxiety*, Hillsdale, NJ: Erlbaum, pp. 77–116.

Bear, D.M., and Fedio, P. (1977), 'Quantitative analysis of interictal behavior in temporal lobe epilepsy', *Archives of Neurology*, **34**, 454–67.

Bentall, P., Claridge, G.S., and Slade, P.D. (1989), 'The multidimensional nature of schizotypal traits: a factor analytical study with normal subjects', *British Journal of Clinical Psychology*, **28**, 363–75.

Berlyne, D.E. (1960), *Conflict, Arousal, and Curiosity*, New York, NY: McGraw-Hill.

Blake, M.J.F. (1967), 'Relationship between circadian rhythm of body temperature and introversion—extraversion', *Nature*, **215**, 896–7.

Blake, M.J.F. (1971), 'Temperament and time of day', in W.P. Colquhoun (ed.), *Biological Rhythms and Human Performance*, London: Academic Press, pp. 109–48.

Brebner, J., and Cooper, C. (1974), 'The effect of a low rate of regular signals upon the reaction times of introverts and extraverts', *Journal of Research in Personality*, **8**, 263–76.

Brebner, J., and Cooper, C. (1978), 'Stimulus- or response-induced excitation', *Journal of Research in Personality*, **12**, 306–11.

Brebner, J., and Cooper, C. (1985), 'A proposed unified model of extraversion', in J.T. Spence and E. Izard (eds.), *Motivation, Emotion, and Personality*, Amsterdam: North-Holland, pp. 219–29.

Buchsbaum, M.S., and Pfefferbaum, A. (1971), 'Individual differences in stimulus intensity response', *Psychophysiology*, **8**, 600–11.

Buchsbaum, M.S., Haier, R.J. and Johnson, J. (1983), 'Augmenting and reducing: individual differences in evoked potentials', in A. Gale and J.A. Edwards (eds.), *Physiological Correlates of Human Behavior: Individual differences and psychopathology*, London: Academic Press, vol. 3, pp. 120–38.

Claridge, G.S. (1967), *Personality and Arousal*, Oxford: Pergamon.

Claridge, G.S. (1985), *Origins of Mental Illness*, Oxford: Basil Blackwell.

Claridge, G.S. (1987), 'The schizophrenias as nervous types — revisited', *British Journal of Psychiatry*, **151**, 735–43.

Colquhoun, P., and Folkard, S. (1978), 'Personality differences in body-temperature rhythm, and their relation to its adjustment to night work', *Ergonomics*, **21**, 811–17.

Connolly, J.F., and Gruzelier, J.H. (1986), 'Persistent methodological problems with evoked potential augmenting—reducing', *International Journal of Psychophysiology*, **3**, 299–306.

Courchesne, E. (1985), 'Event-related potentials correlates of the processing of novel visual and auditory information in autism', *Journal of Autism and Developmental Disorders*, **15**, 55–76.

Courchesne, E., Kilman, B.A., Galambos, R., and Lincoln, A.J. (1984), 'Autism: cognitive processing of novel information measured by event-related potentials', *Electroencephalography and Clinical Neurophysiology*, **59**, 238–48.

Courchasne, E., Lincoln, A.J., Kilman, B.A., and Galambos, R. (1985), 'Autism: processing of novel auditory information assessed by event-related brain potentials', *Journal of Autism and Developmental Disorders*, **15**, 55–76.

Craig, A., Davies, D.R., and Matthews, G. (1987), 'Diurnal variation, task characteristics, and vigilance performance', *Human Factors*, **29**, 675–84.

Crider, A., and Augenbraun, C.B. (1975), 'Auditory vigilance correlates of electrodermal response habituation speed', *Psychophysiology*, **12**, 36–40.

Dimond, S.J. (1970), *Neuropsychology*, London: Butterworths.

Dimond, S.J., and Beaumont, J.G. (1973), 'Difference in vigilance performance of the right and left hemisphere', *Cortex*, **9**, 259–65.

Duffy, E. (1951), 'The concept of energy mobilization', *Psychological Review*, **58**, 30–40.

Duffy, E. (1962), *Activation and Behavior*, New York, NY: Wiley.

Endler, N.S. (1989), 'The temperamental nature of personality', *European Journal of Personality*, **3**, 151–65.

Eysenck, H.J. (1947), *Dimensions of Personality*, London: Routledge & Kegan Paul.

Eysenck, H.J. (1957), *The Dynamics of Anxiety and Hysteria*, London: Routledge & Kegan Paul.

Eysenck, H.J. (1967), *The Biological Basis of Personality*, Springfield, IL: Charles C. Thomas.

Eysenck, H.J., and Eysenck, M.W. (1985), *Personality and Individual Differences: A natural science approach*, New York, NY: Plenum Press.

Eysenck, H.J., and Eysenck, S.B.G. (1964), *Eysenck Personality Inventory*, San Diego, CA: Educational and Industrial Testing Service.

Eysenck, H.J., and Eysenck, S.B.G. (1976), *Eysenck Personality Questionnaire*, San Diego, CA: Educational and Industrial Testing Service.

Eysenck, H.J., and Levey, A. (1972), 'Conditioning, introversion—extraversion and the strength of the nervous system', in V.D. Nebylitsyn and J.A. Gray (eds.), *Biological Bases of Behavior*, New York, NY: Academic Press, pp. 206–20.

Eysenck, M.W. (1982), *Attention and Arousal: Cognition and performance*, New York, NY: Springer.

Fahrenberg. J. (1967), *Psychophysiologische Persönlichkeitsforschung* [Psychophysiological Research in Personality], Göttingen: Hogrefe.

Folkard, S. (1975), 'Diurnal variation in logical reasoning', *British Journal of Psychology*, **66**, 1–8.

Folkard, S. (1990), 'Circadian performance rhythms: some practical and theoretical implications', *Philosophical Transactions of the Royal Society*, London, B327, 543–53.

Gale, A. (1987), 'Postscript: arousal, control, energetics and values — an attempt at review and appraisal', in J. Strelau and H.J. Eysenck (eds), *Personality Dimensions and Arousal*, New York: Plenum Press, pp. 287—316.

Gray, J.A. (ed.) (1964), *Pavlov's Typology*, Oxford: Pergamon.

Gray, J.A. (1982), *The Neuropsychology of Anxiety*, Oxford: Clarendon Press.

Gruzelier, J.H. (1983), 'Left- and right-sided dysfunction in psychosis: implications for electroencephalographic measure', *Psychiatry*, **13**, 192—5.

Gruzelier, J.H. (1984), 'Hemispheric imbalances in schizophrenia, *International Journal of Psychophysiology*, **1**, 227—40.

Gruzelier, J.H. (1985), 'Schizophrenia: central nervous system signs in schizophrenia', in J.A.M. Frederick (ed.), *Handbook of Clinical Neurology. Vol. 2: Neurobehavioural Disorders*, Amsterdam: Elsevier, pp. 481—521.

Gruzelier, J.H. (1987), 'Cerebral laterality and schizophrenia: a review of the inter-hemispheric disconnection hypothesis', in A. Glass (ed.), *Individual Differences in Hemispheric Specialisation*, London: Plenum, pp. 301—30.

Gruzelier, J.H. (1989), 'Lateralization and central mechanisms in clinical psychophysiology', in G. Turpin (ed.), *Handbook of Clinical Psychophysiology*, New York, NY: Wiley, pp. 135—74.

Gruzelier, J.H. (1990), 'Brain localisation and neuropsychology in schizophrenia: syndrome and neurodevelopmental implications', in H. Hafner and W.F. Gattaz (eds.), *Search for the Causes of Schizophrenia*, Berlin-Heidelberg: Springer-Verlag, vol. 2, pp. 301—20.

Gruzelier, J.H., and Flor-Henry, P. (eds.) (1980), *Hemisphere Asymmetries of Functions in Psychopathology*, New York, NY: Elsevier.

Gruzelier, J.H., and Manchanda, R. (1982), 'The syndrome of schizophrenia: relations between electrodermal response, lateral asymmetries and clinical ratings', *British Journal of Psychiatry*, **141**, 688—95.

Gruzelier, J.H., Eves, F.F., and Connolly, J.F. (1981), 'Habituation and phasic reactivity in the electrodermal system: reciprocal hemispheric influences', *Physiological Psychology*, **9**, 313—17.

Gruzelier, J.H., Burgess, A., Stygall, J., Gillian, I., and Raine, A. (in press), 'Hemisphere imbalance and syndromes of schizotypal personality'.

Haier, J.R., Sokolski, K., Katz, M., and Buchsbaum, M.S. (1987), 'The study of personality with Positron Emission Tomography', in J. Strelau and H.J. Eysenck (eds.), *Personality Dimensions and Arousal*, New York, NY, and London: Plenum Press, pp. 251—67.

Hebb, D.O. (1955), 'Drives and the C.N.S. (Conceptual Nervous System)', *Psychological Review*, **62**, 243—54.

Hecaen, H. (1964), 'Mental symptoms associated with tumors of the frontal lobe', in J.M. Warren and K. Akert (eds.), *The Frontal Granular Cortex and Behavior*, New York, NY: McGraw-Hill, pp. 335—52.

Horne, J.A., and Östberg, O. (1976), 'A self-assessment questionnaire to determine morningness—eveningness in human circadian rhythms', *International Journal of Chronobiology*, **4**, 97—110.

Horne, J.A., Brass, C.G., and Petitt, A.N. (1980), 'Circadian performance differences between morning and evening "types"', *Ergonomics*, **23**, 29—36.

Howard, R. (1989), 'Evoked potentials and psychopathy: a commentary on Raine', *International Journal of Psychophysiology*, **8**, 23—37.

Humphreys, M.S., and Revelle, W. (1984), 'Personality, motivation, and performance: a theory of the relationship between individual differences and information processing', *Psychological Review*, **91**, 153—84.

Itil, T.M., Mucci, A., and Eralp, E. (1991), 'Dynamic brain mapping methodology and application', *International Journal of Psychophysiology*, **10**, 281—91.

Jutai, J.W. (1989), 'Psychopathy and P3 amplitude: a commentary on Raine', *International Journal of Psychophysiology*, **8**, 17—22.

Kemali, D., Galderisi, S., Maj, M., Mucci, A., and Di Gregorio, M. (1991), 'Lateralization patterns of event-related potentials and performance indices in schizophrenia: relationship to clinical state and neuroleptic treatment', *International Journal of Psychophysiology*, **10**, 225–30.

Kerkhof, G.A. (1985), 'Inter-individual differences in the human circadian system: a review', *Biological Psychology*, **20**, 83–112.

Kleitman, N. (1963), *Sleep and Wakefulness*, Chicago, IL: University of Chicago Press.

Kopp, M., and Gruzelier, J.H. (1989), 'Electrodermally differentiated subgroups of anxiety patients and controls. II: Relationships with auditory, somatosensory and pain thresholds, agoraphobic fear, depression and cerebral laterality', *International Journal of Psychophysiology*, **5**, 65–75.

Lacey, J.I. (1967), 'Somatic response patterning and stress: some revisions of activation theory', in M.H. Appley and R. Trumbull (eds.), *Psychological Stress: Issues in research*, New York, NY: Appleton-Century-Crofts, pp. 14–56.

Lader, M.H., and Wing, I. (1966), *Psychological Measures, Sedative Drugs and Morbid Anxiety*, London: Oxford University Press.

Liddle, P.F. (1987), 'Schizophrenic syndromes, cognitive performance and neurological dysfunction', *Psychological Medicine*, **17**, 49–57.

Liddle, P.F., and Barnes, T.R. (1990), 'Syndromes of chronic schizophrenia', *British Journal of Psychiatry*, **157**, 558–61.

Liddle, P.F., Barnes, T.R. Morris, D., and Hague, S. (1989), 'Three syndromes in chronic schizophrenia', Symposium on Negative Symptoms in Schizophrenia, *British Journal of Psychiatry*, **155**, (supplement 7), 119–220.

Lindsley, D.B. (1960), 'Attention, consciousness, sleep and wakefulness', in J. Field (ed.), *Handbook of Physiology. Section: Neurophysiology*, vol. 3, pp. 1553–93.

Lishman, W.A. (1968), 'Brain damage in relation to psychiatric disability after head injury', *British Journal of Psychiatry*, **114**, 373–410.

Luria, A.R. (1966), *Higher Cortical Functions in Man*, London: Tavistock Publications.

Luria, A.R. (1973), *The Working Brain*, Harmondsworth: Penguin.

Magoun, H.W. (1963), *The Waking Brain*, Springfield, IL: Charles C. Thomas.

Malmo, R.B. (1959), 'Activation: a neuropsychological dimension', *Psychological Review*, **66**, 367–86.

Mangan, G.L. (1982), *The Biology of Human Conduct: East–West models of temperament and personality*, Oxford: Pergamon.

Martin, I. (1960), 'The effects of depressant drugs on palmar skin resistance and adaptation', in H.J. Eysenck (ed.), *Experiments in Personality*, London: Routledge & Kegan Paul, vol. 1, pp. 197–220.

Matthews, G. (1988), 'Morningness–eveningness as a dimension of personality: trait, state, and psychophysiological correlates', *European Journal of Personality*, **2**, 277–93.

Mecacci, L. (1979), *Brain and History: The relationship between neurophysiology and psychology in the Soviet Union*, New York, NY: Brunner/Mazel.

Mecacci, L. (1984), 'Looking for the social and cultural dimension of the human brain', *International Journal of Psychophysiology*, **1**, 293–9.

Mecacci, L., and Zani, A. (1983), 'Morningness–eveningness preferences and sleep-waking diary data of morning and evening types in student and worker samples', *Ergonomics*, **26**, 1147–53.

Mecacci, L., Scaglione M.R., and Vitrano, I. (1991), 'Diurnal and monthly variations of temperature and self-reported activation in relation to sex and circadian typology', *Personality and Individual Differences*, **12**, 819–24.

Mecacci, L., Zani, A., Rocchetti, G., and Lucioli, R. (1986), 'The relationship between morningness–eveningness, aging and personality', *Personality and Individual Differences*, **7**, 911–13.

388/ *John H. Gruzelier and Luciano Mecacci*

Morihisa, J.M., and Duffy, F.H. (1986), 'Focal cortical arousal in the schizophrenics', in F.H. Duffy (ed.), *Topographic Mapping of Brain Electrical Activity*, Stoneham, MD: Butterworths, pp. 371—82.

Moruzzi, G., and Magoun, H.W. (1949), 'Brain stem reticular formation and activation of the EEG', *Electroencephalography and Clinical Neurophysiology*, **1**, 455—73.

Myrtek, M. (1984), *Constitutional Psychophysiology*, New York, NY: Academic Press.

Nebylitsyn, V.D. (1972a), *Fundamental Properties of the Human Nervous System*, New York, NY: Plenum Press.

Nebylitsyn, V.D. (1972b), 'The problem of general and partial properties of the nervous system', in V.D. Nebylitsyn and J.A. Gray (eds.), *Biological Bases of Behavior*, New York, NY: Academic Press, pp. 400—17.

Nebylitsyn, V.D., and Gray, J.A. (eds.) (1972), *Biological Bases of Behavior*, New York, NY: Academic Press.

Niwa, S., Ohta, M., and Yamazaki, K. (1983), 'P300 and stimulus evaluation process in autistic subjects', *Journal of Autism and Developmental Disorders*, **13**, 33—42.

Oades, R.D., Walker, M.K., Geffen, L.B., and Stern, L.M. (1988), 'Event-related potentials in autistic and healthy children on an auditory choice reaction time task', *International Journal of Psychophysiology*, **6**, 25—37.

Oades, R.D., Stern, L.M., Walker M.K., Clark, C.R., and Kapoor, V. (1990), 'Event-related potentials and monoamines in autistic children on a clinical trial of fenfluramine', *International Journal of Psychophysiology*, **8**, 197—212.

O'Gorman, J.G. (1977), 'Individual differences in habituation of human physiological responses: a review of theory, method, and findings in the study of personality correlates in non-clinical populations', *Biological Psychology*, **5**, 257—318.

Ornitz, E.M. (1985), 'Neurophysiology of infantile autism', *Journal of the American Academy of Child Psychiatry*, **24**, 251—62.

Powell, G.E. (1979), *Brain and Personality*, London: Saxon House.

Prescott, J., Connolly, J.F., and Gruzelier, J.H. (1984), 'Augmenting/reducing phenomena in the auditory evoked potential', *Biological Psychology*, **19**, 31—44.

Pritchard, W.S. (1986), 'Cognitive event-related potential correlates of schizophrenia', *Psychological Bulletin*, **100**, 43—66.

Pritchard, W.S., Raz, N. and August, G.J. (1987), 'Visual augmenting/reducing and P300 in autistic children', *Journal of Autism and Developmental Disorders*, **17**, 231—42.

Raine, A. (1989a), 'Evoked potentials and psychopathy', *International Journal of Psychophysiology*, **8**, 1—16.

Raine, A. (1989b), 'Evoked potential model of psychopathy: a critical evaluation', *International Journal of Psychophysiology*, **8**, 29—34.

Raine, A. (in press), 'The Schizotypal Personality Questionnaire (SPQ): a scale for the assessment of schizotypal personality based on DSM-III-R criteria', *Schizophrenia Bulletin* (in press).

Raine, A., and Venables, P.H. (1988), 'Enhanced P3 evoked potentials and longer P3 recovery time in psychopaths', *Psychophysiology*, **24**, 191—9.

Reiman, E.M., Raichle, M.E., and Butler, F.K. (1984), 'A focal brain abnormality in panic disorder, a severe form of anxiety', *Nature*, **310**, 683—5.

Reivich, M., Gur, R., and Alavi, A. (1983), 'Positron emission tomographic studies of sensory stimuli, cognitive processes and anxiety', *Human Neurobiology*, **2**, 25—33.

Revelle, W., Amaral, P., and Turiff, S. (1976), 'Introversion—extraversion, time stress, and caffeine: effect on verbal performance', *Science*, **192**, 149—50.

Revelle, W., Anderson, K.J., and Humphreys, M.S. (1987), 'Empirical tests and theoretical extensions of arousal-based theories of personality', in J. Strelau and H.J. Eysenck (eds.), *Personality Dimensions and Arousal*, New York, NY, and London: Plenum Press, pp. 17—36.

Revelle, W., Humphreys, M.S., Simon, L., and Gilliland, K. (1980), 'The interactive effect of personality, time of day, and caffeine: a test of the arousal model', *Journal of Experimental Psychology: General*, **109**, 1−31.

Rosadini, G., Cogorno, P., Marenco, S., Nobili, F., and Rodriguez, G. (1991), 'Brain functional imaging in senile psychopathology', *International Journal of Psychophysiology*, **8**, 271−80.

Roth, W.T., Pfefferbaum, A., Horvath, T.B., Berger, P.A., and Kopell, B.S. (1980), 'P3 reduction in auditory evoked potentials of schizophrenics', *Electroencephalography and Clinical Neurophysiology*, **49**, 497−505.

Rusalov, V.M. (1979), *Biological Bases of Individual-psychological Differences*, Moscow: Nauka (in Russian).

Rusalov, V.M. (1989), 'Object-related and communicative aspects of human temperament: a new questionnaire of the structure of temperament', *Personality and Individual Differences*, **10**, 817−27.

Sackeim, H.A., Gur, R.C., and Saucy, M.C. (1982), 'Functional brain asymmetry in the expression of positive and negative emotions: lateralization of insult in cases of uncontrollable emotional outbursts', *Archives of Neurology*, **39**, 210−18.

Schooler, C., Buchsbaum, M.S., and Carpenter, W.T. (1976), 'Evoked response and kinesthetic measures of augmenting/reducing in schizophrenics: replications and extensions', *Journal of Nervous and Mental Diseases*, **163**, 221−32.

Shagass, C., and Roemer, R. (1991), 'Evoked potential topography in unmedicated and medicated schizophrenics', *International Journal of Psychophysiology*, **10**, 213−24.

Skinner, B.F. (1938), *The Behavior of Organisms: An experimental analysis*, New York, NY: Appleton-Century-Crofts.

Stelmack, R.M., and Michaud-Achorn, A. (1985), 'Extraversion, attention, and habituation of the auditory evoked response', *Journal of Research in Personality*, **19**, 416−28.

Stelmack, R.M., Achorn, E., and Michaud, A. (1977), 'Extraversion and individual differences in auditory evoked response', *Psychophysiology*, **14**, 368−74.

Stern, R.M. (1966), 'Performance and psychological arousal during two vigilance tasks varying in signal presentation rate', *Perceptual and Motor Skills*, **23**, 691−700.

Strelau, J. (1983), *Temperament−Personality−Activity*, London: Academic Press.

Strelau, J. (1991), 'Are psychophysiological/psychophysical scores good candidates for diagnosing temperament/personality traits and for a demonstration of the construct validity of psychometrically measured traits?', *European Journal of Personality*, **5**, 323−42.

Strelau, J., and Eysenck, H.J. (eds.) (1987), *Personality Dimensions and Arousal*, New York, NY, and London: Plenum Press.

Stelau, J., Farley, F.H., and Gale, A. (eds.) (1985−6), *The Biological Bases of Personality and Behavior* (2 vols.), Washington, DC: Hemisphere.

Thayer, R.E. (1967), 'Measurement of activation through self-report', *Psychological Reports*, **20**, 663−78.

Tucker, D.M., and Williamson, P.A. (1984), 'Asymmetric neural control systems in human self-regulation', *Psychological Review*, **91**, 185−215.

Tucker, D.M., Antes, J.R., Stenislie, C.E., and Bernhardt, N. (1987), 'Anxiety and lateral cerebral functions', *Journal of Abnormal Psychology*, **87**, 380−83.

Waters, W.F., MacDonald, D.G., and Korenko, L. (1977), 'Habituation of the orienting response: a gating mechanism subserving selective attention', *Psychophysiology*, **14**, 228−36.

Wilson, G.D. (1990), 'Personality, time of day and arousal', *Personality and Individual Differences*, **11**, 158−68.

Zani, A., Rossi, B., Borriello, A., and Mecacci, L. (1984), 'Diurnal interindividual differences in the habitual activity pattern of top level athletes', *Journal of Sports Medicine and Physical Fitness*, **24**, 307−10.

Zuckerman, M. (1979), *Sensation Seeking: Beyond the optimal level of arousal*, Hillsdale, NJ: Erlbaum.

Zuckerman, M. (ed.) (1983), *Biological Bases of Sensation Seeking, Impulsivity and Anxiety*, Hillsdale, NJ: Erlbaum.

Zuckerman, M. (1987), 'A critical look at three arousal constructs in personality theories: optimal levels of arousal, strength of the nervous system, and sensitivities to signals of reward and punishment', in J. Strelau and H.J. Eysenck (eds.), *Personality Dimensions and Arousal*, New York, NY, and London: Plenum Press, pp. 217–31.

PART VII
The Interactionist Approach

15/ Models of person–situation interactions

Joop Hettema
Tilburg University, The Netherlands

Douglas T. Kenrick
Arizona State University, USA

Introduction

Vincent Van Gogh and Paul Gauguin both had a try at the business world before becoming painters. The extroverted and charming Gauguin was quite successful but left his high-paying job, the introverted and maladjusted Van Gogh was a failure and was fired by his own uncle. Despite their differences, both committed their later years to the frugal artistic life. Gauguin lived with a beautiful Polynesian woman, but left her, as he left other women. Van Gogh, on the other hand, lived with only one woman for a short time, but she left him to return to prostitution. The lives of these two men illustrate several aspects of person–environment interactions: each man had a different effect on the people around him, each man chose work and life environments that were somewhat different, and each man meshed differently with his social surrounds. The goal of this chapter is to describe the different types of person–environment interactions, and to show how they are, or can be, viewed from different theoretical perspectives.

This chapter will proceed in four general sections. First, we will briefly review the person–situation controversy. Next, we will review some of the proposed methodological solutions to problems raised by that controversy. Following this, we will delineate the different types of person–situation interaction. We will then consider how those interactions are treated from a biological and from a cognitive/social learning perspective, before, finally, we consider how a biosocial framework can integrate the different perspectives on persons, environments, and their interaction.

The person–situation controversy

Personality psychologists have always insisted that their subject should be viewed from the vantage of the entire functioning person in his or her natural habitat. Yet, the field has historically been divided into two disciplines. One describes persons, often using trait descriptions such as active or passive, dominant or submissive, aggressive or peaceful, extraverted or introverted. The other discipline refers to the same behavioural characteristics, but attributes them to the situation. Thus, some situations provoke activity, others passivity, some dominance, others submission, and so on. The two approaches reflect a more general antithesis within the field of psychology, variously described as clinical versus experimental (Dashiell, 1939), psychometric versus experimental (Bindra and Scheier, 1954), and correlational versus experimental (Cronbach, 1957). The 'two disciplines of scientific psychology' can be characterized by different origins, different theories, and different methods.

Most classical theories of personality originated either in the clinic or in the experimental laboratory. Clinically oriented theories (such as, Freud's, Rogers's, and Kelly's) have been derived from contacts with patients and are primarily concerned with how the characteristics of individuals contribute to their psychological adjustment. The theorists tend to adopt an organismic position, emphasizing the interrelatedness of everything the individual does, and the fact that each act he or she performs can only be understood against the background provided by his or her other acts. In these theories, the emphasis is on the total individual, the consistency of his or her behaviour across different situations, and stability over time.

Experimentally oriented theories, on the other hand, (such as, Watson's, Hull's, and Skinner's) are derived from laboratory studies in which behaviour is studied as a function of systematically manipulated environmental conditions. These theorists adhere to a field orientation that is primarily concerned with the inextricable unity between a given behavioural act and the environmental context in which it occurs. For a field-oriented psychologist, it makes little sense to try to understand a given form of behaviour without specifying in detail the field within which it occurs (cf. Hall and Lindzey, 1970). Experimental theories stress the plasticity of personality, the person's responsiveness to environmental conditions, and the situational specificity of the person's behaviour.

In the mid-sixties, the gap between these two viewpoints led to a reconsideration of the basis of the field of personality psychology (see also Forgas and Van Heck, Chapter 16 in this volume). Psychologists working in either the psychometric or the psychodynamic tradition came to realize that empirical findings generally failed to redeem the promises raised by carefully constructed models and sophisticated methodology. The behaviours of individuals in personality studies did not seem to manifest consistencies over time and over different situations that would have supported the organismic theories. The problem of trans-situational consistency, in particular, became the target of the critics.

Hartshorne and May's (1928) classic study of the nature of character seemed to some observers to provide a perfect example of the lack of consistency in behaviour. By means of self-reports and observations, those authors collected data concerning honesty in children in a number of different settings. While honesty demonstrated much consistency over situations as long as opinions were concerned, it proved to be less consistent with respect to overt behaviour as the situation changed more. A detailed replication by Nelsen, Grinder, and Mutterer (1969) showed essentially the same results: only 35—43 per cent of the total variance in the correlation matrix could be accounted for by the first component. Nelsen *et al.* (1969) concluded that 'The findings of this study . . . support the Endler & Hunt (1966) contention that neither persons nor situations alone account for major behavioural variance. Thus, future theory and research . . . must take into account interactions as well as main effects' (p. 278).

Another much-cited example is a study by Kogan and Wallach (1964) on risk-taking behaviour. These authors found little relationship between different personality traits and the amount of risk subjects were willing to take in practical decision-making situations. In this study, the nature of the situation turned out to be a much better predictor of behaviour than the personality traits studied. Later reviews seemed to cast serious doubt on the generality of trait measures and suggested a large (but usually unknown) influence of situation variables (Hunt, 1965; Petersen, 1965).

The milestone critique was Mischel's (1968) book *Personality and Assessment.* Reviewing a host of empirical studies, Mischel noted that behaviours reflecting a trait in one situation were often poorly correlated with behaviours reflecting the same trait in a different situation. On the basis of those results, he raised serious questions about the practical utility of personality measures:

> In sum, the data reviewed on the utility of psychometrically measured traits, as well as psychodynamic inferences about states and traits, show that responses have not served very usefully as signs of internal predispositions . . . These conclusions for personality measures apply, on the whole, to diverse content areas including the prediction of college achievement, job and professional success, treatment outcomes, rehospitalization for psychiatric patients, parole violations for delinquent children, and so on. In light of these findings it is not surprising that large-scale applied efforts to predict behavior from personality inferences have been strikingly and consistently unsuccessful. (Mischel, 1968, pp. 145—6).

Mischel went on to look for the causes of the failure. Rather than attributing the problems to methodological flaws, he directed his main attack at the theoretical framework underlying classical personality assessment. He was especially critical of 'global personality dispositions': broad behavioural dispositions that manifest themselves across time and different conditions. In Mischel's view, the case for global dispositions was very weak, since individual behaviour becomes inconsistent as soon as there is even a slight change in the situation. He therefore advocated a social behaviourist approach that emphasized the study of situational determinants of behaviour.

Mischel's attack called forth many reactions (Alker, 1972; Block, 1977; Epstein, 1977; Hogan *et al.* 1977; Stagner, 1976). His criticisms were taken not only as an attack on the prevailing personality paradigm, but also as an invitation to abandon the field altogether. But before reaching that conclusion, a more systematic exploration of the different paradigms was necessary. Instead of correlational studies, person × situation experimental designs were used to compare the two approaches (cf. Endler and Edwards, 1986; Endler and Magnusson, 1976). In the person × situation experimental design, persons and situations are both conceived as independent variables. The interactions studied are between different causes of behaviour, rather than between causes and effects (cf. Endler, 1988). A well-known example is that of self-report studies using the S-R questionnaire (Endler and Hunt, 1966; Endler *et al.* 1962). With this technique, data can be collected on the behaviour of individuals in a series of situations and sorted according to different reaction variables (trait indicators). Each individual reports the intensity of every response for every reaction variable in each situation. With ANOVA, the total variance obtained is then distributed according to the major sources of variance: persons, situations, and reaction variables. The relative contribution of each facet can be estimated by the calculation of variance components.

Studies using the person × situation experimental design have been reviewed, for instance, by Bowers (1973), Sarason, Smith, and Diener (1975), and Furnham and Jaspars (1983). A review of 11 studies by Bowers (1973) revealed that, on the average, the main effect of persons accounted for 13 per cent of the variance, whereas the main effect of situations accounted for 10 per cent. Person × situation interactions took the lion's share, at 21 per cent of the variance. Sarason *et al.* (1975) examined 53 studies involving 87 separate analyses of variance. In their review, person effects were significant in 31 per cent of the cases, whereas situation effects reached significance in 66 per cent. Person × situation interactions were significant in 60 per cent of the analyses. Later, Furnham and Jaspars (1983) analysed the results of 24 studies. They found that for 17 of those studies the person × situation interaction variance exceeded the person variance, whereas in 19 studies it exceeded the variance due to the situation factor.

Unfortunately, person—environment ANOVA studies have some serious limitations. Since the samples of persons, situations, and responses used in these studies were not representative, there is no way to say how much variance each accounts for under natural circumstances. Because of systematic bias in different kinds of data, and the models used for data analysis (cf. Furnham and Jaspars, 1983), it is hard to draw unequivocal conclusions about the superiority of any of the basic personality models. Yet, two conclusions can be drawn. First, there is abundant evidence that, in a specific situation, not all persons show the same behaviour. Second, a specific person does not show the same behaviour in different situations. So, neither intra-situational consistency — the basis of the situationist model — nor cross-situational consistency — the mainstay of the personologist model — is supported by these reviews.

Conditional trait models

One way out of the person—situation controversy would be to stop debating whether consistency exists and to begin exploring the circumstances under which consistency will and will not occur (cf. Bem and Funder, 1987; Diener and Larsen, 1984; Funder and Dobroth, 1987; Kenrick and Funder, 1988). This is tantamount to allowing restrictions with regard to the range of convenience of the model studied, by developing conditional models. This strategy has been applied to each of the terms of possible interaction in a search for relatively consistent persons, for relatively consistent responses, and for environments that induce more or less consistency.

One approach is based on the notion that trait consistency is not a general phenomenon but restricted to a sub-group of the population. For instance, Bem and Allen (1974) studied individual variations with respect to consistency on specific traits. They asked each subject to indicate how consistent he or she would be on friendliness or conscientiousness. Their results partly confirmed the hypothesis that people who said they were more consistent on a given trait would also be more predictable. Kenrick and Stringfield (1980) replicated the Bem and Allen (1974) study and extended it to a broader domain of traits by getting each subject to pick his or her most consistent dimensions from a list based on Cattell's 16PF. In addition, they introduced 'observability' ratings in which subjects indicated whether or not each trait would be publicly visible to other people. They obtained the best predictions for consistent and highly observable subjects (see also Amelang and Borkenau, 1982; Baumeister and Tice, 1988; Cheek, 1982; Kenrick and Braver, 1982; Koestner *et al.*, 1989). Although this version of the moderator approach has shown some promise, there are also disadvantages. In addition to limiting predictions on a given trait to only a sub-set of the population, it is not embedded in a more general theoretical framework (cf. Kenrick and Dantchik, 1983; Rushton *et al.*, 1981).

A second approach has elaborated the idea that situations differ with respect to their power to elicit classes of acts predictably (Wright and Mischel, 1987), or to induce the same behaviour in different people (Price and Bouffard, 1974; Schutte *et al.*, 1985; Snyder and Ickes, 1985). Powerful situations are assumed to lead everyone to construe the particular events the same way, to induce uniform expectancies regarding the most appropriate response pattern, to provide adequate incentives for the performance of that response pattern, and to require skills that everyone has to some extent. Conversely, weak situations are not uniformly encoded, do not generate uniform expectancies concerning the desired behaviour, do not offer sufficient incentives for its performance, or fail to provide the learning conditions required for successful genesis of the behaviour (cf. Mischel, 1973). In powerful situations, persons are assumed to act more according to the situationist model, whereas in weak situations persons will act more according to the personologist model. A study by Hettema, Van Heck, Appels, and Van Zon (1986) suggested that different indices of situational power are not always congruent: situations construed in the same way are not necessarily the ones evoking the same behaviour in persons acting in them. More research is needed to establish and test the criteria discriminating between powerful and weak situations. To be more generally useful, the distinction has to be embedded in an explicit theory explaining the connections between powerful versus weak situations on the one hand and specific personality types on the other.

A third conditional trait approach focuses on the specific behaviours that are more or less consistent across situations. According to Mischel (1968, 1973; see also Endler and Edwards, 1986), consistency is to be expected particularly with structural variables like abilities and cognitive competency. As Spearman noted in 1927, correlations among intelligence tests are virtually always positive, and thus there is every reason to assume intelligence to be highly consistent across situations. It should be noted, however, that recent studies of practical intelligence have raised some doubt concerning consistency in daily life situations (cf. Sternberg and Wagner, 1986). In contrast to the case with intelligence, little consistency is usually found with social-emotional behaviours studied with the aid of S-R questionnaires, such as anxiety (Ekehammar, 1974; Endler and Okada, 1975; Ender *et al.*, 1962; Van Heck, 1981), hostility (Endler and Hunt, 1968; Van Heck and Van der Leeuw, 1975), and dominance (Dworkin and Kihlstrom, 1978).

Consistency has also been studied as a function of the mode of measurement used to obtain the data. The results suggest that not every mode provides the same results. For instance, Van Heck and Van der Leeuw (1975) compared self-reports with ratings of others. They asked their subjects to rate their own behaviour as well as the behaviour of their best friend in a number of different situations. Their results showed ratings to be more consistent across situations than self-reports. More recently, Van Heck (1988) compared self-reports, observations of overt behaviour and physiological reactions of subjects confronted with anxiety-provoking situations. In this study, trans-situational consistency was low for each of the three modes. Self-reports obtained the highest value, followed by physiological reactions, whereas overt behaviour showed no consistency at all. Along similar lines, one of us (Hettema, 1988) collected self-reports via questionnaire, physiological reactions via film, and observations made during role-playing in simulated situations. Care was taken to present the same situations in each of the modes studied. As in Van Heck's (1988) study, observations showed low trans-situational consistency, but physiological reactions were more consistent than self-reports. These results suggest that response modes have considerable effects upon consistency obtained in person—situation studies. Research by Moskowitz, however, has suggested that self-reports, ratings, and behavioural observations do tend to converge with sufficient aggregation (for example, Moskowitz, 1990).

To summarize this section, the conditional trait approach has been relatively successful in identifying conditions in the person, the situation, the behaviour studied, and the mode of measurement that will enhance or lower consistency across situations. However, this approach has some severe drawbacks. First of all, it offers only partial explanations; that is, it only explains those behaviours of those persons in those situations that are consistent, leaving the other conditions unexplained. In addition, these findings have proliferated without an adequate theory explaining why, when, and how consistency is to be expected. Finally, none of the studies mentioned can explain the substantial interactions found in person—situation studies. For that purpose, new models, explicitly linking the person and the situation, are required.

Defining person—situation interactions

One lesson of the person—situation debate is that personality is infinitely more complex than we once assumed. Personality psychologists need sufficiently complex models to encompass this complexity. Although the conditional approach may not have solved all our problems, it offers a part of a framework for conceptualizing person—situation interactions in a systematic way. For instance, the notion of differential consistency makes us realize that some persons may be more consistent across a wide range of situations than others. Also, the same person may at times be more consistent than at other times. Likewise, the concept of situational power reminds us that human ecology is not homogeneous and that some situations put stricter demands upon us than other situations. A systematic consideration of these different factors could provide us with a more comprehensive view of possible person—situation interactions. For instance, what kind of interaction will emerge when a relatively consistent person meets a powerful situation? And what if that same person meets a weak situation?

In addition, the notion that some behaviours exhibit more consistency than others may offer a basis to conceptualize interactions further. What does it mean that cognitive-intellectual variables show more consistency than social-emotional variables? Perhaps cognitions — exhibiting more trans-situational consistency — fit better into a personologist conception, whereas emotions are better studied in a situationist framework. What does this mean for the conceptualization of interactions? And what about the differences in consistency found with different modes of measurement? Do they refer to different behavioural systems, reacting differently to situational demands?

In order to answer the various questions about the interaction of individual traits and situational constraints, it is essential to adopt a heuristic framework that jointly considers persons and situations. Interactionist theorists have distinguished several types of interaction. These can be divided into six categories: static person—environment mesh, choice of environments by persons, choice of persons by environments, transformation of environments by persons, transformation of persons by environments and person—environment transactions — mutual transactions in which both persons and environments change over time. These different types of interaction are considered below.

Type I: Static person—environment mesh

Some environments are well suited to particular individuals but poorly suited to others. For instance, Paul Gauguin was successful in the business world, whereas Van Gogh was not. Conversely, some persons are better suited to particular environments than to others. This type of interaction assumes that there are relatively consistent traits of persons and relatively consistent features of environments, and is depicted in Figure 15.1. Cronbach's work with 'aptitude-treatment interactions' exemplifies an approach that considers the issue of person—environment mesh (Cronbach, 1967; Cronbach and Snow, 1977). Within this approach, it is assumed that a child's school success is predicted best by knowing how the child's aptitudes mesh with the particular educational environment he or she confronts.

Type II: Choice of environments by persons

People and environments sometimes randomly confront one another, but not always. People sometimes go out of their way to choose environments to fit their personal

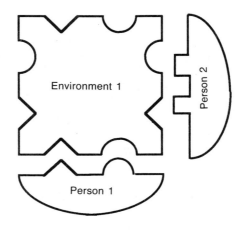

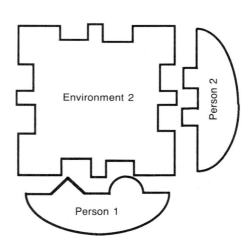

Figure 15.1 Type I: static person—environment mesh

characteristics. Gauguin's artistic inclinations led him to abandon the business world, for instance. This type of interaction also assumes relatively consistent features of environments and persons. As depicted in Figure 15.2, we assume that people often bypass nearby or convenient environments for others that seem more suited to their personal characteristics.

Type III: Choice of persons by environments

Not all environments are accessible to all persons. For instance, not every student who wishes to enter a doctoral programme in nuclear physics, or to play music at

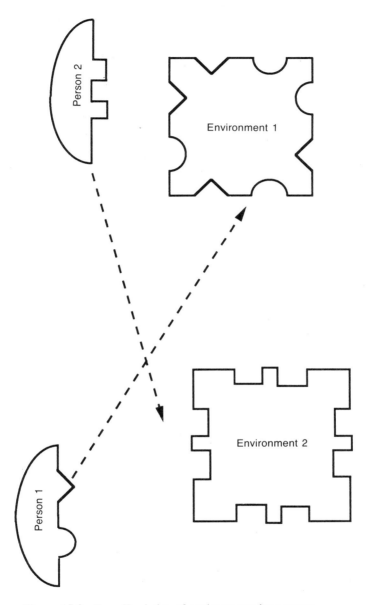

Figure 15.2 Type II: choice of environments by persons

New York's Lincoln Center for the Performing Arts, is permitted to. As in the case of graduate entrance examinations, people must often demonstrate some evidence of environmentally suited traits in order to open gates to particular environments. This type of interaction (depicted in Figure 15.3) assumes, like the first two, that

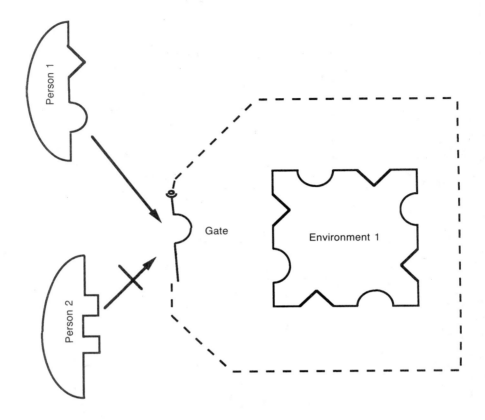

Figure 15.3 Type III: choice of persons by environments

people have relatively static traits, and that environmental gates are sometimes rigidly keyed (as in the case of graduate school admission).

Type IV: Transformation of environments by persons

As Murray (1938) suggested some time ago, persons have the need as well as the capacity to 'transform in a certain direction an existing unsatisfying situation' (p. 123). With regard to social situations, Secord (1977) noted that persons not only avoid some situations and enter others, but also modify situations to suit themselves: 'Most of the time they are either modifying or creating situations that facilitate things they want to do' (p. 46). Aggressive children can turn a peaceful playground into a battleground in short order, for instance (Rausch, 1977).

Figure 15.4 depicts a change in environment that might occur after repeated exposure to the two types of person depicted in Figure 15.1. In this case, the environment is shown to become more flexible; that is, as assimilating both types

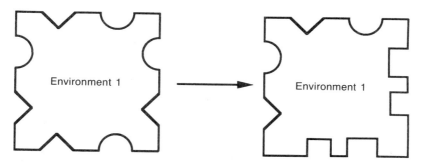

Figure 15.4 Type IV: transformation of environments by persons

of people. It is also possible that some people could change an environment in such a way that it is no longer compatible with the people who were earlier suited to it.

Environment transformation assumes that a person has consistent intentions or goals, and that the person is inherently active and goal-directed (cf. Endler and Magnusson, 1976; Pervin, 1983). Situations, on the other hand, must be somewhat modifiable for this type of interaction to occur, and 'weak situations' lend themselves more to such transformation. In this type of interaction, behaviour is governed by the principle of equifinality: the tendency of the person to reach a particular end state, relatively independently of his or her starting position (cf. Hettema, 1979, 1989).

The type of coherence stressed in environment modification is goal coherence; that is, the characteristic pattern of goals a person will pursue if confronted with different situations. The importance of individual goals has been recently stressed by Pervin (1983; Pervin and Furnham, 1987), and Wakefield (1989), and provides a cornerstone of several classic formulations of interactions (for example, Lewin, Murray).

Type V: Transformation of persons by environments

Persons have an inherent tendency to take account of situational demands and contingencies as well as to learn from experience. As a result, they adjust their behaviour to meet the requirements imposed by the situation. At a simple level, this type of interaction takes the form of different settings eliciting different pre-existing traits in people (Kenrick *et al.*, 1990). Over the long haul, repeated exposures to the same environmental pressures will change a person's characteristics (Newcomb *et al.*, 1967). Graduate students, at least the successful ones, learn to modify their undergraduate 'study for quizzes' repertoire in favour of spending time in the research laboratory. Figure 15.5 depicts a change that might occur after Person 2 has had numerous occasions to interact with environments of both the types in Figure 15.1. In this case, the person is shown to have been somewhat more compatible with one type of situation, but somewhat less compatible with another. Students from

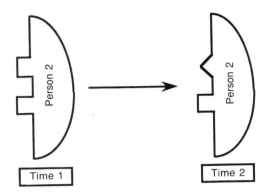

Figure 15.5 Type V: transformation of persons by environments

conservative homes who went to the liberal Bennington College environment might illustrate this type of interaction (Newcomb *et al.*, 1967). Adopting some liberal political beliefs might well make such people more compatible with the college environment, but less compatible with their family environments. This type of interaction assumes that personal traits are to some degree modifiable, and that situations are sometimes relatively powerful.

Type VI: Person–environment transaction

Transactions refer to mutual changes in persons and environments over time (cf. Endler and Magnusson, 1976; Overton and Reese, 1973). A simple example is depicted in Figure 15.6. In this case, certain features of the environment have changed to assimilate a person's traits, whereas certain features of the person have changed to accommodate the environment. Most successful marriages probably involve these types of reciprocal change. The notion of a transaction can include much more complex interplays between persons and environments over time. For instance, love relationships involve sequenced changes in which certain traits are required at one phase, and others are required later on. At the courtship phase, for instance, a certain degree of conscientiousness and emotionality are required to prove one's love. Once a bond has been formed, partners may well tolerate a degree of absent-mindedness and lateness that would have been unthinkable at the earlier phase. And the passionate emotions that served so well in fusing a bond might actually become a hindrance to living and working together on a day-to-day basis (Kenrick and Trost, 1987).

To allow for transactions to occur, persons as well as situations have to be conceived as modifiable and flexible. Clearly, transactions may include several behavioural aspects, including acts, goals, thoughts, feelings, motivational states and the like. Endler and Magnusson (1976) especially emphasized cognitive processes in the person

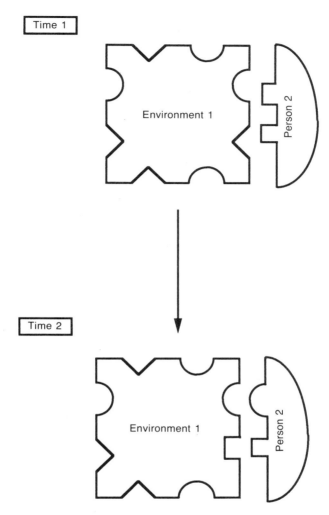

Figure 15.6 Type VI: person—environment transaction

interpreting and reinterpreting environmental events. More recently, however, they have granted a more central position to emotion and motivational states in the transaction process (cf. Endler, 1983; Magnusson, 1988, 1990). Emotions are currently assumed to exert powerful effects upon other behavioural systems by directing attention (Mandler, 1980), providing information (Lazarus *et al.*, 1982), assessing outcome likelihood (Scheier and Carver, 1982), signalling the state of the world (Frijda, 1985), and integrating behaviour (Leventhal, 1984). Also, emotions have the unique capacity to alter the state of the person as well as of the situation (Hettema, 1991). In person—environment transactions, feelings can be assumed to occupy a central position, and, accordingly, feeling coherence is emphasized here as a primary source of individual differences in behaviour.

Figures 15.1—15.6 provide a descriptive framework for organizing different types of interaction. How are such interactions to be incorporated into an explanatory theory? In the following sections, we consider how interactions have been understood from biological, cognitive/social learning, and biosocial perspectives.

Biological, social, and biosocial models of interaction

There have been a number of attempts to conceptualize interactions within different theoretical models. Some of these attempts have been confined to specific aspects of behaviour, like anxiety, stress, or learning. Other attempts have been more comprehensive. Thus far, no dominant theory has been widely accepted as *the* theory of person—situation interaction. Endler (1983) suggested that interactionism must be seen as a model, not yet a theory. Interactions have been extensively considered from two points of view: the biological and cognitive/social learning perspectives. We will discuss each of these in turn, followed by a discussion of the biosocial perspective, which attempts to integrate aspects of the other two.

Biological models

Ultimately, biological models of person—situation interactions are based on evolutionary theory. Personality is conceived of as the result of the two major processes of evolution: variation and selective retention (see Loehlin and Rowe, Chapter 13 in this volume). At the level of individuals, behaviour geneticists have studied the heritability of behaviour. Family, twin, and adoption studies have suggested that at least some of the variance in human behaviour is genetically determined (Plomin, 1986; Rowe, 1989). For instance, one recent study suggested that heredity accounted for 56—72 per cent of the phenotypic variance in altruism, empathy, nurturance, aggression, and assertiveness (Rushton *et al.*, 1986). Studies in this area have generally found that approximately 50 per cent of the variance is associated with additive genetic influence. Accordingly, Goldsmith (1983) has warned that theories of personality development ignore the action of genetic factors at some risk.

Genes influence behaviour through their effects on the development and functioning of physiological mechanisms (cf. Plomin *et al.*, 1980). Genes control the production of proteins, which in turn exert profound influence on behavioural structures and processes via the nervous system and the production of behaviourally relevant hormones and neurotransmitters. Because genetic programmes depend upon inputs from the environment, and because they are keyed to changes in the environment, it makes no sense to consider genes without considering environmental inputs. Accordingly, behaviour geneticists have given serious consideration to person—environment interactions.

Temperament has been suggested as one mechanism for regulating interactions between genetic programmes and the environment. Strelau (1985) has formulated a regulation theory of temperament, according to which temperamental mechanisms regulate inputs from the environment and from internal events. Eliasz (1990) advocated the study of temperament in connection with specific situations using S-R questionnaires. Earlier, Thomas and Chess (1985) proposed an explicit interactional conception of temperament, using the concept of 'goodness of fit' to indicate the balance between the properties of the environment and the individual's characteristic style of behaving. Thus, extraverts seek out stimulating social situations (Furnham, 1981) that fit with their temperamental dispositions. Buss, Gomes, Higgins, and Lauterbach (1987) found clear links between standard dimensions of temperament and the use of specific sorts of manipulation tactics. Along the same lines, Van Heck, Hettema, and Leidelmeijer (1990) studied person—situation mechanisms as a function of temperament, and identified several associations.

Findings of this type reflect gene—environment interactions (Plomin, 1986): differential effects of environments on individuals of different genotypes. Plomin, DeFries, and Loehlin (1977) proposed three different types of genotype—environment interaction. Passive interactions occur when a person's environment fits with the genetic predisposition because his or her parents (who share the same genes) also control the environment. This would seem to be a special case of what we called static person—environment mesh. Reactive interactions occur when the environment responds differently to persons who have different genotypes. Responses can be either positive, enhancing genetic predispositions, or negative, counteracting dispositions, as, for instance, in reactions to aggression. Finally, active interactions occur when individuals seek environments to match their genotypes. All interactions mentioned have the effect of sorting different genotypes into different environments (cf. Scarr and McCartney, 1983). The interactions emphasized in biological models have been discussed earlier under Types I—III (person—environment mesh, choice of environments by persons, or choice of persons by environments).

The biological conception of interaction assumes that a person's behaviour is consistent. Genes control behavioural variation and continue to do so during ontogenetic development (cf. Rowe, 1989). The conception of the environment is akin to the view developed in ecological realism (cf. Gibson, 1979): a specific environment offers specific 'affordances' in response to specific behaviours. In an ultimate sense, person—environment interactions are at the heart of the evolutionary model. Darwinian theory assumes that genes (and the behavioural tendencies coded by genes) are selected to match particular environments.

Cognitive/social learning models

In contrast with biological models, social models of person—situation interaction are concerned primarily with person characteristics that are acquired, especially through social learning (see Cervone and Williams, Chapter 8 in this volume). From a learning perspective, the environment is conceptualized in terms of discriminative and reinforcing stimuli that guide behaviour. Learning processes contribute to personality development in a gradual and systematic way. Repetition and practice serve to establish habits in the learner that affect his or her subsequent behaviour in the same environmental conditions.

Direct reinforcement has a powerful influence on behaviour, but people also learn a great deal without any direct rewards, by observing the consequences of other people's diverse behaviours. Social learning has been emphasized by Rotter (1954) and Bandura (1969, 1986). These models focus on cognitive functions in learning or the social context in which it occurs. The processes described by social learning theorists leave behind products in the individual that are the basis of subsequent behaviour. Those products are of a cognitive nature, such as the cognitive social learning person variables described by Mischel (1973). According to Mischel (1973), individual differences take the form of differences in cognitive construction competencies, encoding strategies, outcome expectancies, outcome values, and self-regulatory systems. Cantor and Kihlstrom (1987) have elaborated this position extensively, and integrated it with laboratory studies of cognition in their consideration of personality as social intelligence.

These classes of cognitive variables attain a coherent mode of thinking in the individual, and they underlie key patterns on his or her behaviour. Thus, thought coherence is the major principle guiding behaviour in this conception. Social models of person—situation interaction tend to favour a subjective conception of the environment; that is, the situation as perceived (cf. Endler and Magnusson, 1976), or appraised by the individual (cf. Stattin, 1984) — an idiographic conception of the situation (cf. Pervin, 1976). For instance, Magnusson (1988) and his co-workers studied specific groups of individuals, sexes, and ages, with respect to the subjective situational characteristics associated with anxiety (such as demand of achievement, accidents) and with respect to the expected consequences (such as separation, personal inadequacy, guilt).

Bandura (1978) has considered person—situation interaction in terms of reciprocal causation: just as environmental events determine individual behaviour, so the individual determines his or her environment (cf. Endler and Magnusson, 1976). Reciprocal causation implies that processes of feedback are an essential part of behaviour. It involves the types of interactions that we discussed under Types IV— VI above (transformation of environments by persons, transformation of persons by environments, and person—environment transaction). Within the cognitive social learning model, individuals are conceived as active, purposeful agents, who interpret information from the environment about conditions and events and who act in the frame of their own systems of thoughts, values, goals, and emotions (Magnusson, 1990).

In contrast to biological models, social models are based on more proximate explanations of person—situation interactions. Persons are conceived primarily as flexible and modifiable. Thus, there is relatively more emphasis on interactions in which persons change to fit the requirements of environments. As we have noted, cognitive social learning theorists have also considered transactions with the notion of reciprocal determination.

Biosocial models

Biosocial models of person—situation interactions are based on the conviction, that, by themselves, the biological and social approaches to personality are insufficient. Since personality psychology is concerned with the whole organism, solutions that focus only on temperament, only on learning, or only on cognition are inherently handicapped. This is especially true to the extent that biological and social factors interact in non-additive ways (cf. Hettema and Kenrick, 1989).

Biosocial models of person—situation interaction assume that innate biological mechanisms as well as acquired social mechanisms are both necessary to explain behaviour at any given moment. Genes do not construct an organism that is insensitive to outside pressures. Instead, they code for programmes that respond to both the objective environment and our subjective and individual interpretation of that environment. Our genetic differences act by making some of us more sensitive to particular sights and smells, by biasing some of us to learn and remember particular events, by producing hormones that make some of us more prone to anger, anxiety, and so on (Kenrick, 1987).

A critical component of the biosocial model is the proximate—ultimate continuum. Some explanations focus on the immediate present determinants of behaviour. These immediate influences include biochemicals currently in the bloodstream, as well as cognitive schemas that determine ongoing attention to and encoding of particular stimuli in the present environment. Ultimate explanations involve the background or historical conditions that influence the immediate causes. Evolutionary explanations are most ultimate — focusing on the adaptive significance of responding to certain environmental stimuli with particular responses (like increasing appetite at the taste of sugar, and spitting out foods that taste bitter).

Cognitive learning concepts address behavioural variations in more proximal terms. Going one step back, current responses to attended stimuli are influenced by previous learning experiences. Conditioning and modelling processes address the way environmental contingencies shape our responses as we are developing. One person views a mathematics test as a horrible threat and another views it as a joke, because of previous experiences that are stored in long-term memory. Modern learning theorists have found that learning is likewise linked to more ultimately based biological constraints. Just as there are differences between species in the things they are programmed to learn, so there are differences within our species. Some of those differences are related to personality. For instance, Eysenck and Rachman (1965) produced evidence that emotional adjustment is related to heritable differences in autonomic arousal, which in turn cause neurotic individuals to condition anxiety to new situations more easily. At the opposite extreme, sociopathic prisoners are low in arousal, and do not learn to avoid punishment very well. However, if they are given a dose of epinephrine, which disrupts learning in sociopaths, they begin to avoid punishment in the normal fashion (Schachter and Latané, 1964). Thus, learning experiences connect back to physiological predispositions.

Innate as well as socially acquired behavioural structures each contribute to the adaptation of individuals to their environment. According to Hettema (1979), in the short term, people use acquired concepts and rules to structure the environment as well as to modify the environment to suit themselves. At the same time, however, innate physiological mechanisms are activated to cope with unexpectedness, frictions, and disturbances. Through learning and conditioning, both types of behavioural structure become connected with particular situations. As a consequence, a complex behavioural system is established to deal effectively with that type of situation in the long term.

In Hettema's (1979, 1989) conception, the major structures governing behaviour are of a strategic and a tactical nature. For instance, a teacher may specify goals and sub-goals, like commitment and understanding, to be attained during a lesson. In addition, he or she may use specific means, like explaining, giving examples, and asking questions, to attain these goals. Goals and means are major parts of the teacher's strategy. However, during class, the students' reactions may reveal a complete lack of understanding, thus invalidating strategic expectations. In that case, according to the model, the teacher's state may change, yielding emotional expressions, increased effort, or persistence. Those reactions are conceived as tactical responses enhancing control. While strategies are viewed as crystallized products of social learning and experience, tactics are directly connected with emotional and motivational states of an innate nature. Thus, in sum, individual adaptation comes about as a product of innate and acquired mechanisms in interaction with concrete situations. Accordingly, the conception of person–situation interactions is multifarious, involving cognitive representations and transformations, physiological and biochemical reactions, as well as overt instrumental and expressive behaviours (cf. Hettema, 1979, 1989).

Likewise, the biosocial interactionist perspective adopted by Kenrick conceives of personality development in multicausal terms (Kenrick, 1987; Kenrick *et al.*, 1985). Environmental events (the focus of traditional learning models), cognitive representations (the concern of more recent social learning models), and physiological predispositions (the mainstay of the biological model) are all necessary, but not sufficient as explanations of individual differences. Consider the case of depression (Kenrick *et al.*, 1985). According to this model, a person will not become depressed unless he or she has an unpleasant experience of a particular sort (like a loss of status or a social rejection). In addition, the person has to pay cognitive attention to that experience, and to interpret it in certain ways ('it was my fault'). However, even a series of negative events that an individual accepts blame for may not lead to depression if that individual has a high physiological threshold for such a response. Thus, depression is conceived of as the result of environmental events, cognitive appraisal, and organismic factors. A similar model has been applied to gender differences in social behaviours like aggression (Kenrick, 1987). Presumably, those differences are based ultimately in genetic differences that code for morphological and hormonal distinctions between the sexes. However, the biological differences can be amplified or dampened by learning experiences that lead to particular cognitive responses to ongoing events. Differences can also be amplified by construction of particular environments by society (such as military camps and karate classes aimed mainly at boys) and selection of those environments by individuals with particular traits (for example, muscular, dominant, high-testosterone boys may selectively choose to play aggressive sports).

In stressing all these explanations as well as their connections, biosocial models are necessarily more complex than either biological or social models. Accordingly, all of the types of interaction come to the fore in the context of biosocial models. On the basis of their biological endowment, some environments will be better suited to particular individuals than other environments. Individuals will select specific environments and reject others. In turn, they will also be subjected to selection by specific environments. They will modify environments to suit their preferences. Confronted with powerful situations resisting modification, they will be modified through learning. And, finally, they will establish a workable balance through transactions with their environment. Biosocial models are thus, almost by definition, interactionist.

Concluding remarks

A quarter of a century after the onset of the person—situation debate, it no longer seems appropriate to ask who was right in the debate between the personologists and the situationists. Instead, it is more fruitful to build on the information obtained with studies of the person—situation type. The nature of situations, the types of person, the behaviour studied, as well as the mode of measurement used have a considerable, but interactive, impact upon behavioural consistency.

Earlier studies of person—situation interactions concentrated on static interactions. The interactions considered were of the statistical sort, as defined in the ANOVA model. That model was not adequate for studying reciprocal relationships between persons and situations. Studies of mechanistic interaction were usually directed at single traits as a function of persons, situations, and modes of expression. For instance, interactions were identified with traits ranging from anxiety to hostility, from dominance to depression, from conformity to honesty (Furnham and Jaspars, 1983).

Mechanistic interactions have been characterized by Endler (1983) as snapshots rather than movies. Accordingly, later studies have focused on dynamic person—situation interactions; that is, the ongoing process in which persons select situations and are selected by them, in which they affect situations and are affected by them. Studies of dynamic interaction are usually not confined to single traits. Instead, they have scrutinized divergent behaviours within sub-systems of personality, like acts, goals, feelings, and cognitions. In what is now called classic interactionism the fundamental feature was the dynamic, continuous, and reciprocal process of interaction between the individual and the environment. Modern interactionism in Europe is also centrally concerned with the interaction among sub-systems of the individual (cf. Magnusson, 1988).

Depending on their focus of interest, modern interaction models have emphasized interactions between acts and goals, or between emotion and cognition (Hettema and Van Heck, 1987). Of particular interest are interactions between biological and social factors as emphasized in the study of adaptation (Hettema, 1989), adjustment (Magnusson, 1988), and coping with stress (Henry and Stephens, 1977; Vingerhoets, 1985). Studies of that type have the potential to shed new light on the interplay of genetic and environmental factors. The ultimate goal of models of person—situation interactions may well be to provide a more definite answer to questions concerning the nature—nurture controversy.

Thus, over the years, interactionism in personality psychology has evolved from a criticism of the classical organismic and dispositional approaches into a new paradigm for the study of personality. A major feature of that paradigm is the notion that individual behaviour is always a function of processes between persons and situations, rather than of persons *per se*. Those interactive processes connect different theoretical perspectives along the proximate—ultimate continuum. Modern inter-actionist models are thus more comprehensive in scope than the traditional models of behaviour. Interactionist models have also suggested new insights into the structure of personality. A mainstay of interaction models is the notion that, through interaction, personality is crystallized to yield coherent recurrent patterns of behaviour rather than solid consistency across situations.

By developing interactionist models, then, the field of personality psychology is moving closer to the traditional ideal of an integrative discipline that connects all the other branches of psychology. The interactionist perspective necessarily includes cognition, learning, development, and behaviour genetics. Finally, interactionism links personality psychology not only with environmental psychology, but also with evolutionary psychology envisioned by William James over a century ago.

References

Alker, H.A. (1972), 'Is personality situationally specific or intra-psychically consistent?', *Journal of Personality*, **40**, 1—16.

Amelang, M., and Borkenau, P. (1982), 'In search of persons with traits: Intraindividual variability, moderator scales, and differential predictability', unpublished manuscript, University of Heidelberg, Germany.

Bandura, A. (1969), *Principles of Behavior Modification*, New York, NY: Holt.

Bandura, A. (1978), 'The self-system in reciprocal determinism', *American Psychologist*, **33**, 344—58.

Bandura, A. (1986), *Social Foundations of Thought and Action: A social cognitive theory*, Englewood Cliffs, NJ: Prentice Hall.

Baumeister, R.F., and Tice, D.M. (1988), 'Meta-traits', *Journal of Personality and Social Psychology*, **56**, 571—98.

Bem, D.J., and Allen, A. (1974), 'On predicting some of the people some of the time: the search for cross-situational consistencies in behavior', *Psychological Review*, **81**, 506—20.

Bem, D.J., and Funder, D.C. (1978), 'Predicting more of the people more of the time: assessing the personality of situations', *Psychological Review*, **85**, 485—501.

Bindra, D., and Scheier, I.H. (1954), 'The relationship between psychometric and experimental research in psychology', *American Psychologist*, **9**, 69—71.

Block, J. (1977), 'Advancing the psychology of personality, paradigmatic shift or improving the quality of research', in D. Magnusson and N.S. Endler (eds.), *Personality at the Crossroads: Current issues in interactional psychology*, Hillsdale, NJ: Erlbaum, pp. 37—63.

Bowers, K.S. (1973), 'Situationism in psychology: an analysis and a critique', *Psychological Review*, **80**, 307—36.

Buss, D.M., Gomes, M., Higgins, D.J., and Lauterbach, K. (1987), 'Tactics of manipulation', *Journal of Personality and Social Psychology*, **52**, 1219—29.

Cantor, N., and Kihlstrom, J.F. (1987), *Personality and Social Intelligence*, Englewood Cliffs, NJ: Prentice Hall.

Cheek, J.M. (1982), 'Aggregation, moderator variables, and the validity of personality tests: a peer-rating study', *Journal of Personality and Social Psychology*, **43**, 1254—69.

Cronbach, L.J. (1957), 'The two disciplines of scientific psychology', *American Psychologist*, **12**, 671—84.

Cronbach, L.J. (1967), 'Instructional methods and individual differences', in R. Gagne (ed.), *Learning and Individual Differences*, Columbus, OH: C.E. Merrill Books, pp. 23—39.

Cronbach, L.J., and Snow, R.E. (1977), *Aptitudes and Instructional Methods*, New York, NY: Irvington.

Dashiell, J.F. (1939), 'Some rapprochements in contemporary psychology', *Psychological Bulletin*, **36**, 1—24.

Diener, E., and Larsen, R.J. (1984), 'Temporal stability and cross-situational consistency of affective, behavioural, and cognitive responses', *Journal of Personality and Social Psychology*, **47**, 871—83.

Dworkin, R.H., and Kihlstrom, J.F. (1978), 'An S-R inventory of dominance for research on the nature of person—situation interactions', *Journal of Personality*, **46**, 43—56.

Ekehammar, B. (1974), 'Interactionism in personality from a historical perspective', *Psychological Bulletin*, **81**, 1026—48.

Eliasz, A. (1990), 'Broadening the concept of temperament: from disposition to hypothetical construct', *European Journal of Personality*, **4**, 287—302.

Endler, N.S. (1983), 'Interactionism: a personality model, but not yet a theory', in M.M. Page (ed.), *Nebraska Symposium on Motivation*, Lincoln, NE: University of Nebraska Press, pp. 155—200.

Endler, N.S. (1988), 'Interactionism revisited: a discussion of 'On the role of situations in personality research', in S.G. Cole, R.G. Demaree, and W. Curtis (eds.), *Applications of Interactionist Psychology: Essays in honor of Saul B. Sells*, Hillsdale NJ: Erlbaum, pp. 179—88.

Endler, N.S., and Edwards, J.M. (1986), 'Interactionism in personality in the twentieth century', *Personality and Individual Differences*, **7**, 379—84.

Endler, N.S., and Hunt, J.McV. (1966), 'Sources of behavioral variance as measured by the S-R Inventory of Anxiousness', *Psychological Bulletin*, **65**, 336—46.

Endler, N.S., and Hunt, J.McV. (1968), 'S-R inventories of hostility and comparisons of the proportions of variance from persons, responses, and situations for hostility and anxiousness', *Journal of Personality and Social Psychology*, **9**, 309—15.

Endler, N.S., and Magnusson, D. (eds.) (1976), *Interactional Psychology and Personality*, Washington, DC: Hemisphere.

Endler, N.S., and Okada, M. (1975), 'A multidimensional measure of trait anxiety: the S-R

Inventory of General Trait Anxiousness', *Journal of Consulting and Clinical Psychology*, **43**, 319—29.

Endler, N.S., Hunt, J.McV., and Rosenstein, A.J. (1962), 'An S-R Inventory of Anxiousness', *Psychological Monographs*, **76** (17, whole no. 536), 1—33.

Epstein, S. (1977), 'Traits are alive and well', in D. Magnusson and N.S. Endler (eds.), *Personality at the Crossroads: Current issues in interactional psychology*, Hillsdale, NJ: Erlbaum, p. 83—98.

Eysenck, H.J., and Rachman, S. (1965), *Causes and Cures of Neurosis*, London: Routledge & Kegan Paul.

Frijda, N.H. (1985), 'Toward a model of emotion', in C.D. Spielberger, I.G. Sarason, and P.B. Defares (eds.), *Stress and Anxiety*, Washington, DC: Hemisphere, vol. 9, pp. 3—16.

Funder, D. and Dobroth, K.M. (1987), 'Differences between traits: properties associated with interjudge agreement', *Journal of Personality and Social Psychology*, **52**, 409—18.

Furnham, A. (1981), 'Personality and activity preference', *British Journal of Social and Clinical Psychology*, **20**, 57—68.

Furnham, A., and Jaspars, J. (1983), 'The evidence for interactionism in psychology', *Personality and Individual Differences*, **4**, 627—44.

Gibson, J.J. (1979), *The Ecological Approach to Visual Perception*, Boston, MA: Houghton Mifflin.

Goldsmith, H.H. (1983), 'Genetic influences on personality from infancy to adulthood', *Child Development*, **54**, 331—55.

Hall, C.S., and Lindzey, G. (1970), *Theories of Personality*, New York, NY: Wiley.

Hartshorne, H., and May, M.A. (1928), *Studies on the Nature of Character. I: Studies in deceit*, New York, NY: Macmillan.

Henry, J.P., and Stephens, P.M. (1977), *Stress, Health, and the Social Environment: A sociobiologic approach to medicine*, New York, NY: Springer.

Hettema, P.J. (1979), *Personality and Adaptation*, Amsterdam: North-Holland.

Hettema, P.J. (1988), 'Method specificity in person—environment interactions', paper presented at the IVth European Conference on Personality in Stockholm.

Hettema, P.J. (ed.) (1989), *Personality and Environment: Assessment of human adaptation*, Chichester: Wiley.

Hettema, P.J. (1991), 'Emotions and adaptation: an open-systems perspective', in C.D. Spielberger, I.G. Sarason, Z. Kulcsár, and G.L. Van Heck (eds.), *Stress and Emotion: Anxiety, anger, and curiosity*, New York, NY: Hemisphere, vol. 14, pp. 47—63.

Hettema, P.J., and Kenrick, D.T. (1989), 'Biosocial interaction and individual adaptation', in P.J. Hettema (ed.), *Personality and Environment: Assessment of human adaptation*, Chichester: Wiley, pp. 3—29.

Hettema, P.J., and Van Heck, G.L. (1987), 'Emotion—cognition interactions in personality', *Communication and Cognition*, **20**, 141—70.

Hettema, P.J., Van Heck, G.L., Appels, M.T., and Van Zon, I. (1986), 'The assessment of situational power', in A. Angleitner, A. Furnham, and G.L. Van Heck (eds.), *Personality, Psychology in Europe: Current trends and controversies*, Lisse, The Netherlands: Swets & Zeitlinger, vol. 2, pp. 85—99.

Hogan, R., De Soto, C.B., and Solano, C. (1977), 'Traits, tests, and personality research', *American Psychologist*, **32**, 255—64.

Hunt, J. McV. (1965), 'Traditional personality psychology in the light of recent evidence', *American Scientist*, **53**, 80—96.

Kenrick, D.T. (1987), 'Gender, genes, and the social environment: a biosocial interactionist perspective', in P.C. Shaver and C. Hendrick (eds.), *Review of Personality and Social Psychology*, Newbury Park, CA: Sage, vol. 7, pp. 14—43.

Kenrick, D.T., and Braver, S.L. (1982), 'Personality: idiographic and nomothetic!: a rejoinder', *Psychological Review*, **89**, 182—6.

Kenrick, D.T., and Dantchik, A. (1983), Interactionism, idiographics, and the social psychological invasion of personality. *Journal of Personality,* **51**, 286—307.

Kenrick, D.T., and Funder, D.C. (1988), 'Profiting from controversy: lessons of the person—situation debate', *American Psychologist,* **43**, 23—34.

Kenrick, D.T., and Stringfield, D.O. (1980), 'Personality traits and the eye of the beholder: crossing some traditional philosophical boundaries in the search for consistency in all of the people', *Psychological Review,* **87**, 88—104.

Kenrick, D.T., and Trost, M.R. (1987), 'A biosocial theory of heterosexual relationships', in K. Kelley (ed.), *Males, Females, and Sexuality: Theory and research,* Albany, NY: State University of New York Press, pp. 59—100.

Kenrick, D.T., Montello, D.R., and MacFarlane, S. (1985), 'Personality: social learning, social cognition, or sociobiology?' in R. Hogan and W.H. Jones (eds.), *Perspectives in Personality,* Greenwich, CT: JAI Press, vol. 1, pp. 201—34.

Kenrick, D.T., McCreath, H.E., Govern, J., King, R., and Bordin, J. (1990), 'Person—environment intersections: everyday settings and common trait dimensions', *Journal of Personality and Social Psychology,* **58**, 685—98.

Koestner, R., Bernieri, F., and Zuckerman, M. (1988), 'Trait-specific versus person-specific moderators of cross-situational consistency', *Journal of Personality,* **57**, 1—16.

Kogan, N., and Wallach, M.A. (1964), *Risk Taking: A study in cognition and personality,* New York, NY: Holt.

Lazarus, R.S., Coyne, J.C., and Folkman, S. (1982), 'Cognition, emotion and motivation: the doctoring of Humpty-Dumpty', in J. Neufeld (ed.), *Psychological Stress and Psychopathology,* New York, NY: McGraw-Hill, pp. 218—39.

Leventhal, H. (1984), 'A perceptual—motor theory of emotion', in K.R. Scherer and P. Ekman (eds.), *Approaches to Emotion,* Hillsdale, NJ: Erlbaum, pp. 271—91.

Magnusson, D. (1988), *Individual Development from an Interactional Perspective: A longitudinal study,* Hillsdale, NJ: Erlbaum.

Magnusson, D. (1990), 'Personality development from an interactional perspective', in L.A. Pervin (ed.), *Handbook of Personality: Theory and research,* New York, NY: Guilford Press, pp. 193—222.

Mandler, G. (1980), 'The generation of emotion: a psychological theory', in R. Plutchik and H. Kellerman (eds.), *Emotion: Theory, research and experience. Vol. 1: Theories of emotion,* New York, NY: Academic Press, pp. 219—43.

Mischel, W. (1968), *Personality and Assessment,* New York, NY: Wiley.

Mischel, W. (1973), 'Toward a cognitive social learning reconceptualization of personality', *Psychological Review,* **80**, 252—83.

Moskowitz, D.S. (1990), 'Convergence of self-reports and independent observers: dominance and friendliness', *Journal of Personality and Social Psychology,* **58**, 1096—106.

Murray, H.A. (1938), *Explorations in Personality,* New York, NY: Oxford University Press.

Nelsen, E.A., Grinder, R.F., and Mutterer, M.L. (1969), 'Sources of variance in behavioral measures of honesty in temptation situations: methodological issues', *Developmental Psychology,* **1**, 265—79.

Newcomb, T.M., Koenig, K.E., Flacks, R., and Warwick, D.P. (1967), *Persistence and Change: Bennington College and its students after twenty-five years,* New York, NY: Wiley.

Overton, W.F., and Reese, H.W. (1973), 'Models of development: methodological implications', in J.R. Nesselroade and H.W. Reese (eds.), *Life Span Developmental Psychology: Methodological issues,* New York, NY: Academic Press.

Pervin, L.A. (1976), 'A free-response description approach to the analysis of person—situation interaction', *Journal of Personality and Social Psychology,* **34**, 465—74.

Pervin, L.A. (1983), 'The stasis and flow of behaviour: toward a theory of goals', in M.M. Page (ed.), *Personality: Current theory and research,* Lincoln, NE: University of Nebraska Press, pp. 1—53.

Pervin, L.A., and Furnham, A. (1987), 'Goal-based and situation-based expectations of behaviour', *European Journal of Personality*, **1**, 37—44.

Petersen, D.R. (1965), 'Scope and generality of verbally defined personality factors', *Psychological Review*, **72**, 48—59.

Plomin, R. (1986), 'Behavior genetic methods', *Journal of Personality*, **54**, 226—61.

Plomin, R., DeFries, J.C., and Loehlin, J.C. (1977), 'Genotype—environment interaction and correlation in the analysis of human behavior', *Psychological Bulletin*, **84**, 309—22.

Plomin, R., DeFries, J.C., and McClearn, G.E. (1980), *Behavior Genetics: A primer*, San Francisco, CA: Freeman.

Price, R.H., and Bouffard, D.L. (1974), 'Behavioral appropriateness and situational constraint as dimensions of social behavior', *Journal of Personality and Social Psychology*, **30**, 579—86.

Rausch, M.L. (1977), 'Paradox, levels, and junctures in person—environment systems', in D. Magnusson and N.S. Endler (eds.), *Personality at the Crossroads: Current issues in interactional psychology*, Hillsdale NJ: Erlbaum, pp. 287—304.

Rotter, J.B. (1954), *Social Learning and Clinical Psychology*, New York, NY: Prentice Hall.

Rowe, D.C. (1989), 'Personality theory and behavior genetics: contributions and issues', in D.M. Buss and N. Cantor (eds.), *Personality Psychology: Recent trends and emerging directions*, New York: NY: Springer-Verlag, pp. 294—307.

Rushton, J.P., Jackson, D.N., and Paunonen, S.V. (1981), 'Personality: nomothetic or idiographic?: a response to Kenrick and Stringfield', *Psychological Review*, **88**, 582—9.

Rushton, J.P., Fulker, D.W., Neale, M.C., Nias, D.K.B., and Eysenck, H.J. (1986), 'Altruism and aggression: the heritability of individual differences', *Journal of Personality and Social Psychology*, **50**, 1192—8.

Sarason, I.G., Smith, R.E., and Diener, E. (1975), 'Personality research: components of variance attributable to the person and the situation', *Journal of Personality and Social Psychology*, **32**, 199—204.

Scarr, S. and McCartney, K. (1983), 'How people make their own environments: a theory of genotype—environment effects', *Child Development*, **54**, 424—35.

Schachter, S., and Latané, B. (1964), 'Crime, cognition, and the autonomous nervous system', in D. Levine (ed.), *Nebraska Symposium on Motivation*, Lincoln, NE: University of Nebraska Press, vol. 12, pp. 221—73.

Scheier, M.F., and Carver, C.S. (1982), 'Cognition, affect, and self-regulation', in M.S. Clark and S.T. Fiske (eds.), *Affect and Cognition*, Hillsdale NJ: Erlbaum, pp. 157—83.

Schutte, N.A., Kenrick, D.T., and Sadalla, E.K. (1985), 'The search for predictable settings: situational prototypes, constraint, and behavioral variation', *Journal of Personality and Social Psychology*, **49**, 121—8.

Secord, P.F. (1977), 'Social psychology in search of a paradigm', *Personality and Social Psychology Bulletin*, **3**, 41—50.

Snyder, M., and Ickes, W. (1985), 'Personality and social behavior', in G. Lindzey and E. Aronson (eds.), *Handbook of Social Psychology* (third edition), Reading, MA: Addison-Wesley, vol. 2, pp. 883—948.

Spearman, C.E. (1927), *The Abilities of Man*, New York, NY: Macmillan.

Stagner, R. (1976), 'Traits are relevant: theoretical analysis and empirical evidence', in N.S. Endler and D. Magnusson (eds.), *Interactional Psychology and Personality*, Washington, DC: Hemisphere, pp. 109—24.

Stattin, H. (1984), 'Developmental trends in the appraisal of anxiety-provoking situations', *Journal of Personality*, **52**, 46—57.

Sternberg, R.S., and Wagner, K.R. (eds.), (1986), *Practical Intelligence: Nature and Origin of Competence in the Everyday World*, Cambridge: Cambridge University Press.

Strelau, J. (1985), 'Temperament and personality: Pavlov and beyond', in J. Strelau, F.H.

Farley, and A. Gale (eds.), *The Biological Bases of Personality and Behaviour*, Washington, DC: Hemisphere, p. 1, pp. 25—43.

Thomas, A., and Chess, S. (1985), 'The behavioral study of temperament', in J. Strelau, F.H. Farley, and A. Gale (eds.), *The Biological Bases of Personality and Temperament*, Washington, DC: Hemisphere, vol. 1, pp. 213—25.

Tucker, D.M., Antes, J.R., Stenslie, C.E., and Barnhardt, T.M. (1978), 'Anxiety and lateral cerebral function', *Journal of Abnormal Psychology*, **87**, 380—3.

Van Heck, G.L. (1981), 'Anxiety: the profile of a trait', unpublished doctoral dissertation, Tilburg University, Tilburg, The Netherlands.

Van Heck, G.L. (1988), 'Modes and models in anxiety', *Anxiety Research*, **1**, 199—214.

Van Heck, G.L., and Van der Leeuw, E. (1975), 'Situatie en dispositie als variantiecomponenten in zelfbeoordeling en beoordeling van de ander' [Situation and disposition as components of variance in self-ratings and ratings of others], *Gedrag, Tijdschrift voor Psychologie*, **4/5**, 202—14.

Van Heck, G.L., Hettema, P.J., and Leidelmeijer, K.C.M. (1990), 'Temperament, situatievoorkeuren en situatie-transformaties' [Temperament, situation preferences, and situation transformations], *Nederlands Tijdschrift voor de Psychologie*, **45**, 1—16.

Vingerhoets, A.J.J.M. (1985), *Psychosocial Stress: An experimental approach: Life events, coping, and psychobiological functioning*, Lisse, The Netherlands: Swets & Zeitlinger.

Wakefield, J.C. (1989), 'Levels of explanation in personality theory', in D.M. Buss and N. Cantor (eds.), *Personality Psychology: Recent trends and emerging directions*, New York, NY: Springer-Verlag, pp. 333—46.

Wright, J.C., and Mischel, W. (1987), 'A conditional approach to dispositional constructs: the local predictability of social behavior', *Journal of Personality and Social Psychology*, **35**, 1159—77.

16/ The psychology of situations

Joseph P. Forgas
University of New South Wales, Australia

Guus L. Van Heck
Tilburg University, The Netherlands

Both organism and environment will have to be seen as systems, each with properties of its own, yet both hewn from basically the same block. Each has surface and depth, or overt and covert regions ... the interrelationship between the two systems has the essential characteristic of a 'coming-to-terms'. And this coming to terms is not merely a matter of the mutual boundary or surface areas. It concerns equally as much, or perhaps even more, the rapport between the central, covert layers of the two systems. It follows that, much as psychology must be concerned with the texture of the organism or of its nervous processes and must investigate them in depth, it also must be concerned with the texture of the environment as it extends in depth away from the common boundary.

(Source: Brunswik, 1957, p. 5)

Introduction

Is human behaviour the product of more or less autonomous dispositions within the person, or are our reactions governed by external, situational forces beyond our control? This age-old debate is not without its deep philosophical and ideological connotations. In analysing human action, philosophers since time immemorial have tended to emphasize either the internal, autonomous, 'free' character of the acting individual or the unmistakable situational regularities in action, consistent with the external determination of behaviour. Skinner (1971) was one of the more radical representatives of this latter philosophical tradition in recent psychology.

As the epigraph by Brunswik suggests, any understanding of personality processes is inextricably linked with the study of situations, and the way personality and situational factors interact in determining behaviour. Although interest in situations has a venerable history in psychology and in the social sciences in general, there has always been a significant bias towards explaining behaviour in terms of dispositions residing within individuals. The aim of this chapter is to provide a comprehensive overview of the significance of a psychology of situations for modern

418

personality theory. The first part of the chapter will consider the impact of 'situationism' on contemporary personality research, and the emergence of interactionist formulations in particular. Next, we shall discuss some of the major conceptualizations of situations in psychology and the other social sciences. Then some of the most important ecological and cognitive approaches to situations will be evaluated, followed by a brief overview of empirical research on people's implicit representation of various social situations. We shall conclude with a discussion of individual differences in situation representations, and the links between situation cognition and behaviour.

The situationist perspective on personality

For most of its history, personality research was based on strong dispositional assumptions, seeking to produce a predictive theory of behaviour first in typological terms, and later in trait terms. Such dispositional models implied that a person's beliefs, feelings, intentions, and typical ways of behaving could be condensed into a limited set of broad personality traits. Traits were assumed to be sufficiently stable and consistent to be powerful predictors, not only of general behavioural trends across time and situations, but also of single acts in concrete situations. Consequently, personality research has been largely a 'quest for such underlying broad dimensions', leading to the construction of 'hundreds of tests designed to infer dispositions, and almost none to measure situations' (Mischel, 1973, p. 153).

The last few decades, however, have seen a period of crisis and critical self-examination in personality psychology. By the late 1960s, serious doubts had arisen about the usefulness of the 'pure trait' model. The lack of success by personality measures in predicting behaviour in specific situations contributed much of this critical attitude. It is interesting that very similar concerns about trait-based predictions were expressed several decades earlier, to little effect. Reinhardt (1937) was among the first to note that the 'reliability of predictions as to future behaviour . . . when based solely upon a personality classification . . . depends not upon the constancy of individual purpose alone . . . but also upon the continuance or recurrence of the same type of situation' (p. 492). Similar doubts were expressed by a group of psychologists concerned with assessment:

> It is easy to predict precisely the outcome of the meeting of one known chemical with another known chemical in an immaculate test tube. But where is the chemist who can predict what will happen to a known chemical if it meets an unknown vessel? How can a psychologist foretell with any accuracy the outcome of future meetings of one barely known personality with hundreds of other, undesignated personalities in distant, undesignated cities, villages, fields and jungles . . . ?. (OSS Assessment Staff, 1948, p. 8)

Such concerns were voiced with increasing frequency (cf. Peterson, 1968; Vernon, 1964), but it was Mischel's (1968) book *Personality and Assessment* that stimulated the most debate. Mischel (1968) reviewed impressive evidence showing that correlations between behaviours supposedly predicted by the same personality trait were usually less than 0.30 across situations. In attempting to explain these results, Mischel suggested that on virtually all non-intelligence-related, dispositional measures, substantial changes occur in personal characteristics longitudinally over time and, especially, across seemingly similar settings cross-sectionally. For that reason, only modest links — labelled 'personality coefficients' by Mischel — should be expected between behaviours that supposedly reflect the same trait, and between scores on trait questionnaires and non-self-report measures of the same trait.

What followed was an upsurge of the old debate about the relative value of situationist and personological models which first took place in the 1930s (for example, Hartshorne and May, 1928; Newcomb, 1929). Once again, the question of cross-situational consistency in behaviour was at the centre of the controversy, and the attack on the trait model elicited a plethora of reactions (for example, Bowers, 1973; Endler and Magnusson, 1976; Epstein, 1979; Hettema and Kenrick, 1989). Some defended the generality of trait-related behaviours across situations by accusing Mischel of unfair selectivity in his review of the literature (Craik, 1969; Hogan *et al.*, 1977). Others proposed the study of behaviour in aggregated form (for example, Epstein, 1979) or suggested various other reconceptualizations of the trait model (see Schmitt and Borkenau, Chapter 2 in this volume). Still others suggested a paradigmatic shift by introducing alternative, non-dispositional models.

For a growing number of researchers, situationism emerged as a prominent non-dispositional model by the early seventies. In his critical review, Mischel (1968) pointed at the strong situational control of behaviour and, within a social learning perspective, argued that in predicting behaviour the emphasis should be on observable, specific stimulus conditions, rather than on broad, intrapsychic dispositions: 'social behaviour theory seeks order and regularity in the form of general rules which relate environmental changes to behavioural changes' (Mischel, 1968, p. 150). This situationist critique was no doubt also influenced by the positivist *Zeitgeist* in psychology, and the growing success of situationist behaviour therapies in clinical psychology, formerly a client-branch of personality research.

As a result of the person—situation debate, many personality psychologists left the field or joined social psychologists and behavioural clinicians in a situationist attack on personality (Hogan and Emler, 1978; Kenrick and Dantchik, 1983). In this period attention also shifted to social cognition and attributions, and to research in laboratory situations which severely constrained the operation of personality differences. In their enthusiasm for the situationist approach, some researchers seemed not to realize that the strength of situational effects in experimental research also does not generally exceed a correlation of 0.30−0.40 (cf. Funder and Ozer, 1983).

With hindsight, it is now possible to present a more detached appraisal of the strengths and weaknesses of the situationist position (Krahé, 1990). The early emphasis on reinforcement principles implied a rather narrow understanding of the concept of situation, 'concentrating on just one out of a great variety of potentially relevant defining features' (Krahé, 1990, p. 18). Regarding the situationist assumption that individual differences within a situation are largely due to measurement error, Krahé points out that social learning theories do allow for individual differences due to cognitive personality variables (for example, Mischel, 1973; see also Cervone and Lloyd Williams, Chapter 8 in this volume). Moreover, situationists often mistake the situational antecedents of behaviour for an explanation of the observed relationship (Bowers, 1973). Situationism also tended to misidentify the S-R model with a 'neutral' methodological strategy, that is, the experiment (cf. Bowers, 1973). Eventually, in a clarification of his position, Mischel (1973) also seemed to back away from an extreme situationist stance, suggesting that the evidence he reviewed 'should not be misread as an argument for the greater importance of situations than persons' (p. 259).

Situationism thus served as a necessary and warranted corrective to trait psychology. However, radical 'situationism has gone too far in the direction of rejecting the role of organismic or intrapsychic determinants of behaviour' (Bowers, 1973, p. 307). Ultimately, both the trait and the situationist positions appear misleading. Instead, an approach stressing the interaction of the person and the situation emerged as a paradigm that is both conceptually balanced and empirically feasible (Bowers, 1973; Pervin, 1981).

Situations in interactionist models

Interactionism also has extensive antecedents in personality psychology. Interest in interactional models can be traced back at least to the 1920s and 1930s (cf. Ekehammar, 1974; Endler and Edwards, 1986). More than half a century ago authors like Angyal (1941), Kantor (1924, 1926), Lewin (1936) and Murray (1938) were already focusing on the complex interplay of the organism and the environment, approaches that we shall discuss in more detail shortly. These earlier formulations share with more recent models the theoretical position expressed in the formula $B = f(P,E)$, stating that behavioural variation is a joint function of personal and environmental (situational) variables.

One research paradigm within this tradition is the so-called variance components approach (for example, Olweus, 1977), investigating variable reactions to situations using questionnaires organized in a stimulus-response format (for example, Endler *et al.*, 1962). This S-R format has been used to study situational variability in anxiety, hostility, friendliness, and several other personality traits. Such S-R questionnaires measure behavioural reactions in a series of situations, such as 'You are going to meet a new date' or 'You are getting up to give a speech before a large group' (Endler *et al.*, 1962). This approach makes it possible to determine the proportion of behavioural variance attributable to situations, responses, and persons, and the interactions among them. Of course, the same variance components model also applies if, instead of S-R questionnaire data, observations of behaviour or psychophysiological reactions are recorded in different laboratory or natural settings (for example, Van Heck, 1981). Table 16.1 illustrates this sort of approach and the results it generates. Compare, for instance, this outcome with Bowers's (1973) meta-analysis, including

Table 16.1 Mean percentages of variance components for each component of reported responses to situations obtained with different Dutch versions of an S-R anxiety questionnaire

Source	Administration	
	First	Second
Persons (P)	13.0	17.0
Situations (S)	11.9	10.5
Response variables (R)	12.1	12.2
P × S	21.9	22.2
P × R	9.0	10.2
S × R	2.7	2.0
P × S × R	3.1	3.5
Residual	26.2	22.4

Note: $N = 136$.
Source: Van Heck, 1981.

18 comparisons, which showed that the average variance due to persons was approximately 13 per cent, variance due to situations approximately 10 per cent, and variance due to person × situation interactions around 21 per cent. Thus, the results in Table 16.1 clearly demonstrate that the interaction between persons and situations is the largest source of variance next to the error term.

Person—situation interaction can also be studied using other methods, such as the correlational strategy, and the person × treatment (situation) experimental design (cf. Endler and Edwards, 1986; Endler and Magnusson, 1976). The correlational approach provides the most direct test of the relative consistency hypothesis, stating that there is a monotonous, linear relationship between a person's position on latent personality dimensions, and his or her positions on scales which serve as indicators for this trait (Magnusson, 1976). This implies that, with respect to a certain type of behaviour, stable rank orders of individuals across situations and trait indicators should exist. Classic studies on the nature of character by Hartshorne and May (1928; see also Schmitt and Borkenau, Chapter 2 in this volume) illustrate this approach.

These authors used self-report and observational data to study honesty in children in a number of different settings. They found considerable consistency in opinions on moral issues, yet moral behaviour showed little consistency as the situation was changed. This need not mean that behaviour is characterized by capriciousness (Mischel, 1973). Rather, such outcomes indicate the existence of an interactive relationship between person and situation in affecting behaviour. A replication of the Hartshorne and May study (Nelson *et al.*, 1969) showed similar results, leading these authors to conclude that 'the findings support the ... contention that neither persons nor situations alone account for major behavioral variance. Thus, future theory and research ... must take into account interactions as well as main effects' (p. 278). In general, the correlational approach has found relative consistency for structural variables (such as, abilities, cognitive competency), for similar situations, and for longitudinal consistency, but little or no evidence for cross-situational consistency with respect to personal and social variables (cf. Endler and Edwards, 1986, p. 382).

In person × situation experimental designs, person and situation variables are both independent variables, with the size of the interaction effect reflecting their degree of interdependence (cf. Endler, 1988). Typical studies within this tradition are the aptitude-treatment interaction studies looking at instruction effects (cf. Cronbach and Snow, 1975), and the anxiety studies based on Endler's (1983) interaction model of anxiety. In Endler's anxiety studies it is found that in order for a person × situation interaction to occur in producing changes in state anxiety, it is necessary for the threatening situation to be congruent with the facet of trait anxiety being investigated (for example, fear of physical danger, interpersonal anxiety, or evaluation anxiety).

Another, more cognitive approach to interactionism has been developed by Mischel and his colleagues over the past two decades (Wright and Mischel, 1987, 1988). In his cognitive social learning formulation, Mischel (1973) proposed that instead of traits, person variables should emphasize such measures as cognitive construction competencies, encoding strategies, personal constructs, plans, outcome expectancies, and subjective stimulus values. In Wright and Mischel's (1987, 1988) more recent model, traits are conceived of as conditional probabilities that a particular action will be evoked by a particular environmental state. In contrast to the classic, relatively context-free conceptualizations of traits, dispositional constructs here are viewed as clusters of if-then propositions.

In most of these approaches to the interaction of persons and situations, as Endler (1983) pointed out, we still seem to be dealing with static snapshots rather than full-length movies. Although structural analyses do have their use — for instance, if the interest is in predictation rather than in understanding (cf. Diener *et al.*, 1984) — they do not enable us to explain the process of interaction. However, it is precisely the study of the dynamic process of mutual influence between person and environments that had been initially advocated by Kantor, Lewin, Murray, and other originators of the interactionist position. Modern interactionism has been increasingly sensitive to the dynamic aspects of the person—situation relationship (see Hettema and Kenrick, Chapter 15 in this volume).

Such a dynamic interactionist model is concerned with the ongoing process of how persons affect situations and are affected by them. The tenets of such an approach were spelled out by Endler and Magnusson (1976) some years ago. Thus, interactionism has four features:

1. Actual behaviour is a function of a continuous process or multidirectional interaction (feedback) between the individual and the situation that he or she encounters.
2. The individual is an intentional active agent in this interaction process.
3. On the person side of the interaction, cognitive factors are the essential determinants of behaviour, although emotional factors do play a role.
4. On the situation side, the psychological meaning of the situation for the individual is the important determining factor (cf. Endler and Magnusson, 1976, p. 968).

Although these assumptions were further elaborated by Endler (1983), unfortunately, no suitable methodology for the study of these unfolding, reciprocal transactions has been offered (see, however, Hettema and Kenrick, Chapter 15 in this volume). With the addition of emotional and motivational factors to basic cognitive strategies, Endler's approach comes close to Mischel's (1973) original list of important personological variables.

Interactionist models tend to focus on the psychological meaning of situations, paying less attention to the role of the objective situation in behaviour (Endler, 1983). Researchers typically focus on comparisons between subjective situational characteristics associated, for example, with anxiety (such as demand for achievement, accidents, etc.), and their perceived consequences (such as separation, personal inadequacy, guilt, etc.) (Magnusson, 1988). Others, such as Endler (1983), Mischel (1973), and Pervin (1976), also point to the need to study people's subjective plans, projects, goals, strategies, and rules of behaviour (see also Hettema and Kenrick, Chapter 15 in this volume). There is probably a complementary need to investigate the role of objective, environmental aspects of situations as cues for behaviour, as well as how and why persons choose the situations they encounter.

It is thus clear that in order to develop comprehensive theories of person—situation interactions, it is essential that we first address the problem of how situations may be defined, described, classified, and analysed. In the next section we shall look at some of the problems in the definition and classification of situations, and we will also survey the major alternative approaches developed for study of situations both in psychology and in related disciplines.

Situations in psychology

What is a 'situation'? How can we define such a complex and ambiguous term in a way that makes it amenable to scientific research? Despite the widespread use of the concept of situations in psychology, a clear definition of this term continues to remain elusive. Situations can be conceptualized in a variety of ways, as most reviews suggest (for example, Edwards, 1984; Forgas, 1979a, 1982; Magnusson, 1981; Van Heck, 1984, 1989). Because of the inherent complexity and ambiguity of the term, some theorists see little point in the continued use of this concept. For example, Cottrell (1970) writes that 'I sometimes suspect that the utility of [this term] is quite as great in preserving an illusion of understanding as it is in conveying genuine comprehension' (p. 68). One source of difficulty is that 'often the concept of situation is left undefined, and frequency it is used interchangeably with the concepts of stimulus and environment' (Pervin, 1975, p. 8).

Fortunately, in a practical sense stimuli, patterns of stimuli, and situations do not appear to us without order. As Kelly (1955) pointed out earlier, perceived regularity in the environment is a necessary prerequisite for directed behaviour. The human ability to discern and symbolically represent recurring, typical situations and episodes lies at the heart of orderly social behaviour (cf. Mead, 1934). To the extent that order and regularity can be observed in the environment, it is possible to arrange patterns of stimuli and events along dimensions, and to group them into homogeneous categories on the basis of common characteristics. Indeed, this approach has proved to be among the most fruitful in the construction of reliable and meaningful models of situational domains (Forgas, 1979a, 1986, 1988).

Apart from a definition of situations in terms of specific temporal and spatial boundaries, the psychological literature suggests a number of different ways of characterizing situations. These may include situation descriptions based on: (1) objective ecological dimensions (such as geographical characteristics, meteorological variables, and architectural features); (2) behaviour settings (natural patterns of environment/behaviour match); (3) organizational structure (size, hierarchy systems, number of supervisees, etc.); (4) the personal and behavioural characteristics of inhabitants; (5) psychosocial features and organizational climate (such as relationship, personal-development, and system-maintenance dimensions); and (6) reinforcement properties (cf. Moos, 1973). But situations have also been described and categorized in terms of other features such as norms (for example, Price and Bouffard, 1974), rules (for example, Argyle, 1977), feelings (for example, Mehrabian and Russell, 1974), expectancies (for example, Lazarus, 1966), goals (for example, Hettema and Hol, 1989a; Pervin, 1981), and other person-specific or objectively defined characteristics or components such as tasks, roles, needs, skills, or acts (cf. Magnusson, 1981). Most of these strategies are based on a rich tradition of earlier work on situations in psychology going back several decades. Concern with situations played a particularly important role in S-R theories, and in the work of *Gestalt* and phenomenological psychologists.

Situations in learning and conditioning research

The contemporary situationist position may be seen as but the latest reincarnation of the environmentalist principles of traditional learning theory, principles that have also been assimilated into contemporary social learning formulations. Even though radical conditioning and learning theories were among the first to emphasize the external, situational determination of behaviour, it is remarkable that systematic research on situations has never been part of the behaviourist agenda. Instead, the elusive search for general laws of learning led behaviourists to focus their attention almost exclusively on unrepresentative behaviours elicited in unrepresentative situations (in the laboratory), and often leading to unrepresentative results (Seligman, 1976).

Early radical behaviourism as represented by Watson and Guthrie was mainly concerned with atomistic stimulus-response chains instead of global situations, in essence fragmenting 'the physical environment into discrete, quantifiable stimuli' (Tuan, 1972, p. 250). The satisfying and annoying effects of environments were first explicitly recognized by Thorndike, although his conception of the situation was still atomistic and external. The beginnings of a global, cognitive, and even interactive conceptualization of situations first emerged in Tolman's later works

(Tolman, 1949). In addition to allowing for the possibility of internal representations, or 'cognitive maps' of situations, Tolman was also among the first to recognize the important role of motivation and goals in situation representations.

Perhaps the most consistently global and interactive conceptualization of situations in early behaviourist research is associated with Kantor (1924, 1926), who proposed that the individual should be studied as 'he interacts with all the various types of situations which constitute his behaviour circumstances' (p. 92). Kantor also incorporated the important distinction between the external, ecological situation and its internal representation by the actor in his model, and suggested in his later 'interbehaviourism' that individuals are not mere 'reactors' to situational changes, but genuinely 'interact' with situations.

Learning theorists were thus among the first to pay serious attention to environmental, situational regularities in behaviour, partly as a historical reaction to Wundtian introspectionism. Their conceptualization of situations evolved from early, atomistic and ecological approaches to later, more molar and representational models. However, at no time did behaviourist research seriously deal with the study of representative situations, an omission that contributed much to the eventual failure of the strict behaviourist paradigm (Seligman, 1976). By assuming that all stimulus-response chains essentially obey the same laws that can be recreated in the laboratory, learning theorists managed to ignore that which should have been the focus of their attention: the study of representative situations typical of the organism's natural environment.

It was not until the advent of social learning theory that interest in global situations was rekindled. For example, Rotter (1955) remained within the learning theoretical tradition in defining situations objectively, yet allowing for the importance of subjective representations: 'Behaviours, reinforcements and situations may be defined in objective terms, although their significance and systematic formulae are concerned with constructs relating to personal or acquired meaning' (1955, p. 260). Rotter (1955) was also influential in emphasizing the need for the systematic description and classification of situations, a task that remains as important today is it was almost four decades ago.

Ultimately, it was Egon Brunswick who, perhaps more than any other psychologist, claimed a central place for the study of situations in our discipline. In arguing for a 'representative design' he suggested that 'proper sampling of situations and problems may in the end be more important than proper sampling of subjects, considering . . . that individuals are probably on the whole much more alike than are situations' (p. 39). Representative design in research should involve the careful sampling of typical life situations relevant to the organism, in contrast with conventional systematic designs based on the study of arbitrarily selected variables in *ad hoc* settings, such as the laboratory. His classification of situations in terms of their relationship to the actor (distal, proximal, and central), and their observability (overt vs. covert) remains one of the more influential taxonomies to date. The evolution of S-R conceptualizations of situations thus clearly shows a gradual shift from atomistic, physical, and reductionistic approaches to more global and subjective definitions.

However, all along there has been an alternative, more phenomenological tradition in dealing with situations. We shall look at these approaches next.

Phenomenological approaches to situations

Just as the extremely reductionist and atomistic formulations of radical behaviourists such as Watson were a reaction to Wundt's emphasis on consciousness, in due course a holistic, *Gestalt* psychology arose to correct the balance once again. By insisting on the wholeness of human experience, *Gestalt* psychologists such as Wertheimer, Köhler, and Koffka recognized the difference between objective, physical, and subjective, psychological situations, and also understood the interactive nature of the person–situation link. As Koffka (1935) wrote, 'G is the geographical environment. It produces BE, the behavioural environment; in this, and regulated by it, RB, real behaviour, takes place, and parts of it are revealed in PHB, phenomenal behaviour' (p. 40).

There are unmistakable links between this approach, and Lewin's (1936) classic 'field theory', perhaps the first comprehensive model in which an actor's representation of the psychological situation is accorded central place. As Mischel (1969) suggested, although Lewin told us about the environment's role long ago, his impact seems to have been more on textbooks than on personality theorists. The major contribution of Lewin's theory is its emphasis on the phenomenal situation, the actor's 'life space', as the ultimate influence on behaviour. It is not the objective, external situation that matters, but the situation as seen and understood by an actor: 'the situation must be represented in a way that is "real" for the individual in question, that is, as it affects him' (1936, p. 25). Sociologists studying cultural adaptation came to remarkably similar conclusions, as Thomas's (1928) classic pronouncement illustrates: 'if men define situations as real, they are real in their consequences' (Thomas, 1929/1966, p. 522). Lewinian field theory also regarded situations as holistic. A person's understanding of the surrounding situation, or phenomenal field, including his or her actions within it, are an indivisible whole.

The interaction between the person and the environment was also very much in the focus of Murray's (1938) seminal theories. As he suggested, 'the conduct of an individual cannot be formulated without a characterization of each confronting situation, physical or social ... the organism and its milieu must be considered together, as a single creature–environment interaction being a convenient short unit for psychology' (Murray, 1938, pp. 39–40). Murray's characterization of situations in terms of their satisfying or inhibiting potential ('press'), and individuals in terms of their need states, created a coherent conceptual system where both individuals and situations could be described in terms of a common set of features. Indeed, Murray also proposed a tentative two-dimensional classificatory system, distinguishing between situations in terms of positive–negative and mobile–immobile press. There is a clear similarity between this taxonomic system and later dimensions such as evaluation and potency, found to underlie a wide range of social phenomena, including perceptions of social situations (cf. Forgas, 1979a, 1982, 1991a). It is unfortunate that Murray's calls for the ingrated classification of persons and situations remained largely unheeded.

Others such as Angyal (1941) were also strongly influenced by Lewin and the *Gestalt* tradition, and sought to develop a unified theoretical system emphasizing the inseparability of person and situation. With Lewin, Angyal believed that it is the subjective, perceived situation that is critical, since 'every person has his own personal world consisting of objects, the content of which is highly individualistic and not comparable with the content they have for another person' (Angyal, 1941, p. 160). In proposing a phenomenological theory of personality, others, such as Jessor (1956), suggested that 'the development of an adequate psychological data language to describe the environment' (p. 178) was an essential task in the quest for such a theory. Ultimately, the phenomenological approach led to the emergence of self-theories, such as Rogers's (1951) humanistic perspective. Within this framework, the objective situation — Koffka's 'geographical environment' — all but disappears. Situations are thus seen as part of the phenomenal field of individuals, where a person is by definition the best source of information not only about him or herself, but also about his or her meaningful environment: 'the organism reacts to the field as it is experienced and perceived. This perceptual field is, for the individual, reality' (Rogers, 1951, p. 484).

Situations in symbolic interactionist theory

The symbolic interactionist approach developed by Mead in a sense represents a sophisticated synthesis of the behaviourist and phenomenologist models. Thus, Mead's social behaviourism (only later to be called symbolic interactionism) was an 'attempt to correct many of the crudities of early behaviourist psychology . . . [he] believed that the scope of behaviourism could be extended to include the neglected introspective phenomena' (Desmonde, 1970, p. 57). In emphasizing the uniquely symbolic, cognitive nature of human behaviour, Mead suggested that individual personality and consensual representations of social situations are both constructed in the course of social interaction. Social behaviour is thus partly predetermined by the situation, and is partly constructed by the actor, reflecting the dual nature of persons as incorporating both the thoroughly socialized 'Me', and the subjective and creative 'I'.

Situations are thus social objects, continuously created and redefined in social interaction: in every episode, 'we find that the situation is partially structured by past definitions, it has already been defined in terms of role scripts and normative expectations. At the same time, the episode is always open, it is subject to reinterpretation and . . . the creation of new accounts and meanings' (Brittan, 1973, p. 84). It is the unique ability of humans to engage in symbolic processes that allows them to create and distil consensual representations about situations that makes social life possible. Accumulated social expertise in familiar situations lies at the core of the socially determined 'Me' — yet the creative 'I' can always monitor, redefine, and reassess social situations.

Situations in symbolical interactionism thus have a dual nature — they are 'givens', part of the existing consensual social structure; at the same time, they are also processes, the continuous re-creation and modification of shared meanings in the course of interaction. Thus, symbolic interactionists 'repudiate the notion that man is a passive neutral agent . . . Man is both actor (the "I"), and acted upon (the "Me"), both subject and object' (Stone and Farberman, 1970, p. 9). It is this duality, the 'contradiction between determinancy and indeterminancy in Mead's overall point of view' (Kuhn, 1970, p. 72) that is the theory's greatest strength as well as weakness. The limited impact of symbolic interactionism on empirical psychology has much to do with this ambiguity, as well as the problems encountered in translating Mead's ideas into a reliable empirical methodology. Yet Mead's theory comes perhaps closest to capturing truly the dual, objective and subjective, nature of psychological situations, leading some to suggest that his is the only genuinely 'social' psychology: 'symbolic interactionism will emerge as the dominant perspective for the future. Psychoanalysis, learning theory and field theory will ultimately be laid to rest in the vast graveyard of social science theory' (Stone and Farberman, 1970, pp. 19−20). Whether this optimistic prediction will come to pass or not, symbolic interactionism certainly provides one of the most useful and sophisticated approaches to situations that should be of direct interest to contemporary personality researchers.

Situations in psychology: some preliminary conclusions

As this brief review suggests, concern with situations has a long tradition both in psychology and in sociology. However, situational analysis remained a minority preoccupation in both disciplines, despite recurring criticisms of the cross-situational consistency assumption underlying much of mainstream research. Although Brunswik's (1956) calls for the representative study of situations had limited impact, several clear lines of evolution can be discerned. As we have noted earlier, 'the concept of situation emerged from the concept of stimulus in psychology, with a gradual shift from the atomistic to the holistic, from the physical to the social, and from the objective (external) to the subjective (perceived) situation' (Forgas, 1979a, p. 68).

Perhaps most clear-cut has been the shift in interest from decontextualized, *atomistic* stimuli to the study of *holistic* situations, from the molecular to the molar level of analysis. There is also a discernible change in perspective away from purely *physical* aspects of the environment to the study of situations as impregnated with *social* meaning, as Barker's (1968) work on behaviour settings illustrates (see below). Another emerging distinction concerns *potential* as against *actual* situations: the first exist independent of the actor as a determinant of behaviour, while actual situations involve the constructive enactment and redefinition of pre-existing situation scripts. Most studies look at pre-existing, potential, and consensual situations, while research on the dynamic aspects of action in actual situations remains relatively rare. Perhaps the most pervasive change has occurred in the shift in interest from the external, objective situation — Murray's alpha press — to the subjective, perceived situation — Murray's beta press. It seems that the 'essential conceptual distinction is between the objective, outer world as it affects the individual, and the subjective world, the environment as the individual perceives and reacts to it' (Ekehammar, 1974, p. 13). Thus, one important aspect of situations is that they embody shared socio-cultural expectations about appropriate forms of behaviour, a question we shall examine next.

The social and cultural aspects of situations

As the above overview suggests, situations are not merely physical, environmental, and even psychological entities. In a fundamental sense, situations are also group products, the elementary building blocks of cultural and social systems, consensually created and maintained by interacting individuals. Concern with situations has never been the exclusive prerogative of psychologists. The quest to understand social behaviour in terms of the delicate interplay between social norms, rules, and structures and the creative, constructive behaviour of individuals has inevitably led scores of social scientists to deal with situational regularities in behaviour. We shall briefly consider the social and cultural aspects of situations next.

Situations in cultural sociology

Max Weber is perhaps the foremost representative of the cultural sociology approach. Weber's work is profoundly psychological in orientation, taking meaningful, situated, individual behaviour as its basic unit of analysis, and seeking to understand the 'subjective meaning which seems to the actor himself or to the observer an adequate ground for the conduct in question' (Weber, 1947, p. 100). 'Elective affinity' is the term used by Weber to describe the process whereby individuals selectively accept and internalize those aspects of an ideational system and situational rules that are relevant to their condition. In analysing different 'ideal' types of human action, Weber distinguished between traditional (habitual), affective (emotion-governed), value-oriented (*Wertrational*), and goal-oriented (*Zweckrational*) types of action. This taxonomic system largely depends on the subjective meanings individuals attach to their behaviours, and in important ways also anticipates more recent taxonomies of social situations. Weber's understanding of the socio-cultural context of social action offers a more sophisticated and enlightening analysis than do, for example, Marx's popular, yet in comparison crude, economic deterministic ideas about culture and society. Weber's concern with how subjective meanings are created, maintained, and negotiated in social situations also served as one of the foundations of micro-sociological research on situated behaviour (Garfinkel, 1967; Goffman, 1974).

The definition of the situation

On the basis of Weber's pioneering work, the way social actors come to understand and define situations also played a major role in Thomas and Znaniecki's classic studies of cultural adaptation. According to Thomas (1923), preliminary to 'any self-determined act or behaviour there is always a stage of examination and deliberation which we may call the definition of the situation' (p. 41). It is in the course of defining the situation that social actors make sense of and interpret cultural and behavioural precedents, and create their own unique reactions to them. In other words, the 'individual does not find passively ready situations exactly similar to past situations; he must consciously define every situation . . . in order to control social reality for his needs, [he] must develop not a series of uniform reactions, but general *schemes* of situations; his life-organization is a set of rules for specific situations, which may even be expressed in abstract formulas' (Thomas, 1928/1966, p. 29). Recent suggestions by Mischel and others on studying individual differences in terms of 'situation interpretation schemes' was thus clearly anticipated by Thomas. In his work on cultural adaptation, Thomas even distinguished between typical 'personality' types (such as the Philistine, Bohemian and Creative types) in terms of their characteristic ways of defining and dealing with situations. Predating the recent situationist debate by several decades, Thomas recognized that 'behaviour patterns and the total personality [are] . . . overwhelmingly conditioned by the types of situations and trains of experience encountered by the individual' (Thomas, 1928/1966, p. 154), and 'as long as definitions of situations remain constant and common we may anticipate orderly behaviour reactions' (p. 166). Thus, Thomas was among the first to recognize clearly the crucial role that small-scale situations and social episodes play not only in the construction of personality, but also in making up the larger social order.

It is perhaps unfortunate that far too little attention has been paid to these pioneering attempts to understand person–situation interactions in contemporary personality theory. Situational analysis as proposed by Thomas was not adopted by mainstream sociologists either, for much the same reasons that prevented psychologists from embracing this approach. As Ball (1972) suggests, 'both sociology and psychology, in their conventional forms, as does everyday life, operate with what may be called the *personal consistency assumption* . . . situations are taken as given, unproblematic, essentially epiphenomenal to the conduct which is to be explained' (pp. 65–6). It is paradoxical that attempts to redress the long-standing neglect of situational influences on behaviour in personality research were often rooted in social learning theory (Mischel, 1968), while in sociology it was phenomenologists who most consistently championed the cause of situational analysis (Douglas, 1973).

The role of a shared cultural experience in the definition of situations was even more strongly emphasized by Thomas's collaborator, Florian Znaniencki, and their followers. For example, Waller (1970) suggested that 'many persons living together . . . have mapped out clearly the limitations of behaviour inherent in the social situations most common in their culture. From their experience has arisen a consensus of what is, and what is not thinkable in those situations. We may refer to these group products as definitions of situations' (p. 162). In a similar vein, Schutz (1970) suggested that a 'system of folkways establishes the standard in terms of which the in-group "defines the situation". Even more: originating in previous situations defined by the group, the scheme of interpretation that has stood the test so far becomes an element of the actual situation' (p. 80). It is thus such a system of consensually shared recipes, or 'scripts' to use a more contemporary term (Abelson, 1981), that lies at the core of what we see as stable individual personalities and social systems. Our research on the cognitive representations of social episodes offers one empirical avenue along which to explore the nature of such implicit situation models (cf. Forgas, 1979a, 1983a, 1983b, 1988).

Situations in microsociology

Contemporary microsociological theories also owe much to this situationist tradition in sociology (cf. Garfinkel, 1967; Goffman, 1974). The dramaturgical model of Goffman carries situational analysis to its extreme: he is no longer concerned with how people come to understand and define situations. Rather, it is the situation that defines the actor. Like Macchiavelli's Prince, Goffman's social actors have 'no internal specifications. Rather, situations specify them ... Goffman has also adopted the specific unit of investigation derived from Macchiavelli's conception of social life — the episode' (Lyman and Scott, 1972, pp. 20–2). Goffman's theatrical analogy implies that situations are defined by clear-cut, consensual rules, and the actor's main concern is to interpret the applicable script correctly in order to stage a creditable social performance. Acquiring and implementing the appropriate performance strategies is what skilled behaviour in various situations is all about; we may call such a 'natural unit of social organization in which focused interaction occurs as focused gathering, or an encounter, or a situated activity system' (Goffman, 1963, p. 7). Violating situational conventional not only leads to loss of face, but also threatens the fragile social structure that sustains encounters: 'the process of mutually sustaining a definition of the situation ... is socially organized ... it is to these flimsy rules ... that we owe our unshaking sense of realities .... To be awkward or unkempt, to talk or move wrongly, is to be a dangerous giant, a destroyer of worlds' (1963, p. 81). The analysis of situational rules lies at the heart of Goffman's work, and he is much less concerned than Weber, Thomas, or Schutz with how actors experience and interpret situations.

Such a reification of the situation is perhaps taken even further in the work of ethnomethodologists such as Garfinkel (1967). For these researchers, the achievement of coordinated situated interaction is intrinsically problematic. Their methods are directed at discovering the applicable situational rules, often by systematically disrupting particular events. As Garfinkel (1967) writes, 'it is my preference to start with familiar scenes and ask what can be done to make trouble ... and to produce disorganised interaction [which] should tell us something about how the structures of everyday activities are ordinarily and routinely produced and maintained' (p. 37). It is paradoxical that ethnomethodology, while most directly concerned with the study of naturalistic situations, has relatively little to contribute to a *psychology* of situations. Because it reduces all social behaviour to instances of rule-following, the psychological aspects of perceiving, constructing, and maintaining situations receive little attention.

As even this by necessity brief review shows, there has been a respectable tradition of interest in the social and cultural character of situations. The cultural sociology of Max Weber, W.I. Thomas and Florian Znaniecki on the one hand, and Mead's symbolic interactionism on the other, provide the two major theoretical influences on this work. Indeed, it can be argued that it is the recognitions of the 'fundamental importance of the question of situationalism and transsituationalism that has most distinguished phenomenological sociologies from absolutist (structural) sociologies' (Douglas, 1973, p. 35). Just as in psychological theorizing, there appears a dualism in sociological approaches to situations, emphasizing either (1) the actor's perception, interpretation, and definition of the situation, or (2) the culturally determined and shared aspects of situations.

It seems, then, that the study of situations has always been part of psychology and sociology, even though it never received the kind of mainstream attention it deserves. If the complex interplay between person and situation is to be understood, it will be necessary to develop suitable techniques for the empirical measurement of how people understand and represent molar social situations. 'The establishment of the dimensions of situations which are relevant for social behaviour is in a far more primitive state than the parallel study of personality', suggested Argyle and Little (1972, p. 28) some twenty years ago; unfortunately, their conclusion remains as valid today as it was then. The need to rectify this state of affairs was the major motivation underlying several influential research programmes aimed at the empirical description and analysis of situations, based on either ecological or cognitive principles.

Ecological approaches to situations: the study of behaviour settings

The conceptual framework

Unlike the social and cultural theories considered above, ecological approaches to situations focus on the objective environment of molar behaviour that exists independent of the psychological process of any particular individual. Such research is directly relevant to various applied issues to do with privacy, personal space, territory, crowding, home environments, institutional environments, cities, communities, etc. (for example Altman, 1975; Barker, 1968; Stokols and Altman, 1987). The ecological context of behaviour thus includes both the social and the physical components of everyday settings for goal-directed, purposive behaviour (Barker, 1968; Schoggen, 1989).

The basic environmental unit in Barker's (1968) ecological psychology is the behaviour setting. The essential properties of a behavioural setting are as follows: (1) standing extra-individual patterns of behaviour with specific temporal-spatial coordinates; (2) constellations of non-behavioural (physical, geographical) setting elements; (3) the fact that the physical-geographical-temporal environment is circumjacent to and synomorphic with the standing patterns of behaviour; and (4) the interdependence within a given behaviour setting of the various configurations of physical and behavioural attributes (see also Schoggen, 1989). The term 'synomorphy' in Barker's analysis denotes the interdependence between environment and behaviour, as recurring patterns of activity conform to the shape and requirements of the physical milieu. Thus, behaviour settings are essentially miniature social systems whose basic function is to carry out so-called setting programmes (Wicker, 1979).

For example, a behaviour setting such as a public lecture includes elements such as the chairperson's introducing the speaker, the speaker delivering his or her talk, and the audience sitting quietly (or laughing and applauding, or whatever the case may be). To facilitate the programme, behaviours of people and arrangements of physical objects within the boundaries of the setting are highly coordinated. The members of the audience stop conversing when the chairperson approaches the lectern. All of the seats in the lecture face the front so that those in attendance can see and hear the speaker. The boundaries of the setting are both physical (the walls of the lecture hall) and temporal (the scheduled hour and day of the lecture) (Wicker, 1979, pp. 755—6). Other examples of behaviour settings are the chemist's or drugstore, the meeting of the school board, a pop concert, etc. Behaviour settings are self-regulating systems. When essential components are missing or persons are not functioning properly, then corrective inputs will be given.

In 1947, Barker and his colleagues (Barker, 1965, 1968; Barker *et al.*, 1978) established a field station in Oskaloosa (800 inhabitants; called Midwest), Kansas, for the purpose of studying such situations. Their questions were: What goes on in the lecture hall, the drugstore, the school board meeting, the concert hall, and all the other settings of the town? They sought to answer these questions through the careful and painstaking analysis of behavioural episodes, the fundamental molar units of the behaviour stream. In doing so, they focused on the links between the physical and geographical environment and observable standing patterns of behaviour within each setting. This approach clearly differs from theories where the focus is upon the situation as it exists for a given person at a given time (such as Murray's 1938, environmental beta press or Lewin's 1936, 'psychological environment'). In Schoggen's words: 'the ecological environment is not equivalent to the psychological environment, which necessarily refers to the subjective representation of the objective environment by a given person at a particular time. In contrast, the ecological environment has a durable existence in the objective, preperceptual world independent of the psychological processes of any particular person' (Schoggen, 1989, p. 3). Thus, the description of a lecture (cf. Wicker, 1979) with its behaviour patterns (speaking, listening, applauding, chairperson, speaker, audience, etc.) and its physical-geographical-temporal properties (lecture hall, lectern, microphone, seats, etc.) emphasizes the observable, objective environment regardless of its psychological significance for any particular pupil. From the nature of its setting, much ongoing behaviour can be predicted without any further assumptions about the intrapsychic aims, motivations, or personalities of the actors (Stern, 1970). In a similar vein, Gibson (1979) defines 'affordances' as what the physical and social environment offers, provides, or furnishes. Thus, while the organism depends on its environment (for example, other persons afford interpersonal interactions and a terrestrial surface affords support), the environmental does not depend on the organism for its existence. Gibson's views are thus similar to those of Barker: 'both are concerned with the objective, preperceptual environment that exists out there independent of the psychological processes of any particular observer or actor' (Schoggen, 1989, p. 304).

Behaviour setting surveys

The most extensive surveys of behaviour settings stem from the Barker group's own work. In two small towns, Midwest (USA) and Yoredale (UK), all behaviour settings belonging to common genotypes such as auction sales, libraries, worship services, etc. were identified and described in full detail (see Barker, 1965, 1968; Barker and Schoggen, 1973; Barker *et al.*, 1978). The aim of these surveys was to represent the total quality of life in these two communities, including the range of habitats, behaviour opportunities, and obligations, the degree of autonomy of behaviour settings, the freedom of movement for children, etc. For instance, in Midwest free movement for children included 78 per cent of all 884 behaviour settings, whereas in the case of the 758 behaviour settings in Yoredale the corresponding figure was 68 per cent. A comparison between the two communities also revealed that children and persons aged 65 and older in Midwest occupied positions of leadership and responsibility more frequently than did their English counterparts. Such data suggest that quality of life was very different in the two communities.

Studies of behaviour settings can provide a useful tool of situational analysis. Analyses of behaviour settings have been used to study community programmes, churches, hospitals, schools and classrooms (Barker *et al.*, 1978; Stokols and Altman, 1978). The study of behaviour settings can help to maintain the quality of life in isolated communities (Bechtel, 1982), and to analyse adaptation to environmental change (Harloff *et al.*, 1981). Typically, such studies show that behaviour is indeed strongly regulated by particular settings such as a cafeteria, a hallway, or a hospital ward.

Behaviour settings studies revealed the highly structured nature of the ecological environment (cf. Kaminski, 1986), and the approach has also been useful in measuring the impact of change on a community. Nevertheless, such descriptive studies of environments and behaviours in entire communities are rather scarce. Several reasons can be given for this state of affairs. One reason may be that the behavioural settings approach tends to neglect transitions between settings, and fails to provide adequately for responses that do not 'belong' to the setting (Kaminski, 1986). The required heavy investment in time and material to identify all behaviour settings in a community is another deterrent (see also Wicker, 1979). Ultimately, the behaviour settings approach is based not on a genuine psychological construct, but on a pre-psychological concept (Kaminski, 1986). Collecting large amounts of data with no theoretical underpinnings appears not to be to everybody's taste.

We would like to point to two other weaknesses of the approach. First, while descriptions of particular behaviour settings may have very high ecological validity, they often lack generality. What happens in Clifford's Drugstore or Midwest's Elementary School Faculty Meeting may not greatly increase our knowledge of drugstores or faculty meetings in general. As a consequence, survey findings are often doomed to stand alone. Second, the cognitions of setting occupants are completely neglected in the behaviour settings approach.

A somewhat related approach may be based on the insider perceptions of human environments (cf. Moos, 1973). A good example of this is the work of Pace and Stern (1958; Stern, 1970) on college climates. These authors developed an assessment instrument called the College Characteristics Index (CCI) consisting of 300 statements about the college environment. The different statements refer to curriculum, teachers, classroom activities, student organizations and interests, campus rules and regulations, administrative policies, physical features of the campus, etc. Using Murray's views on needs and presses as a theoretical framework and using the CCI as an assessment instrument, Pace and Stern (1958) found that the 'personalities' of college environments could be described in ways paralleling the 'personalities' of people. Unlike Barker's approach, the work of Pace and Stern introduces perceived presses in the description of the environment, while consistent with the Barker tradition, the assessment focuses on very concrete instances (such as Fort Wayne Bible College, Vassar, or Northeast Louisiana State College; and not on colleges in general).

Cognitive approaches: situations in the mind

Situations, scripts and prototypes

In contrast with the ecological strategy, cognitive concepts such as scripts, as proposed by Abelson (1981), provide an alternative paradigm to the study of situations. According to Abelson (1981), scripts refer to stylized, everyday situations and describe stereotyped, appropriate sequences of events in particular contexts (such as restaurants, drugstores, faculty meetings, college classes). Unlike behaviour settings, scripts are cognitive structures in the minds of actors as well as observers. While the script concept has been mainly used to study the information-processing consequences of scripted behaviour sequences (cf. Bower *et al.*, 1979), several related concepts have been proposed for the study of cognitive representations about global situations. Work on cognitive situation prototypes (Cantor, 1981; Cantor *et al.*, 1982; Hettema, 1979; Van Heck, 1984, 1989) and research on social episodes (Forgas, 1979a, 1981, 1982, 1983a, 1983b, 1988) provide two such complementary research strategies.

The concept of cognitive situation prototypes (for example, Cantor, 1981; Cantor *et al.*, 1982; Eckes and Six, 1984; Hettema, 1979; Van Heck, 1984, 1989) was developed to study situations in terms of their shared psychological meaning. As such, it allows the careful scrutiny of so-called canonical situations, situations that according to Block and Block (1981, p. 87) are 'consensually defined, consensually constructed, or consensually accepted'. Canonical situations (cf. the alpha press of Murray, 1938) are distinct from functional situations (cf. Murray's beta press). The latter, according to Block and Block (1981), represent the environmental context as it is effectively understood by the individual. The canonical form of situations refers to the psychological demand-quality or structure of the situation as specified by widely established categories of objects, concepts and relations, rules, standards, and normatively provided expectations.

The categorical-prototype analysis is based upon the prototype model developed by Rosch (1978). This model emphasizes the human tendency to group elements of the world, such as objects, people, or psychological events, into categories in terms of their non-unique, overlapping features, allowing categorization on the basis of patterns of 'family resemblances' (Rosch, 1978). According to this position, 'knowledge about any given category is structured around, and represented in, long-term memory as a prototype that captures the meaning of the category' (Cantor *et al.*, 1982, p. 35). The prototypical member of a category is represented by an ideal pattern of features, with each feature assigned a weight according to the degree of association with the category. Thus, situation prototypes function as standards around which more or less divergent exemplars are clustered. Consequently, situation prototypes may be operationally defined in terms of consensual attributes lists, and should have an organizing effect on the way people process the complex flood of environmental information. Although idiosyncratic prototypes are conceivable (cf. Eckes and Six, 1984), attention has mainly focused on the study of consensual prototypes.

Cantor *et al.*, (1982) studied situations within four broad categories, viz, social, cultural, stressful, and ideological, and at three levels of abstraction (for example, 'being in a social situation'; 'being at a party'; 'being at a birthday party'). For each cell in this 4 (categories) × 3 (levels of abstraction) matrix, subjects generated prototypical attributes. It was found that situational prototypes consisted of a combination of physical characteristics of the situation, characteristics (traits) of people in the situation, feelings associated with the situation, and behaviours associated with the situation. A similar approach was followed by Eckes and Six (1984). The most extensive study using this approach has been carried out by Van Heck (1984, 1989). This work aimed at the development of a general and exhaustive taxonomy of situations, which reflects the degree of orderliness in the layperson's everyday, 'natural' categorical knowledge about situations.

Van Heck took as his point of departure the 'lexical' approach (see Hofstee and DeRaad, Chapter 3 in this volume; Ostendorf and Angleitner, Chapter 4 in this volume). This approach posits that most of the socially relevant and salient personality and environment characteristics have been encoded in the natural language. Thus, the starting point was the natural-language dictionary as a source for situation concepts. A dictionary search produced a more or less exhaustive set of the everyday terms people use to describe their environment. Only nouns that refer to situations that can be objectively perceived (that is, with high consensus) were chosen. Those nouns were selected that could be meaningfully substituted into the following sentence frame: 'being confronted with a . . . situation'. After elimination of synonyms and archaic terms, a pool of 263 situation terms was formed with concepts at an intermediate level of abstraction.

The next step was towards the construction of consensual attributes lists for each situation. To compose a pool of situational attributes, a sample of 160 subjects, well-balanced with respect to sex, age, and socio-economic status, were interviewed, using Flanagan's (1949) critical incidents approach. In free descriptions of situations, subjects generated the essential characteristics of the 263 situation concepts. Content analysis of the taped interviews (total duration exceeding 200 hours, with the number of situation descriptions exceeding 4,000) resulted in a pool of 659 separate attributes belonging to the following content categories: (1) context; (2) location/physical environment; (3) objectively discernible characteristics of the physical environment; (4) persons; (5) objectively discernible characteristics of the persons concerned; (6) actions and activities; (7) objects/equipment; and (8) temporal aspects.

In the next stage of Van Heck's (1984, 1989) taxonomic study, the situation concepts were presented to a new group of subjects ($N = 744$). They were asked to give prototypicality ratings per situation concept for all the 659 identified situational attributes. Each situation was described by four subjects, viz, a male below the age of 30, a male above the age of 30, a female younger than 30, and a female older than 30. Situations were then correlated in terms of their prototypicality ratings and the resulting matrix was factor analysed. Ten situation factors were identified (see Table 16.2). The results of this general taxonomy of situations have since been successfully used in the construction of situation-specific means-ends questionnaires (so-called SRS questionnaires; cf. Hettema and Hol, 1989a; see also Van Heck *et al.*, 1990) and of situation-specific Big Five questionnaires (Van Heck, 1991), in designing role plays (Hettema and Hol, 1989b), and in the development of films representing everyday life situations for research purposes (Hettema *et al.*, 1989), suggesting the extensive utility of this approach in interactionist research.

Cognitive representations of social episodes

As we have seen, one of the most fruitful approaches to the study of representative situations is the cognitive-perceptual strategy. As Endler and Magnusson (1976) suggested,

> situation perception can be regarded as legitimate a research field as, for example, person perception. The traditional methods, rating scales, questionnaires, the semantic differential technique, and so forth, that are used for data collection in person perception can also be applied in studies of situation perception . . . In our opinion, research in this field of situation perception is one of the most urgent and also one of the most promising tasks for psychology. (pp. 967–9)

Several researchers have successfully employed these methods in questionnaire studies of situation perception (for example, Ekehammar, 1974; Endler *et al.*, 1962; Moos, 1973; Pervin, 1976). Such studies of perceived situational dimensions often find

Table 16.2 Situation factors and sample situations from Van Heck's (1984, 1989) situation taxonomy

Factor	Factor label	Sample situations
1.	Interpersonal conflict	Blackmail, murder, intimidation, fight, attack, boycott, obstruction, accusation, teasing, quarrel, physical violence, punishment, criticism, conflict, provocation, protest, interruption, intrigue, deceit, manipulation, etc.
2.	Joint working; exchange of thoughts, ideas, and knowledge	Lecture, test, job application, examination, interview, appointment, talk/conversation, judgment, instruction, work, job, cooperation, report, discussion, negotiation, deliberation, exchange of thoughts, therapy, lesson, phone call, etc.
3.	Intimacy and interpersonal relations	Pregnancy, death-bed, seduction, declaration of love, divorce, offer of marriage, gossip, wedding, courtship, flirt, visit, acquaintance(ship), etc.
4.	Recreation	Reception, dancing-party, inauguration, celebration, dinner, jubilee, reunion, feast, concert, diversion, show, game, etc.
5.	Travelling	Motor tour, transport, farewell, arrival, walk, traffic, queue, collision, etc.
6.	Rituals	Funeral, cremation, religious ceremony, etc.
7.	Sport	Contest, match, race, etc.
8.	Excesses	Fornication, obscenity, orgy, drinking-bout, gambling, etc.
9.	Serving	Housekeeping, nursing, breakfast, meal, etc.
10.	Trading	Bankruptcy, market, auction, fair, sale, exhibition, etc.

that 'what is striking is the extent to which situations are described in terms of affects (e.g. threatening, warm, interesting, dull, tense, calm, rejecting) and organized in terms of similarity of affects aroused by them' (Pervin, 1976, p. 471). Similar conclusions have been reached in other studies, generally supporting Zajonc's (1980) claim that connotative, affective dimensions often play a crucial role in reactions to social stimuli.

In our continuing research programme we have been mainly concerned with the way people cognitively represent familiar interaction situations, or 'social episodes', and how such representations are shaped by cultural and individual differences. For our purposes, we may define social episodes as 'cognitive representations of stereotypical interaction sequences which are representative of a given cultural environment, . . . constitute natural units in the stream of behaviour, [and] individuals . . . have an implicit cognitive knowledge and understanding of the episodes practiced in their milieu' (Forgas, 1979a, p. 15). This definition is clearly based on some of the psychological and sociological models of situations reviewed above. Our investigations looked at the way such common, recurring social episodes are cognitively represented by individuals, groups, and sub-cultures. As Pervin (1976) pointed out, 'we know little about the dimensions people use to perceive and organise situations or about the process of person—situation interaction' (p. 465). In these studies, the procedure typically involves collecting a representative range of commonly practised episodes within a given milieu, selecting the most common and typical situations from such a list, and then obtaining a reliable empirical measure of the perceived psychological similarity or relatedness between this group of episodes. This information can be readily obtained in the form of direct similarity ratings, sorting procedures, or bipolar scales by a representative group of subjects familiar with the interaction routines studied (for a summary of these procedures, see Forgas, 1979b, 1982). Such judgments can then be subjected to analytic procedures such as multidimensional scaling (MDS) in order to uncover the structure implicit in subjects' cognitive representation of situations.

In several studies, we found that a limited number of connotative rather than descriptive dimensions typically define such episode spaces. Commonly, it is characteristics such as pleasantness, feelings of self-confidence, of anxiety, or of tension, or perceived intimacy and friendliness that define people's cognitive representation of social situations (Forgas, 1976, 1978, 1979a, 1982a, 1983a, 1983b). Surprisingly, in most of these studies the number of common and recurring social episodes reported are quite limited. In fact, most interactions seem to occur within the confines of a limited number of common, prototypical situation 'themes' (usually 20—40). In well-established, close groups or relationships, the range of shared interaction situations is probably even smaller. Examples of such shared episode scripts may include events such as 'having breakfast together', 'Saturday morning shopping', 'dinner party with friends', or 'going to see a movie together'.

What sorts of variable influence our representations about social episodes? Cultural and sub-cultural factors seem to play a major role. For example, in one study perceptions of typical interaction episodes were compared between Chinese students in Hong Kong and Australian students in Sydney (Forgas and Bond, 1985). The structural and dimensional differences in situation representations between these groups were highly significant, and could be meaningfully related to known cultural differences between the two cultures. In addition, individual demographic, personality, and attitudinal variables were also related to episode perceptions in a culture-specific pattern. In other studies we also explored the effect of membership in different sub-cultures on situation representations. When comparing the perception of episodes in a group of British housewives and students (Forgas, 1976), we found not only that there were structural differences in their cognitive representation of episodes, but that the position of individual episodes within the episode space was also influenced by sub-cultural differences (Forgas, 1976, 1979a). Thus, housewives had an overall less complex episode domain than students, and saw social situations involving contact with others (such as going to the pub, dinner parties) as intrinsically more anxiety-arousing than did students.

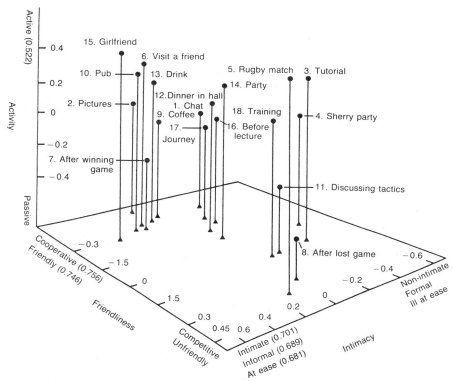

Figure 16.1 Three-dimensional model of the implicit representation of social episodes by members of an intact sports team, showing the bipolar scales used to label each dimension (Source: after Forgas, 1981)

Later studies also showed that small groups engaging in regular interaction, such as academic groups or sports teams, also tend to develop their unique system of cognitively representing social situations. When comparing the perceived episode spaces of members of two rugby teams (Forgas, 1981), we found that a homogeneous team that was more cohesive and friendly also tended to have a more subtle, complex, and better-differentiated representation of social situations than did members of a less cohesive and more heterogeneous team. Thus, we were able to show empirically that implicit representations of social situations are significantly and meaningfully shaped by the sub-cultural and group experiences of individuals. Figure 16.1 shows a three-dimensional model of the implicit representation of social situations by members of the more cohesive and homogeneous group.

Individual differences in episode representations

Apart from such cultural, sub-cultural, and group influences on situation cognition, both psychological and sociological research suggests that individual differences also play a major role in such representations (cf. Mischel, 1973). In fact, it may be argued that 'the personality of each individual could be understood in terms of the patterns and stability of change in feelings and behaviors in relation to a defined group of situations . . . this approach might serve as the basis for the future development of a taxonomy of situations, and behaviors in situations' (Pervin, 1976, p. 465).

In several studies, we sought to explore the role of individual differences in situation representations, a topic central to recent personality research. In one such study, subjects were members of a small, academic group at a British university, who were involved in a long-standing pattern of close collegial interactions (Forgas, 1978). The group contained faculty members, graduate students, and other staff. Shared situations included regular encounters with each other both inside and outside the department, such as participating in a seminar, having tea or coffee together, going to a dinner party, or going to the pub. A representative list of such typical episodes was first obtained from members of the group, who were able to list with a considerable degree of agreement their most common and recurring interactions. Next, each pair of episodes was rated for overall similarity as well as on a number of bipolar scales, and these data were analysed using a multidimensional scaling (MDS) programme. The resulting episode space was defined by four, largely connotative dimensions, such as perceived anxiety, feelings of involvement, evaluation, and social vs. task characteristics (see Figure 16.2).

What sorts of individual difference are most likely to influence such perceptions? In the academic group we studied, status was perhaps the most salient feature differentiating between group members. Would faculty members, research students, and other staff have significantly different representations of the same episodes? To test this possibility, the mean dimension weights (indicating how much each subject relied on each episode dimension in his or her cognitive representation) between faculty, staff, and students were compared. Results showed significant differences. Evaluation was most important to faculty members, anxiety was the most salient episode dimension to general staff, and students saw episodes mainly in terms of their social- or task-orientation (Figure 16.3). Further analysis showed that an individual's sociometric position in the perceived group structure was also significantly related to his or her unique style of perceiving social situations (for a summary of the MDS procedure used in these studies, see Forgas, 1979b).

The aim of subsequent studies was to expand these results, by demonstrating empirically that a significant relationship also exists between personality and the way people habitually perceive and interpret interaction episodes (Forgas, 1983a). On the basis of a free-response diary study, typical interaction situations in a student milieu were identified. A second group of subjects was then asked to (1) indicate their perception of these episodes, and (2) complete a battery of personality measures. Cognitive representations of episodes were based on four implicit dimensions (self-confidence, evaluation, seriousness, and involvement). A canonical correlation analysis of episode perception style (each subject's reliance on each episode dimensions) and personality characteristics (as measured by a battery of scales)

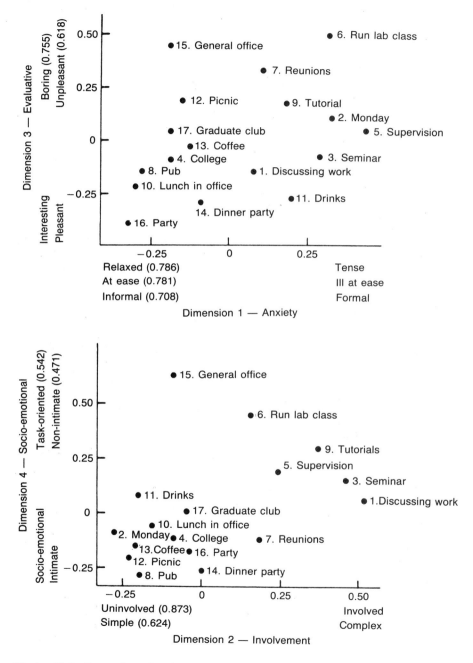

Figure 16.2 Perception of social episodes by members of a close-knit academic group, showing the bipolar scales used to lable each dimension (Source: after Forgas 1978)

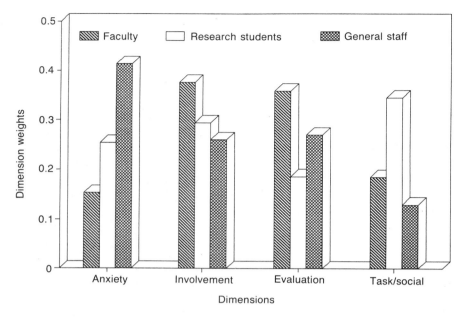

Figure 16.3 Relationship between social status and episode perception: differences between high-status (faculty), intermediate-status (research students), and low-status (general staff) individuals of the kinds of feature they implicitly rely on in perceiving social situations in an academic group (Source: after Forgas, 1978)

revealed two characteristic ways of seeing episodes. Introverted males who scored high on fear of negative evaluation and scored low on assertiveness and social competence predominantly thought about social episodes in terms of how self-confident they felt in them. The second group consisted of more extraverted, competent, and high self-monitoring subjects, who scored low on the feelings of inadequacy scale and thought about social episodes predominantly in terms of the evaluative and involvement dimensions (see Table 16.3).

These results confirm that a person's strategies in cognitively dealing with social situations are indeed significantly related to stable personality dispositions. It is likely that strategic representations of interaction situations would also be significantly related to global measures of a person's social skills. We examined this hypothesis as a follow-up study (Forgas, 1983b). Again, natural episodes were collected in a diary study, followed by separate ratings of representative episodes, and an assessment of each subject's level of social skill using a battery of measures. For this group, social anxiety, evaluation, and perceived intensity were the critical features differentiating between episodes. When comparing the episode perception styles of subjects who scored high or low on the combined social skills measures, we found that socially skilled subjects primarily relied on the evaluation and intensity dimensions in their representations of episodes, while low-skilled subjects discriminated between

Table 16.3 A canonical correlation analysis of the relationship between individual difference measures and a person's characteristic way of cognitively representing social situations

Variables	Canonical variate no. 1	Canonical variate no. 2
Rc—eigenvalue	0.478*	0.281*
Rc—canonical correlation coefficient	0.692	0.527
First set of variables: subject's episode perception style, or dimension weights on four INDSCAL dimensions		
1. Self-confidence	1.052	0.192
2. Evaluation	−0.341	1.211
3. Seriousness	0.056	−0.323
4. Involvement	−0.104	0.878
Second set of variables: subject's sex, and personality measures		
1. Sex of subject (1 = female, 2 = male)	0.658	−0.107
2. Eysenck Personality Inventory, neuroticism	0.211	−0.352
3. Eysenck Personality Inventory, extraversion	−0.940	0.549
4. Watson and Friend fear of negative evaluation	0.872	−0.252
5. Watson and Friend social anxiety and distress	0.335	−0.005
6. Janis and Field feelings of inadequacy	0.206	−0.645
7. Snyder Self-Monitoring Scale	−0.113	1.133
8. Rathus Assertiveness Scale	−1.250	0.337
9. Social competence in situations	−0.719	0.904

* Significant at ≤0.01 level
Source: after Forgas, 1983a.

episodes primarily in terms of the anxiety dimension, as indicated by their mean subject weights (Figure 16.4).

The results of a subsequent canonical correlation analysis of episode perception variables and individual differences measures largely confirmed the results of the first study. Males who were socially anxious, unassertive, introverted, and relatively unskilled were most prone to represent social episodes cognitively in terms of the anxiety they entail. On the other hand, subjects who had a more differentiated and critical perception of episodes, primarily relying on the evaluation and intensity dimensions, turned out to be extraverted, self-confident, high on self-monitoring, and more socially skilled. These results again suggest that there is a close link between particular episode perception styles, and enduring personal characteristics. The fact that situation-perception strategies were significantly related to overall level of social skill may also have important implications for the practice of social skills training and therapy.

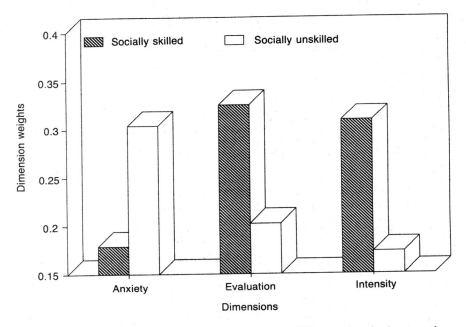

Figure 16.4 Social skills and episode perception: mean differences in episode perception style between high- and low-skilled subjects (Source: after Forgas, 1983b)

What does this series of studies (for a more extensive review, see Forgas, 1979a, 1979b, 1982, 1988, 1991) tell us about the cognitive representation of social situations? Perhaps most notable is the finding that people's social behaviours largely occur within the framework of a limited number of prototypical situations, about which members of a culture, sub-culture, or group have increasingly subtle and differentiated consensual cognitive representations. The dimensions underlying such situation representations are also few in number, and can be reliably established through the analysis of a variety of judgmental data. Interestingly, such implicit representations of situations tend to be largely based on affective, connotative reactions, rather than objective, denotative features of situations. We have also found that the structure, complexity, and coherence of such implicit situation maps can be meaningfully related to a whole range of cultural and individual characteristics.

These studies also have direct implications for clinical or counselling psychology. Evidence that social skills or lack of social skills is significantly related to episode perception suggests that dysfunctional situation perception may be an important aspect of social maladjustment (Forgas, 1983b). In future studies we also aim to analyse the dynamic, unfolding strategies different people use in their definition of social situations, an approach long advocated by classic theorists in psychology and sociology. We also plan to investigate the role of a person's affective state in their definition and representation of situations, following recent evidence for affective influences on a wide variety of judgmental and behavioural phenomena (cf. Forgas, 1991a, 1991b, 1992; Forgas and Bower, 1987).

Personality and situation preferences

What are the likely behavioural consequences of the kind of individual differences in situation perception surveyed above? And more generally, what sorts of link exist between personality traits and individual preferences for particular situations? The evidence so far considered clearly shows that people do have subtle and reliable cognitive representations about typical situations available in their milieu, and that cultural and personal factors have a major impact on such representations (Forgas, 1982; Van Heck, 1989). One consequence may be that individuals avoid some situations and enter others. Moreover, people may modify situations to suit themselves, and create situations that facilitate particular behaviours (Secord, 1977). According to Mischel (1977), 'some of the most striking differences between persons may be found not by studying their responses to the same situation but by analyzing their selection and construction of stimulus conditions' (p. 248). Such individual differences in situation selectivity are in fact quite compatible with traditional trait theories (cf. Diener *et al.*, 1984). Indeed, it is likely that 'one's choice of the settings in which to live one's life may reflect features of one's personality: An individual may choose to live his or her life in serious, reserved, and intellectual situations precisely because he or she is a serious, reserved, and thoughtful individual' (Snyder, 1983, p. 310).

Evidence for the role of personality factors in situation selectivity comes from a range of studies (cf. Snyder, 1983). For instance, extraverts tend to seek out stimulating social situations (Furnham, 1981), and sensation seekers choose sensation-providing leisure situations (Zuckerman, 1974). Authoritarians have a preference for authoritarian educational settings (Stern, 1970), and those who are internally controlled like situations in which outcomes are determined by their own skills (Krahé, 1990). High-reactive individuals also tend to prefer less stimulating situations, whereas low-reactive persons show the opposite tendency (Strelau, 1983). Further, high self-monitoring individuals seem eager to enter clearly defined situations, but avoid vaguely defined situations (Snyder, 1983). Low self-monitors, in turn, are virtually unaffected by the degree of clarity of the situation. Such situation selectivity seems clearly consistent with the kinds of perceptual difference in situation representations that we found between introverted and extraverted, and high- and low-self monitoring, persons above (Forgas, 1983a, 1983b, 1988).

In other studies, Diener *et al.*, (1984) also report that need for order predicted preference for routine, familiar situations, while extraversion correlated with preference for social-recreational activities. Generally, extraversion, sociability, and affiliation appear positively correlated with time spent in preferred situations and negatively correlated with time spent in imposed situations. This pattern seems consistent with results suggesting that avoidance and anxiety play a crucial role in the way less socially skilled persons tend to represent situations cognitively (Forgas,

1983b). However, the links between personality and situation selectivity are far from universal: for example, scores on some scales of Jackson's (1974) PRF showed no links with situation preferences.

Temperament may also have a significant influence on situation preferences. In a recent study of temperament by Van Heck *et al.*, (1990) it was found that male adolescents with high scores on sensation seeking reported a preference for excesses. High scorers on disinhibition and experience seeking had a high appreciation of interpersonal conflict situations and a markedly lower preference for relatively quiet situations that focus on joint working and sponsored teaching. High scores on thrill and adventure seeking reported a more pronounced preference for interpersonal conflicts than did low scorers. Impulsivity was negatively linked with recreation, and positively linked with sport and excesses. Emotionality was related to a preference for serving, and extraversion was negatively correlated with situations such as judgment, exam, lesson, etc. The study by Van Heck *et al.*, (1990) is a good illustration of active genotype—environment interactions (cf. Plomin, 1986), which occurs when individuals seek out environments to match their genotypes.

Persons and situations reciprocally affect each other because at 'any moment the individual selects, interprets, and treats the situational information and transforms it into behaviour, which in the next step of the process becomes an important facet of the situational information for the individual' (Magnusson, 1980, p. 24). These complex transactions occuring at the interface of the person and the situation have been specifically addressed by Hettema (1979, 1989) in a model where personality is conceived as an open system, existing in mutual interaction with its environment. Situation selection as well as situation transformation assume that an individual has a definite preference for specific situations at the expense of others, that is, each individual has his or her own preference order for situations of different types. A recent study by Hettema and Hol (1980b) has provided evidence supporting this notion. It was shown not only that individuals have a clear preference for situation orders, but also that these orders remain invariant when the actual situation in which they find themselves is changed.

Summary and conclusion

In this chapter we have attempted to survey the various historical and contemporary approaches to the study of situations, and discussed some of the most promising empirical techniques relevant to this task. We started this discussion by considering the impact of situationism on recent personality research. Clearly, a better understanding of how individuals perceive, represent, and react to situations must lie at the heart of any truly interactionist conceptualization of personality. According to Kenrick and Dantchik (1983), modern interactionism emphasizes that: (1) individuals select environments to play out personal characteristics; (2) personal characteristics can reciprocally alter the environment; (3) neither personality nor situational factors alone are sufficient to predict behaviour — both must be considered jointly; and (4) an individual's responses to situations in a particular domain are idiosyncratic. Consistent with some prior approaches, these points highlight the intentional and active character of situated behaviour, and the idiosyncratic nature of how particular individuals react to and behave in situations.

At the start of modern interactionism advocates of an idiographic approach to the analysis of situations (such as Pervin, 1976, 1977, 1981) had a major impact on the discipline. Recently, however, researchers seem more in sympathy with Block and Block's (1981) statement that the ultimate goal of interactional psychology is prediction. In order to realize this goal, 'the characteristics of the normatively described, consensually perceived, canonical situations must be defined independently of any one person' (Block and Block, 1981, p. 88). As did others, in our own research (considered above) we also attempted to emphasize the intersubjective and normative character of situation descriptions (for example, Forgas, 1979a, 1982, 1991a; Hettema, 1979; Van Heck, 1984, 1989). This entails treating situations as elements of a public domain, and taking as our point of departure the many subtle discriminations that people belonging to a particular group or (sub-)culture may make with respect to the continuous flow of events. A good example of such an approach is the study of situation representations across different cultural groups (cf. Forgas and Bond, 1985).

Interactionism is by definition a more complex theoretical framework than are classical intrapsychic theories of personality. Interactionist models not only carry the burden of conceptualizing the structure of personality, but also need to represent the structure of situations, as well as the dynamic interplay between these two classes of variables. As we have seen, from the initial situationist critique of classical personality paradigms in the 1960s, it has taken the discipline several decades to come to grips with the many issues involved in person—situation relations. Many important questions had to be first considered: What are the major elements in an interactionist model of personality? Can we make use of classical or modified trait conceptions? How should we conceptualize the situation? And, last but not least, what basic conception is needed with regard to person—situation transactions?

Contributions to the resolution of these questions have emanated from different sources, reflecting different perspectives. The rediscovery of the long history of interest in situations in psychology and sociology provided particularly useful pointers towards a coherent conceptualization of situations, as we have tried to argue here. As a result, we may now be at the threshold of a new age in personality research, as we can begin to see the emerging contours of a new mainstream interactionist paradigm. This must also include a more sophisticated and complex understanding of intrapsychic variables, now comprising emotional and motivational elements in addition to concern with cognitive representations and processing styles (cf. Forgas, 1992). The situation model used has also evolved towards a more realistic conceptualization of situations as cultural, physical, and social entities, with a clear internal structure and definable cues and features.

Cognitive representations of situations, according to Hettema (1979), play a major role in the strategical choices people make with respect to the conversation or transformation of the behavioural context. Evidence for such a link is also provided by several of our studies reviewed above (Forgas, 1981, 1982, 1983a, 1983b; Van Heck, 1984, 1989). Future theories of situated behaviour need to focus on such cognitive representations of situations much more than has been the case so far. In particular, we believe that the concept of cognitive situation prototypes and the concept of social episodes can be successfully used in such endeavours. Indeed, recent work by Mischel and others clearly suggest that such an approach, focusing on the cognitive processes underlying perception and definition of situations, is likely to be one of the focal issues in personality research over the next decades (cf. Carson, 1989). We are therefore cautiously optimistic that the next decade will witness a burgeoning of research dealing with the person–situational interaction, as part of the gradual reorientation of personality psychology.

Authors' note

Support by the Australian Research Council and the German Research Foundation (DFG) to Joseph P. Forgas for some of this work is gratefully acknowledged.

References

Abelson, R.P. (1981), 'The psychological status of the script concept', *American Psychologist*, **36**, 715–29.

Altman, I. (1975), *The Environment and Social Behavior: Privacy, personal space, territory, and crowding*, Monterey, CA: Brooks/Cole.

Angyal, A. (1941), *Foundations for a Science of Personality*, Cambridge, MA: Harvard University Press.

Argyle, M. (1977), 'Predictive and generative rules models of P × S interaction, in D. Magnusson and N.S. Endler (eds.), *Personality at the Crossroads: Current issues in interactional psychology*, Hillsdale, NJ: Erlbaum, pp. 353–70.

Argyle, M. and Little, B.R. (1972), 'Do personality traits apply to social behaviour?', *Journal for the Theory of Social Behaviour*, **2**, 1–35.

Ball, D.W. (1972), 'The definition of the situation: some theoretical and methodological consequences of taking W.I. Thomas seriously', *Journal for the Theory of Social Behaviour*, **2**, 61–83.

Barker, R.G. (1965), 'Explorations in ecological psychology', *American Psychologist*, **20**, 1–14.

Barker, R.G. (1968), *Ecological Psychology: Concepts and methods for studying the environment of human behavior*, Stanford, CA: Stanford University Press.

Barker, R.G. and Schoggen, P. (1973), *Qualities of Community Life: Methods of measuring environment and behavior applied to an American and an English town*, San Francisco, CA: Jossey-Bass.

Barker, R.G. and associates (1978), *Habitats, Environments, and Human Behavior: Studies in ecological psychology and eco-behavioral science from the Midwest Psychological Field Station, 1947–1972*, San Francisco, CA: Jossey-Bass.

Bechtel, R.B. (1982), 'Contributions of ecological psychology to the evaluation of environments', *International Review of Applied Psychology*, **31**, 153–67.

Block, J. and Block, J.H. (1981), 'Studying situational dimensions: a grand perspective and some limited empiricism', in D. Magnusson (ed.), *Toward a Psychology of Situations: An interactional perspective*, Hillsdale, NJ: Erlbaum, pp. 85–102.

Bower, G.H., Black, J.B. and Turner, T.J. (1979), 'Scripts in memory for text', *Cognitive Psychology*, **11**, 177–220.

Bowers, K.S. (1973), 'Situationism in psychology: an analysis and a critique', *Psychological Review*, **80**, 307–36.

Brittan, A. (1973), *Meanings and Situations*, Boston, MA: Routledge & Kegan Paul.

Brunswik, E. (1956), *Perception and Representative Design of Psychological Experiments*, Berkeley, CA: University of California Press.

Brunswik, E. (1957), 'Scope and aspects of the cognitive problem', in H. Gruber, R. Jessor and K. Hammond (eds.), *Contemporary Approaches to Cognition: The Colorado Symposium*, Cambridge, MA: Harvard University Press, pp. 5–31.

Cantor, N. (1981), 'Perceptions of situations: situation prototypes and person–situation prototypes', in D. Magnusson (ed.), *Toward a Psychology of Situations*, Hillsdale, NJ: Erlbaum, pp. 229–44.

Cantor, N., Mischel, W. and Schwartz, J.C. (1982), 'Social knowledge: structure, content, use, and abuse', in A.H. Hastorf and A.M. Isen (eds.), *Cognitive Social Psychology*, New York, NY: Elsevier/North-Holland, pp. 33–72.

Carson, R.C. (1989), 'Personality', in M.R. Rozenzweig and L.W. Porter (eds.), *Annual Review of Psychology*, **40**, Palo Alto, CA: Annual Reviews, pp. 227–48.

Cottrell, S.J. (1970), 'Some neglected problems in social psychology', in G.P. Stone and H.A. Farberman (eds.), *Social Psychology through Symbolic Interaction*, Waltham, MA: Ginn-Blaisdell, pp. 63–70.

Craik, K.H. (1969), 'Personality unvanquished', *Contemporary Psychology*, **14**, 147–8.

Cronbach, L.J. and Snow, R.E. (1975), *Aptitudes and Instructional Methods*, New York, NY: Irvington.

Desmonde, W.H. (1970), 'The position of George Herbert Mead', in G.P. Stone and H.A. Farberman (eds.), *Social Psychology through Symbolic Interaction*, Waltham, MA: Ginn-Blaisdell, pp. 55–62.

Diener, E., Larsen, R.J. and Emmons, R.A. (1984), 'Person × situation interactions: choice of situations and congruence response models', *Journal of Personality and Social Psychology*, **47**, 580–92.

Douglas, J.D. (ed.) (1973), *Understanding Everyday Life*, London: Routledge & Kegan Paul.

Eckes, T. and Six, B. (1984), 'Prototypenforchung: Ein integrativer Ansatz zur Analyse der alltagssprachichen Kategorisiering von Objekten, Personen und Situationen' [Prototype research: an integrative attempt towards the analysis of everyday categorizing of objects, persons, and situations], *Zeitschrift für Sozialpsychologie*, **15**, 2–17.

Edwards, J.M. (1984), 'Situational determinants in behavior', in N.S. Endler and J.McV. Hunt (eds.), *Personality and the Behavioral Disorders* (second edition), New York, NY: Wiley, vol. 1, pp. 147–82.

Ekehammar, B. (1974), 'Interactionism in personality from a historical perspective', *Psychological Bulletin*, **81**, 1026–48.

Endler, N.S. (1983), 'Interactionism: a personality model, but not yet a theory', in M.M. Page (ed.), *Nebraska Symposium on Motivation*, Lincoln, NE: University of Nebraska Press, pp. 155–200.

Endler, N.S. (1988), 'Interactionism revisited: a discussion of "On the role of situations in personality research" ', in S.G. Cole, R.G. Demaree and W. Curtis (eds.), *Applications of Interactionist Psychology: Essays in honor of Saul B. Sells*, Hillsdale, NJ: Erlbaum, pp. 179–88.

Endler, N.S. and Edwards, J.M. (1986), 'Interactionism in personality in the twentieth century', *Personality and Individual Differences,* **7**, 379–84.

Endler, N.S. and Magnusson, D. (1976), 'Toward an interactional psychology of personality', *Psychological Bulletin,* **83**, 956–74.

Endler, N.S., Hunt, J.McV. and Rosenstein, A. (1962), 'An S-R Inventory of Anxiousness', *Psychological Monographs,* **536**, 1–31.

Epstein, S. (1979), 'The stability of behavior. I: On predicting most of the people much of the time', *Journal of Personality and Social Psychology,* **37**, 1097–126.

Flanagan, J.C. (1949), 'A new approach to evaluating personnel', *Personnel,* **26**, 35–42.

Forgas, J.P. (1976), 'The perception of social episodes: categorical and dimensional representations of two different social milieus', *Journal of Personality and Social Psychology,* **34**, 199–209.

Forgas, J.P. (1978), 'Social episodes and social structure in an academic setting: the social environment of an intact group', *Journal of Experimental Social Psychology,* **14**, 434–48.

Forgas, J.P. (1979a), *Social Episodes: The study of interaction routines,* London: Academic Press.

Forgas, J.P. (1979b), 'Multidimensional scaling: a discovery method in psychology', in G.P. Ginsburg (ed.), *Emerging Strategies in Social Psychology,* Chichester: Wiley, pp. 53–88.

Forgas, J.P. (1981), 'Social episodes and group milieu: a study in social cognition', *British Journal of Social Psychology,* **20**, 77–87.

Forgas, J.P. (1982), 'Episode cognition: internal representations of interaction routines', in L. Berkowitz (ed.), *Advances in Experimental Social Psychology,* New York, NY: Academic Press, vol. 15, pp. 59–101.

Forgas, J.P. (1983a), 'Episode cognition and personality: a multidimensional analysis', *Journal of Personality,* **51**, 34–48.

Forgas, J.P. (1983b), 'Social skills and the perception of social episodes', *British Journal of Clinical Psychology,* **22**, 195–207.

Forgas, J.P. (1986), 'Episode representations in intercultural communication', in Y.Y. Kim and W.B. Gudykunst (eds.), *Theories in Intercultural Communication,* Beverly Hills, CA: Sage, pp. 186–212.

Forgas, J.P. (1988), 'Cognitive representations of aggressive situations', in A. Campbell and J.J. Gibbs (eds.), *Violent Transactions,* Oxford: Basil Blackwell, pp. 41–58.

Forgas, J.P. (1991a) 'Affect and cognition in close relationships', in G. Fletcher and F. Fincham (eds.), *Cognition in Close Relationships,* Hillsdale, NJ: Erlbaum.

Forgas, J.P. (1991b), *Emotion in Social Judgments,* Oxford: Pergamon.

Forgas, J.P. (1992), 'Affect in social judgments and decisions: a multi-process model', in M. Zanna (ed.), *Advances in Experimental Social Psychology,* New York, NY: Academic Press.

Forgas, J.P. and Bond, M.H. (1985), 'Cultural influences on the perception of interaction episodes', *Personality and Social Psychology Bulletin,* **11**, 75–88.

Forgas, J.P. and Bower, G.H. (1987), 'Mood effects on person perception judgments', *Journal of Personality and Social Psychology,* **53**, 53–60.

Funder, D.C. and Ozer, D.J. (1983), 'Behavior as a function of the situation', *Journal of Personality and Social Psychology,* **44**, 107–12.

Furnham, A. (1981), 'Personality and activity preference', *British Journal of Social and Clinical Psychology,* **20**, 57–68.

Garfinkel, H. (1967), *Studies in Ethnomethodology,* Englewood Cliffs, NJ: Prentice Hall.

Gibson, J.J. (1979), *The Ecological Approach to Visual Perception,* Boston, MA: Houghton Mifflin.

Goffman, E. (1963), *Behaviour in Public Places,* Glencoe, IL: The Free Press.

Goffman, E. (1974), *Frame Analysis,* Harmondsworth: Penguin.

Harloff, H.J., Gump, P.V. and Campbell, D.E. (1981), 'The public life of communities: environmental change as a result of the intrusion of a flood control, conservation, and recreation reservoir', *Environment and Behavior,* **13**, 685–706.

Hartshorne, H. and May, M.A. (1928), *Studies in the Nature of Character. Vol. 1: Studies in deceit*, New York, NY: Macmillan.

Hettema, P.J. (1979), *Personality and Adaptation*, Amsterdam: North-Holland.

Hettema, P.J. (ed.) (1989), *Personality and Environment: Assessment of human adaptation*, Chichester: Wiley.

Hettema, P.J. and Hol, D.P. (1989a), 'The assessment of behavioral strategies', in P.J. Hettema (ed.), *Personality and Environment: Assessment of human adaptation*, Chichester: Wiley, pp. 87−103.

Hettema, P.J. and Hol, D.P. (1989b), 'An empirical study of interpersonal behavior in simulated situations', in P.J. Hettema (ed.), *Personality and Environment: Assessment of human adaptation*, Chichester: Wiley, pp. 177−85.

Hettema, P.J. and Kenrick, D.T. (1989), 'Biosocial interaction and individual adaptation', in P.J. Hettema (ed.), *Personality and Environment: Assessment of human adaptation*, Chichester: Wiley, pp. 3−29.

Hettema, P.J., Van Heck, G.L. and Brandt, C. (1989), 'The representation of situations through films', in P.J. Hettema (ed.), *Personality and Environment: Assessment of human adaptation*, Chichester: Wiley, pp. 113−27.

Hogan, R. and Emler, N.P. (1978), 'The biases in contemporary social psychology', *Social Research*, **45**, 478−534.

Hogan, R., DeSoto, C.B. and Solano, C. (1977), 'Traits, tests and personality research', *American Psychologist*, **32**, 255−64.

Jackson, D.N. (1974), *Personality Research Form Manual*, Goshen, NY: Research Psychologists Press.

Jessor, R. (1956), 'Phenomenological personality theories and the data language of psychology', *Psychological Review*, **63**, 173−80.

Kaminski, G. (ed.) (1986), 'Ordnung und Variabilität im Alltagsgeschehen: Das Behaviour Setting Konzept in den Sozial- und Verhaltens-wissenschaften' [Order and variability in everyday life: the behaviour settings concept in the social and behavioural sciences], Göttingen, Germany: Hogrefe.

Kantor, J.R. (1924), *Principles of Psychology. Vol. 1*, Bloomington, IL: Principia Press.

Kantor, J.R. (1926), *Principles of Psychology. Vol. 2*, Bloomington, IL: Principia Press.

Kelly, G.A. (1955), *The Psychology of Personal Constructs*, New York, NY: Norton.

Kenrick, D.T. and Dantchik, A. (1983), 'Interactionism, idiographics, and the social-psychological invasion of personality', *Journal of Personality*, **51**, 286−307.

Koffka, K. (1935), *Principles of Gestalt Psychology*, New York, NY: Harcourt Brace Jovanovich.

Krahé, B. (1990), *Situation Cognition and Coherence in Personality: An individual-centred approach*, European Monographs in Social Psychology, Cambridge: Cambridge University Press/Paris: Editions de la Maison des Sciences de l'Homme.

Kuhn, M.H. (1970), 'Major trends in symbolic interaction theory in the past twenty-five years',in G.P. Stone and H.E. Farberman (eds.), *Social Psychology through Symbolic Interaction*, Waltham, MA: Ginn-Blaisdell, pp. 70−83.

Lazarus, R.S. (1966), *Psychological Stress and the Coping Process*, New York, NY: McGraw-Hill.

Lewin, K. (1936), *Principles of Topological Psychology*, New York, NY: McGraw-Hill.

Lyman, S.M. and Scott, M.B. (1972), *The Sociology of the Absurd*, New York, NY: Appleton-Century-Crofts.

Magnusson, D. (1976), 'The person and the situation in an interactional model of behaviour', *Scandinavian Journal of Psychology*, **17**, 253−71.

Magnusson, D. (1980), 'Personality in an interactional paradigm of research', *Zeitschrift für differentielle und diagnostische Psychologie*, **1**, 17−34.

Magnusson, D. (ed.) (1981), *Toward a Psychology of Situations: An interactional perspective*, Hillsdale, NJ: Erlbaum.

Magnusson, D. (1988), 'On the role of situations in personality research: an interactional perspective', in S.G. Cole, R.G. Demaree and W. Curtis (eds.), *Applications of Interactionist Psychology: Essays in honor of Saul B. Sells*, Hillsdale, NJ: Erlbaum, pp. 155−78.

Mead, G.H. (1934), *Mind, Self and Society*, Chicago, IL: University of Chicago Press.

Mehrabian, A. and Russell, J.A. (1974), *An Approach to Environmental Psychology*, Cambridge, MA: MIT Press.

Mischel, W. (1968), *Personality and Assessment*, New York, NY: Wiley.

Mischel, W. (1969), 'Continuity and change in personality', *American Psychologist*, **24**, 1012−8.

Mischel, W. (1973), 'Toward a cognitive social learning reconceptualization of personality', *Psychological Review*, **80**, 252−83.

Mischel, W. (1977), 'On the future of personality measurement', *American Psychologist*, **32**, 246−54.

Moos, R.H. (1973), 'Conceptualizations of human environments', *American Psychologist*, **28**, 652−65.

Murray, H.A. (1938), *Explorations in Personality*, New York, NY: Oxford University Press.

Nelson, E.A., Grinder, R.F. and Mutterer, M.L. (1969), 'Sources of variance in behavioral measures of honesty in temptation situations: methodological analyses', *Developmental Psychology*, **1**, 265−79.

Newcomb, T.M. (1929), *Consistency of Certain Extrovert−Introvert Behavior Patterns in 51 Problem Boys*, New York, NY: Columbia University, Teachers College, Bureau of Publications.

Olweus, D. (1977), 'A critical analysis of the "modern" interactionist position', in D. Magnusson and N.S. Endler (eds.), *Personality at the Crossroads: Current issues in interactional psychology*, Hillsdale, NJ: Erlbaum, pp. 221−33.

OSS Assessment Staff (1948), *Assessment of Men*, New York, NY: Holt, Rinehart & Winston.

Pace, C.R. and Stern, G.G. (1958), 'An approach to the measurement of psychological characteristics of college environments', *Journal of Educational Psychology*, **49**, 269−77.

Pervin, L.A. (1975), 'Definitions, measurements and classification of stimuli, situations and environments', *Educational Testing Service Research Bulletin*, **23**, Princeton, NJ.

Pervin, L.A. (1976), 'A free-response description approach to the analysis of person−situation interaction', *Journal of Personality and Social Psychology*, **34**, 465−74.

Pervin, L.A. (1977), 'The representative design of person−situation research', in D. Magnusson and N.S. Endler (eds.), *Personality at the Crossroads: Current issues in interactional psychology*, Hillsdale, NJ: Erlbaum, pp. 371−84.

Pervin, L.A. (1981), 'The relation of situations to behavior', in D. Magnusson (ed.), *Toward a Psychology of Situations: An interactional perspective*, Hillsdale, NJ: Erlbaum, pp. 343−60.

Peterson, D.R. (1968), *The Clinical Study of Social Behavior*, New York, NY: Appleton-Century-Crofts.

Plomin, R. (1986), 'Behavior genetic methods', *Journal of Personality*, **54**, 226−61.

Price, R.H. and Bouffard, D.L. (1974), 'Behavioral appropriateness and situational constraints as dimensions of social behavior', *Journal of Personality and Social Psychology*, **30**, 579−86.

Reinhardt, J.M. (1937), 'Personality traits and the situation', *American Journal of Sociology*, **2**, 492−500.

Rogers, C.R. (1951), *Client-Centered Therapy: Its current practice, implications and theory*, Boston, MA: Houghton Mifflin.

Rosch, E. (1978), 'Principles of categorization', in E. Rosch and B.B. Lloyd (eds.), *Cognition and Categorization*, Hillsdale, NJ: Erlbaum, pp. 27−48.

Rotter, J.B. (1955), 'The role of the psychological situation in determining the direction of human behaviour', in M.R. Jones (ed.), *Nebraska Symposium on Motivation*, Lincoln, NE: University of Nebraska Press, pp. 345−68.

Schoggen, P. (1989), *Behavior Settings: A revision and extension of Roger G. Barker's ecological psychology*, Stanford, CA: Stanford University Press.

Schutz, A. (1970), *On Phenomenology and Social Relations*, ed. H.R. Wagner, Chicago, IL: University of Chicago Press.

Secord, P.F. (1977), 'Social psychology in search of a paradigm', *Personality and Social Psychology Bulletin*, **3**, 41–50.

Seligman, M. (1976), 'The generality of laws of learning', *Psychological Review*, **77**, 406–18.

Skinner, B.F. (1971), *Beyond Freedom and Dignity*, New York, NY: Knopf.

Snyder, M. (1983), 'The influence of individuals on situations: implications for understanding the links between personality and social behavior', *Journal of Personality*, **51**, 497–516.

Stern, G.G. (1970), *People in Context: Measuring person–environment congruence in education and industry*, New York, NY: Wiley.

Stokols, D. and Altman, I. (eds.) (1987), *Handbook of Environmental Psychology*, New York, NY: Wiley.

Stone, G.P. and Farberman, H.E. (eds.) (1970), *Social Psychology Through Symbolic Interactionism*, Waltham, MA: Ginn-Blaisdell.

Strelau, J. (1983), *Temperament — Personality — Activity*, London: Academic Press.

Thomas, W.I. (1923), *The Unadjusted Girl*, Boston, MA: Ginn.

Thomas, W.I. (1928/1966), 'Situational analysis: the behaviour pattern and the situation', reprinted in *W.I. Thomas on Social Organisation and Social Personality*, ed. M. Janowitz, Chicago, IL: University of Chicago Press, pp. 154–67.

Tolman, E.C. (1949), 'The psychology of social learning', *Journal of Social Issues*, **5**, Supplement Series No. 3.

Tuan, Y.F. (1972), 'Environmental psychology: a review', *Geographical Review*, **62**, 1–12.

Van Heck, G.L. (1981), 'Anxiety: the profile of a trait', Ph.D. thesis, Tilburg University, Tilburg, The Netherlands.

Van Heck, G.L. (1984), 'The construction of a general taxonomy of situations', in H. Bonarius, G.L. Van Heck and N. Smid (eds.), *Personality Psychology in Europe: Theoretical and empirical developments*, Lisse, The Netherlands: Swets & Zeitlinger, vol. 1, pp. 149–64.

Van Heck, G.L. (1989), 'Situation concepts: definitions and classification', in P.J. Hettema (ed.), *Personality and Environment: Assessment of human adaptation*, Chichester: Wiley, pp. 53–69, 241–59.

Van Heck, G.L. (1991), 'The Big Five: traits or tendencies in situations?', paper presented at the Invited Workshop on the Development of the Structure of Temperament and Personality from Infancy to Adulthood, Wassenaar, The Netherlands, 17–20 June.

Van Heck, G.L., Hettema, P.J. and Leidelmeijer, K.C.M. (1990), 'Temperament, situatie-voorkeuren en situatie-transformaties' [Temperament, situation preferences, and situation transformations], *Nederlands Tijdschrift voor de Psychologie*, **45**, 1–16.

Vernon, P.E. (1964), *Personality Assessment: A critical survey*, New York, NY: Wiley.

Waller, W. (1970), *The Sociology of Teaching*, New York, NY: Wiley.

Weber, M. (1947), *The Theory of Social and Economic Organisation* trans. A.M. Henderson and T. Parsons, ed. T. Parsons, Glencoe, IL: The Free Press.

Wicker, A.W. (1979), 'Ecological psychology: some recent and prospective developments', *American Psychologist*, **34**, 755–65.

Wright, J.C. and Mischel, W. (1987), 'A conditional approach to dispositional constructs: the local predictability of social behavior', *Journal of Personality and Social Psychology*, **53**, 1159–77.

Wright, J.C. and Mischel, W. (1988), 'Conditional hedges and the intuitive psychology of traits', *Journal of Personality and Social Psychology*, **55**, 454–69.

Zajonc, R. (1980), 'Feeling and thinking: preferences need no inferences', *American Psychologist*, **35**, 151–75.

Zuckerman, M. (1974), 'The sensation seeking motive', in B. Maher (ed.), *Progress in Experimental Personality Research*, New York, NY: Academic Press, vol. 7, pp. 79–148.

PART VIII
Epilogue

17/ Future prospects

Guus L. Van Heck
Tilburg University, The Netherlands

Gian-Vittorio Caprara
University of Rome 'La Sapienza', Italy

Introduction

The field of personality is nowadays alive and well. During a period of self-criticism and decreasing confidence in the possibilities of the sub-discipline, many personality psychologists went to social psychology or some applied field. Recently, however, there have been numerous signs that a new generation of personality psychologists is bringing a sense of an infusion of new blood into the field (cf. Pervin, 1990, p. 725). In the introduction chapter of their book, *Personality Psychology: Recent trends and emerging directions*, Buss and Cantor (1989, p. 11) formulated this new *élan* as follows: 'the present generation of personality psychologists is not mired in the problems of the past, but rather extracts the best from the past while pushing optimistically towards the future'. This revival of personality psychology, which has, according to Kenrick and Dantchik (1983, p. 300), 'risen from its funeral pyre adorned with new and colorful plumage', is not restricted to the USA. The steady growth of the European Association of Personality Psychology (EAPP) and the recent establishment of the *European Journal of Personality* are valid signs of a development whose main features are a sense of excitement and vitality (cf. Pervin, 1985).

The question should be posed of *why* there is this revival. Why this striking optimism expressed by so many workers in the field? Finding the proper answers to this question is important, because it can give us some indication whether this renaissance of personality psychology is only a temporary upsurge or the precursor of a long flourishing period. To answer this question properly, it is not sufficient to look simply at the number of papers published or the number of conferences organized. One has to look carefully at the content of those publications and at the specific topics conferences focus upon.

Surveying the chapters presented in this volume, we have the idea that personality has changed. Now, no longer has one to sigh 'Where's the person in personality psychology?', as Carlson quite rightly did in 1984. Now, no longer has one to fear that personality psychologists will turn their back on the study of individual differences and human individuality, because of their conviction that the study of personality is unable to produce more than trivial insights. The issues that modern personality psychology is dealing with are far from trivial. For instance, health is not trivial, and it has now been shown that personality psychology can contribute to an understanding of disease-proneness, likely physiological mechanisms, and successful forms of intervention. According to Friedman (1990), there is solid evidence for associations between individual personality differences, emotional reactions, health-related behaviours, physiological responses, and diseases. For instance, it has been demonstrated convincingly that personality plays a substantial causal role in the aetiology of, for instance, coronary heart disease and cancer (Contrada *et al.*, 1990).

Work is not trivial either, and it has been shown that personality psychology can contribute substantially to this field. Individual difference variables have been investigated as components or mediators of stress appraisals or moderators of the stress—outcome relationship within the context of work. Such studies show that personality moderates the relationship between job characteristics and employee well-being (see, for example, Cox and Ferguson, 1991). Aggression and youth delinquency are no trivial phenomena either. Recently, carefully conducted longitudinal studies have brought to light the complex interplay of personality variables and other psycho-social risk factors in developing these forms of maladapted behaviour (for example, Magnusson, 1988).

Apparently, it is quite easy to demonstrate that personality is relevant in different applied fields. However, not only in applied fields but also in basic research, personality psychology has an increasing impact. In the preceding chapters of this book, there are many examples of the fact that basic personality research is dealing with crucial issues. Many chapters show that personality psychology is, step by step, acquiring the status of a cumulative science. For instance, there is a growing convergence in describing personality. Perhaps for the first time, there are combined efforts to come to a standard set of basic personality factors (see Ostendorf and Angleitner, Chapter 4 in this volume; Hofstee and DeRaad, Chapter 3 in this volume).

Basic personality theory has moved more and more to considering interactionist models of the person and the situation (for example, Endler, 1992; see also Forgas and Van Heck, Chapter 16 in this volume; Hettema and Kenrick, Chapter 15 in this volume). Not everybody, however, will be content with the tempo of this development (for example, Endler, 1992); on the other hand, nobody will deny that there is such a development. For instance, there is a growing recognition that traits are conditional. 'Any given personality might not express itself except in the right environments. For example, a competitive individual may not become physiologically aroused if there is no one or nothing for him to compete with. It is hard to overemphasize the importance of person—environment "fit" ' (Friedman, 1990, p. 289). Furthermore, more and more persons underline the view that cognitions should no longer be treated in some sort of vacuum, isolated from other aspects of human functioning, such as affect or goal-setting and motivation (see Cervone and Williams, Chapter 8 in this volume; Kreitler and Kreitler, Chapter 9 in this volume).

Moreover, recent developments in behavioural genetics have made clear that the main dimensions of personality are deeply rooted in the biological endowment (for example, Buss, 1990; Loehlin and Rowe, Chapter 13 in this volume; Plomin and Rende, 1991; Strelau and Plomin, Chapter 12 in this volume). However, developmental studies also make clear that this endowment is characterized by extreme flexibility and plasticity under the influence of the environment (see Hettema and Kenrick, Chapter 15 in this volume).

So, it follows that personality now plays, besides a *moderating* role influencing the relationship between crucial variables in everyday life functioning, also a crucial role as a *unifying* factor, bringing together and integrating the different parts of the puzzle. It is our strong belief that personality psychology can play this role of *integrator* with increasing success when we turn our attention to complex phenomena — thoughts, feelings, actions and reactions. We very much agree with Magnusson's (1992) strong plea for giving priority to the study of the complexity of relevant factors in the process of individual functioning instead of pursuing the control of single variables or isolated processes. In focusing on the phenomena themselves, personality psychology should not run away from the complexity of human functioning, but should incorporate this complexity in its models. There is now an abundance of signs that point to the fact that personality psychology is seriously accepting this challenge. As Pervin (1990, p. 724) noted:

> what is striking is the diversity of theoretical perspectives emphasizing such concepts as hierarchical organization; patterns of relationships among variables; dynamic processes and open systems; equipotentiality and equifinality; integrated and conflicted relationships among the parts; nonlinear relationships; goals and self-regulative or self-corrective mechanisms; and adaptive functions or competencies.

The greater appreciation of the complexity of the personality domain, convincingly demonstrated in the preceding chapters, unavoidably leads to a revision of traditional paradigms and methods.

Whereas deterministic models may be appropriate for explaining single variables, they are unlikely to make sense of *macro* phenomena such as thoughts, emotions, motivations and behavioural strategies, which are multidetermined and result from a variety of factors reciprocally interacting in non-linear, probabilistic, hardly predictable ways. Greater appreciation of *time* will lead to a better understanding of individual functioning in terms of transitions and continuous transformations. Greater appreciation of *organization* will result in a better understanding of thoughts, feelings and actions as the expressions of the various transitory forms of order and equilibrium.

The epistemology of complexity

In the last two decades, the solidity of the Popperian construction which dominated the previous two decades has been more and more frequently the target of criticism, which has gone far beyond the revolution of Kuhn, the revision of Lakatos, and the speculations of Laudan (see Caprara and Van Heck, Chapter 1 in this volume).

In some cases, the criticism is extremely radical, as, for instance, in the epistemological anarchy of Feyerabend (1975). In these cases, no hope is ultimately left for any superordinate idea of scientific rationalism, of progress of knowledge, and of unity among sciences. Also, the most sophisticated and advanced methodologies cannot be considered to be valid in some absolute sense, safe from degenerations that often depend on factors (institutional, ideological) other than the rational principles which apparently regulate scientific work.

In other cases, as in Morin (1977, 1982, 1986, 1991), the dissatisfaction with what has been neglected or prejudicially eliminated from scientific activity by classical science leads to an *epistemology of complexity*, which is characterized by the readmission by the investigating subject of those factors upon which scientific progress depends and, as a consequence, by the full reintegration of psychological and social knowledge within science. In a world that is dramatically changing, in the face of the collapse of traditional ideologies and the re-emergence of archaic conflicts, scientists cannot give up reflection on reality in its various manifestations. Moreover, they cannot escape the sense of frustration which derives from the inability of science to manage and confront its own progress. In this regard, Morin's epistemology of complexity addresses a variety of issues connected with the praxis and ethics of scientific work that tries to deal with *complexity* and to extend our *knowledge about knowledge*. In this perspective, knowledge is characterized primarily by its multidimensional character, in the sense that it is inseparably psychical, biological, psychological, and cultural. Many elements of Morin's (1977, 1980, 1986, 1991) speculations make his contribution particularly valuable for a personality psychology which, compared with the past, pays more attention to the *multidimensionality of phenomena*, the *pluralism of methods*, and the dialogue which takes place and develops in time between the individual and the environment, precluding both from remaining the same. Among these elements, *the reintroduction of the subjective into scientific knowledge, the complementarity of comprehension and explanation, the notion of complexity*, the antagonism and the synergy between *order* and *disorder*, and *the systemic paradigm* appear to us particularly relevant.

The need for knowledge about knowledge implies not only an epistemology of the observer's system. It implies the reintegration of scientists with the object of their discipline. However, the readmission of the subject and the observer into knowledge does not imply the reintroduction of old subjectivism; rather, it expresses *the need to examine objectively the subjective components of knowledge*. In this sense, in Morin's formulation, the idea of researchers who introduce 'finitude' into research represents the historical condition of the scientist and, at the same time, the expression of the complexity of science.

Related to the readmission of the subjective and private into knowledge is the reconciliation in terms of *the complementarity of comprehension and explanation*. Whereas the aim of explanation is to provide a logical demonstration, comprehension may and must participate in all processes of knowledge, making intelligible all that is permeated with subjectivity. Morin's idea is that every human language is at the same time metaphorical (analogical) — that is, potentially comprehensive — and propositional (logical) — that is, potentially explicative. It follows that the relationship between the two terms is one of interdependence, in the sense that comprehension contains a part of explanation and vice versa. This 'dialogical relationship' between comprehension and explanation has to be considered in the light of a *theory of complexity*, since it may ultimately result in terms of complementarity as well as of antagonism and opposition, depending on time periods, cultures, and individuals. Currently, the too-great disjunction between a culture which pretends to eliminate comprehension and a culture which, on the opposite side, pretends to eliminate explanation has to be viewed as one of the main limitations of both technical and humanistic cultures.

As regards the notion of complexity, according to Morin, the most obvious limit of classical science is due to the crisis of the traditional principle of explanation, which claims clarification of the real nature of phenomena, starting from simple elements. Simplification is applied to these phenomena by disjunction and reduction: objects are separated from each other, from their environment, and also from their observers. What is different and varied is reduced by accumulation and quantification. The result is that reductive thought has conceded 'reality'; not to a whole, but to elements; not to qualities, but to measures; not to real beings, but to propositions which can be formulated and put into mathematical terms. However, one cannot approach complex problems with simple solutions. One cannot pursue the explanation of complex phenomena by isolating and separating them from the context to which they belong. Moreover, one cannot mutilate reality by neglecting its contradictions, just because they oppose our efforts to penetrate it. To go beyond simplification and reductionism implies the establishment of a dialogue between order, disorder, and organization, which constitute, according to Morin, the ingredients of complexity.

In characterizing the concept of *order*, Morin underlines the necessity for overcoming the idea of deterministic laws. In this respect, the idea of *determination* is more radical and more profound than the idea of *laws*. Order allows us to understand that bond. Variances, constancies, and regularities depend on singular and variable conditions, which imply a whole series of *determinations* that escape every form of determinism and are characterized by 'transformative' and 'evolutionary' meaning. The concept of order implies a continuous process of interactions and, above all, leads to the recognition of the idea of *organization*; for it is precisely the latter which brings and produces order.

The notion of *disorder*, on the other hand, is also very valuable. Disorder is characterized by an objective pole and a subjective pole. The former is due to the intervention of determined elements which tend toward transformation and agitation, such as dispersions, collisions, irregularities, instabilities, discontinuities, and errors. The latter is due to uncertain and indeterminate conditions experienced as such with regard to the complexity of reality. Thus, disorder is a 'macro-concept', which implies very different realities united by the fact that they always involve some sort of change.

It is important to point out how disorder (which continuously activates disorganization and threats of disorganization) cooperates, by virtue of the changes it produces in many evolutionary processes, with order in creating organization.

This implies the need to capture the way a dialogue between order and disorder may take place through interaction processes. Both order and disorder, in fact, would be absolutely restrictive and limiting if considered in isolation. Absolute order would ultimately imply a lack of innovation and progress; disorder would be impotent in consolidating new processes and fully inadequate with respect to building an organization.

Here, it is obvious that the speculations of Morin (1977, 1980, 1986, 1991) have relevance as regards the current debates in personality psychology on the continuity–discontinuity issue, multicausality, and equi- and hetero-finality. Equally relevant is his criticism and his revision of the concept of 'system'. According to Morin, the theory of systems has notable limits, essentially because it remains bound to a simplified and reductive analysis. The new systemic paradigm, however, implies attention to unity (whole–parts) and to diversity (one–various), to the interplay of antagonist phenomena, and to the way diversity organizes unity, which in turn organizes diversity. This leads to attempts to capture the complex relationships which develop within and among systems; where the *all* may represent more than the *whole* in the sense that it is much more than a global reality; and where the *parts* may represent more than the *whole* in the sense that progress is due also to small unities and not necessarily to the constitution of greater wholeness. The system is characterized by antagonistic forces, which can be neutralized and repressed, or utilized in a constitutive way. In various ways and continuously processes are generated which perpetuate, develop, and renew the system by means of new and spontaneous aggregations. *Being, existence*, and *life* appear as emerging qualities which imply the consideration of a whole series of processes like 'shadowy areas', 'leaks between the expressed and unexpressed', and 'black holes', which exist within every biological, anthropological, and social whole.

Here, the concepts of *organization* and *interaction*, which have been neglected by the classical theory of systems, become fundamental. According to Morin, in fact, systems are mostly constituted by actions between complex units, which are modulated by interactions. Whereas the concepts of *system* and *organization* are indissolubly connected, the latter is placed at the centre of the paradigm; it determines the coherence and the rules of interaction, and it allows for the reorganization of the system that tends to disorganize itself. Finally, it has the quality of reorganizing itself permanently.

We do not believe that within the context of this chapter it is convenient to explore further in detail all the various facets of Morin's (1977, 1980, 1986, 1991) speculations which may have relevance for personality psychology. With this epistemological digression our intention — as in the first chapter of this volume — is to call attention to the pervasiveness of certain questions and notions at certain times across different disciplines, as well as to the relevance of pursuing in psychology too a sounder knowledge of the meta-disciplinary roots of knowledge. As a matter of fact, reflection on complexity pertains not only to the social sciences; rather it is firmly grounded in the natural sciences (see Nicolis and Prigogine, 1987).

Evolution, diversification, instability, and *irreversibility* are properties of phenomena which have imposed a new vision of knowledge in biology and in physics, much earlier than in the social sciences.

The coexistence of various kinds of phenomena imply a pluralistic view of the physical world in which *micro* and *macro* phenomena justify different forms of explanations, deterministic and probabilistic, according to different transitions from one level to another which may take place in time. Small fluctuations may start great changes, whereas significant deviations may remain unnoticed. The same *micro* elements may end in different *macro* phenomena, depending on sequences, combinations and effects, largely affected by chance.

Different forms of order result from the self-regulatory properties of systems, and from the multiple mutations and selections that derive from transactions among systems. Whereas the capability to moderate fluctuations is a property of self-regulatory systems, the rupture of stability, continuity and order may give access to new opportunities and may result in a precondition for the emergence of new forms of functioning and equilibrium:

With regard to the actual debate on complexity, one may have the impression that most personality psychology nowadays is far removed from any metatheoretical concern. This can be a serious impediment to the progress of the discipline; for excessive simplification may lead to the amputation of important aspects of the object of investigation, when incautious or premature quantification makes us blind in the face of phenomena which emerge in time and through aggregation, when reification of the object of study completely distracts us from questioning how the intentions and the concepts of the observer may determine what is ultimately investigated. In the following paragraph, we come back to these issues, taking a closer insight into what is going on in the field of personality psychology.

Models, concepts, and methods to cope with complexity

Since Freud and McDougall, two models, no matter whether explicitly acknowledged or not, have dominated the field of personality psychology: the *mechanistic* model and the *teleological* model. Most theories, especially those from the early stage of development of the discipline, have been tributary to one or the other or to both models, since the two are not necessarily competing or mutually exclusive, but rather instrumental to a focus on different aspects of personality. Whereas the mechanistic model has provided a guide to investigate the basic elements and processes of personality as part of the natural world, the teleological model has moderated the reductionism and physicalism of the former, preserving the dignity of wholeness and subjectivity as objects of study.

The open-system model today seems to constitute the point where the two models come to a confluence which also represents their solution. Personality is not a machine, nor a predestined entity, but a self-regulatory system permanently interacting with other systems. The notions of self-regulation and interaction imply potentialities as well as properties; they represent the cornerstones of the construction of personality.

Since the very beginning, personality has relied upon some self-regulatory properties of the individual. Its development is marked by a progressive extension of these faculties. From the very beginning, too, more and more complex interactions with the environment have laid the foundations of personality and accompanied its development. Today, the most accredited paradigm is that of a *dynamic interactionism* which views both the individual and the environment as open systems in a relationship of tight reciprocity (see Hettema and Kenrick, Chapter 15 in this volume). The individual system of beliefs, feelings, and behaviours has equal dignity with the biological system and the environmental system in the dialogue which develops among them. This is different from paradigms which have generally treated biological and environmental factors as independent variables and have relegated conduct, and the affective and cognitive processes which support it, to the role of dependent variables.

In modern interactionism, affective and cognitive processes and their derivatives figure as interacting variables capable of acting significantly on biological and environmental factors. From this, a new view develops regarding the importance of biological and environmental factors in personality and the role individual constellations of cognitions, affects, and behaviours play in modulating exchanges between the organism and the environment, and thus, in selecting and creating the conditions for their further development. Organism and environment provide the elements and the basic conditions for constituting a psychic organization. Furthermore, it is this emerging organization which largely modulates the action of the former and their relationships in the course of ontogenesis.

With regard to this reciprocal determination of biological, socio-environmental, and psychological elements, the area of the emerging *processes of intermediation* is the one which fits best with the notion of personality. It is above all the study of the various constellations or individual patterns which seems able to reconcile the research on complexity and coherence of conduct with the development of general regularities. In this context, Magnusson (1990) has urged a revision of the traditional *variable-oriented* approach in favour of a *person-oriented* approach, which places the wholeness of the person at the centre of interest.

The examination of individual constellations, more than the study of single variables, can explain how various elements are intertwined and how various intertwinings are transformed in the flow of reciprocal determination. Single variables, processes, mechanisms, or behaviours have little meaning outside the constellation they contribute to define, and outside the network and the sequence of exchanges they contribute to maintain and to develop. The examination of what primes a particular behaviour cannot be separated from the examination of the effects it produces on other behaviours, nor from the effects it produces on other persons, nor from the effects of others' reactions on its perpetuation or transformation. This evidently leads to a revision of the static form of interactionism of the first generation, reinstates the importance of *time* as the dimension along which phenomena can be captured, from their emergence to their dissolution and through all their transformations, and places new emphasis on the relationships among systems and on the mechanisms of equilibrium and change which derive from them and which modulate them. Furthermore, this leads to a revision of what the units of investigation should be (variables or patterns), of ways of operationalization and quantification methods, and of treatment of data.

In certain cases, significant deviations from what is generally expected remain practically unnoticed or are fully normalized. In other cases, marginal deviations can be amplified via aggregation and, thus, pave the way to significant modifications in the relationships with others, which in turn become associated with significant modifications in the beliefs, goals, and behaviours of the individual. Patterns are more relevant than single variables; aggregations of micro-deviations may make more sense than single significant deviations. Thus, it is necessary to go beyond specific behaviours to grasp the different meanings they may assume as part of different individual and interpersonal constellations. Furthermore, it is necessary to account for the processes which, through mechanisms of attribution, classification, and interiorization, ensure the conditions for the development and consolidation of various behavioural styles and strategies. In this view, *longitudinal research* appears to be the necessary successor of the traditional cross-sectional strategy.

The *multicausality of phenomena* and the circularity of causal processes have led to a revision of the traditional notions of *continuity* and *stability* of conduct, since what appears to be relevant is not so much conduct *per se* as the role it plays in the individual's constellation of relationships with the environment. In dealing with continuities and discontinuities, we have to deal with forms of complexity which remind us of Morin's lesson on the organization that emerges from the interplay of order and disorder, as well as on the impossibility of tracing sharp distinctions between phenomena which are antagonistic and synergistic at one and the same time.

The notions of *transformation* and of *emergence* are complementary to the notion of *interaction* in bringing sense into the gradual construction of personality. Transformation concerns both the components and the functions of apparently the *same* psychological repertoire which derives from the dialogue with the environment. Development has to be understood as a succession of *crises* rather than of stages; a succession in which the order that is achieved is immediately put at stake by new forms of disorder, which impose in turn the achievement of new forms of order. The notion of *crisis* is not *per se* incompatible with the notion of *stage*, but the former reflects better than the latter the idea of the dynamism and unstable equilibrium of living systems in which structures, processes, and behaviours constantly emerge, transform, and vanish.

The notion of *continuity* is contiguous to the notion of *stability*; and this in turn to the notion of *coherence*. In all cases, it is a matter of the object as well as of the assumed perspective which lead us to notice continuity or discontinuity, stability or instability, coherence or lack of coherence. On the one hand, discontinuities do not necessarily imply a lack of connectedness between early and later development; on the other hand, apparent instabilities do not imply a lack of coherence of behaviour across various situations. Apparent continuities or stabilities may be instances of discontinuities or change not yet revealed.

Regarding the *object*, it makes a difference whether one refers to structures and processes or to behavioural outcomes, whether one refers to basic factors or manifest behaviours, and whether one refers to style (temperament) or to competence or skill. Because of 'heterotypic continuity', a common latent variable can account for behaviours which may appear different. Furthermore, because of 'equifinality', similar behaviours may be due to different structures and processes.

Regarding the *perspective*, it makes a difference whether one takes the perspective of the *actor* or the perspective of the *observer* of behaviour. Whereas 'ipsative continuity' may account for meaningful constant relationships among intra-individual variables of behavioural organization (cf. Emde and Harmon, 1984), 'socially attributed continuity' may account for the perception of identity, stability, and coherence that others derive from individual performance in spite of its transformations and in the face of different behaviours. In this respect, given the fact that, for instance, aggression is often reported as one of the most stable dimensions of personality (Huesmann *et al.*, 1984; Olweus, 1979), one should question which of the above kinds of continuity or stability is more appropriate to the understanding of apparent constancy of conduct across times and situations. In this regard, one may have the impression that a point that has been completely neglected is the way others' expectations of constancy may preclude any possibility of the individual being different.

In moving towards a more specific analysis of structures and processes, the picture which results from the number of variables in play and from their aggregations, combinations, and integrations reveals levels of complexity which disclose new ways to approach traditional issues — for example, the role of genes in the make-up of personality, and the role of individual differences in describing personality. Prolonged gene–environment interactions in the course of ontogenesis place further emphasis on the plasticity of the brain and give extreme flexibility and variability to behaviour. The genotype may shape individual responsiveness to environmental influences. However, this responsiveness changes with age and may have a different impact in changing the environment itself, in selecting and producing new environments. As a consequence, the variability accounted for by genes, environment, behaviour, and their interactions change at different times.

The notion of *fitting* moves attention from the individual and from the environment to the qualities of the *exchanges* which take place between the two. The person is influenced by the environment which, in turn, is profoundly modified and influenced by him or her. On the environmental side, what is expected and what is offered in terms of care, solicitousness, and support appears crucial. On the individual's side, what happens in terms of modulation of affects, development of cognitive structures, and ability to satisfy requests and expectations of the environment appears crucial.

Thus, the study of development of personality becomes closely intertwined with the study of development of emotions, motivations, and cognitions. In this regard, the study of individual differences may form a bridge between personality psychology as the sphere of molar phenomena and research on more basic processes and mechanisms (Caprara, 1987). On the one hand, close scrutiny of individual differences leads to focusing on their ingredients and on how their development gradually takes place on the basis of the combinations and transformations of these ingredients. In this way, the study of individual differences may provide a vehicle for capturing the foundations and the building blocks of personality as a constellation of dispositions. On the other hand, the systematic use of individual differences in experimental research as amplifiers of more general regularities and more subtle cause—effect relationships provides new avenues towards the generalizability of hypotheses to be tested, and towards the propositions of new hypotheses.

A better understanding of the basic processes that sustain and mediate the interaction of the individual with the environment is made possible by close scrutiny of how certain responses are linked to certain situations during development and evolve into stable and coherent strategies for coping with the variety of situations.

More precise predictions and more accurate interventions are made possible through the articulation of general hypotheses or laws, and by taking into account the various values which determine relationships among phenomena in different individuals.

Ultimately, it is unavoidable that the study of personality and individual differences returns to the lexicon as the origin of all limitations and all potentialities in describing and in pinpointing the multiple aspects of individual functioning.

In the light of emphasis on complexity, exciting new avenues may be able to throw further light on personality psychology.

On the side of *structures*, emphasis on complex rather than simple forms of personal organizations, could, in part, be captured by the use of circumplex models. The scrupulous and detailed investigation of all possible declinations of main constructs as they have sedimentated throughout the history of the culture may reveal promising directions for identifying and investigating the more basic ingredients to which the various constructs refer.

The logic of *simple space, simple structure* can be substituted by the logic of *complex space, simple structure*. Focusing on the intertwining of basic components to reveal factors deriving from their combinations can unfold the complexity of personal dispositional organizations, as well as recomposing most of the discrepancies in the identification and naming of dispositions deriving from the logic of simple space.

On the side of *processes*, attention to the micro-perturbations which may evolve into significant variations with the passing of time, call for renewed interest in transformations and intermediations rather than in mere outcomes. Moreover, more attention should be paid to evolutionary processes, in line with a logic of prediction and prevention rather than with a logic of mere control and intervention.

In conclusion, we firmly believe that the role of personality psychology is to function as a bridge between the *micro* and the *macro* phenomena, between basic processes and total functioning. In this respect, an area that should receive more attention than it has done thus far is where *interactions, shifting of levels,* and *transformations* take place. Much remains to be done here.

However, because we believe that personality psychologists can discipline their ambitions and can resist being seduced by the public to operate beyond their means, we have reason to be optimistic.

References

Allport, G.W. (1937), *Personality: A psychological interpretation*, New York, NY: Holt.
Buss, D.M. (1990), 'Toward a biologically informed psychology of personality', *Journal of Personality,* **58**, 1–16.
Buss, D.M. and Cantor, N. (eds.) (1989), *Personality Psychology: Recent trends and emerging directions*, New York, NY: Springer-Verlag.
Caprara, G.-V. (1987), 'The disposition–situation debate and research on aggression', *European Journal of Personality,* **1**, 1–16.
Carlson, R. (1984), 'What's social about social psychology? Where's the person in personality research?', *Journal of Personality and Social Psychology,* **47**, 1304–9.
Contrada, R.J., Leventhal, H. and O'Leary, A. (1990), 'Personality and health', in L.A. Pervin (ed.), *Handbook of Personality: Theory and research*, New York, NY: Guilford Press, pp. 638–69.
Cox, T. and Ferguson, E. (1991), 'Individual differences, stress and coping', in C.L. Cooper and R. Payne (eds.), *Personality and Stress: Individual differences in the stress process*, Chichester: Wiley, pp. 7–30.
Emde, R.N. and Harmon, R.J. (1984), 'Entering a new era in search for developmental continuities', in R.N. Emde and R.J. Harmon (eds.), *Continuities and Discontinuities in Development*, New York, NY: Plenum Press.
Endler, N.S. (1992), 'Interactionism revisited', *European Journal of Personality,* **6**.
Feyerabend, P.K. (1975), *Against Method: Outline of an anarchist theory of knowledge*, London: New Left Books.
Friedman, H.S. (1990), 'Where is the disease-prone personality?: conclusion and future directions', in H.S. Friedman (ed.), *Personality and Disease*, New York, NY: Wiley, pp. 283–92.
Huesmann, L.E., Eron, L.D., Lefkowitz, M.M. and Walder, L.O. (1984), 'The stability of aggression over time and generations', *Developmental Psychology,* **20**, 1120–34.
Kenrick, D.T. and Dantchik, A. (1983), 'Interactionism, idiographics, and the social-psychological invasion of personality', *Journal of Personality,* **51**, 286–307.
Lewin, K. (1935), *A Dynamic Theory of Personality*, New York, NY: McGraw-Hill.
Magnusson, D. (1988), *Individual Development from an Interactional Perspective*, Hillsdale, NJ: Erlbaum.
Magnusson, D. (1990), 'Personality research — challenges for the future', *European Journal of Personality,* **4**, 1–17.
Magnusson, D. (1992), 'Back to the phenomena', *European Journal of Personality,* **6**, 1–14.
Morin, E. (1977), *La méthode. Vol. I. La nature de la nature* [The Method. Vol. I. The Nature of Nature], Paris: Seuil.
Morin, E. (1982), *La méthode. Vol. II. La vie de la vie* [The Method. Vol. II. The Life of Life], Paris: Seuil.
Morin, E. (1986), *La méthode. Vol. III. La connaisance de la connaisance* [The Method. Vol. III. The Knowledge of Knowledge], Paris: Seuil.

Morin, E. (1991), *La méthode. Vol. IV. Les idées. Leur habitat, leur vie, leur moeurs, leur organisation* [The Method. Vol. IV. The ideas: Their Habitat, their Life, their Customs, their Organization], Paris: Seuil.

Nicolis, G. and Prigogine, J. (1987), *Exploring Complexity. An introduction*, Munich: Piper GmbH.

Olweus, D. (1979), 'Stability of aggressive reaction patterns in males: a review', *Psychological Bulletin,* **86**, 852−75.

Pervin, L.A. (1985), 'Personality', *Annual Review of Psychology,* **36**, 83−114.

Pervin, L.A. (1990), 'Personality theory and research: prospects for the future', in L.A. Pervin (ed.), *Handbook of Personality: Theory and research*, New York, NY: Guilford Press, pp. 723−7.

Plomin, R. and Rende, R. (1991), 'Human behavioral genetics', *Annual Review of Psychology,* **42**, 161−90.

Subject index